History of
Mexican Literature

SOR JUANA INÉS DE LA CRUZ, 1651-1695

Mexico's greatest lyricist (painting by Cabrera)

CARLOS GONZÁLEZ PEÑA

History of Mexican Literature

Third Edition

Translated by
GUSTA BARFIELD NANCE *and*
FLORENE JOHNSON DUNSTAN

SOUTHERN METHODIST UNIVERSITY PRESS • DALLAS

Library of Congress Catalog Card Number 68-24078

First edition, 1943
Second edition, 1945
Third edition, revised and enlarged, 1968

The third edition is translated from
Historia de la literatura mexicana,
ninth edition, by special arrangement
with Editorial Porrúa, S.A., México, D.F.

PRINTED IN THE UNITED STATES OF AMERICA
BY THE SOUTHERN METHODIST UNIVERSITY PRINTING DEPARTMENT
AT DALLAS, TEXAS

Translators' Foreword

CARLOS GONZÁLEZ PEÑA's *Historia de la literatura mexicana*, the most authoritative single volume in its field, was selected for translation into English because of the need for a clear interpretation of Mexican thought to American readers. No other work of its nature and scope is now available.

The author was a fellow of the Mexican Academy, a member of the faculty of the National University of Mexico, and an editor of Mexico City's leading newspaper, *El Universal*. He remains a recognized authority on Mexican language and literature, and his *Manual de gramática* is used as a text in Mexican high schools. His *Historia de la literatura mexicana*, widely studied in schools and universities in many countries, was first published in 1928. Over the next quarter-century González Peña continuously revised the text, preparing eight editions before his death in 1955. A novelist and essayist as well as a scholar, he presented his material with individuality and narrative skill and constructed a living picture of each important author, using the events of the writer's life and the development of his work as supplementary parts of the full portrait.

The Ninth Edition of *Historia de la literatura mexicana,* published in 1966 by Editorial Porrúa of Mexico City, has been brought up to date by means of an Appendix prepared by Aurora Ocampo de G., Ernesto Prado Velázquez, and D. María del Carmen Millán. Using this Ninth Edition as the basis of their Third Edition, the translators have tried to keep the book's distinctive flavor, retaining, so far as possible, the author's style, which is very Mexican and at the same time personal. Though Spanish scholars may regret to see the familiar titles of Mexican books translated into English, the purpose for which this book is intended—the presentation of Mexican thought and character in a way intelligible to American readers—seemed to require such translation. The policy has not been followed, however, with absolute consistency, some titles being left in Spanish; these, in the main, are either titles that practically translate themselves for American readers, or those for which no suitable idiomatic equivalents could be found. In hazarding the title translation of several works inaccessible to them, the translators have been keenly aware of the possibility of errors. They have appended, however, a list of the original titles.

In the long task of preparing this work, the translators wish to acknowledge indebtedness to the author for his encouragement and co-operation in regard to their first two editions; to George Bond and the late John H. McGinnis of Southern Methodist University, Henry Nash Smith of the University of California, Angel Flores (formerly of the Pan American Union's Division of Intellectual Co-operation in Washington and now at Queens College), Virginia Huerta Jones of Mexico City, and Concha Romera James, formerly of the Pan American Union, for their invaluable suggestions on the earlier editions; and to Allen Maxwell and Margaret L. Hartley, of Southern Methodist University Press, for assistance in preparing the manuscript of the Third Edition for publication.

G. B. N.
F. J. D.

Dallas, Texas
Decatur, Georgia
November 6, 1967

Introduction to First Edition

THE PRESENT WORK appears at a most auspicious moment. A definite public awaits it—intelligent readers who despite their monolingual limitation are eagerly seeking a fuller understanding of our neighbors to the south. The translators of this *History of Mexican Literature* must be thanked, first of all, for their magnanimous service in bringing this essential material to the studious men and women of Anglo-America. They must be thanked, too, for having chosen the right book. González Peña's *History of Mexican Literature* is, beyond any doubt, the most sober, best rounded work on the subject. It is not the definitive analysis one might wish for, one that delves into the economic, social, and political factors which ultimately determine cultural phenomena. González Peña's book does, however, present the men and women who with their literary creations enriched the cultural heritage of Mexico, and it provides a general critical evaluation of these creations and of the multiple fluctuations determining the ebbs and flows of genres. From it the student may acquire a fair grasp of the entire field of Mexican letters. And this is no meager help. All that can be wished is that, encouraged by the warm reception given González Peña's work, the translators will bring to English readers the literary histories of other Latin American countries.

It cannot be overemphasized that the present work will inspire confidence in its readers: for we have here a Mexican who has been teaching and writing about the literature of his native country for several decades. His *History* is written from within, i.e., from the vantage point of one who knows the psychological and social climate which produced Mexican literature. Taine's *History of English Literature*, interesting and revealing as it is, remains, above all, an outside job. It is English literature seen through the eyes of a Frenchman,

vii

and consequently full of certain errors and distortions which could not possibly have befallen an intelligent English critic. This generalization is less true of course in the case of concentrated analysis where spiritual affinity plays such a preponderant role, imbuing the remarks of an André Gide, for example, with such keenness in discussing Dostoyevsky. But for the purposes of a survey like the present *History of Mexican Literature*, it is much safer to have a Mexican, and especially one of the stature of González Peña, for a guide.

Here, then, is a fine *History of Mexican Literature*, brightly illuminating the course of friendly inter-American relations. Knowledge of the cultural heritage of each of our neighbor American nations is the first essential step to hemispheric solidarity. Here one has been taken in the right direction.

ANGEL FLORES

Washington, D.C.
November 6, 1943

Mexican Publishers' Note

FOR SOME twenty-five years Don Carlos González Peña revised each new edition of this manual, which has proved to be useful not only as a text for scholars but as a source of information and study for the general reader.

Since the author's death—a great loss to Mexican letters—we have continued to publish new editions to which our technical department has added biographical and bibliographical data and made minor corrections, leaving intact the critical judgments and evaluations of the author. To bring the work up to date and make it as complete as possible, we have added an appendix (Appendix A) to this edition, listing the most recent writers and their works without discussing the different genres or repeating classifications and characteristics. Included in this are Mexican writers whose recent work definitely belongs to the history of our letters, and writers of other nationalities who have resided for a long time in Mexico and have made contributions to our literature.

The documentary source for Appendix A is the research conducted by two investigators from the Center for Literary Studies of the National Autonomous University of Mexico, Aurora Ocampo de G. and Ernesto Prado Velázquez, in collaboration with the director of the Center, D. María del Carmen Millán. Ernesto Prado Velázquez made the selections, adaptations, and synthesis of the material.

Contents

The Sixteenth Century

The Beginnings

MEXICAN literature uses the Spanish language and is, in fact, a branch of Spanish literature. But it differs from the literature of Spain because of the distinctive character which the Mexican national spirit has given it.

The intellectual history of Mexico begins with the work of the first Spanish colonists. On August 13, 1521, the Conquest was completed by the occupation of Tenochtitlán, the ancient metropolis of the Aztecs; immediately, on the still smoldering ruins, the conquerors began the reconstruction of that city, the future capital of New Spain. After they had laid down the bases of political organization and provided for immigration from Spain, there remained the much more complex and difficult task of incorporating the Indian nations into the framework of Spanish culture—the task, that is, of creating a civilization.

The program of the conquerors involved one prime objective: the conversion of the Indians to the Christian creed and moral standards —which was, by its nature, a work of religious character. But conversion required both an understanding of the Indians and the ability to teach them. First, it was necessary for the clergy to establish intimate contacts with the natives, to become familiar with their language, customs, and character, to investigate their history and traditions, to fathom their inmost nature. Along with this, it was essential to create in the Indians themselves sentiments and ideas which would link them psychologically with the new forms of civilization. Such was the work assumed by the missionaries—a labor of gigantic proportions if one considers the triple aspect of investigation, evangelization, and instruction; the extreme difficulty of dealing with people speaking different languages and all antagonized by the harshness of the Conquest; and, finally, the small number of men who started this work, as compared with the millions of beings to whom intellectual, moral, and religious instruction had to be given.

If the undertaking was exceptional in magnitude, exceptional were the men who accepted the task and carried it to completion. They combined the ideal of poverty with a kindliness that won the confidence and affection of the conquered; perseverance, with a culture that enabled them to be both apostles and teachers; heroism, with spiritual and physical vigor.

Their influence was not only religious but highly social. It extended, through the evangelical organization, over a vast territory and often afforded protection and relief to the natives. In the cities the missionaries did not confine their activities to the churches, but built schools nearby. While they taught the fundamentals, they also inculcated aesthetic ideas and trained students in the industrial arts so that they could earn a livelihood. These schools were the centers from which civilization spread throughout New Spain. They can be considered the cradle of Mexican culture, primarily because of the efforts and activities of the teachers, rather than the diligence of the students.

THE FIRST SCHOOLS

To Friar Pedro de Gante (1479-1572), of Flemish origin and a relative of Charles V, one of the three Franciscans who arrived in Mexico in 1523, goes the glory of having established the first educational institution in America: the School of San Francisco de México, which he directed with amazing ability and steadfastness for half a century. In that school were gathered almost a thousand students, many of them from the Indian aristocracy. They were given elementary instruction in religion and the rudiments of learning. Later, Latin, music, and singing were taught. At a still later time, a school of industrial arts and crafts was opened for adults, and from it emerged sculptors, painters, engravers, needleworkers, stonecutters, tailors, carpenters, and shoemakers. Not content with all this, the great Franciscan founded a children's hospital within the school and sustained and expanded it in spite of all obstacles.

The first bishop of Mexico, Friar Juan de Zumárraga, saw the need for a school of higher learning, which would provide something more for the Indians than rudimentary instruction and training in useful crafts and would foster the development of exceptional individuals. Consequently, on January 6, 1536, he founded the Academy of Santa Cruz de Tlaltelolco. Sixty native pupils were enrolled on opening day. In addition to religion and ethics, the following subjects were taught: reading, writing, Latin grammar, rhetoric, philosophy, music, and Mexican medicine (herb lore). The teachers—all Franciscan monks— were remarkable men and included among their number such famous scholars as Friar Andrés de Olmos, the linguist; Friar Bernardino de Sahagún, the historian and ethnologist; and the French friars Arnaldo de Basacio and Juan Focher, the latter a Doctor of Laws from the University of Paris.

This school produced native teachers who taught the Nahuatlan language to the Spaniards and informed them concerning Indian history, religious rites, and social customs. It also produced amanuenses, collaborators, and printers who made possible the great historical and philological works of the sixteenth century.

In the meantime, a new class had arisen—the mestizos, who were generally the illegitimate offspring of Spaniards and Indians. Many such children, disowned by their fathers and abandoned by mothers who were unable to support them, had been either killed or left to their fate. In order to aid this class, Don Antonio de Mendoza, the viceroy, founded the Academy of San Juan de Letrán. This institution served the double purpose of offering a refuge for mestizo foundlings and of providing a training school for teachers who were to organize other such schools. Three clerics appointed by the king directed it: each of these, in turn, served one year as rector of the school, while the other two performed separate duties—one taught in the school and, on certain days, instructed the people of the community in religious doctrine, with the aid of his most advanced pupils; the other gave lessons in Latin grammar and conducted some of his pupils to the university for more advanced studies there. At that time there were two types of students in the school: some, not possessing outstanding ability, were eligible to remain only three years and were given an elementary education and a training in some trade; others—six in number—were selected for unusual excellence at the end of each school term and were allowed to pursue a seven years' literary course.

To complete the summary of Mexican education in its earliest phase, mention should be made of the schools established for creole children, that is, children of European parentage who had been born in the New World. These were private schools because creoles were not allowed to attend the schools for Indians and mestizos. Spanish instructors, to whom fees were paid, taught the fundamentals. Dr. Cervantes de Salazar, during the early years of his residence in Mexico, was one of the outstanding teachers.

The Augustinian monks were the first to establish schools where both Spanish and creole children were taught. The school at Tiripitío was opened in 1540, and the Academy of San Pablo in 1575. The latter was founded by Friar Alonso de la Veracruz, who assembled a good library as well as a collection of maps, globes, and scientific instruments that was remarkable in its day.

About the same time, in 1573, the Academy of Santa Maria de Todos Santos was established, and provision was made for ten scholarships to be given to poor young men of outstanding ability. This gave new impetus to the diffusion of culture, which had been greatly accentuated by the arrival of the Jesuits in 1572. These men, according to Don Carlos Pereyra, assumed "the role of spiritual advisers to the best classes and instructors to the youth of those classes," and they "took into their hands the highest symbols of moral power in this new society." After overcoming serious obstacles, the Jesuits founded, on January 1, 1573, the Academy of San Pedro and San Pablo; and, in 1575 and 1576, the seminaries of San Miguel, San Bernardo, and San Gregorio. Having enrolled more than three hundred students in the first of these schools, they inaugurated secondary education on October 18, 1574, with great ceremony. But the pupils showed such outstanding proficiency—those between the ages of twelve and fourteen "composed excellent Latin pieces in prose and verse and recited them in public"—that soon thereafter, on October 19, 1575, the Jesuits instituted still more advanced studies, including philosophy.

By the end of the sixteenth century, the Academy of San Pedro and San Pablo—then called the *Colegio Máximo*—was occupying its own ample and substantial building, the one now standing. Meanwhile, the seminary of San Gregorio had been set aside exclusively for the Indians; and, in 1583, the schools of San Miguel and San Bernardo had been united under the name of San Ildefonso.

In their effort to promote knowledge among the creoles through the *Colegio Máximo,* the Jesuits competed successfully with the University of Mexico (to be described later). They gave considerable impetus to the study and appreciation of classical literature; and textbooks of Cicero, Virgil, Ovid, and Martial were published by their press. They also extended their activities beyond the capital, establishing schools at Pátzcuaro, Valladolid, Oaxaca, Puebla, Veracruz, and Guadalajara. Realizing, too, their evangelical duty (which they were later to accomplish in the vast mission field extending from California almost across the continent), they undertook the study of the native languages. For this purpose, they established a seminary in the village of Tepozotlán, a practical school for learning the Indian languages, particularly the Nahuatlan and the Otomí.

THE FOUNDING OF THE UNIVERSITY

The University of Mexico antedates the earliest of the Jesuit schools. Within twenty-five years of the Conquest, public instruction in Mexico City had progressed to the extent that a need was felt for a university. Advanced studies were not then taught in any school in the New World. Indians, mestizos, and creoles were educated in separate schools. Many young people went to Spain to complete their education, but such a course was not open to everyone. The City of Mexico petitioned for "a university of all the sciences where the natives and the sons of Spaniards might be trained in the Holy Catholic faith and taught other branches of learning"; and the viceroy, Don Antonio de Mendoza, took the first step toward creating a university by endowing it with some cattle ranches of his own. He may therefore be considered the founder of the university—all the more so since he, not satisfied with his own efforts and realizing that only the king would be able to establish the university on a firm basis, joined with representatives of the city, the church, and the religious orders in petitioning the Spanish monarch for the formal founding of the university with the necessary endowment.

The court must have been somewhat slow in acting upon the viceroy's request, for the royal reply came during the rule of Don Luis de Velasco, Mendoza's successor. The Emperor Charles V, King of Spain, by decrees prepared in Toro on September 21, 1551, and signed by the prince (afterward Phillip II), ordered the establishment of the University of Mexico, endowing it with a thousand pesos of gold from the mines each year, besides the income from the ranches given by Mendoza, and granting to it (with some limitations which were later withdrawn) the same privileges and tax exemptions which the University of Salamanca enjoyed. In 1555, at the request of the king, the pope confirmed the establishment of the university and the privileges granted, bestowed the control on the Spanish monarchs as the founders, and, at a later date, gave the title of Pontifical to the university.

The university was officially opened January 25, 1553, in the presence of the viceroy, the *Audiencia* (a high court appointed by the Spanish king), judges, and churchmen. High mass was celebrated in the Seminary of San Pablo; two members of the *Audiencia*, Don Antonio Rodríguez de Quesada and Don Gómez de Santillana, were named rector and dean, respectively; and a brilliant procession marched to the first building occupied by the university, the one standing today at the corner of Seminario and Moneda streets.

The first session was inaugurated June 3 with a Latin oration by Dr. Cervantes de Salazar. Actual instruction began on a different date in each department—from June 5 to June 24—so that the viceroy and *Audiencia* could attend each of the exercises in a body. The professorial chairs were held by men from the already established Mexican schools. Among the outstanding members of the faculty were: Alonso de la Veracruz, the learned Augustinian; Dr. Cervantes de Salazar, whose name is intimately connected with the colonial culture of that day; Don Juan Negrete, a Master of Arts from the University of Paris; and Dr. Frías de Albornoz, a disciple of the famous attorney Diego de Covarrubias. The first subjects taught were theology, sacred literature, canon law, decretals, laws and legal principles, the arts, rhetoric, and grammar. Medicine was soon added; and, after half a century, the Nahuatlan and Otomí languages were also taught.

Thus was this great institution established; it continued to exist nearly three hundred years.[1] Although it experienced many ups and downs and cannot always be spoken of with approval, its founding, nevertheless, must be regarded as one of the high points in the history of Mexican culture.

---

[1] The University of Mexico was closed in 1833, but reopened the following year. After other troubles, it was completely shut down in 1865. The National University was opened in 1910.—Translators' note.

THE FIRST PUBLISHERS

Along with the schools and the university, another important cultural agency was the printing press. Mexico City has the honor of being the first city in America to establish a press. Viceroy Mendoza and Bishop Zumárraga ordered a completely equipped printing press from Juan Cromberger, a famous printer of Seville, and it reached Mexico City in 1536, according to García Icazbalceta. At first, it was probably used only for printing leaflets (giving the A B C's) and other needed materials, but in 1537 a book was issued. This—the first book printed in America—was San Juan Clímaco's *The Spiritual Ladder for Reaching Heaven,* which had been translated from Latin by Friar Juan de la Madalena.

The press was installed in the House of the Bells, on the southwest corner of the streets which are now known as Moneda and Licenciado Verdad. Juan Pablos (born Giovanni Paoli), an Italian from Brescia, Lombardy, had charge of it. On February 17, 1542, he was given citizenship; in May of the following year he was granted land for a dwelling, in the San Pablo district; and in 1548 he obtained the exclusive right to operate as printer and bookseller. He renewed this permit in 1554. Antonio de Espinosa, however, protested so successfully against these privileges that in 1559 he was permitted to establish a press. There is no record of Pablos' activity later than 1560. Probably he was succeeded in the House of the Bells by Pedro Ocharte, who published many books in the native languages and produced famous editions of other works for more than thirty years.

Other presses were established by Pedro Balli, in 1575, and Antonio Ricardo, between 1577 and 1579. Although Ricardo, or Ricciardi, a native of Turin, Italy, was successful in Mexico City, he moved his press to Lima, thus introducing the art of printing in Peru. Enrico Martínez, the originator of the drainage system for the Valley of Mexico, and Melchor Ocharte, son or relative of Pedro, were also early Mexican printers.

Throughout the century the activity of the Mexican press was remarkable. Although the bulk of the published material consisted of certificates, catechisms, lexicons and grammars written by the friars, prayer books, liturgies, mass books, psalters, and antiphonals, there were also some few books on law, medicine, history, and natural, military, and nautical science.

A listing of all works printed in the sixteenth century can be found in *Mexican Bibliography of the Sixteenth Century,* by Joaquín García Icazbalceta, a new edition of which was published by Agustín Millares Carlo in 1954.

In the following sections, the intellectual activities of that time, though they were not essentially literary in character, will be discussed briefly. Since the problem of language is in the forefront, it will be discussed first.

THE PHILOLOGISTS

The chief obstacle encountered by the missionaries was the strangeness and variety of the native languages: they were not only radically different from European tongues but fundamentally different from each other. Don Carlos Pereyra has correctly said, "New Spain was a Babel of tongues; one was as different from the other as Russian is from French, or Spanish from Basque." The missionaries' program required, first, the learning of the Indian languages, then a thorough understanding of the Indians' way of thinking, and, last, the writing of books that would give all the necessary information to the missionaries who would come later.

Friar Pedro de Gante and his companions, Juan de Tecto and Juan de Ayora, having arrived August 30, 1523, soon after the occupation of Tenochtitlán, initiated this work. It is said that they first tried to learn the Nahuatlan language by "becoming children with the children." They would take part in games, write down the children's expressions with utmost care, and later assign to these the most suitable Spanish equivalents. Perhaps the friars did begin in this crude way, but they soon found a better method. They heard that two sons of a Spanish widow (who had come to Mexico at the beginning of the Conquest) had learned the native language from children of their age. The mother permitted her elder son, Alonso, to become the constant companion of the friars. He served them ably as interpreter and preached their sermons to the natives. When he reached the required age, being strongly drawn toward the religious life, he assumed the Franciscan habit; he became the famous linguist known as Friar Alonso de Molina.

Molina represents, with regard to language, the first tie between the missionaries and the Indians. When schools were opened and developed, the task of the friars was made easier by native students who excelled in Spanish and Latin. Within a short time the missionaries acquired exceptional skill in speaking the Indian languages and used them in preaching to the Indians. Gante, Motolinia, Sahagún, and Mendieta became proficient linguists. Besides achieving greatly in other fields, they and their co-workers became the creators of American philology.

The work of these men should be estimated, not only in terms of its intrinsic value but also in terms of the exceptional conditions under which they worked. "Today," says García Icazbalceta,

the study of a number of languages, perhaps of one only, enhances greatly the reputation of a scholar, who almost always finds some existent work on which to base his studies; but at that time, with no aid whatsoever, the missionaries had to learn or, rather, divine a whole language from the very bottom; one of them might even undertake to master five or six languages that had no common relationships and no known alphabets. At the present time, such work is usually done in the tranquillity and seclusion of the study; then it was carried on in the fields and forests, on the roads, and under the open sky by ill-clothed men weary from ecclesiastical duties, hunger, and sleeplessness.

He adds,

The missionaries did not undertake this serious task to gain personal fame; they did not compare the languages or treat them in a scientific manner. They did try to adjust all of them to the Latin standard, but they were primarily interested in the practical point of being able to deal with the natives. In achieving this end, they also laid a solid foundation for the magnificent edifice of language that was later to be constructed.

Friar Andrés de Olmos, who arrived in Mexico in 1524, is chronologically the first of the philologists. He mastered several dialects of the Chichimecas, among whom he worked, and compiled grammars and lexicons of the Nahuatlan, Huastecan, and Totonacan languages. All his works, including some important historical treatises, have been lost excepting his *Mexican Grammar*, which was completed in 1547, but was not published until 1875, when Rémi Siméon printed it in Paris.

Alonso de Molina, mentioned above as interpreter and instructor of the friars, is also noted for his philological work. His *Castilian-Mexican Vocabulary* was printed in 1555; this was revised, enlarged, and reprinted in 1571 with his *Mexican-Castilian Vocabulary*. His *Mexican Art,* a grammar, was published in the same year. He died in Mexico City in 1585, having devoted fifty years of his life to preaching.

A number of other philologists deserve mention. Maturino Gilberti, a French Franciscan, who came to Mexico in 1542, mastered Tarascan and wrote a *Vocabulary* and *Grammar,* published in 1558 and 1559, respectively. Juan Bautista de Lagunas, a Franciscan born in New Spain, explained the character of the Tarascan language in an *arte,* a brief dictionary, and other works, all published in one volume in 1574. Francisco de Cepeda (1532-1602), a Dominican of La Mancha, learned several languages in the province of San Vicente de Chiapa and in 1560 published a work called *Arts of the Chiapanecan, Zoquean, Tzendal, and Chinantecan Languages.* Juan de Córdoba (1503-1595), a Dominican of noble birth, previously a soldier under Charles V in Flanders and Germany, was the author of a *Zapotecan Vocabulary* and an *arte* of the same language, both published in 1578. Antonio de los Reyes, another Dominican, who came to Mexico from Spain in 1555 and who died in 1603, studied the Mixtecan language and described it in an *arte,* published in 1593. Francisco de Alvarado, a member of the same order and a native of Mexico, published a *Vocabulary of the Mixtecan Language* the same year. A Jesuit, Padre Antonio del Rincón, descended from the native Tezcucan kings, is credited with a *Nahuatlan Arte,* which was printed in 1595, about six years before his death. Last of these early philologists was Friar Luis de Villalpando, author of a Mayan *arte* and vocabulary.

Religious Literature

Apart from lexicons and grammars, most of the books published in Mexico during the sixteenth century were of religious character. Some of these were for the instruction of the Indians, some were prayer or liturgical books, others contained church regulations, while a few dealt with the ideals of asceticism and the lives of saints.

The most common of the religious books were *doctrinas* or catechisms. The earliest of these was written by Friar Pedro de Gante in the Nahuatlan language and printed in Antwerp in 1528. Members of the different orders composed similar books in Tarascan, Huastecan, Zapotecan, Mixtecan, Otomí, and other languages or dialects. If the numerous catechisms in the Nahuatlan language are a criterion, the friars must have achieved quick results in teaching the natives how to read.

Friar Bernardino de Sahagún prepared, under the title of *Christian Psalmody*, a collection of songs for the Indian fiestas. Padre Gaona published in the Nahuatlan language *Colloquies Concerning the Peace and Tranquillity of the Soul*, a work noted for purity of diction, according to his contemporaries. Friar Maturino Gilberti wrote in the Tarascan language his *Spiritual Treasure* and his famous *Dialogue Concerning Christian Doctrine*, which was withdrawn from circulation by the Council of the Indies, the supreme body governing all the colonies of Spain. The Dominican Friar Antonio de Hinojosa published his *Life and Miracles of the Glorious San Jacinto* in 1597. This work is no longer extant, but according to Remesal it was a delightful book and contained much Latin and Spanish poetry written by natives of Mexico. Last of these works to be mentioned here is the copious collection of *Sermons* by the Augustinian Friar Juan de la Anunciación. This was written in Nahuatlan.

Very great, indeed, is the wealth of linguistic data which the missionaries have left to posterity; yet it is thought that only a fraction of their work is now known. Innumerable documents still remain unedited; and of those that have been published, many are now lost —destroyed by constant use or by the passage of time. Apart from their philological value, the surviving works possess—as Icazbalceta says—great historic interest: some of the *artes* or grammars of the native languages contain important facts about the Indian races, and the *confesonarios* (handbooks for priests) include much curious data regarding superstitions and customs of the Indians. Discussing the enormous work accomplished by these missionary-pioneers in slightly more than half a century, Icazbalceta says with justice that the linguists—though little is known about them—deserve a place of highest honor in the history of Mexican literature.

Scholastic Philosophy

As one type of religious literature, scholastic philosophy requires attention. This branch of learning, completely decadent but still commanding interest in the sixteenth century, was represented in Mexico by the great Augustinian, Alonso de la Veracruz, member of the first faculty of the University of Mexico and founder of the Academy of San Pablo.

Born in 1504, a native of Caspueñas, in the diocese of Toledo, he bore the family name of Gutiérrez. His wealthy parents gave him a thorough education in Alcalá and Salamanca, and from the latter university he received a degree in theology. After being ordained as a priest, he taught in Salamanca a course in *artes*, as philosophy was then called. Urged by Friar Francisco de la Cruz, he decided to abandon his professorial chair and go to Mexico. He arrived July 2, 1536, and in the city of Veracruz assumed the habit of the Augustinians, thereupon taking the name of that city as his surname.

In 1540, when the Augustinians established their school at Tiripitío in Michoacán, he was sent there to teach philosophy and theology and to learn the Tarascan language. He founded several monasteries in that region and worked hard in the interest of his order. In the absence of the venerable Don Vasco de Quiroga, he presided over the bishopric of Michoacán, and in 1553 he was appointed professor of scholastic philosophy in the University of Mexico. When he joined the faculty, he had already completed and given to the printer his *Recognitio Summularum* and *Dialectica Resolutio,* published in 1554, and his *Physica Speculatio,* published in 1557. At that time, Icazbalceta says, the strongly entrenched dialectics of scholasticism had been converted "into a foolish concern for disputation defended by puerile and empty arguments," and the difficulty of its intricate doctrines had increased to such an extent that seldom might there be found a student with sufficient intellectual vigor to escape from its labyrinth. A reformation of the system was badly needed, and in this Father Veracruz timidly took the lead in his books. He proposed to remove the excessive encumbrances from dialectics. At all events, however, even though he did prune some of the superfluous foliage, "he did not venture to apply the sickle to the rank weeds." Scholastic doctrines were not appreciably clarified in his writings; on the contrary, in what he called physics, "he is as obscure as the other members of his school; he fills pages with metaphysical conjectures, which at that time took the place of true experimental physics." But if his works did not bring about the reform of which he dreamed, "they are noteworthy for their purpose and because they reveal a less servile spirit than that generally shown by teachers in that epoch."

The three works mentioned above, along with the *Speculum Conjugiorum* (1556), a work in which Father Veracruz tried to solve the intricate matrimonial problems of the Indians, were reprinted in Spain; and the *Physica Speculatio* was also reprinted in Milan at the end of the sixteenth century.

Father Veracruz was a learned and remarkably industrious person who, endowed with a singular sense of the practical and a courageous spirit of independence, intervened in some of the most complicated religious problems of his day. In 1561, he went to Spain to aid in solving the conflict between the bishops and the monastic communities. On his return to Mexico in 1573, he refused high honors and positions because he wanted to devote his time to teaching and preaching. Besides founding the Academy of San Pablo, he served several times as provincial of his order and he wrote various theological works which were not published and which perhaps have been lost. He received many honors before his death in June, 1584, at about eighty years of age. Even if his work, as well as that of the philosophical school which shaped it, did come to naught, he was, nevertheless, a representative man of his age.

Scientific Works

This brief account of cultural activities in the sixteenth century would be incomplete if the published works of scientists were not listed.

In the field of law, Dr. Vasco de Puga published in 1563 his *Cedulario* (a book of legal forms), which was the first digest of laws in America and is of great importance to the early history of the Conquest.

Of the observational sciences, medicine was especially cultivated. Dr. Francisco Bravo's *Opera Medicinalia* was published in 1570. Alonso López de Hinojoso's *Suma y Recopilación de Cirugía* (*Summary and Abridgment of Surgery*) appeared in 1578; Agustín Farfán's *Brief Treatise on Medicine* was published the year following; and the first part of *The Problems and Marvelous Secrets of the Indies*, by Dr. Juan de Cárdenas, was issued in 1591. All these books are now considered devoid of scientific value, but they are interesting because they reveal the status of the natural sciences at the time. Also, as early documents, they contain unique data of no little significance in the history of Mexico.

Lastly, Dr. Diego García de Palacio's two books on military affairs—*Military Dialogues* (1583) and *Nautical Instruction* (1587)—should be mentioned. The first, intended as a textbook of military science, consists of a series of conversations between two Spaniards, a Biscayan who had taken part in the Italian wars and a Montañan who had fought in the Indies. *Nautical Instruction,* which is probably no longer extant, must have had some merit, at least in diction, for the Royal Spanish Academy used it in compiling its *Dictionary of Authorities.*

Leaving at this point the nonliterary works of the sixteenth century and entering now the field of literary history proper, the next chapter will be concerned with the early historians and chroniclers. Following chapters will deal with the beginnings of poetry and drama.

II

Historians and Chroniclers

To spanish historians and official chroniclers, the exploration of America and the Conquest of Mexico furnished fascinating material. Also, some of the conquistadors—including the most renowned of them all—prepared reports of the events in which they had participated, narrating their own exploits and describing the new and marvelous sights they had seen in the Western World. The missionaries, in their turn, having come into intimate contact with the Indians and having pierced the secret of their speech and traditions, filled volumes with rare data on the origins of the natives, their ancient religion and customs, their laws, the physical and social world in which they lived, and the characteristics of the different races. Lastly, rivaling the missionaries and giving proof of the friars' successful efforts to advance learning, appeared the native chroniclers—Indians, taught by the friars—who, as Icazbalceta has said, undertook "with admirable zeal the task of preserving all that they had learned from their elders."

History, therefore, flourished with exceptional brilliance in the sixteenth century. And it is not the least of the merits of this activity —especially from the religious standpoint—that the attitude of the authors was generous and unselfish. The missionaries themselves sought no materialistic end and perhaps not even fame. Even their contemporaries did not know the extent of their work. For over two centuries many great works of the period were buried—in effect, lost—in dusty archives; and only in recent years have they been published and studied. Today the world recognizes their immense value as faithful and unique accounts of one of the most dramatic periods in the history of civilization.

With two groups added to the three that have already been suggested, the chroniclers of the Conquest will be discussed below under five headings.

COMPILERS

Pedro Mártir

This group comprises those who wrote about the New World without having actually visited it. The first, Pedro Mártir de Anglería, was the father of American history. He was born in Arona, near Anghiera, in the duchy of Milan, on February 2, 1457, and went to Spain in 1487. A humanist and writer, he occupied high positions under the Catholic monarchs and Charles V. Having been named Chronicler of the Indies in 1510, he wrote his *De Orbe Novo*, a History of the New World, divided into eight parts. This was published at Alcalá in its entirety for the first time in 1530, four years after his death in Granada.

Pedro Mártir shared with the men of his century an immense interest in the newly discovered continent. He was eager to read the news; he studied the diaries, sea charts, and narratives of the first navigators and conquistadors, with whom he made personal contact. "For this reason," says Icazbalceta, "his books contain much information that may be sought in vain elsewhere." His wise spirit penetrated to the bottom of things; he discovered relationships and understood consequences.

He is not an eyewitness, but his great faculty for isolating the truth makes his work deserve a considerable degree of confidence. As Las Casas has said, "If his books contain any falsehoods, these ought to be attributed to the difficulty of verifying incidents which occurred at so great a distance, and, especially, to haste and carelessness in writing." Since he did not intend his works for the public, he never attempted to revise or correct them. Written at various times and in different places, they suffer from lack of plan and from some few contradictions. In spite of all defects, however, they stand as one of the unique documents for the history of the New World.

De Orbe Novo carries the story of the Spanish conquest down only to the death of Cristóbal de Olid in Honduras.

López de Gómara

Concerning the second of this group, Francisco López de Gómara, little information is available. A member of a distinguished family, he was born in Gómara, in the province of Soria, in 1511, and died there about 1566. He occupied the chair of rhetoric in the University of Alcalá, was ordained as a priest, went to Rome, and on his return to Spain entered the service of Hernán Cortés as private chaplain, accepting that post in 1540, when the conqueror returned from the New World. At that time, intending to flatter his master, he began to write his *General History of the Indies*. He accompanied Cortés on his expedition to Algeria; and, when Cortés died, he served under the conqueror's son, Don Martín. Nothing further is known of him, not even the year or place of his death.

Never having been in America, Gómara drew the material for his book from the narratives of Cortés and other conquistadors and from information furnished by sailors and travelers. He divided his history into two parts: in the first, he described the discovery and conquest of the Indies in general, up to 1552, omitting New Spain; in the second, he dealt exclusively with the Conquest of Mexico. Although he was a man of evident scholarly training, he departed from the conventions habitually followed by the humanists in portraying great deeds and was able to achieve genuine originality. Except when he was discussing his idol, Hernán Cortés, he weighed information carefully and was judicious in his appraisals, idealizing neither the conquerors nor the conquered. His style is easy and agreeable. But his chronicle contains numerous errors; and its one great defect— bluntly attacked later by Bernal Díaz del Castillo—is that it seems to have been written solely as a eulogy of Cortés and entirely overlooks the part played by Cortés' soldiers.

The first edition of Gómara's work was published in Zaragoza in 1552. This was followed in 1553 and 1554 by another edition in Spain and one in Antwerp; shortly afterward, it was translated into Italian, French, and English, and disseminated throughout Europe. The work, however, was proscribed by edict of the Spanish king in 1553—almost as soon as it appeared—and its distribution prohibited in the mother country. Because of this fact and the singular popularity of Bernal Díaz' famous history, Gómara's work was forgotten until 1727, at which time, the ban having been lifted, the scholarly Don Andrés González Barcia included it—though sadly mutilated—in his *Collection of Primitive Historians of the West Indies*. Only one edition of

Gómara's work—likewise mutilated—has been issued in Mexico; this was a two-volume edition, published in 1826 by Don Carlos María de Bustamante. Until recently the edition considered to be the best modern one was that published in *Primitive Historians of the Indies,* in the *Biblioteca de Rivadeneyra;* but the one which is now considered the outstanding edition was published in Mexico in 1943 by Editorial Robredo, with introduction and notes by Joaquín Ramírez Cabañas.

Herrera and Solís

Don Antonio de Herrera y Tordesillas (1549-1625), third of this group, was official Chronicler of the Indies and of Castile. From his pen came the *Décadas* [ten books] *or General History of the Deeds of the Castilians on the Islands and the Mainland of the Atlantic,* published in 1601 and commonly known as *General History of the Indies.* This work tells the story of the New World from the discovery up to 1554. Compiled by a humanist, pompous and with scarcely any critical sense, a man who never set foot in the New World, the book draws its material chiefly from *The Chronicle of New Spain* by Cervantes de Salazar.

Herrera's successor as Chronicler of the Indies, Don Antonio de Solís (1610-1686), also depended upon the experience of others for his knowledge of the Conquest. His *History of the Conquest of Mexico* was famous in its day, but—in the judgment of Icazbalceta—it is "a high-flown eulogy of Cortés; a beautiful piece of literature, perhaps, but not the history of the Conquest that the Spanish people desired in vain for long years."

CONQUISTADORS

This group comprises, for the most part, soldiers who, temporarily exchanging their swords for pens or turning to literature in their last days, narrated the exploits in which they had been actors or witnesses.

Cortés

Hernán Cortés (1485-1547), the first of these, had no intention of writing a history of his achievements when he composed his long letters to Emperor Charles V between 1519 and 1526. There are five of these, and they are known under the title of *Cartas de Relación sobre el Descubrimiento y Conquista de la Nueva España (Letters Reporting the Discovery and Conquest of New Spain)*. They have the freshness characteristic of letters and the vigor of an eyewitness account. Though their language is simple and colloquial, they produce an effect of magnificence because of the nature of the events described. The style is not that of a soldier but is clear and polished, a characteristic that reflects the author's study of the humanities at Salamanca. The *Letters* have been compared to Caesar's *Commentaries*. Cortés differs from Caesar, however, in his sympathy for the conquered people and in the delight with which he describes not only the military expedition—which he directed from the time of his arrival at Cozumel until his journey to Honduras—but also the institutions, people, customs, and folkways encountered in those fabulous countries. These elements make his letters doubly interesting, and they arouse the imagination so much by the description of marvelous but most real incidents that sometimes they seem like fiction.

The letters have had a remarkable history. Soon after they were written, the second, third, and fourth were published in Spain and were read avidly throughout Europe. They were translated into Italian and Latin before the end of the sixteenth century. Archbishop Lorenzana published them in Mexico in 1770, and a French translation of this edition appeared in 1778. But the first and fifth letters were lost for over two hundred years and finally were found in the Imperial Library in Vienna. In 1852 the first complete collection was published in Madrid, when Don Enrique de Vedia included it among the great Spanish works in the *Biblioteca de Rivadeneyra*.

Fernández de Oviedo

Gonzalo Fernández de Oviedo y Valdés (1478-1557), second of this group, took up the writing of history in his old age, when he was appointed Chronicler of the Indies. A native of Madrid, he had participated in the siege of Granada, fought under Gonzalo de Córdoba in Italy, and served in the Indies, after 1513, as a soldier and as warden of the fortress of Santo Domingo in Haiti. The first part of his *General and Natural History of the Indies* was published in Seville in 1535; but the two remaining parts—one of which dealt with the Conquest of Mexico—were not published during his lifetime, probably because of the efforts of his enemy, Las Casas. These were finally published by Amador de los Ríos during the years 1851-55. Oviedo's voluminous work contains useful data but is of no value for historical criticism.

Bernal Díaz

Concerning the remarkable life and deeds of the famous captain Bernal Díaz del Castillo, third of these chroniclers, history records little beyond what is included in his own writings. He was born in 1492—the memorable year of the discovery of America—at Medina del Campo, and in 1514 he came to the New World as a soldier under Pedrarias Dávila, governor and captain-general of Darién (Panama), the man who a short time later became the cruel executioner of Vasco Núñez de Balboa. Having received permission to go to Cuba, Bernal Díaz remained there three years under Diego Velázquez. After taking part in the expeditions of Hernández de Córdoba and Juan de Grijalva, he enlisted under Hernán Cortés, at whose side he became eyewitness and actor in the fabulous adventures of the Conquest, from the embarkation at Santa María, on February 18, 1519, to the disastrous expedition to Honduras. At last, worn out by the hardships of the 110 battles in which he fought, he retired to Santiago in Guatemala, where he served as *regidor* (alderman) and lived in comparative poverty to an advanced age. The date of his death is not known.

At the age of seventy, without any documents and with only his prodigious memory to draw on, Bernal Díaz began his history of the Conquest. Just as he was beginning to write, copies of the chronicles by Paulo Giovio, López de Gómara, and Gonzalo de Illescas came into his hands; and, finding that all these chronicles had a tendency to give exclusive credit to Cortés for the daring feats of the Conquest and had nothing to tell about the merits of his companions, the old soldier, gloomy and resentful, expanded the original plan of his work to include not only the story of the Conquest but also corrections of the errors and erroneous tendencies of those who wrote only from hearsay. He finished his work in 1568 and called it *The True History of the Conquest of New Spain.* Two copies were made and probably corrected: one was sent to Spain for printing—an unrealized dream; the other stayed in Guatemala as a precaution against loss of the first.

This marvelous and unique chronicle captivates as much by its powerful and rough style as by its dazzling and picturesque contents.

Because of his naturalness of expression, his passionate love of truth, and the living warmth in his pages, Bernal Díaz gives the impression of being not an author who narrates and comments, but an old soldier talking directly to the reader and telling his adventures in a familiar and impressive way. "This chronicle," says Pereyra,

> is formed of the stuff that makes immortal books; it was written with dominating passion, flashing imagination, and the will that concedes nothing to the infirmities of the body or the crushing griefs of the soul. It is history par excellence; it is the only kind of history that deserves to live; it is history in the etymological sense: the testimony of deeds accomplished.

Without detracting from the merits of Cortés, Bernal Díaz retrieves for himself and his comrades the glory that belongs to them. Scenes and characters surge into his pages. The conquistadors march past as living men. He speaks dispassionately and sometimes with sympathy and praise of the conquered. He paints the real battles that he fought. And with emotions stirred by the strange, new world that he saw, he makes the Indians themselves, their customs and ways, spring to life.

For long years this matchless chronicle remained unpublished. The first edition was printed in Madrid in 1632 by Friar Alonso Remón, who, having found the original manuscript—the one used by Herrera in his *segunda década* (second book)—and recognizing its merit, decided to save it from oblivion. Unfortunately, however, Remón did not reproduce the original faithfully. He introduced falsehoods and was guilty of making changes, omissions, suppressions, and capricious interpolations. His version was translated into the principal modern languages and for many years was the only known text. In 1904, the Mexican historian Don Genaro García obtained an exact and complete copy of the original autographed manuscript from the Municipal Archives of Guatemala and prepared a new edition from this. Neither his edition nor Remón's, however, gives Bernal Díaz' original text in its completeness: Remón corrupted his, and García followed a text that had been prepared for the printer and changed considerably, presumably by the author himself. When a third copy of the *True History* became available, Editorial Robredo published, in 1939, an edition entitled *True History of the Conquest of New Spain*, in three volumes, with introduction and notes by Joaquín Ramírez Cabañas. More recently, Editorial Porrúa published, in their *Biblioteca Porrúa*, two editions—one in 1955 and the other in 1960—authorized by Joaquín Ramírez Cabañas, of the work originally published by Editorial Robredo.

"*The Anonymous Conquistador*"

The fourth of these chroniclers is an unknown man whom Clavijero was the first to call "The Anonymous Conquistador." His work, a curious document, was written soon after the Conquest and, under the title of *Relazione d'un gentiluomo di Ferdinando Cortés*, included in the third volume of the collection published in 1556 by Juan Bautista Ramusio, the celebrated Venetian traveler and publicist. Although brief, this account of the conditions in New Spain is priceless. No Spanish version is known, and doubtless the work would have been lost if Ramusio had not translated it into Italian. Don Carlos María de Bustamante, with some lightness, presumably without having seen the original and certainly without producing any proof, stated that the author was the poet Francisco de Terrazas. This statement has never been verified, and, in reality, there exist no data either to prove or disprove it.

It is now generally agreed that the Anonymous Conquistador was a companion in arms of Cortés and that, being more impressed by the life and customs of the Indians than by the incidents of the war, he wrote a picturesque account of their culture. According to Clavijero,

His description is quaint and accurate. Without mentioning the events of the Conquest, he tells what he saw in the temples, the homes, the tombs; he describes the weapons, clothes, food, drinks, etc., of the Indians; he clearly depicts the architecture of their temples. If his work were not so brief, it would have no equal among the descriptions of Mexican antiquities.

Ternaux-Compans translated Ramusio's version into French. The first Spanish version was made by García Icazbalceta, who published it in Volume I of his *Collection of Documents for the History of Mexico* (1858).

Suárez de Peralta

The fifth in this group is Juan Suárez de Peralta, a man fond of equine sports and possessing great knowledge of everything connected with horses and horsemanship. He would not figure among these annalists had it not been for the discovery of an interesting manuscript which the Spanish bibliophile Don Justo Zaragoza found, covered by the dust of three centuries, in the provincial library of Toledo, and published in 1878 under the abbreviated title *Historic News of New Spain*.

Suárez de Peralta was born in Mexico City sometime between 1535 and 1540. His father, one of the first colonists of New Spain and close friend and favorite of Hernán Cortés, is presumed to have been the Juan Suárez who was a brother of Doña Catalina, Cortés' first wife; at any rate, it is known with certainty that he was the first *encomendero* (government agent) at Tamazulapa. Suárez de Peralta probably spent his youth in Mexico, living the idle, carefree, and boisterous life of a conquistador's son. With other such boys he no doubt shared his delight in horsemanship, an art cultivated then as now by every gentleman, including the Viceroy Don Luis de Velasco, who, he said, "was a very graceful man on horseback." With the flower of Mexican youth, he took part in the spectacular and ruinous fiestas given in honor of Don Martín Cortés, second Marquis of the Valley, on the latter's arrival in 1563. About this time, he married the daughter of the conquistador Alonso de Villanueva Tordesillas. He was eyewitness to the conflicts and tragic incidents that resulted from the residence of Cortés' son in New Spain. With his property diminished or himself worn out, perhaps, by the troubles of that agitated period (which he was later to summarize in one of his books), he emigrated to Spain in 1579.

There, in Seville, during the following year, Suárez de Peralta published his *Tratado de la Caballería de la Gineta y Brida (Treatise on Two Styles of Horsemanship: La Gineta and la Brida)*, and he composed his *Libro de Alveitería (Book of Veterinary Science)*, which is still unpublished in the National Library at Madrid. He remained in Spain until 1589, the year in which he completed his *Treatise on the Discovery of the Indies and Their Conquest* and Don Luis de Velasco II was named viceroy. It is presumed that he returned to Mexico because of his friendship for the viceroy, but there is no definite information on that point or concerning the place and date of his death.

"If Bernal Díaz del Castillo," observes Artemio de Valle-Arizpe, "is the captain of the chroniclers, Don Juan Suárez de Peralta is the brilliant standard-bearer because of the agreeable simplicity of his writings and the salty tang of his style, full of movement and charm." Certainly he occupies an exceptional, perhaps unique, position among the chroniclers of New Spain. Though, as he himself said, he "had little grammar but much delight in reading history and meeting learned people," he had the happy knack of describing vividly everything he saw in the dramatic epoch in which he lived. So far as style is concerned, his work reveals a great natural gift: the ability to use with distinctive art the everyday, spoken language of the creoles and to make his pages reflect the vivid impressions of an observer curious about not only the great political events but the details of living, the customs of the people of his day. From the philological, psychological, and historical points of view, his *Historic News of New Spain* is a delightful book; for one who wants to penetrate into the intimacies of private life in the viceroyalty and see the social customs of that day, there is no book like it.

Suárez de Peralta's historical treatise, which deals with the history of the New World from "the origin and beginning of the Indies and the Indians" to the time of Viceroy Don Martín Enríquez, is of uneven value. When he writes of things he saw, the events of his own day, he is beyond praise; but when he presents material drawn from hearsay or from his limited reading, he is mediocre, at times inaccurate, and often repeats badly what others had already said well. His sole interest, obviously, was in contemporary life. If he hardly interests us when he describes the Indies or the customs and idolatries that the conquistadors encountered, he nevertheless has no equal in picturing the reign of the second viceroy and the life of that time. Without losing his simplicity and naturalness, speaking with the accents of an actual spectator, he stirs deep feelings when he tells the story of the rebellion attributed to the second Marquis of the Valley, and, especially, when he describes the execution of the Avila brothers. Equally moving and picturesque are the chapters narrating the landing of John Hawkins at San Juan de Ulúa and the capture of the English pirates.

Baltasar de Obregón

Lastly, mention should be made of Baltasar de Obregón, born in Mexico City in 1544, author of a *History of the Ancient and Modern*

Discoveries of New Spain (not published until 1924, although it was written in 1584), and whom Padre Mariano Cuevas calls "the first historian of Mexican manners and customs."

MISSIONARIES

By far the largest group of the early chroniclers belonged to religious orders. They were principally missionaries who took time from their rigorous task of evangelization to gather valuable data on the history and ethnography of Mexico. Fortunately, they put into writing not only what they learned from observation but all they gleaned from oral tradition in their daily contacts with the Indians. With the help of the natives, they also attempted to interpret the ancient hieroglyphics, the only written records left by the primitive peoples of Mexico.

Las Casas

Friar Bartolomé de las Casas, the first of this group, was born in Seville in 1474 and died in Madrid, at the age of ninety-two, in 1566. Son of a soldier who had accompanied Columbus on his first voyage to the New World, he studied in Salamanca and voyaged to the Indies in 1502. For eight years he was engaged in farming on the island of Haiti. It was not, however, his destiny to till the soil, but to protect those who did. Accordingly, he embraced the priesthood in 1510 and, in Cuba, dedicated himself to missionary work. In 1514, indignant at the system of *repartimientos* (which involved the parceling out of Indians for forced labor) and believing that the conquerors treated the natives unjustly and tyrannically, he determined to devote his life to their protection and defense. Renouncing his lands, he protested in behalf of the Indians before the civil and the ecclesiastical authorities of Spain. He instigated investigations, devised new systems of colonization, and attempted unsuccessfully to establish colonies. Indefatigable, he traveled back and forth between the New and the Old World. To his tenacity are credited the New Laws, which checked the unbridled cruelty of the conquerors. A Dominican after 1523, bishop of Chiapas when he was seventy years old, preaching as much by example as by word, involved continually in lawsuits and arguments, threatened, persecuted, hated, loved, he lived for one idea: to erect above the ruins of oppression the Indian's right to a free life.

Because of this, his figure, fighting and ardent, stands brilliantly against the horizon of the dramatic sixteenth century. Because of this, he belongs to the history of human liberty, rather than to the history of literature.

Las Casas wrote three books: *History of the Indies,* which deals with events from Columbus' voyage to 1520 and was first published in 1875-76; *Historia Apologética* (published in 1909), a supplement to the former; and the famous *Brief Report of the Destruction of the Indies,* which was addressed to Emperor Charles V, was printed in Seville in 1552, and caused a tremendous sensation. Modern criticism questions the historical value of Las Casas' work; it considers him a fanatical theorist who, pledging himself to demonstrate that the Indians were models of virtue until they were corrupted by the Spaniards, launched himself into a realm of fancy, without bothering to consider facts. It should be insisted, however, that he was the champion of a cause, not a historian. "No doubt he exaggerated," Don Justo Sierra says,

the natural goodness of the Indians and the wickedness of their exploiters, but not so much as others have. But, even so, the men who blacken the picture of evil for a good purpose are necessary in periods of crisis, for through them a remedy, even though it may be inadequate, is hastened.

Motolinia

Friar Toribio de Benavente (Motolinia), the second of this group, was a native of Benavente, in Zamora. His real name was Toribio Paredes, but, following the custom of the day, he changed it for the name of his native town when he took the habit of St. Francis in the Province of Santiago. He was already a renowned preacher and confessor when he was ordered to leave for New Spain with the first twelve Franciscans sent to the New World. Under the leadership of Friar Martín de Valencia, they disembarked at Veracruz in May, 1524, and, barefooted, began the long journey to the City of Mexico. En route, they stopped to rest at Tlaxcala. According to Mendieta, it was market day, and they were astonished "at seeing as great a multitude of people as they had ever seen in one place"; consequently, they "thanked God joyfully for the huge harvest that lay before them." The natives, walking behind the friars and wondering at their humble manner and threadbare clothes, exclaimed, *"Motolinia! Motolinia!"* which in their language meant "poor one" or "poor ones." Not knowing the meaning of the word, Friar Toribio asked a Spaniard what it meant. Upon hearing the meaning, he declared, "This is the first word that I know in their language, and that I may not forget it, it shall be my name henceforth."

The friar's work in the new country was like that of many of his illustrious companions: it consisted of learning the native language, engaging with fiery zeal in the work of evangelization, and—so far as possible—protecting the Indians from oppression. Referring to the Indian name adopted by Toribio, as well as to the remarkable man who bore it, Bernal Díaz writes:

It means "the poor friar," because whatever he was given, he gave in the name of God to the Indians, and often went hungry, and wore tattered clothes, and walked barefooted, and preached continually; and the Indians loved him greatly because he was a holy man.

Tireless and fiery was Motolinia's life in New Spain. Hardly had he arrived and assumed his work as *guardián* (superior of Franciscan monasteries) at the side of Friar Martín de Valencia, when Cortés led his expedition to Honduras, and it fell to Motolinia's lot to be the principal actor in the terrible struggle, beginning in 1525, with the criminal and despotic *Audiencia*. With Cortés absent, the appetites and cupidities of his men were unloosed. When these stern men abused their power, it was the Franciscans who defied them and disregarded hatred and persecution, calumnies and threats, to protect the Indians. Motolinia himself says,

The friars put on patience as a shield against the insults of the Spaniards; and when the latter became angry and accused the friars of endangering the country by taking sides with the Indians, the friars, to lessen the anger of their countrymen, answered patiently: "If we did not defend the Indians, you would soon have no one to serve you. If we favor them, it is to preserve them so that you will have someone to work for you. In defending and teaching them, we are really serving you and easing your consciences; for, when you took charge of them, you also became responsible for teaching them. You care for nothing except that they work for you and give you everything they possess."

And he added, like a stroke of lightning, "The souls of these Indians cost Jesus Christ no less than those of Spaniards and Romans . . .!"

Motolinia was a man of action as well as words. In April, 1529, to prevent the *Audiencia* from imprisoning the principal Indian chiefs and their families, he gave refuge to them in his monastery at Huexot-zingo. His determined attitude and his firmness in resisting oppression and injustice sometimes gave his enemies an opportunity to slander him. In August of the same year, he was falsely accused of conspiracy. If the charge contained any element of truth, the reason for it, as Ramírez says, "would be the intolerable despotism and disorder in the government of the royal officials."

The activities of Motolinia as missionary and bringer of civilization extended beyond New Spain to Guatemala, Nicaragua, and Yucatán. Acquainted with the languages and customs of the Indians, intense and fearless, he traveled hundreds of miles on foot (he confessed that he walked over a thousand miles on the trip from Mexico to Nica-ragua), and there was no village where he did not preach, say mass, teach and baptize children and adults. Strong and robust, he was continually busy on his ceaseless apostolic journeys. Of the difficulties of travel, he wrote:

Some villages are high in the mountains; others are in the depths of valleys. It is therefore necessary for the friars to go up into the clouds (some of the mountains are always covered with clouds) and at other times to go down into the abysses, and, since the land lies deep and in many places is muddy and slippery, walking is difficult. Consequently, the poor friars cannot travel these paths without great effort and fatigue.

He established several convents, one of them at Atlixco. He also took the principal part in the founding of Puebla, which he called the City of the Angels; he had a hand in laying out the city and said the first mass there on April 16, 1530. He was the sixth provincial of his order in New Spain and *guardián* of Texcoco and Tlaxcala. A man of great and remarkable virtues, not the least being his humility and limitless love for humanity, he was indefatigable in his perseverance and ac-tivity—of all the missionaries he "was the one who covered the most ground." He died, laden with years and in the fragrance of sainthood, in the convent of San Francisco de México on August 10, 1568, and was buried there. He had arrived with the first of the Franciscans, and he outlived them all. "He is," as Icazbalceta wisely says, "the most admirable and the most representative of the Spanish missionaries of the sixteenth century."

It would be difficult to make an exact and complete bibliography of Motolinia's works. The following are attributed to him: *War of the Indians of New Spain, Highway of the Spirit, Treatises on Spiritual and Devotional Matters, Christian Doctrine in the Mexican Language, The Coming of the First Twelve Fathers and What They Achieved Here, Memoranda, History of the Indians of New Spain, Letter from Friar Toribio de Motolinia and Friar Diego de Olarte to Don Luis de Velasco, Viceroy of New Spain, Regarding the Tributes Paid by the Indians Before Their Conversion* (signed in San Francisco de Cholula on August 27, 1554), and *Letter to Emperor Charles V* (dated January 2, 1555, at Tlaxcala). Only the last four of the above-mentioned works are known today; the sole information about the others has been preserved by the historians. A good part of the contents of the *Memoranda* (published in Mexico in 1903 by Don Luis García Pimentel) may also be found in his *History of the Indians of New Spain*. In regard to the letters, the one addressed to the viceroy was published by Ternaux-Compans in his *Voyages,* and the other was included by Friar Daniel Sánchez García in his edition of the *History of the Indians of New Spain* (Barcelona, 1914).

The *History* is Motolinia's most important work, the only one that in breadth and quality deserves the name of literature. It was published, incomplete and under another title, in Lord Kingsborough's *Antiquities of Mexico* (1848), but the first complete text was printed by Don García Icazbalceta in Volume I of his *Colección de Documentos para la Historia de México*. It is thought that the *History* is the oldest book written about New Spain. Motolinia began to write it in 1536, when he was *guardián* at Tlaxcala, doing the work in leisure hours when he should have been resting. It was written without any desire for literary fame, and he intended that his name should not be connected with it. "If this report," he wrote to the Count of Benavente, "should leave the hands of Your Illustrious Lordship, I beg of you two things, for the love of Our Lord: first, that this be attributed to a minor friar, without any name being given. . . ." The work is divided into three parts: the first deals with the religion, rites, and sacrifices of the Aztecs; the second, with their conversion to Christianity and their manner of celebrating the festivals of the

Church; the third, with the temper and character of the Aztec nation, its system of chronology and astronomy, together with information concerning some of the cities and the most abundant products in the country.

As historian, Motolinia is distinguished by two qualities: truthfulness and discretion. He was far from being credulous, and he used great caution. He affirmed nothing (except in regard to miraculous happenings, in which he believed with lovable frankness) unless he had been convinced through personal experience. He wrote with graceful facility and naturalness. People, customs, and landscapes are painted with sobriety and eloquence. He had—and this is extraordinary—a profound political insight: in 1540 he anticipated the prophecy that the Count of Aranda was to make two centuries later regarding the destinies of the colonies of America. Nevertheless, his work has the fault common to the works of most of the sixteenth-century chroniclers: it lacks plan and orderliness. He included information about all that he observed and found most interesting, but his work is at times incoherent and confused because he brusquely cuts the thread of his narrative to insert an anecdote. Notwithstanding, his *History* is an arsenal of data; and, in regard to Aztec antiquities, Motolinia is considered an authority of the first rank. Further information about him is found in the excellent *Life of Motolinia* by José Fernández Ramírez, in the *Collection of Mexican Writers* published by Editorial Porrúa.

Sahagún

The third of this group, Friar Bernardino de Sahagún (born Bernardino Ribeira), took the name of his native town, Sahagún, in the kingdom of León, where he was born probably in the last year of the fifteenth century.

He studied in Salamanca. He was of fine appearance; his portrait, preserved in the National Museum, reveals him as a type of delicate, spiritual beauty. While very young, he took the habit of St. Francis in the old university city where he had been a student. He came to New Spain in 1529 with nineteen other friars brought over by Friar Antonio de Ciudad Rodrigo, and immediately consecrated himself, with ardor and intelligence, to the study of the Nahuatlan language. During the voyage to America, he had already begun his study with some Indians who, having been taken to Spain by Cortés, were being returned to their own land by order of the Emperor. Having arrived in Mexico, he continued to study until he knew the language perfectly.

The first years of his residence in Mexico were spent in the monastery of Tlalmanalco, and it was at this time that he made his expedition to Popocatépetl and Ixtaccíhuatl. Pursuing the duties of his order, he walked through the Valley of Puebla and Michoacán. It is supposed that he served as *guardián* of the monastery of Xochimilco. The longest and perhaps most fertile period of his life, however, was spent in the school of Santa Cruz de Tlaltelolco. Shortly after that school was founded in 1536, he became professor of Latin, his students being young Indians of the leading native families, and he remained in that position until 1540. Years later, probably in 1570, he returned to the school and, dedicating himself to teaching, administrative work, and historical studies, remained there until the day of his death. He died in the cloister of San Francisco de México on February 5, 1590.

Sahagún did a tremendous amount of writing, and a bibliography of his work is hard to establish. "He spent nearly fifty years in writing," Icazbalceta says,

and he not only wrote many works but gave divers forms to them, correcting, amplifying, re-editing, sometimes extracting sections or disconnected parts and issuing them as distinct books. He wrote now in Spanish, now in Nahuatlan; and sometimes he added a Latin version or gave two forms to the Nahuatlan.

His books reflect the three fields of his activities: evangelism, philology, and history. Of the religious type, he wrote: *Epistles and Gospels for the Sabbath in the Nahuatlan Language, Sermons, Evangeliarum, Epistolarium et lectionarium,* a *Life of San Bernardino of the Seine as Written in the Chronicles of the Order* (translated into the Nahuatlan language), *Daily Exercises in the Nahuatlan Language, Manual for the Christian, Christian Doctrine in Nahuatlan, Treatise on the Theological Virtues Written in the Nahuatlan Language, Book on the Coming of the First Fathers and the Talks They Had with the Priests of the Idols, Catechism of the Christian Doctrine, Christian Psalmody,* and many separate treatises on diverse questions, such as *Post-baptismal Talks to Children, Spiritual Light, Spiritual Guidance,*

Precepts for Married People, Hindrances to Marriage, Doctrine for Physicians, etc., etc. In the field of philology, the following works are on record: an *arte* of the Nahuatlan language; a *Trilingual Dictionary: in Castilian, Latin, and Nahuatlan;* and a *Calepino* (Latin dictionary), which is not extant and probably formed a part of his *History.*

All this enormous output is, in a sense, unknown. Of the whole group, the only work published during Sahagún's life was the *Christian Psalmody.* Some of the other works exist in manuscript, but many have been lost and are known only through the references made to them by historians.

The *General History of the Things of New Spain* is Sahagún's outstanding work. Presenting a prodigious pageant of the customs, beliefs, and arts of the ancient Aztecs, the book is an encyclopedia rather than a real history; it is, in the words of Icazbalceta, "an inexhaustible treasury of information" concerning the principal Indian race.

The author spent a great part of his life in writing this book. Having planned the book, he was transferred in 1557 to the town of Tepeapulco; and there, from the lips of aged Indians and from four of his former students at Tlaltelolco, he obtained much of the information he wished to record. This furnished the basis for the first version of his history, which he completed in about two years. After going to Mexico City to attend a meeting of the Chapter of his order in 1560, he returned to Santiago Tlaltelolco and gathered around him a group of eight or ten Indians who were "very proficient in their language and in the antiquities of their race." With these and four or five trilingual students, he shut himself up in the school and for more than a year corrected and expanded what he had written at Tepeapulco, making a new and complete copy "even though it was almost illegible because it was written with such haste." This was the second version of the work. Later he was transferred to a monastery of his order in the City of Mexico, and there for three years he went over and over his work, dividing it into twelve books and each book into chapters and some of the chapters into shorter sections. When a suitable copy was made, it was further edited and added to by various Indian scribes, who completed their part in 1569. This was the third manuscript or text. According to Icazbalceta, it "comprised the

Nahuatlan text of the work, and seems to have been definitive—at least, its author so regarded it."

Having finished the history to this point, the hardworking friar asked that some monks be designated to pass on it. The critics concluded that the book was of much value and that the Spanish version, which probably had already been begun, should be completed. Someone in the Chapter, however, protested against spending money on scribes to do the clerical work, saying that this was contrary to the Franciscans' vow of poverty. Consequently, the author was directed to dismiss his assistants, but was left at liberty to write as much as he pleased. But since he was then seventy years old and his hands trembled so that he could not write, the work remained unfinished for more than five years. In an effort to get aid, Sahagún drew up a summary of the *History* and sent it to Spain in 1570 by Friars Miguel Navarro and Jerónimo de Mendieta. In a "Notice to the Reader," in one of the prologues accompanying the summary, he stated:

The Spanish version and the glossaries are not complete because I have not been able to do more without assistance. If the necessary aid is given me, it can all be finished in a year or so; and, certainly, if it were finished, it would be a treasury for one who wished to know many worthy things, to be well-informed, and to learn easily this language with all its secrets. It would be a work of great value to both New and Old Spain.

Meanwhile, although the *History* had not been printed, it was known to many monks because in the same year, 1570, the Provincial, Friar Alonso de Escalona, took the separate sections of the work and "scattered them throughout the province." It is a miracle that they were not lost then and there, and, also, that three years later Friar Miguel Navarro (having returned to Mexico as *Comisario*) was able to collect every one of the parts and place them again in the hands of the author in 1574. Finally, in the following year or early in 1576, the new *Comisario*, Friar Rodrigo Sequera, arrived in Mexico with an order from Juan de Ovando, president of the Council of the Indies, for a copy of the work, the summary of which interested him. Sequera ordered the author to complete the translation and make a new copy in two columns, one in Nahuatlan and the other in Spanish. This was the first manuscript to be written in both languages, and the fourth version of the *History*.

As painful as the composition of the *History* was the fate that pursued it. Ovando having died in 1575, the Council of the Indies ordered that all originals and copies of the *History* be collected and sent to Spain; and the King repeated the order in July, 1578. Sahagún, touched, thinking perhaps they were asking for his book in order to print it, had written to the monarch on March 26 of that year saying that he understood both from the viceroy and from the *Comisario* that they had sent the four volumes of the work; but, he added, "If they did not send them, I humbly beg Your Majesty to inform me so that a new copy may be made and this opportunity may not be lost, nor the memorable things of New Spain left to oblivion."

Poor Sahagún! The opportunity was already lost; the oblivion lasted more than two centuries, and even today it partly exists.

Philip II passed the author's letter on to the Council, and on September 18 that body ordered coldly, "By this decree let the Viceroy send whatever remains there, both copies and originals. Let him send all, without leaving any copy there."

What motivated such an extreme and absurd order? What happened to the various manuscripts of Sahagún's work? What was done with the different versions? The copy sent by the viceroy in 1578 arrived at its destination. But what became of it? Likewise, it seems evident, according to Icazbalceta, that the copy in Nahuatlan and Spanish ordered by Father Sequera in 1575-77 was carried off by him. But since Ovando, who had requested it, was then dead and it could not be delivered to him, what happened to *it*?

These are enigmas of Mexican literary history that have never been solved.

For two centuries the work of Sahagún remained forgotten; but in 1779 Don Juan Bautista Muñoz, having been named Historian of the Indies and commissioned to write the "General History of America," began a search for Sahagún's work, and he learned that a copy of it existed in the Franciscan monastery of Tolosa, in the province of Cantabria. He went there in April, 1783, armed with a royal order, and secured the old manuscript, a folio containing only the Spanish text of the twelve books. It corresponds to none of the manuscripts mentioned by Sahagún, nor does it bear his signature. According to Icazbalceta, "The original from which this Spanish part was copied might well have been Father Sequera's manuscript, which in all probability is the one to be found today in the Laurenziana Library in Florence."

From this Tolosan manuscript, the first three published editions of Sahagún's work were made: the first, that of Don Carlos María de Bustamante, was published in Mexico in 1829-30; the second, Lord Kingsborough's, was included in the collection already cited; and the third, that of Don Ireneo Paz (1890-95), was a reproduction of Bustamante's text. All are defective. Bustamante made the mistake of publishing the twelfth book by itself in 1829, in a quarto volume; later he published the eleven remaining books in three volumes. He made serious alterations and suppressions, and scattered puerile comments throughout. Nevertheless, he is entitled to credit for being the first published of Sahagún's great work. More recently, an excellent five-volume edition of the *General History of the Things of New Spain* has been published by Don Pedro Robredo (Mexico, 1938). Profiting by the studies made by Paso y Troncoso, Jourdanet, Rémi Siméon, and Seler, Robredo corrected the errors and filled in the gaps in Bustamante's and Kingborough's editions.

In 1956 Editorial Porrúa published a new edition of Sahagún's *General History,* edited by Padre Angel María Garibay K., who revised the text, basing his revisions on the Florentine manuscript, corrected the spelling of Nahuatl words, divided the history into marginal paragraphs to facilitate locating material, and wrote a fourth volume containing abundant material which extends the scope of Sahagún's work.

Cervantes de Salazar

Francisco Cervantes de Salazar, fourth of this group, a man possessing many titles to fame in the history of Mexican literature, was born in Toledo, in either 1513 or 1514. He studied the humanities in his native city and canon law at Salamanca. While very young, he performed official duties of unknown nature in Flanders, and served as Latin secretary to Cardinal García de Loaysa on his return to Spain. Proof that he enjoyed fame as a Latin scholar even at that time is supplied by a volume printed in 1546 at Alcalá de Henares by Juan de Brocar. It is entitled *Works That Francisco Cervantes de Salazar Has Made, Glossed, and Translated,* and is divided into three parts. The first includes a "Dialogue on the Dignity of Man," which was begun by Master Hernán Pérez de Oliva and completed by Cervantes de Salazar, who dedicated it to Cortés. The second part contains the "Apology for Idleness and Work" by the prothonotary Luis Mexía, to which Cervantes de Salazar prefixed an original introduction, "Argument and Morality of the Work," and which he elaborated in scholarly notes. The last part comprises the famous "Introduction to Wisdom," written in Latin by Juan Luis Vives and translated into Spanish by Cervantes de Salazar.

The publication of this volume seems to have brought neither fame nor money to Cervantes de Salazar. In 1550 he was teaching rhetoric in the University of Osuna; but in the same year or the following, seeking to find employment that would furnish him a living, he emigrated to Mexico.

Modest were his first activities in Mexico; he earned his bread by teaching Latin grammar in a private school. But on the founding of the university—whose studies he inaugurated with a Latin oration on June 3, 1553—he became professor of rhetoric with the meager salary of 150 pesos annually. Student and professor at the same time, he studied the arts and theology with Friar Alonso de la Veracruz, and was graduated as licentiate and Master of Arts "because of ability" on October 4, 1553. In June of the following year, he was examined for the bachelor's degree in canon law; and then, choosing an ecclesiastical career, he received the sacred orders in 1555 before finishing his theological studies, which, nevertheless, he did complete, receiving in due succession three degrees: those of bachelor, licentiate, and doctor.

In April, 1559, he was named chronicler for the City of Mexico by the City Council. After he had made, in 1562, a trip to the mines of Zacatecas, he obtained a canonship in the Archbishopric of Mexico, taking possession of the office on March 16, 1563. But the ecclesiastical calling for Cervantes de Salazar must not have been very strong, for Archbishop Moya de Contreras accused him in a letter of being "frivolous and changeable" and of not being accredited with "honesty and chastity." Having come to the New World as a layman, he probably became a priest by force of circumstances. He doubtless enjoyed the university atmosphere and literary activities more than the shepherding of souls. In addition to rhetoric, he taught decretals and was elected rector of the university in November, 1567. He was holding the latter position the year before his death, which occurred between September and November, 1575.

Besides such books as the *Dialogues* and the *Imperial Tomb* (which will be discussed later), the principal work that entitles Cervantes de Salazar to be considered as historian is his *Chronicle of New Spain*. Though it is certain that he wrote this at the command of the City Council and that the chronicler Antonio de Herrera (who plagiarized it to a great extent) and the bibliographer González Barcia had examined it, the work was considered lost for a long time. The original, or a copy, was sent by the author to Spain in 1567 with a request to the king for the post of Royal Chronicler; but the book, until recently, was unidentified. It was catalogued as an anonymous manuscript in the National Library of Madrid, and the honor of discovering and identifying it has been claimed by two persons: the eminent polygrapher Don Francisco del Paso y Troncoso and the distinguished American scholar Mrs. Zelia Nuttall. The former stated that he made the discovery in 1908; the latter reported to the Congress of Americanists in London, in 1912, that she found the manuscript the year before. Be that as it may, the facts are that the only complete edition of the *Chronicle* is the one published in 1914 under the auspices of the Hispanic Society of America; and that Paso y Troncoso, who, in turn, undertook the publication of the work, printed only the first volume. The two remaining volumes were published in 1936 by the National Museum of Mexico.

The original plan of Cervantes de Salazar was to write a general chronicle of the Indies, dividing it, in imitation of Gómara's work, into two parts: the first was to include everything that happened from the time of Columbus until the conquest of Yucatán, at least; and the second was to give the history of the conquest of New Spain. It is presumed that the author never wrote the first part; and it cannot be definitely concluded that he finished the second part, since the extant portion is incomplete. The fragment of the *Chronicle* consists of six books, the first two describing New Spain and giving an account of its discovery, the other four telling of the conquest of Mexico from the arrival of Cortés at San Juan de Ulúa until he sent Villafuerte and Sandoval to the "Southern Sea" (i.e., the Pacific Ocean). The narrative is broken at this point; of Chapter 34 (the last chapter in Book VI), only the heading remains.

Cervantes de Salazar's *Chronicle of New Spain,* nevertheless, is of the greatest importance, and some critics would even consider it the most valuable historical account of its kind for an understanding and evaluation of the events it describes. In regard to the plan and execution of the work, Cervantes de Salazar suggests the professional man of letters who not only knows what he wishes to say but can express his thoughts artistically; as to style, his clear and vigorous prose reveals he was an accomplished writer.

The principal sources Cervantes de Salazar used in writing his *Chronicle* were the *Letters* of Cortés (whom he had known in Spain); the memoirs of Alonso de Ojeda and Andrés de Tapia, captains in Cortés' army, who took part in nearly all the battles and expeditions led by the conqueror; the *Memoranda* of Motolinia; and the work of López de Gómara, which he always had before him. Without considering some secondary sources, the chief circumstance worth mentioning in this connection is the fact that he lived in the City of Mexico for twenty-five years shortly after the Conquest and had the opportunity to talk with persons who had taken an active part in it; from them he received useful and rare information which he used wisely.

Mendieta

Friar Jerónimo de Mendieta, the fifth of this group, was born in the City of Vitoria, Spain, in 1525, and had the peculiar distinction of being the last of the forty children who were the fruit of the three marriages of his prolific father.

During his early youth, he assumed the habit of the Franciscans in the monastery of Bilbao. He came to New Spain in 1554. In the cloister of Xochimilco, where he was sent, he studied the arts and theology. He gave himself over to the study of the Nahuatlan language, and so thoroughly did he master it that even though he was a stutterer in his native tongue, his words flowed rapidly and smoothly when he preached to the Indians in their language. He stayed some time in Tlaxcala and in Toluca, and between 1564 and 1567 he spent a year traveling through the tropics in the vicinities of Teutitlán, Tlatlauquitepec, and Hueytlapan. He enjoyed great prestige in his Chapter. In 1570 he returned to Spain and lived in the monastery of his native town. At that time he engaged in an interesting corre-

spondence with Don Juan de Ovando, a member of the Council of the
Inquisition, who, recognizing Mendieta's natural ability and knowledge of affairs in the Indies, sought information from him. In these
letters Mendieta expounded original points of view concerning
the social status of the colony and suggested means of improving
conditions there. As a true Franciscan he showed himself to be a
sympathizer with the Indians, for whose well-being and defense he
struggled. "The tone of his correspondence," writes Icazbalceta,

reveals the force of his character: he addressed the King with the same freedom that he would show in talking with a minor official, or perhaps with
greater freedom. The letter he wrote the King in 1565 was an outline of
everything that would weigh on the royal conscience for neglecting the government of the Indies. I doubt that any public official today would tolerate
without an indication of anger the terrible series of charges that he hurled
at the greatest monarch of that century.

In 1573 Mendieta returned to Mexico charged with the task of
writing in Spanish a complete report of the conversion of the Indians.
In spite of his being diligent, it took him twenty-five years to prepare it. He was made *guardián* of his order at Xochimilco, Tepeaca,
and Huexotzingo; he had charge of the monastery of Tlaxcala and
served twice on the governing committee of his order. He showed
himself to be zealous in maintaining efficiency and purity among the
Franciscans. Though he was naturally fiery and energetic, he was, in
his social behavior, long-suffering and restrained. So great was his love
of the Indians, and his desire to protect them, that he was occasionally
unjust to the Spaniards. He was almost eighty years old when he
succumbed to a painful disease on May 10, 1604, and was buried in
his monastery.

Besides the *Letters*—which Icazbalceta published in Volume I of
his *Nueva Colección de Documentos para la Historia de México*
(1886)—the only work which, according to available information,
Mendieta wrote was the *Ecclesiastical History of the Indians*. This
book remained unknown and unpublished for more than two centuries—in fact, until 1870, when it was printed in Mexico through
the efforts of Icazbalceta.

Mendieta divided the *History* into five books. In the first he tells
"of the introduction of the Gospel and Christian faith into Haiti and

the neighboring islands that were discovered first," and discusses the discovery of America, the grant of the Apostolic See, the faint success that the preaching of the gospel had had in the Indies, the rebellion of the Indian chief Enrique, and the Spaniards' cruel treatment of the Indians. The second book treats "of the rites and customs of the Indians of New Spain in their pagan worship." The author was, he said, inspired in writing this by a work—now lost—by Friar Andrés de Olmos and by the writings of Motolinia. In the third book, he describes "the manner in which the faith in our Lord Jesus Christ was introduced and established among the Indians." The fourth deals with "the advancement of the natives and their conversion," the coming of the Dominican and Augustinian friars, the founding of the Province of Michoacán, and the journeys of the missionaries. He tells how the Indians were taught in the school at Tlaltelolco and praises their ability and ingenuity; he discusses the *repartimientos* and abuses of the Spaniards, showing their disregard of their monarchs' orders favoring the Indians; and, finally, after describing the plagues and calamities that the conquered race suffered, he lists the provincials and *comisarios* of his order, the bishops of the different dioceses, items of interest about the Franciscans who wrote in the indigenous languages, and ends with an invective against the Spaniards for the harm which their excessive cupidity did to the spreading of the Gospel and to the cause of good government. His last book, divided into two parts, is an extraordinary repertory of biographical sketches of the missionaries.

The *Ecclesiastical History of the Indians*, in the opinion of Icazbalceta, is a work of singular merit: "The elevated spirit of uprightness and justice dominant in it, the vigor and freedom with which it is written, the clear thinking and good diction heighten the value of the simple, terse narrative, making it delightful reading." If "Mendieta is not an original writer in the strict sense of the word, he shows much originality in the statement of facts and opinions, and deserves a very distinguished place among our historians."

Durán

The Dominican Friar Diego Durán, the sixth of this group, is a man about whom little information has been preserved other than the brief and belittling statement made by the chronicler of his province,

Dávila Padilla, who said: "He was a native of Mexico who wrote two books, one of history and the other of the ancient customs of the Indians; he was sick a great deal and died in 1588."

The learned Mexican Don José Fernando Ramírez, however, thinks Durán was "one of the first fruits of the legitimate marriages of Spaniards to the daughters of the country"; and he concludes that the year of Durán's birth cannot have been later than 1538, seventeen years after the Conquest, since there is evidence for placing it in that year or earlier.

Friar Diego spent his long life in useful activities. From his own words it seems that he was one of the most ardent propagators of the gospel in the sixteenth century; and his writings likewise show his natural gifts as a diligent investigator and conserver of traditions and historical records. Though the negligence of historians and chroniclers is responsible for there being few traces of his passage through life, time has been kind to the great Dominican by preserving for this generation what was perhaps his only book, the *History of the Indies of New Spain and the Islands of the Mainland*. From the manuscript found in Madrid, Ramírez had a copy made; he then arranged the material in order, polished the crude prose, and published the first volume in Mexico in 1867. The entire work, however, was not published until 1880.

Durán's *History*, completed in 1581, is divided into three parts: the first includes the history of Mexico from ancient times up to the Conquest and ends with the expedition of Cortés to Honduras; the second contains information about the Aztec gods, rites, festivities, and temples; and the last, though describing especially the Aztec calendar, continues the story of the festivities, mentioning those observed monthly.

In writing the *History*—a work of authentic and strongly primitive nature—Durán used as source and framework an old historical compendium originally prepared by an Indian in his own language and known today as the *Codex Ramírez*. Probably Durán also made use of other history or old records. But it is evident that the material was almost exclusively Indian, taken from the ancient historic paintings (hieroglyphics) of the natives and from the memoirs written by Indians after they had learned to use alphabetic characters; and that he was also steeped in the oral traditions of the natives and Spaniards who had survived the Conquest. Hence the great value of his book, which, as Ramírez says, is "a history essentially Mexican with Spanish features." Harsh, rough, and awkwardly written, the work compensates the reader by "the substance it contains"; perhaps it would be unreadable if it were not for Ramírez' patient editing of the monstrous text as found in the manuscript.

In summary, the value of Durán's book can be stated in Ramírez' words:

This work is individual in that it gives us a living picture of the Aztecs; we see them move, we hear them talk, we understand their feelings, and just as though we were living in their midst, we can appreciate their good and bad qualities, the strength and weakness of their institutions and governments. The author, in spite of his crude language, is admirable in his knowledge of people. No one has depicted the nature of the Indian more discerningly; furthermore, he enters into minute details concerning the religious and civil practices, the public and private customs and habits which other writers have disdained as inappropriate material for serious history but which give his book some of the interest possessed by autobiographical writings.

Acosta

A native of Medina del Campo, Spain, where he was born about 1539, Father José de Acosta, the seventh of this group, became a Jesuit very early in life and lived for many years in Peru. In 1586 he was in Mexico, and from there returned to Spain, where he held important posts. He lived his last years in Valladolid, composing excellent Latin sermons, and died in 1600.

His *Natural and Moral History of the Indies* was printed in Seville in 1590; and the remarkable popularity that the work enjoyed is proved by the fact that, besides going through six Spanish editions, it was immediately translated into Italian, French, German, English, and Dutch, and included later, in Latin, in Theodorus de Bry's *America*.

The first four books of Acosta's work comprise what he calls the natural history of the Indies: going back to remote antiquity, he discusses the origin of America and its inhabitants; next, making use of a great quantity of data acquired through direct observation, he concerns himself with the atmospheric phenomena and geographical peculiarities of the New Continent; he then mentions the different metals and their exploitation, and is the first to describe the process of mining silver by the use of quicksilver; and, lastly, he discusses the animals and plants characteristic of the Indies. He treats the "moral history" in the last three books. The idolatry, social and political organization of the Incas and Aztecs, and a special history of the Aztecs from the time of the ancient inhabitants to the death of Montezuma are presented in a delightful series of short, clear-cut chapters characteristic of Acosta's style.

As a rule, posterity is not mistaken when it concedes continuous praise to a writer. Acosta is a classic: the best balanced, the most restrained and elegant of the chroniclers of the Indies, and a model writer of didactic prose whom the Academy has rightfully included among the authorities on the language.

As historian, Acosta has been highly praised; but he has also been accused of plagiarism. The first to make this accusation was Dávila Padilla, who, in his *Chronicle of the Dominican Province of Mexico* (1596), said, referring to Durán, that "he was quite ill and his works had not won fame although a part of them were published in the *Natural and Moral Philosophy* of Father Josef Acosta, to whom Father Juan de Tovar had given them." The accusation of plagiarism has been confirmed by Antonio de León, Kingsborough, and such outstanding Mexican historians as Ramírez and Orozco y Berra. The discovery of the *Codex Ramírez* proved, in effect, that if Acosta did not plagiarize Durán, whose work he possibly did not know, he certainly did appropriate, without alluding to the source, the narrative of the anonymous Indian chronicler, following it "almost" to the letter.

But even if Acosta did plagiarize—a practice quite common among the chroniclers of the sixteenth century—who can deny that there are to be found in his *History*, among other qualities, real merit and beauty, both in content and in style?

Torquemada

Friar Juan de Torquemada, the last of this group, came to Mexico when he was a child. At the age of eighteen or twenty, in February, 1583, he took the habit of St. Francis in the monastery of San Francisco, of which he later became *guardián*. He died suddenly in the choir loft of the church of Tlaltelolco in 1624, and his body was carried with great pomp to his monastery, where he was buried.

Nothing more is known of the life of Torquemada. The man remains unknown, but not so his historical work, which, besides that of Acosta, was the only chronicle of the Indies that was known in printed form to his contemporaries. While centuries were to pass before the old manuscripts of Motolinia, Sahagún, and Mendieta were brought to light, Torquemada's work enjoyed the honors of public attention at the beginning of the seventeenth century. His *Indian Monarchy,* which was completed in 1612, was published three years later. It, however, does not excel or even equal the works of his predecessors. On the contrary, because it is to a great extent a mere reflection and frequently a compilation of the earlier chronicles, it is considerably inferior to them. A copious and tedious book, filled with dull digressions (if "the useless part were deleted, the bulk would be reduced by one half," according to Icazbalceta), it is a motley bazaar in which wares belonging to other writers are displayed. Torquemada plundered Motolinia's *Memoranda* and possibly the writings of Friar Andrés de Olmos; and, in a shameless way, he pillaged entire chapters from Mendieta's *Ecclesiastical History of the Indians,* disfiguring these from time to time to make them pass for his own and deleting invariably all that Mendieta had written in favor of the Indians and against the conquistadors.

INDIAN CHRONICLERS

This group comprises Indian historians: the first flower of the Hispanic civilization in the New World. Crude and spontaneous, they produced unique psychological documents by means of which one can directly penetrate the Indian's mind. In this lies their originality and chief merit.

The Codex Ramírez

When the large monastery of San Francisco de México was destroyed in 1856, Don José Fernando Ramírez found the invaluable manuscript known as *El Anónimo o Códice Ramírez (The Anonymous or Codex Ramírez),* the latter title being added later in memory of the discoverer.

The Codex, a single volume bound in vellum, contains a "Report of the Origin of the Indians of New Spain, According to Their Legends" and three fragments belonging to other works. One of these depicts incidents relative to the history of Montezuma I; the second describes events of the Conquest from the arrival of the Spaniards at Texcoco up to the surrender of Mexico; and the last, although included in this volume, seems to have no connection with the others.

The author of the "Report"—according to Ramírez, who calls him The Anonymous One—seems to have been a native layman who wrote in his mother tongue. Ramírez bases his conclusions on the following:

first, the various etymologies and translations, though some are erroneous, which he gives to the Nahuatlan names; second, the praise and peculiar esteem with which the author speaks of the Aztecs; third, the laconicism with which he mentions, without justifying, the slaughter of the Indians by the Spaniards at Cholula; fourth, the horrible description of Alvarado's cruelty to the Mexican nobility, which the author does not vindicate in any way but attributes mainly to the covetousness of the conquistadors; fifth, the indifference and even contempt with which he speaks of Montezuma in the description of the emperor's tragic death, charging this to the Spaniards also; and, lastly, other statements scattered throughout the narrative that are likewise unfavorable to the Spaniards.

The conjecture that the author was a layman is based on his severe treatment of the churchmen, whom he reproaches for their indolence and neglect of Christian instruction, comparing them unfavorably with the priests of the ancient pagan religion.

It is thought that the "Report" was written about the middle of the sixteenth century; and, according to Chavero, it is an extensive interpretation of some hieroglyphic codex of the ancient Aztecs and was made in conformity with the purest tradition.

The work is all the more important because it served as a nucleus for the chronicles of Durán, Tezozomoc, and Acosta. Shortly after it was written, it must have been quite popular. The Jesuit Tovar translated it into Spanish; and Father Acosta, without indicating its origin, included it in his *Natural and Moral History of the Indies*. One copy, or perhaps the original, served as a basis for the *History* of Durán, who, in contrast to Acosta, did not limit himself to reproducing it but also augmented it with numerous details and traditions gathered from his contemporaries, so that it formed a volume five or six times as large as the anonymous narrative itself. Finally, Tezozomoc had it before him as he wrote, was guided by it, and, like Durán, augmented it considerably, enriching it with data of his own gathering. There are, according to Don Alfredo Chavero,

four chronicles: the *Codex Ramírez* and those of Durán, Acosta, and Tezozomoc, which are in reality one, presenting the only true source for writing the history of the powerful Aztec empire, which the daring Tenoch laid the foundation for and the cowardly Montezuma allowed to crumble.

The only edition of the *Codex Ramírez*—included in the same volume with Tezozomoc's *Mexican Chronicle*—was published in Mexico by Don José María Vigil in 1878.

Tezozomoc

Second of this group is the famous Indian historian—the son of Cuitláhuac, the next to the last Emperor of the Aztecs—who at baptism adopted the name of Don Hernando de Alvarado Tezozomoc. Little information is available about his life. Orozco y Berra infers that he was born a few months before or after the death of his father in 1520; and from a passage in his *Chronicle*—originally written in Spanish—it is deduced that he composed this work at an advanced age, in about 1598.

The *Mexican Chronicle* should have two parts, according to the original plan of the author; the first was to tell the story of the Aztecs up to the coming of Cortés; the second, to recount the events of the Conquest. The last part has been lost, or perhaps it was not written. Lord Kingsborough published the first part in 1848 in his *Antiquities of Mexico;* Ternaux-Compans published a French translation of it in 1853; but the only edition made from the original manuscript is that published in 1878 by Vigil, to which reference has been made.

The *Mexican Chronicle* should have two parts, according to the enly language; his phrases are often forced and obscure; occasionally, he omits words necessary for the completion of the meaning and uses expressions in a manner entirely different from accepted usage. Orozco y Berra attributes this to the fact that Tezozomoc was fighting against the difficulty of expressing his thoughts, conceived in his own language, in the Spanish language, with which he was not thoroughly familiar. His work also shows serious chronological defects because he did not know how to adjust accurately the dates of the ancient

Aztec calendar with those of the corrected Gregorian calendar. His Indian origin is shown in the frequent invectives he hurls "against the great devil and superstition Huitzilopochtli" as though he were fearful of seeming to be a poor Christian or still bound to the abhorred beliefs of his elders.

In his completely indigenous character, however, lies the greatest attractiveness of Tezozomoc. "All that is written about ancient history, by those belonging to the race and by outsiders," Orozco y Berra says,

> has more or less the artificial form which the classics of the different epochs have given to this branch of human knowledge, being completely removed at times from the true and peculiar pattern of the native races; each writer has displayed his own talent instead of giving a true picture of the subject he is sketching. But Tezozomoc's *Chronicle* presents legend in its pristine simplicity; it has the flavor of those stories handed down from remote times by savage peoples, transmitted from generation to generation with a certain luster of the prodigious and fantastic; it paints the deeds and customs of the heroes with a certain nobility united with simplicity, which is one of the charms Homer gives to the characters of the *Iliad*; it tells the causes and results of the wars, allowing whatever there was of grossness, arbitrariness, and injustice in the conduct of the monarchs of the Triple Alliance to stand revealed. The dialogues are natural, harsh, and slovenly in style, characteristic of the people to whom they pertain. To summarize, it is tradition, true tradition, which the Aztec priests preserved in their schools and required their pupils to learn by heart.

Written about the same time as Durán's *History of the Indies,* Tezozomoc's *Mexican Chronicle* was inspired by similar sources, as has been mentioned already — especially by the "Report" of the Anonymous Chronicler. If throughout the work of Durán we perceive the emotion of the mestizo as he interprets the aboriginal race, in Tezozomoc's work we discern the trembling and throbbing soul of the Indian.

Ixtlilxóchitl

As Tezozomoc gives the Aztec interpretation of history, so Don Fernando de Alva Ixtlilxóchitl, the third of this group, represents the Tezcucan. He was descended from the Tezcucan kings, being the great-grandson of the last ruler and of Doña Beatriz Papantzin, daughter of the Aztec emperor Cuitláhuac. Born about 1568, he studied in the school of Santa Cruz de Tlaltelolco. When he was an old man, he served as interpreter for the Court of the Indies; and he died in 1648, an octogenarian.

Various *Relaciones* (reports) are ascribed to Ixtlilxóchitl. The first of these were originally written in the Nahuatlan language, were approved by the Town Council of Otumba in 1608, and include information about the Toltecs and Chichimecas, the ordinances of Netzahualcóyotl, and the colonists. But his principal work is the *History of the Chichimecas,* on which he worked during the declining years of his long life. Probably forming a part of a general history of New Spain which the author, according to a vast plan, had in mind, the *History of the Chichimecas* begins with the Indian traditional conception of the creation of the world and continues up to the Conquest, ending abruptly in the last chapter with a description of the first attack Cortés made against Mexico City, although most of the events of this siege are missing.

Concerning this historian, Icazbalceta has said:

Oh, that he had written less with more thoroughness and attention to chronology. It is almost impossible to follow him in the labyrinth of his *"relaciones,"* which are usually no more than variations of the same theme, but variations that cannot be easily reduced to a perfect system.

Nevertheless, the sources which inspired Ixtlilxóchitl give extraordinary value to his works. These sources were the hieroglyphic pictures of the ancients and the old stories and songs of the Indians. From the hieroglyphics he learned the most important events; and in the songs he found numerous details about the deeds and lives of the upper classes. Because of this—in the judgment of Chavero—the works of Ixtlilxóchitl deserve consideration; but, since they reflect only the Tezcucan interpretation of history, one should compare them with the Aztec versions of Tezozomoc and Durán in order to obtain the whole story.

Ixtlilxóchitl's works were published in Kingsborough's collection; the *History of the Chichimecas* and *Relación de Pobladores (Report of the Colonists)* were translated into French by Ternaux-Compans; but the best edition of his complete works is the one published in Mexico in 1891-92 under the editorship of Chavero.

MINOR CHRONICLERS

Occupying a place secondary to that of the chroniclers already discussed in this chapter are three historians whose names will be mentioned here. The first of these, Friar Agustín Dávila Padilla (1562-1604), a Dominican and native of Mexico, was a notable pulpit orator and archbishop of Santo Domingo. His *Historia de la Provincia de Santiago de México de la Orden de Predicadores (History of the Dominican Province of Santiago, Mexico)* was published in Madrid in 1596. A disciple of his, Friar Hernando de Ojea, came to New Spain about 1582, and wrote a *Religious History of the Province of Mexico.* The last of the three is Don Diego Muñoz Camargo, a Tlaxcaltecan mestizo, who was an interpreter for the Spaniards and a diligent investigator of the antiquities of his country. He was born, according to Torquemada, in the first years of the Conquest, in either 1526 or 1530, and died at an advanced age toward the end of the sixteenth century. His only known original work, the *History of Tlaxcala,* has survived as a fragment; this was printed in Mexico in 1892, with notes by Chavero.

III.

Prose and Poetry

MEXICAN literature written solely for enjoyment was not extensive during the sixteenth century. The novel, which was so very popular in Spain in the form of the romance of chivalry, was practically unknown in Mexico. That these romances were early forbidden to the Indians is evidenced by a decree of April 4, 1531, which prohibited Spaniards from bringing to the colonies "light or profane historical romances such as *Amadís* and others of its kind because reading these is an evil exercise in which the Indians should not engage." The worst part was that the prohibition of this "evil exercise" affected in reality Spaniards and Creoles as well, and for a long while they had access to "profane literature" only through contraband.

The epoch was a rude one. The anonymous translator of the Latin book *Meditatiunculae,* the Spanish version of which was made at the request of the second wife of Hernán Cortés, said, in the dedication to his translation—written in the first third of the century at Cuernavaca, "the most delightful and peaceful village of New Spain":

Willingly, I did my best in the translation of this book, but do not be surprised if my language does not flow so smoothly as that of some Castilian rhetoricians, for the necessity of spending so much time in this uncivilized country where the language of the Indians is spoken more often than the Spanish and where one has no standing unless he is a barbarian among the barbarians, causes one to forget the elegance of the Castilian language . . .

Prose, as might be expected, was scarce. It was cultivated, at the best without any special attention being given to matters of style, by the friars in their chronicles, grammars, and prayer books; but none of these men, be it said, wrote for the mere pleasure of writing.

LITERARY PROSE

The *Dialogues* of Cervantes de Salazar is considered the only prose work of this century that can be classed as literature, but it was written in Latin and for use in the university.

"The rebirth of letters at the end of the fifteenth century," says Icazbalceta,

brought with it the necessity of purifying the Latin language, which had been barbarously corrupted during the Middle Ages. The modern languages, not very well developed at that time, were viewed with scorn by the scholars, who considered Latin as the universal and exclusive means of communication among themselves. The professors sternly prohibited the use of any other language in the schools and appointed spies among the pupils to denounce those who dared to use the vulgar tongues even in the privacy of the home; hence the necessity for adapting the Latin language to familiar usage when at each step there arose the difficulty of finding words for new objects and occupations unknown to antiquity. With the purpose of supplying this deficiency and preventing the students, who were corrupted by the barbarisms that filled the instruction books, from employing and inventing intolerable expressions, the professors decided to edit some dialogues similar to the Manuals of Conversation in which the authors attempted to use classical phrases, but, where these were lacking, supplied phrases as best they could, according to the rules of the language. The most scholarly turned to the Greek for aid in this impossible task of infusing life into a dead language and adapting it to new times and customs.

The most famous work of this genre was Luis Vives' *Dialogues*, on which Pedro de Mota wrote a commentary. Not satisfied with Mota's commentary, Cervantes de Salazar, before coming to Mexico, had written one of his own. When the University of Mexico adopted Vives' *Dialogues*, Cervantes de Salazar, in the capacity of professor of Latin there, published a new edition, adding his own commentary, along with Mota's, and seven additional dialogues, of which the last three—*Academia Mexicana, Civitas Mexicus interior,* and *Mexicus exterior*—succeeded in rescuing from oblivion this effort of the learned humanist and thus came to occupy a deservedly important place in Mexican literature.

Under the title of *Mexico in 1554*, Icazbalceta translated these three dialogues into polished Spanish prose and published them in an annotated edition in 1875. They are, according to the editor, invaluable historical documents. The first describes the university and contains rare data about its founding and constituents. In the second, the interlocutors travel through the resplendent city erected on the ruins of Tenochtitlán, the city which Cervantes de Salazar called famous and of which he often said that it seemed appropriate for "the world to learn from me, rather than from another, of its grandeur and majesty." The last paints the surroundings of the capital.

The dialogues have the academic tone characteristic of the dead language in which they are written. Undoubtedly, Cervantes de Salazar was no artist; but—and this seems sufficient—he was a resident of Mexico City: a resident who transmitted his vision of the city to us. He takes the reader through the streets and shows him the rows of houses which have the solidity of fortresses; he is enraptured before the original royal palace; he pictures the broad plaza where fairs and markets are held and every kind of merchandise is to be had; he describes the drains and many canoes on the picturesque canals, which do not suffer in comparison with those of Venice; he silhouettes, throughout the narrative, the monasteries and churches; in company with the personages of the dialogue, he takes the reader to the beautiful neighboring sites of Tacuba, Chapultepec, Coyoacán; and, finally, from the heights the characters view the marvelous panorama of the Valley of Mexico, which calls forth their highest praise.

If Juan Pablos, the printer of the *Dialogues,* is to be believed, Cervantes de Salazar "described Mexico City and its vicinity so learnedly and completely that he seemed to be placing the scene before one's eyes rather than to be giving mere description"; however, some reservations should be made, since, in the judgment of his eminent Spanish translator—who is an authority on the subject—there is to be noted in the work a "certain propensity to exaggerate the merit of what actually existed."

EARLY POETRY

Poetry received more attention than prose from the very first, and as time passed, it was cultivated enthusiastically. It was taught at the university and was in special demand at commemorations and fiestas. All the prejudice and distrust that the directors of public welfare felt toward the extravagant stories of Palmerines and Amadises changed, it would seem, to warm welcome when they dealt with the sonorous rhymes in the old Castilian manner or with the Italian forms that Garcilaso and Boscán had used successfully in Spain.

Some Latin poems included in the book entitled *Manual for Adults*, printed in Mexico in 1540, were formerly regarded as the first poetry produced in New Spain; they were signed by Cristóbal Cabrera, native of Burgos, who came to Mexico when he was quite young and was serving as an apostolic scribe in 1535. Verses had been composed, however, not in Latin but in Spanish, prior to 1540. The honor of primacy belongs to the Christmas carols in Spanish which appear in the *auto* (short, symbolic religious play) *Adam and Eve*. Excepting the carols, this play was written in Nahuatlan and was presented in 1538 at the festivities with which the Tlaxcaltecans celebrated the Day of Incarnation, as shown by allusions in Motolinia's writings. But if the field of popular poetry—which was mainly anonymous—be considered, among the first Castilian verses known in New Spain should be placed the satires and lampoons that the conquistadors themselves directed against Cortés in Coyoacán to give vent to their resentment at being insufficiently favored when the spoils were divided.

Later, in 1559, without abandoning its occasional character but assuming a form correct and very modern for that era, Mexican poetry entered a new phase. The impetus for this was the celebration of the funeral rites of Emperor Charles V in the church of San Francisco. There was erected a very magnificent tomb, which Cervantes de Salazar described in detail in the booklet he published the following year under the title of *Imperial Tomb Erected by the Great City of Mexico for the Obsequies of the Invincible Emperor Charles V*. On this tomb, a work of excellent architecture and "a marvel to all who saw it," were many inscriptions in prose and verse, in Latin and Spanish. Although the chronicler does not reveal the identity of the authors of these inscriptions, some critics think they came from the pen of Cervantes de Salazar himself. Others, on the contrary, contend that he wrote the Latin and not the Spanish. The latter are few in number and are written in sonnets and eight-line stanzas, an interesting fact from which the conclusion may be drawn that the first elegant expressions of Spanish poetry in America were in the Italian manner. The eight-line stanzas are quite heavy, while the sonnets reveal facility in versification, beautiful and correct language, and a lack of noble ideas: characteristics showing that the author was influenced by the fashionable literature of his time.

A phenomenon singular and worthy of mention is the fact that the superabundant production of poetry—which has always been characteristic of Mexico—began to show itself even in the sixteenth century. Though only a small amount of poetry from that period is extant, there is reason to believe, nevertheless, that poets or persons with poetic aspirations were quite numerous. In the literary contest held in 1585 during the third provincial Mexican Council, three hundred poets took part, according to Bernardo de Balbuena, who was one of the laureates. If the numerical eloquence of such an assertion be not convincing, further evidence is found in a certain colloquy by the Mexican dramatist Fernán González de Eslava, who has one of his characters say, "There are more poets than dung." The *gracioso*, however, after saying this, adds the following advice to his interlocutor concerning the slight pecuniary rewards from poetry: ". . . Look for some other occupation: you will earn more in one day making adobes than in one year writing sonnets."

Perhaps there is some extravagance in the playwright's idea of the number of versifiers; but, nevertheless, everything points to the fact that the writing of poetry reached a high point in New Spain during the second half of the sixteenth century.

Marvelously, the ancient city of Tenochtitlán rose again from its ruins. Attracted by the lure of wealth, new people surged into the city and increased its population. Parallel with material enrichment, work along cultural lines began to bear fruit. With southern exaggeration Eugenio de Salazar speaks of

> Los edificios altos y opulentos
> De piedra y blanco mármol fabricados,
> Que suspenden la vista y pensamientos;[1]

and Bernardo de Balbuena, referring to the university and comparing it with the universities of Alcalá and Louvain, declares the latter could be esteemed

[1] The buildings, high and opulent,
Made of stone and white marble,
Which cause unspeakable amazement.

> . . . de tener las aulas llenas
> De más borlas, que bien sería posible,
> Mas no en letras mejores ni tan buenas.[2]

This glowing praise would lead one to believe that the Spanish culture transplanted to the capital of the viceroyalty was flourishing there in full glory. Mexico, says Balbuena, is

> donde se habla el español lenguaje
> más puro y con mayor cortesanía.[3]

Concerning everything which the human mind embraces, he further says:

> los gallardos ingenios desta tierra
> lo alcanzan, sutilizan y perciben . . .[4]

The new nascent race, the creole youth, was distinguished by intelligence and alertness, and the scions of the ancient Indian stock revealed remarkable talents in various branches of learning. As to literary studies, it is obvious that instruction in the classroom was beginning to bear fruit, not the least of which was a delight in versification.

COURT POETS

Undoubtedly, the splendor and brilliance of the Golden Age in Spanish literature influenced Mexican culture of that era, although, in regard to books, the number brought to Mexico was not extensive. Some influence, also, must have been exerted by the few but illustrious Spanish writers who came to New Spain in the sixteenth century. Three of these poets—Gutierre de Cetina, Juan de la Cueva, and Eugenio de Salazar—and the question of their influence on Mexican literature will be discussed here.

---

[2] . . . for having lecture halls filled
With more doctors' bonnets—which might well be possible—
But not superior in learning, nor so good.

[3] Where the Spanish language is spoken
with the greatest purity and courtesy.

[4] The excellent minds of this land
perceive, master, and refine it . . .

Gutierre de Cetina

Gutierre de Cetina came to Mexico in 1546, when he was about twenty-six years of age, accompanying his uncle Gonzalo López, Procurator General of New Spain. Of a noble and well-to-do family, he had been born in Seville in 1520 and had been educated in his native city, where he was taught the Latin classics from his early youth. As a soldier, though "on a pilgrimage more passionate than military"—as Don Francisco A. de Icaza aptly says—he followed the King through Spain, Italy, and Germany. He became the friend of Hurtado de Mendoza, Jorge de Montemayor, the Prince of Ascoli, and the Princess Molfetta; and he was enamored of Countess Laura de Gonzaga, to whom he sang in his verse. His exact reasons for coming to America are unknown. Before his coming, however, he had won recognition as a poet and was one of the outstanding representatives of the Italo-Spanish school initiated by Garcilaso and Boscán. His literary work, consisting of sonnets, madrigals, *epístolas, canciones,* and a few prose pieces, had already been completed. The product of youth, written between his twentieth and twenty-sixth years, they were, nevertheless, finished works.

It is impossible to determine in detail the literary influence of Cetina's residence in Mexico; even the data concerning his literary activities in New Spain are unavailable. In his known writings there is no allusion to America except in the celebrated *Paradox in Praise of Horns,* which was probably composed before he left Spain. Pacheco, his biographer, asserts that Cetina, while in New Spain, wrote a volume of morality plays, but this is unknown today. Withal, and considering the poet's essentially dynamic genius, it is reasonable to suppose that he did not remain idle during his eight years' residence in Mexico, especially since his position and circumstances—and, presumably, the state of mind created by his amorous memories of the years just past—must have been favorable for writing poetry.

In the National Library of Madrid there is an old, incomplete manuscript entitled *Garlands of Varied Poetry,* which was compiled in Mexico in 1577. It contains 330 poems by 31 authors; 78 of these are by Cetina, who has the largest representation of any one author. Is it not possible that some of the seventy-eight were composed in Mexico and that many others like the ones preserved in this anthology have been lost?

Be that as it may, no trace remains of whatever Cetina may have written in Mexico; neither is there any information about his residence here except the story of the romantic adventure that ended his restless career. On the night of April 1, 1554, in Puebla of the Angels, Hernando de Nava, son of a conquistador who came to New Spain with Narváez, treacherously stabbed the poet while he was under the window of Doña Leonor de Osma. Fatally wounded, Cetina gallantly refused to tell the name of his assailant. Nava, however, was sentenced; and, though he was not executed, he did not entirely escape punishment for his crime, for on July 7 of the same year, in the Plaza Mayor of Mexico City, his right hand was cut off. Three years later, in 1557, one of his accomplices asked for pardon, and his petition makes plain that Cetina had died of his wound.

The life of Cetina was, it seems, as short as it was unfortunate; the brilliant courtier who, in erotic dissipation, traveled through Italy, the friend of scholars and princes, the lover of Countess Laura de Gonzaga, fell mortally wounded in an obscure city beneath the window of a woman whom, perhaps, he did not love and who probably did not love him. With his works scattered and unknown for centuries, his literary fate might have been equally unfortunate had it not been rescued from oblivion by a madrigal, the most beautiful in the Spanish language:

> Ojos claros, serenos,
> si de un dulce mirar sois alabados . . .[5]

Cueva

Juan de la Cueva, in contrast to Cetina, left a literary record of his sojourn in New Spain. A Sevillian also, born presumably in 1550, he came to Mexico when he was about twenty-five years of age with his brother Claudio, who was later named archdeacon and inquisitor. By documentary evidence and by making use of the poetry Cueva composed shortly after his journey, Icaza has fixed the time of the residence of the poet in New Spain as being from October, 1574, to the first months of 1577.

From his childhood Cueva had read and translated the Latin clas-

---

[5] Eyes beautiful and serene,
if you are praised for a sweet look . . .

sics, and his early poetry shows Petrarchan and other Italian influences which he later repudiated. It is certain that he was not famous when he came to Mexico; most of his lyric poetry, it is thought, was written after that time. Regarding his plays, which constitute his chief claim to fame, it seems that none was written before his arrival in the New World, since the first was presented in Seville in 1579, two years after his return to Spain, and the others were successively presented there until 1581. His remaining works, in which he attempted the most diverse poetic genres, can be dated between the time of his return to Spain and 1609, after which every trace of his existence has disappeared.

As Icaza says, several of the poems included in Cueva's *Works,* published in 1582, had already appeared in *Garlands of Varied Poetry* —the manuscript compiled in 1577 and to which reference has been made—and belong, therefore, to his early youth. Most of his poetry has been preserved in manuscript form in the Library of the Ecclesiastical Chapter House of Seville. From the diligent critic and commentator already cited—who has written the highest praise of Cueva, saying that "in his collections of verse, he anticipates all later Spanish poetry perhaps more clearly than he anticipates the Spanish theater, of which he was a precursor"—we learn that Cueva, during his short stay in Mexico, wrote two kinds of poetic compositions:

In the first, he describes and paints whatever claims his attention in the new lands in order to acquaint his friends in Spain with it or to discuss it with his new friends in Mexico; in the second, he reminisces and sings with more sincerity and hopeless nostalgia than sensitiveness and true poetry.

This first kind is excellently illustrated in the long *Epistle* Cueva wrote to the lawyer Laurencio Sánchez de Obregón, first *corregidor* (magistrate over the Indians) of Mexico, in which he describes what he saw and felt in Mexico City. Effusively, with warmth and enthusiasm, he depicts the city; his eyes are enraptured by nature, and he speaks of the strange fruits and flowers:

> Mirad aquestas frutas naturales,
> El plátano, mamey, guayaba, anona . . .[6]

[6] Look at these natural fruits,
The plantain, mamey, guava, annona . . .

His attention is attracted by the native cookery, which has lasted to the present day and is original with the Mexican people:

> Que un pipián es célebre comida,
> Que al sabor dél os comeréis las manos . . .[7]

Like the chroniclers—though in a different way—he was interested in the characteristics and picturesque customs of the Indians, of whom he speaks poetically:

> Dos mil indios (¡oh, extraña maravilla!)
> Bailan por un compás a un tamborino
> Sin mudar voz, aunque es cansancio oílla . . .[8]

During the early part of his visit, as the *Epistle* states, the poet must have felt deeply the enchantment of the new land where the clouds "distil gold":

> Vivo en mi libertad y gusto mío . . .
> mi voluntad me rige y me gobierna,
> y del que así no vive burlo y río . . .[9]

But, at last, homesickness seems to have engulfed the poet completely; this is revealed in a sonnet to his brother, a sonnet which expresses the reverse of all the paradisaical enthusiasms previously possessing him:

> Los alegres placeres han huído
> y el descanso que siempre nos seguía,
> Claudio, desde el postrero y cierto día
> que partimos del dulce y patrio nido . . .[10]

[7] The *pipián* is a famous dish,
The taste of it makes your mouth water . . .

[8] Two thousand Indians (oh, strange marvel!)
Dance to the beat of a drum,
Without varying the sound, though it deadens the ear . . .

[9] I live without restraint, according to my taste . . .
My own will rules and governs me.
I scoff at anyone who does not live so . . .

[10] Happiness has slipped away
And peace, too, which always followed us,
Claude, until that certain day
When we departed from our dear home . . .

The homesickness probably did not last long. The poet returned to Spain in 1577.

Salazar

Eugenio de Salazar was a lesser poet than either Cetina or Cueva; nevertheless, because of his longer residence in New Spain, his prominent position, and his university activities, his poetry exercised a greater influence on the poetic atmosphere of Mexico and offers a brighter reflection of Mexican life than theirs.

Born in Madrid about 1530, he attended the universities of Alcalá and Salamanca and received a degree in law from the University of Sigüenza. In 1557 he married Doña Catalina Carrillo—the chaste Dulcinea of his innumerable amatory verses—and had two children by her. After carrying out commissions in Spain and holding an important post in the Canary Islands, he was made *oidor* in Santo Domingo and later prosecutor for the *Audiencia* of Guatemala, in which capacity he was transferred to Mexico in 1581, where he also became *oidor*. In 1591, he received the doctor's degree from the University of Mexico; finally, Philip III appointed him to the Council of the Indies, on which he was serving in 1601. The date of his death is not known.

Of incomparable grace and refinement in his prose letters—according to Menéndez y Pelayo—Eugenio de Salazar was very fecund and skilful in writing verse.

There are doubtless in the enormous quantity of verse found in his *Miscellany of Poetry*—still unpublished for the most part—many mediocre and insignificant passages in which informality degenerates into slovenliness and conjugal tenderness into prosaic domesticity; but there is in the amatory part, that is to say in the numerous poems written in "contemplation of Doña Catalina Carrillo, his beloved wife," a pure affection, upright, sincere, very human, and a hundred leagues from Petrarchan monotony; and in the descriptive part, much magnificent and highly-colored diction, and a definite effort to give local and American color to his landscapes . . .

In his preoccupation with local color, Salazar followed in the footsteps of Juan de la Cueva. Two of his works showing this tendency were included in the *Examination of a Spanish Library of Rare and Queer Books;* the first is a poem in eight-line stanzas describing the lagoon of Tenochtitlán, and the second is the *Epistle* in tercets, addressed to Fernando de Herrera, giving an attractive picture of the high state of culture which the City of Mexico had attained in both the scientific and literary realms.

In résumé: it is probably true that the residence of these three poets in New Spain during different periods of the sixteenth century contributed, as Menéndez y Pelayo assumes, "to the development of the good literary practices disseminated by the schools of Salamanca and of Seville." If Cetina left hardly a trace of his footprints in Mexico, Cueva and Salazar, on the other hand, anticipated Balbuena, through whom Mexican poetry became fully American.

EULOGISTS OF MEXICO

Balbuena

Unlike the court poets of the foregoing discussion, who were only birds of passage, the first writer of this group, Bernardo de Balbuena, is bound to Mexican literary history with the closest ties.

He was born in Valdepeñas on November 20, 1568.[11] When very young, he was brought to Mexico, where he pursued his studies under the protection of his uncle Don Diego, canon of the cathedral. With a precocious mind and a natural talent for writing, at the age of seventeen he won his literary spurs, being triumphant in the literary contest held in 1585, to which allusion has been made. In 1607, having reached manhood, he returned to Spain and there received the degree of Doctor of Theology from the University of Sigüenza. He was named abbot for the island of Jamaica in 1608 and bishop of Puerto Rico in 1620; he attended the meeting of the provincial synod in Santo Domingo; he presided over a meeting of the synod in his diocese in 1624. His death occurred in 1627.

The three known works of Balbuena are: *The Grandeur of Mexico,* published in Mexico in 1604; *The Golden Age in the Forests of Erifile,* a collection of eclogues printed in 1608; and *Bernard, or The Victory of Roncesvalles* (1624), a heroic poem written in no less than

---

[11] Recently, the hypothesis has been suggested that Balbuena was a native of New Spain. Don Victoriano Salado Alvarez, in a well-documented study (*A Great Mexican Poet Restored to His Country*), maintains that the author of the *Bernard* was born and educated in Guadalajara (Jalisco).—Author's note.

five thousand stanzas. Since the last two works have no place in Mexican literature, only *The Grandeur of Mexico* will be discussed here.

This is a poem describing the capital of New Spain during the closing days of the sixteenth century. In the following octave, the author summarizes the main points of the eight divisions of the poem:

> De la famosa México el asiento,
> Origen y grandeza de edificios,
> Caballos, calles, trato, cumplimiento,
> Letras, virtudes, variedad de oficios,
> Regalos, ocasiones de contento,
> Primavera inmortal y sus indicios,
> Gobierno ilustre, religión y estado
> Todo en este discurso está cifrado.[12]

Balbuena, as he himself says, aspired to paint Mexico in all its aspects: the material and external, the spiritual, the social, and the political; and, in fact, he succeeds in doing so, drawing upon his prodigious verbal exuberance, his remarkable descriptive power, his incomparable wealth of color and fantasy.

Enraptured, he walks through the then new capital. The city, "soothed by a gentle and fresh breeze," rises above the clear lagoons. He pictures towers, domes of churches, marvelous windows. Under a magnificent sky appear, here and there, rows of poplar trees and gardens "containing various plants and beautiful fruits." Through the streets and highways throng droves of beasts, carriages, and carts, large and small; a motley crowd goes from one part of the city to another: muleteers, officials, builders, *"cachopines,"* noblemen, courtiers, clergy, friars, men, women; all different in color, nationality, and language. The streets are like a chessboard; the glossy waters "glow in flames of beauty"; the rising towers threaten to conquer the clouds, and the city, the flower among cities, is the glory of the

---

[12] The site of the famous City of Mexico,
The origin and grandeur of buildings,
Horses, streets, social intercourse, manners,
Literature, virtues, variety of occupations,
Pleasures, occasions of joy,
Immortal spring and its tokens,
Illustrious government, Church and State—
All are included in this discourse.

West. Sweet is the speech of the affable and courteous people. The ladies are the very picture of beauty, besides being chaste and modest, and the men are subtle and amorous.

The horses please the poet greatly. In the third canto, he speaks at length of the fine, spirited horses of perfect breed, differing in color, markings, and build—horses with restless feet and fiery natures. He tells how the trappings, crests, and ornaments heighten their briskness, and describes the skilful and beautifully erect horsemen.

In Mexico, the poet says, exquisite things are made: jewelers, lapidaries, watchmakers, botanists, glaziers, goldsmiths, iron founders, engravers, actors, sculptors, and architects work without ceasing. Poets are not lacking, poets who penetrate and reveal all things. Athens had not so many learned men; in fact, betasseled doctors as great in science as in dignity swarm in hosts.

In summer, when the jasmine blooms and fancy runs free, fiestas are never wanting. The city of the sixteenth century—which many suppose to have been somewhat gloomy—is filled with festivities: there are evening parties, visits, masquerades, walks, hunting parties, musicals, balls, frolics . . .

Reading his effusive eulogies, which, for the most part, coincide with those of his contemporaries, one might believe that whatever Balbuena paints, thinks about, and praises relative to the grandeur of Mexico, is a work of his fancy, a product of his naturally ostentatious and dazzling manner; but, in refutation, the reliable opinion of Icazbalceta is offered. The great historian thinks that the poet "did not need to invent what did not exist," and that his work—with "certain reservations"—deserves, without regard for its literary value, to be esteemed as a historical document.

In the judgment of Menéndez y Pelayo, "If it were necessary to set a date for the birth of American poetry, properly speaking, the date of the publication of this book would be the accepted one." It is "a species of poetic topography." "Although the landscape, with its richness and luxuriance, has no more than a conventional and approximate value, and is, so to speak, forced into a literary mold, nevertheless, in Balbuena's torrent of descriptions, the prolific vigor of Mexican springtime is felt."

Almost forgotten during the long years after the first edition was made by Ocharte in 1604, *The Grandeur of Mexico* was not reprinted even in incomplete form until the nineteenth century, when five editions were published: three in Madrid in 1821, 1829, and 1837, one in New York in 1828, and the fifth in Mexico in 1860. In 1927 the Society of Mexican Bibliophiles published a facsimile of the original edition—now the only complete edition in print—with Balbuena's celebrated letter to Dr. Antonio de Avila y Cadena, Archdeacon of New Galicia, and the *Apologetic Compendium in Praise of Poetry*: both important documents as mirrors of the personality and artistic nature of the poet.

Terrazas

Only fragmentary information is available concerning Francisco de Terrazas, another of the eulogists of Mexico. In the "Canto of Calliope," whch is a part of the sixth book of *The Galatea*, Miguel de Cervantes Saavedra, the famous author of *Don Quixote*, wrote two octaves praising ingenious Americans, including one Mexican:

> De la región antártica podría
> Eternizar ingenios soberanos,
> Que si riquezas hoy sustenta y cría
> También entendimientos sobrehumanos.
> Mostrarlo puedo en muchos este día,
> Y en dos os quiero dar llenas las manos:
> Uno de Nueva España y nuevo Apolo,
> Del Perú el otro, un sol único y solo.
> 　Francisco el uno de Terrazas tiene
> El nombre acá y allá tan conocido
> Cuya vena caudal nueva Hipocrene
> Ha dado al patrio venturoso nido . . .[13]

"Who was this Francisco de Terrazas?" Icazbalceta asks. "What

[13] It should be possible to immortalize
Superior minds of the antarctic region—
That region that today sustains such riches
And creates also superhuman intellects.
I can show you this in many today,
And I wish you to receive two such men gladly:
One of New Spain, who is a new Apollo;
The other of Peru, a sun unique.
　The first, Francisco de Terrazas, has
A name known here and there.
His genius has given a new Hippocrene
To his lucky native land.

did he write that his name should be 'known here and there'? If he published nothing, as it appears, where did Cervantes get the notice of his existence? And what did he see in his writings to cause him to praise Francisco thus?" According to documentary evidence, Terrazas is the earliest Mexican poet. Information about his life and fragments of his work were fortunately discovered by Icazbalceta in Baltasar Dorantes de Carranza's *Brief Report*.

Francisco de Terrazas was the first-born son of the conquistador of the same name who came over with Cortés as his majordomo. It is known that the elder Terrazas died in 1549 while he was *alcalde ordinario* (justice of the peace) in Mexico City. Regarding the son, the date of his birth is unknown, but it is supposed that he died about the end of the sixteenth century or the beginning of the seventeenth. From Cervantes' reference to him, it is concluded that he was still living in 1583, the year in which *The Galatea* was written; and the erudite Icazbalceta even conjectures that the poet had probably gone to Spain—where Cervantes became acquainted with him—"because it was a common occurrence for the sons and grandsons of conquistadors to go to the court seeking recompense for the services of their fathers or grandfathers."

Be that as it may, Terrazas was known and acclaimed in Mexico and in Spain; and, moreover, according to the testimony of Dorantes de Carranza, Terrazas "wrote excellent poetry in the Tuscan, Latin, and Castilian languages." That he should write in Latin was not unusual; that language was studied in the schools, and many persons mastered it and even wrote verse in it. But that he wrote in Tuscan gives rise to two conjectures: the first, that Terrazas probably had been to Italy, where he would have had the opportunity of learning that language; the second—and seemingly the more credible—that Tuscan was taught him by Gutierre de Cetina himself, of whom perhaps he was a disciple, whom he imitated, and with whom he is supposed to have had intimate contact.

The first known works of Terrazas were the three sonnets published in Gallardo's *Ensayo (Essay)* and taken from *Garlands of Varied Poetry,* the famous manuscript already cited, which also contained two other sonnets by Terrazas. The fact that one of these sonnets definitely shows the influence of Cetina caused Menéndez y Pelayo to assume that Terrazas could easily have been the friend or disciple of the author of the "Madrigal." Such an assumption is well founded. Cetina came to Mexico in 1546. Terrazas, whose father had died in 1549, was then perhaps about the age of Cetina, who was twenty-six years old; and it would be taking little for granted to suppose that they knew each other, since the nephew of the Procurator General of New Spain and the son of a conquistador and *alcalde ordinario* were in the same social class. Would it be, then, illogical to suppose that the influence of Cetina on Terrazas was not limited to poetry but that perhaps Cetina taught him the Tuscan language, of which, undoubtedly, the lover of Countess Laura de Gonzaga was master? If so, it follows that Terrazas, without leaving New Spain, could have written "excellent poetry" in the Tuscan (although, to be sure, there is no proof of this); it also follows that in 1577, when the anthology of poetry was compiled, he must have been already famous and, perhaps, about fifty years of age.

Furthermore, considering the fact that the *cancionero* (anthology of poetry) was in circulation in Spain during the first part of the seventeenth century (Andrés Faxardo of Seville owned a copy in 1612), is it not reasonable to suppose that a copy was taken there from Mexico soon after the anthology was compiled, and that Cervantes knew the work of Terrazas through this *cancionero* and not through personal contacts with the poet, who then was probably over sixty years old and who, apparently, did not publish his poems?

Because little is known of Terrazas and because his work has been preserved only in fragments, it is difficult to form an exact opinion about the poet.

Of the three sonnets published by Gallardo, one begins: *"Dejad las hebras de oro ensortijado . . ."* (Forsake those golden ringlets . . .) and is suggestive of Cetina; the second has not been republished because of its lewdness; and the third is dedicated *"a una dama que despabiló una vela con los dedos"* (To a lady who put out a candle with her fingers).

Terrazas, however, aspired to the composition of poems more worthwhile than these. There is attributed to him a work entitled *Sea and Land*, which Muñoz Camargo cites in his *History of Tlaxcala*, and in which are related the deeds of Cortés and his companions during the expedition to Honduras. And incidentally, inserted in the narrative of Dorantes de Carranza are fragments of a long poem, *The New*

World and Its Conquest, which was unfinished at the death of the poet. This poem, written in octaves, was inspired by Ercilla and, though circulated in manuscript form, must have enjoyed great favor with Terrazas' contemporaries. Alonso Pérez, in an extravagant epitaph inscribed on the tomb of the poet, compared Terrazas with Cortés, the hero whose deeds he sang, and with an unknown poet (whom Dorantes de Carranza identifies as Arrázola), saying,

> Francisco de Terrazas, Fénix solo
> Unico desde el uno al otro polo.[14]

Truly, it is not easy to confirm such hyperboles. The fragments mentioned above, which were included in Carranza's *Brief Report,* along with quotations from the aforementioned Arrázola and from one Salvador de Cuenca, and which Icazbalceta succeeded in identifying, lack both unity and coherence.

In the tone and with the grandiloquence characteristics of the type, Terrazas begins *The New World and Its Conquest* in this manner:

> No de Cortés los milagrosos hechos,
> No las victorias inauditas canto
> De aquellos bravos e invencibles pechos
> Cuyo valor al mundo pone espanto . . .[15]

He refers, in one of the fragments, to the expedition of Francisco Hernández de Córdoba to the Guanajos Islands. In another fragment, he compares Cortés to Xerxes and emphasizes the fact that the army which undertook the conquest was small; he describes an unusual instance of sharkfishing—also mentioned in Andrés de Tapia's *Report* —and gives, finally, the speech Don Hernando made to the Indians of Cozumel through Melchorejo, the Indian army interpreter. But of all these fragments, in the present irremediable condition of the poem, the only one which possesses the unity of a complete episode is

[14] Francisco de Terrazas, solitary Phoenix,
 The only one from pole to pole.
[15] Not of Cortés and his mighty deeds
 Nor of the extraordinary victories
 Of those brave and invincible hearts
 Whose valor amazes the world, do I sing . . .

the charming story of the love of Huitzel and Quetzal. This delightful tale shows that Terrazas had more talent as an idyllic poet than as a writer of epics. Although his sonnets are facile and elegant, his fragmentary poems show that while he composed with ease, he lacked vigor and polish. He is to be regarded as a man of culture, informed as to the literary movements of his epoch; and there must have been a reason for the extravagant praise accorded him by his contemporaries in spite of the fact that in his only known work conceived on a large scale, he does not reveal more than "mediocre ability," as Icazbalceta says.

The works of Terrazas which are in the *Garlands of Varied Poetry* (1577) and in the *Brief Report* of Dorantes de Carranza, along with others found later, were published in 1941 by Antonio Castro Leal, under the title, *Poetry, Francisco de Terrazas* (Editorial Porrúa).

Saavedra Guzmán and Villagrá

That the story of the Conquest was a literary incentive for both genuine and pseudo poets and moved them to attempt to put into verse the remarkable deeds which are told in the stirring and rude prose of the early chroniclers is demonstrated not only by Terrazas' incomplete poem, *The New World and Its Conquest,* but by other works that are poems in name only, such as those of Saavedra Guzmán and Villagrá, who were also eulogists of Mexico.

Antonio de Saavedra Guzmán was a Mexican by birth, like Terrazas; but, unlike the latter, he was not a poet. Son of one of the first colonists and great-grandson of the first Count of Castelar, Don Juan Arias de Saavedra, he married a niece of Jorge de Alvarado, a captain in Cortés' army and a brother of the celebrated Don Pedro. He devoted himself—though this is not evident in his work—to the study of *belles lettres*, especially to poetry and history, and it is said that he fully mastered the Nahuatlan language. He was *corregidor* of Zacatecas, *visitador* in Texcoco; and toward the last of the sixteenth century, he went to Spain, probably because of some claim; but what became of him and whether he returned to Mexico are not known.

Seven years he had spent in collecting the data for *El Peregrino Indiano (The Indian Pilgrim)*, but during the seventy days then required for the crossing over to Spain, he inflicted on the Muses the torture of composing this poem, which he printed in Madrid in 1599 prefaced with laudatory sonnets that such illustrious persons as Espinel and Lope de Vega had apparently felt no hesitancy in writing.

Through 2,039 octaves, Saavedra aspired "to record for posterity the valiant deeds of Hernán Cortés and of the others who conquered New Spain." Written to the "rocking of the vessel" (which doubtless impaired the versification), his work begins with the expedition Cortés organized in Cuba and ends with the imprisonment of Cuauhtémoc. It is—as Icazbalceta ironically says—"a veracious account of the war, ornamented with parleys of the Indians, harangues by Cortés, battles, tempests, and love affairs of the Indians—all insignificant." A multitude of allegorical personages, wild beasts, and horrible monsters intervene in the action. Lucifer has no small part in the formidable tempest that strikes the ships of Cortés. The nature of the work can be inferred from the foregoing statements.

In view of what has been said, it seems incredible that there should be differences of opinion concerning the value of such a book. But Prescott considers the author more chronicler than poet; Ticknor, more poet than chronicler; Clavijero maintains that the poem "should be classed as history since it is poetic only in form"; and our worthy canon Beristáin compares it with nothing less than Lucan's *Pharsalia*. Truly, it would not be presumptuous to say that none of these critics ever waded through the endless octaves of this venerable piece of literary archeology.

Captain Gaspar de Villagrá, the last of these versifiers of the Conquest, was not inferior to Saavedra Guzmán in the writing of prolix poems in the form of rhymed chronicles; on the contrary, he surpassed him. His *History of New Mexico*, printed in Madrid in 1610, consists of thirty-four cantos in blank verse, in which he casually inserts writs, royal decrees, and other documents. Because of its rare qualities, this book was reprinted by the National Museum of Mexico in 1900.

DEVELOPING ANTAGONISMS

Independent of its artistic significance, the poetry of the sixteenth century reveals a development or tendency which the historian cannot allow to pass unnoticed; namely, the growth of a conflict that deeply stirred that newly formed society: the antagonism between the *peninsulares* (those born in Spain of Spanish parents) and the creoles (those born of Spanish parents in the Indies), a conflict which not only had immeasurable social and political influence—because in it were the germs of the movement for independence—but also affected greatly the literary development of New Spain.

The sons of the country did not willingly accept the practice of granting to the *peninsulares* the highest political offices, especially those to which the creoles felt they had a greater claim. This rivalry was keen among the descendants of the conquistadors who felt they deserved certain privileges because of the services of their ancestors.

The quarrel surely began during the time of the Conquest when the companions of Cortés registered complaints against him, accusing him of seizing material advantages and appropriating all the glory of that prodigious undertaking; and, as has been mentioned, the resonant prose of Bernal Díaz flowed from the pen of the old soldier for the one purpose of counteracting Gómara's excessive praise of Cortés.

Generally speaking, however, in the beginning there was little strife connected with the colonizing of the conquered lands; but with the passing years and the disappearance of the first beneficiaries, conditions changed. The granting of estates by the king ceased, incomes were diminished or mortgaged, and families increased. At the end of the sixteenth century, many sons and grandsons of the conquerors were actually in want. Thinking themselves aristocrats, they refused to earn a living through work they considered beneath them, and they disdained both agriculture and commerce, which brought security and riches to those Spaniards who engaged in them. Ever aspiring to public posts, the impoverished creoles saw these snatched away from them by the "newcomers" appointed by the king.

"Oh, Indies!" exclaimed Dorantes de Carranza in wrathful censure. "Mother of foreigners, shelterer of outlaws and delinquents, common home for unnaturalized newcomers. . . ." And Terrazas, in one of the fragments of his unfinished poem, cried out in a similar tone against New Spain:

> Madrastra nos has sido rigurosa
> Y dulce madre pía a los extraños . . .[16]

A similar note is found in the fifteenth canto of Saavedra Guz-

---

[16] You have been a rigorous stepmother to your own
And a sweet, merciful mother to strangers . . .

mán's *The Indian Pilgrim*. Moreover, not only the descendants of the conquistadors but all the creoles, as well, felt this antagonism toward the *peninsulares* who were successful financially in America or were enjoying bureaucratic favor. A well-known sonnet by an anonymous poet illustrates their indignation:

> Viene de España por el mar salobre
> A nuestro mexicano domicilio
> Un hombre tosco sin algún auxilio,
> De salud falto y de dinero pobre.
>   Y luego que caudal y ánimo cobre,
> Le aplican en su bárbaro concilio,
> Otros como él, de César y Virgilio
> Las dos coronas de laurel y robre.
>   Y el otro que agujetas y alfileres
> Vendía por las calles, ya es un conde
> En calidad y en cantidad un Fúcar:
>   Y abomina después el lugar donde
> Adquirió estimación, gusto y haberes,
> Y tiraba la jábega en Sanlúcar.[17]

The extent of the influence of this antagonism on the social and literary history of New Spain cannot be given in a brief account. If in the common activities of life, the road open to the creoles was not broad and unobstructed, it is natural to assume that their opportunities in literature were likewise restricted.

It is singular that, while history showed such richness and fecun-

---

[17] There comes from Spain over the briny sea
To our Mexican domicile,
A man uncouth, without any aid,
Poor in health, and lacking in money.

And as soon as he gains wealth and assurance,
Others like him, in their barbarous council,
Decorate him with the two crowns
Of oak and laurel, Caesar's and Virgil's.

Another such one who sold
Laces and trinkets in the street
Now is a count in rank and a Fugger [merchant prince] in riches:

And then he despises the place
Where he acquired his reputation, his tastes and possessions,
And he squanders his wealth in Sanlúcar [a Spanish seaport].

dity in the sixteenth century, poetry was distressingly sterile. Notwithstanding the numerous poets to whom contemporaries refer; notwithstanding the eulogies of Eugenio de Salazar, for whom in New Spain "resounded the song of the delightful Muses" in such form and manner that all kinds of poetry—even the most opposite types, without a single omission—were composed in these remote lands; notwithstanding the grandiloquent and hastily formed ideas of Balbuena, who seriously stated that here were flourishing "the most eminent men of all branches of science," true "marvels in ability" and "in sacred and profane literature," men whose keen intellects comprehended and refined everything—notwithstanding all this, the fact remains that in New Spain during the sixteenth century, regardless of our determination to find him, no poet was born, or bred, or flourished here in such a manner that he illuminated the native soil with the brilliance of his inspiration. Terrazas continues to be little known; and the only poets known definitely as such, namely, Balbuena and Alarcón, found it necessary to leave New Spain before writing much poetry.

In his letter to the Archdeacon Don Antonio de Avila y Cadena, which was inserted in *The Grandeur of Mexico,* Balbuena uses some phrases that seem to supply the necessary corrective to the fulsome praise he had given the writers of Mexico. Referring to various works, which he had already written or was considering writing, he says, "If some day they should deserve to be published, they shall enjoy the privilege of being sent or taken to Spain." Speaking of *The Grandeur of Mexico,* he adds: "In the meantime, I wish to see what reception it will get from the world."

These revealing words indicate that in the New World, hardly propitious for poetry, the poets, toiling desperately in pursuit of glory and a more favorable atmosphere, turned ardently toward the Old World. And what a small world was that in which the singer of the grandeur of Mexico hurled his poem beyond the seas, eagerly awaiting its reception by "the world"!

IV

The Theater

THE FIRST dramatic performances in New Spain were of religious character. The missionaries wished, through the use of entertaining devices, to attract the Indians, who were accustomed to numerous bloody religious rites, and to replace the pagan festivals with others no less spectacular but embodying Christian morals and dogma. Realizing, too, the immense value of the drama for teaching objectively the mysteries of the Christian religion to the multitudes they were trying to convert, they began to arrange and present sacred productions.

RELIGIOUS DRAMA

At first, the friars partially modeled their plays on the Spanish *autos sacramentales*. They themselves either composed or adapted the pieces, or, if the plays were not original, they translated the borrowed material into the language of the hearers, with the aid of Indian students from the school of Tlaltelolco. The subjects of the plays were taken from the Scriptures; Indians were trained to act the parts, with boys perfoming the feminine roles. Since the temples were inadequate for such productions because of their limited capacity, chapels with many naves had to be built, with the entrances left uncovered so that the multitude occupying the ample atria could see the ceremonies. And as this arrangement in the course of time also proved inadequate, the performances were finally given in the open air, being introduced as digressions in pageants and forming only a part of the entire program.

In this way, dramatic performances came to occupy a secondary place in religious fiestas, the order of which was as follows: beneath a bright, blue sky the procession began to march; priests carried the holy sacrament under the pallium, and the faithful bore the images on magnificent litters. Everywhere crosses and banners were in evidence, and lighted candles were in thousands of hands. The way was strewn with flowers; blossoms fell in a shower of petals on bystanders, and triumphal arches made of flowers were raised here and there. Erected at regular intervals were chapels with elaborately decorated altars and altarpieces, on which the sacred host was placed while it was honored by songs and dances. The procession then resumed the march, and on the same day—if time permitted—or on one of the following days, if the procession were formed again, many dramatic productions such as pantomimes representing sacred episodes or religious plays in the Nahuatlan language were presented on raised stages or "platforms."

The first and most brilliant fiesta of this kind in New Spain was celebrated by the Tlaxcaltecans on Corpus Christi Day in 1538. Motolinia gives a colorful and naïve description of it. The procession took place on Thursday, June 20; then later, on St. John the Baptist's Day, June 24, four plays were presented: the first depicted the annunciation of the birth of St. John the Baptist to his father Zacharias; the second, the annunciation to Mary; the third, the visit of Mary to Elizabeth; and, lastly, the birth of St. John.

The most important of all these presentations was doubtless the performance of the play *Adam and Eve* by the Tlaxcaltecans themselves on the Day of the Incarnation, of which Motolinia writes in great detail. The uniqueness of the setting should be mentioned first. "The dwelling of Adam and Eve was so adorned," the chonicler says, "that it seemed indeed a paradise on earth with various fruits and flowers, some of which were natural, while others were artificial ones of feathers and gold; in the trees was a great variety of birds, from the owl and other birds of prey to the smallest of birds. . . ." Elevated in the center was the Tree of Life, and near it, the Tree of the Knowledge of Good and Evil. When the procession arrived at this place, the play began, adhering closely to the biblical text. Stained by sin, Adam and Eve finally went forth from paradise, exiled and weeping. Three angels carried each of them away. With sword in hand, a cherub remained to guard the entrance. When the sinners reached the earth, angels showed Adam how to till the soil and gave Eve spindles for weaving.

And, consoling the disconsolate, the angels went away singing, in an organ-like chant, the following carol:

"Para qué comió
La primer casada,
Para qué comió
La fruta vedada.

"La primer casada,
Ella y su marido,
A Dios han traído
En pobre posada,
Por haber comido
La fruta vedada."[1]

The Spanish lines of this carol and the Nahuatlan verses that conclude the play are the poems referred to in Chapter III as being the oldest verse known to have been written in New Spain.

In character, these primitive plays were, in their picturesque simplicity, didactic and moral rather than literary. Other pieces emphasize the same qualities. For instance, the Indians of Tlaxcala gave a fiesta on Corpus Christi Day in 1539 to celebrate "the peace between Emperor Charles V and the King of France"; and, after a sham battle, three plays were presented. The first dealt with the temptation of Christ by Lucifer, who came disguised as a hermit but did not succeed in covering two of his appurtenances—his horns and hoofs. After trying to conquer Our Lord by enumerating and offering to Him all the pleasures and riches of New Spain and of the entire world (especially the wines, of which the Spaniards and Indians were equally fond), he suffered the most shameful defeat. Christ having responded to his offers with the command, "Get thee behind me, Satan," the Devil sank down into Hell with the other demons; and, immediately, angels, seeming to descend from Heaven, brought food for the Master, put it on a table, and began to sing. Presented in the plaza (like the first), the second play was inspired by the legend of St. Francis preaching to the birds, and was staged with simple and delightful ingenuousness.

Of the same nature were the other religious performances given in

[1] "Why did the first wife eat the forbidden fruit? She and her husband have brought God to a poor lodging place because the first wife ate the forbidden fruit." [The angels' song prophesies Christ's incarnation. The "poor lodging place" is the stable at Bethlehem.]

New Spain in the course of the sixteenth century and immediately following. In passing, the play called *Juicio Final (The Final Judgment)* should be mentioned. It was written in the Nahuatlan language by the learned friar Andrés de Olmos and was presented sometime between 1535 and 1548 in Mexico City, in the chapel of San José de Naturales, before Viceroy Mendoza, Bishop Zumárraga, and a large gathering. There is also a record of one scriptural play with a tragic ending; this was performed in Etla, a town in Oaxaca, on Corpus Christi Day in 1575. Lastly, mention should be made of representations, which were probably given in pantomime, of the Passion. These were organized by Friar Francisco de Gamboa in Mexico City during the last years of the century and were produced on Fridays in the chapel of San José as a part of the sermon; likewise, plays, or *neixcuitilli* (a Nahuatlan word meaning "model" or "example"), which the historian Torquemada introduced, were presented on Sundays. He either wrote or directed the writing of these; their production became customary for more than a century, and from them, it is said, the Indians derived the pantomimes they still continue to present.

Undoubtedly, in view of the geographical range of these religious performances, it can be presumed that such plays were numerous, although only a few are now extant. Three, which Paso y Troncoso published in both the original Nahuatlan and a Spanish translation, are: the anonymous play *Adoration of the Kings,* which, by the first half of the sixteenth century, was being given in the fiestas of the village of Tlacomulco; the *Comedy of the Kings,* written at the beginning of the seventeenth century by Agustín de la Fuente; and the *Destruction of Jerusalem,* an anonymous seventeenth-century play that was inspired by a Provençal text.

Very slight, if any, is the literary value of all these productions. Unpolished in style, static and incongruent in action, the plays often contain absurd statements in which geographical and historical errors commingle. Nevertheless, they are invaluable documents for the study of the early Mexican theater.

In the meantime, while the friars were introducing among the Indians the celebration of the Corpus Christi with religious and secular festivities, the Spaniards, on their part, continued to observe this fiesta in the new dominions as they had in Spain.

The first reference to these observances is found in the record of the acts of the City Council of Mexico City on January 9, 1526. From this and other similar records it is known that in the reconstructed city on the occasion of the Corpus Christi fiesta, a procession was formed of officials—both Indians and Spaniards—of the various crafts, who were preceded by alcaldes and the images of their patron saints; that among the "officiating craftsmen" bitter and often prolonged disputes arose regarding the place in the procession each would occupy; that such disagreements were not uncommon among the civil officials themselves, since the question concerning who had the right to carry the pallium caused sharp discord between members of the municipal government and the *Audiencia;* and, finally, as was the custom in Spain, that the last place in the procession was occupied by the giants and probably by the popular *tarasca* (dragon).

Theatrical performances certainly had a definite place in these festivals. Proof of this is found in Mendieta's statement that Bishop Zumárraga "had forbidden, for just causes, the profane dances and hardly decent plays that were given in the general procession of the Corpus Christi fiesta . . ." And Zumárraga himself, in the appendix he added to a treatise by Dionisio Cartujano on the reverent and devotional manner in which processions should be held, affirmed that it was a

matter of great shame and irreverence for men wearing masks and women's clothing to go before the Sacred Host dancing with obscene and lascivious gestures, making noises that interfered with the singing of church hymns, representing worldly triumphs like that of the god of love, so very indecent that even immoral persons were embarrassed at the sight. . . .

On the other hand, the appeal of these spectacles must have been great, for the decree of the prelate was observed only until his death in 1548. After that date, the Ecclesiastical Council permitted dances and dramatic representations in the Corpus Christi fiesta; furthermore, years later, it encouraged them by offering "a piece of jewelry of gold or silver worth at least thirty *escudos* for the best performance arranged for presentation on Corpus Christi Day," a recompense which was doubtless in addition to the rewards already offered to authors by the municipal government. Ultimately, the Third Mexican Council, held in 1585, prohibited the giving of these performances and profane songs in the churches, regardless of the nature of the festivities, but made an exception of anyone who wished "to present sacred history, or other sacred material beneficial to the soul, or devotional hymns, provided he would present himself to the bishop for examination one month beforehand."

Documents are not available for a study, step by step, of the evolution and development of sacred and secular dramatic performances in Mexico during the sixteenth century. Referring to the religious productions, Icazbalceta, the scholarly investigator of the early Mexican theater, thinks that here, probably, as elsewhere, these were given first in the churches with the clergy enacting the roles, and later in the streets with professional actors producing them in the manner in which secular plays were performed in the seventeenth century.

The street performances were given on temporary platforms built for the occasion and with the elementary scenic devices of that day; and not only were they used in the celebration of the Corpus and other religious festivals but also on the arrival of viceroys and on similarly important occasions.

Examples of the use of these representations are found in the records pertaining to two famous festivals: the one given in the cathedral on December 8, 1574, on the occasion of the placing of the pallium on Archbishop Don Pedro Moya de Contreras; and the other in 1578, a program of festivities organized for the reception of relics sent to Mexico by Pope Gregory XIII.

In the first of these representations was a play entitled *Spiritual Betrothal of Pastor Peter and the Mexican Church*, by Presbyter Juan Pérez Ramírez. Son of a conquistador, he was born in Mexico about 1544; he knew the Nahuatlan and Latin languages, studied canon law, and was considered a man of ability and a good poet in the Spanish tongue. He is recognized as the earliest Mexican dramatist. His *Spiritual Betrothal* has a simple plot; it symbolizes, in the manner of the pastoral, the prelate's mystic betrothal to the church, and the theological and cardinal virtues are introduced as allegorical figures, along with the "simpleton," who was included to please the masses. Episodic in nature, the work of Pérez Ramírez is distinguished, nevertheless, by facility in versification, clever manipulation of the farcical element, and especially by the judgment and moderation with which the author handles the comic element represented by the simpleton—

this last being a characteristic which was to reappear later in the plays of Don Juan Ruiz de Alarcón.[2]

That the sacred and secular were intermingled in these celebrations is revealed in a peculiar incident that happened at the above-mentioned fiesta. In addition to the play, a very amusing *entremés* (interlude) was presented in the cathedral. This *entremés* was greatly enjoyed by the audience and dealt with a revenue officer or constable who was extorting pledges for the payment of the *alcabala* (tax on sales); and since this was given at the time of the establishment of the *alcabala* in New Spain, the civil authorities felt that they were being alluded to and ridiculed. Thereupon the archbishop received severe censure from the viceroy and *Audiencia,* who accused him of intentionally insulting them, when, in reality, the little play had been brought over from Castile, where it had been popular. The incident caused a turbulent lawsuit, resulting in the arrest of three men: Juan de Victoria, who had produced the play with the aid of the choirboys; Hernán González (de Eslava), an evangelical clergyman, who had arranged for the performance; and Francisco de Terrazas, an outstanding poet to whom were attributed certain couplets—displeasing to the authorities—that were found one morning nailed to the church door.

Of greater solemnity and ostentation was the festival held four years later, in 1578, on the occasion of the reception of the relics which Pope Gregory sent to the Jesuits of the province of Mexico.

The fiesta was announced by a magnificent parade of students on horseback, dressed in rich uniforms and grouped according to the Spanish, English, or Turkish costumes they were wearing. One, dressed in silk and gold and mounted on a white charger with elaborate trappings, was the leader. Wearing full regalia, the king-of-arms carried on a golden spear the placard announcing the festival. With music of kettledrums and trumpets, the parade ended in the Plaza Mayor, and the placard was affixed to a rich canopy of one of the windows of the *Ayuntamiento* building. A brilliant pageant followed. Two lofty triumphal arches with appropriate inscriptions in several languages were erected. Under these arches, the dances already mentioned were performed. In other arches were angels, Indians, and sym-

---

[2] The manuscript of the *Spiritual Betrothal* and some interesting notices concerning its production are in the National Library. The text of the play was published by Don José María Vigil in his unfinished *Historical Research in Mexican Literature.*—Author's note.

bolic figures who recited poetry. And, also, on the first six days of the eight-day celebration, sacred plays were given, the outstanding one being the *Triumph of the Saints*, a five-act tragedy performed by the students. The authorship of this work is unknown, although several writers are supposed to have collaborated in composing it. The theme was Diocletian's persecution of the church and the splendor of that institution during Constantine's reign. Among the characters were: Pope Sylvestre, Diocletian and Constantine, Dacian (the governor of the province), President Chromacio, St. Peter, St. Dorotheus, St. John, and St. Gorgonio, the gentlemen Albinio and Olimpio, a messenger and his secretary, two local officers, the Church, Faith, Hope, Charity, Paganism, Idolatry, and Cruelty.

The type of subject matter and the unusual mixture of characters suggest that the literary value of the play must have been slight. Nevertheless, its effect on the audience was remarkable. A Jesuit, author of a letter written in 1579 (which contains the foregoing information), states that the tragedy produced "an unheard-of sensation, tears, and the conversion of many." The religious force of the play—as well as the childlike simplicity of the listeners—must have been great, for the writer of the letter affirms that "it was sufficient to convert Turks had they been present."

By way of summary, the foregoing discussion shows that Mexican drama in the beginning comprised only occasional pieces (productions without dialogue or written in crude language for the purpose of evangelizing the Indians) and secular comedies presented as interludes at religious festivals. It is thought that plays brought from Spain were produced for the enjoyment of the Spaniards and creoles and were alternated with plays written by members of the growing colony. Indications are that there was some dramatic activity in Mexico during the sixteenth century. Concerning Cetina, his biographer states that during the poet's residence in Mexico, he composed a "book of morality plays in prose and verse," which, however, is unknown today. Eugenio de Salazar, in his letter to Fernando de Herrera, includes "tragedy and comedy" among the genres cultivated at that time; and Balbuena, also, alludes to theatrical spectacles. Whatever is said in this connection, however, is mere conjecture. In fact, apart from the data already noted, no sixteenth-century Mexican dramatists or their works can be named saved one: González de Eslava. It will be recalled that though Alarcón was born during that century, his plays were written in the seventeenth.

GONZÁLEZ DE ESLAVA AND HIS COLLOQUIES

In 1610, several years after the death of the author, the Augustinian Friar Fernando Vello de Bustamante published the *Spiritual and Sacramental Colloquies and Sacred Poems* of Presbyter Fernán González de Eslava.

Little or nothing is known of Eslava. Icazbalceta, to whom goes the credit for having reprinted the *Colloquies* and thus saving them from oblivion, thinks, with some basis for his conclusion, that Eslava was born in Andalusia, probably in Seville. That he was famous in his time is deduced from the opinions recorded by Vello de Bustamante in the first edition, the inclusion of some of his poems in the unpublished manuscript of 1577—mentioned in Chapter III—and the fact that he wrote poems of praise to accompany the publication of works by his distinguished contemporaries. In the judgment of Menéndez y Pelayo, Eslava was "a writer of the greatest facility and depth of thought; prodigal, but not discerning, in his witticisms; rich in his malicious and biting references to contemporary events; an excellent poet, especially in his *quintillas* [five-line stanzas]; firm and sound in his theological doctrines."

His colloquies are sixteen in number, and were probably written in Mexico between 1567 and 1600. Though similar in inspiration to the *autos sacramentales,* they differ from them in structure and subject matter. The dialogue is colloquial; the plot is simple; comic touches, which often approximate the grotesque, are abundant; the characters, when not allegorical, are surprisingly real; and, in trying to illustrate theological theses, the dramatist explains and reasons in a manner easily understandable to his audience of both Indians and Spaniards—though often at the risk of sacrificing the dignity and lofty tone which his theme demands.

The colloquies can be classified, according to the dominant theme, as religious and moral, or historical and occasional. All are in one act and in verse, except two: the "Colloquy on the Consecration of Archbishop Moya de Contreras," which is written in prose and verse, in seven divisions, and is singularly similar in subject matter to Pérez Ramírez' *Spiritual Betrothal*—already cited; and the "Divine Forest," which is also written in prose and verse and is in two acts. All the colloquies are of religious character; and it is worthy of note that the author is awkward when he attempts to write symbolically about secular affairs; as, for example, when he tries to represent the seven sacraments by the seven forts constructed by Viceroy Enríquez. Similarly unfortunate is the conversation of Fortitude, Faith, and Understanding in the colloquy celebrating the arrival of the Count of Coruña, and the handling of the characters of Contentment, Time, Hope, Saint Michael, Saint Gabriel, and Saint Raphael in the colloquy honoring the arrival of Don Luis de Velasco.

The characteristics of Eslava's colloquies indicate that he belongs to a tradition earlier than that of Lope de Vega; his "Divine Forest" is still regarded as a brilliant allegorical conception, revealing an undeniable and uncommon poetic talent. Interesting as valuable documents for the study of the Mexican theater in the sixteenth century, the *Colloquies,* in addition to their literary value, are highly significant to the linguist and the historian. In them is reflected the early creole speech, rich in Andalusian expressions and influenced by the Nahuatlan language. In them, also—above all, in those written for special occasions—because they abound in what is today called "local color," the historian may find information concerning the customs and the manner of thought and feeling of the inhabitants of New Spain, as well as allusions to contemporary events which reveal authentic data for the understanding of Mexican life at that time. A new edition of the *Colloquies,* with an introductory prologue which contains all the latest information on the poet, has been made by José Rojas Garcidueñas, in the *Collection of Mexican Authors* (Editorial Porrúa, 1958).

The religious poetry of Eslava forms the second part of the volume containing his colloquies. His songs, ballads, and carols—"verses of a song-writer," according to Menéndez y Pelayo—are in the literary tradition of Friar Ambrosio Montesino, Juan López de Ubeda, Damián de Vega, and the great Valdivieso, and equal at times the best written by these poets. As has been said, Vello de Bustamante rescued Eslava's works "from the oblivion in which carelessness and the death of his dear friend had left them." Furthermore, he promised, in 1610, to print soon the "more human works" of the author, but either he failed to do so or the edition was lost.

Ruiz de Alarcón

Don Juan Ruiz de Alarcón y Mendoza's birth prior to 1581, in Real de Minas, Tasco, justifies his being included in this discussion of early Mexican dramatists. He was of a well-to-do and ancient family. His grandfather, Don Hernando de Alarcón, probably under the protection of the first viceroy, had established himself in New Spain. The future dramatist was, indeed, of distinguished lineage: through his father, Don Pedro Ruiz de Alarcón, he was a descendant of a Cuenca family that had been elevated to the nobility in the twelfth century; through his mother, Doña Leonor de Mendoza, he was of even more illustrious ancestry, for the house of Mendoza gave to Castile its first admiral and to Mexico its first viceroy and to literature such noted figures as Chancellor López de Ayala, Marqués de Santillana, Jorge and Gómez Manrique, Garcilaso de la Vega, and Hurtado de Mendoza.

Alarcón's childhood was probably uneventful. It is presumed that the financial status of the family was good or at least moderate; his father was operator of the royal silver mines of Tasco and of high social position. Destined for the career of letters, in 1594 Alarcón entered the University of Mexico, where he studied the liberal arts and both canon and civil law. At that time the university was at the height of its early splendor—judging from the eulogies of Cervantes de Salazar—but, nevertheless, the university centers of Spain had a great attraction for young students of New Spain. For this reason or some other, young Alarcón was sent to Spain in 1600. By August 15 of that year he was in Seville. He must have gone from there to Salamanca, for two months later, on October 25, he obtained the bachelor's degree in canonical law from the University of Salamanca; and from the same institution, he was graduated as a bachelor of civil law on December 3, 1602. As an incentive to study, a Sevillian relative of his, Gaspar Ruiz de Montoya, gave him an annual allowance of 1,650 *reales*—a fact suggesting that by this time the Alarcón family was impoverished. And another bit of evidence that substantiates this supposition is that the poet suddenly abandoned his studies, left Salamanca, and went to Seville, where, in order to make a living, he was, in 1606, practicing law without a license. Under such circumstances, it was natural that he should think of returning to his homeland. His parents and his brother Pedro were still living in Mexico.

His native land perhaps offered to the ex-student of Salamanca two bright prospects: the hope of continuing and completing his interrupted studies and the possibility of securing a position from persons of influence.

The return to the Indies became, it seems, his chief desire. His resources were meager, but help was not lacking: a citizen of Jerez de la Frontera, dying in 1607, left him a legacy of four hundred *reales* to be used for the journey. This small sum was not supplemented by other gifts; and because of this, the poet conceived the idea of crossing as a servant of Friar Pedro Godínez Maldonado, Bishop of New Cáceres in the Philippines, who was leaving during that year with a fleet of merchant ships bound for New Spain. Alarcón asked permission from the *Casa de Contratación* (House of Trade), but the projected voyage came to naught because the ships were used to pursue Dutch pirates. Not discouraged, Alarcón determined to depart one way or another. In the following year—1608— in April, he again asked for a permit to make the voyage; and not for himself alone—as would be supposed—but for himself and his three servants. It is doubtful that he was able to afford these servants on the pitiful income of a "pettifogger," as we now say; rather, it is thought that such apparent ostentation had no other purpose than to increase his resources through the sale of the extra permits.

Finally, he realized his dream; on June 12, 1608, probably as a member of the retinue of Friar García Guerra, Archbishop of Mexico, he embarked on the fleet of merchant ships of Don Lope Díez de Aux Almendáriz. Accompanying him was an individual whom he described as servant and secretary, and on the same ship Mateo Alemán, celebrated author of the picaresque novel *Guzmán de Alfarache*, was traveling. Two months later Alarcón again saw the shores of his native country, for the fleet arrived at San Juan de Ulúa on August 19. Granted that he accompanied Frier Guerra as a member of the latter's retinue, he approached Mexico City by way of the Tlaxcala road. Here he must have found the home he had left—perhaps intact, maybe dilapidated, but certainly impoverished. His arrival, however, coincided with a great event: the ceremony on September 17, 1608, celebrating the newly constructed drainage system of the Valley of Mexico. Viceroy Don Luis de Velasco was in charge and was assisted by the new arrival, Friar Guerra.

What did Alarcón do on returning to his native land? The truth is that his hopes were realized only in a small way, and, for the most part, vanished.

He was graduated as a licentiate of laws by the University of Mexico on February 21, 1609. But he did not receive the doctorate, in spite of the fact that, because of his poverty, the usual ceremony was waived. On the graduation of his friend Brician Díez Cruzate, however, he wrote the *vejamen,* or traditional academic satire. From 1609 to 1613, Alarcón applied successively for the chairs of Legal Principles, Decretals, and Legal Codes, but he received no appointment. Unfortunate in his efforts to get academic employment, he was no more successful in his aspirations to public office. His physical deformity handicapped him in securing such posts. The only service he was permitted to render was as lawyer to the Royal *Audiencia* of Mexico.

For the good of letters and the glory of the dramatist himself, this series of disappointments should be celebrated. What would have been the literary career of Alarcón had he remained in New Spain? Thanks should be given to the nobility who forsook him; thanks, also, to the famous university which did not receive him! In 1612, Friar Guerra died without having materially aided Alarcón, and his hopes of receiving a bureaucratic position from the viceroy failed. Perhaps—why not make the supposition since he had already written some of his comedies?—his desire to win literary fame, which would make it easier for him to find a place at the court, caused him to decide to return to Spain. At any rate, he left Mexico the last of May, 1613. At the end of that year, he was in Madrid. Documentary evidence shows that he was in Seville in 1615. From that date, his literary life begins: a gloomy and bitter life of fierce, active struggle that consumed his best years and lasted until old age, when, finally estranged from the Muses, he eked out an existence in the colorless labors of officialdom.

Alarcón's genius must have been great; otherwise, he, who in reality was a stranger and had written little in comparison with his rivals, could not have succeeded in imposing his own personality on that dynamic, confounding, and changing world—the theatrical world of Madrid—dominated by the great Lope de Vega.

No one was attacked so severely as was Alarcón; no one was so

ridiculed and reviled as was he. The choice minds in that wonderful
moment of the Golden Age took arms—entirely unjustly, of course
—against him. They chaffed him, above all, for his physical deformity; he was a hunchback and also had a deformity of the chest and
a rough beard, which was probably dark brown. Because of his
appearance, he was unmercifully derided by such important writers—
vying with each other—as Góngora, Quevedo, Lope de Vega, Tirso
de Molina, Vélez de Guevara, Salas Barbadillo, Antonio de Mendoza,
Montalván, Suárez de Figueroa . . . He was called the "monkey poet,"
"Mr. Moneybag," "Mr. Cucumber," and "embryonic man," "the
poet with a trunk on his back," and "the original humbug." They
said, "He has a ball in front and in back in order to revolve,"
and they compared him with the dwarf Soplillo. And the *regidor*
Juan Fernández addressed to him the well-known *quintilla:*

> Tanto de corcova atrás
> y adelante, Alarcón, tienes,
> que saber es por demás
> de dónde te corco-vienes
> o adónde te corco-vas.[3]

But with dignity, hiding his bitterness in serenity, the poet responded to such taunts through one of his characters in *Walls Have
Ears:*

> En el hombre no has de ver
> la hermosura o gentileza:
> su hermosura es la nobleza;
> su gentileza, el saber.[4]

His aristocratic pretensions—characteristic of the creoles of New
Spain—were also ridiculed. It has been indicated that he was of noble

[3]Alarcón, you are so curved in the front
and hunched in the back
that it makes no difference
whether you are going
or coming.

[4]Thou shalt not look for beauty
and gentility in man's physique:
his beauty lies in nobility of soul;
his gentility, in wisdom.

ancestry, but Spanish writers objected to his placing "Don" before his name, a title in common use today. "He woke up one morning a Don," writes Suárez de Figueroa. "The nicknames of Don Juan grow like mushrooms . . ." says a censure attributed to Quevedo. "I assure you that he has his humps full of titles. Take note that the *D* is not for *Don* but is a reflection of his shape."

Answering this, Alarcón had one of his leading characters in *The Proof of Promises* say:

> Si fuera en mí tan reciente
> la nobleza como el DON,
> diera a tu murmuración
> causa y razón suficiente;
> pero si sangre heredé
> con que presuma y blasone,
> ¿quién quitará que me endone
> cuando la gana me dé?[5]

What more! Even his manner of being affable and courteous, his friendly and genuinely American mien gave ground for satire. At times, moreover, his rivals and envious persons went beyond words. On the presentation of *The Antichrist*, they poured ill-smelling oil on the footlights with the purpose of interrupting the performance. The play was presented in the midst of hissing, suffocation, and sneezing; and the production would have been irremediably ruined had it not been for the courage of the actress playing the leading role. Because of this prank—according to a letter by Góngora—the arrest of Lope de Vega and Mira de Mescua was ordered.

The fact that he was the victim of such attacks is proof in itself of his merit. The comedies of Alarcón commanded respect. They interested the Queen. No longer did he have to wait for the coveted official favor which, gratifying to his ambition, proved harmful to his poetic inspiration. In 1623, during the fiestas in Madrid cele-

---

[5] If the nobility in me
were as recent as the *Don,*
there would be sufficient cause
and reason for your complaint;
but if I inherited
noble blood,
Who can prevent me from calling myself Don
when I so desire?

brating the marriage contract between Charles Stuart, Prince of Wales, and Doña María of Austria, Infanta of Castile, the author of *The Truth Suspected* was designated to write the customary Descriptive Eulogy. Wishing to gain favor with his superiors, pressed for time, and lacking the ability—he, who so much needed it!—to write this kind of occasional and eulogistic rhetoric, he brought together some of his friends to aid him in fulfilling this great duty, and each wove an octave with him. The result was a very imperfect piece ("a labored poem, son of several fathers," Pérez de Montalván said), which brought a shower of cutting and droll epithets down upon the author.

But some day recognition was destined to come to this poet who, while awaiting that day, had composed, in the guise of entertainment and time-killers, such excellent comedies! On June 17, 1626, through the influence of the president of the Council of the Indies, Don Ramiro Núñez Felipes de Guzmán, Alarcón obtained the post of temporary teller of the council, an appointment which was made permanent on June 13, 1633. Confined to a bureaucratic life, busied with the mercantile affairs of America, and perhaps deeply, very deeply, disappointed in the literary life, Don Juan Ruiz de Alarcón y Mendoza abandoned, at least ostensibly, literary pursuits. Silent, meditative, he lived in seclusion in his home. Some time before he had become the father of an illegitimate daughter, Lorenza de Alarcón, by Doña Angela Cervantes. "Toward the end of his life," writes Alfonso Reyes, "he lived with a certain ease on Las Urosas Street; he had a coach, servants, and money for his friends." He died in Madrid on August 4, 1639, and was buried in the parish church of San Sebastián.

In comparison with the luxuriant opulence of the work of Lope de Vega, or with that of Calderón, or even with Tirso's, the dramatic output of Alarcón is small in number of titles; counting the doubtful ones and those written in collaboration with others, his plays hardly number thirty-five. He published two volumes of plays: the first in 1628, including eight pieces; the second in 1634, containing twelve. To this total of twenty should be added four others that are considered original and authentic. The influence of Lope de Vega and Tirso is seen in his *The Man Who Resembled Himself, The Unfortunate Pretender, The Cave of Salamanca,* and *Industry and Fate.* Character development is dominant in the following: *The Truth Suspected, Walls Have Ears, Proof of Promises, To Change for the Sake of Improvement, The Examination of Husbands, There Is No Evil That Does Not Bring Good, The Favors of the World*. Among the most dramatic of his plays are: *The Antichrist, Cruelty for the Sake of Honor, The Weaver of Segovia* (second part), *Whoever Chooses Evil, Evil Destroys, Guilt Begets Punishment and Insult Provokes Vengeance*, and *The Master of the Stars*. His plays of the heroic type include: *The Winning of Friends, Privileged Ones, Everything Is Chance*, and *Friendship Penalized*. Only one of his plays, *The Pawns of a Deception*, has an intricate plot. His *The Trick of Melilla* is filled with theatrical devices.[6]

The limited fecundity of Alarcón is explained partly by the hardships of his life. It is explained also by the evident hostility of the public, to whom, in the prologue of one of his comedies, he gave the name of "wild beast"; and, in issuing his printed works, he wrote: ". . . Treat them [the plays] as you are accustomed to, not as is just, but as you wish; for, since they have already survived your hisses and now have only to outlive your rancor, they fearlessly look at you with scorn."

But that which not only explains but justifies this limited fecundity is the very nature of his work, which, far from improvisation, is essentially a product of calm reflection and deliberate polish. If he began by imitating Lope, he ended by creating a type of comedy unmistakably his own. In addition to entertaining, he purposed to enlighten and to teach. "Proud and discreet, observant and thoughtful," Pedro Henríquez Ureña remarks, "his cruel social experience caused him to adopt a practical code of ethics whose precepts are evident throughout his plays." He lashed at vices: ingratitude, slander, lying, inconstancy. He exalted virtues: piety, sincerity, gratitude, loyalty. He did not achieve his moral purpose directly by obvious preaching; it is implicit in the story, enveloping and illuminating it. He was incomparable in the art of creating character, being careful of logical development without omitting human frailties. He combined penetrating psychological analysis with minute observation of customs. With respect both to content and to manner—the artistic

---

[6] This classification was made by Hurtado and González Palencia in their *History of Spanish Literature* (Madrid, 1921).—Author's note.

form of the plays—the qualities of Alarconian comedy are unique and exceptional in Spanish literature. The poet concerned himself with organic structure as well as style; he developed his plots with proportion and harmony. Frugal by nature, he avoided useless plots and characters. His acts and scenes are lively and short; his dialogues, brief; his monologues, concise. Without many lyrical flights, his verse is limpid and elegant, his language beautiful in its simplicity and purity.

Having experimented with several types of drama, Alarcón created a type which is indisputably his own: the moral comedy of manners. Having as a remote ancestor the Latin Terence, to whom the critics say he shows great resemblance, Alarcón directly influenced Corneille, was a precursor of Molière, and was the progenitor of Moratín's theater; it may even be affirmed that, because of his influence on both French and Spanish literature, Alarcón is the fountain from which modern comedy flows.

The great dramatist was born and educated in Mexico; but he lived a little more than half of his life in Spain and died there; he carried on his literary career in Spain, and his comedies deal with Spanish subjects. Should he be considered as Mexican? Was he, rather, Spanish?

For a long time he was regarded as a Spanish writer; now Mexico asserts the right to consider as her own this great universal figure of letters.

The thesis concerning the Mexican characteristics of the illustrious writer is relatively new: it dates from 1913 when, in a memorable conference, the Hispanic-American critic, Don Pedro Henríquez Ureña, maintained that Alarcón "rightfully belongs to Mexican literature and represents in a consummate manner the spirit of the Mexican people."

In support of this statement, Alarcón's singularity within the Spanish drama of that epoch has been pointed out. The first to notice it was a contemporary, Montalván, who said: "He constructs them [his plays] with such novelty, ingenuity, and 'strangeness' that there is not one of his comedies which does not contain much to be admired . . ." Alluding to this same quality, Fitzmaurice-Kelly says: "Individuality so greatly marks the genius of Ruiz de Alarcón—the strangeness of which Montalván speaks—that he is almost better appreciated abroad than in Spain." And stressing the "personal note," the "equilibrium" of Alarcón, he further declares that these qualities place him "somewhat apart from the two or three most eminent Spanish dramatists." The reading of Alarcón will show that he was truly a figure apart from the other great playwrights of the Golden Age.

But, granting that he differs from his Spanish contemporaries, does Alarcón's work show any peculiarly Mexican qualities? Henríquez Ureña has drawn a parallel between several qualities of his plays: discretion and frugality, deliberate development and proportion—no agitation and no giddiness—and "the discreet sentiment, veiled tone, and twilight hue" noticeable in Mexican poetry. He has also shown that Alarcón is Mexican in his concise observations, unexpected repartee, numerous witticisms, and courteous manners.

Alarcón's moral purpose and meditative temperament illumine with pale light and tinge with gray melancholy this aesthetic world which, drawn with clear and firm lines, is more regular and serene than that pictured by the Spanish dramatists but lacks their richness of color and form.

Other angles of the situation merit consideration. When Alarcón left for Spain in 1600, he had spent his childhood and early youth, including a good part of his university years, in the land of his birth, and his personality was already formed; "having already lived"—as Alfonso Reyes expresses it—"the first twenty years of his life in a distinctive atmosphere at the age when psychological development is largely determined." Probably by that time he had begun his literary career, writing his first plays—not his best, to be sure, but those which show the distinctive traits of his genius. Hartzenbusch offers many reasons to support his statement that *The Unfortunate Pretender, Guilt Begets Punishment,* and *The Cave of Salamanca* were written by 1599, while Alarcón was still in Mexico and was attending the University of Mexico. He also says that *Industry and Fate* and *Whoever Chooses Evil, Evil Destroys* were written in 1600 and 1602, respectively, and consequently should be considered as belonging to the period in which the poet studied at Salamanca, although the former may have been written in Mexico. A parenthesis may be inserted in Hartzenbusch's chronological table of Alarcón's life from 1602 to 1616—or, rather, the period of the dramatist's wretched existence in Seville before his return to Mexico sometime between 1608 and 1613—in which he places the comedy *The Man Who Resembled Himself*. This play, however, may have been written—and even Menéndez y Pelayo admits the possibility of this—after Alarcón's return to his native land, since the first scene refers to the inauguration of the drainage project of Mexico City, which the poet may have attended. It may also be assumed that during the same period or a little later the *Proof of Promises* was written, because the magician Don Illán, one of the characters of the play, was inspired—according to Fernández Guerra's conjecture—by the strange personality, completely shrouded in mystery, of the scientist Enrico Martínez, inventor of the drainage system of the Valley of Mexico.

If, then, Don Juan Ruiz de Alarcón was born and educated in Mexico, where he spent his first twenty years; if his literary calling was revealed and the first fruits of his art matured there; and if, lastly, this art, both then and in its later development, was markedly different from that dominant in Spain in the same period, and if it reveals, furthermore, characteristics of perception and expression that are peculiarly Mexican, then obviously Alarcón should be regarded as a Mexican dramatist.

True, the frame of colonial poetry was small and ill-proportioned for a dramatist of such greatness and perfection, as Menéndez y Pelayo says. But the fact that the figure did not fit the frame does not keep it from belonging to Mexico. As we have already seen, a newborn society could not, and did not, offer an atmosphere favorable to letters. Mexican poetry in the sixteenth century was reduced to mere rhetorical stammerings, a few occasional verses, and the profile of one poet (Terrazas) little known today. In the theater, which was confined to the narrowest limits, we have only one minor figure: González de Eslava. Even the illustrious work of the chroniclers remained, for the most part, unpublished for two centuries . . . And as if to compensate us for this distressing indigence, there appears against the background of Spain of the Golden Age—the only background capable of containing him—the proud, lofty, solitary, and very Mexican figure of Don Juan Ruiz Alarcón!

The Seventeenth and
Eighteenth Centuries

Decadence and Reaction

T HE sixteenth century was a heroic period in the history of Mexican letters. Along with the attempt to transplant a culture appeared a creative urge not only *not* lacking in originality, but, on the contrary, overflowing with it. Corresponding to the material force required for the subjugation of the new dominions was a spiritual vigor, giving tremendous impetus to the establishment of advanced European culture in the New World. Beside the temple was erected the school. Evangelization was extended to the circumference of the vast territory. Teaching reached extraordinary heights; educational plants were multiplied; and public instruction was carried to the highest degree, culminating in the university. With the study of the past and of the Indian languages, new branches of history and philology were opened up. Classroom studies and perhaps also, though to a lesser extent, the influence of writers coming over from Spain promoted the cultivation of letters; and though poetry did not progress beyond the formless imitations written by innumerable competitive versifiers, the New World did produce, nevertheless, side by side, writers of recognized merit who were suffocated by the environment, such as Terrazas, and brilliant creative geniuses such as Ruiz de Alarcón and Balbuena, who added luster to Spanish literature. The printing press turned out books in such great profusion that a copious bibliography was formed. In short, the capital of New Spain, rising proudly over the ruins of Tenochtitlán, became the emporium of civilization in America.

TRANSITION

Considering the irrepressible force of this creative impulse, it was to be expected that the movement would spread and become still more resplendent in the next century. And something of the kind did happen, in effect, in the first part of the new century; New Spain, particularly its metropolis, continued the unusual development, especially along material lines; the city was transformed, beautified; new architectural monuments were erected; painting reached its height. But it might be said that such was the magnitude of the effort expended that finally weariness prevailed, and stagnation followed the many activities.

The sixteenth century transmitted to the seventeenth its literary spirit together with its ideas and forms. The writers of the former century were still active at the beginning of the new. In his native city Alarcón was writing some of the plays which were later to bring him fame and renown. There were also Spanish writers who, like Cueva and Salazar, came to America and here continued their literary activities; one of these, Mateo Alemán, the author of *El Pícaro Guzmán de Alfarache (The Rogue)*, was a member of the retinue of Friar García Guerra, came to Mexico in 1608, and finished and published in 1609 his *Castilian Orthography*. He continued in the service of the prelate; and, on the death of the latter, published the memoir entitled *Events in the Life of Don Friar García Guerra, Archbishop of Mexico* (1613), which includes some curious items about life in New Spain, and a *Funeral Oration,* commemorating the death of the viceroy-archbishop, whose memory the author zealously praised and defended as a loyal protégé. These are probably Alemán's last works. Perhaps he died in Mexico, but the date and circumstances are unknown. During this same period, the poet Luis de Belmonte Bermúdez also lived in these lands; his *Life of Father Ignacio de Loyola,* a poem composed in double *quintillas* (five-line stanzas), was printed in Mexico in 1609, and contains a *Eulogy* written by Mateo Alemán, which is of interest in the study of that novelist. Another Spanish poet, Diego Mexía, while traveling in the interior of New Spain, translated Ovid's *Heroides*.

Notwithstanding, just as the social order of the seventeenth century soon became different from that of the preceding century, so literary tendencies began to show distinctive features.

GONGORISM

The Golden Age of letters was coming to an end in Spain. The great Renaissance ideal, which depended on reviving the beauty of the ancient classics, had attained maximum splendor in the work of Friar Luis de León. The limit of human perfection having been reached in this respect, to persist in carrying the imitation of the Greek and Latin poets to excess necessarily meant decadence. The germ of this decadence, which was widely propagated and infected all literary activity in a complete and fatal manner, was *Gongorism* or *culteranismo*. The cult was called by both names: the first, *Gongorism,* being derived from its supreme pontiff, the genial Don Luis de Góngora; the second, *culteranismo,* from its attempt to represent everything refined and cultured, in opposition to the vulgar, and to school itself in the disciplines that constituted the literary culture of that day—i.e., the classics.

In an effort to point out new paths for poetry, Gongorism attempted, in substance, the following: to mold the Spanish on the Latin, introducing not only many Latin words but also, in servile imitation of that language, serious syntactical changes; to replace the direct meanings of words by figurative senses; to employ artificial metaphors, involving subtle relations and almost imperceptible meanings in the metaphorical terms; and to multiply, finally, the allusions to classical mythology. In this way, Gongorism, or *culteranismo,* converted poetry into a cultural tidbit, making it impossible for the uninitiated to understand it, and creating, in antithesis to simple and clear expressions, a new manner of speech so far removed from natural and current usage, so queer and obscure, that no one, regardless of effort, could understand it.

Soon another artifice of speech was united with Gongorism: *conceptismo* (the cultivation of affected or exaggerated conceits), a formula which tended to distil and subtilize not only the external form but the concept, the idea itself. Both schools, having the same purpose, soon joined forces to such an extent that, with the passing of time, it was difficult to distinguish the *culteranos* from the *conceptistas,* since both were equally guilty of obscurity, artificiality, and emptiness.

When *culteranismo* appeared in Spain, it encountered opposition from eminent persons, who lashed it furiously; but nothing was able for long to hold in check that epidemic which appeared contemporaneously in many European literatures. It spread rapidly. The literary innovation of Góngora—the tricks minus the man—ended by infecting all literature with its lamentable symptoms and thereby plunging the brilliant Golden Age in fatal decadence.

It follows that since the literary modes of Spain were immediately echoed in America, the rank weed of Gongorism soon found here extensive soil for reproduction. It might even be said that not only was this style accentuated by Mexican writers, who carried it to the ultimate limits of ridiculousness and emptiness, but Gongorism became so deeply rooted in New Spain that it continued unabated here after it had almost disappeared in the land of its origin, having been swept away by the restorers of "good taste."

Further, as we shall see later, *culteranismo* infected poetry written in both the Latin and Spanish. But it did not stop there: it invaded history, and some historians—though not at all outstanding ones—delighted in this verbal ostentation; it completely infested religious literature, which was indeed voluminous but of no artistic value; and it even produced bombastic preachers who, by the spoken word rather than by the pen, set themselves to propagate this diseased style. No one was willing to be understood. And though it was in the latter part of the seventeenth century that Don Pedro Muñoz Camargo published his "Magnificent Elevation of the Bethlehem Rose from the Best American Jericho and Congratulatory Action Because of Its Happy Transplantation, Newly Erected in the Sacred Religion by His Holiness the Pope Innocent XI Which Was Celebrated with Religious Sacraments in This Noble City of Mexico by the Venerable Dean and the Most Esteemed Nuns in the Chapel of This Metropolitan Holy Church," the eighteenth century could boast with equal propriety of the publication of a work with a similarly remarkable title, a little book of prayers which was very popular and was entitled, "Mystic Towel or Sweet Exercise for Drying Off Christ, Our Fallen Savior, Dampened by the Black Waters of the Brook Kidron." These titles are sufficient to indicate the contents of such works. If it is recalled that titles of this kind were not rare but quite numerous, it will be easily understood how this literary vice, which was assiduously cultivated in order to replace real talent by wordy emptiness, led to the curious result of the total disappearance of intelligence in literary efforts.

But was Gongorism the principal cause of the decadence of Mexican literature? Or was the inferiority of Mexican letters in that period—and the strange spread and persistence of *culteranismo*—the result of other influences no less ostensible, but more profound?

THE CAUSES OF DECADENCE

New Spain was not entirely devoid of talent. Apart from the exaggerated claims made by Salazar and Balbuena, to which reference has been made, it is well to remember that Dr. Juan de Cárdenas, in the sixteenth century, stated, in referring to the creoles, that they had "keen and refined talent" and their

speech was so polished, courteous, and interesting, with so many preambles, refinements, and rhetorical features, which were neither studied nor artificial but were natural, that one might easily believe a Spaniard born in America had lived all his life at court or in the company of persons of gentle and discreet speech.

Furthermore, Friar Juan de Grijalva, in the seventeenth century, said: "Generally speaking, the minds [of the creoles] are so keen that at eleven or twelve years of age, the children know how to read, write, and count; they know Latin and write poetry as did the famous men of Italy."

Discounting those statements of the clergy that show childlike credulity, but taking into account the unanimity of all available testimony, it would seem evident that capacity and decided literary ability were not lacking in Mexico during that era. Nevertheless, such would be of little service when conditions were far from being favorable for the creation of an intellectual atmosphere, and when, because the country was in a formative stage and its attention was of necessity directed to its material development, conditions conducive to literary efforts did not exist. "A narrow and dwarfed world" was the name given to New Spain by Bernardo de Balbuena in his *Epistle* to the Archdeacon of New Galicia. And he added,

Although the country is vast, it is not densely populated, and outside this rich city [of Mexico], almost all is barren and exhausted as far as letters, good taste, intellectual pleasure and curiosity are concerned, because material profit and love of money have dominated the minds of the people.

Probably there was little incentive for the creoles to follow difficult and unprofitable literary pursuits. "The majority," says Dr. Antonio de Peralta Castañeda in the prologue to the *History of Tobias* (1667), "vacillate from necessity, become discouraged through lack of rewards and even of a living, and die in oblivion, the usual fate of scholars." Only with the aid of the church and while enjoying the benefits of an ecclesiastical post was it possible for a writer to devote himself to letters. This explains why the majority of writers in New Spain during the two last centuries of the Viceroyalty were priests or monks and why the literature of that time had a distinctly cloistral aspect. In the sixteenth century, the authors belonging to the monastic orders, busy in the work of civilizing the Indians, were the great historians, the great ethnologists, the great linguists; in the second half of the seventeenth century and in the first part of the eighteenth —with rare exceptions—the minds of the monks were sterilized by the use of an artificial and hollow rhetoric in theological and devotional books, which were far distant from the pure fountains of the Spanish mystics of the Golden Age and were so numerous that they constituted 70 per cent of the works printed in Mexico during that period.

If the material obstacles opposing the natural and luxuriant development of creole talent were insuperable, the social picture of Colonial Mexico likewise presented nothing that would promise intellectual stimulation and growth.

The quiet and monotonous life offered no incentive to literary activity. The Colony was isolated from all foreign influence, and, therefore, even more than Spain, it was shut off from the European Renaissance. Censorship prevented books from coming in without previous strict examination, with the result that few books were imported. Neither could books be printed in Mexico without permits. Thus, far from all foreign inspiration and shackled at home by lack of liberty, the mind had no chance for free flight.

Further, it was not possible for one to react against and overcome this strict control, and the stagnation of culture became more and more complete with the passing of the years. "Philosophy, history, literature, all the sciences," as Don José María Vigil has said, "were living in peaceful partnership with theology." The university, which by its very nature should have created select groups—the university, which from its beginning, as Justo Sierra remarks, was almost completely alien to the powerful intellectual currents of the Renaissance—was "immured intellectually," continued to be so, and, according to the keen judgment of that eminent thinker, was a school adhering to the word (always the Latin word, too) rather than the idea, a school where the word was "the proverbial shuttle which moved back and forth ceaselessly in an infinite warp of dialectical concepts."

What, then, could be expected? Without liberty, in lethal isolation, and in the midst of a sordid fanaticism which the Inquisition was charged vigilantly to maintain, what could be the fate of letters in Mexico if not the same as that which befell literature in Spain during the epoch of decadence which culminated in the disastrous reign of Charles II, the last of the Austrians?

THE REFORM

With the advent of the Bourbon dynasty, a reinvigorating spirit was felt in Spain. Something of this was reflected in America.

The reformation was slow, however, and did not become manifest in the intellectual field until the middle of the eighteenth century. With the weakening of censorship—or in spite of it—new ideas penetrated the quiet, motionless atmosphere of the Colony.

Reaction against the classical was begun in literature; this movement was developed in their schools by the Jesuits, among whom then flowered the best writers of Latin poetry as well as the first great Mexican historian. The expulsion of the Jesuits retarded, but did not entirely check, the cultural movement in Mexico. Open opposition surged against scholasticism; an illustrious Mexican, Benito Díaz de Gamarra (1745-1783), introduced modern philosophy with his chief work *Elementa Recentioris Philosophiae*, which was published in 1774. The physical sciences had a zealous cultivator and propagandist in the learned Father José Antonio Alzate (1729-1790). Contemporaries of Alzate and tireless workers were these other eminent Mexicans: Don Francisco Javier Gamboa, jurisconsult and geologist; Don Joaquín Velázquez de León, geodesist and astronomer; Don Antonio León Gama, astronomer, geographer, and archeologist; Don José Ignacio Bartolache, mathematician; and Don José Ignacio Mociño, botanist.

In 1784 appeared the first regular periodical, *La Gaceta de México (The Mexican Gazette)*. In this—a periodical intended to be principally informative—as in the irregular publications that had preceded it and those which came after Alzate's time, appeared articles on geography, natural history, geology, medicine.

The College of Mines was founded in 1792, and associated with it were such outstanding men as Don Fausto Elhúyar and Don Andrés del Río. The latter wrote the best work on mineralogy in the Spanish language. In view of the activities of the college and, in general, the scientific development observed in Mexico during his visit there, Baron von Humboldt could make the statement that the ardor with which the capital of New Spain was then embracing the study of the exact sciences "was much greater than the devotion to the study of the ancient languages and literature."

But if, in fact, the status of literature in the Colony during the latter part of the century did not correspond to the splendor which the Jesuit humanists and historians were giving to it in their exile, the plastic arts, on the other hand, were undergoing a period of remarkable activity. In 1783, the Academy of San Carlos was founded. Architecture flourished. This was an epoch in which great buildings were erected under the direction of the prominent Spaniard Tolsa and the Mexican Tresguerras.

After an extensive period of stagnation, New Spain experienced a definite intellectual renaissance as the Viceroyalty was drawing to a close. This was closely allied to the slow but certain development of new political ideas. Along with the introduction of eighteenth-century European philosophy and literature through the medium of books or through men who, imbued with new ideas, came for the first time—or returned—to New Spain, new forms of social organization were outlined; and aspirations which had long been dormant received definite impetus so that soon these ideas resolved themselves into action on the part of the citizenry. These forces brought about the events which resulted in the creation of a new nation at the beginning of the next century.

VI.

Poetry

THE chief factors in the spread of Gongorism were the conditions under which poetry was written in the sixteenth century and the pedantic education given to those who were to produce poetry.

Strictly speaking, popular poetry did not exist in Mexico, for Mexican poetry was, from the beginning, scholarly: it was born and nourished in the classrooms; it was cultivated, in leisure time, by persons of academic background who held good or fairly good civil or ecclesiastical positions. Inveterately occasional, limited to celebrating accessions or deaths of monarchs, arrivals of viceroys, dedications of shrines, canonizations of saints, and literary contests arranged for these purposes, poetry lacked spontaneity and sincerity; it was forced and made to order; and, instead of the free play of inspiration, it represented the patient application of the mind to mere rhetorical exercises which, for the most part, fitted into the intellectual system in which the minds themselves were formed—a system that developed only the verbal faculty and a skill in dialectics. Out of these conditions, the *culterano* (euphuistic) mode developed.

THE EUPHUISTIC MODE

The poets and pseudo-poets who employed the euphuistic manner liked not only the forced subtlety and extravagance characteristic of it, but, equally well or even more, the rhetorical gymnastics which accompanied it. Queer metrical combinations were the order of the day. As to sonnets, not to mention other forms, there were simple, double, and triple ones, with refrains or repetitions continuous, linked together, or retrogressive, and with acrostics or with ritornelle. Nor was the example of the Greco-Latin classics sufficient to restrain such aberrations. Bad taste not only infested the domains of Spanish versification, but spread also into Latin verse. In his *Poetics* "for the use of young students"—which was composed in Mexico in 1605, before the advent of affectation—Father Bernardino Llanos included, along with sacred doctrine and classic precepts, numerous grotesque inventions: the cento (poetic medley), the labyrinth, the anagram; also, the *pangramatón* and the *metronteleón*, requiring, respectively, the use in one line of all the letters of the alphabet or of all the parts of speech; and, lastly, formulas for composing Latin poems that sound like Spanish—this being but an anticipation of the beloved Gongoristic ideal that struggled, conversely, to produce Spanish verses that sound like Latin.

Thus, dedicated to such small, sterile practices for the clever, the poetasters in both languages were congratulated for their extravagance; and Gongorism, on gaining ascendancy, made its followers appear utterly ridiculous. One of these was Friar Juan de Valencia, a member of the order of the Merced, who was on the governing committee of his order and who died while he was *comendador* (prefect) in the monastery of Veracruz in 1646. He performed two feats, both quite useless: the memorizing of a Latin dictionary, the *Calepino*, and the writing of a eulogy of Saint Teresa which was composed of 350 Latin couplets in retrogressive verses so that they could be read backward as well as forward. So arduous and difficult was the composition of this eulogy that the Jesuit Canal, a great Latinist, almost lost his mind when he, in turn, tried to imitate this undertaking by writing in retrogressive couplets a eulogy on the above-mentioned *Teresiada* by Valencia. Perhaps the Licentiate Francisco Ayerra y Santa María, in concocting his famous cento from the works of Góngora, really lost his mind—at least, those who try to read his work run the risk of losing theirs. It is well to notice, in this connection, that the centos, whether Latin or Spanish, enjoyed singular favor in those days and that their artifice consisted in drawing material for new poems from the work of any selected author. Góngora, as well as Virgil, suffered from this desecration. Furthermore, the illustrious founder of Gongorism had bewitched the verse-makers of New Spain to such an extent that they placed him on the same altar with the classical writers; and there Don Luis, between Homer and Horace, was read, commented upon, and even memorized in the schools.

As in the good old days of González de Eslava (or even more recent times), there was a plethora of versifiers in Latin and Spanish. Beristáin, in his *Library of Northern Spanish America,* mentions more than one hundred. In 1623, there was published in Mexico a *Garland of Erudite Latin Verse in Honor and Praise of the Two Most Beautiful Flowers and Saintly Virgins, Lucía and Petronila,* to which a large number of poets contributed. Literary contests were held frequently. In the contest which was sponsored by the University of Mexico in 1682 in honor of the Immaculate Conception, and which Sigüenza y Góngora described in his work entitled *Triunfo Parthénico (Parthenic Triumph),* the compositions numbered more than five hundred, and sixty-eight of them won prizes.

POETS OF THE *Triunfo Parthénico*

Considering the large number taking part in the contest and the fact that among the winners, apart from poets of renown, were doctors of philosophy, licentiates, holders of bachelors' degrees, and prelates—persons, in fact, who had won degrees representing high standards of scholarship—it might be thought that New Spain, in the last years of the seventeenth century, was a luminous and fragrant garden of the Muses. Nothing could be less true. Not only were good taste and good poetry absent from such a medley, but good sense and literary decorum as well. The *Triunfo Parthénico* is a brothel filled with freaks and oddities hateful to common sense. If there is some talent present occasionally, it becomes deformed on the rack of ridiculous subtleties or is hidden in the bombastic rubbish of empty words; generally speaking, however, ideas are lacking, and it would seem that such a distressing, rhetorical barbarism could have been executed only by idle quacks in an intellectual vacuum.

Why pause, then, to study in detail each and all of the versifiers of the *Triunfo Parthénico,* who represent—individually and collectively —the zenith of Mexican Gongorism? It will suffice to point out a few and to mention in passing their peculiar characteristics which give them a family resemblance.

Luis de Sandoval y Zapata was one of the group; he was of an illustrious Mexican family and, according to Father Florencia, "the equal of the best poets of his century." He wrote a *Miscellany of Poetry to Our Lady of Guadalupe,* of which the following sonnet celebrated by his contemporaries is an example. In this poem, he compares—Pimentel says—the transformation of the flowers into the image of the Virgin with the metamorphosis of the mythological phoenix:

> El astro de los pájaros expira,
> Aquella alada eternidad del viento,
> Y entre la exhalación del movimiento
> Víctima arde olorosa de la pira.
>
> En grande hoy metamórfosi se admira
> Mortaja a cada flor; más lucimiento
> Vive en el lienzo nacional aliento
> El ámbar vegetable que respira.
>
> Retratan a María sus colores:
> Corre cuando del sol la luz las hiere
> De aquestas sombras envidioso el día.
>
> Más dichosas que el fénix morís, flores;
> Que él, para nacer pluma, polvo muere
> Pero vosotras para ser María.[1]

Sandoval also published in 1645 a *Panegyric on Patience*—and probably he foresaw that much of the same would be needed to read it.

Juan de Guevara, another represented in the *Triunfo Parthénico*, a Gongorist as remarkable as Sandoval, was chaplain of the monastery of Saint Inés and had a reputation as a poet, so much so that in 1654

---

[1] The astral bird expires,
That winged eternity of the wind,
And in the ashes lies
The fragrant victim burning on the pyre.

Today a greater miracle is
To be seen as a shroud to each flower:
A national spirit lives on the canvas
Which breathes the vegetable amber.

Their colors depict Mary;
The day, in envy of their hues,
Disappears when the light of the sun plays upon them.

But, flowers, you will die a more blessed death than the Phoenix,
For he becomes as dust to be a bird again,
But you will be Mary.

the university honored him by electing him secretary of its literary contest in praise of the Virgin Mary. He wrote a poetic medley and many sacred poems. He is remembered, however, for his connection with Sor Juana Inés de la Cruz, with whom he collaborated in the play *Love Is a Labyrinth*, the second act of which he composed.

José López Avilez (chaplain and page master of Viceroy Friar Payo Enríquez de Rivera) versified in abundance and obtained from Sigüenza y Góngora the title "the great father of the Muses and the favorite of academic literary contests." This great father of the Muses published in 1669 a worthless folio of Latin poems in praise of the Virgin of Guadalupe.

Another of these Gongorists, Francisco Ayerra y Santa María, licentiate, secular presbyter, and chaplain of Jesús María, was a native of Puerto Rico, but should be considered Mexican because Mexico was the scene of his literary activity. Besides being an "elegant Latinist, an admirable poet, an acute philosopher," and the possessor of a multitude of perfections, he was considered by the collector of the *Triunfo Parthénico* "an erudite encyclopedia of flowery letters." His claims to fame, however, have been effectively canceled by posterity, which remembers only his celebrated and freakish cento of lines extracted from Góngora's works.

Pedro Muñoz de Castro, bachelor of arts and presbyter, appears to have been a person of keen and fertile intellect, in the judgment of both Sigüenza and Beristáin. He was indefatigable. He specialized in the coining of titles. He made them extraordinary. See one of them, which will suffice—and more than suffice—to explain the personality of such an author: "Echoes from the Caves of Mount Carmel and Resounding Sad Bleats from Rachel's Sheep in the Sheepfold of Elijah, the Carmelite Sun, Whose Ardent Rays Melted into Tears His Daughters, the Carmelite Nuns of Mexico, Who Mourn the Loss of Their Beloved Benefactor, His Excellency, Sr. Don Fernando de Lencastre Noroña y Silva, Late Viceroy of New Spain" (1717).

Lastly, Don Carlos de Sigüenza y Góngora, the pride and glory of the culture of New Spain—perhaps in his time the sole representative of it—should be included, as a poet, in this brief enumeration. His historical works will be discussed in Chapter VIII; here his ability as a poet and critic will be mentioned. As a critic—as has already been seen—he was an easy prey to flattery; he was also inconsistent. He severely condemned affectation in speech. "To write of a dead woman," he said in the prologue to his *Western Paradise,*

that her face—instead of revealing sadness and faded graces—glowed with the red of a blush or the color of crimson roses, which made her peaceful face unbelievably beautiful; and to use all this circumlocution only to say that she kept in death the coloring she had in life—what is this except for the author to condemn his own book to oblivion, especially if the whole work is written in such a style?

Though he was not a *culterano* by conviction, Sigüenza poured out the copious flood of his praise on the Gongoristic poets of the *Triunfo,* and he himself became more and more affected, although it must be admitted that he was guilty of this only in verse and doubtless believed that extravagance and nonsense, so inadmissible in plain prose, conveyed elegance and were a necessary aid to poetry.

His "*Canción*" (song), which was included in the *Triunfo Parthénico* and which took the first prize at the university, is as abstruse, empty, bombastic, and tasteless as are all the other poems of the collection. Neither his sacred-historical poem about the Virgin of Guadalupe, entitled *Indian Spring* (1668), which was written in seventy-nine wretched octaves, nor his composition praising San Francisco Javier is to be recommended. The Lord did not call him to be a poet, surely; he belonged on a different road.

THE RULE AND THE EXCEPTIONS

Of all the throng of Gongoristic versifiers, perhaps the only one who deserves to be remembered and esteemed is the Jesuit Matías de Bocanegra. Born in Puebla at the beginning of the seventeenth century, he was respected by viceroys and bishops as much for his ability as a poet as for his knowledge of letters and theology. But only one of his poems—which is quite superior to most of what was written in his time—rescues him from oblivion. This is the *Allegorical Song of Disillusion,* a moving parable in which the poet proposes to show the excellences of the religious life, which, austerely and calmly, in silence and in solitude, disregards the worldly pleasures and dissipations that bring only disillusion and bitterness. A work commendable, according to Menéndez y Pelayo, "for the fluency of its poetry as well as for the delicacy of its mystical meaning," the *Allegorical Song* was popular at the time it was written and was imitated frequently by various poets in the seventeenth and eighteenth centuries.

The scourge of Gongoristic versifiers invaded, in full deification of affectation, all fields of writing. Everything was versified copiously: in verse, the biography of Friar Payo Enríquez was presented; in verse were told the lives of saints aplenty; woven in short sibylline lines were descriptions of funeral processions, royal festivals, and voyages.

The poets of New Spain, during the seventeenth century, resembled a flock of jangling magpies. But, in the midst of all this discord, suddenly a melodious voice was heard: it was the Tenth Muse who was singing.

Juana Inés de Asbaje

Juana Inés de Asbaje—such was the name the blessed nun bore in worldly life—was born in a farmhouse in San Miguel Nepantla, in the territory of Amecameca, on November 12, 1651.

Her precocity presaged the robust strength of her genius. At three years of age, without the knowledge of her mother, she began her studies.

. . . My mother having sent my sister, older than I, to one of those so-called "friends" to be taught to read, I followed her as a prank; and, on hearing the lesson given to her, I became fired with the desire to learn to read; deceiving the teacher, I said that my mother wished me to receive a lesson also.

Whatever the lesson was, it must have been easy for a pupil of such ability. In two years, says her biographer Father Calleja, she had learned "to read, write, count, and perform all the quaint intricacies of pretty needlework."

She had been born with the natural gift of expressing herself in verse. Before she was eight years old, she had composed a *loa* (a commendatory introduction) for the Corpus Christi festival. In the meantime, her intellectual curiosity continued to grow. She heard that in Mexico City there were a university and schools in which the sciences were studied.

. . . And as soon as I heard this, I began to beseech my mother with urgent and persistent entreaties to allow me to change my manner of dress [the future nun proposed to disguise herself as a man] and go to Mexico City in order to study and to attend the University while living in the home of some relatives. She did not permit me to do so—and quite rightly—but I satisfied my desire by reading many different kinds of books belonging to my grandfather, without letting punishments or reprimands stop me.

Juana Inés was eight years old when she moved with her parents to the capital of New Spain. Here all wondered, as she said, "not so much at my talent as at the memory and information I had at the age when it seemed that I had hardly had time to learn to talk." Twenty lessons from the bachelor Martín de Olivas were sufficient for her to acquire a mastery of Latin. She had not only ability, but the will to work. When she wished to acquire new knowledge, she adopted the harsh practice of setting a time limit for herself by cutting her hair; if her hair grew out before she accomplished her purpose, she cut it again, since she did not think it appropriate "that a head so devoid of knowledge should be covered with hair, which is a most desirable adornment."

She was beautiful with spiritual and profound beauty, which is quite evident and unforgettable in the portrait Cabrera made of her when she was a nun. Since she was intelligent as well as beautiful, her fame spread and soon she became prominent at court as a lady-in-waiting to the wife of the viceroy. The latter was quite flattered by the many poems that the poet dedicated to her. A little later, astonished at the intelligence Juana Inés seemed to possess and desiring to test her, Viceroy Marqués de Mancera called to his palace all the professors at the university and also all scholars in Mexico City who were learned in the arts and sciences. The young girl appeared before an assembly of about forty theologians, scripturists, philosophers, mathematicians, historians, humanists, and poets. And "just as"—in the words of the viceroy—"a royal galleon would defend itself from smaller sloops which were attacking it, so did Juana Inés extricate herself from the questions, arguments, and rejoinders that all, each in his field, propounded."

While living in the palace of the viceroy, she was not only admired for her rare intellectual gifts, but courted for her beauty. Strangely enough, however, at this time she suddenly determined to embrace a monastic existence.

Considering the spirit and customs of her age, such a resolution was not extraordinary, but for those who are acquainted with one element of her lyrics—perhaps the best part of her poetry: the love element—there is concealed in that important and possibly dramatic moment of her life a mystery that perhaps will never be solved. Was a hidden passion, perhaps a disappointment in love, the motive that impelled her to enter a cloister? She offered an explanation, certainly, of the motive which caused her to take that step, by saying:

> I became a nun, recognizing that the profession had aspects (I am speaking of the accessory, not the essential things) repugnant to my intellect; but withal, in view of my complete distaste for marriage, taking the vows seemed the least undesirable and most reasonable choice I could make. For the sake of the assurance of salvation, that being of the first and greatest importance, I yielded up all the foolish desires of my being: the wish to live alone, to have no obligatory duties that would deprive me of freedom to study, and no community gossip to disturb the restful silence of my books.

But the heat of the flame which burns in some of the poet's verses is sufficient to indicate that she made the foregoing statements after she became a nun, with the purpose of keeping her real reason secret, and not while she was contemplating taking the vows.

It is certain, however, that on August 14, 1667, when she was not quite sixteen years of age, she entered the convent of Santa Teresa la Antigua, Viceroy Marqués de Mancera and his wife witnessing the ceremony. But the poet could not long endure the austere life of the order; she became ill and left the convent on November 18. But her decision was irrevocable: a little more than a year later, on February 24, 1669, she entered the convent of San Jerónimo, this time to remain for the rest of her life.

In the shadow of the cloister, she lived among her books, maps, and musical and scientific instruments, consecrated to study. But such consecration could not always be constant or tranquil. Once her Mother Superior, "very saintly and candid," ordered her to abstain from study as a sinful thing. In view of her health, physicians, on another occasion, made the same recommendation. But since she had a strong will and since her consuming love of books and her desire for knowledge constituted her reason for living, she devoted nearly all of her time in the convent to study.

Toward the close of her life, events forced her to depart from the path she had been obstinately following. It happened that she challenged some statements made by Father Vieyra, a famous preacher, thereby giving an opportunity to Don Manuel Fernández de Santa Cruz, Bishop of Puebla—who assumed the pseudonym of "Sor Filotea" —to address to her a stupid letter in which, after flattering her for the above-mentioned challenge, he exhorted her to lift her eyes to heaven and give up secular learning in order to consecrate herself entirely to religion. "You have wasted much time," concluded the bishop, "in the study of philosophers and poets; now it is right that you should give up books and devote your time to perfecting yourself."

Literary history owes much to the impertinence of "Sor Filotea"; if his letter had not been written, the best document on the life and psychology of the poet would be lacking. This document is the valuable letter which Sor Juana sent in reply to the Bishop of Puebla, a letter in which she gave the most complete data now available on her life, her character, her literary inclinations, and the difficulties arising from these, and in which, further, with the most noble integrity, she declared herself in favor of the education of women and maintained her right to question the sermon with which she had disagreed.

Very deep, however, must have been the effect produced on the mind of the illustrious nun by the bishop's warning that she should consecrate herself entirely to religious matters and completely separate herself from secular things. For, shortly thereafter, she ordered sold, for the benefit of the poor, the four thousand volumes in her library, as well as her musical and scientific instruments and her maps. She made a general confession and signed with her blood two protestations of her faith. In the solitude of her cell, there remained only devotional books, the reading of which she interrupted frequently with the rigors of cruel penances. In the fervor of such mystic ardor, Sor Juana had spent two years when an epidemic of malignant fever desolated Mexico City and invaded the convent. Impelled by a great love, the poet then nursed her sick sisters, and, being stricken in turn, she fathomed the secret of death on April 17, 1695, at the age of forty-four years.

That the genius of Sor Juana Inés de la Cruz, as Menéndez y Pelayo observes, should appear in such a disastrous literary epoch has something of the supernatural and extraordinary about it.

The same qualities which isolated her and placed her above the writers of her time kept her from perishing in such an atmosphere.

Traits distinctive of her personality were restlessness of spirit, shown in her never-ceasing eagerness for learning and investigating, breadth of culture, vigor of mind, powerful imagination, and a boundless depth of feeling that could fraternize with honesty only.

Although she could not keep from paying tribute to the prevailing bad taste, she possessed innate qualities that prevented her from being dominated by it. In her prolific works there are, indeed, occasional poems and verses written on request, in which affectation runs parallel with overrefinement of thought. She made concessions, also, to the current style in her fantasy *A Dream* by imitating Góngora's *Solitude;* and she even surpassed him in extravagance and obscurity in her *Allegory of Neptune*. But, in spite of these lapses, she never wholly surrendered to Gongorism, and she should not be classed with the occasional versifiers of her time. Her euphuistic tendency had something of literary virtuosity in it; but it was not a genuine and sincere manifestation of her genius, which was essentially clear and direct. On the other hand, her poetic instinct was too well developed for her to limit herself to the artificial combinations that were pleasing to those who lacked such instinct; furthermore, she had too many worthwhile things to say to take exclusive delight in that sonorous vacuum which pleased those who pretended to be wits; in short, she belonged, because of her culture, to the sane literary tradition of the preceding century.

Even if Sor Juana's poetry is not always devoid of affectation—even if it sometimes has a complicated and subtle ingenuity which approaches the *conceptismo* style—her best poems reveal the influence of no school, portray her own unique personality, and have "enduring and absolute poetic value," as Menéndez y Pelayo says. These are the works that make her the major poet of her epoch and place her among the greatest poets in the Spanish language.

Disregarding the many occasional poems and euphuistic imitations, Sor Juana's purest vein is to be found in her beautiful carols, in which, according to Manuel Toussaint, she "seems to sing with the voice of an angel," and, above all, in her poems of mysticism and of human love.

"Sor Juana's poems of worldly love," in the judgment of Menéndez y Pelayo, "are the most gentle and delicate that have ever come from the pen of a woman." There is such eloquence in them—Sor

Juana succeeds so easily in using the right word at the right time (the true touchstone of sincerity in love poetry)—that the suspicion, well founded, indeed, has been voiced that a passion, as fervent as it was mysterious, must have filled the life of the matchless poet. The amorous demands, the soft cooing, the painful complaints, the jealous raptures, the grief broken with sobs are not, and could not be, artificial and feigned experiences: they have the incontestable accent of truth.

Among the most notable of her secular poems are: the "Ballad of Absence"; the "Lyrics"; the sonnets "To the Rose," "O Shadow, Stop," and the one written on the death of the Duke of Veragua; and her famous *redondillas* (seven-syllable quatrains) *"Hombres necios . . .,"* which are very popular today.

Because of having felt human love so very deeply, Sor Juana was likewise fitted to soar to the very highest in the expression of divine love. Referring to what he considers the most beautiful of her spiritual poems, the songs interpolated in *The Divine Narcissus*, Menéndez y Pelayo says,

They are so beautiful and pure, and, generally speaking, so free from affectation and *culteranismo* that they appear to belong to the sixteenth rather than to the seventeenth century and to be the work of some disciple of San Juan de la Cruz and of Friar Luis de León rather than the work of a nun of the New World.

Sor Juana wrote little prose; however, that which she did write shows mastery of that medium, also. The *Athenagórica*, which contains her criticism of Father Vieyra, the *Reply to Sor Filotea*, and two works of a devotional character constitute her only known prose work.

But, following in the footsteps of Calderón, she showed outstanding ability in the drama. *The Obligations of a Home* is a beautiful cloak-and-sword comedy. Less fortunate is *Love Is a Labyrinth*, which is weakened by euphuism. As has been stated, Juan de Guevara collaborated with her on the second act of this play, but in the other acts there are many beautiful passages that are obviously the work of Sor Juana. The religious plays *The Divine Narcissus, Saint Hermenegildo,* and *Saint Joseph's Scepter*—which are of brilliant Calderonian inspiration—and the *Praise of the Immaculate Conception* comprise, in addition to the plays already mentioned, the dramatic works of the nun.

Excepting the *Allegory of Neptune,* printed in 1680 or 1681, and the carols, which were printed soon after they were written, the works of Sor Juana were first circulated in manuscript form. Don Juan de Camacho Gayna began to collect these manuscripts, and the first volume of her poems was printed in Madrid in 1689 under the long and unfortunate title of "The Castalian Flood of the Unique Poetess, the Tenth Muse, Sor Juana Inés de la Cruz, Professed Nun in the Monastery of San Jerónimo of the Imperial City of Mexico; Who, in Various Meters, Idioms, and Styles, with Elegance, Subtlety, Clarity, and Ingenuity Furnishes Useful Poems for Teaching, Recreation, and Delight." The second volume was published in Seville in 1692, and the third and last in Madrid in 1700, after the death of the poet. Of these volumes other editions were printed in Madrid, Barcelona, Valencia, Zaragoza, and Lisbon during the seventeenth and eighteenth centuries. Few in number, incomplete, and inferior are the nineteenth-century editions of her works. Her poems, filled with gross errors, appeared in anthologies, periodicals, and reviews. And except for the excellent selection by Don Manuel Toussaint (*Sor Juana Inés de la Cruz, Obras escogidas,* Mexico, 1928) and the beautiful edition of the sonnets (*Sonetos,* Mexico, 1931), prepared and annotated by Xavier Villaurrutia, it could be affirmed, until recently, that the public did not know the original, authentic, and complete text of the poems of the Tenth Muse.

Fortunately, Dr. Alfonso Méndez Plancarte undertook the publication of the *Complete Works* of Sor Juana, in four volumes entitled *Personal Lyric, Christmas Carols and Sacred Letters, Sacred and Secular Theater,* and *Prose* (Foundation of Economic Culture, 1951-57). The first three volumes were prepared by Dr. Plancarte and, after his death, the fourth was completed by Alí Chumacero and Alberto G. Salceda.

The Last Stages of *Culteranismo*

In the first half of the eighteenth century *culteranismo,* which had reached its height in the previous century, became completely decadent. Even before the corruption of taste had become general, it can be said that true poetry had disappeared. No influence was exercised by Sor Juana—that is, by the strong and individual works in which she departed from the literary mode dominant in New Spain. On the contrary, Gongorism continued its reign, becoming more and more hazy and degenerate until it disappeared in the middle of the century.

Among the inferior versifiers of this period, two poets of unequal merit will be discussed here. The first of these, in chronological order, is Don Miguel Reyna Zeballos, a lawyer of the *Audiencia* of Mexico, who published in 1738, under the title of *The Eloquence of Silence*, a life of San Juan Nepomuceno. Reyna Zeballos was more of a *conceptista* than a *gongorino;* and although his book may by its title be a symbol of the virtue which he and his colleagues ought to have respected, it can be honestly said that his verse is vigorous. The second, Francisco Ruiz de León, a native of Tehuacán de las Granadas, was a better poet than Reyna Zeballos. Apart from the volumes of poetry which he left in manuscript form, the following have been published: in 1755, a heroic poem, *Exploits of Hernán Cortés: Triumphs of the Faith and Glory of Spanish Arms;* and, in 1791, in Bogotá, perhaps after the author's death, the religious poem entitled *Sweet Myrrh for the Encouragement of Sinners*. The *Exploits of Hernán Cortés,* containing twelve cantos written in octaves, presents the history of the Conquest of Mexico from the expedition of Juan de Grijalva to the imprisonment of Cuauhtémoc. Of the many poor efforts at writing epic poems praising Hernán Cortés, this may be considered the most interesting, although it hardly rises above the mediocre. Suffering from the worst vices of the Gongoristic school, of which he was the last representative in New Spain, Ruiz de León was, nevertheless, an able poet, skilful and occasionally profound. In his work the religious inspiration is superior to the heroic; in the *decimas* (ten-line stanzas) of his *Sweet Myrrh,* which tells of the grief of the Virgin Mary at the foot of the cross, are some moving passages written with such spontaneity and simplicity that it would not be too much to say that his work, though it is euphuistic, reveals glimpses of the new school, pseudo-classicism, which was to follow *culteranismo.*

THE CLASSICAL REACTION

The reaction against affectation—which had dominated Mexican poetry during almost all of the seventeenth century and part of the

eighteenth—was initiated about the middle of the latter century by
two concurrent causes that produced the same effect: the efforts of
the Jesuits, who, in their studies, tried to restore classical taste, with
its harmony, proportion, and clarity, not only by explaining but by
translating and imitating the great Latin poets; and the influence of
the Spanish neo-classicists who, at the accession of the Bourbons, had
transplanted French taste to Spain. Among the latter were: Luzán,
a strong and determined teacher; Father Isla, a writer of elegant and
smooth prose, merciless in his attitude toward pompous preachers; and
Don Nicolás Fernández de Moratín, a meticulous poet; and, later,
Cadalso, a refined and comprehensive writer, Iriarte and Samaniego,
authors of fables, and the effeminate Meléndez Valdés.

The movement in Mexico merely followed the literary mode of
Spain. But just as Mexican writers, imitating Gongorism, had gone
far beyond its original creators, so the new school carried the reaction
against Gongorism to the extreme opposite and was guilty of a new
and vicious exaggeration: *prosaísmo,* the extreme of prosy dulness.
The eccentric and undecipherable euphuists were followed by clumsy,
prosaic poets; the excess of poetic language, by none at all; obscurity,
by blatant vulgarity. And it was not until the dawn of the nineteenth century that the needed equilibrium was achieved in the person
of a little-known Franciscan monk, a genuine neo-classic poet, Friar
Manuel de Navarrete, who effectively represents neo-classicism among
Mexican writers. Another poet, a contemporary of his, Sartorio, reflects extreme *prosaísmo.* The contrast between the two is remarkable.

Sartorio

Don José Manuel Mariano Aniceto Sartorio was born in Mexico
City on April 17, 1746, and died there on January 28, 1829. His
father was Italian and his mother Mexican. In spite of his poverty, he
received a good education; he was a student at the School of San
Ildefonso, where he held a scholarship until the expulsion of the
Jesuits in 1767. He studied Latin and various living languages; he
became a priest and was distinguished as a preacher because of his
fine command of words; but he never advanced beyond the rank of
a mere *presbítero,* although he held numerous posts: he was rector
of a school, professor, president of learned societies, synodical exam-

iner of the Archbishopric of Mexico, censor of theatrical works, books, and periodicals.

Sartorio's life, modest and simple as well as long and laborious, was divided between professional duties and the cultivation of letters. He was of a humble, tranquil, and gentle nature until he was shaken by the coming of a grave event: the War of Independence. Sympathizing with the revolutionary party, Sartorio refused—thereby disobeying viceregal mandates—to convert his pulpit into a political weapon against liberty. This aroused the suspicions of the authorities and culminated in an order by the attorney-general of the Inquisition for his arrest, from which fate he was saved by the Countess of Regla. He thus acquired political prestige: he participated, as elector, in the popular elections of municipal officials, granted under the Spanish Constitution of 1812; and, when Independence was gained, as a member of the Provisional Assembly he signed the act of emancipation on September 28, 1821. On this same memorable date, he preached at the thanksgiving service held in the Cathedral of Mexico City. Because he was a friend of Iturbide, who had decorated him with the Cross of Guadalupe, he saw that he was in danger of being exiled when Iturbide's government fell; but political passions, always violent, were curbed in the presence of the merits of the old priest, and he was allowed to end his days in peace.

Many of Sartorio's original works and translations, among them twenty volumes of sermons, remained unpublished during his lifetime; and he published only a few prayer books, two or three sermons and as many letters, some religious pamphlets, and a few "Lyrics" in praise of Charles IV, which won a prize offered by the university. The posthumous edition of his *Sacred and Profane Poems* was printed in Puebla in 1832 and fills seven thick volumes in octavo.

In his copious poetic work, two styles are noticeable: one, familiar and circumstantial; the other, mystical, or, to be more exact, *mariana*, i.e., in the traditional manner of the poems celebrating the Virgin Mary.

Sartorio's style is invariably prosaic in his informal work. In the above-mentioned seven volumes of poetry are to be found—writes Luis G. Urbina—

décimas written on request, sonnets on familiar themes, octaves of felicitation, insipid epigrams, *redondillas* for collecting alms, extravagant epitaphs, shallow fables, songs for awakening the novitiates on the day of their profession, trivial poems to persons and animals—to noble ladies, mothers superior of convents, the Archbishop, the Viceroy, a dog named Mono, in celebration of "a parrot's victory," to housewives, to the naked poor, to an old woman who asked the poet for verses; all truly naïve poems. Several of these trifles were written in Latin verse; the remainder, in mediocre Castilian. They can be described as childish scribblings on a pupil's slate.

In his compositions of a religious character, Sartorio, though trying to maintain the dignity proper to the type, does not show so much prosiness as in his secular poetry; nevertheless, he is never free from it, excepting only in the poems which, with Italian vivacity, flow from his pen in praise of the Virgin Mary. Urbina speaks of these as "delightful hymns of holy love, flowing from the purest mystic fountain"; poems which are "still slovenly, but never dull, nor inferior, nor trivial," and which reveal "a true poet who is not exempt from the artificial rhetoric of his epoch but is expressive, sincere, restrained by a profound sentiment, and glowing with the fires of inspiration."

Sartorio, however, was not, and could not be, the one to receive the torch of poetry as it fell from the hands of Sor Juana Inés de la Cruz in the last days of the seventeenth century. The poet to whom this honor belongs and who, because of it, should be considered the restorer of lyric poetry in Mexico was Friar Manuel de Navarrete.

Navarrete

In 1806 there began to appear in the *Mexican Daily* some beautiful anacreontic lyrics in which were combined the musical clarity of Garcilaso in expressing emotion and Virgilian serenity in describing nature. There were such grace and elegance in these lyrics that the poet far surpassed other poets of his time: he was a marvelous flower in a desert.

The mystery of his incognito aroused curiosity concerning the personality of the singer; his poems achieved such popularity that the Arcadia, a literary society that drew to its bosom the most enthusiastic advocates of neo-classic taste, named him its *mayoral* (head shepherd) by virtue of his being the chief poet of New Spain.

The author of these anacreontic odes was Friar José Manuel Martínez de Navarrete. Of a noble but poor family, he was born in

Zamora, Michoacán, on June 16, 1768. He studied Latin in his native city and came to the capital when he was quite young. He decided to become a monk; and at nineteen years of age, he went to Querétaro, where he entered the Franciscan monastery of San Pedro y San Pablo. There he was made a novitiate; he perfected his Latin studies in the monastery of Pueblito; he studied philosophy for three years in the cloister of Celaya; and, returning to Querétaro, he completed his theological courses and was made professor of Latin in the monastery of his order. He taught in the convent of Valladolid (now Morelia); having been ordained as a priest, he preached in Ríoverde and Silao about 1805; later, he became the parish priest of San Antonio Tula (1807); and finally was made *guardián* of the monastery of Tlalpujahua, where he died on July 19, 1809.

A man of extreme simplicity and modesty, Navarrete was as lovable as he was timid, and was pleasing and attractive in appearance. But since his religious life was drab and without incident, his poetic biography is more interesting than his personal one.

His poems were published in Mexico City in two volumes entitled *Poetic Interludes* (1823). Apparent in much of his work is the influence of Meléndez Valdés, the most popular and pleasing of the Spanish neo-classicists of that time. Nevertheless, the Latin background of Navarrete, his familiarity with old Castilian poetry, particularly with that of Garcilaso and Lope, and, above all, the fact that he was a born poet of rich sensibility and natural gifts, which he refined and polished, gave to his literary personality the vigor and prestige no mere imitator can ever attain.

"He had," says Menéndez y Pelayo, "the sense of proportion and harmony, revealed not only in each verse, but in each complete poem," a quality which "is the clear indication of essentially poetic organization." His language was "naturally pure and ample enough, without ostentation or seeming effort." He was, therefore, very different from almost all the other Mexican poets of the seventeenth and eighteenth centuries.

The influence of Meléndez Valdés is most conspicuous in Navarrete's amorous poetry, especially in those erotic odes which might be interpreted as reflecting on the character of the humble Franciscan if it were not for the fact that such carnal praises of Clori and Clorila, Phyllis and Anarda, instead of representing true passion and sensuality, are transparent rhetorical artifices to which the innocent friar resorted, following the tendency of his poetic school.

Precisely because of this insincerity, the amorous poems of Navarrete are the least consistent and beautiful of his poetry. They are surpassed, undoubtedly, by the poems in which he gives free rein to his quiet love of nature, and by his poems of moral and religious character.

Some critics claim that Navarrete's poems are sometimes too long, that his inspiration is intermittent and uneven, and that occasionally he does not escape *prosaísmo*. Conspicuous in his works, nevertheless, are spontaneity, freshness, sensitive delicacy, picturesqueness, and—as Menéndez y Pelayo observes—"a certain melancholy fervor which is like the faint dawn of romanticism."

With its combination of good and bad qualities, the poetry of Friar Manuel de Navarrete represents—along with that of Sor Juana Inés de la Cruz—the highest point reached in Mexican colonial lyric poetry. In its relationship to its own epoch, it exemplifies the maturity of neo-classicism, the tradition in which the style of the poets of the revolutionary period was formed.

VII.

The Humanists and the Theater

I F ANY literary tradition is outstanding in Mexican literature, it is the classical. The Greco-Latin culture was given predominance from the early days of the founding of the first schools by the missionaries; it was strengthened later in the university; and it found, lastly, learned proponents and propagandists among the Jesuits.

From the end of the sixteenth century, Latin was cultivated as much as Spanish. In Latin were written laudatory epigrams, inscriptions, mottoes, and couplets for the adornment of monuments, tombs, and triumphal arches. Almost all literature intended for teaching purposes was written in Latin; and, as already mentioned, Latin versifiers were as numerous as Spanish—both being equally infected by the cult of *culteranismo.*

Reacting against the dominant literary decadence, the Jesuits, by cultivating good Latin poetry and by translating the classics, brought about the most important humanistic movement that American culture records. The appearance of the renowned humanists of the eighteenth century constitutes an important occasion in Mexican letters.

"A type of academic literature that is always tinged with the artificial and false," is Menéndez y Pelayo's comment on the works of the writers who carried humanism to its extreme perfection; and perhaps it is due to this academic flavor, as much as to the disuse of the Latin language, that their works lie today in oblivion. But, as this same critic argues, it is essential to distinguish

between the centos and mosaic pieces, called academic verse—which have no value other than that of more or less useless mental gymnastics, and the abuse of which can become pernicious—and the truly poetic Latin verses composed by worthy poets who were, at the same time, learned humanists. These latter were accustomed to think, feel, and read in a foreign tongue that was to them not a dead language, but living and real, since they studied, taught, and communicated with scholars in it, and found it easier, more natural, and more adequate for expressing their inspiration than their own tongue.

THREE DISTINGUISHED HUMANISTS

Three great humanists represent the full flowering of Latin poetry in New Spain: Abad, Alegre, and Landívar.

Abad

The first of these, Father Diego José Abad, was born of a rich family on July 1, 1727, on an hacienda near the village of Jiquilpan, Michoacán. After receiving his early education there under private teachers, he entered the school of San Ildefonso de México, where he was an outstanding student. In 1741 he joined the Jesuit order as a novice at Tepozotlán. Later, as a professor of rhetoric, of philosophy, and of both canon and civil law in schools in Zacatecas and Mexico City, he became known as a mentor of youth because of his reforming zeal. He fought scholasticism in philosophy and Gongorism in literature. He devoted his entire life to study and to teaching. At the time of the expulsion of the Jesuits, he was rector of the school at Querétaro. He emigrated to Italy; and in Ferrara, the place he chose for his residence, he continued the literary tasks that brought him prominence and honor. He died in Bologna on September 30, 1779.

Father Abad published or left manuscripts of various works of scientific character. He also translated into Spanish some of the *Eclogues* of Virgil. But his great renown as a humanist is based on his Latin poem *De Deo,* the first part of which is a theological treatise in hexameters and the second part a *"Cristiada,"* or life of Christ. Of this work, which he began while he was in Querétaro, different editions were printed even before the poem was finished. The definitive edition in forty-three cantos, dedicated to the youth of Mexico, was published at Cesena in 1780.

In the opinion of Menéndez y Pelayo, the Latin of Father Abad is not entirely pure because of the neologisms required by his subject and the Gongoristic habits that he could not entirely avoid. Though

others surpass him in diction and harmony, he excels in greatness of thought and doctrine, in the lyrical quality of the frequent apostrophes with which he breaks the solemnity of the didactic material, in the power of sustained flight into the highest realm of thought, in the gentleness and grace of some of his descriptions, and—as a characteristic quality of style—in a certain sententious and grave conciseness.

Alegre

Padre Francisco Javier Alegre, the second of the humanists, is considered the greatest Mexican Latinist.

He was born in Veracruz on November 12, 1729. In the school of San Ignacio de Puebla, he studied rhetoric and philosophy, and at seventeen years of age became a Jesuit, taking his vows in Tepozotlán. Like his contemporary Abad, his greatest delight was in study; theology, history, and particularly classical literature were the objects of his loyal devotion. For some time he lived in Havana; from Cuba he went to Mérida and became professor of canon law in the school there. Later he was called to Mexico City to continue the history of the province which Father Florencia had begun. At the expulsion of the Jesuits, he was exiled to Bologna in 1767. His love of literature sweetened the last years of his life in exile. His death occurred on August 16, 1788.

Father Alegre left many works in either printed or manuscript form. Among his literary compositions are: a short epic poem on the conquest of Tyre by Alexander the Great (1775); Latin translations of the *Iliad*, printed in Bologna (1776), and of the *Batrachomyoachia*; Spanish translations of some of Horace's satires and epistles, and of the first three cantos of Boileau's *Art of Poetry*; and some original Latin poems, among which one deserves to be pointed out, the eclogue "Nysus," which was translated into Spanish by Bishop Pagaza. His previously unpublished works were issued in Mexico by Icazbalceta under the title of *Opúsculos inéditos latinos y castellanos del P. Francisco Javier Alegre* (1889).

As a Latin prose writer, Alegre compares favorably, because of the classic purity of his diction, with Melchor Cano or any of the finest theologians of the Renaissance, according to Menéndez y Pelayo. Likewise, if the merits of verse and diction only be considered, his version of the *Iliad* "is doubtless one of the monuments of Latin academic poetry"; however, when compared with the original, his version appears to be more Virgilian than Homeric. His epic on the conquest of Tyre and his incidental poems may be considered as mere exercises in style, preparatory to his translation of the *Iliad*; and of the few Spanish poems, the best is his free rendering of Boileau, which is graceful, smoothly flowing, and elegant, and is enhanced by excellent notes in which the translator reveals his wide knowledge as well as the flexibility and breadth of his taste.

Landívar

Because of the place of his birth, the last of this group, Father Rafael Landívar, cannot in the strictest sense be called Mexican, yet his turn of mind and his poems show that he very largely belongs to Mexico. Furthermore, this country—for which he professed great love—played a part in shaping his intellectual development. There is so much of the Mexican soul and landscape in his *Rusticatio Mexicana* that this poem cannot be omitted from a history of Mexican literature. Born in Old Guatemala (which then belonged to the viceroyalty of New Spain) on October 27, 1731, Landívar came to Mexico when he was quite young. He was hardly nineteen when he took the Jesuit vows in 1750 at Tepozotlán, where he taught philosophy. Later, he taught rhetoric and poetry in the Seminary School of San Jerónimo de Puebla. He was in Guatemala when the order for the expulsion of the Jesuits was given. He went to Italy, and died in Bologna on September 27, 1793.

Landívar was—in the judgment of Menéndez y Pelayo—"one of the most excellent poets among the modern Latinists." Because of his descriptive power, he would occupy first place among all American poets in that genre if he had written in Spanish. At any rate, because of the American local color which characterizes his work, the *Rusticatio* deserves a place between *The Grandeur of Mexico* by Balbuena and the *Poetic Miscellany* by Bello.

The *Rusticatio Mexicana*, written in Latin hexameters and comprising fifteen cantos and an appendix, is, in contrast to Virgil's *Georgics*, which inspired it, more than a bucolic poem: it is a vast and exquisite picture of nature and country life in America. The first three cantos form a series of marvelous frescoes in which the poet mirrors Mexican lakes, the eruption of Jorullo, and the cataracts of Guatemala. He describes, next, the flowery countryside of Oaxaca, the production of cochineal and the purple dye obtained from the murex, and the sowing, cultivation, harvest, and manufacture of indigo. He depicts the interesting habits of beavers and the different ways of trapping them. His muse tarries to consider life in the mines and the mining of silver and gold. He describes the cultivation of sugarcane. In a succession of pictures of delightful rustic flavor, he paints great herds, and flocks. Mexican springs furnish him abundant descriptive material. He writes about the birds, Mexican birds: the turkey, the *chachalaca* (chatterbox), the thrush, buzzard, wild pigeon, and mockingbird. For contrast, he draws attention to the wild beasts of the American forests. And, finally, the bucolic poet further adds to the attractiveness of his poem by dropping his role of naturalist and telling of some popular pastimes: cockfights, bullfights, the game of the greasy pole, and handball. He concludes the poem with an appendix concerning the Cross of Tepic, describing the valley and city by that name, and ends with an exhortation to Mexican youth:

> . . . Tú, empero, a quien eleva
> genio sutil sobre la plebe ruda,
> de la vida anticuada te desnuda,
> y vístete el ropaje de la nueva . . .[1]

Very few among the cultivators of neo-Latin poetry, according to Menéndez y Pelayo, had such genial and fresh inspiration as Landívar, or such wealth of descriptive imagination and such variety of poetic resources as are found in this poem.

The two earliest editions of the *Rusticatio Mexicana* were made in Italy: the first in Modena in 1781, and the second—notably enlarged because it is complete and definitive—in Bologna, in 1782. Several parts of this work have been translated into Spanish: the description of the cockfights, by Don José María de Heredia; the first canto, "The Lakes of Mexico," elegantly paraphrased by Bishop Pagaza; and the second canto, "The Jorullo," by Don Rafael Dávalos Mora. But complete translations of the poem have not been made until fairly recently. Father Federico Escobedo made a magnificent Spanish verse translation with scholarly notes, under the title of *Mexican Georgics;* and Don Ignacio Loureda made a literal prose version called *Rustica-*

---

[1] . . . You, however, whom subtle genius
Raises above the common herd,
Take off the customs of yesterday
And clothe yourselves with the new.

ción Mexicana, and printed it along with the original Latin. Both translations were published in Mexico in 1924.

Much later, in 1942, the National University published a new translation—in prose—of the poem, by Octaviano Valdés, with the title *Through the Fields of Mexico.* This last translation is, perhaps, the one which best reflects the spirit of Landívar's work.

OTHER MEXICAN HUMANISTS

Among other Mexican humanists worthy of mention are two Jesuits: Juan Luis Maneiro (1759-1802), who wrote in clear Latin prose a work entitled *Lives of Illustrious Mexican Men;* and Agustín de Castro (1728-1790), author of *The Exploits of Cortés,* an unfinished epic poem about Hernán Cortés, and other works which, apparently, he left in manuscript form, including a Spanish translation of Phaedrus' *Fables,* Seneca's *Troades,* and various poems by Anacreon, Sappho, Horace, Virgil, and Juvenal.

Further, the humanistic movement was not lacking in dull writers, such as Don José Rafael Larrañaga, native of Zacatecas, who translated all the works of Virgil into Spanish verse. This translation was published in Mexico in 1787, in four volumes; and if it cannot be recommended for elegance, at least it should be commended for being strictly literal.

THE THEATER

During the seventeenth and eighteenth centuries, dramatic art continued the course of development initiated in the sixteenth century. Unquestionably, the productions were better and more numerous than in the preceding period, and Mexican plays were presented along with the Spanish works then in vogue. Don Luis González Obregón mentions the existence of a *casa de comedias* (playhouse), which was in use by the end of the sixteenth century; and in the seventeenth century there was also a theater in the palace of the viceroy where plays were given on the saints' day of the viceroys, on the days for swearing allegiance to the king, and on other state occasions. By the year 1673, Mexico had a theater with a permanent company functioning normally; it was located in the Royal Hospital. When it was destroyed by fire in 1722, it was succeeded by the Old Coliseum, where, until the middle of the eighteenth century, quite a few actors won fame. In 1752, construction was begun on the New Coliseum, called today the Principal Theater, which was opened the following year.

Important facts are available about the buildings and theatrical companies; but, unfortunately, information about the plays and authors is too incomplete to give an accurate conception of the Mexican dramatic literature of that time.

Among the dramatists of the seventeenth century may be cited the names of Juan Ortiz de Torres, Jerónimo Becerra, and Alfonso Ramírez Vargas, who composed religious plays and *loas*. Two writers of comedies were Agustín Salazar y Torres and Eusebio Vela. Salazar y Torres, a Spaniard by birth, came to Mexico when he was a child. He probably composed some theatrical pieces here. Later he returned to Spain and there made his mark as a playwright. Speaking of Eusebio Vela, Beristáin says, "This dramatic poet, if not equal to the Lopes and the Calderóns, is certainly superior to the Montalvans and Moretos in the decency of his jests." He was a native of New Spain, where he lived and developed his talents. Fourteen of his plays are known by name, but all of them, though some were printed, are probably lost. Judging by their titles—*The Deceiver Deceived; Maddened by Insults, Calmed by Jealousy; The Achievement of Great Happiness Through the Dangers of Love*—it is to be presumed that Vela was influenced by the playwrights of the Golden Age.

The Mexican theater of the following century reached no higher development than that of the seventeenth century. The Presbyter Don Manuel Zumaya composed a drama, *Roderick* (1708), and an opera, *Parthenope* (1711), both of which were presented in the Viceregal Palace; Don Cayetano Cabrera Quintero, also a presbyter, wrote *Frustrated Hope* and *The Rainbow of Salamanca*; and Francisco Soria had three plays produced, *Duke William of Aquitaine, Mexican Magic,* and *The Genevieve*. . . . It is safe to say that neither Thalia nor Melpomene was particularly moved by the works of these writers.

VIII.

History

HE events of the Conquest, the problem of delving into the origin, history, and customs of the Indians, as well as the desire to know the Indian languages and dialects in order to hurdle the linguistic barrier between them and the natives, shaped the work of the missionaries and soldiers who created the great historical and philological works of the sixteenth century. Though following new plans, their successors did not lessen such activities during the next two centuries.

Except for Vetancourt, who walked in the footsteps of his predecessors, the field of history was almost completely dominated in the seventeenth century by the chroniclers of the ecclesiastical provinces. There were only a few writers—of whom López de Cogolludo is an example—who devoted themselves to the composition of other kinds of history, or, like Sigüenza y Góngora, besides reviewing particular events, dedicated themselves to collecting materials which would facilitate the task of future historians.

During the eighteenth century also, the chroniclers of the ecclesiastical provinces worked earnestly. But, thanks to the previous works of Sigüenza and no less to those of Boturini, there appeared historians who, like Clavijero and Veytia, could add method to scholarship; and these, guided by the true critical spirit, succeeded in making the great syntheses of Mexican history before the Conquest.

Paralleling history, philology was persistently cultivated during this period. The Golden Age of linguistics had been—as was natural— the sixteenth century, for in that century the first contact had been made between the civilizing missionaries and the Indians; but later the members of the religious orders did not cease in their efforts to extend their intercourse with the natives by increasing their own knowl-

edge of the indigenous languages and dialects. Therefore, they continued writing grammars, dictionaries, and catechisms. To the Nahuatlan language, knowledge of which was preferred above any other at
first, and to the other languages investigated during the first century
of the Conquest, there was added the study of new languages such as
the Timucoanan, Mame, Masahuan, Mayan, Cahitan, Tepehuanan,
and Tarahumaran; and to the names of early philologists, there were
added others no less illustrious: Friar Francisco de Pareja, Friar
Jerónimo Larios, the French Franciscan Friar Gabriel de San Buena-
ventura, and the Jesuit Father Horacio Carochi.

The six outstanding historians and linguists of this period will be
discussed first, and briefer mention will be given to the chroniclers
of the ecclesiastical provinces, other historians, and to the bibliographers at the close of the eighteenth century, whose investgiations
are of such great value to literary history.

The Chief Historians and Linguists

Vetancourt

Friar Agustín de Vetancourt, the first of this group, was born in
the City of Mexico in 1620 and took the Franciscan habit in Puebla;
he was parish priest of the church of San José of the Natives, chronicler of his province, and general commissioner of the Indies. His life,
dedicated equally to his work in the ministry and to literary endeavors, ended in 1700.

Possessing a thorough knowledge of the Nahuatlan language, he
published an *Arte (Grammar)* of that language in 1663 and also some
writings of religious character in both the Spanish and Nahuatlan.
The work for which he is now known is his *Mexican Theater: Short
Description of the Typical Historical, Political, Military, and Religious
Events in the New World* (Mexico, 1698).

The *Mexican Theater* is divided into four parts: the first is a treatise on the natural history of Mexico; the second deals with political
events from the most remote time up to the arrival of the Spaniards;
the third gives information about military affairs, from the discovery
of the New World until the fall of Tenochtitlán; and the fourth part
is the "Chronicle of the Province of the Holy Evangel," supplemented
by the "Franciscan Calendar."

Vetancourt, in respect to ancient history, did no more than synthesize the information contained in Torquemada's *Indian Monarchy*, bringing it up to date. But he surpasses Torquemada because of the sobriety of his clear and natural style, and his work can be much more easily read than Torquemada's. His best passages are in the last part of the *Mexican Theater*, or, rather, in the "Chronicle of the Province of the Holy Evangel" and the "Calendar"—admirable books which give an eloquent picture of the great civilizing work accomplished by the Franciscans. Also, in some of the pages, history is colored and pervaded by a pleasing flavor of intimacy with the lives and deeds of many worthy friars whose memory would not have come down to us if this zealous and faithful chronicler had not lived and written.

Sigüenza y Góngora

The second of this group, Don Carlos de Sigüenza y Góngora, must necessarily be mentioned in the study of almost every aspect of the Mexican culture of his time.

He was born in 1645 in the City of Mexico. In 1660, while still a youth, he assumed the Jesuit cassock and in 1662 took the first vows in the school of Tepozotlán. Shortly thereafter, he severed his connections with the Jesuits, but by the time of his death on August 22, 1700, he had been reinstated in the order, as is demonstrated by the fact that the Jesuits of the *Colegio Máximo* conducted an elaborate funeral for him. For eighteen years he was chaplain in the Hospital del Amor de Dios and also almoner for the Archbishop of Mexico, Don Francisco de Aguiar y Seijas; in both positions he practiced piety and brotherly love, harmonizing these with the supreme passion of his life: study and scientific investigation.

Don Carlos was, indeed, a loyal servant of culture. He was especially learned in physics, astronomy, and mathematics and was quite proficient in languages, history, and the antiquities of the Indians; in philosophy he was hostile to the Aristotelian system and was an advocate of Descartes' ideas, which inspired his writings and purged them of heavy scholastic jargon. He was chosen—in a competition with other scholars—professor of mathematics in the university (1672); he was royal cosmographer, by appointment from Charles II; and in 1693 he accompanied Don Andrés de Pes, admiral of the Barlovento

Armada, on a scientific expedition charged with exploring the Gulf of Mexico. His fame crossed national frontiers and increased more and more in his own country, where he was surrounded with admiration and respect.

Because of the breadth of his knowledge, this Mexican savant was able to write extensively on varied subjects. Nevertheless, only twelve of his works were published, all of these in the seventeenth century; the others—since it was a financial impossibility for the author to get them printed—remained unpublished.

Sigüenza's published works, in chronological order, are: *Indian Spring: Sacred-Historical Poem to Holy Mary of Guadalupe* (1668), *Glories of Querétaro* (1680), *A Theater of Political Virtues for the Instruction of a Prince* (1680), *Philosophical Manifesto Against Comets* (1681), *Parthenic Triumph* (1683), *Western Paradise* (1684), *Misfortunes of Alonso Ramírez* (1690), *Astronomical and Philosophical Terms* (1690), *Trophy of Spanish Justice* (1691), *Historical Account of the Activities of the Barlovento Armada* (1691), *Winged Mercury Bearing the News of the Recovery of the Provinces of New Mexico* (1693), *Eastern Evangelical Planet: Sacred Laudatory Epic* (1700).

Reference has been made in Chapter VI to Sigüenza's poetic works. Outstanding among his books of scientific character is *Astronomical and Philosophical Terms*, a reply to the criticism that Father Kino, a German Jesuit, had made of the famous *Philosophical Manifesto Against Comets*, which Sigüenza wrote to dispel the alarm occasioned by the appearance of a comet in November, 1680, and to combat the popular and erroneous theory that comets announce calamities. So far as his historical works are concerned, doubtless the most important of the few he published is the one entitled *Misfortunes Which Alonso Ramírez, Native of San Juan, Puerto Rico, Suffered at the Hands of English Pirates Who Captured Him in the Philippine Islands As He Was Sailing Alone, Without a Compass, for the Coast of Yucatán.* This book, written in clear and fluent prose, shows that Sigüenza was one of the few good prose writers of New Spain in the seventeenth century; and because of its truly romantic character, it is considered, besides being a great work of history, the first Mexican novel.

It is quite possible that the best of the historical works of Sigüenza y Góngora are among those which he left unpublished and which are known today only by hearsay. These include: *History of the Chichimecan Empire, Genealogy of the Mexican Kings, Calendar of the Months and Fiestas of the Mexicans,* and *Theater of the Grandeurs of Mexico. . . .* "If there were anyone in New Spain who would finance the printing . . .," Don Carlos said bitterly in the prologue of his *Western Paradise,* "there is no doubt that I would publish several works whose composition has stimulated in me a great love for my country, and in which would be found the most singular information. . . ."

Besides producing his original works, Sigüenza served history by his investigations and by assembling the copious collection of Mexican documents that he accumulated in twenty-eight volumes and bequeathed to the *Colegio Máximo.* So great was his love of historical documents that when a fire broke out in the Cabildo Houses on June 8, 1692, he did not hesitate to risk his life in order to save the precious manuscripts, old and modern, that were deposited in those buildings. Furthermore, equally great was his generosity: he co-operated with the Italian traveler, Gemelli Carreri, by permitting Carreri to use his own studies freely in compiling all the Mexican data needed for the latter's work entitled *Around the World,* which was printed in 1700 and translated into various languages—one part, the section dealing with Carreri's visit to Mexico, being translated into Spanish by Don José María de Agreda y Sánchez. Under the title *Voyage to New Spain,* Don José's translation was published by the Society of Mexican Bibliophiles in 1927. Lastly, it will not be too bold to affirm that today Mexican history owes more to Sigüenza the collector than to Sigüenza the historian; for, just as the investigations and documents of Boturini were to serve Veytia as the source for the composition of his *Ancient History of Mexico,* so the rich treasury of documents collected through the efforts and wisdom of Don Carlos de Sigüenza y Góngora was the starting point for Clavijero's masterly and immortal work by the same title.

Clavijero

Until the eighteenth century mere chroniclers were the only writers dealing with the ancient history of Mexico and the Conquest. The first great Mexican historian who, by combining scientific method with profound critical insight and solid learning, was to present a marvelous picture of both the Aztec civilization and the accomplishments of the conquistadors, was the abbot Don Francisco Javier Clavijero.

Of an illustrious family, Clavijero was born in the port city of Veracruz on September 9, 1731. His father, Don Blas Clavijero, a native of the City of León, Spain, had received a most thorough education in Paris and had come to New Spain to take charge of the government of the provinces of Tetziutlán and Xicayán in Mixteca. His mother, Doña María Isabel Echegaray, came from Biscay and was a distinguished woman, numbering among her relatives the wife of a viceroy of Mexico.

Because of his father's work, Clavijero spent his childhood in the country. While he was being educated in his own home, contemplation of the natural beauty of his native land and constant contact with the Indians and observation of their customs and languages contributed to the awakening of his desire to be a historian. He studied Latin in Puebla, and philosophy and theology in the schools of San Jerónimo and San Ignacio. At an early age he became a Jesuit novice, and, on February 13, 1748, was vested with the cassock in Tepozotlán. Like the other great Jesuits of his time, he was distinguished by his broad and deeply rooted culture, the foundations of which had been laid by the time he was seventeen years old. Far from confining himself to theology, he extended his knowledge to the exact sciences, physical and natural. His artistic inclinations were shaped by music, and his excellent literary taste was nourished by the study of the classics, both Latin and Spanish. He was, furthermore, adept in languages: in addition to Greek and Latin, he knew Hebrew and possessed perfect mastery of the principal European tongues; of the indigenous languages, he wrote and spoke Nahuatlan, Otomí, and Mixtecan, and knew the grammatical rules of twenty other languages and dialects of the Indians.

Like Abad and Alegre, Clavijero was an innovator in philosophy and letters. Knowing the new trends of thought, familiar with Descartes and Leibnitz, and nurtured in an intellectual discipline as strange as it was odious to other men of his time and place, he struggled in the Jesuit schools of San Ildefonso de México, Valladolid, and Guadalajara to destroy the prevalent and antiquated procedures by "clearing away the rank weeds of Aristotelianism and thereby directing his pupils to a more rational system of scholastic philosophy." This spirit of philosophical modernity stands out in his *Dialogue Between Philateles and Paleophiles*. Likewise in the literary field, the wholesome desire for reform which inflamed Clavijero was evidenced in his writing and in his teaching in the schoolroom, where he attempted to rout the presumptuous and vacuous Gongoristic style and to bring sacred oratory back to sanity by combating the pompous preachers.

Clavijero was occupied with these worthwhile undertakings in the school of Guadalajara when the decree of expulsion was issued. Having been escorted to Veracruz, he embarked, with his companions in exile, on October 25, 1767. So great was his eagerness for knowledge that in the midst of a difficult voyage—interrupted by a serious illness that necessitated his disembarking at Havana for treatment—he began the study of navigation, physics, and astronomy on the warship which carried him to Europe. On arriving in Italy, he lived, successively, in Ferrara and Bologna. His life was, from then until his premature death—which occurred in Bologna on April 2, 1787—an inspiring example of consecration to learning. With his eyes focused on his native land, he began the composition of the work which was to bring him universal renown: the *Ancient History of Mexico;* and, eager to combat the errors and falsehoods that foreign writers such as Pauw, Buffon, Raynal, and Robertson had fostered in regard to Mexico, he supplemented his *History* with the admirable *Dissertations*.

Clavijero was well prepared to write the *History:* from his youth he had familiarized himself with the languages, customs, and character of the Indians, as well as with nature, which he had found opportunity to study while roaming through the regions governed by his father. Later, his conscientious study of the indigenous languages, his reading of the old chronicles, and the minute examination he made of the rich collection of documents gathered by Sigüenza y Góngora and preserved in the library of the *Colegio Máximo*—together with the resultant training he received in the interpretation of the Indian hieroglyphics—enabled him to filter and give scientific consistency to his original impressions. But, even so, having begun this work in a foreign country "to serve as best he could his native land and to spend his leisure time profitably during his exile," he found the endeavor such that only his tenacity and wisdom were capable of carrying him through his difficulties.

He groped about in libraries and archives, collecting data—often going from place to place on foot, because of lack of money; he consulted and acquired books, occasionally spending for them money he needed for food; and, speaking of books, he was able to say that "few were published, either at home or in foreign lands, on the antiquities of Mexico, which he had not studied." After such a quantity of material had been assembled and examined closely, the author began his work. He overlooked nothing in his effort to attain perfection—in a letter to the historian Veytia, he says that he tried to attain "the greatest conciseness, the greatest clarity, and, above all, the greatest impartiality and fidelity in narration," along with "the purest and most appropriate diction."

Truly, Clavijero succeeded in his efforts. The *Ancient History of Mexico* is admirably proportioned. He divided it into ten books, and begins by describing the geography of the Valley of Mexico. Next, he discusses the people who inhabited the Valley before the coming of the Aztecs. He tells of the departure of these from Aztlán and of their wanderings to the place where they settled permanently. He presents a picture of the political and military life of the Aztecs and of the other leading tribes of the Valley. He delves into their inner life: religion, customs, culture, social organization, and sources of activity and wealth. He establishes, for the first time, the chronology of the indigenous peoples. He ends the work with the story of the Conquest, describing the arrival of the Spaniards and their activities up to the siege of Mexico City and the imprisonment of Cuauhtémoc, by means of which the destruction of the Aztec empire was completed. In the *Dissertations*, which serves as an amplification of his history and which, generally, has a polemic tone, Clavijero discusses, explains, and clarifies questions such as the origin of the Indians of America, geographical peculiarities of Mexico, the physical features, moral principles, culture, and religion of the Aztecs, and the geographical limits and population of the Valley.

Clavijero has been accused of exaggerating sometimes and of creating imaginary interpretations of hieroglyphics; but it is universally recognized that—for well-assimilated knowledge, a rigorous method which does not exclude an agreeable style, precision and exactness that harmonize with a subtle and penetrating judgment—the work of the Mexican historian is unique in its kind.

Having written the original text in Spanish, Clavijero was obliged to translate it into Italian, and in that language, under the title *Storia Antica del Messico,* the first edition was published in Cesena in 1780-81. Two Spanish translations of the Italian text are known: that of Don José Joaquín de Mora, printed in London in 1826, and that of Dr. Francisco Pablo Vázquez, Bishop of Puebla, which was published in Mexico in 1853. Soon after its publication, the *History* of Clavijero won high renown; and translations into English (1787) and German (1789-90) appeared before the first Spanish translation. In 1945, the first Castilian edition of the original text, under the editorship of P. Mariano Cuevas, S.J., who also wrote the prologue, was published in four volumes in the *Collection of Mexican Authors* (Editorial Porrúa).

This first Castilian edition, revised by Antonio Castro Leal, and with the addition of the ninth *Dissertation,* which deals with "The Origin of Venereal Disease," was reprinted in 1959, in the same *Collection of Mexican Authors.*

The *Ancient History of Mexico* is the principal work of Clavijero. Apart from this, there should be cited his *History of Old or Baja California,* which was published for the first time in Italian, in Venice (1789), after the author's death. This was translated into Spanish by Presbyter Don Nicolás García de San Vicente and was published in Mexico in 1852.

Boturini

The fourth of this group of writers, the Italian cavalier Don Lorenzo Boturini Benaduci, Señor de la Torre y de Hono, was more important as an enterprising collector of documents pertaining to Mexican history than as a historian.

He was born about 1702 in the Villa de Sondrio, Bishopric of Como, and came to New Spain in 1736, empowered by the Countess of Santibáñez to collect an annuity which was due her as a descendant of Montezuma.

After visiting the shrine of Guadalupe, he conceived the idea—as a pious and scholarly gentleman—of dedicating himself to collecting documents which would confirm the miracle of the Virgin's appearance there. He began his work, and after six years of investigations, hardships, and expenses—wandering through cities and villages, often unable to find shelter and food, traveling on rough and out-of-the way roads, occasionally walking fifty or sixty miles in search of some data, overcoming the mistrust of the natives, confronting and removing obstacles in his way—this energetic Italian succeeded in making the most splendid collection of Mexican documents that is known today. It comprised "twenty volumes of manuscripts, the majority by Indian writers, and a surprising number of charts on Indian paper, animal skins, and cotton cloth, adorned with figures, characters, and hieroglyphics," besides some rare printed books. And even if these did not confirm the apparition of the Virgin—as the investigator proposed at the outset—all are important for the writing of the history of Mexico.

In a hermitage on the hill of Tepeyac, he dedicated himself to a patient study of this material. It was his misfortune, however, to promote at this time the coronation of the Virgin of Guadalupe—because of his deep devotion—and, later, to start a public subscription to carry out this plan. The new viceroy, the Count of Fuenclara, surprised that a foreigner should assume such authority, made Boturini the victim of base persecution: he had him indicted and imprisoned; he confiscated his "museum" and exiled him to Spain in 1744.

The hapless Boturini, after having fallen into the hands of English pirates at Gibraltar and having undergone many hardships, finally reached Madrid. The Mexican historian Don Mariano Veytia offered him shelter there. The Italian gentleman succeeded in persuading the Council of the Indies to recognize his innocence and even to recompense him for his mistreatment, with the result that the king named him historiographer of the Indies with an annual salary of a thousand pesos—which was probably never paid—and ordered him to return to Mexico to claim his papers, which certainly were never returned to him.

Doubtless his unhappy memories of New Spain influenced Boturini in his decision to remain in Spain; devoting himself to historical labors that he did not complete, he lived in poverty and obscurity in Madrid until his death about 1756.

Boturini's works are: *Idea of a New General History of North America,* published in Madrid in 1746, together with the "Catalogue" of his "museum"; and the *Chronology of the Principal Nations of North America,* which was presented to the Council of the Indies in 1749 and which, not having been published, is probably lost.

Judging by the *Idea of a New General History of North America,* which Icazbalceta classifies as a book written "in fantastic and pompous style" and of little value, Boturini did not possess gifts that would lead one to suppose he could use adequately, as historian, the treasures he had gathered as a collector. Nevertheless, Veytia, in his *Ancient History*—as will be seen in the next few paragraphs—used these advantageously. Had it not been for this fortunate circumstance, the efforts of the illustrious but unlucky Italian would have gone for nothing: his marvelous collection of manuscripts was stored in the secretariat of the Viceroyalty, where neglect, carelessness, cupidity, and rats partially destroyed it; much mutilated, it was transferred to the library of the university; and the remains of it are now in the National Museum.

Veytia

Don Mariano Fernández de Echeverría y Veytia, the fifth of this group, is the historian who shares with Clavijero the honor of having been the first to write the ancient history of Mexico. He was of the old manorial family of Veytia and was born in Puebla on July 16, 1718.

He was noted for his precocity. At the age of fifteen, he received the bachelor's degree in philosophy from the University of Mexico; at nineteen, he was a lawyer. In 1737, his father, who was senior *oidor* of the *Audiencia* of Mexico, sent him to the Spanish court to arrange "many and important affairs." When he had finished this business, Veytia went to the village of Oña, became alcalde, solicitor, and permanent councilman, and lived with his paternal grandmother. He traveled in Spain, Portugal, Italy, France, England, and Morocco, and wrote his impressions of his travels in a diary which has not been published. He made three voyages to New Spain and traversed its principal provinces. He received the Cross of St. James in Madrid in 1742, and made his profession as a Knight of the Order in Puebla in 1768.

His fondness for history moved him to collect ancient documents. Among these were various narratives, written by the Aztecs, which he considered authentic and which differed from those published by the Spanish chroniclers. Convinced by this fact that a true history of these ancient people still remained to be written, he conceived the idea for his future work. He was preparing to attack that work when the cavalier Boturini, exiled from Mexico, arrived in Madrid. Veytia took him into his home, "where," he says, "he stayed for two years, and during that time, under such intimate conditions, we developed a strong and true friendship that lasted to his death." Through his friendship and intercourse with Boturini, Veytia acquired much historical data. "The first light," he says generously, "that I had on this material and the little knowledge that I possess of it now, I owe to his verbal instruction and to the documents he collected with such painstaking efforts."

While Boturini remained in Spain, Veytia returned to Mexico in 1749 and established his residence in Puebla, inspired by the thought of continuing his work. He wanted to write the ancient history of Mexico in accordance with a new criterion of impartiality, distinguishing the fabulous from the true, and evading every preconceived idea, since, as he affirmed,

among the ancient native writers who wrote in hieroglyphics and the modern ones who interpreted them, there were men of different nationalities who, through jealousy and the ambition to glorify their own people, were inclined to misrepresent events that were unfavorable to their nation and to paint with brighter colors those that were favorable.

The task was enormous. For its accomplishment, in addition to the documentation which he already possessed, Veytia examined minutely Boturini's collection, which was in the Secretariat of the Viceroyalty, following carefully the suggestions of its former owner. Also, he had other codices and manuscripts copied, and he assembled still more material through research in libraries and archives. With all this at hand, he began his book—but he had hardly begun when the news of Boturini's death caused him such grief that he was on the point of abandoning it. But, feeling that it would be a pity for "antiquities so precious" to be lost, he took up the work again, "stealing the time from the many laborious tasks" which were overwhelming him. He had finished a great deal of his cherished work at the time of his death in Puebla on April 9, 1779.

Although incomplete, Veytia's *Ancient History* was published in 1836, in three volumes, with notes and an appendix by Don Francisco Ortega. It covers the period from the earliest occupation of the Valley to the middle of the fifteenth century. The first book deals with the location of New Spain, the origin of its first inhabitants, the calendar, the first migrations, the legend of Quetzalcóatl, and the history of the Toltecs and their monarchy. The second tells of the coming of the Chichimecas and the founding of their empire, also of other tribes and the establishment of their monarchies in the Valley during that epoch. The third book was supposed to describe the deeds of the Emperor Netzahualcóyotl, his wars and conquests, his laws and government; the great progress of the Aztec nation, its laws, kings, customs, and religion; and, lastly, contemporaneous events occurring in the republic of Tlaxcala and other provinces. But Veytia did not go beyond the seventh chapter and was hardly able to develop, even in an incomplete way, the first part of his proposed plan, that is, to tell the story of the Poet King (Netzahualcóyotl). Ortega, in the appendix, continued the *History* up to the time of the capture of Mexico City by the Spaniards and to the death of Cuauhtémoc, drawing upon the works of Torquemada and Clavijero for material.

The style of Veytia is natural and easy, although, on occasion, it is prolix; his documentation is admirable. From the critical point of view, Prescott thinks that this historian surpasses all his predecessors. Veytia gave special attention to the Tezcucan dynasty; and, for this reason, his *Ancient History* complements to a certain extent Clavijero's work, which was devoted principally to the Aztec civilization.

Besides the *Ancient History*, two other works of Veytia have been printed. One was published by his son, Friar Antonio María de San José, under the title of *Bulwarks of Mexico*, and is the history of the four most famous Mexican virgins: the Ladies of Guadalupe, los Remedios, la Piedad, and la Bala. The other is a *History of Puebla*, published in that city in 1931. Among the unpublished works of this illustrious historian are various treatises and dissertations, and a translation of the *Provincial Letters* of Pascal.

Cavo

The last of this group of historians was Father Andrés Cavo, another Mexican Jesuit who was banished to Italy. He was born in

Guadalajara on January 21, 1739; he became a Jesuit, was ordained as a priest, and was working in the missions for unbelievers in 1767 when, because of the decree of expulsion, he was forced to embark at Veracruz for Italy. He established his residence in Rome; there he renounced his vows and left the Order, but in spite of this fact, he was not allowed to return to his native land. He was living in Rome as late as 1794. The date of his death is unknown.

Father Cavo was a peaceful, quiet, and studious man. His only known work is the *Civil and Political History of Mexico*, which he left in manuscript form. This might have been lost if a copy of it had not been found in the library of the Bishop of Tanagra by Carlos María de Bustamante, who published it in Mexico, in 1836, under the title *Three Centuries of Mexico under Spanish Government*, and—it is to be presumed—made some alterations.

Cavo is the only Mexican historian who treated the extensive period of Spanish domination. Nevertheless, far from being a history of this period, the *Three Centuries*—if we use the false title that the publisher gave this work—comprises rather the annals of Mexico City, written without the least pretense and dealing mainly, as Icazbalceta observes, with the elections of mayors and councilmen, annotated year by year with lamentable prolixity.

Father Cavo's book covers, in strict chronological order, the period from 1521 to 1766. Bustamante added a *Supplement* to it, bringing it up to 1821 and inserting some important documents.

Ecclesiastical Chroniclers and Minor Historians

Historical literature was especially enriched during the seventeenth and eighteenth centuries by the chronicles of the ecclesiastical provinces, which had been established in New Spain as soon as the Conquest was completed. These are rightly regarded as historical sources of inestimable value. Although limited to the narration of the activities of the different Orders and dealing with the lives and deeds of their members, whether obscure or outstanding, these chronicles are rich treasuries of information for a study of the beliefs and customs during the colonial period; and sometimes they are the only documents giving the history of certain regions. The principal chroniclers will be listed below, according to the Orders to which they belonged.

The Augustinians had the following as chroniclers: Friar Juan

González de la Puente, whose *Chronicle of Michoacán* was printed in 1624; Friar Francisco Burgoa (1605-1681), an Oaxacan, who, in addition to various religious works and an *Itinerary from Oaxaca to Rome and from Rome to Oaxaca*—which he did not publish—wrote the *Historical Palaestra, or History of the Province of San Hippolytus of Oaxaca* (1670), and the *Geographical Description of North America and the New Church in the Western World* (1674); and Friar Diego de Basalenque (1577-1651), a Spaniard from Salamanca, author of a *Chronicle of Michoacán* (1673).

The Dominicans were represented by Friar Juan de Grijalva, a native of Colima, Mexico, born in 1559, a writer characterized by simplicity and good taste, who wrote the *History of Saint William, Duke of Aquitaine* (1620) and the *Chronicle of the Province of Mexico* (1624); and by Friar Antonio Remesal, from Galicia, who, in 1613, went to Guatemala and wrote the *History of the Province of Saint Vincent of Chiapa and Guatemala,* published in Madrid in 1619.

Among the Franciscans were Friar Alonso de la Rea, who was born in Querétaro in 1624 and who wrote the *Chronicle of the Province of Saint Peter and Saint Paul of Michoacán* (1643); and Friar Antonio Tello, who, in the middle of the seventeenth century, wrote the *Miscellaneous Chronicle of the Spiritual and Temporal Conquest of the Holy Province of Jalisco,* which was published more than two centuries later, in Guadalajara, in 1891.

The *Dieguinos* had as chronicler Friar Baltasar de Medina (1600-1670), a native of Mexico City, whose *Chronicles of the Province of Saint Diego of Mexico* was published in 1681 and 1682.

Lastly, the Jesuits were represented by Father Francisco de Florencia, who was born in Spanish Florida in 1620 and died at the end of the century. He was rector of the *Colegio Máximo* and wrote only the first part of the *History of the Province of the Society of Jesus in New Spain* (1694). Years later his work was not only continued but entirely revised by the illustrious Father Francisco Javier Alegre, who produced the finest religious chronicle of New Spain: a work of abundant documentation, excellent for its plan and style. The first three volumes of the completed work were not printed until 1841, at which time Bustamante published them in Mexico City, many years after the death of the author; and the last volume remains unpublished.

To the religious chroniclers listed, these other historians should be added: Gil González Dávila, who, in his *Ecclesiastical Theater of the Churches in the Indies,* gathered together much information that is interesting if not always exact; the Spanish Franciscan Friar Diego López de Cogolludo, author of a *History of Yucatán,* which was printed in Madrid in 1688; the jurisconsult Don Matías de la Mota Padilla (1688-1776), who wrote a *History of New Galicia,* which was not printed until 1856; the Franciscan Friar Joaquín Granados, Bishop of Sonora and Durango, who died in 1794, the father of a mixed-up book called *American Afternoons;* Don José Antonio Villaseñor y Sánchez, native of Mexico and royal cosmographer, who wrote the *American Scene: General Description of the Districts and Provinces of New Spain* (1746); Don Francisco Sedano, a bookseller who was born in Mexico about 1742 and died in 1812, and who left in manuscript form *News from Mexico* (published by Icazbalceta in 1880), a collection of curious items gathered by the author in the course of his life and classified in alphabetical order; and, finally, Presbyter Cayetano Cabrera y Quintero, who patiently wrote the weighty and voluminous history known as *Coat of Arms of the City of Mexico.*

The value of these works, if considered separately, is unequal; but if they are considered in the aggregate, their value is great because of the information they contain. They give an idea of the developments in New Spain during the seventeenth and eighteenth centuries, and are, in the opinion of some critics, the only sources for Mexican colonial history.

BIBLIOGRAPHERS

Notwithstanding the fact that literary activity was considerable from the beginning of the Conquest, no one, until the dawn of the eighteenth century, attempted to collect biographical and bibliographical data on the writers, except the chroniclers of the ecclesiastical provinces who devoted some space to information about the lives and works of the missionaries distinguished in literature. Apart from these chronicles, then, no one was interested in that type of material which is so very necessary in the formulation of judgment about the literature of the epoch and in the facilitation of research studies.

The first writer to be interested in American bibliography was

León Pinelo, from Lima. His *Epitome,* published in Spain in 1629, was unsatisfactorily expanded in 1737 by the collector and editor Don Andrés González Barcia. Pinelo's book was a dry catalogue of books and manuscripts, without biographical references; furthermore, it did not deal exclusively with Mexican literature. So little was known at that time of Mexican letters and culture that a humanist, the erudite Dean of Alicante, Don Manuel Martí, in his *Latin Letters* —published in Madrid in 1735—showed complete ignorance of the intellectual status of New Spain. In one of these letters, desiring to persuade a certain young man that he should continue his studies in Rome instead of Mexico City, Martí asked him what benefit he could derive from that city which was a vast literary desert, where there were neither teachers nor pupils, where none studied and none wished to study because all despised learning. "What books will you examine?" he asked. "What libraries will you frequent? Searching for such things there is a waste of time. . . ."

Mexican literary history owes much to the contemptuous words of the Dean of Alicante. They stirred the anger of Eguiara who, on seeing his country thus abused, decided to attempt the first bibliographical effort in Mexican letters. His work and that of Beristáin, his young contemporary, will be briefly discussed here.

Eguiara

Born in the City of Mexico toward the close of the seventeenth century, Don Juan José de Eguiara y Egurén studied in the royal school of San Ildefonso; he became doctor, rector, professor, and chancellor of the university; and he was considered learned in letters, canon and civil law, philosophy, oratory, and mathematics. He held important ecclesiastical positions and was named Bishop of Yucatán, but he gave up the bishopric for reasons of health and dedicated himself to his work entitled *Mexican Library.* In this he intended to prove, by publishing the biographies and works of the many writers of New Spain, how utterly false had been the statements of the famous Dean.

Eguiara also wrote and published a great deal of theological material in both Latin and Spanish, but he was afflicted with the bad taste of his epoch, showing himself to be a perfect Gongorist. The only work for which posterity remembers him is the *Library,* on which he labored vigorously and which he printed on his own press. Impatient to see the work published, he did not wait until he had completed the manuscript but gave the first volume to the press in 1755. That thick volume in folio must have been the first and only volume of this important work, for no other is known to have appeared before the author's death in Mexico City on January 29, 1763. It dealt with writers whose names began with A, B, and C, and carried a kind of introduction divided into twenty chapters, to which he gave the title of "Foreword"; in this, after explaining his plan and refuting Martí, he sketched, in a high-flown and pedantic style, the development of Mexican culture from its beginning.

Eguiara's *Library* abounds in serious defects: it is written in Latin, which makes it practically useless today; the titles of the works are poorly translated into Latin; and the authors are presented alphabetically according to their Christian names and not their surnames. He does not have any critical sense, and simply because his work is intended as a piece of refutation, he adopts a high panegyrical tone. Nevertheless, and in spite of its incompleteness, Eguiara's work represents a worthwhile effort. It deserves credit, above all, for having stimulated the production of another and far more successful work: Beristáin's bibliography.

Beristáin

Originally from Puebla, where he was born on May 22, 1756, Don José Mariano Beristáin y Souza studied in his native city, received the bachelor's degree in philosophy from the University of Mexico, and went to Spain with the Bishop of Puebla, Fabián y Fuero, who was archbishop-elect of Valencia. In Valencia Beristáin received the degree of doctor of theology and was regent of the academies of philosophy. He became professor of theology in the University of Valladolid; and, after many vicissitudes, he returned to his native land rewarded with the canonship of the Cathedral of Mexico. Literary societies and academies honored him with various titles, and he was given important positions. Beristáin was a versatile and servile man. He opposed the movement for Independence in the pulpit and in the press, but he cannot be given credit for being loyal to his convictions. He had none, probably, in politics: his shamelessness was so great that after preaching, in 1812, a sermon on swearing to observe the Constitution, which he called a "sacred book," he did not hesitate to preach another sermon opposing the Constitution when he learned in 1814 that the king did not wish to swear to abide by it. Beristáin suffered an attack of apoplexy in the pulpit of the Cathedral of Mexico a short time thereafter, and died on March 23, 1817.

Mexican letters are indebted to Beristáin for his *Library of Northern Spanish America*, or "Catalogue and information concerning the literary figures who, having been born, or educated, or having reached literary maturity in Northern Spanish America, have published some work or have left material prepared for publication." The *Library* was published in Mexico City in three volumes in 1816, 1819, and 1821, respectively, and reprinted by Padre F. H. Vera in Amecameca in 1883, also in three volumes. Writing in Spanish and following a better plan than Eguiara did, Beristáin spent twenty years in preparing this work, which contains information on approximately four thousand writers! It suffers from one major defect —the changing and abridging of the titles of the works included. Its style frequently leaves much to be desired; and from the critical point of view, it hardly commends the good taste of Beristáin. But, rich in data, it is the only biographical and bibliographical dictionary that Mexico possesses; and on that distinction is based the reputation that it enjoys.

The Epoch of
Independence

IX.

Changing Conditions

In the three centuries since the Conquest, New Spain had been transformed. From the union of the two races—the Spanish and the Indian—which the Conquest had brought together, a new ethnic group had sprung: the mestizo. In addition, the creoles—that is, the Spaniards born in America—had multiplied rapidly until another powerful social group was formed. From the mixture of all these elements, Mexican society was born: a heterogeneous organism certainly, but one which, as Don Justo Sierra has said, "had been forming from the seventeenth century, and continued to develop in the eighteenth, a separate entity," an entity showing visible signs of becoming a nationality. For a long time these tendencies had been evident; but because of the growth of the society which was then reaching maturity, they were accentuated during the era of the "enlightened despotism" of the Bourbons.

When the Marqués de Croix, in the celebrated proclamation issued immediately after the expulsion of the Jesuits, declared that vassals were born "to be silent and to obey," it may be said that in reality they were silent and did obey, but at the same time, privately, they discussed the situation and exchanged opinions. The comments, the spirit of unrest then dominant, the sentiment for resistance which was making itself felt, and even the insurrections that were occurring spasmodically were quite revelatory of a growing impatience with the status quo and a strong desire to change it.

The spirit of independence lying deep within the social mass began to pulsate.

Various events contributed powerfully toward the awakening of this spirit of independence during the reign of Charles III: the creation of the colonial army; the financial and administrative reorganization by the inspector Gálvez, which resulted in a considerable increase in royal revenues; and the ostensible aid given by the Spanish government—because of the pressure of internal politics—to the American colonies fighting for their independence against England. The first of these placed in the hands of Mexicans the necessary instrument of liberty—arms; the second accentuated in them the feeling of protest; the third caused them to see that independence in itself was feasible and legitimate.

The clear-sighted plan, almost prophetic, which the Count of Aranda prepared in 1783—a plan recommending to the king that he divest himself of all his possessions on the mainland of America—was an augury of the approaching conflict. The policy of greater isolation of the colonies, which was inaugurated to forestall the struggle, was pushed vigorously; and, above all, the administrative work of two illustrious viceroys, Bucareli and Revillagigedo, delayed the inevitable denouement. Serious events, however, finally brought on the conflict.

THE EDUCATED CLASS

The creoles and mestizos together formed the educated class of New Spain.

The Indians, who, in the early days of the Conquest, thanks to the zeal of the missionaries, had become the beneficiaries of culture and produced such men as Ixtlilxóchitl and Tezozomoc, were gradually excluded from the cultural current. Almost outside the current, also, were the Spaniards who came to Mexico; these were, for the most part, either government officials or crude men of business whose one mission in America was the holding of government posts or the building of fortunes.

Apart, then, from the other classes, the creoles and the mestizos—principally the former—developed a culture. From these as a nucleus came the most eminent figures which adorn the early history of Mexican letters: the greatest dramatist of the sixteenth century, the worthiest poet of the seventeenth century, and the humanists, historians, philologists, and poets who, during those two centuries, gave Mexican culture a national character of its own.

Mention has already been made of the intellectual renaissance which began in the middle of the eighteenth century, a renaissance that was felt in literature with the advent of neo-classicism; in philosophy with the initial opposition to scholasticism; in science with the introduction of experimental studies, which culminated in the founding of the College of Mining; and in the plastic arts with the establishment of the Academy of San Carlos and the architectural activities that reached their greatest splendor in the magnificent works of Tolsá and Tresguerras.

Nevertheless, the Inquisition watched vigilantly and tried to limit intellectual expansion. It made every effort to throttle thought: its function had been reduced to destroying prohibited books in order to keep New Spain in spiritual isolation from the rest of the world. In spite of this, these "prohibited books" (which were the best of that period) were smuggled into the country and read widely, and through them were diffused the new ideas propagated by the French Revolution.

The beginning of an intellectual emancipation, which was the forerunner of political freedom, made itself felt. Mexican thought—below the surface—was restless; a mordant fermentation was not long in revealing itself.

LITERARY ACTIVITY

There is no doubt that the expulsion of the Jesuits retarded the development which was so brilliantly making itself felt in letters. If such works as those of an Abad, an Alegre, and a Landívar could be produced in Latin, it is possible that similar ones would have been written in Spanish. The sudden exile of so many worthy and irreplaceable persons—the closing of the Jesuit schools, which, unlike the university with its backwardness and vegetative nature, were centers of intellectual activity—meant necessarily a serious setback for culture. Although the arts and sciences remained, it was not easy to supply by improvisation that which had formerly been developing under guidance. For a while, then, the creole youth of New Spain lacked coherent and energetic direction; and, because of this, the following generations were weakened.

Certainly, at the beginning of the nineteenth century the neo-classic renaissance had not yet been consummated. *Culteranismo* and *conceptismo*, as persistent heritages, continued to exist in an anemic and occasional literature despite the influence of the rhetoricians of the school of Luzán and the favor shown to the verse of Meléndez

Valdés and the elder Moratín and to the prose of Feijóo and Cadalso. Bombastic preachers predominated in the pulpit; and along with the involved and empty rhetoric of Gongoristic character that fought extinction, *prosaísmo* had begun to thrive.

The production of books had decreased; few were printed; and almost none were literary. The genre which thrived was the periodical. In the capital of New Spain, the *Gaceta de México (Mexican Gazette)* was founded in 1784 and continued until 1809. It contained, besides information of uncertain value, articles on geology, medicine, botany, current events, art, and poetry. Material of a scientific character was published over the signatures of such learned men as Don Antonio León y Gama and Don Andrés del Rio. But neither in the *Gazette* nor in any other periodical did there appear a literary figure of outstanding importance. Literature experienced a strange inactivity.

Nevertheless, as always, there was a plethora of versifiers. On the occasion of the unveiling of the equestrian statue of Charles IV—the work of Tolsá—on December 9, 1803, the popular muse strained herself in song, and the learned poets also participated, taking advantage of that special and superlative event. Ever ready to flatter, but somewhat late in getting started on this occasion, Don Mariano Beristáin de Souza, Canon of Mexico City, came forward to commemorate this singular occasion. On November 24, he hastily convoked a literary contest. In spite of the press of time, approximately two hundred poets took part, which was a considerable number. Many of the compositions that were entered in the contest were published by Beristáin himself in 1804, under the title of *Songs of the Mexican Muses*. It is unfortunately necessary to add, however, that these songs, which were preceded by a pretentious dedication by the erudite bibliographer, combined common and vulgar prosiness with a pompous and overcharged style that was as unintelligible as it was empty.

This collection of rhymes gives no evidence that the neo-classic doctrines, proclaimed some time before, had produced any results. But the richest product of these ideas in Mexico, Navarrete—a poet whose turn of mind, style, and literary background belonged to the eighteenth century—did not make himself known until 1806, when some of his poems were published in the *Diario de México (Mexican Daily)*.

Neo-Classic Flowering

Only a year before, in 1805, the first daily newspaper published in New Spain had been founded by Don Carlos María de Bustamante and Don Jacobo de Villaurrutia. "The *Daily* was," according to Don Nicolás Rangel, "a clear reflection of the life of the City, not so much in its official aspect as in the daily commonplace details and intellectual phases." In it, immediately, a new literary generation found refuge, the short-lived and slightly retarded generation which neo-classicism had brought into being. This brilliant publication became the vehicle and, at the same time, the propeller of great activity in letters. Until its discontinuance in 1817, approximately 120 poets and certainly no smaller number of prose writers, according to the estimate of Don José María Lafragua, contributed to the *Diario de México*.

Besides Navarrete, others who appeared in this daily and who rendered special devotion to poetry were: Ochoa, Castro, Sánchez de Tagle, Barquera, Quintana del Azebo, Lacunza, and Mendizábal. They paid homage to Spanish neo-classicism, which was still in vogue at that time, though it was beginning to decline in Spain. It was an artificial and sentimental type of poetry, depicting saccharine lovers and false shepherds and shepherdesses, such as Parthenio, Clorila, Anarda, Sylvia, and Dalmiro, who sigh and weep deplorably—porcelain figurines on stages illuminated with a rosy hue.

This sudden eruption of shepherds and shepherdesses in the somewhat decadent Mexican letters gave rise, in 1808, to the formation of the Arcadia, a literary society similar in every way to European literary societies of the same name. Such an institution was destined to breed and stimulate pastoral poetry. The first "head shepherd" of the Arcadia was Friar Manuel de Navarrete; and other versifiers and poets joined under the names of shepherds—Damón, Batilo, Anfriso, Dametas, Mirtilo.

In that same year (1808) Don Juan Wenceslao Barquera began the publication of the *Inexpensive Weekly of Curious and Erudite Information*. His object was "to make more accessible, by means of a small periodical, the learning which is usually found in voluminous and rare works." An indication that European culture was then penetrating Mexican life is seen in the fact that some French and English works were published in translation in the *Inexpensive Weekly* in its departments dealing with literature, education, hygiene, ethics, etc.

THE THEATER

So far as dramatic art is concerned, handbills of the period show that the plays presented were, for the most part, Spanish dramas of the seventeenth and eighteenth centuries—possibly a greater number from the latter century—along with some translations from the French theater and a few from the English. Available information indicates that the majority of these plays were lacking in literary importance. There should be mentioned, however—to show that, in spite of the taste in vogue, all were not worthless—some memorable performances: Shakespeare's *Othello,* in 1806; Moratín's *The Café,* in 1806, and his *The Maidens' Consent,* in 1808, which was remarkably successful.

Mexican authors soon showed an interest in dramatic activity. Ochoa, Guridi y Alcocer, Barquera—among the authors known today —wrote for the stage; but, unfortunately, their plays were not published, and only the titles have survived. Prior to 1808, contests in the writing of *sainetes* (one-act farces) and comedies were promoted by individuals and by periodicals; and there was even a contest for a "national tragedy," the subject matter to be taken "from the antiquities of this hemisphere, a field unknown to Europeans." From this tournament one work resulted, doubtless the first of its kind; it was called *Xóchitl,* but whether it was produced is unknown. Two of the winning farces, however, were presented: *El blanco por fuerza (White by Necessity)* by Don Antonio Santa Ana, and *The Miserable Deceived One, or The Maiden of the Half Almond* by Don Francisco Escolano y Obregón. Also, two other Mexican works—hardly comedies—were produced in 1806: *The Pettifogger* and *The Mexican Woman in England.* It is known, too, that during this time there was being cultivated in Mexico a type of drama known as the *coloquio* (colloquy)—later designated as the pastoral—which was given not only in the theaters of the city proper but also on improvised stages in the suburbs. None of these is extant; and perhaps this fact is not to be deplored, for a subscriber to the *Mexican Daily,* in criticizing a certain Mexican play, *The False Nuncio from Portugal,* which he had seen, affirmed that it was "the worst of our very bad comedies."

The political events of 1808 scarcely disturbed the placid and rather infantile development of letters. While the theater was twaddling, in January of 1809 occasional poetry had something with which to busy itself. In the contest sponsored by the Royal and Pontifical University "to solemnize the ascension to the throne of the August and Beloved Monarch Don Fernando VII," many Arcadians participated and produced sonorous and laudatory poems.

Colonial poetry was in its last stage. Literature, like society, was on the eve of transformation: everything was pointing toward the year 1810.

THE REVOLUTION

The events preceding the movement for Independence were vital and fast-moving: in 1805, the defeat of Trafalgar loosened the ties of Spanish colonial control; in 1808, the Spanish War of Independence erupted in the mother country, resulting in two incidents that were to have immense repercussions in America: the mutiny of Aranjuez, which affirmed the popular sovereignty against the absolute power of the kings; and the creation of assemblies which organized the rebellion against the French invaders and, by stirring the people themselves to action, fostered the ideal of nationalism, along with that of popular sovereignty.

In less than two years, these powerful external factors—uniting with internal elements that had been developing the movement for emancipation—brought matters to a head in Mexico. On September 16, 1810, in the village of Dolores, the priest Don Miguel Hidalgo y Costilla proclaimed Independence.

From its beginning until its consummation in 1821, amid bloody vicissitudes, the Revolution wrought great changes in Mexican society. These changes naturally influenced the literature which was developing and was directly affected by the stirring events agitating the country; they stamped on literature a new character, a political one, which dominated all writing during the epoch. Proclamation, edicts, manifestoes, and speeches appeared both for and against the insurgent movement. The prose writers were, almost exclusively, political writers; and poetry assumed qualities in harmony with the warlike atmosphere.

PAMPHLETS

Pamphlets and handbills played an important part as a medium for propaganda during the Revolution. Pamphlets especially were innumerable and were written in varied styles and by diverse writers; they ranged from those well written and discriminatingly prepared for cultured readers, to those that were homely and coarse, but skilfully written in the language of the people in order to influence their thinking.

The series was inaugurated in 1810 by a bulletin entitled: *Prediction of Happiness in America and Rightful Rejoicing in Mexico, the Natural and Proper Expression of Feeling on the Part of a Spanish American Because of the Happy Arrival on These Shores of His Excellency, Don Francisco Javier Venegas, Viceroy, Governor, and Captain General of New Spain*. As the title indicates, this work is a litany of praise for the new governor.

When the storm of the Revolution broke out with fury, a flood of pamphlets was directed chiefly against the movement's initiator. These were notorious for their impudence, grossness, and acrimony. There were not lacking, however, those of a temperate viewpoint which advised peace, union, concord, and the permanent erasure of such odious names as "*gachupines*" and "creoles"; nor those of a certain theological aspect in which an effort was made to point out the "erroneous, absurd, and heretical statements" comprising the manifesto published by Hidalgo; nor, lastly, those in which admonition, diatribe, and political preaching were disguised and invested with certain literary characteristics, the author providing a story element, principally by means of dialogue, and confining the debate to imaginary persons who served as his mouthpieces. In one of the leaflets, a cleric is represented as coming in the darkness of night to the palace of Santiago and asking to speak to the "night patrol of the loyal and valiant Indians" in order to persuade them that they should fight in the ranks of the king; in another, a woman, Mariquita, converses with a soldier; in a third, an erudite and ultrafashionable woman enters into a conversation with "Don Felipe"; and in still another, "a dragoon, a maker of tortillas, and her husband, Pascual," talk with each other. The ingenuity of the royalists in their antirevolutionary propaganda was sharpened and increased; passion overflowed in the pamphlets—not only those composed in the popular form of dialogues, but also those in the form of letters, discourses, memorials, warnings, and proclamations. *Patriotic Letters of a Father to His Son on the Conduct He Should Observe Toward the Insurgent Corrupters; Christian-Political Memorial Pointing Out How Much New Spain Should Fear Lack of Unity; Enlightenment of the Indians, Making Them See Their Indebtedness to the Spaniards*: such were the titles of several of these pamphlets, some of which were signed, while others were anonymous. They had become quite numerous during the last days of 1810.

The pamphleteer squall, notwithstanding, subsided between 1811 and 1812. Of this period there is one entitled: *New Encounter of the Valiant Numskull Don Quixote with His Squire Sancho on the Shores of Mexico, a Dialogue in Verse between Master and Servant, for Instruction concerning the History of the Present Revolution, in Which Likewise Is Ridiculed the Accursed Project of Hidalgo and His Followers.* In the furious writing campaign conducted by the royalists, obviously, verse played as great a part as prose.

The royalist group wrote the vast majority of these leaflets, in fact. The insurgents lacked the means for publicity, and they resigned themselves in the beginning to various proclamations and periodicals edited and printed amid the turmoil of the conflict with great effort. But in 1811 there appeared on the scene a revolutionary pamphleteer, one who was more talented and capable than any of those of the opposing party: Fernández de Lizardi. The temporary liberty of the press, granted by the no less temporary Spanish Constitution of 1812, gave a weapon to the friends of Independence in the very capital of the viceroyalty.

After two years of popularity, this new type of writing lost its appeal, and only a few pamphlets were published from 1813 to 1819. But the freedom of the press, re-established in May, 1819, resuscitated what had been a passing fancy, and in 1820 more than five hundred pamphlets were published on various subjects: constitutional government, freedom of thought, social questions, humorous themes, theatrical criticism, and petitions to the authorities. The insipid character of many of these is indicated by titles as picturesquely ridiculous as *A Witty Morsel for the Busiest Author* and *Tripe and Pulque for the Consumption of Father Soto.* In brief, some of the last pamphlets of the viceregal era stirred up again the ashes of rancor on the eve of independence, though, certainly, at that time the question of Independence was no longer a source of discord in a society already con-

vinced of the necessity of achieving freedom. The embrace of Acatempa[1] was next.

THE PRESS

The status of the press in Mexico from the beginning of the century to 1808 has already been discussed.

The Revolution of 1810 gave rise to the insurgent press. The liberators, recognizing the formidable power of the press for propaganda
purposes, founded their own periodicals. Though devoted particularly
to the publication of proclamations, platforms, manifestoes, and military communiqués, these also contained poems and articles fiery with
civic ardor.

Between 1810 and 1812 the royalists, who were carrying on their
counterrevolutionary propaganda especially by means of pamphlets,
began to publish some periodicals; but these were short-lived and
were weeklies, for the most part. Beristáin published his *Dialogues
between Philopatro and Aceraio* and *The True American Illustrator*,
the latter being a reply to the insurgent periodical of the same name;
Don Fermín Reigadas published *The Critic*; Don Ramón Roca, the
Friend of the Country and a literary review of brief existence, the
Mexican Museum. Finally, there were royalist publications with such
queer names as *The Curious Public and the Lay Speaker* and *The
Parrot of the City*.

Freedom of thought, granted by the Constitution of Cádiz, provoked in Mexico an unexpected as well as fleeting expansion of journalism in 1812. The *Mexican Daily* joyously hailed "the freedom of
the press, the real foundation of political and civil liberty." Fernández de Lizardi, as has been previously mentioned, soon launched
a weekly called the *Mexican Thinker*. Simultaneously, Don Carlos
María de Bustamante founded another containing clever revolutionary propaganda: *Playthings*. Vain flapping of the wings of a liberty
more illusory than real! It passed quickly; far from being a precious
right, the grant of freedom turned out to be a clever snare. Those
who had availed themselves of this newest privilege found themselves
in prison or in flight.

After 1813, periodical activity decreased. From a literary view-

[1] Iturbide and Guerrero met at Acatempa February 15, 1821. The uniting of the rebel
forces and the viceregal army followed.—Translators' note.

point, there should be noted a new periodical, the *General News,* which appeared in 1815; it contained articles on literary and scientific questions and the most outstanding poetry in an epoch hardly propitious to the Muses.

ORATORY

At the beginning of the War of Independence, representatives from Mexico went to Spain to the Cortes assembled at Cádiz. It was there, for the first time, while struggling for the rights and in the defense of their country, that Mexicans practiced political oratory. Among those distinguished in this were Don Miguel Guridi y Alcocer, deputy from Tlaxcala, who was an ardent and convincing orator; Don Miguel Ramos Arizpe (1755-1843), deputy from Coahuila, an illustrious patriot and supporter of constitutional government, who suffered imprisonment in Spain during the triumph of absolutism; and Don Antonio Joaquín Pérez Martínez (1773-1829), who—unlike Arizpe, in that he was loyal to Spain—was president of the Cortes which Ferdinand VII dissolved in 1814, and obtained the bishopric of Puebla through his devotion to the re-established traditional government.

Sacred oratory, which had been decaying since the eighteenth century to such an extent that its exponents were castigated by Father Isla in his *Friar Gerundio of Campazas,* was converted into a political weapon for the Revolution. An outstanding writer of sermons against the insurgents was Friar Diego Miguel Bringas y Encinas, a Franciscan and chief chaplain in the army of Calleja; his "Sermon on the Reconquest of Guanajuato," delivered in December, 1810, may serve as a model of this type. An emulator of Bringas y Encinas in his hatred of the insurgents was Don José Mariano Beristáin de Souza, the scholarly bibliographer, whose unique political inconsistencies in the pulpit are well known and whose "Palm Sunday Sermon," delivered in Mexico City in 1815, is unexcelled in intemperate incoherence, Jesus Christ, Barabbas, Hidalgo, and Ferdinand VII being cited indiscriminately.

INDEPENDENCE AND NATIONALISM

At the end of ten years of fighting, independence was finally consummated by means of "The Treaty of the Three Guarantees," which was drafted by Iturbide and Guerrero in the village of Iguala. This was recognized by the last viceroy, O'Donojú, in the Cordova treaties; and the entrance of the Army of the Three Guarantees into Mexico City on September 27, 1821, marked the beginning of a new era in Mexican history. After three centuries, New Spain was freed from Spanish rule; sovereignty passed into the hands of Mexico, which had now become a free nation.

Though Independence was realized in the political order, national consciousness nevertheless was yet to develop. Favoring Independence were a vast majority of all classes and even a considerable number of those who had fought it. The movement originated in passion, but at long last it had crystallized into a dominant idea. And, for that reason, when unexpected events suddenly produced the Revolution, in the heat of the fight the national spirit was formed and developed—the spirit that, jubilantly seizing upon independence, knew how to preserve and defend it.

Literature, as has been seen, was of necessity close to the Revolution; in fact, the Revolution left a deep imprint upon it. If during the colonial epoch literature in New Spain had been a kind of "*mester* of the clergy"—an almost exclusive patrimony of ecclesiastics, a development by this group without immediate contact with the popular mind—its form and character underwent profound modifications in the period under review. In the heat of the struggle, political literature was born, but with emphasis on action and passion rather than form; the press developed and followed new paths; parliamentary oratory was born in the Cortes of Cádiz at the same time that sacred oratory was abandoned because of its servile subjection to authority. But, apart from these political developments, which perhaps are extraneous to literature proper although they are interesting as revelations of the period, there appeared in Mexican letters, coinciding with the struggle for Independence, a superlatively important phenomenon: the awakening of the national spirit.

This nationalistic sentiment—which, as will be shown later, animated lyric poetry—began in the theater and culminated with the appearance of the first Mexican novel; and it was to become, after Independence, a spiritual force directed toward giving to literary production in Mexico an even more unmistakable and characteristic expression.

Poetry

HE poets of the latter part of the eighteenth century continued
writing in the nineteenth. During the first decade of the new
century, lyric poets did no more than continue the forms, imitate the
models, and nourish themselves with the ideas which had prevailed
in the preceding literary movement: between the last echoes of Gongorism and the new prosaic manner, Spanish pseudo-classicism, controlled by cold and rigid preceptors, struggled to obtain a dominant
position.

The outbreak of the war silenced the lyric poets. Ingenuous
pseudo-classic eroticism disappeared; the religious muse became almost
mute; and only satire—discreetly hiding itself in order to be able to
speak at all—survived. Instinctively, poetry assumed a revolutionary
aim. The fable and the epigram appeared. Elegance of style was almost entirely absent; beauty of language and excellence of versification were lacking; the sole purpose of poetry was to propagate ideas
for the rebellion, evading, wherever possible, censorship by the authorities. Except for these manifestations, poetry was silent. In 1816,
an event unusual amid the commotion of that epoch, namely, a literary contest sponsored by the tireless Beristáin to celebrate the return of the Jesuits, brought poetry into prominence for the moment.

Notwithstanding, in the course of the War of Independence, just
as seeds germinate because of the heat of the earth, lyric poetry was
transformed from the bucolic and amatory type to the heroic. This
change was brought about by the events of the war, but its literary
fruition came through the influence of three great Spanish poets
whose spirit and muse, inspired by the patriotic and civic fervor
aroused by the French invasion of Spain and the dawn of constitutional government, were in harmony with the thought and sentiment

of the people of Mexico in the whirl of the first revolution. These poets were Don Manuel José Quintana, Don Nicasio Alvarez de Cienfuegos, and Don Juan Nicasio Gallego. Like the Mexican poets, they sang of liberty and fatherland, exalting the heroes and, in stormy strophes, sweeping tyranny away.

About 1812 the heroic type of verse—principally in José Quintana's style—conquered Mexican lyric poetry, and royalists as well as insurgents adopted it. And by the time the movement begun in Dolores had been consummated, a new type of lyric was being produced by the principal Mexican poets.

By way of summary, the two phases of poetry during this period are: first, at the beginning of the century, the Gongoristic taint, pseudo-classicism, and *prosaísmo*; and second, before, during, and after the Revolution, a nationalistic aspect, as evidenced by the representation of Mexican types and customs, by satirical and political objectives in fables and epigrams, and by heroic manner and civic ardor.

POETS OF THE TRANSITION

Ochoa

Chronologically and from the literary viewpoint, Don Anastasio María de Ochoa y Acuña is the poet of transition between the late eighteenth-century poets and those of the epoch of Independence. By his literary education, he belongs to the eighteenth century and is, above all, a humanist; but by the special characteristics of his poetry, in which the lighthearted portrayal of Mexican customs prevails, he belongs to the period when, amidst the songs of the civic singers of the first revolution, the laughter of Periquillo[1] was heard.

A native of Huichapan, where he was born on April 21, 1783, Ochoa studied Latin in the City of Mexico with Dr. Juan Picazo; philosophy in the School of San Ildefonso; and canon law at the University of Mexico, about 1803. He attended the Theological Seminary in 1813 and was ordained as a presbyter in 1816. From 1817 to 1827 he served as curate in several places in Querétaro. In 1828 he returned to Mexico City to devote himself entirely to letters, and he died there on August 4, 1833, during an epidemic of cholera.

---

[1] A character in Fernández de Lizardi's novel *El Periquillo Sarniento.* See Chapter XI.— Translators' note.

His witty poetry appeared in the *Mexican Daily* in 1806 under two pseudonyms: "Atanasio de Achoso y Ucaña" and "The One-Eyed Man." He was famous for his delightful humor. In 1808 he became a member of the Arcadia—to which reference has been made —under the name of "Damón," which he later changed to "Astanio." He was a winner in the literary contest sponsored by Beristáin in 1816 to celebrate the return of the Jesuits.

So far as serious poetry is concerned, Ochoa cannot be considered a poet of great inspiration, though his work is characterized by clarity and ingenuity. He wrote verse with ease and correctness, and his vocabulary was extensive and adequate. Occasionally artificial in conformity with the vogue of his time, to which he paid tribute, he was, nevertheless, more often inspired by Spanish poetry of the Golden Age and reflected its influence.

He was much more popular in his poetry of a lighter vein, which he seems to have preferred and in which he had no rival in his epoch. From this standpoint, he was a precursor; and inasmuch as his amusing poems are genuinely Mexican, it may be said he is the originator of a certain picturesque nationalism in poetry. Adopting Iglesias as his model in the rondelet and epigram and "Tomé of Burguillos," that is, Lope de Vega (whom he imitated and even parodied on occasion), as his master in the sonnet, Ochoa did not hesitate—as Urbina wisely observes—to draw upon other masters such as Baltasar de Alcázar, Góngora, and Quevedo. Ochoa was in verse, as Fernández de Lizardi was in prose, the best painter of Mexican social life during the latter part of the colonial regime and the beginning of the era of Independence. The types that he delineated and the delightful scenes he described are not inferior to those which are to be found in the *Periquillo*.

Ochoa is also outstanding as a humanist. He made a translation of Ovid's *Heroides* in hendecasyllables; these are "very exact and at times poetic," according to Menéndez y Pelayo, "with a certain easy abandon of style which is a good imitation of the suave and tender manner of the original and is quite pleasant as long as it does not degenerate into slovenliness." Likewise, he translated *Bajazet* by Racine; *Virginia* by Alfieri; *Penelope*, a Latin tragedy by the Jesuit Father Andrés Fritz; *The Lectern*, or *Lutrin*, by Boileau; some cantos of *Télémaque* into octaves; and many other works which were never published. Spanish translations of some fragments from Abad's poem *De Deo* and of Father Remond's Latin elegies appear in the edition of Ochoa's poetry. Lastly, in the field of drama, Ochoa made an arrangement of Beaumarchais's *Eugénie,* and wrote two comedies which were not published and a tragedy, *Don Alfonso,* which was successfully produced. A general collection of his poetry was published in New York in 1828 under the title of *Poesías de un mexicano (Poetry by a Mexican).*

Castro

Don José Agustín de Castro, like Ochoa, was a figure of the transition period.

Very few biographical data are available on this poet, who should not be confused with Agustín Castro, a Jesuit of Veracruz. Agustín de Castro, a native of Michoacán, was, in 1786, a notary in the ecclesiastical tribunal of his region; and, between 1791 and 1797, he was chief notary of the Tribunal of Justice and chief vicar of the bishopric of Puebla. In 1809, he was in the capital of New Spain, probably performing some official task.

He contributed to the *Gazette* and *Mexican Daily* and achieved a fair reputation. He published in three volumes his *Miscellany of Sacred and Profane Poems* (1797-1809). In this collection there are many short poems; religious *loas;* three miracle plays; lives—in verse —of Saint Augustine, Saint Francis of Assisi, and Saint Louis Gonzaga; a prose work entitled *Private Exhortation to a Novice;* a few translations of Latin poets, of Horace in particular; and two short works for the theater: *The Cobblers* and *The Charro.*

Castro was—in the opinion of Luis G. Urbina—a presumptuous and prosaic poet, especially in his religious poetry, though he did employ in his secular poetry "pleasing gallantry, sententious dialectics, and the affected elegance of the Calderonian fables." He is defective in his prosody and abundant in provincialisms and awkward constructions; but, nevertheless, he is interesting because of his obvious stand for literary emancipation and his marked preference for the national and indigenous. In several compositions he makes literary use of the jargon of the common people and the *charros;* and in many of his satires, he portrays the prevailing spirit of the epoch. This tendency, consonant with the spirit that heralded Independence, was accentuated much more in his dramatic works; his little play, *The Cobblers*, is the first attempt made in the nineteenth century to present on the stage speech, characters, and customs that are genuinely Mexican.

Don Andrés Quintana Roo

Don Andrés Quintana Roo belongs to the political more than to the literary history of Mexico. Born in Mérida on November 30, 1787, he made a brilliant beginning in his studies in the Theological Seminary of that city; and in 1808 he continued his studies at the University of Mexico, where he received the bachelor's degree in liberal arts and canon law. To obtain a license in law, he practiced as assistant in the law office of Dr. Agustín Pomposo Fernández de San Salvador, a prominent jurisconsult; and in the home of the latter, he met the one who became the dramatic and fiction-like love of his life: Doña Leona Vicario.

The War of Independence and his remarkable romance with Doña Leona filled his youth. Ardently championing the cause of liberty, he devoted himself to it, body and soul. The pen was his best weapon, and with it he fought in the insurgent camp by publishing two famous periodicals: *American Patriotic Weekly* and *American Illustrator*. As a deputy to the Congress of Chilpancingo, he presided over the National Constituent Assembly which drew up the Declaration of Independence, and he wrote the manifesto which was issued to the nation with the Declaration. First alone, and later in the company of Doña Leona Vicario—who, as an insurgent also, had been in prison and had escaped from prison to marry him—Quintana Roo suffered the series of cruel vicissitudes which the Congress experienced. Footsore, hungry, miserable, and sustained only by their high patriotism, for more than a year this couple wandered through rugged mountains. In a cave of wild beasts, Doña Leona bore her first child, a daughter. When they were pursued and surrounded in March, 1818, Quintana Roo wanted to escape, but the fear of his wife's falling into the hands of the royalists and being shot moved the illustrious patriot to surrender.

Quintana Roo was one of the most eminent figures in the War of Independence, and after it was won he devoted himself to politics; the parliamentary tribune, journalism, and important positions in the government absorbed his attention until his death in Mexico City on April 15, 1851.

Being an upright man possessing great civic virtues, Quintana Roo was—as Menéndez y Pelayo observes—"more of a magistrate and politician than poet; but even if he was not an inspired poet, his thought was elevated, his versification noble and correct, his tone serious, as suited his particular kind of talent." These characteristics are explained by his classical education: he was a Latinist who had drunk from the fountains of Cicero and Horace. His prose—all of it in manifestoes, proclamations, and discourses—did not exclude, though it was fiery and vehement, noble seriousness and harmony. In his poems of simple and severe refinement, he is revealed as a discriminating cultivator of the language. But this revolutionary poet, who was almost alone in singing for his country, had his eyes turned toward ancient Rome; and his literary erudition triumphed over his spontaneity.

Though he was influenced, as were the other members of his group, by the Spaniard Quintana, the spirit which animates his poetry is, notwithstanding, characteristic of the epoch in which it was produced. To date, his works have not been collected; and the same fate suffered by his prose works—which are of occasional character and of purely historical value, and are scattered throughout the periodicals in which they first appeared—has extended to his poems, of which few are known today.

Don Francisco Manuel Sánchez de Tagle

Not one but three literary epochs comprise the long and busy life of Don Francisco Manuel Sánchez de Tagle: the last decade of the eighteenth century, the period of Independence, and the turbulent post-Independence era up to the middle of the nineteenth century.

A native of Valladolid, Michoacán, having been born there on January 11, 1782, and the son of a prominent family—his father was related to the Marquises of Altamira—he was a brilliant student in the School of San Juan de Letrán de México; and he was named professor in that school, at the age of nineteen, by Viceroy Iturrigaray. A graduate in philosophy and theology of the university and an authority on classical and modern languages, he became famous for his encyclopedic interests. He was a man of remarkable moderation;

and this, together with his culture and background, helped him to avoid the danger of shipwreck in the midst of political squalls and to win the respect of all parties. The colonial government recognized him; on the entrance of the Army of the Three Guarantees, he became a member of the Supreme Provisional Governmental Assembly, having been called to help in drafting the Act of Independence. Holding a high seat in Congress and important positions in the state, he lived until Mexico was invaded by the United States, which so greatly disheartened him as to cause his death in Mexico City on December 7, 1847.

His poetry reflects the dominant tendencies in each of the three epochs mentioned. In the first, he was a neo-classicist, a disciple and imitator of Navarette, whom he succeeded in 1809 as "Head Shepherd" of the Arcadians. He was as much influenced by Meléndez Valdés as he was restrained by the literary rules then in vogue; and while classical, his poems of that period have a vague Gongoristic sound. In the second epoch, political events and the example of Quintana and Cienfuegos gave inspiration to his verses. He was influenced in the third period by the constant fluctuations of civil discord, and he was almost a romanticist. He sang of love, sorrow, religion, and fatherland. Odes, amorous songs, elegies, patriotic songs, and stanzas of philosophical inspiration comprise his numerous works. Steeped in eighteenth-century culture, he followed closely the literary movement of the nineteenth century; he translated Rousseau, Metastasio, and Lamartine.

The poet himself destroyed some of his poems, but the remaining ones were published posthumously in Mexico City, in 1852, under the title *Poetic Works*.

Don Francisco Ortega

Don Francisco Ortega is reputed to have written the most correct and purest poetry of his time.

He entered the literary field victoriously by winning in the literary contest promoted in 1816 by Beristáin. He was from a noble family, being a descendant of the Counts of the Valley of Oploca. Born in Mexico City on April 13, 1793, he became an orphan while he was quite young; his godfather, a canon, sheltered him; and perhaps his literary tastes were developed by the educated woman who cared for him during his childhood. He studied Latin and philosophy in the Palafoxiano Seminary of Puebla, and there he began the study of canon and civil law while he was earning his living and making his first literary attempts. He continued his studies in Mexico City, though he did not receive the law degree. Perhaps his poverty and his decided taste for letters were responsible for this failure. In 1816, after winning Beristáin's literary contest, he obtained a minor appointment in the Treasury Department, thus becoming the first of the type—later common enough and inevitable—of the Mexican writer forced to accept a bureaucratic appointment in order to sustain himself. After holding minor posts during the latter part of the viceregal regime, he entered politics in 1822 and was elected deputy to the first national congress, in which, being an ardent republican, he opposed Iturbide and resisted his imperial designs. In his poetry Ortega commented on the events of the turbulent civic life of that period; his muse fought in the press for political ideas. Hardly is there a picturesque incident worthy of mention in his entire life. His death occurred in Mexico City on March 11, 1849. Ortega—aside from his literary work—served as deputy or senator in several sessions of Congress; he held various posts in the government and the position of sub-director of the ephemeral Institute of Ideological Sciences and Humanities. The drafting of the famous *Organic Bases* of 1841[2] is attributed to him.

Ortega was, above all, a patriotic poet. No one among the poets of his generation mastered the technique of versification as he did. He was precise, circumspect, and also a little cold. In him, reason prevailed over imagination; and academic dignity often restrained his enthusiasm. Nevertheless, his ode "To Iturbide on His Coronation" is a violent invective. Because he was both churchman and patriot, his inspiration was not always political; religion plays no little part in his work. His best poem is on a theological subject, "The Coming of the Holy Spirit"; and Menéndez y Pelayo thinks that "the style of Ortega in sacred poetry is very similar to that of such poets as Lista, Reinoso, and Roldán of the Sevillian school at the end of the eighteenth century, though Ortega's poetry, perhaps, is fresher and less rigid." Ortega also wrote amatory poetry of the pastoral kind in the

[2] The "constitution" that governed Mexico for a brief time after the fall of President Bustamante.—Translators' note.

style of Navarrete and Meléndez Valdés. His poem "To the Eyes of Delia" (the name behind which the poet concealed his innocent and chaste love) is one of his most pleasing works.

Ortega was not a stranger to the theater. Among his poems published in 1839 was a patriotic drama with musical accompaniment, *Free Mexico,* which had been staged in 1821. He left other plays unpublished, including a version of Alfieri's *Rosmunda.* He brought to light, also, the unpublished and incomplete work of Veytia, to which he added an appendix. And, finally, besides collaborations for periodicals, dissertations, and essays on various subjects, Ortega gave further aid to literature by making his home a meeting place for men of letters.

MINOR POETS

The following minor poets should be mentioned. Don José Mariano Rodríguez del Castillo, founder of the Arcadia, was a mediocre but skilful poet who approached the style of Navarrete in erotic and pastoral ballads. He was, according to Henríquez Ureña, one of the most exquisite prose writers of the era of the *Mexican Daily.* Very prosaic and vulgar, although not lacking in elegance on occasion, is the work of Don José María Villaseñor y Cervantes, author of *Festive Acclamations of the Town of Jalapa to Ferdinand VII* and some verses dedicated to the statue of Charles IV and commemorating the oath of "The Beloved King." He also wrote an allegorical melodrama, *The Glory of the Nation Through Its King and Its Union,* which was presented in Mexico City during the ceremony of the taking of the oath to the Constitution. His early convictions did not prevent him from becoming later an ardent panegyrist of Independence in his poem *Liberty* (1827), which was composed on the anniversary of the *grito de Dolores.*[3] In the period of transition between Gongorism and *prosaísmo* is found Don Juan Wenceslao Barquera, who was more of a politician and prose writer than a poet and whose contact with the Muses was fortunately infrequent. He was the author of the odes "To Ferdinand VII" and "To Liberty." Don Ramón Quintana del Azebo was also a member of the Arcadia and an indefatigable contributor to the *Mexican Daily.* "His versifica-

[3] The war cry of Independence raised at Dolores by Hidalgo and his followers.—Translators' note.

tion," according to Henríquez Ureña, "is euphonious, and his diction has a certain purity," although none of his compositions is worthy of inclusion in an anthology. A fecund and prolific versifier as well as a tireless imitator was Don Juan María Lacunza, whose work abounds in biblical allusions. It is claimed that he made a verse translation of the Psalms. Don José Ignacio Basurto also wrote poetry with ease and correctness, and was an agreeable storyteller in spite of the occasional absurdities in his work. In 1802, he published *Moral Fables for the Profit and Entertainment of the Children in the Elementary Schools.* A fabulist also, lacking in literary discipline but not in ingenuity and wit, Don Luis de Mendizábal used the fable for subversive propaganda in the *Daily;* his apologue "The Ass, the Horse, and the Mule" caused a sensation in those stirring times. Hopelessly prosaic, even though his tales do contain a few sparkling passages, the work of Don Mariano Barazábal belongs with that of the other fabulists of this period. Lastly, Don Joaquín María del Castillo y Lanzas (1781- 1878), a native of Jalapa, a diplomat, politician, and journalist, has enjoyed the most lasting fame among these minor poets. He is noted for only one poem, "To the Victory of Tamaulipas," which was composed in imitation of the poem that Olmedo wrote to celebrate the victory of Junín.[4] Under the title of *Ocios juveniles (Juvenile Pastimes)*, Castillo y Lanzas published his poetry in Philadelphia, in 1835.

[4] A decisive battle during the wars of independence. Fought near Lake Junín, Peru, on August 6, 1824.—Translators' note.

XI

Prose

FROM colonial times Mexico had been a land of many poets, but it was not until the struggle for Independence that numerous prose writers appeared. Times were turbulent; to propagate ideas was the principal objective. And for this a supple instrument was required, a type of writing far from the artificial structure and intentional obscurity that had been favored for many years.

Even more than verse, prose underwent an almost complete transformation at the beginning of the century. The change was brought about by the teachings of neo-classicism, which had been received and propagated in the schools from the middle of the preceding century; by the examples of such popular Spanish writers as Father Isla, Feijóo, Jovellanos, and Cadalso, and even—in a smaller degree and through a very few individuals—by the influence of the French writers who were beginning to be read; and finally, by the influence of the daily journals, whose appearance practically coincided with the beginning of the revolutionary era. These influences made the prose of this period fundamentally different from that of the past.

This does not mean that the Mexican prose writers of this period had lost all resemblance to their immediate predecessors. Even though the bombastic Gongoristic manner had almost disappeared, prose still fell occasionally, through force of circumstance, into rhetorical pomp and grandiloquence. And although the familiar tone bordering on vulgarism was used, and abused, and political writers showed a tendency toward brief, simple, direct argumentation, the inevitable vices of pompous scholastic reasoning were not lacking.

In spite of all—and this is the important thing—prose took on a new form. It became more like everyday speech than the old academic type had been. It may be said that not only was prose emancipated, but its scope was broadened. Emerging from the genres which had confined it—history, hagiography, prayer books—prose now animated such new types as political oratory, periodical articles, travel stories, and novels.

POLITICAL WRITERS

The writers who, at the outbreak of the Revolution of 1810, dedicated their energies either to combating or promoting the Revolution belong more properly to the political than to the literary history of Mexico. Some few, like Mier and Guridi y Alcocer, have left truly literary work in their autobiographies and travel stories, but a great part of the writings of these two and of their contemporaries has little value as literature, notwithstanding the fact that it reflects to a great extent the life of that time. The prose writers were preeminently political writers; and the pen, more than the sword, was their weapon.

Fernández de San Salvador

The first of the group of political writers of this epoch was Dr. Agustín Pomposo Fernández de San Salvador (1756-1842), one of the most devoted adversaries of Independence.

Of a distinguished family, a supposed descendant of European nobility and native chieftains, attorney for the Royal *Audiencia* and the *Illustre Colegio,* Don Agustín Pomposo held one of the most important positions in the viceroyalty. He was rector of the university three times, and, furthermore, was "an industrious and very pious man"—according to Beristáin. He declared himself at the outset a determined supporter of the Spanish government and fought bitterly the insurgent cause. A useless fight since he suffered defeat in his own home! While his son Manuel was dying in the war, in 1813, fighting on the side of the revolutionaries, his niece, Doña Leona Vicario, was prosecuted by the viceregal government, having been accused of giving aid to the insurgents. Reference to her story was made in the preceding chapter. Escaping from prison, she joined on the battlefield a man who had been an assistant in her uncle's office, Don Andrés Quintana Roo.

Though he was not a poet, this austere lawyer had tried to write poetry before the crisis of 1810. He wrote a poem entitled "America

Bewailing the Untimely Death of Her Beloved, Her Father, Her Joy, and Her Delight, the Excellent Sr. Don Bernardo de Gálvez, Count of Gálvez." Fortunately, he abandoned poetry and, at the outbreak of the Revolution, took refuge in plain, facile prose. He published such productions as *The Deeds of Hidalgo, a New Type of Quixote, Doer of Wrongs,* etc. (1810); *Disillusionments by Which the Insurgents of New Spain, Seduced by the Freemasonry Agents of Napoleon, Learn the Truth About the Catholic Religion and Experience* (1813); *The Christian Standard Presented to the Insurgents of America* . . . (1814), etc.

He was a scholastic logician, a clumsy and colorless prose writer.

Maldonado

Dr. Francisco Severo Maldonado, the second of this group, enjoyed a unique career in the pitiless political fight of that epoch. He was born in Tepic in the latter part of the eighteenth century, and his death occurred in 1832. Other writers of his kind, in the struggle for Independence, were distinguished for participating on one or the other side: the insurgent or the royalist. But Maldonado—perhaps the only exception—is known for having fought on both sides and for having allied himself finally with the winning side. He inaugurated Mexican political inconsistency.

Maldonado was, according to Mora, "a man of vast learning, of no small capacity, and of an unheard-of arrogance and presumption." He was a priest in Mascota, Jalisco, at the beginning of the Revolution of 1810; and, when Hidalgo occupied Guadalajara in November, he founded the first insurgent periodical, the *American Warning.* This did not prevent him, after the suppression of the insurrection and his pardon in 1811, from founding another periodical, the *Guadalajara Telegraph,* for the royalists. Thus the same pen which called Hidalgo a "new Washington," "a great soul full of wisdom and kindness," had no qualms at stigmatizing him afterward as "an infamous and impudent sybarite, a Sardanapalus without honor and without shame." He who in November was calling the insurgents "our brother liberators," the next February was calling them "bands of highwaymen. . . ."

Assuredly Maldonado was lacking in the greatest endowment of a political writer: honest convictions. For that reason, the value of his work is lessened, though his prose was written with fluency and vigor and his observations often were those of a thinker and sociologist. It is said that he was one of the first in New Spain to study and enjoy the science of economics; and it is known that in his last years he professed a social doctrine similar to that of Fourier, though certainly this versatile journalist was completely ignorant of the latter's work.

Maldonado's work was rather limited and, apart from journalism, consisted of a *Contract of Union for the Republic of the United States of Anáhuac* (1823) and of a book, now lost and probably quite odd—according to available information—called *The Triumph of the Human Species.*

Cos

The Zacatecan political writer, Don José María Cos, was distinctly upright morally and apparently had literary ability. He received his doctorate from the Royal University in 1805; taught grammar, rhetoric, philosophy, theology, and Latin in the Tridentine Seminary of Guadalajara; and served as parish priest in several places in Zacatecas and Jalisco.

He was performing the duties of a curate in Burgo of San Cosme when the insurrection began, in which, without taking sides, he was involved from the outset. Ultimately being forced to take sides, because of the inconsistencies of the viceroy, "he chose that of the Revolution as the just one," according to Bustamante.

Dr. Cos was "a man of great ability, of fecund ingenuity in literary artifices," Alamán says. This was demonstrated sufficiently by his activity after he presented himself to the Council of Zitácuaro in November, 1811. Without constituents or resources, he founded the second insurgent periodical, the *National Illustrator*. For this, he himself built the press, and carved the type from rough pieces of wood; for ink, he used a mixture of indigo and oil in printing the first numbers of the journal. Following that publication, which was improvised in the heat of the struggle, he published another periodical that really was a guide to thinking during the dramatic epoch in which it appeared: the *American Illustrator*, in which, as has been said, he had Quintana Roo as a collaborator.

Cos belongs almost entirely to political history; to literary history, however, belongs the journalist, author of manifestoes and proclamations in which—a curious fact—this man so ardent, vivacious, irritable, violent, reveals himself, during his last years, as a firm and persuasive thinker, one who, having recourse to rhetoric, nevertheless can give his prose sincere human warmth and vibrancy. His death occurred in 1819.

Barquera

Don Juan Wenceslao Barquera, who was born in Querétaro on April 22, 1779, was also a journalist and political writer. He studied Latin, philosophy, and jurisprudence; and in 1809, he received from the university his first degrees and from the *Audiencia* the license to practice law. At the beginning of the century, he participated in the literary movement of which the Arcadia was the center. He was an enthusiastic contributor to the *Mexican Daily,* which he directed for some time and in which he carried forward a skilful campaign in favor of Independence, mocking the censorship of the Inquisition and the viceregal government. Fervently serving the insurgent cause, he dedicated himself not only to writing but to participation in politics: he was a member of the famous secret society, the *Guadalupes,* which did so much for liberty that the Inquisition suppressed it. When Independence was gained, he was the first orator to honor the insurgent heroes in the popular assembly (1827); he occupied high positions in the judiciary and in Congress; he worked for education. He died in the City of Mexico on February 25, 1840.

As an occasional and prosaic rhymer, Barquera made slight contribution to poetry; but he was gentle and sensitive in his prose work, *Salutation to Spring.* This was dedicated to Navarrete and was accordingly permeated with pastoral artifices dear to the neo-classicists. In his civic orations, he showed forcefulness and character without the use of rhetorical ornamentation. Barquera wrote extensively on varied subjects: law, politics, agriculture. He left, according to Beristáin, three plays in manuscript form that are no longer extant; but his most important works, individual and copious, are found in journals, principally in the *Mexican Daily,* from 1805 to 1816.

Mier

Perhaps the only political writer of literary importance during this epoch was Friar Servando Teresa de Mier.

Because of his travels, activities, and unusual adventures, Meir's life would make an interesting picaresque novel. He was born in Monterrey on October 18, 1765, of a family of ancient lineage. Though he had no inclination for the cloister, he assumed the habit of the Dominicans at Mexico City when he was sixteen; he studied in the school of Portacoeli, took the lesser orders, and entered the priesthood; and at twenty-seven years of age he was a doctor of theology and enjoyed fame as an eminent preacher. He preached his famous sermon on the Virgin of Guadalupe on December 12, 1794, before the viceroy, archbishop, and *Audiencia*; and the archbishop, considering some of his statements regarding the apparition of the Virgin as daring and even impious, caused Mier to be denounced from the pulpit. Later, he had him imprisoned and prosecuted, and finally condemned him to ten years of exile in Spain with retirement in the convent of the Caldas, near Santander, and to permanent disqualification as teacher, preacher, and confessor. Mier was also deprived of the title of doctor.

This marked the beginning of the remarkable Dominican's impassioned existence—and also of his principal business and supreme art: flight. "He used evasion and the act of disappearing," Alfonso Reyes notes, "with the mastery of a ghost, and something magical seems to float through the story of his life."

Mier disembarked at Cádiz in 1795. He was imprisoned in the convent of the Caldas, and from there he made his first escape. He was caught and imprisoned in the convent of Saint Paul, in Burgos, where he remained until the end of 1796. In order to receive a fair trial, he asked permission to go to Madrid to appear before the Council of the Indies. He was ordered to a convent in Salamanca; he took a different road; he was captured and confined in the Franciscan convent of Burgos, from which—a second time—he escaped, reached the frontier, and took refuge in Bayonne, arriving there in 1801, on the "Friday of Sorrows" (the second Friday before Easter). On the following day, he participated in a public dispute with the rabbis in the synagogue. He went to Bordeaux and then to Paris, where he opened a school for the teaching of Spanish; he translated Chateaubriand's *Atala* and published a dissertation combating Volney, for which he was rewarded with the parish of Saint Thomas. With the idea of secularizing himself, he went to Rome in 1802; he achieved this, in addition to receiving some honors from the Pope. On his return to Spain, he was again arrested because of a satire he wrote in defense of Mexico. He was taken as a prisoner to the Toribios of Seville in 1804, and from there he made his third escape. He was again seized and sent to prison. For the fourth time he escaped. He lived for three years in Portugal, where the Spanish consul made him his secretary and Pius VII named him Domestic Prelate in recognition of his efforts in converting two rabbis. With the beginning of the war between Spain and France, in 1809, he again entered Spain, this time as a military priest and chaplain of the battalion of volunteers from Valencia. He took part in bloody fights. In Belchite he was a prisoner of the French; but—of course—he escaped and presented himself to General Black, who recommended him to the Assembly at Seville because of his distinguished services. The Regency of Cádiz granted him an annual pension of three thousand pesos as a bishop of Mexico, a pension which Mier would not accept.

Learning of the revolt of Hidalgo, Mier immediately went to London to work through the press for the independence of Mexico. In London he met Mina, who influenced him to undertake the famous but unfortunate expedition of 1817 and who accompanied him in the venture. He became a prisoner of the royalists when the Fort of Soto la Marina was captured, and he was taken in chains to the City of Mexico, where he was imprisoned in the cells of the Inquisition. Since his trial had not been concluded when this tribunal was dissolved in May, 1820, and since, furthermore, he was considered a dangerous man ("His unswerving and dominant passion," asserted his inquisitors, "is independence by revolution, which he has unfortunately inspired and fomented in both Americas by means of his poisonous and venomous writings"), he was sent to Spain in December. But lo, again utilizing his singular abilities, he escaped in Havana! This was his last escape, the sixth. He went to the United States. When Independence was established, he tried to return to Mexico in February, 1822. Again prison awaited him; he had hardly arrived at Veracruz before he was imprisoned in the Fort of San Juan de Ulúa, which the Spaniards still held. He was freed by the First Constituent Congress, of which he became a deputy from his native region. On arriving in Mexico City in July, he learned that Iturbide had been crowned emperor, an act for which he reproached Iturbide in a private audience during which he gloried in his republican creed. Considered a foe to the empire, he had to suffer further imprisonment, the last; on August 28, he was incarcerated with other deputies who were suspected of conspiracy. The republican revolt of February, 1823, finally gave him liberty.

He did not lose his freedom again, but so little time for living remained! Re-elected to the Constituent Congress on December 13, he gave his celebrated speech "on the prophecies," in which he pleaded for a centralized republican form of government and urged that, in any case, a federalized system, if adopted, should be moderate. Victoria, the first president, gave him quarters in the National Palace, and the nation pensioned him in 1824.

Mier was, beyond question, an unusual man, even up until his last moment. When he saw that death was near, on November 15, 1827, he invited his friends to be present at his viaticum, which was administered the following day. The ceremony was splendid, with a procession of representatives from the citizenry, the monasteries, and the schools, together with a company of infantry and a military band. The Minister of Justice and Ecclesiastical Affairs, Ramos Arizpe, presided. Before receiving the sacrament, the patient delivered a copious and eloquent discourse to explain and justify his life and opinions. A few days later, on December 3, he died. The Vice-President of Mexico, Don Nicolás Bravo, presided at the elaborate funeral, and Friar Servando Teresa de Mier was buried in the shrine of Santo Domingo, another place of confinement in which he did not find rest.

These details of Mier's life have been given because he was typical of his epoch: like his contemporaries, he was a man of action, not a thinker. Without a knowledge of his life, it would be impossible for one to understand his principal work, the *Memoirs,* a fitting title under which the *Apology and Story of His Life* was published in a modern edition, with a prologue by Alfonso Reyes. The first part of this book deals with the mishaps and legal proceedings which pursued the Dominican because of his sermon on the Virgin of Guadalupe, and the second part tells of his experiences in Europe from his arrival at Cádiz in 1795 until his escape to Portugal.

This work is an expression of deep restlessness; it is made up of memoirs which are as much like an imaginative novel as a book of travels; it is written in a smooth and at times nervous style by a genius who is now serious, now gay, always delightful, and often witty; and it constitutes the best book in the literary baggage of Mier. His remaining work, besides the above-mentioned sermon and his letters and articles on religious and political controversies, is the *History of the Revolution of New Spain,* which he wrote and published in London in two volumes, in 1813, under the pseudonym of "Don José Guerra." Nearly all of the first edition of this work was lost by shipwreck, but it was reprinted in Mexico in accordance with a resolution adopted by the Chamber of Deputies in 1922. Perhaps the merit of the *History*—which seems to follow no definite plan, being formless and confusing—lies in the fact that it was the first on this particular subject. The extremely restless genius of Mier was unable to confine itself to the systematic discipline of a historian; he was, above all, a fighter, a combatant. Thus, rather than a history, this work is a sort of political allegation; as a political discourse which is also literary, it presents the physiognomy of this remarkable person —a subtle scholastic thinker in whom was stirring the radiant and fiery love of liberty of the French encyclopedists—a man who was a forerunner of Independence, an active worker for it, and, in the last years of his life, a representative, as Alfonso Reyes observes, of "the first vacillations of the constitutional era," in the agitated and bloody struggle between federalism and centralism.

Guridi y Alcocer

The last of this group, Don Miguel Guridi y Alcocer, was not of the same temperament as Mier, but resembled him in his activities as a writer. He was born in San Felipe Ixtacuiztla, Tlaxcala, on December 26, 1763, and died in the City of Mexico on October 4, 1828. He was student and professor in the Palafoxiano Seminary in Puebla, a doctor of theology and canon law, a graduate in law of the Illustrious and Royal School of Mexico, and he served as curate in the dioceses of Puebla and Mexico. Elected in 1810, by his native province, as a deputy to the Cortes of Spain, he went to the Peninsula, where he remained for two years and became an outstanding member of the Cortes, being its president at one time. Returning to Mexico, he held, between 1813 and 1821, important ecclesiastical positions. When the Revolution triumphed, he was a member of the Provisional Congress; he was a signer of the Act of Independence, was a deputy in the first two congresses, and was elected prebendary of the metropolitan diocese.

Numerous were the intellectual activities of Guridi y Alcocer. In addition to being prolific as a preacher (it is estimated that from 1791 to 1820 he preached sixteen hundred sermons), he was prominent as a parliamentary orator, both in the Spanish Cortes and in the Mexican Congress, where he showed himself to be an enthusiastic panegyrist of the liberties resulting from the constitutional regime. It is said that he wrote a *Course in Modern Philosophy,* and also that he published in 1805 a *Latin Grammar.* Though somewhat limited and mediocre as a poet, he did not fail to pay tribute to the lyric; an ode and a sonnet by him are included in the *Songs of the Mexican Muses,* Beristáin's anthology, which was discussed in Chapter IX. He also composed a *Discourse on the Evils of Gambling,* which has enjoyed the distinction of being reprinted recently.

Nevertheless, Guridi y Alcocer wrote only one work that can be considered literary: *Notes on His Life,* which he wrote during the latter part of 1801 and the early part of 1802; this was published in 1906 by Don Luis García Pimentel. Guridi's story is less varied and colorful than Mier's *Memoirs,* but it is of vital interest as a picture of manners and customs and, above all, as "a human document." Under the influence of Rousseau, Guridi y Alcocer used himself as a subject for introspection; he depicted the vices, passions, and virtues which he thought he had; he related—purposely following his model—exploits and adventures from which roguery and cynicism were not excluded; and he frequently analyzed his own social background. The book is written with restraint and simplicity, and often with beauty of style. His prose reveals that in 1801 the Spanish models of neo-classicism had already achieved a complete transformation of taste.

THE BIRTH OF THE NOVEL

At the beginning of the nineteenth century, within the period of Independence, there burst forth in Mexico a literary genre which, though old in the world, had had few cultivators here.

This is a phenomenon: the tale, so very genuine, so very characteristic of Spanish literature from its origin, was not written in New Spain. And, so far as the novel itself is concerned, only the germ of it is to be found in colonial literary history. The following is a brief summary of the available information.

Francisco Bramón, a graduate and, later, chancellor of the University of Mexico, published in 1620 *The Linnets of the Immaculate Virgin*, a pastoral romance in the style of Cervantes' *Galatea*. Antonio Ochoa, a licentiate and presbyter of Puebla, is said to have written a novel in 1662; but only the title of this is known, *Deeds of Fernando or Fernando's Fall*. Sigüenza y Góngora published, in 1690, *Misfortunes of Alonso Ramírez*, a historical narrative, which, because of its romantic aspect, would seem to be a novel but in reality is not. There are no other novels or novelists in seventeenth-century Mexican literature. The eighteenth century is even more barren than the seventeenth, though two names should be mentioned. Marcos Reynel Hernández, student and then professor of theology in the Tridentine Seminary of Mexico, composed a nonsensical mystic work with certain novelistic aspects: *The Pilgrim with a Guide and Universal Medicine for the Soul* (1750). José González de Sancha, a priest, wrote, in 1760, in a polished style with no signs of mysticism, a novel entitled *Fabian and Aurelia*, which—according to Pimentel—deals with "light" and "indecent" love affairs.

In reality, as has been said, there was no colonial novel. The Mexican novel was developed coincidentally with the insurgent movement. It is worthy of note that without literary antecedents in its native soil or marked foreign influence, the novel in Mexico appeared full-grown and was profoundly Mexican from the first. Fernández de Lizardi created it.

Fernández de Lizardi

Journalist, novelist, *costumbrista* [portrayer of common life], writer, poet, and dramatist, Don José Joaquín Fernández de Lizardi —more commonly known by the pseudonym of "The Mexican Thinker"—was the most important and most popular literary figure in Mexico during the first third of the nineteenth century.

He was born in the City of Mexico November 15, 1776, of a family in modest circumstances; and it was with difficulty that he managed—following the custom in vogue—to take courses that would prepare him for a literary career. He spent his childhood and first school years in Tepoztlán, where his father was physician for the Jesuit Seminary. He returned to Mexico City to study Latin; and he later entered the School of San Ildefonso to study philosophy, but he never succeeded in obtaining the bachelor's degree from the university. The poverty of his parents forced him to leave school. Little is known of his youth. It is thought that he lived in Tepozotlán for some time. In 1805 or 1806, he was married in Mexico City. Perhaps during that time—though this is not confirmed—he wrote for the *Daily,* which had just been founded. His appearance in literature dates from 1808 when he published a poem called "A Polonaise in Honor of Our Catholic Monarch, Fernando VII."

It is hardly strange that the author of the "Polonaise" should already be, at the beginning of the insurrection of 1810, in spiritual sympathy with that movement. As an official deputy in Tasco in 1812, when Morelos entered that city, he surrendered all arms, munitions, and powder to the rebel. For this act, he was taken to Mexico City as a prisoner, but he was soon freed, his course of action being considered justifiable.

At that time the feverish love of publicity, which he never lost, was burning in him. Self-taught, nourished by reading forbidden books that propagated the ideas of the French encyclopedists, he began to publish his first pamphlets by 1811. When the freedom of the press, instituted by the Constitution of Cádiz, was proclaimed, Fernández de Lizardi established in Mexico City his celebrated periodical, the *Mexican Thinker,* and proved himself to be an able and intrepid worker for liberty. His criticism of Viceroy Venegas caused his arrest when the freedom of the press—as fleeting then as always—was suppressed. But in prison the journalist continued to write; in addition to being turbulent, he was persuasive and tenacious. He ceased to publish the *Mexican Thinker* in 1814, but soon it was succeeded by other publications: *Cupboard of Trinkets* (1815), *Entertaining Moments* (1819), the *Electric Conductor* (1820). Besides journals, the indefatigable Lizardi edited pamphlets and books. By 1820 he had completed the books that brought him fame. He was widely read; he was everywhere discussed. He became more and more a fervent literary propagandist: in 1820, he organized the Public Reading Society, which supplied books and periodicals by subscription; in 1821, he was again imprisoned because of a certain satiric and jocose dialogue; in 1822, he defended the Free Masons, for which he was excommunicated; the following year, he produced another periodical, the *Brother of the Parrakeet*; in 1824, he published *The Conversations of the Churl and the Sacristan*; and, lastly, in 1826, he made a final effort at establishing a periodical, the *Weekly Mail from Mexico*.

His last years—during which he was ill with tuberculosis—were spent in respectable poverty and continued activity, the committee named to recompense the servants of Independence having assigned to him the salary of a retired captain. He was also the editor of the *Government Gazette*. He died in his natal city on June 21, 1827.

Fernández de Lizardi was, above all, a journalist, and his social and literary qualities should be considered from that viewpoint. Without preoccupation with style, without seeking beauty of form or artistic sentiment, he followed the most direct path to his object, which was, essentially, to bring about reforms in the political realm and to improve social conditions. He held to these aims in periodical articles and in books; and in both types of writing, his attitude was substantially the same.

To the journals and miscellaneous periodicals that he founded and supported, there should be added—among "The Thinker's" typically journalistic works—his pamphlets, of which there are more than two hundred on varied subjects. In language always easily understandable and full of popular flavor, with admirable good sense and no unusual number of ideas—neither his thought nor his culture was very deep —he succeeded in touching the heart of the people. The cause of liberty owed much to him: in dangerous and difficult times when censorship was alert, Fernández de Lizardi, with wisdom and ingenuity, using now irony and now sarcasm, but more often maintaining himself on a plane of serenity, became the most forceful propagandist for Independence. But at the same time that he was a political writer, he was even more of a moralist. Within him, the curious observer and the analyst of the social life of his time took their stand beside the patriot.

There is no doubt that the moralizing and didactic tendency predominated in Fernández de Lizardi as a novelist. His four works of fiction are: *El Periquillo Sarniento (The Mangey Parrakeet)*, *Little Miss Quixote and Her Cousin*, *Don Catrín de la Fachenda (Don Dandy the Windbag)*, and *Sad Nights and Happy Days*.

The *Periquillo* is a picture of Mexican life during the latter part of the viceregal epoch. It relates the adventures of a lively youth, half a rogue (or a rogue and a half), who is forced by circumstances to lead an irregular and carefree existence; but, like the protagonists of the Spanish picaresque novels of whom he is a direct descendant, Periquillo shows certain traits of honesty, goodness, and generosity which finally redeem him. He frequents the various circles of Mexican society, now in the center of a respectable home, now in student circles, and again in a religious atmosphere. The death of his parents leaves him alone and helpless; bad company leads him to the *hampa* [the underworld of vagabonds and criminals]; he becomes a gambler and a cheat; he is familiar with prisons; he serves—like Lazarillo— several masters. He marries and loses his wife. He has various adventures, including a voyage to Manila that ends in shipwreck and the life of a castaway on a desert island. At last, he returns to Mexico, where, after many experiences, he is converted to an honorable and peaceful life. The incorrigible rover risks his neck again in holy matrimony, has children, and—to show himself a good Christian and a lover of good, and to prevent his children from surrendering to vice and from "taking only the bad example of their father, perhaps with the foolish hope of reforming late in life as he did"—he writes in autobiographical form his vagabond history and finally dies, leaving all those around him full of tenderness, unction, and consolation.

Edifying digressions are numerous in this novel—there is almost no episode without a moral; typical, too, are the innocuous attempts to display Latin erudition by the insertion of verses and apothegms. Fernández de Lizardi fights vice, ridicules bad habits, and on occasion subversively attacks the existing government. His eye is quick to see the depths as well as the surfaces of things: he reproduces atmosphere, creates types, describes episodes pleasingly; and, though he does not stir the reader deeply, he is interesting, convincing, and humorous. For this reason, the *Periquillo* is incomparable as a picture of that epoch. It is the best museum of Mexican customs during the decline of the viceregal period.

Without adornment or finery, plain and facile, "The Thinker's" prose accomplishes its purpose; that is, it entertains while it teaches. He describes soberly and analyzes sparingly, without shrinking from the crudest realism. No one has surpassed him in depicting the spirit of Mexican life, so that not only chronologically, but also from the viewpoint of national development, he is the first Mexican novelist.

The *Periquillo* attained, from the time of its first appearance, remarkable popularity. It was published for the first time—though incomplete because of censorship by the viceregal government—in 1816, and a second edition soon appeared. In the third edition (1830-1831) the novel was published in its entirety; and, since then, more than fifteen other printings have been made.

Little Miss Quixote and Her Cousin (1818) was almost as popular as the *Periquillo*. It is a moral and didactic novel showing the influence of Rousseau, and may be called the companion book to the *Periquillo*, though it is greatly inferior. If in his first novel Fernández de Lizardi intended to "criticize the customs of misguided men and to ridicule their grossest vices," in the second he proposed "to apply soap and water to the women." Consequently, he presents two women: one, a product of "a common and perverted education"; the other, a product of "a rearing which was moral and free from the most common prejudices." In the contrast—declares the novelist—"will be found the moral of the satire, and in the fate of both young women the teaching of the book—that is, the warning to fear evil and the admonition to do good works." The story, however, is so very inane and contains such frequent digressions that it is soporific and should be considered mainly as a curious document on Mexican customs.

The Life and Deeds of the Famous Cavalier, Don Dandy the Windbag is the third and last of Lizardi's novels. It was published posthumously in 1832 and is a picaresque story of the same style and flavor as the *Periquillo*, but it differs from the latter—apart from plot and incidents that are naturally different—in that it has for its protagonist a distinct social type: the *catrín*, or fop, of colonial times.

Of an entirely different nature is Lizardi's *Sad Nights and Happy Days* (1818); this is composed of autobiographical dialogues in which, inspired by the famous and popular *Melancholy Nights* of Cadalso, "The Thinker" relates his sufferings during the War of Independence. Although artificial, this work has a singular importance and constitutes a landmark in Mexican literary history: it is the first fruit in Mexican letters of the influence of European "pre-romanticism."

Fernández de Lizardi also wrote poetry. His inspiration certainly was not very elevated, nor his versification especially pure and clear.

His poetic inspiration was—as Luis G. Urbina picturesquely expresses it—"a muse who did not disdain to traverse, with unkempt locks, the worst parts of Mexico City and to share the intimate life of the social outcasts and the *catrín* in order to understand and vividly depict them"; because of this conception of poetry, Lizardi seems to be a precursor of Guillermo Prieto. His incurable moralizing tendencies naturally found their proper medium in the versified fable; and as a fabulist, he was one of the last stragglers after the camp of *prosaísmo*. These stories, following the style of the day, were definitely influenced by the Spaniards Iriarte and Samaniego, especially the latter. The *Fables* of "The Thinker" were published in 1817.

As if to omit no type of literary activity, Lizardi also wrote for the stage. His original plays are: the second part of a very popular melodrama, *The Sensitive Negro* (1825); the miracle play called the *Auto Mariano* [The Virgin Mary's play] *to Commemorate the Miraculous Appearance of Our Mother and Lady of Guadalupe*; and a pastoral drama, *The Happiest Night, or The Reward of Innocence*. Two plays in verse that are attributed to him but have not been published are: *The Tragedy of Father Arenas*, in four acts, and *El Unipersonal don Agustín de Iturbide*, a monologue in hendecasyllabic verse. Perhaps these unknown works were of no better quality than the known ones. The plays of this most Mexican novelist do not recommend him as a dramatic writer.

Of rich "folkloric" and historical content, the enormous work of Don José Joaquín Fernández de Lizardi—journalist, novelist, poet, dramatist—has been reduced, according to the estimate of posterity, to the novel. And even in this genre "The Thinker" was able to create only one book outstanding today: the *Periquillo*. A popular-priced edition of this classic was published in 1959 by Editorial Porrúa in their collection, "That All May Know." It has a prologue written by Jefferson Rea Spell, who prepared a volume combining *D. Catrín de la Fachenda* (Don Dandy the Windbag) and *Sad Nights and Happy Days*, which was published in Porrúa's *Collection of Mexican Authors* in 1959.

From the Consummation of Independence to 1867

XII

Classicists and Romanticists

THE POLITICAL STRUGGLE

BY THE War of Independence, Mexico had gained her freedom from Spain. But she still had to free herself from the colonial regime, and this was the cause of the uninterrupted and tragic struggle which fills one of the most dramatic cycles of Mexican history: the period from 1821 to 1867.

Two forces were in conflict: one force that, in effect, desired to preserve colonial rule, and another that sought to destroy it. The struggle lasted for nearly half a century. With the Regency established,[1] strife between the two parties appeared in the first Constituent Congress. Since Spain had adopted a conservative constitutional monarchy, with a Bourbon as sovereign, and had rejected the Treaty of Cordova, the first question to be considered was: Should the new regime headed by a prince of a ruling house that was not Spanish be upheld—or should a republic be proclaimed? This was, in reality, only a secondary phase in the already confused conflict of principles then dominant; for then, as always, the form of government mattered less than the forces controlling it. The first *caudillo* [soldier-politician] had appeared: Iturbide. The people adored him; the army supported him. Through the prestige of arms, he imposed his authority on the Congress; a sergeant, Pío Marcha, proclaimed him Emperor. The army thereby intervened for the first time in politics. It was only a short time until it intervened again, for in October of that same year—1822—a general, Santa Anna, proceeded to proclaim the Republic.

With regard to the Republic, the struggle between the parties was

[1] A provisional government, administered by a committee of five.—Translators' note.

193

reduced to the question: Would the government be centralized or federal? The conflict between centralization and federalism served only to mask the two real issues: the conservation of privileges, the abolition of privileges. Those who, for the most part, possessed special privileges, that is to say, the conservatives, chose centralism. The *puros*—those who were opposed to the riches and privileges of the church and the old Spanish party, and who had been infected by a desire to imitate the United States—declared themselves to be federalists.

A general was the first president. From then on, the contest for the presidency was settled among generals by recourse to arms. Pedraza succeeded Victoria; Guerrero, by insurrection, overthrew Pedraza. Another uprising put Bustamante in the chair. A succession of systems, men, and crises followed. Mexico passed from federalism to centralism, from centralism to federalism. One constitution followed another. Civil war raged incessantly—insurrections, rebellions, "manifestoes," a dizzy succession of men in power. An interruption occurred: a foreign war, an unjust war of aggression—the American invasion of 1847, which resulted in the first dismemberment of Mexican territory. Civil war and anarchy followed before the land could recover from the losses incurred in that unequal struggle. A dictatorship that did not seem to be temporary—it was declared to be indefinite—was established. But the Revolution of Ayutla in 1855 overthrew Santa Anna, who unlawfully attempted to retain his power with the aid of the conservative party. The struggle became implacable, bloody, without quarter. The reform party, having promulgated the Federal Constitution of 1857 and having carried on the terrible conflict commonly known as "The Three Years' War," seemed to be firmly entrenched in power. Then the threat of the Tripartite Alliance appeared. The danger of this triple European intervention soon vanished, leaving only the French as a real threat. The conservative party used the French intervention in order to remain in power. Conservatives and liberals, in the last act of the tragedy, adopted new names—names given them by the struggle created around a dream of empire: imperialists and republicans. The last act was brief; the drama of Querétaro[2] was its epilogue.

[2] The Emperor Maximilian was captured at Querétaro May 15, 1867.—Translators' note.

"With the Empire, with the war that was officially called 'The Second War of Independence,' " writes Don Justo Sierra,

ends the long period of Mexican Revolution, begun, in reality, in 1810 but reaching its final stage in 1857. In the last great phase of this struggle of more than half a century, Mexico lost—either on the field of battle or as a direct result of the war—over three hundred thousand men, but acquired a soul, a national unity. There had been conflict everywhere; if it had been possible to spray the blood over the entire country, inch by inch, the land would have been covered with a mist of blood. Mexico was fertilized by blood.

With the restoration of the Republic in 1867, Mexico—at least in the realm of politics—was freed from the colonial regime.

THE STATUS OF LETTERS

Without scanning the political scene, it would be impossible to explain the nature of Mexican literature in this period. Ideas and forms, personalities and schools: all seem to be linked with politics. If literature itself had been political in the former epoch, in this period the politicians were the writers. It can be said that because of its influence on letters, politics determined not only the activities of writers but, even more, the tenets of the literary schools.

The political struggle, so far as the principles in conflict were concerned, was conducted for the greater part on the rostrum and in the press; and it engendered also a new activity in letters: the writing of contemporary history. The battle was drawn in the parliamentary precincts, in the newspapers, in the pages—vibrant with eloquence and never free from passion—of the political historians who reviewed the very scenes that they witnessed and took part in.

With the exception of history and the political literature that was published in periodicals and pamphlets, the status of literature, strictly speaking, was precarious at the beginning of the period of Independence. After Fernández de Lizardi, there is a long period of silence in the realm of the novel. The drama—apart from isolated manifestations of diverse value—was hardly cultivated actively during the latter part of this period. As for poetry, the situation was far from encouraging. A contemporary, Don José Bernardo Couto, affirmed that "the noise of arms and the revolution which has rocked the land since 1810 has left rest for no one." The struggle overshadowed everything. Couto himself complained of "the invasion of political and economic studies, which demanded the attention of many and almost choked the delicate plant of literature." Poetry, he said, was in a "miserable state." "One must agree," he adds, "that we have retrogressed rather than progressed."

Of the eminent poets of the preceding period, Ortega and Sánchez de Tagle were still living and writing. Quintana Roo had become silent; in reality, he had written but little poetry ever. And to these lyric voices was added that of a foreigner, the great Cuban poet, Don José María de Heredia, author of the famous ode "To Niagara" and of "The Teocalli of Cholula."

Heredia was born in Santiago, Cuba, in 1803. While still young, he accompanied his parents to Florida, to Haiti, and to Venezuela. He studied philosophy in Caracas and law in Havana, and came to Mexico in the early part of 1819 with his father, who had been named crime commissioner and who died in Mexico in 1820. After Heredia returned to his native country, he was condemned, in 1823, to perpetual exile because he had taken part in a conspiracy for Cuban independence. Having emigrated to New York, he published there the first collection of his poetry in 1825. In that same year, he accepted an invitation from President Victoria to return to Mexico. He occupied several official posts, serving as an employee in the Secretariat of State, a judge in Cuernavaca, and a member of the legislature from the state of Mexico, where he established his home and married a Mexican girl. He died in Mexico City in 1839.

The revolutionary storm whirled Heredia through a varied career within a short time. As he himself said, he had been, "with more or less luck, a lawyer, soldier, traveler, professor of languages, diplomat, journalist, magistrate, historian, and poet before reaching twenty-five years of age." His versatility made him prominent in Mexico. A second and enlarged edition of his poetry was issued in Toluca in 1832. Heredia inspired beginning writers with his counsel; he edited various journals; certainly he influenced the propagation of new romantic trends, since he was an admirer of Chateaubriand and had translated and imitated Young, Lamartine, and Foscolo. But—though he contributed to the movement—Heredia was not the restorer of Mexican poetry in this epoch. That title belongs jointly to Pesado and Carpio. The purpose and impelling force of the restoration were affirmed also by the Academy of Letrán.

THE ACADEMY OF LETRÁN

Originally this was a voluntary society of young men who formed what might be called the first Mexican literary Bohemia. In a room in the old School of San Juan de Letrán, there lived, as a hermit, the young lawyer, Don José María Lacunza. That room—as Guillermo Prieto describes it in his *Memoirs of My Times*—

properly could be called a cell, with its high windows, its bare tiles, and its wooden screen in the doorway. It was completely filled with books, without any vacant space except that occupied by a narrow table that it would be calumny to call a desk. In one end of the room, opposite the table, was a small, lonely cot in keeping with the makeshift character of the place. A white wooden table completed the furnishings; and on it, either provoking or giving evidence of the appetite of the owner, was a tin dinner pail and a clay pitcher of fresh water.

Lacunza, after defending a brilliant thesis in philosophy, had dedicated himself to the natural sciences, learned several languages by himself, and become known as a literary figure because of an ode on the invasion of Barradas.[3] He had taught or substituted in all the chairs of the school; he had a prodigious memory; he was a remarkable dialectician; and he nourished one single passion—to devour books.

Of his few friends, several gathered regularly in his room; among these were his brother Juan Nepomuceno, Manuel Toniat Ferrer, and Guillermo Prieto, all of whom were immature poets. They would arrive at his door at a fixed hour with their "rolls of verses in their pockets." The authors would read their compositions in turn; some of those present would ask for the floor in order to point out the defects in the poems they had heard—the comments caused great merriment at times—and each composition was corrected or approved by a strict vote of the majority. "Those literary exercises," says Prieto, "had ostensibly the aspect of a game; but, in reality, thanks to the wisdom of Lacunza, they were valuable courses of study, usually directed by him." Because of these meetings, such ancient names as those of Horace and Virgil, Herrera and Friar Luis lived again, and with these

---

[3] Barradas commanded the expedition sent by Spain to reconquer Mexico in 1828.—Translators' note.

were mingled the names of poets whose fame was already spreading beyond Europe: Goethe and Schiller, "Ossian" and Byron.

These literary exercises lasted for more than two years, and one afternoon in June of 1836—according to Prieto—these young men resolved valiantly to form a society that should bear the name of the famous school, to inaugurate this at once, and to invite literary friends to become members, provided that each candidate received the unanimous approval of the group. Almost immediately a quietness fell upon the little group. The opening speech was delivered by José María Lacunza. A sliced pineapple, sprinkled with sugar and fraternally divided among those present, formed the menu of the inaugural banquet, which was rendered more enjoyable by noisy improvisations. In that unique body there were no rules. For everyone aspiring to be a member, it was sufficient that he present a composition in verse or prose and that this composition be approved, with the provision that, when it was read, the author should name his defenders and should hand over his work for debate.

Who would have prophesied that from this "child's play" would emanate one of the most serious, sustained, and vigorous impulses that Mexican literature has ever received! In the Academy of Letrán was incubated the generation which later filled half a century of the history of Mexican literature. A little old man knocked at the door; the young founders, by acclamation, elected him president: he was Quintana Roo. Carpio and Pesado entered later "as worthy representatives of classical literature"; likewise, Don Francisco Ortega and Don Alejandro Arango y Escandón became members. Other members were: Fernando Calderón, Rodríguez Galván, the future fighting Bishop Munguía, Don Ignacio Aguilar y Marocho, Gorostiza, and Ignacio Ramírez. The last of these adopted the pseudonym of "The Necromancer" and, under the disguise of a mad Jacobin, scandalized the learned group by denying the existence of God; it was he who later became the doctrinaire of the War of Reform.

From 1836 to 1856 the Academy had its weekly meetings in the School of Letrán; there discussions were held, theses sustained, and principles determined. Free criticism exercised its noble, purifying influence. Studies of grammar and pronunciation, especially, were made to eliminate habitual vulgarisms. The Academy democratized literary studies by bringing writers together without any distinction as to age, ability, political or religious opinions. The Academy "having been born"—as Guillermo Prieto says—

of four poor students, and being open, without discrimination, to nobles and learned men who, in turn, might yield their places to office apprentices, book clerks, or vagabonds like Ramírez, a spontaneous evolution took place in which knowledge, light, inspiration, and genius won a noble and generous supremacy.

But the greatest and most important achievement of this movement was, undoubtedly, "its definite tendency to Mexicanize literature and free it from the influence of other literatures by giving it a distinctive character." Writers of novels, poems, legends, and dramas imposed upon themselves national themes whether they were dealing with colonial matters or events before the Conquest, or were depicting customs or types or landscapes.

When the Count de la Cortina began his sharp attacks in *El Zurriago (The Whip)*, a periodical of rough and beneficial satire rather than of grammatical and literary value, and another Spanish poet, Don Casimiro del Collado, along with Don José María Lafragua, founded in 1841 *El Apuntador (The Observer)*, a publication of literary and theatrical criticism, the active members of the Academy of Letrán did not disdain to contribute to the press: Prieto edited a journal, *El Domingo (Sunday)*, in which appeared his first efforts as a *costumbrista* [a delineator of everyday life]; and Rodríguez Galván compiled the volumes which, under the title *Almanac for Mexican Young Ladies*, appeared successively in 1837, 1838, 1839, 1840, 1841, and 1843. These annuals contained literary works in verse and prose, and were, in a way, precursors of the elegant "Friendly Gifts" of Cumplido.

Within and without the Academy of Letrán, in literature as well as in politics, were two factions: one that upheld tradition and one that aspired to set it aside. The facts seem to indicate that the significance of romanticism and classicism was at that time more political than literary. Without exception, the writers who were active in the conservative party were classicists; with few exceptions, the romanticists were affiliated with the liberal party. Among the classicists were persons who, in the main, belonged to the higher social classes, had strict training and solid literary education, and were polished writers inspired by the ancient Greek models and the Spanish poets of the Golden Age. The second group were, essentially, talented writers without careful artistic preparation, in whom spontaneity predominated over adherence to rules; they were naturally sympathetic toward new foreign forms, but they were not yet capable of assimilating these by giving them naturalization papers in Mexican literature.

ROMANTICISM

The beginnings of Mexican romanticism date from about the year 1830. The first sources, except for Byron, were French. Later, Spanish romanticism influenced it directly through Espronceda and the Duke of Rivas in lyric poetry and García Gutiérrez in the drama.

Some of the poetry written by Fernando Calderón in 1826 and 1827 already had a certain romantic flavor. Rodríguez Galván's poetry, which dates from the early thirties, was openly romantic. A Mexican poet, Castillo y Lanzas, translated Byron. One of Lamartine's *Meditations* was translated into Spanish by Calderón in 1840. In 1838 the first romantic drama was produced: *Muñoz, Inspector of Mexico,* by Rodríguez Galván. Between the following year and 1842, three romantic plays of Fernando Calderón were staged one after another.

Should Mexican romanticism be considered as a mere transplanting of a foreign mode; or did romanticism have here—as in other countries, as everywhere—a reason for existence which obeyed a less external cause?

Few terms have been so variable, so ambiguous in connotation, so vaguely defined as "romanticism" and "romantic." In the eighteenth century, "romantic" was used in France as a synonym for "romanesque," or fictional, a term which—according to Petit de Julleville— had in Rousseau "the sense of the picturesque with a tinge of savage melancholia."[4] Madame de Staël was the first to define it successfully; she maintained that classic poetry, born in imitation of the ancients, is the opposite of romantic poetry, born of Christianity and chivalry. Interpreted thus, romanticism served as a banner in the battle effectively waged in countries of classic tradition, such as France. Romanticism, says Edward Maynial, "was a reaction: against the narrow rule of reason, the free flight of imagination rebelled; against the severity

---

[4] *Histoire de la littérature française.*—Author's note.

of classic taste, the tumultuous complexity of nature; against the fanatical worship of antiquity, the insatiable curiosity of the modern foreign literatures."[5]

But romanticism was not only destructive; it was creative. It broke with common literary rules that were becoming petrified; in opposition to the incessant evocation of classic antiquity, it placed not only medieval subject matter, but modern—and it even used, as themes for drama and poetry, episodes from contemporary history. Above all, against cold reserve it championed the exaltation of emotion. "In classical poetry," Maynial explains, "the poet is absent from his work. In romantic poetry, individualism triumphs; the 'I,' emancipated, is paraded, is described, is confessed."

On the other hand, besides being a literary mode, romanticism was a "sentimental state" which, in a given moment of civilization, had the world for its stage. Beyond literature it spread to all the arts: painting, sculpture, music. It infiltrated the customs of the people; it conditioned, to a certain extent, the modes of seeing, dressing, speaking, feeling. A romantic landscape and romantic finery were viewed in the same manner. Speech, as well as love, became romantic. Especially were imagination and sensibility the accepted fashion.

Precisely, in this form of sentiment—"romantic sentiment"—the literary novelty spread to Mexico almost simultaneously with its enthronement in Europe. The lyrical and subjective element was particularly popular here. It could not have been otherwise. Though Mexico was a country of classical tradition, romanticism did not necessarily have to appear here as a destructive element, as a reaction against classicism. No trace of classicism had appeared in the confused medley of *culteranismo* during more than a century. Neither neo-classicism, which was weak at first and of short duration, nor the subsequent return to the classic forms of the Spanish Golden Age, on the part of such poets as Pesado and Arango y Escandón, constituted a literary movement that, generally and persistently, was capable of generating a revolution in the literature laboriously cultivated after the struggle for political freedom.

By reason of obvious congeniality, the romantic sentiment flourished in Mexico and penetrated literature and customs. The spirit, the

---

[5] *Littérature française moderne et contemporaine.*—Author's note.

atmosphere, and the times were propitious for that sentimental fever. The tempestuous political era, from the consummation of Independence to the tragedy of Querétaro in 1867, was, in essence, romantic: a struggle by the spirit of reform against reigning tradition. Nature, society, the very soul, as Luis G. Urbina has pointed out, "were ready to receive and diffuse the new literary manifestation. We possessed the psychic elements; the manner and expression came to us from without. We had the emotion already; we had had it for many years."

The phenomenon of romanticism is clearly evident from the time of its first appearance in Mexican letters. Calderón was unmistakably romantic; his dramas—because of his open tendency toward literary imitation, which, unfortunately, was not accompanied by the determination to supply his own ingredients—were counterfeited from medieval European materials, but there is in them a personal—an authentically personal—romantic sentiment. This sentiment soon became accentuated in the novel. Orozco y Berra and Díaz Covarrubias were romanticists; Florencio M. del Castillo was also insufferably, madly so. As time passed, romanticism invaded poetry. With the advent of the following period, it found its highest exaltation in Manuel Acuña. It was alive, more than ever, in the novels of Altamirano and in the first stories and first odes of Justo Sierra. It achieved a tempered, intimate, eloquent expression during the epoch of "modernism" in the work of some of the best poets of the latter part of the nineteenth century.

If romanticism did not exist as a reaction against classicism, neither did it show any trace of archeological and historical research into indigenous legends or the colonial past. It was, notwithstanding, an incontestable literary reality as a lyrical and subjective tendency.

There was not in Mexico, properly speaking, any struggle between classicism and romanticism. The two tendencies which opposed each other in politics lived together peacefully in the literary field. They both filled that period, and it seems an extraordinary thing that in the midst of the flaming intensity of the political drama that occupied the half-century of the era of Independence, high and noble spirits should turn their eyes toward an imperishable ideal: that of beauty and art, to build and to create. And they actually built and created, paving the way for the most brilliant period of Mexican letters.

XIII.

Poetry

THE two social tendencies that were in conflict in this tempestuous period were reflected in poetry: the traditional or conservative, represented by the classicists; the reforming or revolutionary, by the first romanticists. The former, generally speaking, were humanists of refined culture, polished and elegant writers, though somewhat cold; in contrast to their immediate predecessors, they disdained weak and ingenious pseudo-classicism in order to imitate the purest ancient models. Their antagonists, almost all of whom were improvisers with insufficient literary preparation, were characterized by mental unrest, spontaneity, and stubborn rebellion against authority; they felt and expressed themselves more freely and revealed a new sensibility in their poetry.

DISTINGUISHED CLASSICISTS

Pesado

Don José Joaquín Pesado is doubtless the most prominent member of this group. He was born in San Agustín del Palmar, Puebla, on February 9, 1801. Having lost his father at an early age, he settled with his mother in Orizaba, where his family possessed considerable fortune and where, under the direction of his mother, he received an excellent education. He was a man of profound religious faith and naturally inclined toward scholarly studies. Being intellectually and spiritually mature at twenty years of age, he dedicated himself to the mastery of the Latin, Italian, French, and English languages as well as his own; he also acquired the rudiments of Greek and delved into theology and the exact, natural, and political sciences, thus acquiring a wealth of serious and solid learning to which he continually added throughout his life. In 1822 he married María de la Luz de la Llave y Segura, the "Elisa" of his verses. He spent his time in cultivating literature, in managing the property he had inherited, and later in public life. Affiliated with those of liberal ideas, he took a conspicuous part in the politics of the state of Veracruz in 1833 and 1834; he was minister of the interior in 1838 and of foreign relations in 1845 and 1846. His political and social ideas, however, gradually changed; he eventually became a member of the conservative party and was recognized as one of its most distinguished writers. Established finally in Mexico City after 1851, he enjoyed an independent and easy life and a singular social position; and, at the reopening of the university in 1854, he was given a doctor's degree and the chair of literature. The Royal Spanish Academy made him a corresponding member; and while he was still active in literary work, he died suddenly on March 3, 1860.

Don José Joaquín Pesado was, above all, a poet; and, as such, he is characterized by his profound Christian sentiment and his classical background. The latter was derived, unlike that of some of his contemporaries and immediate predecessors, not from seventeenth-century classicism, but from the Italo-Spanish classicism of the sixteenth century. If his juvenile poetry is impaired by defects—principally prosodic defects that were common to the poets of his time—the poetry of his mature years is so polished and clear that Menéndez y Pelayo has said, "It is more sustained as a whole than that of any other American poet with whom I am familiar." He further states that one of Pesado's poems, the elegy "Elisa's Guardian Angel," is "worthy of any Spanish poet of the Golden Age."

The poetic work of Pesado includes all types, and in almost all he is uniformly excellent. In the quiet, genuine tenderness of his *Amorous Rhymes*—"The First Impression of Love," "My Beloved at Early Morning Mass," and "The Valley of My Childhood"—he shows the inspiration of Petrarch and Herrera. Though he is more personal, less inspired, and more monotonous in his moral poetry than in his other verse, the perfection with which he writes blank verse is admirable in "The Man" and "The Sepulcher." His descriptive poems are noticeably superior to his moral ones; in addition to originality and perfection of form, they contain a picturesque and delightful Mexican atmosphere. In these, the poet paints "scenes of country and village in Mexico": a village pageant and feast; a bullfight; a cockfight; a market; a serenade; acrobatics and fireworks; "sights and scenes from Orizaba and Córdoba": the peaks of Acultzingo, the fountain of Ojozarco, nomadic flocks, mountains, a storm at night, the summit of Orizaba.

He introduced indigenous elements into Mexican poetry with his collection entitled *The Aztecs*; these are "translations or glosses," according to the poet, of old Indian songs, among which are several attributed to Netzahualcóyotl. In reality, Pesado did not know the indigenous languages, and these are original poems, probably the most beautiful ones that he wrote. The lovely romance *The Princess of Culhuacán* is an example. A pleasing archeological flavor, nevertheless, distinguishes these poems; and, alluding to them, Bishop Montes de Oca has said, "The Mexican bard deserves credit for having studied the history and character of the Aztecs, for having pierced their very souls and thus made them sing in Spanish with the same harmony, sweetness, rhythm, and half-savage fire that they would have used in their native tongue."

In his religious poetry, the muse of Pesado attained high and majestic flights. As has been said, he was essentially a Christian poet. "To conceive beauty, goodness, and true love without religion," he wrote, "is to create lifeless bodies, or cadavers without souls. The moral world would be an arid desert if the divine breath did not vivify it continually." His poem *Jerusalem* and his *Praises to the Most Holy Virgin* are his best in this field.

Pesado was not a stranger to epic poetry, though in this genre he left only two incomplete poems: *Moses* and *Revelation*. In brief, a large part of his work is composed of translations, imitations, and paraphrases. He may be considered, according to Menéndez y Pelayo, as one of the poets who spent most of his time imitating and translating. Following Horace and Virgil, Garcilaso and Andrés Chénier, his poetry abounds in imitations and reminiscences of classical poets— "an instance of the transfusion of ancient poetry into the veins of the new." His direct translations from other languages into the Castilian, also, are numerous and varied. His versions of Theocritus and Sinesius are weak because they are not direct translations; weak, also, is his translation of Manzoni's famous ode "The Fifth of May," because the original is untranslatable; and a little unfortunate are his versions of Lamartine's work. On the other hand, his rendering of Horace is considered excellent, and his versions of some cantos of Tasso's *Jerusalem Delivered* are without equal in the Spanish language. And, lastly, his translations of the Psalms and The Song of Songs, though not direct because he did not know Hebrew, are considered the most finished work that came from his pen; the latter— Menéndez y Pelayo thinks—is an able fusion of the manner of Friar Luis de León with that of the Italian translators of the same poem.

The poetry of Pesado was first published in 1839; a second edition followed in 1849; the third and only complete edition was printed in 1886.

Carpio

The second of the classicists, Don Manuel Carpio, shares with Pesado the credit for sustaining and revitalizing classical poetry in Mexico.

Carpio was born in the town of Cosamaloapan, in the old province of Veracruz, on March 1, 1791. While still young, he was taken by his family to Puebla, where his father died and his family lost their wealth. In the Conciliar Seminary of that city, he studied Latin, philosophy, and theology; and in the library to which he had access through one of his teachers, he buried himself, even in his adolescence, in the reading of Greek and Roman classics and books on religion and ancient history, laying thus the foundation for his literary education. Though he was deeply religious by nature, he did not follow an ecclesiastical career, but chose medicine, which he studied at the University of Mexico, completing his work in 1832. He practiced his profession with nobility, kindness, and enthusiasm all of his life. In his youth he translated the *Aphorisms* and *Prognostics* of Hippocrates; and later he worked for the advancement of medical science as teacher, writer, and active member of learned societies. His habits of study, gentleness, and austere rectitude tended to separate him from politics in the turbulent period during which he lived; he hardly intervened in politics although he was a member of the Legislature of Veracruz and later a representative in the Federal Congress. In his modest home in Mexico City, devoted to his profession and to the cultivation of science and literature, respected and beloved by all, he lived a tranquil life until his death on February 11, 1860. His funeral occasioned sincere public mourning, revealing the love and popularity with which he had been surrounded.

Though Carpio was of an undeniable poetic temperament, the Muses knocked at his door rather late: he was over forty years of age when his first poems were given recognition. Having been collected by Pesado, they were published in 1849.

Carpio—though less perfect in versification and inferior in inspiration to Pesado—had classical taste and a predominantly religious inspiration. "The Bible," Couto has observed, "was for him an everyday book." He knew Greece and Rome through their poets, and the panorama of history held a singular attraction for him. The appeal of the Orient was still greater. From afar and without having known the East, he was enveloped in its mysterious light. Steeped in the love of the Holy Books, the poet constantly turned his eyes toward remote civilizations: Nineveh, Babylon, Syria, Egypt. This explains the epic character of the poems inspired by those sources and the pomp and extravagance of color and light which distinguish them. His style is clear and limpid, although at times weak and prosaic; his versification is easy and varied; and his lavish descriptive powers are remarkable.

Don José Mariá Roa Bárcena has expressed the following opinion of the poet-physician:

Clarity is one of the good qualities of Carpio; but, since defects often result from the excessive use or abuse of good qualities, his great desire to be clear often caused him to be prosaic. Such are his faults: the monotonous manipulation of phrases and turns of speech; the careful search for difficult and rare rhymes and sound effects; excessive details in descriptions; prolixity in his strophes; lack of unity and coherence, a fault that often makes his lines seem admirable as isolated passages but not necessary parts of a beautiful and perfect whole. In the face of these criticisms there should be remembered, in defense of the writer, his tendency toward Greek simplicity; the enviable merit of an individual style which is stamped unequivocably on all of his productions; the facility and good taste with which the scholar reveals his treasure of knowledge; and, finally, his aspiration to achieve the artistic, an aspiration which is not satisfied with the perfection and the effect of the whole, but desires perfection in each detail.

Though Carpio was a classicist, he paid unconscious tribute to romanticism. The romantic sensibility, with characteristic exaltation and vehemence in its tenacious melancholia, appears signally in his ode "The Turk," in which a lover, beside the Bosporus, with turban awry, laments the absence of his loved one.

The majority of Carpio's poems are of religious and historical character. Following these in number are the purely descriptive poems such as *Mexico* and *El Popocatépetl*. He wrote only a few moral poems and even fewer erotic ones. Outstanding among his poems of biblical inspiration are *Belshazzar's Feast* and *The Witch of Endor,* which abound in epic features and Oriental color. Among those of religious inspiration should be mentioned *The Annunciation* and *The Virgin at the Foot of the Cross.* The most pleasing of his historical poems is *Napoleon in the Red Sea.*

Arango y Escandón

Don Alejandro Arango y Escandón, the third of this group, was a poet of the same literary affiliations as Pesado and, like him, a great man of letters.

Born in Puebla on July 10, 1821, of a wealthy family, Arango went to Spain in 1831 and studied the humanities at Madrid. On his return to Mexico in 1836, he studied canon and civil law in the Conciliar Seminary and was graduated as a lawyer in 1844. He held, from that time on, various public positions of importance; he was also head of the Department of Humanities at the university and was prominently active in the conservative party. He was secretary of the Assembly of Notables which created the Empire, and later a member of Maximilian's Council of State. After Maximilian's downfall and after a short exile in Europe, Arango y Escandón, in whom friends and enemies recognized sincere firmness of convictions and great rectitude and probity, returned to Mexico and isolated himself from public affairs, devoting his time to the administration of his estate and to letters. He was director of the Mexican Academy when he died in Mexico City on February 28, 1883.

Possessing genuine culture and refined taste, Arango was essentially a classicist. He was greatly influenced by the Roman poets and the Italo-Spanish poets of the sixteenth century. At sixteen years of age, he knew by memory all of the poetic works of Friar Luis de León, Garcilaso, and Argensola. Friar Luis was his chief model; and from him Arango took not only style and poetic diction but exalted religious sentiment, noble moderation and serenity, and restrained elegance.

Arango strove for perfection; he worked tirelessly on the form of his verse, and in this surpassed his contemporaries. Menéndez y Pelayo considers Arango's two odes "The Immaculate Conception of Our Lady" and "Invocation to Divine Goodness" as "perfect models of noble symmetry, smooth expression, and refined taste"; and the same could be said of his excellent sonnet "Divine Mercy," a favorite with anthologists. This striving toward perfection and the poet's predominantly artistic nature make his work, if not extensive, excellent in quality. All of it is included in two books: the *Poems*, a single small volume, which includes his original productions—odes, erotic poetry, and sonnets of political satire—together with his excellent translations of Luigi Carrer's Italian legends entitled "The Horse of Extremadura" and "Vengeance"; and the *Historical Essay on Friar Luis de León*, first published in the review called *The Cross* in 1855-56, and issued as a book in 1866, which is considered the best work in Spanish on Friar Luis de León. Arango also translated Corneille's *The Cid* and Alfieri's *The Conspiracy of the Pazzi*, but only fragments of these versions are known today.

Ramírez

The fourth member of this group, Don Ignacio Ramírez, commonly known by the pseudonym of "The Necromancer," occupies a unique place in the nexus of politics and letters during this period. He was in poetry an outright classicist, but in politics a firm and implacable destroyer of tradition.

In Ramírez' life are to be found the spirit and turmoil of the War of Reform. Born in the village of San Miguel el Grande, Guanajuato, on June 23, 1818, he began his literary studies in Querétaro, and in 1835 he continued them in the School of San Gregorio of Mexico City, where he was an outstanding student and was awarded the law degree. Always a student, he startled the members of the Academy of Letrán by defending the following thesis: "There is no God; natural beings sustain themselves." Such was his first act of rebellion. He continued to destroy, beginning at the altars. He opposed religion, Spanish tradition, and political and social organizations. At popular assemblies and in the press, he enunciated, in 1846, the ideas that were to form the program of the War of Reform. He was dry, sardonic, destructive, implacable. He had, furthermore, as dreaded weapons, an adamantine will, indisputable talent, encyclopedic knowledge. The first journal that he edited—*Don Simplicio (Mr. Simpleton)*—caused his imprisonment. In the midst of political upheaval, he applied his admirable talents to administration and to teaching: in the Literary Institute of Toluca, he taught law and literature and was the instructor of Altamirano. His learned lectures were heard with enthusiasm and profit in Puebla and in Mexico City. He worked for the governments of several states. He knew well the prisons of Santa Anna. He sat in the Constituent Assembly. He joined Juárez and Ocampo in fighting Comonfort. He contributed, in the storm of the Revolution, to the enrichment of the galleries of the San Carlos Academy. As a minister of justice he was known for his upright character. He suffered imprisonment, persecution, and exile; he experienced the bitterness of proximity to the gallows and the vicissitudes of a wandering life during the tumultuous period which lasted from the Three Years' War, the Intervention and the Empire, until the re-establishment of the Republic; his travels through the country were marked by the appearance of flaming, polemical articles and indignant verse in the columns of the provincial press which still escaped censorship: true dispersion of a literary work which can never be reconstructed! Shortly before the fall of Maximilian, Ramírez was imprisoned in the dungeons of San Juan de Ulúa; as he was being taken to Yucatán, he engaged in debate even while he was suffering from yellow fever. On the re-establishment of the Republic, he became an irreproachable judge on the Supreme Court; he was prominent—he was always accepted as an authority—in scientific and literary centers; yet he suffered persecution under the presidency of Lerdo de Tejada. When Porfirio Díaz triumphed, Ramírez became again, for a short time, minister of justice; still later, he returned to his seat on the Supreme Court for a third time and held it until the day of his death, which occurred in Mexico City on June 15, 1879.

The poetic work of "The Necromancer" is not extensive; it comprises not more than fifty poems. He was a profound humanist, and his refined taste made him a classicist whose style was limpid, polished, and somewhat cold. Occasionally, his poems have a philosophical tone. But at times he becomes excited over politics, and then flashes of hatred and irony appear in his work. Still more often—especially during his later years!—he sings of woman and love. A senile passion —his passion for Rosario, the same Rosario who was the muse of Flores and Acuña—illuminated or, rather, darkened the last years of his life. In a famous sonnet, "To Love," his defenseless old age uttered a pitiful cry. This and other sonnets—"To the Sun," "To My Muse" —his short poem "To Josephine Pérez," a fragment of which, in the opinion of Menéndez y Pelayo, seems to be a translation of one of the most beautiful epigrams of the *Greek Anthology;* and his magnificent tercets "For the Sake of the Dead" and "In Behalf of the Unfortunate Ones," would be sufficient in themselves to give him a prominent place on the Mexican Parnassus.

The works of Ramírez were published in two volumes in 1889. In addition to his poetry, these volumes contain all of his prose that has appeared in collected form: speeches, historical and literary articles, polemical dialogues, and essays on economic, political, and social questions. In prose, as in verse, Ramírez is dry; but at times, instead of being cold, he is sarcastic, fiery, and passionate. His explanations are clear, his reasoning is vigorous, and ideas play an important part in his work. His prose is slow-moving and limited in appeal by its occasional character, for the most part; nevertheless, there are some excellent passages in it.

Roa Bárcena

Although he came to maturity with the poets who sustained the classical tradition against nascent romanticism, Don José María Roa Bárcena—the last of this group—outlived his contemporaries and continued to write until the dawn of the twentieth century.

A native of Jalapa, where he was born on September 3, 1827, he chose a type of work hardly conducive to the cultivation of the Muses: commerce. His artistic inclination, however, lured him along another road; and thus, from his youth, he devoted himself to literary studies and tasks, publishing some of his lyrical and fictional exercises in the local press. In 1853 he went to Mexico City. The struggle between the liberals and conservatives dominated everything at that time. Roa Bárcena allied himself with the conservatives. He was a man of strong religious and political convictions, which he never concealed. With ardor, he took up the battle in the conservative press. He supported Intervention and the Empire; he was a member of the Congress of Notables; but, being more conservative than Maximilian, who in reality was not conservative, he turned against the Empire when he realized that Maximilian did not share the views of the group which had put him in power. He criticized the acts of the government, predicted its downfall, refused to participate in its administration, and set himself against the French regime and the cabinet. And—when the imperial venture ended tragically—after an imprisonment of several months, notwithstanding the fact that the liberal press interceded in his favor by recalling the honesty and firmness of his political convictions, he permanently returned to private life. Dedicating himself to business and letters, he lived to extreme old age, dying in Mexico City on September 21, 1908.

Roa Bárcena's poetic work was extensive and sustained in quality. It is composed of the following: *Diana*, a poem (1857); *Lyric Poems* (1859); *Mexican Legends, Stories and Ballads of Northern Europe, and Other Poetic Attempts* (1862); *Last Poems* (1888-1895); and *A Collection of Castilian Sonnets* (1887), a beautiful anthology, which he published with interesting notes.

Distinguished as he was, Roa Bárcena is not considered a great poet. Others sang with vigor; he was inclined to sing quietly with discretion and grace. Nevertheless, his gifts are worthy of esteem. His complete command of language made his work clear and pure; he wrote verse with correctness; he expressed his thoughts with decorum. In the *Legends*, he used American local color, following and often even surpassing Pesado. The *Xóchitl* and *Princess Papantzin* are among the most finished poems on indigenous subjects in Mexican literature. As a translator, Roa Bárcena was excellent. He made Spanish translations of Horace, Virgil, Schiller, Byron, and Tennyson. Referring to his version of *Mazeppa*, Menéndez y Pelayo says, "Seldom has Byron been so well interpreted in Spanish, and perhaps never better."

The prose of Roa Bárcena is no less abundant than his verse. His prose fiction was published in 1870 under the title *Novels*. This volume contains "Night in the Open," "A Flower in Its Tomb," "Aminta Rovero," "Buondelmonti," and "The Model Villa." Among his later works of fiction are "The Small Launches," "The King and the Clown," and "Battles in the Air." These original stories, together with translations of Hoffmann and Dickens, comprise Roa Bárcena's fictional work, which was published in two volumes of the Agüeros Collection. In this story teller, as Don Juan Valera has said, "the skill, talent, and ability to narrate are heightened by naturalness of style, grace, and beauty of language, which is pure and without the slightest tinge of the archaic." Considering the local color in Roa Bárcena's short stories, Don Manuel G. Revilla is justified in saying that they are "a series of animated pictures, familiar scenes, interiors, views, and landscapes in which throbs a sincere and noble realism"; and, further, that the characters belong among those "who have come within the scope of our own observation" and who seem to be "moving in our own atmosphere and reflecting the traditional customs—which have not yet entirely disappeared—of the Mexico of other days."

As a critic, Roa Bárcena is accredited with excellent biographies of Gorostiza and Pesado, contributions of great value to Mexican literary history. And, to conclude, as a historian he is represented by the following: *Catechism of Mexican History* (1863); *Attempt at a History of Mexico in Anecdotal Form*; and *Memoirs of the North-American Invasion* (1883), an admirable chronicle of that unhappy event. This last work, written in concise prose, unites profound earnestness and straight thinking with austere patriotism. It was reprinted in the *Collection of Mexican Authors*, Porrúa, in 1947.

MINOR CLASSICAL POETS

Among the minor classical poets distinguished not only by their literary training but by their religious inspiration should be included the following:

José Sebastián Segura (1822-1889), brother-in-law and disciple of Pesado, was mediocre and prosaic in his original works, but excellent as a translator. He translated some of the Psalms, some of the works of Horace and Virgil, the first three cantos of *The Divine Comedy*, and a number of poems by French, Italian, and German poets, among them being the "Song of the Bell" by Schiller.

Miguel Jerónimo Martínez (1817-1870), prebendary of the cathedral at Puebla, was a facile poet of mystic inspiration. He destroyed many of his poems; those remaining were published in 1877.

Ramón Isaac Alcaraz (1823-1886) was a poet of refined classical taste whose infrequent lyric flights resulted in beautiful and polished

lines. His poetry was published in two volumes in Mexico City in
1860. *The Seasons* is considered his most characteristic work.

Francisco de Paula Guzmán (1807-1884), an accomplished humanist and translator of Virgil and Tiro, was, in the last years of his
life, a poet of ardent mystical expression.

Don Wenceslao Alpuche (1804-1841), was a poet of Yucatán
whose popularity and influence were purely regional. He cannot be
definitely classified as either classicist or romanticist. Though a friend
of Pesado and Carpio, he differed fundamentally from them and can
be considered a straggler from the previous literary generation. He
followed Quintana as a model; he was a robust and spirited poet. His
patriotic odes and his poem *Hidalgo* are his best works. The poetry
of Alpuche was published in Mérida in 1842.

Not as an original poet but as a worthy humanist, Don Francisco
Gómez del Palacio (1824-1886) of Durango should be included in
this list. He made the best Spanish translation of Tasso's *Jerusalem
Delivered*; this was published in Mexico City the year of the translator's death.

THE FIRST ROMANTICISTS

Calderón

Romanticism appeared in Mexican letters with Don Fernando
Calderón. He was born of Zacatecan parents in Guadalajara on July
20, 1809. His infancy and early youth were spent in his native city,
where he was educated and where he received the degree of licentiate
in law about 1829. Though of noble ancestry (he inherited the title
of Count of Santa Rosa, but never used it), Calderón professed advanced political ideas at an early age. He embraced liberalism permanently, participated in actual fighting in one of the innumerable
revolutions which were then devastating the country, and was seriously wounded in the battle of Guadalupe, waged and won by Santa
Anna near Zacatecas in 1835. For his political opinions he was later
exiled from Zacatecas, where he was living, and fled to Mexico City.

At that time he was already enjoying a growing literary prestige;
his first poems had been written when he was fifteen years old, and
he staged his first play when he was eighteen. His residence in the
capital made it possible for him to deepen and broaden his knowledge

of literature. His pleasing personality won friends in the highest intellectual circles of that era. He cultivated friendly relations with, and received advice and instruction from the celebrated Don José María de Heredia; he plunged assiduously into the activities of the Academy of Letrán and devoted himself completely to literature, writing his lyrical poems in that fecund period of his life and also composing and staging the works which gave him a deserved reputation as a dramatic poet.

Then, with his fortune diminished, he returned to Zacatecas, where he served in various public positions. And in the fulness of manhood, when even greater works could have been expected from his fertile genius, he died in the town of Ojocaliente on January 18, 1845.

Though he was a born poet and showed definite talent at fifteen years of age, his lyrical work is far from being abundant; there are hardly two dozen of his poems. Among these are: "To a Faded Rose," "Recollections," "The Return of the Exile," "Soldier of Liberty," and "The Tyrant's Dream"; the first three are of amorous or elegiac inspiration, whereas the remaining two express patriotic ardor.

Fernando Calderón shares with Rodríguez Galván the honor of being the first Mexican romanticist. He was greatly influenced by the Spanish romanticists Cienfuegos and Espronceda, but he was influenced no less—and that directly—by French romanticism represented by Lamartine. He studied Lamartine, translated two of his *Méditations,* and probably drew from Lamartine the plaintive harmony of some of his own verse. Calderón wrote with ease and beauty, though occasionally his lines are faulty or prosaic. His impetuous spirit—the bewitching quality of his poetry, which was particularly felt in his dramatic work—charmed his contemporaries. He was a representative of the sensibility of his epoch.

Calderón's poetry and dramas were published for the first time in 1844, in Mexico; and this edition was followed by one in 1849, with a preface by Pesado. In 1959 Editorial Porrúa published Calderon's *Plays and Poetry* as a volume in their *Collection of Mexican Authors,* with Francisco Monterde as editor.

Rodríguez Galván

Don Ignacio Rodríguez Galván, the second of this group, was

even more genuinely romantic than Calderón. Galván was born in the village of Tizayuca, in the present state of Mexico, on March 12, 1816. A worthy example of self-education, he gained all of his literary knowledge through his own efforts. He was the son of a farmer in moderate circumstances; and, after his father lost his property during the War of Independence, Galván, barely eleven years old, went to Mexico City to earn his living as a clerk in his uncle's bookstore. Between the reading and the selling of books, his calling was determined. Since he had had no previous intellectual preparation, it is presumed that his training was insufficient and unsystematic. Nevertheless, his ability was such that without the aid of a teacher he learned Latin, French, and Italian; in his leisure time he devoted himself to the cultivation of literature; and in 1840, wishing to live for and by letters, he gave up his employment at the bookstore.

This act did not improve his circumstances. Misery and unhappiness were his lot. To judge by his poems, poverty, sorrow, and desperation were his constant companions. He seemed, also, to possess a mysterious passion which tended to darken his existence. And playing no small part in his life, harrowing his feelings and adding to his own wretchedness, were the misfortunes of his country, which was torn by factions in that tormented epoch during which he lived. Referring to Galván, Zorrilla, the Spanish poet, speaks of "the desperation of the genius who, possessing wings for flight, is lashed to the reef of an evil fortune in an epoch which will never understand him or do him justice until after his death. Belonging to a society without atmosphere for his soul, he can not make the flight he feels capable of." Short was the flight, indeed. In the dawn of his literary renown and with misery and hardships averted, thanks to a modest diplomatic post granted by the government, the poet embarked at Veracruz for South America; on passing through Havana, he contracted yellow fever and death soon claimed his life, young and incomplete, on July 25, 1842.

Such a man was by nature fitted to be the first Mexican romanticist. The leaven of the new literary school fermented spontaneously in that lacerated spirit. In his poetry the chords of the mythological lyre, which had been touched lightly by classicists and neo-classicists, were exchanged for the strings of his own heart. Although he was acquainted with romanticism through his reading—he translated Delavigne, Lamartine, Manzoni, and Monti—he did not theorize about romanticism. He was, in his own being, a romanticist; and, when he began to sing, naturally and passionately, the new poetry was incarnate in him.

Galván's sad life is reflected in his poetry, which was published with his plays in 1851. His poems are vehement, desperate; in them, the curse is more common than the complaint; gentle tears are replaced by terrible sobs; and stern and cruel pessimism is dominant over all. His themes are love, glory, country, faith. But his muse of love is a dishevelled fury who turns angrily on inconstancy, treason, and deceit. His love for his native soil, shown in his frequent historical and legendary passages and in the descriptions of Mexican types and landscapes, is whipped into tremendous curses and prophetic warnings of the misfortunes that threaten the country, and bursts forth into sharp cries of homesickness from the ship which, bearing him away from his native shores, is taking him to his death. Finally, religious faith, deeply rooted and sincere, appears in him at times like a brilliant spark in the midst of much blackness and despair, and lifts him to the purest inspiration in such poems as "The Fallen Angel," "Lenten Candles," and "Eve Before the Body of Abel."

Though his poetry is faulty and prosaic at times, Rodríguez Galván is recognized as an outstanding figure in Mexican lyric poetry. His "Prophecy of Guatimoc," the most beautiful of his patriotic songs, is, in the judgment of Menéndez y Pelayo, "the masterpiece of Mexican romanticism," a work which gives a "full-length portrait of the romantic movement at the happiest moment of its inspiration." In addition, the beautiful ballad entitled "Mora" and the legends "The Insurgent in Ulúa" and "Montezuma's Vision" should be mentioned among his best.

Prieto

The life of the next member of this group, Guillermo Prieto, covers a large part of the nineteenth century, and his literary activities embrace two long epochs in Mexican literature.

He was born in Mexico City on February 10, 1818, and he died in Tacubaya on March 2, 1897. During his long life he was active in politics and public administration, literature and teaching. His literary preparation was meager; from early childhood he had to earn his bread by his own labors. Hurled into the revolutionary tornado, he accepted the plan of Ayutla. He was a deputy to the Constituent Congress. He was an upright secretary of the treasury under Juárez in a troubled epoch. He fought courageously in the press and experienced persecution and exile. The triumph of the Republic in 1867 found him strong and robust, ready to lavish—for many long years— his characteristic energies in parliamentary debates, in the multiple labors of the public press, and in the duties of his position as professor of political economy and Mexican history. In his last days, old and in failing health, with chronic complaints and obscure ailments— some of them real, others imagined—half blind and using as a guide the first person he encountered (he always spoke familiarly to everyone), Guillermo Prieto, carelessly dressed and wearing his wide-brimmed slouch hat, was saluted on the streets of Mexico City as a phantom from a faraway past by the younger literary generation that had developed during the last years of the century.

Prieto was the popular poet par excellence, and, in this respect, he was the successor of a writer whom he resembled singularly, Fernández de Lizardi. Like the latter—or even to a greater extent— Prieto was lacking in literary training, good taste, and artistic sensibility; he also resembled Lizardi in his popular type of humor. It would be difficult to find a more slovenly and plebian poet. "I left school," he wrote in the *Memories of My Times,* "without knowing anything correctly; my parents wanted to dedicate me to books, but first it was necessary to eat. . . ." Sánchez de Tagle and Carpio were his favorite writers, and perhaps the ones who awakened in him the desire to be a poet. His first reading matter was poorly chosen and too difficult for him; he did not know foreign languages and literatures; and in the cultivation of his own, he merely skimmed the surface.

With Lacunza he founded the Academy of Letrán, and from that time his literary sympathies inclined him toward romanticism, although as a romanticist he possessed only the theatrical and external elements and was far from being romantic in sentiment. The earliest of his poems that he mentions—it is now lost—was a religious poem entitled "To Christ Crucified" (1833). This type of subject matter was unusual for him, since he cultivated the sentimental, the amorous, and the heroic by preference. He was, in his first period, grandiloquent and sonorous, with no little artificiality and rhetoric, but he was in tune with the stormy and eminently dramatic historical period with which his youth and maturity coincided. During the difficult years of the War of Reform, later during the stubborn defense of his country against the French invasion, and during the Empire, Prieto was essentially the national poet. The passionate struggle gave flaming words to his muse; his cutting satire lashed the enemy; he spoke to the people in their own language; and his famous couplets—like "The Crabs"—were changed into veritable war songs in the crash of battles.

Guillermo Prieto was certainly "the national poet" because he was of his time and for his time. His supreme originality lies not in the emotion or sentiment of his work—much less in its form—but rather in the picturesque and folklore qualities of his poetry; his position in lyric poetry is the same as that of "The Thinker" in the novel—that is, he is the most national of Mexican poets. His generous Mexican coloring is to be found in that part of his work in which he labored to evoke the great deeds of the heroes of Independence and of the Reform movement and to depict types, customs, and landscapes of his native country: both are illustrated in *El Romancero Nacional (The National Book of Ballads)* and the *Musa Callejera (The Street Muse)*.

Suggesting the anonymous poets of ancient Spanish ballads, Guillermo Prieto's *Romancero* (1885) covers the cycle of Independence from the initial movement of 1808—described in "The Ballad of Iturrigaray"—until the entrance of the Army of the Three Guarantees in 1821, with its procession of *caudillos,* captains, and guerrillas, detailing their fortunes in conspiracies and battles. The collection is broad in scope, spirited, stirring. Altamirano has asserted—doubtless with exaggeration—that this book "is the national epic—in all its features, with its dramatic quality, its picturesque personalities, and with historic truth that does not require the brilliant trappings of the legend in order to be admirable."

When all of his writings are considered, the best and most characteristic work of Prieto is *The Street Muse,* a collection of poems that covers a considerable period of his literary activity. Its publication in Mexico in 1883 made famous his pseudonym "Fidel." In this work, as Urbina has said, the satirist disappears, leaving the dreamer and from time to time the humorist. The poet becomes a genre painter. His palette contains many colors, and he paints—in the open air—real landscapes, night festivals in the city, popular types and customs: the *china poblana* dressed in spangled baize, the *charro* wearing a sombrero adorned with silver, the voluptuous servant girl, the cunning Indian, and the bold guerrilla. Each, using his own jargon, talks in character and moves in his own sphere—the narrow and dirty street, the fruit stand, the barber shop with guitar and gamecock, the house of the neighborhood trouble-maker. Everything is typical and regional, richly vivid and multicolored, with daubs and splotches of unmistakable effect. It is the expression, the manifestation, of a people idealized by the tenderness and imagination of a great poet.

Besides the collections already indicated, the poetic work of Prieto is contained in the volumes entitled *Selected Verse* (1877) and *Unedited Poems* (1879).

As a writer of prose, Prieto is no less prolific and reveals the same qualities and defects that are found in his poetry. His *Memories of My Times*, which deals with the period between 1828 and 1853 and was published in two volumes in 1906, contains the most delightful and picturesque chronicles in existence of the social, political, and literary life of Mexico in that era. A traveler, sometimes for pleasure and sometimes because of necessity, he described his impressions of a wandering life, often with insuperable grace, in *Viajes de Orden Suprema (High-Class Travels)*, 1857, an incomplete work, and *Voyage to the United States* (3 volumes, 1877-1878). His journalistic work is as labored as it is awkward, revealing prodigal humor and undeniable ability in depicting customs; but, with the exception of *The Holy Mondays of Fidel* (1923), his periodical work has not been published in book form. To complete this account, his works of a very different character, which give evidence of his wide activity as a writer, should be mentioned: his *Lessons of Mexican History* and a treatise on political economy.

Valle

Juan Valle, the fourth of this group, was the patriotic poet of the War of Reform. Born in the city of Guanajuato on July 4, 1838, he lost his sight when he was either four or five years of age. A mysterious sensitiveness of spirit guided him in his blindness. From the lips of his brother, the blind child learned the books that molded his character: the Bible, the ancient classics, the Spanish poets of the sixteenth century, and contemporary Mexican writers. At fourteen years of age he became an orphan, and in his grief turned to song. "His blindness made him a poet," comments Zarco.

Juan Valle's first poems appeared in the newspapers of Mexico City in 1854 and attracted wide attention. "Through an extraordinary phenomenon, through a truly prodigious intuition," says Don José María Vigil, "there existed in the blind poet the feeling of plastic beauty, expressed with such vividness and originality, that images stood out naturally and simply against the shadowy background of an incurable melancholy." When he was not quite sixteen, Juan Valle dedicated himself to the literary life. Incapable of directing his pen, he composed mentally with seeming tirelessness; and when his poems were finished and polished, he dictated them. In 1855 he staged in his native city a drama which reveals some of the facts about his life. This play, *Social Mysteries*, was published in a volume with his poems in 1862. Civil war was raging in the country at that time, and if the blind poet was unable to see its bright splendor, he was able to feel its heat. He espoused the democratic cause and served it, if not with the sword, with the lyre. He became "the Tyrtaeus of liberty."

The despicable fury of partisans respects neither the blind nor the poets. Coming into power at Guanajuato in 1857, the conservative group unloosed inhuman persecution against Juan Valle. He suffered all kinds of abuse: in June, 1859, he was led through the streets between bailiffs who incited the populace to stone him for heresy; he was then imprisoned among hardened criminals; and, finally, he was exiled. His journey across the war-inflamed country was dramatic. He took refuge in Morelia. Later, when the liberal party triumphed, he returned to Guanajuato. Shortly thereafter, the French invasion occurred. He fled to Colima and from there to Guadalajara. No thing and no person could subdue his integrity. Faithful to his party—the one which stood for national defense—he suffered with fortitude and resignation. But his physical strength was declining. With a family—he had married his childhood friend, Doña Josefa Aguiar, and had one daughter by her—and without resources or the possibility of taking up arms for his country, the blind poet hid himself permanently in the shadows in which he had lived. His death in Guadalajara occurred either on December 31, 1864, or in January of 1865.

Because of his delicacy of feeling, Juan Valle belongs to the romanticists, but because of certain influences in his literary education, he belongs also to the classicists. In his early poems, principally those of religious inspiration and those intended to depict scenes and personages of the Bible and of ancient history, the influence of Carpio is undeniable. Also, in the few poems he wrote on Indian themes, he walked in the steps of Pesado. But those that display his full originality—and his finest quality, sincerity—are those poems of subjective or autobiographical character in which the poet exalts his tender idealism and paints the state of his soul or the events of his singular life—"My Story," "Your Absence," "Misfortune," and "My Mother's Death." Above all, his individual qualities are evident in his patriotic odes, a genre in which he occupies first place among the poets of his age. His vigorous tercets on "The Civil War" are the best example of this type. Juan Valle wrote poetry with ease; in his work, however, are defects of form, prosaic expressions, and a certain declamatory quality. Who will not admit, nevertheless, that—considering the epoch and existing conditions—the work of the blind poet is almost miraculous?

Isabel Prieto

The cycle of romanticism is closed by Doña Isabel Prieto de Landázuri, the gentle poet whom her contemporaries praised by calling her the twin sister of Sor Juana Inés.

Though Doña Isabel was born in Spain—in Alcázar de San Juan, in the province of Ciudad Real, on March 1, 1833—she was brought to Mexico when she was very young—about five years of age; and it can be said, as Don José María Vigil has stated, "that she belongs to us completely since the influences which molded her temperament and intelligence were Mexican." She spent her childhood and early young womanhood in Guadalajara; there, in the city of Tapatíos,[1] which she loved deeply, she established her home and wrote her first songs; and she left there only when her husband had been appointed Mexican consul at Hamburg and it was necessary for her to accompany him to Germany, where she died September 28, 1876.

Isabel Prieto had an excellent literary education. Though her taste

---

[1] A familiar name applied to the natives of Guadalajara—also to a Mexican dance.—Translators' note.

was formed by the Spanish classics of the Golden Age, the influence, perhaps, of modern foreign literatures that she cultivated and the inspiration born of the heat of the new literary school which was erupting in the Mexican atmosphere made her the first Mexican romantic poetess. She cultivated the lyric and—as we shall see later —the drama. It is useless, surely, to look in her works for the impulses of hate and despair from real or imagined disillusionment exaggerated by a diseased sensitiveness. She depicts the aches of sorrow, the torment of unfortunate love, the struggles between violent passion and inescapable duty; but all this, observes Vigil, is sweetened and made poetic in passing through the filter of a soul "which has its vision fixed on those regions of inextinguishable light where no one is allowed to enter who circumscribes all his aspirations and hopes within the petty circle of our earthly life."

Her muse was heard for the first time in 1851, and she continued to sing her clear and feminine song in the midst of the revolutionary tempest. Now she was mournful, now amusing, and sometimes both melancholy and witty. Though her lyrics were multiform and most varied, Doña Isabel distinguished herself and occupies an indisputable place on the Mexican Parnassus because she expressed maternal love in unmistakable accents. She knew, as Vigil has said,

how to paint, with the hand of a master, those charming pictures of intimate life which recreate the warmth of the domestic hearth, the tranquil family scenes, multiple and varied episodes that are unfolded against a pleasing background and in which stand out the tender and delicate figures of mother and son.

Her characteristic poems of this type are "The Prayer," "Mother and Child," and "To My Son Who Is Giving Alms."

The romantic fervor nascent in Isabel Prieto surged up when she visited the land of Wieland and Heine; and her last poem, the legend of "Bertha of Sonnenberg," is one of the most beautiful of the Mexican romantic poems.

In 1883, Don José María Vigil collected and published in Mexico City Doña Isabel Prieto de Landázuri's original poems, together with her lyric translations of Hugo, Lamartine, and Chénier.

MINOR ROMANTICISTS

The romantic school in this early period included several minor poets, as well as renowned ones, among its enthusiastic supporters. A brief discussion of four of these follows.

Marcos Arróniz (a native of Orizaba who died about 1858) is considered by Pimentel "as a representative of ultraromanticism: a poet of doubt, delirium, and desperation." His poems, which were never collected, appeared in literary publications of that epoch.

Juan Díaz Covarrubias, whose work as a novelist will be discussed in Chapter XIV, wrote imperfect lyric poems, which were printed in 1859 under the title *Pages from the Heart*. He was a poet "of exaggeration and delirium," according to his own statement in his dedication to Zorrilla (though the story of his life, to be told later, gives a different picture of his character). As a poet he was limited "to bemoaning his real and imagined sorrows," hurling cries of mournful, grievous desperation, blaspheming society, and even cursing nature "in that period of youth in which opposing sentiments struggle in the heart without guidance from good sense and prudence."

Pantaleón Tovar (1828-1876), a soldier of his country during the North-American and French invasions, an ardent liberal who was persecuted and banished during the War of Reform, wrote both drama and poetry. Don Justo Sierra sees in his work the influences of the French romantic and socialist school. His verse has not been published in collected form. Luis G. Urbina has selected one of Tovar's sonnets, "To a Child Who is Weeping for Some Flowers," as a typical example of Mexican romanticism.

José María Esteva (1818-1904) was a native of Veracruz whose greatest originality lay in his cultivation of regional poetry depicting the customs of his country (one of his typical poems is entitled "The Rough Countryman"). He wrote three volumes of verse: *Poetry* (Veracruz, 1850); *The White Woman,* a Mexican legend (Havana, 1868); and *Types from Veracruz and Various Compositions* (Xalapa, 1894).

XIV

The Drama and the Novel

CLASSICAL COMEDY

Gorostiza

ALTHOUGH Don Manuel Eduardo de Gorostiza undoubtedly belongs to us by virtue of the fact that he was born in Mexico and lived here after 1824, Menéndez y Pelayo is right in saying that his literary work hardly belongs to Mexico "since, with only one exception, all of his original plays were staged first in Madrid and were written for a Spanish audience, without reflecting in any way the American origin of the poet." Nevertheless, inasmuch as his claims are somewhat similar to those of Ruiz de Alarcón and Balbuena, he should be included in our literary gallery.

Gorostiza was born in Veracruz October 13, 1789. His progenitors were Spaniards of recognized families. His father, Field Marshal Don Pedro Fernández de Gorostiza, had charge of the fortifications of the port. His mother, Doña María del Rosario Cepeda, a lady of rare intelligence, included in her family tree no less a person than Saint Teresa de Jesús. On her husband's death in 1794, Doña María took her children to Spain. In Madrid Don Manuel Eduardo began an ecclesiastical career; but, as he was inclined toward military affairs, he seized the opportunity of becoming a cadet. He was captain of the Grenadiers by 1808; and during the Napoleonic invasion, he fought fiercely and was wounded several times, once by a bayonet thrust in the chest, which left him somewhat deformed in figure. Having attained the rank of colonel, he retired from the army in 1814 and devoted himself to politics and literature. Affiliated with the liberal party, he was one of the most radical orators of the "Fountain of Gold," a patriotic society. He frequented clubs and public meetings; and to his revolutionary prestige was added literary prominence when he presented his first plays, which were acclaimed in the theaters of Madrid.

Ferdinand VII, on regaining absolute power, exiled Gorostiza and confiscated his property. Joining a celebrated group of exiles—among whom were the Duke of Rivas, Martínez de la Rosa, Toreno, and Quintana—he left Spain in 1821. With his family he settled in London, where he led a precarious existence, plying his pen to subsist.

In 1824, when the representative of Mexico, Don José Mariano Michelena, reached London, Gorostiza presented himself as "a stray Mexican who wished to return to the fold of his country" and gave him a petition to the supreme executive of Mexico. In it Gorostiza stated that he had "served the cause of European Liberty first as a citizen and then as a writer" and, as a result, found himself in exile; as a Mexican, though "the ties binding him to the birthplace of his fathers" had been broken, he offered his services to the new Republic. "I ask nothing," he concluded; "having been unable up to this time to be of service to my country, I feel that I have no right to ask anything. But if my country thinks that my feeble talents can be of any use, she may dispose of them and my life as she pleases."

Though it seems clear that Gorostiza's nationalistic enthusiasm had not existed before 1824 and it may be presumed that political spite and poverty impelled him to the present step, what at first sight might seem a selfish maneuver to find relief from his distress sprang, it is certain, from a fervent and loyal desire to dedicate himself wholly to his native land—as was demonstrated sufficiently by his later deeds. His services were accepted by the Mexican government, and various diplomatic missions were successively assigned to him in Europe. He discharged these in a manner very efficient, tactful, unselfish, and patriotic. To show the value of his services in this respect, it is sufficient to mention that it was he who negotiated almost all of Mexico's first treaties with foreign powers, and for this reason he is considered one of the founders of Mexican diplomacy.

In 1833, at the very time when the struggle between the conservatives and liberals was most violent and when the liberals were in power, Gorostiza returned to Mexico after having given to the press in London his famous *Political Primer*. His background as well as his personal accomplishments made him acceptable to the regime, and he soon was serving in various posts: as federal librarian, official in the municipal government, member of the Department of Public Instruction. In 1836 he returned to the diplomatic field as envoy extraordinary and minister plenipotentiary to the United States. The brilliant and most honorable manner in which he fulfilled that difficult mission—when the burning question of Texas was being considered—is recorded in the documents which the Mexican government published in 1837 under the title "Controversies between the Specially Appointed Legation of Mexico and the Department of State of the United States," for which Gorostiza wrote the introduction. "Nowhere can a better conception be gained of the ability, culture, courtesy, and energy of Gorostiza," Roa Bárcena has written, "than in those notes which do honor to Mexico and show to history and posterity the reasonableness and honesty of the conquered and the treachery and poorly disguised abuse of power on the part of the conquering nation." Gorostiza defended the rights of Mexico with dignity and courage; but when, in spite of his protests, American forces violated Mexican territory, he asked for his passport.

His activity in public affairs did not decrease in the years following. He served as minister of finance and of foreign relations and as plenipotentiary for the settlement of the questions which provoked the war with France in 1838. His philanthropic sentiments caused him to found, in 1841, with his own funds, a "House of Correction for Delinquent Youths." A few years later, in 1847, during the North American invasion, "the illustrious diplomat who had upheld in Washington the just cause of Mexico, now resolved to fight for it as a soldier, aspiring to seal his words and writings with his own blood," Roa Bárcena says.

He levied and organized a battalion of artisans called "*Bravos*"; and when the rest of the brilliant army, weakened at Padierna, retired in confusion before the bayonets of the conquerors, this old man of about sixty, strong, brave, and determined as in the days of his youth, placed himself at the head of his national guard in the convent of Churubusco and held back the enemy until the last round of ammunition was exhausted. Then, dauntless still, he waited for the enemy with his arms resting on a gun.

This was the last chivalrous and noble act of his public life. To make his life typical—after it had borne such precious fruits—nothing was lacking except that he should suffer poverty, ingratitude, and oblivion in his old age. He died in quiet obscurity in Tacubaya on October 23, 1851.

A study of Gorostiza's literary work shows that he was an excellent dramatic poet (hardly any of his lyric poetry is known) and that the greater part of his work was written in his youth. His dramatic output consists of the following: six original plays, *Pardon for All, Customs of Yesteryear, Tit for Tat, or Men and Women, Little Don Diego, Bread and Onions with You,* and *Don Boniface*; and four adaptations, *The Gambler* (from Regnard), *The Intimate Friend* (from a French *vaudeville*), *You Bring Bad Luck If You Come Alone* (from Calderón)—Gorostiza retitled it *Woman Also Has a Secret*—and Rojas' comedy entitled *What Women Are Made of.* To these should be added an adaptation of Lessing's *Emilia Galotti,* which Gorostiza staged in Mexico City but which remains unpublished, and other recastings and rearrangements which filled his time as impresario and enthusiastic supporter of the theater. Some of these arrangements are: *The Godmother*; *Pauline, or Who Pulls the Wires?*; *The Daughter of the Clown*; *Estela, or Father and Daughter*—besides *A Valuable Predicament* and *A Society Wedding* (this last is a translation from Scribe), which were published under a pseudonym and have been attributed to him. Without distinction, such works are included in the collections entitled *Original Plays* (Paris, 1822), *Selected Plays* (Brussels, 1825), *Supplement to the Selected Plays* (Paris, 1826), *Works of D. Manuel Eduardo de Gorostiza* (Mexico, 1899-1902), each vying with the other in inaccuracies. And even other works, occasional pieces and arrangements not collected, have been mentioned as products of Gorostiza's pen. One volume, entitled *Select Drama* and containing three of his comedies—*Pardon for All, Little Don Diego,* and *Bread and Onions with You*—has been published by Porrúa in the *Collection of Mexican Authors.* Armando de María y Campos wrote the preface and included some biographical and bibliographical notes which contain some new data.

In Spanish drama Gorostiza occupies a place between Moratín and Bretón de los Herreros; he is—in his own way—a follower of the one and a forerunner of the other. Without a doubt, he was the most important figure of the Madrid stage during the short period of his activity.

Gorostiza, an agile versifier for whom technique held no secrets, perfected the Moratinian type of comedy, introducing a variety of metrical combinations. Action is neither abundant nor varied in his dramas, and high moral teachings are lacking. Instead, his plays offer fluent dialogue, clever and varied characters, and accurate descriptions of the customs of the age. *Pardon for All* is considered his best play. Alongside it rank the following: *Customs of Yesteryear,* for originality and good motivation; *Little Don Diego,* for sparkling cleverness; and *The Gambler,* for its study of character. In the judgment of Menéndez y Pelayo, "The principal merit of Gorostiza, which causes his simple comedies—almost childish in structure—to please many readers and also to be pleasing on the stage when they are well produced, lies in the sprightliness and quick movement of the dialogue, the abundance of comic elements, and a continuous innocent, kindly, and infectious gaity that permeates the whole, dispelling irritation and boredom."

Perhaps if the circumstances of his life had been different, Gorostiza would have been an even better playwright. He practically abandoned the theater in 1820. After he had dedicated himself to the service of his country in the field of diplomacy, he wrote only one original drama, *Bread and Onions with You,* which was published in London in 1833. Later, when he was living in Mexico, except for the one-act play already cited, *Don Boniface*—written in prose like the former and also, like it, possessing less literary value than his plays in verse—the poet devoted his dramatic ability, not primarily to renewing his personal triumphs, but to bringing about the stimulation of the Mexican stage through acting as impresario and furnishing his troupes of actors with translations and arrangements of plays by other writers.

ROMANTIC DRAMA

The influence of romanticism in Mexico was felt earlier in the theater—though it faded quickly—than in the field of lyric poetry. Two poets attempted romantic drama in Mexico: the one, drinking from European fountains and taking subjects and inspiration from them; the other, trying—with little success—to popularize the new genre by dramatizing themes of remote colonial history. Both wrote lyric poetry that was discussed in Chapter XIII.

Calderón

The first of these poets, Don Fernando Calderón, is more out-standing as a dramatist than as a lyric poet. In the opinion of Menén-dez y Pelayo, Calderón's plays have "not only beautiful lines, but dramatic interest, good taste, spontaneous passion, noble and gentle-manly feelings, which he himself possessed and easily transferred to his characters."

Calderón was inspired early in his life to write for the theater. His first play, called *Reinaldo and Elvira,* was presented in Guadala-jara in 1827. This was followed by *Zadig; Zeila, or the Indian Slave; Armandina; Politicians of the Day; Ramiro, Count of Lucena; Iphi-genia; Hersila and Virginia,* all of which were produced in the thea-ters of Guadalajara and Zacatecas between 1827 and 1836. None of these, however, is extant; and the only known works, those on which the dramatic reputation of Calderón rests, are the following: two dramas of chivalry, *The Tournament* (1839) and *Herman, or the Return from the Crusade* (1842); one historical drama, *Ann Boleyn* (1842); and one comedy, *None of the Three.* These four plays belong to the period when the poet was living in Mexico City in com-plete and happy political ostracism; they were staged there with great success, were produced throughout the country, and even crossed the frontiers into South America. The titles indicate the nature of these plays. With the exception of *None of the Three,* a delightful com-edy with a Mexican theme and Mexican local color, in the current style of Bretón de los Herreros, all the surviving plays of Fernando Calderón are on foreign subjects.

Today the objection is raised that Calderón did not create a ro-mantic drama with national elements; but probably in his time no one would have thought of such an objection. For the purposes of poetry—influenced by his voracious reading—he turned to castles, minstrels, mail-clad knights, tournaments and jousts, troubadours, and delicate ladies ready to yield to love; and since none of this ex-isted in Mexico, the poet had to resort to transplanting European ro-manticism with all of its medieval pomp. Perhaps he should not be censured for doing so. It cannot be claimed that the great romanti-cists—Schiller, Hugo, Vigny—invariably created a national drama based on national subjects. Furthermore, over and above this consid-eration, there still remains in the Mexican's favor the fact that he did handle his imported themes with refinement and good taste. He was not limited—as Menéndez y Pelayo observes—to an imitation of Spanish romanticism alone or, in particular, of García Gutiérrez. He was also inspired by the French theater. In general, his dramas of chivalry, as well as his historical play—besides being admirably planned and brilliantly executed—reveal his deep study and copious knowledge of the Middle Ages and of English history in the sixteenth century.

The dramatic ability of Fernando Calderón is obvious. *None of the Three* shows the captivating spirit of the comic poet. This is a well-made play, vivacious, witty, abounding in sparkling situations and characters, and full of interesting references to the atmosphere and life of that period. It can be considered as the first and perhaps the only Mexican representative of the Moratinian comedy developed by Gorostiza and Bretón.

But Calderón's abilities ran more to the dramatic than the comic. His dramas of chivalry have quite typical romantic themes. In *The Tournament*, which is set in England in the eleventh century, the Baron of Bohun is about to marry Isabel, daughter of Baron Fitz, even though she is engaged to Albert, an orphan with whom she has been reared. In vain Isabel tries to prevent her marriage to the Baron, and there is the expected clash between the highborn suitor and the obscure youth she loves. But, in due time, a new character comes to light; she is Lady Arabela, a woman dressed entirely in black. She has just escaped from the prison in which the Baron of Bohun had kept her; she accuses the Baron of murdering her husband and son, and of usurping the fortune and titles belonging to them. In order to establish the truth, she demands of Baron Fitz (Isabel's father) that the question be decided by the "judgment of God," that is, by a duel between the defendant and a knight who comes to her defense. This knight is none other than Albert, who proceeds to kill his rival. The final touch is the disclosure, made by a squire, that Lady Arabela's only son, whom the terrible and infamous Bohun had ordered to be killed, is none other than the avenger, Albert himself. The mother and the son then embrace; and it is not difficult to suppose that Isabel will be married forthwith to the one she has loved all her life.

Sensational incidents of the same kind occur in *Herman, or the*

Return from the Crusade, the scene of which is laid in Germany during the twelfth century. Herman goes on a crusade to Palestine with the promise that his betrothed Sophia will await his return. Years pass and her dying father, fearful that the knight has died and that Sophia will be left unprotected, forces her to marry the Duke Othón. Needless to say, Herman returns, and there occur scenes of mutual recrimination; but, notwithstanding her love for Herman, Sophia remains true to her marriage vows and sends him away forever. Such good resolutions do not prevent the Duke Othón—who has surprised the lovers during a rendezvous in the garden—from having them imprisoned and condemned to death. At this moment Ida, the mother of Herman, appears. Learning the fate awaiting her son, she talks with the Duke, reminds him of his love for her in their distant youth, and reproaches him for seducing her and then abandoning her and their son . . . And he understands at once: the aforesaid son is none other than Herman! Thereupon the Duke hastens to take the boy from the gallows and to recognize him as his own. For his part, the youthful knight, after throwing himself at his father's feet, decides to return to the Holy Land in search of an obscure grave in which to sleep.

Regarding *Ann Boleyn*, the poet did no more than reproduce the tragic episode, following history closely in the development of events and characters; he thus gave to Mexican dramaturgy its most finished historical play.

As a romanticist, Calderón searched for unusual themes for his dramas wherever he could find them and especially for legendary and historical materials. These subjects served only as a pretext for the poet to give free rein to his inspiration. But if the rich verbal dress of his plays reveals him as a splendid and vigorous poet, he is to be admired no less as a dramatist for the ability with which he presents and handles his characters, the technical mastery he often shows in the linking of scenes, the delicate gradation of shades of thought heightened by the magic of verse, and, lastly, the passion, vigor, and overflowing pathos appropriate to the romantic mood. These characteristics make him a unique example in Mexican dramatic literature of the direct and immediate influence of the literary current of romanticism which was extended to America contemporaneously with its culmination in Europe.

Rodríguez Galván

Unlike Calderón, Ignacio Rodríguez Galván, an excellent lyric poet, was hardly a success in the theater.

His stage productions consist of one dramatic sketch, *The Chapel* (1837), and two dramas, *Muñoz, Inspector of Mexico* (1838) and *The Viceroy's Favorite* (1842). All three have violent and savage themes. The sketch deals with the last hours of Alonso de Avila, the celebrated conspirator who was condemned to torture when the conspiracy of the Marqués del Valle was discovered in 1566; *Muñoz* depicts the wild passion of the despotic inspector for the wife of Baltasar de Sotelo; and *The Favorite* is a dramatization of the well-known legend by Don Juan Manuel.[1]

The features which distinguish and even embellish the lyric poetry of Rodríguez Galván—the desperate and somber mood, the fiery rage, the frequent tendency to imprecation—detract from and disfigure his dramatic compositions. Everything in them is frenzied and indecent. The characters, instead of being human, seem to be demon-possessed creatures in perpetual fury. In the accumulation of gloomy scenes, the dramatist does not achieve his desired end. If he had any talent for the theater, he lacked sufficient technical knowledge to write plays that could be staged successfully. He did not have the refinement or the delicacy or the subtle instinct of climax which are found in Calderón. In pursuit of the pathetic, he constantly fell into the extreme and the coarse. If it cannot be denied that occasionally his inspiration shines through passionate scenes and delights us in eloquent passages, it is also true that the mediocrity of the dramatist at times stifles the poet even then.

He is to be credited, nevertheless, with two important contributions: he was the first in his epoch to write for the stage (*Muñoz, Inspector of Mexico* was produced in 1838) and, unlike his undoubtedly superior rival Calderón, he always dramatized national themes with laudable patriotic persistence.

Minor Romantic Dramatists

The dramatic movement initiated in Mexico by the works of Cal-

[1] A Spanish prince and author (1282-1349), a predecessor of Boccaccio in writing stories. —Translators' note.

derón and Rodríguez Galván and by the efforts of Gorostiza as an active, enthusiastic impresario and adapter of foreign plays was certainly not of great importance. Among the few dramatists who succeeded them, three should be mentioned: Carlos Hipólito Serán, a most prolific author of satirical comedies of manners, who wrote *Social Nonentities* (1852); Ignacio Amieva, who wrote *Valentina* and *The Senator's Daughter*; and Pantaléon Tovar, the very versatile author of *Mysteries of the Heart, A Sublime Dishonor, The Glory of Grief* (dramas); *And for What Purpose?* (a comedy of manners); *Heavenly Justice* (a cloak-and-sword comedy); and *Mexican Conspiracy* (a historical play).

If it is certain that all of these works were produced, very few are extant, and, generally speaking, their influence on the Mexican theater has been slight.

The same is true regarding the dramatic work of the poet Doña Isabel Prieto de Landázuri. Don José María Vigil estimates that she wrote fifteen original pieces, comedies and serious plays, the majority of which were in verse—not to count a translation of Victor Hugo's *Marion Delorme*. But only five of her plays were staged: four in Guadalajara—*The Two Are Worse, Gold and Tinsel, The School for Sisters-in-Law,* and *Angel or Ghost?*—and one in Mexico City—*A Lily Among the Brambles.* Her only published plays, *The Two Flowers* and *The Two Are Worse,* were printed in Guadalajara, in 1861 and 1862, respectively. Of these two plays Hartzenbusch speaks with praise; the first is a romantic drama; the second, a comedy in the manner of Bretón de los Herreros.

THE NOVEL

The Mexican novel, little cultivated before the time of Fernández de Lizardi, was developed and popularized in the first half of the nineteenth century, but it did not achieve an artistic form. It was historical and episodic in character; the events were depicted at length and in great detail, but little interest was shown in portraying native customs. The novelists, with rare exceptions, were romanticists; they idealized everything, and there is hardly a figure who in their hands retains any trace of earthy clay. Romanticism invaded fictional prose, and its philosophy was pessimistic. Rare was the writer who did not shipwreck in the *fleuve du tendre.* Tearful sensibility was the vogue.

Orozco y Berra

With Fernando Orozco y Berra the romantic novel appeared in Mexico. He was born in San Felipe del Obraje, State of Mexico, on June 3, 1822. While a small boy, he was taken to Mexico City. He studied philosophy and Latin in the Conciliar Seminary and began the study of medicine, which he concluded in Puebla in 1845. There he practiced his profession, but he was soon attracted by journalism and literature, which he began to cultivate; and, on returning to Mexico City, he dedicated himself altogether to writing. He was a liberal with advanced ideas; he was one of the editors of the *Nineteenth Century* and of the *Republican Monitor*. At his early death on April 15, 1851, he left unpublished several plays and numerous poems. His very few published poems included one exquisite sonnet, "At the Sepulcher of a Little Girl," which was highly praised by Roa Bárcena.

It seems that the life of Orozco y Berra was wretchedly unhappy, and this engendered a bitterness and at times a desperate pessimism which are reflected in his only published novel, *The Thirty Years' War* (1850). This work enjoyed some popularity during his era.

Contrary to the implication of the title, this bulky volume is merely a detailed account of the amorous experiences of the protagonist—presumably the author himself—during the first thirty years of his life. The novel contains, according to the author, "a little of everything, with emphasis on love, love blended with dejection and sadness, the kind of love in style at that time—skeptical, ideal—and with all the rest that the winds from overseas brought us." The protagonist becomes a Don Juan somewhat prematurely: when he is hardly seven years old, he becomes infatuated with a little girl of his own age; during his adolescence, he is the object of the affections of an attractive middle-aged woman whose snare he escapes because of his innocence. But from that time on, he is the victim of successive love affairs, some of them sensual, others pure and idealistic. His sweethearts are Louise, Mary, Angela, Serafina, Lola . . . The net result—including the death of one of his platonic lovers who loves him without hope, and his absolute surrender to a woman who ridicules and despises him—causes Gabriel, on the threshold of maturity, to draw up a balance sheet of his amatory experiences:

Thirty years! And what have I gained? Thirty years of war with women! And what triumph have I achieved? To enjoy oneself in this world, one must harden his heart in crime and close his eyes to justice and modesty. The most innocent and purest pleasures must be bought with money or with tears; and in order to find the money, one must crawl on the ground as a viper.

This is cheap philosophy which reflects no credit on the author.

Apart from being the first amorous novel in Mexican literature, *The Thirty Years' War* lacks outstanding literary merit, though it achieved remarkable notoriety. It is written in slovenly and homely prose; it is prolix, insipid, and tedious; and the development of the theme is not original. The work assumes an autobiographical character since the main events did occur and the amours were those of the author. Although the action is whimsically placed in Burgos and Madrid, the events really occurred in Puebla and Mexico City. Perhaps this change in geography was made because the author hoped, by withholding the "key," to conceal the reality of the actions. This much is certain, however: some of the women to whom allusions are made in the book devoted themselves to the difficult and costly task of removing copies from circulation; and for this reason, *The Thirty Years' War* has become a genuine bibliographical rarity.

Díaz Covarrubias

The novels of Juan Díaz Covarrubias—another of the romanticists—are, from a rigorous literary point of view, mere fictional essays; but they are quite superior to the fiction of Orozco y Berra.

Díaz Covarrubias was born in Jalapa on December 27, 1837. His father, Don José de Jesús Díaz, was an estimable poet, author of ballads on the War of Independence, and, as such, a precursor of Guillermo Prieto. Díaz Covarrubias studied in his native city; and when, on his father's death, he went with his impoverished mother to live in Mexico City about 1848, he enrolled in the School of San Juan de Letrán, where he studied philosophy and the humanities and later took up the study of medicine. While still a student—his life was too short for him to complete his studies—he attracted attention as a novelist and poet. Two sad events, the premature death of his mother and an unfortunate love affair, saddened his youthful muse. Perhaps, also, his deep restlessness of soul resulted from some presentiment of his tragic death—one of the most shameful chapters, not yet forgotten, in the Mexican civil war. Loving the liberal cause, but keenly aware of his humanitarian and religious duty of caring for the sick and wounded of both sides, he was practicing his profession in the camp at Tacubaya, the last stronghold of the liberals, when they were routed by Márquez on April 11, 1859, and he and other young physicians were made prisoners. The fierce leader, violating the rules of warfare, savagely commanded that they be shot, thus covering himself with infamy and destroying—with fratricides' bullets—that poet of twenty-one years, one of the most promising figures of Mexican literature.

A romanticist like Orozco y Berra, and like him also in morbid sensitiveness and in the causes that determined it, Díaz Covarrubias revealed the faculties and the broad vision of a novelist; he lacked, however, the maturity of style and thought that can be obtained only through time and the exercise of artistic disciplines. He also revealed strong nationalistic tendencies; he painted Mexican characters and scenes and devoted many of his pages to Mexican customs.

With the exception of *Impressions and Sentiments* (1857), a collection of articles, stories, and literary fantasies, the prose works of Díaz Covarrubias are all fictional; namely, *The Sensitive Soul* (1859), a novelette; *Gil Gómez the Insurgent, or the Doctor's Daughter* (1859), a historical novel; and *The Middle Class* (1859) and *The Devil in Mexico* (1860), novels depicting Mexican customs.

The love theme, dominant in the works of Covarrubias, bears the unmistakable stamp of romanticism in presentation and treatment. In *The Sensitive Soul*, Luisa is dying of love for Ferdinand and has the good fortune—a thing not rare in this type of story—to see her lover arrive in time to witness her agony and receive a last kiss. *The Middle Class* depicts the rehabilitation of a fallen woman and has an unusual ending: the heroine, Amparo, considering herself unworthy of the generous Román, who offers her marriage, enters a convent. In *The Devil in Mexico*, the author tries to show how passionate illusions can be destroyed by material interests. Enrique and Elena, who believe themselves destined for each other and are consumed with love, separate finally because of sordid financial considerations, and each contracts a marriage of convenience. Lastly, even in his historical novels, the writer holds to his favorite theme. In *Gil Gómez the In-*

surgent, which has for its background the War of Independence, he tells a story of love which, in its overflowing exaltation and pathetic outcome, differs not at all from its predecessors.

The prose of Díaz Covarrubias is fluid and pleasing; its impurities may be overlooked because of the spontaneity and simplicity of the work. His dialogue is natural, his narration is generally smooth, and his description is vivid. Influenced by Lamartine and particularly by the social ideas of George Sand, he seems to be the most genuinely romantic writer of the early Mexican novel. There is to be noticed also in his work the warmheartedness and lack of restraint that influenced Altamirano's conception of the author of *The Middle Class* and led him to say: "He had infinite kindliness, the heart of a child, amid the roar of cannon."

Perhaps none would deny that his work is far from being perfect in substance and in form; that, because of the conditions under which it was produced, it seems a preparatory exercise, a happy augury of better things, rather than a finished product. The reader should remember that this is the work of a novelist twenty-one years old.

It is necessary, also, to take into account the tumultuous epoch of violence in which it was produced and of which its author was a victim and martyr. "Perhaps," he sadly wrote in 1858, several months before his death, in the dedication of one of his novels to the poet Luis G. Ortiz, "there will be many to say that only a child or a madman would think of writing about Mexico in this tragic epoch of social madness and expect to be read by the ruddy light of flames and amid the roar of cannon."

Florencio M. del Castillo

Florencio M. del Castillo, a third romantic novelist, resembled Díaz Covarrubias in his consecration to literature and, also, in his misfortunes. Born in Mexico City on November 27, 1828, Castillo attended the School of San Ildefonso and began the study of medicine; but his literary inclinations, which were definite and early, distracted him, and he became interested in journalism and letters. An ardent liberal, he fought with his pen for the Reformist principles; and when the Revolution of Ayutla triumphed, he became a deputy to the Congress of the Union. He took up arms in defense of his country during the French Intervention; but, having been captured in Mexico City and taken to Veracruz, he was confined in the Castle of San Juan de Ulúa—the invaders hoping that the fatal climate would effect their cruel and inhuman purpose without resort to the firing squad. Within a few weeks, in fact, the young patriot contracted yellow fever and was taken in a dying condition to the hospital of the port. He perished there on October 27, 1863.

Castillo cultivated the novelette and short story. While these genres were, in themselves, literary novelties in Mexico at that time, the subject matter he chose constituted an even greater innovation. Although completely romantic and even more sensitive and saccharine than his contemporaries, the novelist did not limit himself to sentimental love affairs; he tried, rather, to present the conflict of human passions and even gave evidence of being a psychologist and theorizer. Thus, in *Love and Misfortune,* he makes money sway the balance in favor of senile desire, as the determining factor in the action. In *A Crown of Lilies,* he paints the struggle in two souls—a nun and her confessor—between human love, which is drawing them together, and divine love and religious duty, which hold them apart. In *As High as the Sky!* the sexual impotence of the husband, creating in the wife an incestuous passion, which is controlled in time, is the dominant theme. In *Guilt,* he portrays a young girl who is avid for luxury and pleasure and is naturally coquettish; she refuses an honorable lover and becomes a prostitute. The action of his *Two Hours in St. Andrew's Hospital* takes place in the gloomy atmosphere of sickness and death. *Sister of the Angels,* Castillo's longest story, aspires to present a study of self-denial symbolized in one type of woman.

From the foregoing it might be assumed that Castillo surpasses the other novelists of his time in dramatic effects and high purposes, and that he was—as his contemporaries believed—the best Mexican novelist of the day. Nothing would be more erroneous. His dramatic instinct was drowned in sentimental tears. He idealized everything beyond measure. He was insufferably pedantic in his digressions and cheap metaphysics. So fond was he of quotations—a characteristic that reveals his pernicious and undigested half-culture —that he used them over and over again, even in conversation, putting them into the mouth of characters for whom they were not suited. Unlike Díaz Covarrubias, he lacked narrative skill; and his diction, sown with every kind of unpardonable barbarism, does not have—as that of the author of *The Middle Class* does—the virtues of simplicity and spontaneity which would have made his work tolerable despite his other literary defects.

The above-mentioned stories of Florencio M. del Castillo have been published in book form, together with several articles and the short story called "The Rosebud." There have been several editions, the earliest in 1850 and 1872.

Inclán

Luis G. Inclán stands on the border of romanticism and shows some affinity to Fernández de Lizardi in the faithful and minute reproduction of Mexican customs. It should be said that Inclán was not a professional literary man, in the full sense of the term, or even to the degree that it was possible for a man of his environment and epoch to be. He was a countryman by birth—born on the Carrasco ranch, in the jurisdiction of Tlalpan (today a federal district), on June 21, 1816. He attended a primary school and then took a course in philosophy in the Conciliar Seminary of Mexico City; but, feeling that the rancher's life surpassed every other kind of calling, he soon returned to the place where he was born, became master of the ranch, and lived there until 1847, occupying himself with the duties of his calling. The American invasion caused him to decide to move to Mexico City—and behold the result! The ex-rancher invested the proceeds from the sale of his property in a shop for lithographing and printing, and turned publisher—launching into the world many a printed portrait of the saints and many a piece of popular literature, sacred and profane, such as short prayers, long prayers, nine-day prayers, *loas*, ballads, etc. While he was still consecrated to these tasks, taking up the pen whenever business permitted or profit demanded, death surprised him on October 23, 1875.

A writer under such circumstances could not be—and Inclán was not—more than an instinctive worker lacking the artistic discipline which would have restrained his excesses and led him to refine and polish his work. In the field of letters, as on the ranch, Inclán is to be regarded as a natural force in action. And in this respect precisely—in his primitiveness, in his expressive rudeness, in his simple and eloquent self-revelation, without embellishment or compromise—lies the attractiveness of his personality. He wrote only one novel. Who knows whether it was inspired by homesickness for the ranch—or by the desire to provide work for his presses! It was called *Astucia, Chief of the Brothers of the Leaf, or the Cowboy Smugglers of the Bough* (1865).

The kilometric title suffices for indicating the literary quality of this novel in which the writer proposes, as a fundamental theme, to relate the romantic adventures of a group of brave fellows—very gentlemanly individuals—who are supporting themselves by smuggling tobacco but are far from being thieves and bandits; on the contrary, "they pursue and hang without ceremony any robber they find in their path," and "they are loved, respected, and even venerated by all who know them." But, breaking away from this central motive, the book widens its scope and the fictitious action is multiplied and complicated by a thousand details and diversions: the scene is peopled with many types of characters; here and there are landscapes, scenes, and customs which are genuine and typical of Mexican rural life; local color abounds; and the fiction itself has a semblance of reality—an experience felt and lived by a genius who is all simplicity, who says what he means in a style sometimes coarse and inappropriate, but always sincere and superlatively human. He speaks in the language of the folk—the style that the people of Mexico use in their songs, when sorrow or joy makes them sing, and in the tales and fables they tell for amusement.

In this regard—in the portrayal of Mexican qualities—Inclán goes farther than Fernández de Lizardi; that which is disciplined art in the latter is naïve and natural expression in the former. As Don Federico Gamboa has observed, Inclán, in *Astucia,* reproduces Mexican people without being influenced by other writers or models. For this reason, his novel—so questionable from a strictly literary point of view—can be considered a unique document—unique for its description of rural life and for its inexhaustible and still insufficiently explored treasure of folklore, since it preserves, in all completeness, the speech of the people.

Other Novelists

Outside the literary current engendered in Mexico by romanticism is to be found Don Justo Sierra the Elder (1814-1861), an eminent jurisconsult and man of letters, to whom both the journalism and the history of Yucatán, his native state, owe much. He wrote *The Jew's Daughter* and *A Year in St. Lazarus' Hospital*; both are regional novels and were inspired by Dumas and Sue. The first of these novels was reprinted in 1959 in the *Collection of Mexican Authors* (Porrúa) with a prologue by Antonio Castro Leal.

Along with Dr. Sierra, another writer from Yucatán should be mentioned: Don Eligio Ancona (1836-1893), author of historical novels such as *The Cross and the Sword* and *The Count of Peñalva*. And lastly, though lacking in literary merit and enjoying no great fame, the following should be cited: Don Pantaleón Tovar (1828-1876), a fabricator of novels of rhetorical pessimism such as *Ironies of Life* and *God's Hour*, in which, again, the inspiration of Sue appears; the lacrimose Don Aurelio Luis Gallardo (1831-1968), who wrote *Ada, or an Angel's Love*; Don José María Ramírez (1834-1892), who was equally sentimental and declamatory in *A Rose and a Rag*; and Don José Rivera y Río, who, between 1851 and 1861, published *The Mysteries of San Cosme, Fate and Providence*, and *Martyrs and Hangmen*.

XV

History and Other Types of Prose

THIS epoch, more than any other in Mexican history, was impassioned and turbulent. Historians, in the heat of the struggle, were more concerned with the present than the past. All were politicians—actors in the national drama. As annalists and commentators on contemporary events, they could with difficulty evade party bias. They deserve credit, nevertheless, for admirable pages which no one could improve—pages in which the truth often shines with brilliance amid the outbursts of passion.

MAJOR HISTORIANS

Bustamante

Don Carlos María de Bustamante, whose earlier activities were mentioned in Chapter IX, was the first historian to appear in the era of Independence. His tireless activity filled half a century.

He was born in Oaxaca on November 4, 1774. He studied Latin grammar, philosophy, and theology in his native city, and was graduated as a bachelor of arts and studied law in Mexico City. Later, having moved to Guanajuato and Guadalajara, he was admitted to the bar in 1801 by the *Audiencia* of the latter city and held the position of *relator*. In the capital of New Spain, to which he returned for a short time, he devoted himself to law and journalism. At the outbreak of the insurgent movement, he refused at first to unite himself with the national party; but when the freedom of the press was suspended in 1812, he feared imprisonment and went to join Morelos. He was active in the Congress of Chilpancingo. When this was dissolved, he fled to save his life. He applied for amnesty in 1817. While trying to escape from Mexico by embarking on an English frigate at Veracruz, he was caught and imprisoned in the Castle of San Juan de Ulúa, but later was included in the decree of amnesty. When Independence was won, he again became active in politics. From 1824 until his death, he played a prominent part in Congress, except for short intervals, as a deputy from Oaxaca, and he devoted himself earnestly to writing and publishing many of his own works and a number of works by others. The North American invasion greatly disheartened him, and he died in Mexico City on September 21, 1848.

Bustamante's production should be divided into two classes: original works, and works that he merely edited and annotated.

Prominent among his original works is the *Historical Picture of the Mexican Revolution,* the second edition of which, published 1843-46, is considered definitive. The political history of his day is continued in the following: *History of Emperor Don Agustín de Iturbide* (1846), *The Mexican Cabinet during the Second Period of the Administration of President Bustamante* (1842), and *Notes for a History of the Government of General Santa Anna* (1845). Bustamante also wrote *Gallery of Ancient Mexican Rulers* (1821); *Campaigns of General Don Félix María Calleja* (1828); *Mornings along the Alameda in Mexico City* (1835-36), an account of Aztec history up to the arrival of the Spaniards at Veracruz; and, finally, *The New Bernal Díaz del Castillo, or History of the Anglo-American Invasion of Mexico* (1847), which he did not finish.

Foremost among the works edited by Bustamante are those of Gómara, Sahagún, Alegre, and Cavo, which have already been discussed. And to all these should be added the numerous magazine articles, bulletins, and pamphlets on varied subjects that came from his indefatigable pen. The man was a stranger to fatigue—he had a mania for writing. It is estimated that he gave to the press something like 19,142 quarto pages, not counting his unpublished work!

Bustamante was, however, a confusing and most inaccurate writer —at times ingenious, picturesque, and imaginative, even to excess, but more often commonplace to the point of triviality. He is recognized as an honest and sincere patriot, though without fixed principles in politics; this latter characteristic and his credulity—which was proverbial—led him to frequent contradictions and inconstancy. Noticeable in his writings, generally, is lack of plan and of logical development, along with prejudice and inaccuracy in reporting events.

As editor of the works of others, he branded himself as a man of few scruples, by virtue of the fact that he had no hesitancy about altering his texts, suppressing passages, interpolating his own opinions jumbled together with those of the author, or adding notes promiscuously. But, undeniable as his defects are, Bustamante's merits should not be slighted: Mexican history is indebted to him for having preserved abundant material about the national life in which he participated or which he witnessed; and for having published books that, in spite of numerous errors, would perhaps have remained in oblivion had it not been for his generous enthusiasm in making them known.

Alamán

Don Lucas Alamán, another historian of this period, showed himself to be the diametrical opposite of Bustamante, both in literary methods and in temperament. He did not improvise history; he constructed it methodically. There are few writers as consistent and logical, as well prepared and as rigorously disciplined as he was.

A native of Guanajuato, where he was born October 18, 1792, Alamán was the son of Spanish parents whose wealth came from mining. He received a careful education from his childhood, studied the humanities and exact sciences in Guanajuato, and acquired also a practical knowledge of mining. At the beginning of the War of Independence, he witnessed the entrance of Hidalgo into Guanajuato; and when his family fled to Mexico City the same year—1810—he had opportunity to broaden his scientific and literary knowledge in the capital. In the College of Mining, he studied chemistry and mineralogy with the learned Don Andrés del Río; he liked the natural sciences, particularly botany, and he learned several modern languages. From 1814 to 1820 he made a profitable tour of Europe, visiting Germany, England, France, Spain, Switzerland, Italy, and the Netherlands. In Paris he continued his scientific studies in the Collège de France, where he specialized in mineralogy; he studied Greek; he knew and had contact with many eminent persons. Knowing thoroughly the classical languages, being familiar with the English, French, Italian, and German languages and literatures—as well as the Spanish—and possessing broad scientific knowledge and the genuine polish that worthwhile travel can give, young Alamán, before he was thirty, was a distinguished figure in his country and epoch.

His accomplishments contributed largely to the part he was to play in the public affairs of his country. Returning to Mexico in 1820, during the time of the re-establishment of the Constitution of 1812, he was named deputy to the Cortes from the province of Guanajuato, and the following year he sailed for Spain. When Independence was achieved, he made another trip to France and England, in the interest of forming a large mining company, which was finally organized in London; and he returned to his country in 1823, immediately after the downfall of Iturbide. The provisional government named him secretary of state and of foreign relations. From that year on, aligning himself with the conservative party, he participated in governmental and political affairs, except for the intervals during which he devoted himself to literary tasks or to great industrial enterprises in the fields of textiles and mining. While he was minister of foreign relations in the last administration of Santa Anna, death came to him in Mexico City June 2, 1853.

Alamán was a born historian; but, like all the historians of his time, he was a party man, and political feeling profoundly influenced his writings. He produced two works: *Dissertations on the History of Mexico* (1844-52) and *History of Mexico* (1849-52). The *Dissertations* deals with the Conquest, the establishment of the Spanish government prior to the creation of the viceroyalty, the projects undertaken by Cortés, the establishment and propagation of the Christian religion in New Spain, and the founding of the City of Mexico—in addition to a synthesis of the history of Spain from the Catholic Kings to Ferdinand VII and numerous appendices. The *History of Mexico* covers the period from the first efforts toward securing independence, in 1808, up to 1852.

Because of the vigorous and unadorned style that makes Alamán the best prose writer of his epoch; because of the conception and the harmonious realization of the selected plan; because of the wisdom and force of the analysis, the vividness of the episodes, the animation and accuracy of the narrative, Alamán's work has been unanimously recognized as belonging with the most notable works of Mexican literature. But, at the same time, his status as historian has been the subject of constant controversy: no one has been more discussed, attacked, praised, and vilified, not only by his contemporaries, but by posterity. For some (those of his party) Alamán is, as Bassoco said, the one man "who was raised by an austere wisdom above human regards and, always quick to give due praises to virtue, made iniquity fear judgment and censure." For others (those of the opposing party) he symbolizes hatred for the insurgent cause and is, in the words of P. Rivera, "the Bourbon-lover to the death—the reverent steward of the sacred majesty of kings, the loyalty of the colonies to Mother Spain, the kindliness of the viceregal government, and all the ideas and traditions of the Spanish monarchy."

Zavala

Just as Alamán represented the conservative spirit, Don Lorenzo de Zavala stood for radicalism.

A completely restless and rebellious soul, from his early youth he was consumed with the desire for liberty. In the Seminary of San Ildefonso, in Mérida—where he was born October 3, 1788—he studied theology, without any intention of becoming a clergyman. For his master he had a skeptic and a sworn enemy of scholasticism. He secretly read forbidden books, especially those of the French encyclopedists. And at a public function of the school, to the horror of those present, he attacked a statement of St. Thomas.

When he finished his school work in 1807, he was disconcerted and aimless. But the Napoleonic invasion of Spain and the constitutional movement of 1812 gave him an incentive; he was, above all, a fighter, born to hurl himself into combat. He took part in the councils of the "*sanjuanistas*" of Mérida; he delivered excited speeches; he founded and edited journals in which his aggressive zeal yielded to no thing and no person; he occupied a chair—perhaps the first in Mexico—of constitutional law; and with his friends, he began among the Indians persistent revolutionary propaganda, which is considered by some as being the origin of the class war that later devastated the Yucatán peninsula.

When absolutism triumphed in 1814, he was arrested and deported to the Castle of San Juan de Ulúa, where he remained a prisoner until 1817. His enforced idleness in prison was spent in studying English—which he thoroughly mastered—and medicine. When he was finally freed, his activities were somewhat giddy and amazing.

Elected deputy to the Spanish Cortes in 1820, he took part in plots and agitations in Spain, and he also carried on intrigues in the first National Congress of Mexico, in which he proved himself to be an excellent orator. At first he was a friend to Iturbide, but later he became his most bitter adversary. When the Empire fell, he fought for federalism; worked for the establishment of the York Rite (Masonic) lodges; organized the popular party; co-operated in the expulsion of the Spaniards; was governor of the State of Mexico; participated in the insurrection of Acordada; was minister of finance under President Guerrero, and, when the latter was overthrown, went to the United States to evade persecution. He traveled through England, Holland, Germany, Belgium, Switzerland, and Italy, and finally established residence in Paris, where he wrote his *Historical Essay* in 1831. The following year he returned to Mexico, again was governor of the State of Mexico, and was the initiator of the law nationalizing the wealth of the clergy. During the cholera epidemic, his heroic and humanitarian activity deserved the highest praise. Later, in 1834, he went to Paris to represent the Mexican government at the court of Louis Philippe, but he soon resigned in lofty and ringing terms because he was not in accord with the political ideas of Santa Anna.

In its bright intensity, Zavala's life was like a shooting star. How pitiful that it should end in ignominy! A man of extreme passions, confused political ideas, without scruples, he forgot his highest duty —loyalty to his country. As a concessioner of immense areas of colonizable land in Texas—not only because of hatred of his enemies, who were in power, but perhaps for a less forgivable reason, the ambition for wealth—he who had been the champion of liberty began by violating the nation's laws and ended by betraying his country. He joined with the rebellious Texans and signed the Declaration of Independence as a deputy from Harrisburg. Elected vice-president of the ephemeral republic, he accepted and discharged that duty before retiring to his residence at San Jacinto, near Lynchburg, where he died on November 15, 1836.

The life of Zavala explains his personality as a writer. He was a man of superior talent and culture, but he was enslaved by passion. He wrote while fighting, he fought while writing. Rather than a historian, he was a vivid and impassioned chronicler of his period. His style is clear, precise, cutting, full-throated; at times, it strikes fire.

Apart from his unpublished works (there is mention of some *Memoirs*, a *Journey to Switzerland,* and a *Journey to Belgium and Holland,* which have been lost), only two of his works are known: the *Historical Essay on the Revolutions of Mexico* and the *Journey to the United States,* both written while he was abroad. The *Essay* was published in two volumes: the first, in Paris in 1831; the second, in New York in 1832; another edition was issued in Mexico in 1845. The *Journey to the United States,* which was also published first in Paris, in 1834, was reprinted in Mérida, Yucatán, in 1846, with a note on the author's life and writings by Justo Sierra O'Reilly.

In the last-named book—in which, perhaps, the moral genesis of his treason can be traced—Zavala is revealed not only as a vivid narrator of his travels, but also as a man endowed with a keen capacity for observation of people and customs. The *Historical Essay on the Revolutions of Mexico* covers the era from the beginning of Independence in 1808 to the administration of Bustamante, and is, without a doubt, Zavala's best and most characteristic book. But the lack of calmness and systematic plan is certainly a fault. Also, the author does not give due regard to details of names and dates. As Don Alfonso Toro has observed in an excellent study, he lacked "historical perspective" in his view of the epoch of Independence; his estimates or portraits of his enemies in relation to the later events in which the author himself took part are violently partisan and sometimes no more than caricatures. On the other hand, what acute observation and insight many of his pages show! Sometimes he penetrates to the most deeply hidden causes of the drama of Mexican history. Even today, some of the questions that he raised are alive and urgent.

If Zavala can not be ranked with the best Mexican historians, he is doubtless one of the greatest political writers of Mexico.

Mora

A man of advanced ideas and active in politics, Don José María Luis Mora, the last of this group, is, among Mexican historians, unique for deliberation, well-balanced judgment, and comprehensive intelligence.

Born in Chamacuero, Guanajuato, in October, 1794, Mora received his early education in Querétaro; later, in Mexico City, he was a brilliant student at the Academy of San Ildefonso, where he was ordained a priest and received the degree of Doctor of Theology. Liberal by conviction from his youth, he edited, in 1821, the *Political and Literary Weekly*; he was named, in the following year, a member of the provincial deputation of Mexico; and he defied prison by opposing Iturbide. When the Empire fell, he was a deputy from the State of Mexico to the Constituent Assembly, played a brilliant role in it, and was admitted to the bar in 1827. As a member of the Scottish Rite Lodge, he took part in the struggle between the Scottish and York groups; during the alternating triumphs and defeats of his party, he upheld his cause by defending his ideas in the press (*The Recorder*, a periodical founded by him, was noted for its vehemence) and by writing his *Political Catechism of the Mexican Federation* and his *Dissertation on the Nature and Use of Ecclesiastical Income and Wealth*; and he took an active part, during the administration of Gómez Farías, in disputes concerning education. He was—as he said in defining what he understood by the "political march of progress" —an advocate of "the confiscation of the wealth of the clergy; the abolition of the privileges of the ecclesiastical and military classes; the extension of education to all classes—that is, public education, absolutely independent of the clergy; the suppression of the monasteries; the absolute freedom of opinion; the equality of foreigners with natives in civil law; and the use of juries in criminal trials." When his party fell from power, Mora fled with Gómez Farías to Europe and established his residence in Paris. There, living a precarious, almost wretched life, he still found courage to devote himself to literary tasks. When the political situation shifted at home, he went to England in 1847 as minister plenipotentiary from Mexico; but he was suffering from tuberculosis, probably contracted during his years of want, and when the disease grew worse, he went back to Paris, where he died July 14, 1850.

Dr. Mora published two books in Paris: *Mexico and Her Revolutions* (1836) and *Unclassified Works* (in two volumes, 1837). An edition of the first book, with a prologue by Agustín Yáñez, has been published by Porrúa in their *Collection of Mexican Authors*.

As early as 1828 he was collecting material for the first of these books, and he began the composition of it in 1830. According to the plan he outlined, the book was to comprise: first, a statistical account of the general status of the Republic and of each of the states and territories; second, the history of Mexico from the Spanish Conquest to the administration of Santa Anna. The author was not able to carry out his purpose. Of *Mexico and Her Revolutions,* only three parts actually appeared. The first deals with the location, extent, topography, and natural products of the territory; the mining, the industry, and commerce; the administration of Mexico under the Spanish regime; the political and social organization, foreign relations, and revenues of the Republic up to the time when he was writing. The third (the second part never reached publication) is concerned with the conquest and the various efforts to establish Independence. The fourth treats the epoch of Independence up to the death of Morelos. As a historian, Mora is outstanding for the accuracy of his judgment, the reasonableness of his general statements, and his evident desire to avoid political prejudice in the evaluation of events and to maintain always an attitude of serenity and honesty. Lacking the impetuosity of Zavala and the vigorous energy of Alamán, Mora recorded events soberly and precisely and showed himself to be a wise observer. Though incomplete—truncated, in fact—this, his best work, is plainly a classic for the study of Mexican history.

The *Unclassified Works* is a document of inestimable value for an understanding of Mora's interesting political personality. "This contains," he said, "the history of my thoughts, my desires, and my principles of conduct." In the first volume, the author brought together the following: his picturesque and admirable political review of the various administrations of the Republic up to 1837; the writings of the Bishop Abad y Queipo; his dissertation (cited above) on the nature and use of ecclesiastical wealth; and his various plans and works relating to the credit and public debt of Mexico. The second volume contains the writings that he had previously published in the *Political and Literary Weekly* and the *Observer of the Mexican Republic.* In these he stands revealed as a remarkable political writer.

Mora was a profound thinker and sociologist, as well as an eminent historian.

MINOR HISTORIANS

Side by side with the great historians of this period, those of lesser stature should be mentioned.

In the foreground stands Don Luis Gonzaga Cuevas (1800-

1867), a prominent member of the conservative party, whose penetrating essay entitled *The Future of Mexico* (written between 1851 and 1857 and reprinted in 1954 in one volume) is an analysis of the condition of the Republic from the period of Independence to the mutiny of the Acordada in 1828; at the same time, it aspires to be—within the limits of the author's political criterion—a prophecy of the nation's destinies as a consequence of the policy it adopts.

Concise narratives of the events of that epoch were written by the following: Don José María Tornel y Mendivil (1797-1853), a general and politician whose name is well known in the innumerable revolutions of the period; and the conservative politician, Don Francisco de Paula Arrangoiz (died in 1889). The former wrote *Brief Review*, published in incomplete form in 1852; the latter, a work entitled *Mexico from 1808 to 1867*, printed in 1872.

Two historians of particular events should also be mentioned: Don Francisco Zarco (1829-1869), who wrote a *History of the Extraordinary Constituent Congress* (published in 1857 and reprinted in 1956 with a "Preliminary Study" by Antonio Martínez Báez); and Don Manuel Ramírez Aparicio (1831-1867), author of an account of the *Suppressed Convents in Mexico* (1861). Lastly, Don Marcos Arróniz, in whom poetic activities were combined with historical, published an interesting *Biographical Handbook of Mexico* (1857) and a rather picturesque *Traveler's Handbook of Mexico* (1858).

During this period the only Mexican deeply devoted to the study of the remote past was Don José Fernando Ramírez (born in Parral, Chihuahua, May 5, 1804; died in Bonn, Germany, March 4, 1871), the illustrious archeologist and scholar, to whom Mexican culture is deeply indebted. If Ramírez wrote no history, he did preserve precious material for others and established, also, the fundamentals of the ideographic interpretation of the Aztec codices. His great work is fragmentary and scattered, but the following require mention: *Additions to Beristáin's Library* (1898), which completed the basic work of that bibliographer; essays on Motolinia, Nuño de Guzmán, and Pedro de Alvarado; and *Notes and Clarifying Data for Prescott's History of the Conquest of Mexico*. Antonio Castro Leal has published in Porrúa's *Collection of Mexican Authors* the excellent *Life of Motolinia*, by Ramírez, and some important articles he wrote for the

Universal Dictionary of History and Geography (Mexico, 1853-56), which had already been published in book form.

SCHOLARS AND POLITICAL WRITERS

Among the scholars, it is proper to consider Don José Justo Gómez de la Cortina, Count of La Cortina (born in Mexico City in 1799; died there January 9, 1860), a grammarian, philologist, and—in moments of leisure—literary critic and humorous poet. Though he was of Spanish descent and served in the diplomatic corps of Spain in his youth—among other duties he was charged with introducing ambassadors at the court of Ferdinand VII—the greater part of his life was spent in Mexico. This circumstance—along with the fact that he occupied several public positions in Mexico, used a part of his great wealth in promoting Mexican literature and art, and carried on his literary activity in Mexico—justifies his inclusion here. The Count's magnificent home was the literary center for the most brilliant people of Mexico during the first half of the century. He was a man of gentle courtesy and extensive culture, an excellent conversationalist, and a versatile writer. One of his contemporaries, Señora Calderón de la Barca, says, in her *Life in Mexico,* that she saw three of his compositions. The first of these—a pamphlet on earthquakes—was addressed to a lady, and gave a scientific explanation of the causes of earthquakes, interrupted now and then by praises of the lady's beautiful eyes; the second was a burlesque poem about the devil; and the third was a heavy and deep dissertation on the Church Fathers. From this array of subject matter, one can infer a certain literary dilettantism—of elegant tone, no doubt—on the part of the highborn gentleman. Probably Gómez de la Cortina was, more than anything else, a dilettante. In his youth he had begun his literary activities by translating Bouterwek's *Spanish Literature,* which he began to publish in 1829 but left incomplete. Later, in Mexico, he contributed worthless criticism—written "with more ease than ability," in the opinion of Menéndez y Pelayo—to his celebrated literary magazine, the *Whip* (1839), doing his share to "preserve the shell of the classical tradition in the full tide of romanticism."

He wrote *Elementary Ideas on Numismatics* (1843), *Dictionary of Castilian Synonyms* (1845), *Short Dictionary of Technical Castilian Words Used in the Fine Arts* (1848), and *Biography of Pedro*

Mártir de Anglería (1858). But much more than he published, he left unpublished: materials dealing with questions of diplomacy, grammar, linguistics, history, geography, cosmography, and Mexican chronology. Two novels entitled *Leonora* and *Euclea, or the Blind Woman of Trieste* were published in some periodical of that time but are now hopelessly lost.

Another scholar, Don José Bernardo Couto (1803-1862), a jurisconsult and humanist, was a disciple of Mora. He was the restorer of the Academy of San Carlos and a public figure of singular prestige, who took part in varied cultural activities. He wrote a famous *Discourse on the Constitution of the Church* and a scholarly *Dialogue on the History of Painting in Mexico;* he translated Horace's *Ars Poetica* and contributed diligently to the *Universal Dictionary of History and Geography* (10 volumes, Mexico, 1853-56).

As in the preceding period and for the same reasons, political literature flourished in this epoch; its practitioners used the pamphlet, the public platform, and the press. Two periodicals were the bulwarks of the opposing parties—the *Nineteenth Century,* for the liberals; *The Cross,* for the conservatives—and in them the best writers expounded and defended their ideas. Besides Ignacio Ramírez, Prieto, and Altamirano, who have already been mentioned, other liberals who were distinguished as orators or journalists, or both, were: Don Francisco Zarco (1829-1869), a stout debater, an outstanding orator in the Constituent Congress and historian of the same, and the founder of the famous satirical periodical, *Las Cosquillas;* Don Vicente Riva Palacio, poet and novelist, who will be discussed in Chapter XVIII, a man whose genius for epigrams gave no little concern to his adversaries; Don Ponciano Arriaga (1811-1865), a champion of the Constituent Congress; and, lastly, Don Ignacio L. Vallarta (1830-1893), a prominent constitutionalist, who, because of his *Discourse on the Abolition of the Jesuit Order,* was acclaimed one of the most distinguished orators of the Congress.

On the conservative side, in addition to Pesado, Roa Bárcena, Couto, and Arango y Escandón, already referred to, the following played important roles: Don Clemente de Jesús Munguía (1810-1868), Archbishop of Michoacán, a vigorous orator and controversialist, and, to a certain extent, the leader of his party; and Don Ignacio Aguilar y Morocho (1813-1884), a member of the commission which offered the crown of Mexico to Maximilian at Miramar, an author of innumerable political pamphlets and discussions of civil and criminal jurisprudence, and a writer whose keen intellect and wit stand out in the famous satire called *The Battle of Holy Thursday*.

Don Anselmo de la Portilla (1816-1879)—connected in a way with the preceding writers, but worthy of inclusion here for a variety of reasons—was a vigorous journalist from Spain who worked hard to bring about the reconciliation of Mexico and the mother country. Mexican literature owes much to him. He founded the journal *La Iberia* in 1867, and in it published serially his celebrated *Historical Library*, a collection of ancient works—never before printed or very rare—of prime importance for Mexican history. He wrote poetry, novels, history, and literary criticism, and edited not a few periodicals. Various books came from his pen: *The Revolution of Ayutla, Mexico in 1856-1857, From Miramar to Mexico,* and a novel, *Virginia Steward*. On his death, a resolution was presented to the Congress, declaring. "He well deserved the gratitude of Mexico."

From 1867 to 1910

XVI

Literary Development

The End of the Struggle

WITH the restoration of the Republic in 1867, a new era began in Mexican political history. New, also, was the aspect manifested in literary history from that time on.

The victory of the Republic was not bloody. With the defeat of Maximilian, Miramón, and Mejía on the hill of Campanas and the occupation of Mexico City on June 21, the national government under Juárez entered the capital. No more blood was shed after the siege of Querétaro. The political leaders who had participated in the imperial adventure—among them, some writers—suffered the penalty of prison or exile. Shortly thereafter, a general amnesty was decreed. The country at last achieved political unity by recognizing law and order; thus the generating cause of incessant anarchy—of civil war that had lasted without truce for fifty years—disappeared.

Lerdo de Tejada had said to the supporters of Maximilian: "Civil war can and should end with the reconciliation of the parties." But, in reality, there was no reconciliation; instead, one party was eliminated, and the other acquired complete control. Thus was the old struggle ended and peace made possible.

The first years of the republican era were not free from political agitation within the ranks of the victorious party. Juárez had to struggle with a strong opposition and saw his government constantly menaced by military leaders and political bosses. When he died in 1872, Don Sebastián Lerdo de Tejada succeeded him; but the new president was deposed at the very moment when he was flushed with the victory of re-election, and went into voluntary exile. The vice-president, Don José María Iglesias, tried to seize the government, but he also fell when the faction headed by General Porfirio Díaz triumphed. Díaz became president in 1876 and, through successive re-elections, governed the country—except for a brief period of four years—until 1911.

During the long period between 1867 and 1910, Mexico underwent profound changes in the political, economic, and social orders. The situation thus created affected literature in various ways. We point out only the principal result: when public affairs no longer absorbed the energies of writers, intellectual activities were developed for their own sake—apart from political strife, which, in general, had practically ceased. Aided by a prolonged peace, Mexican literature reached its maximum development.

The True Amnesty

Letters had declined—as they always do in time of war—in the decade that ended in 1867. "It was natural," as a contemporary—Altamirano—says,

that all men's minds should fall under the influence of political prejudices; there was hardly a family or individual who did not share in the excitement convulsing the whole nation. Under such circumstances, how could a writer devote himself to the serious work of historic investigation or the delights of poetry, which demand a tranquil mind and a free, untrammeled spirit? True, such a period is the right time for powerful and stirring martial songs to vibrate and for the light of truth to blaze forth from the fire of discussion; but it is perfectly clear, also, that such impassioned poetry and political argument are not the only branches of literature, and that, generally speaking, the shadow of peace is a necessity if men are to give themselves up to the great works of the mind.

He who spoke so wisely in 1869, in the introduction to the famous literary review he founded, was to be the master of two generations in the task of securing the harmony necessary for work along cultural and artistic lines. "The true amnesty," Don Carlos Pereyra says justly, "was offered in the columns of the *Renaissance,* in which those who fought each other on the battle field joined as co-workers." Altamirano himself, "the true comprehensive spirit of his generation," he adds, "declared that while he was living the life of a guerrilla in the forests of the South, fighting against the Empire, he took delight in reciting the beautiful ode with which Roa Bárcena had saluted Maximilian's arrival."

In the spirit of the Mexican people, there was a definite desire to create a culture. Those who "had thrown away the lyre to seize the saber" now reached for it again and began to play. The "deep silence that had reigned in the kingdom of letters" was followed by the musical vibration of active and free life. The press was reborn; from the ashes of the dying fire, it is not strange that a flame should rise now and then, but there was no longer the danger of a conflagration. Political passions were moderated. Letters awakened from their disturbed slumber; "when the struggle ceased," says Altamirano, always magnanimous, "old friends and brothers found each other again." Literary reunions were held; the atmosphere was invigorating. A contagious feeling of brotherhood predominated.

The *Renaissance*—a symbolic and appropriate name—was founded in 1869. It was not only a vehicle of the reviving literary activity, but also a spiritual index of the epoch. Around Altamirano, the leader, were grouped writers old and young, liberal and conservative: beside the revolutionaries Ramírez and Prieto were the imperialists Montes de Oca and Roa Bárcena; side by side with Payno and Riva Palacio were Justo Sierra and Manuel Acuña. The call had been made "to all lovers of *belles-lettres*," to writers of "all political parties." In that literary period unique in nature, and quite new for Mexico, the long-expected spring came—as though conjured up by hope—and the barren garden was suddenly filled with roses. In the pages of the *Renaissance*, all types of writing had a place; all ideas were granted admission. Poetry, criticism, the novel, short stories, history, literary chronicles, theatrical reviews, and translations of great foreign poets, ancient and modern—all were found in that weekly review. And when publication was suspended, well could Altamirano afford to say that all who had collaborated with him in the enterprise "had derived the satisfaction—which public justice would not deny them— of having definitely contributed to a literary movement that was known everywhere." He himself, not without reason, called the results "most extraordinary."

The Mexican Academy

The atmosphere of the period was favorable to the formation of groups and coteries and to the organization of literary societies.

The Academy of Letrán, which had been suppressed in 1856, on the eve of the War of Reform, was succeeded by the Hidalgo Lyceum, which had for its leading spirit Don Francisco Zarco, the journalist, and was revived in later years by Altamirano. Similar in nature to the Hidalgo Lyceum was the Mexican Lyceum, an organization for young writers.

In 1875 the Mexican Academy was founded. It came to be a most vigorous institution solidly established on a permanent basis. Like other academies created at that time in Spanish America, it was established as a link with the Royal Spanish Academy. Considering that more people spoke Spanish outside of Spain than within Spain itself; that there existed, linguistically, a vast Spanish world divided by the ocean; and that, furthermore, in the sixteen republics of Spanish origin and civilization in the New World, the preservation of the language—which was becoming a symbol and synthesis of race—was of equal importance to Spanish Americans and to Spaniards, all of whom were united by the common bond of speech—it was decided to create American academies, autonomous in whatever concerned their internal affairs, but closely connected with the Royal Academy. Such corresponding academies, interrelated with each other and with the parent organization, were to work for the preservation of the common language, bringing forward the expressions that deserved admission to the standard language, taking steps to promote the principles that impede corruption and decay, and, finally, fostering the development of intellectual activities. These growing organizations became a symbol of the intellectual interests that reached beyond frontiers and bound together more than 100,000,000 persons. They represented, and still represent, the spiritual union of the race.

From its beginning, the Mexican Academy shared in collecting material for the *Dictionary of the Language,* having dedicated itself to gathering and evaluating the provincial expressions of the country. It also promoted the important studies of literary history and criticism that constitute the volumes of its *Memorias* published thus far. But it has done something even more valuable: in a broad spirit of co-operation, totally disregarding the winds of politics, it has brought together in one group the most eminent figures of Mexican letters. It has thus accomplished the ideal that was dominant at the time of its origin: the amalgamation of all the forces that must share in the noble task of creating a culture.

Literary Flowering

Under such auspices—moved forward by the intellectual enthusiasm of older writers, who were already famous, and new ones, who were surging with a desire to win fame—the developments begun in 1867 were accentuated more and more throughout the course of the period.

All types of literature flourished. History attained a development and splendor comparable to that reached in past centuries; important works of research and synthesis were brought to completion. In this period, for the first time, novelists succeeded in giving the novel both an artistic form and a national character. Literary criticism developed. In the period from 1870 to 1880, the theater experienced an activity unparalleled in Mexican literary history—an activity without great artistic significance, but at least symptomatic of the strong intellectual currents of the day. Lastly, the lyric, through successive changes, reached its most beautiful and finished form.

Without doubt, poetry was the most important type of Mexican literature in the last third of the nineteenth century and the first decade of the twentieth. Altamirano aspired—as will be seen in the next chapter—to create a national lyric. The dominant romanticism was purified. "The lyric was cleansed of exaggerated sentimentality and falsities," as Luis G. Urbina says, referring to this period; "eyes were again focused on reality, and the estimable tendency toward honest feeling and truthful expression was initiated." Spanish influence continued to be manifest, but already interest in foreign literatures and acquaintance with other models pointed out new courses. The French language and literature, as a result of contact with the invaders, had become better known; English and Italian began to be cultivated. Altamirano first and Justo Sierra later—and with more ardor—accelerated the interest in foreign literatures.

In the meantime, classical poetry was decaying because lyric poetry drew its inspiration almost exclusively from the modern literatures; however, some of the humanists who had belonged to the former period were outstanding in this brilliant epoch. It was destined to decay much more. The hand of Barreda (1824-1881) divorced the new generation from all veneration of the eternal models. That philosopher of the republican era established higher education on the foundation of positivistic ideology; as Antonio Caso has said, he banished "the study of the humanities, classical culture, and those literary principles of antiquity that, transmitted from generation to generation, have created the most exquisite flowers of thought and the highest rewards of the mind." How much damage this unforeseen impulse has done to letters, no one can yet tell.

The poets of the so-called "post-romanticism" of 1870 continued in direct descent until the latter part of the century; then, in those latter days, the spirit of restlessness prevailing in the world produced a lawless reaction similar, in some respects, to romanticism itself. This reaction—joined with the Mexican writer's expanded horizon, his increasingly cosmopolitan culture—gave origin to that complex movement commonly but arbitrarily called "modernism."

MODERNISM

Belated romanticism and French Parnassianism and symbolism were dominant among the various foreign literary influences that shaped modernism and which, far from being dissipated in servile imitation, were absorbed and blended by Mexican poets in accordance with their individual styles. Modernism did not develop into a school. The variety of tendencies it embraced and the diverse manner in which these tendencies were manifested do not permit the modernists to be definitely classified. All of them show a certain family resemblance, but each is, at the same time, distinctive.

Gutiérrez Nájera is considered the precursor of modernism in Mexico. With his name should be associated that of Salvador Díaz Mirón, and, antedating both, that of Justo Sierra. "Knowing our literary idiosyncrasy," Luis G. Urbina said, speaking of Sierra, who had succeeded Altamirano as the intellectual guide of the younger generation,

his advice was always to avoid verbal excesses and to cultivate exactness and intellectual balance. He knew very well that the national literature was in a state of formation, that with each step we took, we were creating an individual design, that our French orientation was serving to separate us definitely from Spanish imitations, and that we were cleansing our dusty images, our stale prejudices, our old Castilian molds in the bath of a new art—the splendid art of French poetry and prose. To purify the style, to make it better and clearer each time, to preserve the essentials of our neo-Hispanic character, in order to open our curiosity to the four winds of the spirit and give new life to ideas and forms in harmony with our cultural and social development: this was the horizon shown to us by the master.

The impulse came, then, from the past. It was established, in its first phase, in the *Azure Review* (1894-96). It reached its highest point in the *Modern Review* (1898-1911).

In modernism, two aspects became evident; the outer, or purely formal; and the inner—the ideology and the feeling—that conditions the outer form. Neither is entirely new. The very traits that are pointed out as distinctive of the modernists are fundamentally romantic: their exalted individualism, which impels them to withdraw into ivory towers, in complete disdain for the rabble; their obsession with death and skepticism; their gloomy pessimism and rebelliousness of spirit, which instils in them a hatred of habitual things and a morbid desire for the new. In regard to form, the idea of matching sense with sound is not exclusive with them, though it is true they have achieved rare and original blendings of tone and color. Without really being innovators, they endeavored to break away from the accepted Castilian verse forms, either by reviving ancient metrical combinations—Spanish and French—or by cultivating verses of nine, ten, twelve, or fourteen syllables—types of verse that were not common, though not without precedent. In their work, the one unquestionable novelty was in rhythm, thanks to the reforms they introduced in the distribution of accents.

Nevertheless, modernism was destined to produce a profound change in Mexican poetry. Among the French influences which shaped it, romanticism—though belated—was the decisive element in some poets; Parnassianism was relatively limited in influence; but symbolism was a much more effective force. In regard to content, symbolism led some poets, according to Puga y Acal,

to suggest, rather than express, ideas and feelings—which as a result, acquired a mysterious exquisiteness—and to increase greatly the range of subject matter, multiplying the phases of life and nature treated in poetry. So far as diction and form were concerned, it caused writers to expand the dictionary, revive words and expressions that had fallen into disuse, coin new ones, and employ old metrical combinations, ballades, and rondels, which had been in vogue in France before the seventeenth century.

The movement encountered serious resistance; many contemporary poets did not accept the new aesthetics. Modernism was certainly guilty of excesses: it was artificial; its eagerness for exotic and novel effects often bordered on the puerile; it fostered a ridiculous "Parisianism" in America; it cultivated "neuroticism" and other "isms" in vogue. But purified, adapted, and incarnated—so to speak—in the Mexican genius, it reformed, enriched, and gave a beautiful and original character to Mexican poetry. It succeeded to the point that a foreign critic—Isaac Goldberg—could say: The modernist movement "signaled the definite entrance of Spanish America into European literary currents."

It should be observed, in addition, that modernism influenced prose, also. It gave to prose beauty, delicacy, fineness of shading, though often accompanied by violations of grammar—a defect that, if it can be considered characteristic of the forerunners and initiators of the "new manner," was nevertheless corrected little by little as the muddy current cleared itself and as the leaders, and the generation that followed, returned to purity of style—a style, furthermore, that was broad, vigorous, and modern.

In the first decade of the twentieth century, Mexican literature reached its height. Though political writing had decayed, other types were more or less successfully cultivated. Culture was more amply diffused than in any preceding period. In the midst of diverse foreign influences, in the midst of literary contacts that might be called cosmopolitan, Mexican literature, far from being denationalized, tended to show more and more an intimate, distinctive, and fully developed individuality.

Just as surely as it marks the end of an era in Mexican history, the year 1910 concludes a cycle—perhaps the most harmonious and brilliant—in the history of Mexican literature.

XVII.

Poetry

THE lyric poets of this period can be classified in four groups: the group formed by Altamirano; the romantic group, under the leadership of Acuña; the classics, still faithful to the Greco-Latin tradition and to the cultivation of the humanities; and the modernists, who brought Mexican lyric poetry to its most brilliant flowering.

ALTAMIRANO AND HIS FOLLOWERS

The blending of classical culture with the literary currents of modern Europe—principally those of France—together with the aspiration to create a genuinely Mexican lyric poetry: this is what Altamirano represented. The force of his example was decisive with the group that he formed and taught, but it was later dissipated in diverse literary channels.

The Master

Don Ignacio Manuel Altamirano was a pure-blooded Indian. He was born in Tixtla (now included in the state of Guerrero) on November 13, 1834. His parents, the humblest kind of people, owned no land and had no surname; they adopted the name of a Spaniard who had sponsored the baptism of one of their forefathers. What could they give their son? The boy, at fourteen years of age, was entirely ignorant of the Spanish language, and he lived a free and half-savage life in the tropical forests of his region, listening to the mockingbird's song in the ceiba trees or bathing his bare feet in some quiet pool near the banana plantations.

Perhaps his destiny was determined by the fact that his father was chosen mayor of the town. When he entered school, the teacher, wishing to ingratiate himself with the new official, placed the lad among the *gente de razón,* the "intelligent people" (i.e., the descendants of European races, as distinguished from the Indians). So alert and robust was the mind of Altamirano that he soon surpassed his classmates; and his further education was assured by a law promulgated by the government of the state, providing that the most promising young Indians of the different communities should be selected by examination and educated at the Literary Institute of Toluca. The boy took leave of his parents and in 1849 went to Toluca, where he studied Spanish, Latin, French, and philosophy, always standing at the head of his class. Given employment as librarian of the institute, he read eagerly the many books that came to hand, often stealing the time from sleep. He studied literature under Don Ignacio Ramírez and wrote at that time his first verses and articles.

The literary development of Altamirano seems almost a miracle— a miracle of genius, willpower, faith. When he left the institute, he found refuge in a private school of Toluca, where he was given room and board in return for teaching French. Then he plunged into a roving life, being equally ready to teach the A B C's in the village schools or to serve as dramatist and prompter for a traveling company of actors. Finally, he went to Mexico City to enrol in the Academy of Letrán, but the Revolution of 1854 drove him away. He headed for the South on foot to join the revolutionists. On returning to Mexico City, he re-entered Letrán to complete his study of law. In the tempestuous year 1857, he divided his attention—as he himself said—"between the contradictions of the Digest, which produced nothing but a deluge of subtleties from the professor, and the vexing arguments of politics, which were agitating liberals and conservatives and inciting the bloodiest of our civil wars." He began to write for the press; and, while continuing his studies, he taught a Latin class. His modest study was sometimes converted into "an editor's office, a revolutionary club, and a literary center." To it flocked the literary youth of the time: Marcos Arróniz, Florencio M. del Castillo, Juan Díaz Covarrubias, José Rivera y Río. With them Altamirano went many times "to the galleries of Congress to applaud the eloquent speeches of Ocampo, Ramírez, Zarco, and Arriaga." At the end of 1857, civil war broke out; and, by January, 1858, the conservatives were masters of the capital. The club then came under the surveillance of the police. Indignant, Altamirano wrote "those alexandrines, 'The Bandits of the Cross,' which were very bad, but which flew on the wings of party spirit throughout the Republic, then agitated by the two parties." One afternoon, he and Manuel Mateos, sitting on the edge of the fountain of Letrán, composed some "atrocious couplets against the reactionary government." His companions engaged in similar labors. The rooms of the School of Medicine and the College of Mining became centers of conspiracy where the revolutionary fire was kept burning. At last, the band of young writers—soldiers and politicians in embryo—was dispersed. They went to the battlefields, to achieve glory or death. The War of Reform had begun.

Altamirano fought in the South. When the Reformist group was victorious, he was elected deputy to the Congress of the Union in 1861; and there, opposing the passage of a law of amnesty and demanding the punishment of enemies "whose skulls should already be bleaching on the *picota*,"[1] he won his first definite and imposing oratorical triumph, and the people lifted him on their shoulders and carried him home. But the end had not yet come. The hard days of the French Intervention and Empire followed; and, again, the fighter and patriot had to prove his devotion by action, by taking up arms for his country.

Upon the re-establishment of the Republic in 1867, Altamirano—the grim revolutionist, the fighter for Reform, the veteran of the wars against the Imperialists and the French—recognized the arrival of a solemn moment, the most beautiful of his life: the moment for beginning to build a culture. With the back pay which the military authorities paid him in a lump sum, he launched a magazine; this was the magnificent review, the *Renaissance*, founded in 1869 to promote letters, almost withered away by strife, destruction, and blood. He attained one of the most remarkable literary careers the history of Mexican literature records: he became the master of two generations; he stimulated and encouraged beginners; he labored actively in the press; he set the tone of literary criticism; he re-estab-

---

[1] A stone column marking the place of executions. It was equipped with rings and hooks to hold the heads of criminals, or other parts of their bodies, for public display.—Translators' note.

lished the Hidalgo Lyceum and founded other cultural societies; he devoted a part of his time to teaching; and he progressed, briefly, through various public posts. Divorced from politics in his last years, he made writing, reading, teaching, and conversing his constant occupations.

In 1889, appointed consul general to Spain, with residence in Barcelona, he left the country that he loved and that owed him so very much. From Barcelona, he was sent to take charge of the consulate in Paris. He visited Italy, filled with fervor and a longing for his own country. A serious illness drove him to seek relief in San Remo, and he died there February 13, 1893. In accordance with his will, his body was cremated and his ashes were sent to Mexico. They rest now in the Rotunda of Illustrious Men, to which they were removed during the ceremonies honoring the centenary of his birth.

Altamirano is the greatest Mexican writer of his time. It would seem that he possessed the burning heat and fertility of his native tropical forest; and yet the artist in him is all deliberation and balance, and, at the same time, highly original and personal. Romantic by temperament, he is classic in expression. He represents self-control, moderation, simplicity; his thought is clear; his style, precise; his sensibility, fine and delicate—he gives, so to speak, the perpetual quivering of his emotion to the marble of classic lines. This romanticist, who had drunk at an opportune time from the clear fountains of the ancients and who had become thoroughly imbued with the modern spirit and culture, constantly turned his eyes to the imperishable models. For this reason, as much through his own work as through his personal attractiveness—for he was always an inspirer, a teacher—he has exercised a beneficial influence on Mexican literature, aspiring to unite in one current, strong and new, and, above all, national, the two literary currents—the classic and the romantic—that had previously been separate and even antagonistic.

His work is rich and varied and includes many diverse types of writing. His prose will be discussed in the next chapter. Though he wrote little poetry, his position in that field is of singular importance.

The poetic work of Altamirano consists solely of one volume, *Rhymes*, the oldest known edition of which is dated 1880. The thirty-two poems brought together there were written prior to 1867. Although the amatory theme is not lacking, the descriptive element predominates. Altamirano wished to give poetry a national stamp—to express, in the purest and best style, the spirit of the race. He thought that the description of landscape was the most effective means of attaining this end. "In the portrayal of nature," as Luis G. Urbina says,

he found the distinctive character of our poetry. If landscape is a state of soul, it is, to him, in its outline and coloring, the means whereby we reveal ourselves mentally and emotionally. The flow of our rivers, the murmur of our forests, the gray placidity of our villages, the indigenous names of our flowers and birds—all this, necessarily, must enter into our poetry, our literature, which would thereby take on a distinctly regional aspect, *sui generis*, and would give us soon a definite American personality.

And his poetry realized this ideal, which, though apparently only external and pictorial, is in reality eminently national. He was the first to give us the feel, the vibration, the color of the section of Mexico where he was born, in verses of extraordinary strength and genuineness. From this point of view, the poems entitled "Flower of the Dawn," "The Orange Trees," "The Bees," "The Poppies," and "To the Atoyac" not only are characteristic, but also represent a new style in our lyric poetry.

Justo Sierra

Justo Sierra was a disciple of Altamirano's and, in turn, when the latter had disappeared from the scene, was also the master of two generations. Poet, political orator, traveler, storyteller, historian, he is rightfully considered one of the great representative writers of Mexican literature in its most brilliant period. He had—as Urueta said on a memorable occasion—"an irresistible magic, a power of attraction and fascination that drew spirits to him naturally, as to a shelter, a place of rest, a strong tower." But never, as Antonio Caso has penetratingly observed, "did the mental corrective of irony or the cautious art of the critic desert him."

Justo Sierra was born in Campeche on January 26, 1848. The love of literature was in his blood; from his father, the novelist and jurisconsult mentioned earlier in this book, he took both name and literary inclinations.

After beginning his studies in Mérida, Justo Sierra went to Mexico City in 1861 to continue them in the Academy of San Ildefonso; he received the law degree ten years later. At old San Ildefonso the poet was revealed. He had brought from his native coast a little poem, *"Playeras,"* inspired by the sound of the sea, and it created a sensation in Mexico City. The literary clubs opened their doors to him. Articles, short stories, novels, and poems came unceasingly from his pen for publication in periodicals. A radical and revolutionist like Altamirano—and, like him, enamored of the beautiful—he contributed regularly to the *Renaissance* in those days of enthusiasm and literary regeneration. His "Sunday Conversations" in the *Republican Monitor* were famous. At the tomb of Acuña, he composed a sorrowful elegy. Just as he was beginning to take part in political journalism, a misfortune, the death of his brother Santiago—a writer like himself and one whom he loved deeply—caused him to draw back suddenly. Then, for the politician, for the journalist, there opened a period of meditation and study. Thinking and studying alone, far from the windy surf of events, he was transformed: the poet of impetuous lyricism, the romantic storyteller, the smooth and easy commentator on the literary scene became the great historian, the profound sociologist, the admirable educator.

Politics carried him several times into the Chamber of Deputies as a member, and he left there the mark of his passing. He was also a judge on the Supreme Court, and he represented Mexico brilliantly at the Hispano-American Congress of Madrid. But his public activities were especially outstanding in the field of education. In the National Preparatory School, the classroom where he taught general history like a master is still called by his name. His abilities raised him to the office of undersecretary of public education; later, as minister of public education and fine arts, he achieved, between 1905 and 1911, a vast and noble work of culture: a work that was crowned by the opening in 1910 of the National University. Having resigned from public office shortly before the triumph of the Revolution, he was sent by President Madero's government to Spain in 1912 as minister plenipotentiary. He had scarcely arrived in Madrid to discharge his mission when he died on September 13, 1912. Mexico honored the great man by restoring his body to the soil of his native land and by giving him a solemn funeral that assumed the proportions of national mourning.

More than a poet, Justo Sierra was a great prose-writer. His poetic inspirations belonged to his youth, and, though he never lost the desire to write verse, he found his muse quite shy after he had reached the border of middle age. He himself, with obvious playfulness, confessed that he did not feel himself to be a poet because of "a certain fundamental inability to unite idea with feeling and both with unfailing lyrical expression." His poems were collected first by Margaret Dorothy Kress in an edition published in 1937 by the National University of Mexico, which later published a monumental edition of his works (1948). Justo Sierra cannot be denied a place of honor in our lyric poetry. According to Luis G. Urbina, the adolescent poet of *"Playeras,"* reaching maturity and eager to find himself,

had followed the French lyric poets, and, attracted by Victor Hugo, had brought to Mexican poetry the apocalyptic visions of his tremendous metaphors, brusque similies, grandiloquent odes, and vast and fiery expression, which destroyed with one blast of wind the tasteful and well-proportioned molds then in vogue.

It was not that *victorhugoism* (Urbina's word) had not previously been introduced to the Mexican Parnassus: it had existed in a certain shapeless way.

But the scintillating antithesis, the dazzling imagination, and the titanic figure of speech appeared first in the odes of Justo Sierra, in those *silvas* that sparkle like red-hot iron beaten on the anvil, in those hendecasyllables and heptasyllables of bronze, in that transcendental philosophy, a little mysterious and a little sibylline, which makes of poetry a prophetic song.

Although suckled by Victor Hugo, the poet of the ode "To God" succeeded in creating for himself an undeniable personality, and perhaps with him begins the direct and insistent influence of the French lyric on Mexican poetry—an influence which, later, was to produce a complete transformation through the work of the modernists.

Among the verses of the illustrious thinker, we would place in the top rank his beautiful and much-discussed poem, "The Blessed Calasanz," which was published in the *Azure Review*; his songs, "To Christopher Columbus" and "On the Deification of the Heroes of Independence"; the tercets, "To the Author of the *Murmurs of the Forest*," "The Bucolic Funeral," and "Autumnal"; the polished sonnets, *"Spirita," "Florencia,"* and "Hannibal"; and, finally, the magnificent translations he made of portions of Heredia's *Les Trophées*.

To this chapter also belongs the prose work of Sierra's youthful years, those fictional tales, genuinely poetic in nature, that were first published in periodicals of the time but were not collected until 1896, when they were issued under the title *Romantic Tales*. "Little poems in prose impregnated with sentimental and delirious lyricism," the author called them. They include a variety of types: some—like "Sea Piece," "Fisherwoman," and "The Siren"—are narratives evoking the atmosphere of his native land; others—like "Nero," "In Jerusalem," "Marie Antoinette"—are flights of imagination to other countries and ages, revealing his wide reading and foretelling the future historian; still others—like "The Romance of a College Student" and the "Confessions of a Pianist"—are really novelettes of romantic hue. The stories found in *Romantic Tales* are important in the evolution of our literature: they represent, along with Altamirano's novels, the exact moment when Mexican romanticism in fiction crystallized into a form appropriately literary and artistic.

Juan de Dios Peza

Juan de Dios Peza was conspicuous among the poets of his time because of one characteristic trait: he stayed strictly within the Spanish tradition. He had no subtleties, no complexities, no difficulties with the stubborn chiseling of form. A natural lyricist, he sang like a nightingale—because that was his natural way of expressing himself. He followed in the footsteps of Campoamor, Núñez de Arce, and Bécquer, and from his youth he succeeded in handling the distinctively Spanish versification with incomparable ease, gracefulness, and beauty.

He was born in Mexico City on June 29, 1852. His father, a prominent member of the conservative party and a high official in the Second Empire, tried to give him a good education. He entered the Preparatory School in 1867 and studied under "The Necromancer" (Don Ignacio Ramírez). Like the sorrowing poet of the "Nocturne," he mistook his road, thinking he was destined for the profession of medicine; but the poverty, loneliness, and desolation that fell upon him—his father in exile and in need—forced him to correct his error. On the point of becoming a physician, he broke away to dedicate his life to literature and journalism. He tried the theater; he became editor of the *Universal Review* and of the *Echo of Both Worlds,* in which he published his first poems. These revealed the spirit of the times and found such favor that soon, during the years 1876 and 1877, Peza was the popular and acclaimed poet of the day, the singer in demand on public occasions. In 1878 he went to Spain as undersecretary of the Mexican legation. His stay in Madrid was very profitable, considering his poetic personality. There he found and purified his style; he nourished his spirit; he was loved and feted; he had intimate contact with the intellectual leaders of city and court; he contributed to the *Spanish and American Illustrated Magazine.* Through the writing of magazine articles and the publication of his anthology, *The Mexican Lyric,* he introduced the poets of his country to Spain. In fine, he developed there a great and sincere love of Spain that he was never to lose.

On his return to Mexico, a family tragedy wounded him to the depths. Then the sonorous poet, hearty, extravagant, and a little rhetorical, who had sung of love and native land, found his true self in sorrow; he became the singer of home and children. His muse, full of resigned sadness, tenderness, and kindness, gave him lordship over a realm that no one today—perhaps ever—will dispute with him: the realm where life had torn him—the realm of home. His *Songs of the Hearth,* a book unique in Mexican lyric poetry, increased his popularity in his own country and even beyond its borders. No other Mexican poet has been so well known abroad; and as proof of this statement, it is sufficient to mention only one of the most beautiful and typical poems of that collection, "Guns and Dolls," which has been translated into German, Portuguese, Italian, Russian, Hungarian, and Japanese.

But it is said truly that there is no fame without bitterness; and when he had become well known, Peza was attacked mercilessly by the critics. New winds were blowing, and they carried lyric poetry into novel paths. But the poet would concede nothing to the new schools. He remained faithful to the Spanish tradition; nevertheless, as he gained in years and experience, he became more and more personal, showing a feeling more his own, and he succeeded in achieving effects as genuine, as full of originality and color as that exemplified in one of his most famous poems, "In My Ward." Styles in poetry had changed, but he never ceased to sing in his own manner. He was always a poet—in the professor's chair, in the public forum, in the editor's chair, and on the benches of Congress: a full-voiced, rhetorical poet when he tried to blow the trumpet note of the epic; a poet of the inner life, all feeling and tenderness, when, in a hushed tone, he wrote the autobiography of his heart. And thus death found him in his native city on March 16, 1910.

Vast was the poetic production of Peza. To show this, the enumeration of the titles of his works is sufficient: *Poems* (1873), *Song to the Native Land* (1876), *Hours of Passion* (1876), *Songs of the Hearth* (1884), *Some Unpublished Verses* (1885), *Complete Poems* (1886), *The Old Muse* (1889), *Patriotic Lyric* (1890), *Home and Country* (1891), *The Harp of Love* (1891), *Memories and Hopes* (1892), *Flowers of the Soul* (1893), *Selected Poems* (1897), *Historical, Traditional, and Fantastic Legends of the Streets of Mexico* (1898), *Monologues and Songs to the Fatherland and Its Heroes* (1900), *Mexican Legends and Traditions* (1900), and *Daisy Petals* (1910).

His prose work includes *Mexican Poets and Writers* (1877); *Charity in Mexico* (1880); *Memories, Relics, and Portraits* (1900), a most pleasant book of anecdotes, containing interesting data for our literary history; and, lastly, *Benito Juárez* (1904).

To conclude, Peza's work for the theater is worth mentioning; he wrote the comedy entitled *The Science of the Home* (1873) and two dramas: *Last Moments of Columbus* (1874) and *An Epilogue of Love* (1875).

Other Poets

The deliberation and moderation praised by Altamirano has a representative in Agustín F. Cuenca, a poet who was born in Mexico City in 1850 and died there in 1884. He was a student in the Academy of San Ildefonso and later in the Conciliar Seminary. In 1870 he entered the School of Jurisprudence to study law, but he interrupted his course quickly in order to consecrate himself to journalism and letters.

Limited in quantity, but exquisite, was the poetic work of Cuenca. It reveals him as a poet of delicate shadings that sometimes reach the subtle; for this reason, some traces of Gongorism, if not *conceptismo,* are thought to show faintly in him. Two elements, the erotic and the descriptive, dominate in his poetry and often intermingle. His amorous compositions—"Rose of Fire," "Carmen," "August Sun"—have a pleasing smoothness and beauty that heighten the subdued melancholy. In some of his descriptive poems—"On the Banks of the Atoyac," "The Lane," and "The Mountain"—without recourse to outward and merely superficial nationalism, he achieves such freshness of vision, such deep and harmonious coloring, and, above all, such sincerity of feeling that they can be considered a true transcription of nature.

In technical mastery, refinement, beauty of sound and of style, Cuenca suggests, in a way, the modernists; Manuel Toussaint, who, in 1920, edited a collection of Cuenca's *Selected Poems*, suspects that he shows a trace of French influence. Having died at the age of thirty-four, Cuenca had no chance to develop fully a personality that, nevertheless, showed itself to be vigorous and original. In 1881 his play, *The Iron Chain*, was published. His work has been thoroughly and intelligently studied by Francisco Monterde in *Agustín F. Cuenca: Prosewriter and Poet of Transition* (Mexico, 1942).

Don Vicente Riva Palacio is a clear and restrained poet, but he was not very productive. His qualities and the essentially national stamp he put on his poetry give him a place in Altamirano's group; three of his sonnets—"The Escorial," "To the Wind," "Old Age"—have merited the honor of inclusion in anthologies. Within this group, likewise, should come José María Bustillos (1866-1899), a disciple of Altamirano, whom he resembled in his descriptive ability, though his work has less color and more inner delicacy and melancholy. His qualities may be seen in such poems as "Hummingbirds," "Close to the River," "In the Night," "Summer Nocturne," and "The Cave of Cicalco," a poem of indigenous inspiration.

The Romanticists

Romanticism with all that it means: exaltation, passion, rebellion —romanticism still rooted in the Spanish tradition of Zorrilla, Espronceda, and Bécquer—had its culmination in a poet who was a romantic in life as well as in poetry, Manuel Acuña.

Manuel Acuña

Manuel Acuña hardly has a biography. Two dates, almost alone, comprise it: August 26, 1849, the date of his birth in Saltillo, Coahuila; and December 6, 1873, the day of his tragic death in Mexico City. Between the one and the other come his first childish writings, his first schooldays in his native city, his decision to come to the capital, in 1865, to begin the study of medicine, a hopeless love affair, his youthful songs . . .

These immortalized him.

Acuña was not a finished poet, but he was a talented one. Before him, there had been poets in Mexico; with him came—briefly—the great poet. He lacked the time to reach his destined place. He had no chance to cultivate his taste, broaden his intellectual scope, achieve full mastery of style. Here and there, in the lyrics of his student days, may be found coarseness, slovenliness, poor diction, and even visible traces of his favorite poets, who, beyond doubt, were Hugo, Espronceda, and Campoamor. But, in spite of all, how personal and fascinating he is, how able to call up images! In all his verses there is a poetic power never before equaled in Mexico—a power that occasionally lifts him to the summits.

He was, by temperament, a morbid emotionalist; by contagion, he became a materialist and a skeptic. Filled with homesickness and faith, he had come from the patriarchal atmosphere of his province; and the flower of his youth opened in a new world where science was being elevated to the category of dogma. He became lost in doubt. Nevertheless, materialism and skepticism could not stifle the pure, simple, superlatively human expression of his feelings. On the contrary, his muse, moving through the dense air of the dissecting room and stopping before the sad, sodden, inert flesh, found somehow the way to turn such material into poetry. And therein lies his originality. In "The Man" and "The Prostitute," the incredulous and desperate student rants and screams; but in "Tears" and "Then and Now," the soul, all tenderness and devotion, calls back the memory of a faithful home, peaceful and far away. Beside the dogmatic materialist in "Before a Corpse" stands the enamored romantic of "Nocturne," essentially spiritual and chaste, and the melancholy dreamer of "Dry Leaves." At the side of the emphatic denier of the hereafter is the hearty humorist of the "Rondelet" and "Country Life."

Two of the aforementioned poems mark the culmination of Acuña's poetic genius and show, too, the conflict of forces—the moral problem—which vexed his troubled soul. The first, "Nocturne," ranks as one of the most beautiful love songs in Mexican poetry. The second, "Before a Corpse," is, in the judgment of Menéndez y Pelayo, "one of the most vigorous works of inspiration that has honored the Spanish poetry of our times"; in it Acuña shows himself to be so much the poet that he "could change the harshest and most desolating doctrine into a flood of immortal harmonies."

His short, sad life was a flash of lightning that illuminates a moment and is gone. When, on an unlucky day for Mexican letters, the young poet—twenty-four years of age—took his own life, Mexico mourned not only the poet who had been, but the poet that might have been.

The poems of Acuña were collected in a posthumous edition that was published the year following his death. The theater owes to him one drama, a play of unrestrained romantic fury: "The Past," which was staged in 1872. His complete works appear in Porrúa's *Collection of Mexican Authors*, with a critical study by José Luis Martínez.

Manuel M. Flores

Manuel Acuña's cry of hopeless spiritual passion was converted by Manuel M. Flores into a cry of sensual desire. The poet of *Passion Flowers* was less versatile and profound than the author of the "Nocturne," but he surpassed Acuña in perfection of style and taste, probably because he attained a full and normal development.

Little is known of the life of Flores; perhaps it burned like a bonfire until it consumed itself. He was born in San Andrés Chalchicomula in 1840. In 1857, he was in Mexico City, studying philosophy in the Academy of Letrán; "he was"—Altamirano tells us—"a youth of sixteen years, dark-skinned, pale, with black eyes and thick curly hair, sad and frail in appearance." He studied little; he confined himself to his room, and there, indolently settling himself, would watch with an absentminded air the spirals of smoke from his enormous German pipe. He was a misanthrope; and, shrouded in mystery, he would write verses—melancholy and passionate poems of love. Soon, he was taking a part in the literary meetings in the room of Altamirano, who thought he saw in the intractable youth a strange resemblance to Tibullus. In 1859, Flores left school, which seemed a prison to him, and abandoned himself to a free and Bohemian life in the company of "two black Andalusian eyes that fascinated and intoxicated." Freed at last from his Circe and finding his literary friends scattered because of the political storm, he became affiliated with the liberal party, fighting for his ideas with pen and sword. Later, serving as a soldier against the French invaders, he was made prisoner and confined in the Castle of Perote. On the re-establishment of the Republic, he served several times as a deputy to the Congress of the Union; and with these activities he concluded his public service. Afterward, his existence, which seems to have been filled with inner torments, vacillated between love and poetry until it was lost in obscurity. He died—poor, blind, and forgotten—in Mexico City in 1885. His poems had appeared three years previously under the title of *Passion Flowers*.

Popular acclaim has given Flores a niche as an erotic poet, and criticism is accustomed to confine itself to this phase exclusively. But he was not solely the singer of Eros, though he was principally concerned with the erotic. There is something more in his poetry than sensual delight and burning lasciviousness: there are sincere and naked sorrow, restrained tenderness, painful remorse, mystical memories, feelings of patriotism, humorous touches. Also, there are exquisite translations and imitations of Byron, Hugo, Lamartine, Shakespeare, Dante, Schiller, Lessing, and Heine; and, though presumably not all of these were direct translations, they show an uncommon literary background, as well as the varied feelings of the author.

Nevertheless, to the public "the erotic bard" means Flores; and there is no lack of reason for the identification. He thought continually about women; he lived for women: they are always present in his poems, sometimes in the dedications—"To Rosario," "To Ramona," "To Clementina," "To Carmen"—sometimes in poems inspired by the prevailing heroines. "Under the purple finery of his poetry," says Luis G. Urbina, "his muse trembles with desire like an aroused Bacchante." His eroticism is not rhetorical and artificial like that of the innocent neo-classic lovers of Phyllis and Amaryllis; it is not simulated and affected like that of some of the romanticists. Urbina himself, who knew Flores, says that "a sensual flame lapped at his inspiration until it consumed it," and the poet "perished in the same fire that blazes in his passionate songs."

In the development of Mexican romanticism, Flores represents a vibrant and rhythmic carnal desire. The sensuality and glow of his poems—"Eve," "Your Image," "Under the Palms," "Come"—give the sensation not only of provoking a feverish ardor in the poet but of communicating that ardor to the atmosphere and surroundings. Under the influence of an insatiable passion, Flores is an admirable painter of tropical landscapes; and nude Eve gives his palette magic colors for painting the night and the dawn.

Certainly, this type of poetry, soft and lascivious, ends by boring us, and the predominance of a single insistent note denies variety of feeling and emotion to the work of the author of *Passion Flowers*. But precisely for that one element—because he is unique in the field of erotic poetry—Manuel M. Flores holds a distinctive place in our lyric poetry.

José Rosas Moreno

José Rosas Moreno represents, in contrast to the preceding poets, a moderate type of romanticism, so mild that he might almost be placed between the classic poets of the former generation and those representing the culmination of romanticism.

Rosas Moreno's life was humble and respectable like his muse. He was born in Lagos, Jalisco, on August 14, 1838, and died there on July 13, 1883. From early youth he dedicated himself to literature, and he was no stranger—no one could be in his time—to politics. He became a liberal and experienced persecution and imprisonment. After the restoration of the Republic in 1867, he served at various times as deputy to the general Congress; he was a well-known figure in the theater; and he held, from time to time, the most inconspicuous public offices. But the greater part of his life he passed in obscurity under difficult conditions, resorting to the composition of school texts for a living. Because of his simple and kindly spirit, he was destined to be the children's poet. He is considered, in fact, the greatest Mexican writer of fables, and his fine tales are the best known and most important of his poetic works.

His lyrics are characterized by grace and gentleness rather than by passion; he wrote verse with ease; he expressed himself with neat clarity. Certainly, we cannot find in him elevation of thought or extreme originality of inspiration. He is a poet in a minor key. In his "Twilight Sadness," "The Mocking-bird," and "Country Life," and especially in the stanzas of "The Valley of My Childhood," may be found the most personal accents of this poet, who was all tenderness and delicate sentiment.

The best collection of Rosas Moreno's poems is *Cluster of Violets,* which was published in 1891.

Minor Romantic Poets

In the current of romanticism, in this period, the following minor poets played a part: Luis G. Ortiz (1835-1894), who had classic tendencies and made many excellent translations of Italian poetry; Josefa Murillo (1860-1898), a sensitive poetess of Veracruz, whose lyre resounded on the banks of the Papaloapan; Laura Méndez de Cuenca (1853-1928), a spirited inspirer of Agustín F. Cuenca, her husband, and herself a poet of pleasant inspiration; Esther Tapia de Castellanos (1824-1897), whose copious works were not always perfect in form; Isabel Pesado de Mier y Celis (1828-1913), much inclined toward doleful complaints; Manuel Caballero (1851-1925), an industrious journalist and a romantic poet when he sang; José I. Novelo, who has published several volumes of lyric poetry: *April* (1936), *Man and Other Poems* (1938), *Last April* (1939), *Last Roses* (1944); Adalberto Esteva (1863-1914); Antonio Zaragoza (1855-1910); José Peón del Valle (1866-1924); Ignacio M. Luchichí; Javier Santa María (1843-1910); and Celedonio Junco de la Vega (1863-1948).

THE CLASSICISTS

This group, small in number, was headed by two poets who were excellent humanists: Montes de Oca and Pagaza.

Montes de Oca y Obregón

Don Ignacio Montes de Oca y Obregón was born in the city of Guanajuato on June 26, 1840. Because he revealed definite talent at an early age, his father, a distinguished lawyer, decided to give him a most careful education. He studied first in England and then in Rome, where he was an outstanding student in the *Colegio Pío Latino Americano* and in the *Academia de Nobles*. At seventeen, the young Mexican spoke seven languages and could write prose and verse, perfectly, in four of them: English, French, Italian, and Latin. Needless to say, he had also acquired a thorough education in the language and literature of his own race, and he added to it continually. Having become familiar with the great Greco-Latin and Spanish models, he was a classicist by principle: "I have held on," he once said, "to the experience of the centuries."

Ordained as priest in the Eternal City on February 28, 1863, and being also a Doctor of Theology and of both canon and civil law, it was natural that he should occupy high ecclesiastical posts. On returning to Mexico in 1865, he was—during the short duration of the Empire—Maximilian's chaplain *de honor*. In 1871, when he was barely thirty, he was consecrated bishop. He served first at Tamaulipas, then at Linares, and, lastly, at San Luis Potosí, of which diocese he remained the head until the end of his life. Death came to him suddenly in New York on August 18, 1921, just as he was returning to his country after a long absence.

Monsignor Montes de Oca had the stateliness and dignity of a Renaissance prelate. A man of keen intelligence, vast culture, and genuine literary ability, he enjoyed solid prestige in his country and in Europe, to which he made innumerable trips and where he lived at various times. From his youth, the "Arcadians" of Rome accepted him as their own, under the pastoral name of "Ipandro Acaico." The Royal Academy of Spain called him to membership; and, among other marks of distinction, gave him the honor of delivering the eulogy of Miguel de Cervantes at the solemn ceremonies held in 1905 to celebrate the tercentenary of *Don Quixote*.

He was a consummate humanist and, at the same time, an illustrious orator and poet. By the force of that combination, he is entitled to rank with the best Mexican humanists of the eighteenth century. He made the first complete Spanish translation of Pindar, the master of the lyric, and also of the pastoral poets Theocritus, Bion, and Moschus. He knew Greek thoroughly and cultivated by preference, according to Menéndez y Pelayo, the strictest and most difficult of the Spanish metrical forms: *octavas*, tercets, sonnets. In his translations, there can be found occasionally some prosaic or rough lines; but, in the manner of a true poet, he always knew how to translate the Greek songs with beauty and grace. "His translations," Don Miguel Antonio Caro has said, "keep that original fragrance that is lost in second-hand translations; and his commentaries reveal the competence of the translator as a Greek humanist." In his original poetry, he is perfectly and undeniably classical, but classical with a dexterity, a beauty of style, a sensitiveness that were not, certainly, common before his time. In particular, there is one form—the sonnet—which he handled like a master and of which he has left abundant examples.

His prose works—and the prose of "Ipandro Acaico" is not inferior to the poetry—fill eight thick volumes of his *Pastoral and Oratorical Works* (1883-1913). In these appear—besides the notable pieces of sacred oratory—beautiful discussions of literature and the funeral orations that were published in a separate edition in the *Collection of Spanish Writers* (Madrid, 1901).

The work of the humanist and poet includes: *Greek Bucolic Poets* (1877); *Odes of Pindar* (1881); *Poetic Pastimes* (1878), this last book containing his original poems from youth to maturity—odes, hymns, songs, elegies, satires, sonnets; the poem *Fiesco*; the *Memories and Meditations of a Pilgrim in the Castle of Miramar*; and, lastly, some translations of Anacreon and of Greek epigrams. In addition, there are the books written during the prelate's last years—an extraordinary evidence of vitality, almost incredible in an octogenarian. From 1914, when he returned to Europe, to the eve of his death, he published *At the Banks of the Rivers: One Hundred Sonnets* (1916); *The Rape of Helen* (1917), a verse translation of a Greek poem by Coluto of Licopolis; *Another Hundred Sonnets by Ipandro Acaico* (1918); *The Argonautica* (2 vols., 1919-20), the epic poem by Apollonius of Rhodes, translated into Spanish verse at the request of the Royal Academy of Spain; *A New Century of Sonnets* (1921); and *Sonetos jubilares* (1921), his last work.

Joaquín Arcadio Pagaza

Monsignor Joaquín Arcadio Pagaza—an emulator of Montes de Oca—was a poet of magnificent inspiration, possessing the greatest and deepest sensibility among our genuine classicists.

Born in the Valley of Bravo (state of Mexico) on January 6, 1839, Pagaza received his elementary education in his native village. His teacher—a priest, who was no ignorant memorizer of the mass, but a genuine humanist—initiated him into the knowledge of Latin and philosophy. Choosing the priesthood as his vocation, Pagaza went to Mexico City and entered the seminary. Ordained a priest in 1862, he served in modest curacies for twenty years. His talents drew him, little by little, from the obscurity he had humbly sought, until he was made bishop of Veracruz on May 1, 1895. From that time on, he lived in Jalapa, where he was busy with religious and literary work up to the time of his death on September 11, 1918.

As the Most Illustrious Monsignor Montes de Oca said in a fine phrase, Pagaza was "a tireless bee in the depth of the cloister of San Camilo, hidden in the woods of the Valley of Bravo. There, during long years, in silence, he had been building panels of fine honey." When he emerged, timidly, from the shadows, he was greeted as a great poet.

Among the Arcadians of Rome he was known by the name of "Clearco Meonio." Already famous as a humanist, he translated Horace and Virgil. Sometimes paraphrasing, sometimes giving a literal rendering, he always made his translations incomparably graceful and beautiful. His success led Menéndez y Pelayo to say that Pagaza "is beyond gainsay one of the most polished classical poets who today adorn Spanish literature." He was not only a translator but an original poet, a metrist with absolute mastery; and in his pure, crystalline verses, besides the delightful form, there is an indefinable sweetness that makes him the best of our pastoral poets.

Pagaza's first and most celebrated work is *Murmurs of the Forest* (1887). This was followed by *Mary: Fragments from a Poem Descriptive of the Tropics* (1890) and *Some Intimate Ballads* (1893). *Horace* and *Virgil,* his great translations from the Latin, were published in Jalapa in 1905 and 1907, respectively. For some years before his death, he was occupied with preparing for publication the *Complete Works* of Virgil, translated into Spanish verse, but he succeeded in publishing only the first volume (1913). Lastly, it should not be forgotten that one of Pagaza's most beautiful original compositions— "Challenge"—appears in the *Literary Crown,* published on the occasion of Archbishop Labastida's Jubilee.

José María Vigil

Don José María Vigil, the eminent and voluminous writer, deserves a place among the well-known humanists, if not among our best classical poets. Born in Guadalajara, Jalisco, on October 11, 1829, he died in Mexico City on February 18, 1909. He studied Latin and philosophy in the seminary at Guadalajara and law in the university of his state. Soon, however, he interrupted his study of law in order to enter the struggle for the liberal cause, of which he was an ardent and sincere supporter. When Santa Anna's regime fell and the Revolution of Ayutla triumphed, he founded in Guadalajara the *Revolution,* a periodical in which he defended the principles of the Reform movement. His early activities were divided equally between politics and letters. He established literary reviews and societies; he taught Latin and philosophy in the State Lyceum for Young Men, thus contributing to the spread of culture in the West. During the Wars of Reform and the French Intervention, he gave strong support, in his country and abroad, to the cause of national independence. When the Republic was restored and he had been elected deputy to the Congress of the Union, he went to Mexico City; and for the remainder of his long, exemplary, and rich life, he was, successively, a justice of the Supreme Court; a journalist and defender of the new constitutional principles in the heated controversies of the day; a scholarly publicist, to whom we owe the printing of Las Casas' *History of the Indies* and Tezozomoc's *Chronicle;* and, lastly, a director of the National Library, a position he held until his death. As head of the library, he began the work—still incomplete—of cataloguing that rich bibliographical treasury.

As poet, historian, dramatist, and critic, Vigil was a prolific writer.

Poetry was, for him, the expression of youth. His collected poems appeared in a bulky volume entitled *Dreams and Chimeras* (1857), which was followed by *Flowers of Anáhuac* (1886) in two volumes, the second containing his plays. His inspiration was not exceptional; and his poems, all of a classical pattern, suffer often from formlessness and *prosaísmo.* His works as a humanist, in his authoritative translations, is worth much more than his original poetry. His Spanish verse translations of the *Satires* of Persius (1879) and of *Thirty Epigrams* of Martial (1899) are considered models of their kind, especially the first, the text of Persius being, according to Menéndez y Pelayo, the "most obscure and enigmatic in all classical Latin." The notes and marginal comments by Vigil are worth as much as the translation itself. Likewise, he made some verse translations of Petrarch and Schiller, and translated Ponsard's *Charlotte Corday.*

Manuel José Othón

Manuel José Othón was fundamentally a classicist despite the complexity of his literary personality.

He was born in San Luis Potosí on June 14, 1858, and died there on November 28, 1906. Though a poet by nature, he was a lawyer by profession; and, practicing law reluctantly, with more resemblance to Don Quixote than to the average judge, he spent his life in small villages in northern Mexico—when he was not in complete retirement in the back country of Coahuila, where he wrote his best verse. Except for an occasional trip to the capital, to which his fame spread quickly and where he was loved and admired, his life was passed in the drowsy quietude of the provinces. He enjoyed the delightful tranquillity of the little towns, but he felt absolute freedom only in the open country. And because of this, his poetic work—as Alfonso Reyes has said—"is innocent and kindly—wholesome as an early-rising country woman, steady as a farmer grown old over his plough, holy and profound as a hymn to God in the remotest depths of a forest . . ."

According to Othón's own confession, he wrote verses from his adolescence. These comprised his first *Poems* (1880), which, with stern severity, he refused to acknowledge throughout the years. If he felt any foreign influence, he hastened to throw it off. "The Muse," he wrote,

must not be a strange spirit who comes from the outside to influence us; she must germinate within us, so that we, feeling her inside our bodies, quickened by the touch of Life itself, searching, loving, caressing, can cry out in the holy rapture of wonder and ecstasy, as the father of the human race before his divine and eternal mate: *"Os ex ossibus meis et caro de carne mea!"*

He declared that the artist should be sincere even to the point of naïveté. "We should express nothing we have not seen—no feeling or thought we have not experienced. If we do so, it will not be our spirit that speaks, and we shall be lying to the world and deceiving ourselves."

The result of this theory of aesthetics was *Rustic Poems* (1902), a book in which an irreproachable mastery of form blends with a marvelous outpouring of feeling.

Othón was, by education and literary tastes, a classicist; by temperament, he was something more than a romanticist: he was a modern. Thus he attained the miracle of satisfying equally the devotees of tradition and the extremists among the lyric poets. In reality, like Díaz Mirón, he came to be an isolated—and magnificent—figure in Mexican poetry, without ties with the past or connections with the present. "He succeeded in finding," as Don Francisco A. de Icaza wisely observes,

what can be called a method of his own, within the rigid orthodoxy of the language; and this accounts for his relations with the American purists, who were more insistent perhaps on correctness of language than the Spanish purists themselves. But he was "a man aware of the exterior world" and he copied nature as he saw it, without turning back to conventional models; and the revolutionaries in matters of art, the rebels against routine, proclaimed him an innovator.

"The poet of the field," to us, means Othón, although he in no way resembles the artificial pastoral poets or the pasteboard singers of nature who worked with a classical yardstick. "He does not paint from memory or in a studio," Icaza insists,

but out in the open air and from nature; a landscape artist with a palette of ample and true colors, he can copy anything, but he is more affected by rugged rocks and twisted old trees than by misty landscapes in the half-tones of twilight. He describes admirably, but his true merit lies, not in describing, but in understanding nature and making it loved and felt.

Othón also wrote stories and plays. For the stage he wrote two dramas in verse, *After Death* (1883) and *What Lies Behind Good Fortune* (1886), a dramatic experiment entitled *The Last Chapter* (1905), and two monologues. His *Complete Works,* in one compact volume, including poetry, short stories, short novels, and plays, were published in Mexico City in 1945.

Minor Classical Poets

Because of his humanistic character, Don Joaquín D. Casasús (1858-1916), translator of Horace and Virgil, Catullus and Tibullus, belongs among the classicists of this period. Likewise, with this group should be mentioned the priest Federico Escobedo (born in Salvatierra, Guanajuato, February 8, 1874; died in Puebla, November 13,

1949). His literary work is extensive and includes original poetry in Castilian and in Latin, as well as translations from the Latin. His first book, *Poetry* (1903), contains the best of his early work in Castilian. According to Francisco González Guerrero, his verses "are fluid, transparent, and musical. They travel the road traveled by Horace, but they follow in the footsteps of Fray Luis de León." That volume was followed by *Deep Trenches* (1918), *Biblical Rhapsodies* (1923), *Ever Old and Ever New* (1927), and *Aromas of Legend* (1940). "The poetry, original and in Castilian, of Padre Escobedo" —concluded the above-mentioned critic—"reveals the virtues and limitations of academic origin: meager inspiration and outmoded forms, and it seems to fit the designation of a nice gray tone." His most eminent work is as a translator; and his translation in verse of the Latin poem of Padre Rafael Landívar, with the title *Mexican Georgics,* is outstanding. Escobedo was known among the Arcadians of Rome as Tamiro Miceneo.

A faithful follower and continuator of a tradition that was fading in his day was Don Enrique Fernández Granados (1867-1920), the sweetest Anacreontic poet. His elegantly chiseled poems are—in Gutiérrez Nájera's phrase—"nectar sipped from Ionic flowers." Fernández Granados' poetry was far from being copious; the most characteristic of his poems are collected in two attractive little volumes, *Myrtles* (1889)and *Daisies* (1891). He also made some beautiful translations from Italian poets.

Lastly, the pastoral poet, Juan B. Delgado (a native of Querétaro, born in 1868; died in Mexico City, June 12, 1923) should be mentioned. He was an Arcadian—like some of the preceding—who, as González Martínez says, "conscientiously polished his work, strove for pure, sonorous, and clear language, and is almost a traditionalist in the matter of form." His work comprises several volumes: *Songs of the South* (1900), *Poems of Trees* (1907), *Paris and Other Poems* (1919), *Under the Beechtree of Títiro* (1920), *The Wandering Song Writer* (1927), and *The Country of Rubén Darío* (1932).

THE MODERNISTS

Modernism covers two periods: the first, the period of the direct, though belated, influence of French romanticism—and also Parnassianism—to which Gutiérrez Nájera and several of the poets of the

Azure Review belong; and, second, the culmination of the movement—under the influence of French symbolism—represented by Nervo in his early work and by the poets of the *Modern Review*.

Gutiérrez Nájera

With Manuel Gutiérrez Nájera, a new era in Mexican letters begins. As Isaac Goldberg astutely observes, he introduced melody into the structure of the language; "after him, the verse of the poets flows more smoothly, more musically; the prose is more agile, more luminous, and gleams with a thousand pregnant suggestions, novel images, and evidences of a varied culture." He played a double role in Mexican literature: that of precursor and of reformer.

Born in Mexico City on December 22, 1859, of a modest middle-class family, he inherited sensibility and tenderness from his mother—a woman of extreme piety—and an inclination toward literature from his father. His mother was his first teacher; and since, presumably, she dreamed of devoting him to an ecclesiastical career, she molded the child's spirit through the study of the mystics: Saint Teresa, Saint Juan de la Cruz, Juan de Avila, Malón de Chaide, Friar Luis de León, and Friar Luis de Granada. Later he studied Latin and then French. Precocious as he was, he sent his first article to *La Iberia* when he was thirteen years old and continued to publish prose and verse there. This was to be his mission: to write and write in the dizzy whirl of the daily press. The bare story of Gutiérrez Nájera's life contains nothing of interest: he was a galley slave to journalism. One by one, he passed through the editorial rooms of the principal periodicals: the *Federalist*, the *National Review*, the *Liberal Party* . . . . Sometimes under his own name, sometimes under different pseudonyms—among these "El Duque Job" (The Duke Job) became famous—he flooded the pages of dailies and reviews with a production most varied, most abundant, most original, and—what is most extraordinary and what no other day laborer of letters could attain—most exquisite. He married, he had children, he was the fashionable writer. He lived by letters and for letters. With Don Carlos Díaz Dufoo, he founded the *Azure Review*, which came to have an influence on the literature of the period similar to that exercised by the *Renaissance* of Altamirano. Wearied by his tremendous literary labors, he laid down his day's work while still young (at thirty-five years of age), dying February 3, 1895, in his native city, from which he had hardly ever ventured forth.

But if the external biography of Gutiérrez Nájera tells us little, how rich and fruitful, on the other hand, is his inner biography!

His first songs—"The Cross," "Mary," "God," "The Faith of My Childhood"—were of frankly religious inspiration: the pristine reflection of the piety instilled by his mother. According to Don Justo Sierra, his best critic, whom we shall follow step by step, there can be noticed in the poet "the desire to conform to the venerated models of sacred poetry that contained touches of eroticism and romanticism, a desire that enchanted the generation belonging to the second third of his century"; it seemed, for a moment, that this sublime youngster might be the successor of Carpio and Pesado. But two disturbing elements marked his poetry: eroticism and "Frenchism." The awkward eroticism of Gutiérrez Nájera was not dressed in classical drapery; it was not an empty imitation of the ancients: it was a reflection of a passion, penetrating and sweet, real and voluptuous. On the other hand, if it is certain that he was influenced by Spanish writers, he did not conform to them but went directly to French sources, through which he came in contact with foreign literatures. Thus was a general change prepared and accomplished. These foreign influences, which made him more refined, more subtle in his ideas, at the same time giving new shadings to his expression, he assimilated in such a manner as to convert them into something personal and exclusively his own. Besides the influence of Bécquer and of Campoamor, he felt the influence of all the French poets from the generation of the romanticists up to his contemporaries, that is, from Hugo, Lamartine, and Musset to Richepin, Rollinat, and Verlaine—including Gautier, Baudelaire, and Coppée. According to Sierra,

In the last six or eight years of his life, having attained complete mastery of himself—writing not in the style of his masters, but in a style they would not have repudiated and that was unique in our literature—the poet, "El Duque Job," realized in his writing what he had dreamed of: the amalgamation of the French spirit and the Spanish form. In full march toward the ideal, with the control already acquired over his genius and expression, he was stopped by death's impious, unforeseen stroke.

The quality predominant in Gutiérrez Nájera is *grace*: "a sort of smile of the soul," Sierra says, which gives to all his poems a light and winged rhythm that, penetrating in impalpable waves, like light, through all the nerves of style, lends them a unique magic that produces on the spirit an impression similar to a difficulty conquered without effort—a difficulty that turns into delight and enchantment.

The manifestations of this gift, which prepared the way for the cultivation of his taste, are distinction, dexterity, and elegance of style, plus an imagination as "great as that of an Athenian," an inner delicacy and tenderness of feeling, and the note of graceful and skeptical humor that often tempers the exaltation of his feeling by light, humorous parentheses. He was essentially a romantic and elegiac poet, but was full of the restlessness of his epoch. To interpret this mood, Mexican lyric poetry needed new and more subtle means of expression, and he succeeded in finding them. The upward flight of his muse, always higher—the integration, so to speak, of his vigorous poetic personality on the road toward perfect expression—can be seen in those of his most celebrated compositions that date between 1880 and his death: "For What Purpose?" "Hamlet to Ophelia," "*Tristissima nox,*" "The Duchess Job," "Monologue of the Incredulous One," "Butterflies," "Whiteness," "Schubert's Serenade," "*Pax animae,*" "My Mourning," "*Non omnis moriar,*" and the *Short Odes.*

At the time of the author's death, all that admirable work remained scattered, but the pledge to save it from destruction "was made at the tomb of the poet." In 1896 his poems were collected in one volume, with a preface by Don Justo Sierra; and between 1898 and 1903 his works in prose were published in two volumes. An edition of the *Complete Poetic Works* of Gutiérrez Nájera, remarkably well organized and corrected by Francisco González Guerrero, was published in Porrúa's *Collection of Mexican Authors* in 1953.

His prose works comprise impressions of the theater, literary and social criticism, travel notes, bits of humor, chronicles, fantasies, and the brief stories assembled under the titles *Fragile Stories* and *Stories the Color of Smoke.* Gutiérrez Nájera's prose, as Goldberg has said, "is, in reality, a kind of poetry, a strange commingling of substance and airiness." In literary journalism, "El Duque Job" created a genre on which he put his most personal stamp and by means of which he exercised a powerful influence on two generations of writers—the chronicle. He also gave a new form to the story, a kind of lyric caprice, undoubtedly of French inspiration, in which the humorist, now frivolous, now bitter, and the poet, inwardly mournful, roam through the fields of reality and fantasy, sometimes rising to planes of transcendental meditation, as in "Rip-Rip" and the "History of a Counterfeit Peso," the major successes of Gutiérrez Nájera in this genre.

Salvador Díaz Mirón

Salvador Díaz Mirón, though wilfully and loftily confined to gloomy isolation, far from literary struggles and cliques, played a significant part among the precursors of modernism. This solitary, this aristocrat, who seemed to live his private life in a fortified tower, far from the rabble and in contemplation of vast horizons, influenced Darío and Chocano in the first stage of his poetic production and, in the second, carried his eagerness for reform to such an extreme that his works reveal him as a personality *sui generis,* not only in Mexican lyric poetry, but in the poetry of the Spanish-speaking world.

A native of Veracruz (born December 14, 1853; died June 12, 1928), the man had a personality no less remarkable than that of the poet. "He was an exceptional being," Urbina defines him,

a figure of knightly legend, endowed with a temperament eager always for action just as his mind was eager for perception. He provoked admiration and dread. He was like an artist of the Renaissance. He would bear comparison with the Italian masters—in the variety of his knowledge, with Leonardo da Vinci; in impulsiveness and valor, with Benvenuto Cellini.

He took part in the parliamentary tribune and the press; he knew prison and exile. But it is doubtful that his existence was ever centered on anything that separated him from his intense, incessant preoccupation with literature.

In his early work he was a romantic, a romantic in whose heightened sensibility there was already the impetuosity of violence. Then, laying aside softness and tears, loves and sorrows, the heroic poet appeared, all arrogance, courage, and brilliance—the poet who summoned up the singer of *Manfred* and the thunderer of *Les Châtiments.* To this epoch belong "To Glory," "*Sursum,*" "To Byron," and "Ode to Victor Hugo." Díaz Mirón's inspiration was burning lava, and his lines have the strength and resonance of a trumpet. But the poet had higher aspirations. Revering purity of language and aspiring to create a new technique, he imposed upon himself the severity of a Cyclopean discipline. His mind, eager for perfection, as Isaac Goldberg has said in a picturesque simile, "was no longer the crater of a volcano, but the atelier of an Olympic sculptor, hewing statues from mountains of marble." To quote Urbina,

Each time he demanded more of himself; he sought an absolute purity and precision of expression. He conceived a technique in which not only each syllable but each letter should have a harmonious setting, so that, combined in the accentual unity of each line, they would attain a rhythmical ideal, a music without opaqueness or dissonances, without hiatuses or cacophonies. And like his prosodic ideal is the verbal one, which would preclude the rhyming of two adjectives, and the syntactical ideal, which would dispense with the article, when possible, in order to approach the Latin style and to give lapidary polish and epigrammatic conciseness to the language.

From such an effort was born *Lascas* (*Chips of Stone*, 1901), the work that Díaz Mirón, haughtily disdaining his previous poetry (never to be forgotten), declared his "only book." In like manner originated his *Splinters and Triumphs,* a work of the same or even greater elaboration, which the poet did not publish, although selections from it are known and have appeared in anthologies. In what can be considered his definitive manner—a style he used until his death—it is thought that Díaz Mirón lost in spontaneity, in communicative and direct emotion, whatever he gained in marvelous plastic and rhythmic richness through increased knowledge. In his desire for perfection, which sometimes made him enigmatic and mannered, he resembled Góngora, to whom he had an obvious kinship. Thus, while he was ascending toward the dreamed-of goal, more and more he was withdrawing from the multitude who were intoxicated with the music of his early poems. And he who had begun as a popular poet was in danger of converting himself into a poet of the decaying aristocracy.

  Mexico paid her last homage to Díaz Mirón by transferring his mortal remains to the capital of the Republic, in order to give them solemn burial in the Rotunda of Illustrious Men.

  The *Complete Poetic Works* (1876-1928) of Díaz Mirón, containing the most complete biography yet written, notes, and a bibliography, were published in 1941 by Antonio Castro Leal, and a later edition was published by Porrúa in the *Collection of Mexican Authors*.

Luis G. Urbina

Luis G. Urbina can be considered in many respects the direct successor of Gutiérrez Nájera.

Born in the City of Mexico on February 8, 1869, he represents, in our literature, a singular instance of intellectual development. It can be said of him that he was his own master and that he showed from his childhood a well-marked personality—the same personality, indeed, that was to be revealed, without substantial alteration, at the end of his fruitful, rich, and multiform literary life.

He was very precocious. Before he was twenty years old, he had made his mark in the field of literary journalism that he was later to dominate completely—first, with the chronicle, light, fine, contemporary, overflowing with wit, humor, and poetry, in which he followed "El Duque Job," although elevating the genre to its highest perfection and giving it an undeniably personal stamp; then, with theatrical criticism, over which he exercised mastery, brilliantly, for more than two decades, holding the chair of literary arbiter in improvisations of real literary beauty; lastly, with his poems, which, alternating with his obstinate, indefatigable labor in prose, reminded the public that the commentator on the daily scene and the theatrical reviewer was also a lofty poet. Poet, chronicler, journalist, critic and historian of literature, he was able to carry on his exemplary activity without wearing out his spirit and without enfeebling in the least the literary quality of work that was produced under pressure most of the time and was, in itself, copious. At the side of Justo Sierra, he worked in the Secretariat of Public Instruction and Fine Arts. For many years he taught literature in the National Preparatory School. In collaboration with Pedro Henríquez Ureña and Nicolás Rangel, he conducted the very important research into literary history that formed the basis for the *Centennial Anthology* (1910); the masterly introduction to this book was his own work. He directed the National Library. He carried out a cultural mission to Argentina, delivering there a series of lectures on Mexican literature which were published under the title *The Literary Life of Mexico* (1917); an edition of this is included in Porrúa's *Collection of Mexican Authors*. And, again away from his own country, he continued his literary work, first in Cuba and then in Spain, writing various books and articles for the press.

Urbina's songs of adolescence appeared in one volume called *Poems* (1890); those of his youth were published twelve years later in *Ingenuas* (1902). Even in these books, Urbina revealed himself as he was—as he would always be. The fundamental characteristic of his whole work is its homogeneity. Ideas and sentiments that inspired his poems could and did vary, according to periods, so that it is possible for us to place the poet within these periods; but the aesthetics that gives shape to them remains the same. Urbina, as González Martínez has said, was revealed in all his splendid integrity from the first, and his later efforts were limited to intensifying his poetic sensibility and to mastering form. Without themes of artificial novelty, without abstruse subject matter, without pedantic subtleties, and with only the old, rich emotional tradition of love, pain, life, and death, he constructed "a work of aesthetic unity that can serve for example and edification to those who wander along barren roads without finding the desired path." As a sincere artist who knew his way from the first moment, he walked imperturbably among the perils of literary fads.

Urbina had in common with Gutiérrez Nájera—apart from certain perceptible but indefinable traits of mind—the music, the humor, and the sadness of his poetry. But he differed from him in that his inspiration was free from foreign influences, his melancholy deeper and more penetrating, and his verse, though musical ("predominantly melodic," according to Icaza) is essentially plastic—the reverse of "El Duque Job's" poetry.

All these qualities are accentuated in *Sunsets* (1910), a book of poems that in essence are identical with his earlier poetry, but more finished, more profound, and of still greater technical mastery. The landscape artist who was already partly revealed in *Ingenuas* comes here to his full splendor; he reaches a high point in the "Poem of the Lake" and, above all, in a form that was his own: the *Vespertinas*, those "little twilight scenes," as Manuel Toussaint defines them, "in which the landscape, a grave and silent collaborator, winds itself about an emotion and inspires poetry by its very presence."

In *Lámparas en agonía* (*Dying Lamps,* 1914), the poet shows himself to be wiser, more autumnal: "He has reached the point where he can talk with Life," González Martínez writes, "about those things that are known only at forty." The tendency toward digression is carried to an extreme; the old irony is sweetened. With this book a cycle in the poet's life is closed. Afterward, absence from his country deepened the meditative attitude, the painful note. His last books—*The Glossary of Ordinary Life* (1916), *The Trickster Heart* (1920), *The Last Birds* (1924), and *The Songbook of the Serene Night,* published in a posthumous edition by the National University of Mexico in 1941—add the bitterness of nostalgia to his distinctive melancholy.

Urbina's prose work is much more abundant than his poetry. It can be said that, without counting the aforementioned volumes of literary criticism, his writings dealing with theatrical and literary events fill a whole epoch of Mexican journalism; furthermore, of that part of his work, little has been collected—only *Lively Stories and Imaginary Chronicles* (1915), *Sick Psyche* (1922), and *Men and Books* (1923). To these should be added the volumes that contain the poet's impressions in foreign lands, especially Spain: *Under the Sun and Facing the Sea* (1916), *Travel Sketches* (1919), and *Lights of Spain* (1924). A two-volume edition containing Urbina's complete poems, with a study by Antonio Castro Leal, was published by Porrúa in their *Collection of Mexican Authors.*

As a prose-writer, Urbina had, besides mastery of form, one distinguishing quality: the art of captivating. His prose is polished, flexible, richly hued, prodigal of images. The art critic seems always full of profound suggestion; and as a commentator on the life of the day, he undoubtedly united a wise, observing spirit with a capacity for emotion, attractive and easily shared, which resolves itself in friendliness.

Amado Nervo

Amado Nervo was born in Tepic (capital of the present state of Nayarit)on August 27, 1870. "My surname," the poet declares in a short autobiography,

is Ruiz de Nervo; my father modified it by shortening it. He was called Amado, and he gave me his name. The result, then, would be Amado Nervo; and this, which seemed to be a pseudonym—many in America believed it to be—and which at any rate is a rare name, was perhaps of no little value to my literary career.

His childhood slipped by in the quiet of his native city. He was the firstborn of seven children, and soon revealed his inclination toward literature. "I began to write while I was still what is called a child; and on one occasion my mother found some verses that I had written secretly and she read them to the whole family assembled around the table. I hid in a corner. My father frowned . . ." He would not frown again for the same reason. Soon thereafter, the precocious artist was left fatherless. His mother, Doña Juana de Ordaz, then decided to send him to the little Michoacán village of Jacona, near Zamora, to study at the school established there—a school famous at that time. Nervo entered that institution in 1884, at the age of thirteen; and there, as his friend Don Perfecto Méndez Padilla says, he passed "the first years of his adolescence studying the Spanish of Cervantes, translating Horace and Virgil, and, at the same time, studying the languages of Shakespeare and Corneille . . ." The following year the Nervo family moved to Zamora. From the Academy of Jacona, in which he had spent two years, the future poet proceeded to the Seminary of Zamora, where, from 1886 to 1888, he pursued the course in sciences and philosophy and, in 1889, devoted himself to studying the first year's work in law; but the law department was abolished by the seminary in 1890, and he remained out of school the whole of that year. His first love, meanwhile, had borne fruit; he produced his first prose pieces and songs. Suddenly, "fascinated by the zeal of the Altar" (as Don Alfonso Méndez Plancarte expressed it), he re-entered the Seminary of Zamora in 1891 and began the study of theology. There the charm of the religious life entered into him, and he engulfed himself in mystical studies and practices, those studies and practices that were to have so much influence in shaping his spirit and his literary personality. He took the road toward the priesthood. His destiny, however, willed that he should be driven to walk profane paths. Compelled by the financial distress of his family, he left the seminary at the end of the year and flung himself into the struggle for existence.

For confronting life, he had only one weapon: his pen. After a short stay in Tepic, to which he returned, he went to Mazatlán.

There he was initiated into journalism; next, he went to Mexico City, where, during the years 1894 to 1898, he became known not only through articles, translations, and chronicles published frequently in the periodicals, but also through his first literary works. In 1895, the publication of a daring novel—*El Bachiller*—inevitably stirred up sharp controversies and established his name. In the following year, a poem recited on the first anniversary of Gutiérrez Nájera's death won popularity for him. Two years later, the appearance of the *Mystics* raised him as a poet. With Jesús E. Valenzuela, he founded the *Modern Review*, which was the banner and the rallying place of the devotees of the new poetry. In 1900 he traveled through Europe—a Bohemian journey, footloose, ecstatic, full of tribulations and struggles, which served to complete and perfect his artistic education. On his return to Mexico, without giving up his literary work, he occupied —briefly—a professor's chair, continued practicing journalism, and in 1905 embraced a diplomatic career, establishing himself in Madrid. He remained there until 1918, when his government called him home at the full height of his literary celebrity and glory. Named minister plenipotentiary to Argentina and Uruguay, he set out for the republics of the Plata, and died suddenly in Montevideo on May 24, 1919. His body was brought in state to Mexico, and he was given the most solemn funeral rites ever accorded any poet in America.

Although he had earnestly desired to reduce his production to "one little tome," "a book single and unique," Nervo wrote a great deal. Twenty-nine volumes form his *Complete Works*, published between 1920 and 1928, in Madrid—under the supervision of Alfonso Reyes—after his death. Besides these, the book called *Poet's Morning* must also be counted. This was published by Don Alfonso Méndez Plancarte in 1938 and contains some authentic scribbling of the poet: a few autobiographical pages; a handful of stories and poems, which assuredly their author never would have given to the press; all this accompanied by the collector's own preliminary study and appendices, which are very valuable for the understanding of Nervo's life and work.

Three stages mark the development of Amado Nervo's poetic production. Belonging to the first are *Black Pearls* (1898), *Poems* (1901), *The Exodus and Wayside Flowers: Lira Heroica* (1902), *The Inner Gardens* (1905). In this period the poet was influenced by French symbolism, but this did not prevent him from revealing even then a fully formed personality, original and very much his own. "I acknowledge only one school," he was to declare later, "that of my own deep and eternal sincerity." He is bold, fastidious; he boasts of the freedom with which he breaks the rules of verse; he delights in subtleties, emotions, words, and rare rhythms. There is in him, underneath the lordly elegance, tenderness and a welling up of feeling. He loves life, and he peers into its mystery. His restless youth, a flower that had opened in the perfumed smoke of the altars, was whipped by doubt and held a long debate between "the cursed flesh that kept him from heaven" and the mystic desires born in his home and altered now in the homesickness for his seminary days. For a moment it would seem that mysticism triumphs. But this mysticism is more literary and external than private and profound; it depends, above all, on the golden brilliance of the liturgy; it speaks to us of the reflection of the candles on the priests' vestments; of missals and breviaries, with the red initials standing out; of gleaming vessels for the Host; of many-hued cathedral windows; of adorned altars, overflowing chalices, lofty domes.

Nervo's second phase comes, it would seem, when he separates himself from the dazzling outer world in order to question the deep inner "I." A love encountered suddenly, in the flesh, gives him tranquillity and serenity; and then his first personality is purified and refined: he turns to naturalness and simplicity. It is the hour of the appearance of *In a Low Voice* (1909) and *Serenity* (1914), the two golden fruits of his maturity, which the autumn sun illuminated. In these books a preoccupation with the beyond is predominant; in them is clarified the pantheistic hope that he had already suggested in the earlier period in *"La Hermana Agua"* ("Sister Water"). The poet had reached, as Rubén Darío expressed it, "one of the most difficult points in poetic mountain-climbing: the level ground of simplicity, which is found between the very high peaks and the very deep abysses." "The pompous style" frightened him, he himself said, though he exaggerated when he alluded to his earlier poetry; "the extravagance of the showy adjectives" dismayed him; he searched for "the discreet tone, the half shading, the soft colors"; he knew, at last, how to say what he wished, in the way he wished; no longer did words drive him; "he had won dominion over them."

He was destined to go even farther along this road in his third period. The sudden breaking off of the love that filled his life, the contemplation of death, and the sorrow before irreparable loss led him to complete resignation and an expression of the most eloquent, if not the purest, asceticism. He aspired to elevate his soul and that of the world with books—as he says playfully, though it is unnecessary to take him literally—"without rhetoric, without method, without technique, without literature." And such are *Elevation* (1917); *Plentitude* (1918), a work written in prose, as if the poet, for greater simplicity, had rejected the artifice of rhyme; and, lastly, *The Lotus Pond*, the final collection of poems that Nervo published during his life. *The Constant Lover* and *The Divine Archer* were published posthumously in 1922.

Nervo's prose work is most varied. In addition to essays, chronicles, and articles, it includes the beautiful study of *Juana de Asbaje* (1910) and several novels and stories. We have said that the literary renown of Nervo began with *El Bachiller*, a short novel of bold naturalism. This was followed by *Pascual Aguilera*, a story of pronounced regional flavor; the novelesque fantasy *The Giver of Souls*; and, finally, the short stories collected under the title *Souls That Pass* (1906). Many years were to pass before Nervo returned to the cultivation of fiction; but in 1916 appeared *The Unselfish Devil*; and other short novels followed in sequence: *The Diamond of Restlessness, A Lie, A Dream, The Sixth Sense, Amnesia,* and *Mysterious Stories*. In this man, who was above all a poet, there was also an original novelist: in the first novels and stories that he wrote (all being of Mexican character, but the stories to a greater degree), Nervo is revealed as a most delicate observer and painter of landscapes; the novels of the second period, with the strong initial nationalism lost, belong entirely to the cosmopolitan writer. His prose is nervous, full of vivacity; the evolution toward purity and simplicity proceeded much more rapidly in it than in his poetry.

José Juan Tablada

José Juan Tablada (born in Mexico City on April 3, 1871; died in New York, August 2, 1945) became one of the staunchest supporters and propagandists of the new aesthetics in the *Modern Review*. As poet, as critic of art and literature, as chronicler, novelist, and journalist, the outstanding trait of his character was restlessness.

He appeared at the right moment, occupying an advanced position among the reformers of the lyric. "His metrical art," Valenzuela says, "grated on the hardened ears of the rhyming rule-makers." "It came from his reading and from his own spirit, complete, polished and cut like a jewel in the style of Théophile Gautier, and made poignant with the aesthetic bitterness of the absinthe of Baudelaire and other French poets after Victor Hugo." It struck the note of the subtle and exotic. His book belonging to that embattled epoch—his best and most famous book of poetry, *The Florilegium*—was published in 1899 and republished in 1904 with notable additions. This was followed, in 1918, by *Toward the Sun and Under the Moon,* in which there is no substantial variation in the poet's aesthetics. The already visible restlessness of his spirit was to drive him later—though with less success—to affiliate himself with the extreme schools of decadence, or what might better be called the present school of poetic confusion. The following are products of this new manner: *One Day,* "synthetic poems"; *Li-Po,* "ideographic poems"; *The Pitcher of Flowers,* "lyric dissociations"; and *The Market,* "Mexican poems."

Tablada's work in prose has been no less abundant than his poetic work. It includes *Parisian Nights and Days,* a book of chronicles; *Hiroshige,* a monograph devoted to the celebrated Japanese painter; *The Resurrection of the Idols,* a novel; *The Market of Life,* memoirs; and, lastly, the *Mexican Plastic Arts* and the *History of Mexican Art.* A prose style that is all energy and color—possessing unquestionable beauty—is his.

Enrique González Martínez

Enrique González Martínez is the last great poet of the modernist movement. A native of Guadalajara, where he was born on April 13, 1871, he studied in his native city and took the degree of Doctor of Medicine. In Sinaloa, he alternated for many years between the practice of medicine and literature. He went to Mexico City in 1911, labored in the press and the classroom, discharged a number of public duties, and finally entered the field of diplomacy. On his return to his native country, after a long residence abroad, he devoted himself exclusively to his literary work. He died in Mexico City, February 19, 1952, and was buried in the Rotunda of Illustrious Men.

Occupying a place between the group typically "modernistic" and the generation that followed, he is a figure in high relief. His poetic autobiography, Pedro Henríquez Ureña has said, "is the history of a perpetual ascent toward greater serenity; but, at the same time, toward sincerity, toward the deepest and most austere concept of life." "The poet," Alfonso Reyes says,

emerges into the world, takes a brief look at nature, glances hastily into books, calls a greeting to men, looks after his daily life a little, and presently slips away, along the paths that he alone knows, to the sanctuary of silence. There all poetry must end, for the soul itself is mute. There he arrives, with the treasury of his visions rifled; he corrects his values; he weighs them; and the soul silently assimilates the new emotions and thus begins to grow into perfection.

In the seclusion of his province, he published his first volumes of poems: *Preludes* (1903), *Lirismos* (1907), *Silénter* (1909), and *The Hidden Paths* (1911). When he came to Mexico City, he was already recognized as a master. Then appeared *The Death of the Swan, Gardens of France* (1915), *The Book of the Strength of Goodness and Illusion* (1917), *Parables and Other Poems* (1918), and *The Wind's Word* (1921). Later, during his long stay in foreign lands, performing various diplomatic missions as representative of Mexico, González Martínez published two more collections of poems, *The Deluded Pilgrim* and *The Secret Signs* (1925). Returning to Mexico, he prepared—as his speech *de recepción* into the Academy—a study of *Some Aspects of Mexican Lyric Poetry* (1932); and he also gave to the press the following new volumes of verse: *Poemas Truncos (Incomplete Poems,* 1935), *Absence and Song* (1937), and *The Deluge of Fire*—a rough draft of a poem—(1938), *Poems* (1940), *Under the Mortal Sign* (1943), *Second Awakening* (1945), *Thistledown in the Wind* (1948), and *Babel* (1949). His complete poetical works up to 1940 were published in three volumes entitled *Poetry*.

"He hammered his own verse," Don Francisco A. de Icaza has said, in synthesis, in a brief evaluation of the poet's personality,

into the perfect Spanish interpretation of the most contradictory foreign poets: Lamartine, Poe, Verlaine, Heredia, Francis Jammes, Samain; and he achieved a technique that distinguishes his poetry today—a technique entirely original and wise in the mechanics of expression. Gonzáles Martínez's poetry is pantheistic. There is one kind of pantheism that, deifying the world, worships it and thereby worships itself. There is another kind that deifies nature and loves it devotedly even in its most humble aspects: this is the pantheism of González Martínez. A melancholy optimist, he feels the transience of pain, which in the normal life is as fleeting as pleasure, and he sings of both, already vanished, with vague melancholy tenderness, for to him the dread-inspiring pain is not a guest, but a wayfarer who stops for the night and, in the morning at the break of day, hastily dusting his sandals, goes away again.

As an explanation of himself, Enrique González Martínez has added to his poetic work one volume in prose entitled *The Unsocial Being: Mystery of a Calling* (1944), a remarkable book of memoirs covering the years from infancy to lyrical maturity; this was followed by a second volume entitled *Peaceful Madness* (1951).

Minor Modernist Poets

Among the poets of the *Modern Review* who were factors in the modernist movement in Mexico, the following are noteworthy:

Jesús E. Valenzuela (born in Guanaceví, state of Durango, December 24, 1856; died in Mexico City, May 20, 1911), founder and director of the *Modern Review* and the Maecenas of the group; a man of unlimited generosity and of open and jovial spirit. He was a poet, but—according to Urbina—he never arrived at absolute mastery of form; "for his ideas, generally beautiful, an attractive dress is ordinarily lacking. The fabric of the dress is rich; the gems are brilliant; but the brocade does not always fall with statuesque majesty, and the diamonds lose no little of their splendor through the poor settings." His poetic work comprises three volumes: *Souls and Incantations* (1904), *Lira Libre* (1906), *Handful of Rhymes* (1907).

Balbino Dávalos (born in the city of Colima on March 31, 1866; died in Mexico City, October 2, 1951), lawyer, diplomat, professor; a poet of solid and broad culture. "He possessed"—in the judgment of Rubén Darío—"a rich vocabulary and an airy elegance of style. He is complex, yet personal. He is a classicist, a romantic, a Parnassian, a symbolist in turn. He had the gift of understanding everything and of pouring out his soul on the impulse of the moment." He made elegant translations of Pierre Louys's *Aphrodite* and Maeterlinck's *Monna Vanna*, as well as other neat versions of French, English, Italian, and Portuguese poets. His original poems are contained in the volume *The Offerings*.

Francisco M. de Olaguíbel (born in Mexico City, November 6, 1874; died in Coyoacán, Federal District, December 14, 1924), orator and journalist. He was preoccupied as a poet with the subtleties and abstruse phases of technique, but he was genuinely romantic in his sensibility and the exuberance of his inspiration. His verses were collected in two volumes: *Bohemian Songs* (1905) and *Roses of Love and Pain* (1922).

Efrén Rebolledo (born in Actopan, state of Hidalgo, July 9, 1877; died in Madrid, December 11, 1929), the author of *Little Jewels* (1907), *Japanese Rhymes* and the *Book of Mad Love* (1916); "an eminent workman rather than an eminent poet," in Nervo's phrase. "Coldly he chisels, polishes, labors. He takes to pieces, he hammers, he links together. He knows many deep secrets of rhythm and rhyme. Verse is his slave." During his roving life as a diplomat, he wrote several works in prose: *The Disenchantment of Dulcinea* (1916), a book of essays; and *Bamboo Leaves* (1910) and the *Saga of Sigrid the Blond* (1922), novels.

Rubén M. Campos (born in the city of Guanajuato on April 25, 1876; died in Mexico, June 7, 1945), who has been a more abundant prose writer than poet. His poetic compositions, published for the most part in the *Modern Review,* are characterized perhaps by the morbidity of the inspiration; but indigenous, musical touches are not lacking. Up to the present, only one volume of his poems has been published: *Pan's Flute.* His fiction, in which the study of psychology predominates, includes: *Claudio Oronoz* (1906), *Atzlán: Land of the Herons* (1935), a volume of *Mexican Stories,* and *Mexican Traditions and Legends.* In the field of literary criticism and literary history, he wrote *The Literary Production of the Aztecs* (1936), *The Literary Folklore of Mexico* (1929), and *The Bar (The Literary Life of Mexico in 1900).* In the field of travel books, he has written *Nomad Wings.* He wrote a handsome monograph on *Chapultepec: Its Legend and Its History.* Finally, his devotion and love for the music of Mexico inspired two works of singular importance: *Mexican Folklore and Music* (1928) and *The Musical Folklore of the Cities* (1930).

Luis Rosado Vega (born in Valladolid, Yucatán, June 21, 1876) was also affiliated with the modernist movement and revealed himself as a poet of lively inspiration tempered and refined into beautiful simplicity in the following volumes: *Sensations* (1902), *Soul and Blood* (1906), and *Book of Illusion and Pain* (1907).

Other Poets

Within the modernist movement, though they did not ostensibly identify themselves with it in a militant manner, are the following lyric poets to whom we should make brief reference:

Manuel Puga y Acal (1860-1930), poet, historian, critic, and journalist. Educated in France, he returned to Mexico imbued with modern French poetry. Much too late, his verses were collected under the title *Lyrics of Long Ago* (1923). Of these, perhaps the most characteristic are the "Sad Ballads" and the poem "Othello before God." He also made some excellent paraphrases and translations of Musset, Baudelaire, Sylvestre, and Rollinat.

Francisco A. de Icaza (1863-1925), though he spent most of his life away from his country, did not lose his Mexican character. His poetry was published in four books: *Ephemeras* (1892), *Remote Distances* (1899), *The Song of the Road* (1906), and *Songbook of the Deep Life and the Fugitive Emotion* (1925)—not counting the translations he made of such German poets as Liliencron, Dehmel, and Nietzsche (1919). "The aesthetic balance, the elegant and restrained expression, which are distinctive of true artists," Urbina says,

give an impression of spiritual nobility, of the aristocracy of feeling, to Icaza's poetic work. But in the depth of this subtle and painstaking goldsmith, this filigree-artist of rhyme, there is—underneath the "covering" of which Santillana speaks—a creole soul, an American soul, with its sweet ancestral languor and its old racial melancholy, both softly tinged with skepticism.

María Enriqueta Camarillo de Pereyra (born in Coatepec, state of Veracruz, January 19, 1875), better known as María Enriqueta, a graceful poet hardly belonging to any school; a robust spirit, all simplicity and tenderness, who captivated by her melodious feminineness. For her, emotion and thought resolved themselves spontaneously into song. Hers is a poetry always sad and sweet—an authentic poetry. Following her first volume, *Voices of My Orchard* (1908), which won for her an outstanding place in our lyric poetry, she published in Spain, where she lived for some years, *Romantic Nooks* (1922) and *Sentimental Album* (1926).

XVIII.

The Novel and the Drama

IN THE second half of the nineteenth century, the Mexican novel reached a height and splendor never before known. No longer did it have, as in the preceding period, the invariable character of a mere experiment or approximation. It found its inspiration in the observation and study of the national scene, though foreign literary currents did not cease to influence it constantly. For the first time, it succeeded in attaining an artistic form; and it offered—within the modes of both romanticism and realism—the most varied aspects: historical, *costumbrista*, psychological, and the political or social thesis.

MAJOR NOVELISTS

Payno

Don Manuel Payno, who belonged to the same stock as his contemporaries, the novelists of the preceding period, extended his activities as a writer to the end of the century.

The home of Payno was the City of Mexico, where he was born June 21, 1810. Beginning in the customhouse as an assistant without salary, he progressed little by little and held various positions in the fiscal branch. In 1842 he was named secretary of the Mexican legation in South America; he traveled through Europe and then went to the United States, commissioned to study the penitentiary system. When war broke out with that nation, he fought for his country, establishing a secret mail service between Mexico City and Veracruz and fighting against the invader in Puebla. On various occasions—the first time in 1850—he was minister of finance, a post in which he was outstanding for honesty and efficiency; he endeavored to bring order into the traditional disorder of the public treasury, and he made an advantageous settlement of the foreign debt. Persecuted by Santa Anna, he emigrated to the United States. At the triumph of the Revolution of Ayutla, as a member of Comonfort's cabinet, he was one of those who took part in the coup d'état of 1857; and Altamirano, in that epoch of furious passions, asked for his head from the rostrum of Congress. Eliminated from politics, he was fated, nevertheless, to suffer persecution during the French Intervention: along with Florencio M. del Castillo, he was imprisoned in Ulúa, accused of conspiracy. Afterward, he acknowledged the Empire. When it fell and the Republic was restored, he was deputy, senator, and professor; he returned to Europe in 1886, as consul at Santander and then at Barcelona. Already an octogenarian, he again occupied a seat in the Senate on his return to Mexico. His death occurred in San Angel, Federal District, November 4, 1894.

Payno was an active journalist: he wrote abundantly and on everything—on political, financial, philological, and historical questions. Nevertheless, his literary claims are limited to the novel. Between 1839 and 1845 he wrote his first pieces of fiction—novelettes and stories. His initial novel, *El fistol del diablo (The Devil's Scarfpin)*, published in the *Scientific and Literary Review* in 1845 and 1846, is the first full-length novel that appeared in Mexico after the works of Fernández de Lizardi.

Like "The Thinker," Payno paints, in this book, the types and customs of the epoch; *The Devil's Scarfpin* is a "veritable depository preserving the records of the customs of the old Mexican society: its language, proverbs, styles of dress, conventions, tendencies," and, in that respect, is a novel genuinely national. Payno resembles Fernández de Lizardi, also, in lack of artistic sense and carelessness of style; but he differs from him in that he is preoccupied not with moralizing but with interesting the reader. He introduces the element of the fantastic; he resorts to a copious, endless series of incidents. With *The Scarfpin*, he inaugurated in Mexico the type of novel commonly called *"de folletín"* (the newspaper serial), the kind that at a later time, issued in separate parts, was to attain a great vogue. To understand what must have been his concept of a work of art, it is sufficient to state that his famous novel was notably augmented in the second edition (1859) and that in the third (1887) it not only acquired further additions but had a complete change of ending.

The serial author ceded his place to the *costumbrista* in *The Man in the Situation,* his second novel, published in 1861. The *costumbrista* appears, too, in *Cloudy Afternoons* (1871), the volume in which he assembled his novelettes and stories—though here the *costumbrista* is to be found, not in the stories themselves, but in the picturesque description of a trip from Mexico City to Veracruz, which is published with them.

Payno returned, however, to his first manner, publishing at the end of his life the work that can be considered his most representative: *The Bandits of Río Frío* (1889-91), two heavy tomes with two thousand and more pages. In this "naturalistic, humorous novel of customs, crimes, and horrors," as the author himself called it (he published it under the pseudonym of "A Wit of the Court"), Payno, following his usual procedure, accumulated a supply of episodes from the fringe of a celebrated criminal case in Mexico. Proportion and moderation are lacking in this prolonged history; the complete absence of concern with style—characteristic of the author—is marked in it. But there is a wealth of character types, many of them authentic, copied from nature; also, one finds direct observation of environment, frequent fidelity in the transcription of popular speech, and a high degree of local color in some of the descriptions. A five-volume edition of this famous novel has been published by Porrúa in their *Collection of Mexican Authors,* and a recent edition of their "That All May Know Collection."

The novels of Payno, it may be said in summary, hold more interest as historical documents for the study of customs and folklore than as literature.

Riva Palacio

Don Vicente Riva Palacio, like Payno, cultivated the serial novel, although in a different manner.

He was born in Mexico City on October 16, 1832. He died in Madrid, November 22, 1896; and forty years afterward (in 1936), his remains were brought to his native city, where they lie in the Rotunda of Illustrious Men. The son of a well-to-do family, he studied in the capital, made a good record as a student, and obtained a degree in law. Presently, he took up arms to oppose the French Intervention and the Empire. With the Intervention concluded and the Empire overthrown, General Riva Palacio, despite his having reached the high military hierarchy, laid down the sword and took up the pen. As journalist and politician, he participated in the revolutions that followed the restoration of the Republic; and when the Revolution of Tuxtepec triumphed, he occupied high governmental posts, though this fact did not prevent him from occasionally inhabiting a prison cell, accused of conspiracy. He was minister of public works, governor of the states of Mexico and Michoacán at different times, judge on the Supreme Court of Justice; and he ended his days as minister plenipotentiary in Spain.

In spite of the fact that no little part of his energies was consumed by military and political life and by his sharp, satirical contributions to the journalism of controversy (it will be remembered that he was the founder of *El Ahuizote*), still a generous portion of his strength was consecrated to letters. He cultivated history, criticism, the drama, and poetry; but his lordship and fief, in which popularity smiled on him for many years, was the novel.

He had a taste for the historical novel and can be considered the creator of this genre in Mexico. He turned up old papers in the archives; he also dipped his hand into his own memories of the war against the Empire and the French; and from a combination of it all, his stories came forth. Instead of Walter Scott, it was Dumas and even novelists of less excellence, such as Eugène Sue and Fernández y González, that must have influenced him. What Riva Palacio cared least about, in the writing of novels, was "literature"; he wished, above all, to entertain, to divert, to interest, with incidents and adventures that were extraordinary, dramatic, at times hair-raising. In depicting his characters, neither psychology nor direct observation engrossed his attention. His tales are prolix, though not to the same extent as Payno's; the subject matter is diluted into numerous episodes; incidents follow each other in prolonged dialogues—and all this in a style easy, sometimes expressive, but often colorless. He seeks, more than anything else, to excite curiosity, to hold the mind of the reader in suspense before the eternal question, "What happens next?" He tried, indeed, to keep within historic truth; and along the edge of the truth he goes, weaving his fiction, indefatigably.

Riva Palacio was, in fact, endowed with great fecundity. Nearly all of his fiction production—which was vast—was written in three years, from 1868 to 1870. In this brief period he produced his first novel *Calvary and Mt. Tabor* (1868), memoirs of the struggles of the Intervention, and memoirs—mainly of colonial inspiration—entitled *Martín Garatuza* (1868), *Nun and Wife, Virgin and Martyr* (1868), *The Two Recluses* (1869), *The Pirates of the Gulf* (1869), and *The Return of the Dead* (1870). Subsequently, he wrote the *Memoirs of an Impostor, Don Guillén de Lampart, King of Mexico* (1872) and his posthumous book—from a literary viewpoint, quite distinct from the preceding—entitled *Stories of the General* (1896), a delightful book, full of Attic wit, which was published in Madrid in the year of the author's death. All of the novels cited have been included in *Collection of Mexican Authors,* published by Porrúa. To find the real Riva Palacio, waggish and sarcastic, it is necessary to look, not in his novels, but in his journalistic writings and, very particularly, in that "gallery of contemporaries" that he published in one volume under the title of *The Zeros* (1882).

In his field, notwithstanding the defects already pointed out, justice requires that Riva Palacio be recognized as first among all those— and they were many—who in his time cultivated the popular novel. He gave no little work to the presses; he entertained three generations; and we should sincerely mark to his credit his spontaneity and the richness of his inventive faculty.

Altamirano

From a strictly literary point of view, the first novelist who appears in the history of our literature is Don Ignacio Manuel Altamirano.

The qualities that distinguish him as a writer (see Chapter XVII) are especially evident in his fiction. He is the first Mexican writer who concerns himself with the technique of fiction. His novels, unlike those of his predecessors, have artistic structure. He devises his plots with a large sense of proportion, unity, and restraint; therefore, his narratives are well wrought and concise, the opposite of the copious and formless stories that were the style in his day. He arranges and harmonizes episodes so that the story moves forward in excellent order, gaining in emotion and interest. To the surroundings and the characters he gives as much prominence as to the plot. His settings are not imagined, but seen and felt; they abound in vivid and striking color. His heroes and even his minor characters, though cast in an idealistic mold and, for the most part, of undeniable romantic aspect, are not always the unvaried product of imagination; they are very human creations, and even, at times, the representation of people whom the author knew and with whose lives he was familiar. This equilibrium of powers is made complete by grace and beauty of style. Altamirano's prose is pure, fluid, vigorous, clear. He narrates with dexterity; he describes with restraint and beauty, using broad strokes; he writes dialogue with vivacity; he is brief, but eloquent, in the picturing of characters.

Altamirano's production in this genre, of which he can be considered the creator from an artistic standpoint, is confined to the following works: two novels, properly speaking, *Clemencia,* published for the first time in the *Renaissance* in 1869, and *El Zarco,* his posthumous work, completed in 1888, but not published until 1901; the quasi-novel—or, rather, delightful long story—called *Christmas in the Mountains* (1870), which he published serially in *La Iberia*; and three fictional narratives. This last group includes "The Three Flowers," a little story of foreign atmosphere, but with a decided flavor of Mexican romanticism, which Altamirano claims to have translated when he was a student, though there are reasons for supposing it to be his own original work. It was published in the *Mexican Mail,* in 1867, under the title "The Sweetheart" and was reprinted under the other title in the *Renaissance*. Also in this group are the two short novels, very Mexican in scene and character: "Julia," which first appeared in the *Nineteenth Century* under the name "A July Night"; and "Antonia." Both were included, along with the other works mentioned above, excepting *El Zarco,* in the two volumes entitled *Winter Tales,* which Don Filomeno Mata published in Mexico City in 1880. Considering the abundance of his powers, much more might have been accomplished by the novelist if he had not lacked the time and the tranquillity—as is shown by the fact that he left two other novels incomplete, though in a fairly advanced stage of composition; these are *Antonia and Beatrice* and *Athena*. The latter was published in 1935 by the National University of Mexico in the volume honoring Altamirano.

Of all these works, the ones that have brought just fame to Altamirano are the first three, *Clemencia, El Zarco,* and *Christmas in the*

Mountains, which have been published, and continue to be published, both in Mexico and abroad. In *Clemencia* and *El Zarco,* the story is concerned with romantic love: the first has for its background the War of the French Intervention in the western part of Mexico; the second is set in the picturesque region of the state of Morelos, where those famous bandits popularly known as *los plateados* (the silver-plated ones) roamed at will. In writing these novels, Altamirano had recourse to his memories of life as a soldier and politician and to his travels through the lands of the south, which he knew well and loved very much. In both books, the painter of customs and landscapes stands out; and if the action is not so vigorous or thrilling in *El Zarco* as in *Clemencia,* Altamirano always, in each of his novels, succeeds in striking the artistic note in narratives of unmistakable Mexicanism. Perhaps because of a deep, innate tenderness, his appeal as a story-teller is even greater in the novelette *Christmas in the Mountains,* that rustic idyl of sane romantic sensibility, which the author laid in a little village of southern Mexico during the civil war—a scene like a pool of clear, sweet water in the midst of the horrors and violent hatreds that the conflict stirred up.

Altamirano is also outstanding as a *costumbrista.* He gave numerous articles and studies of this genre to the periodicals; all of these, polished and revised for the purpose, he intended to assemble in three volumes. Before his death, he published only the first volume, *Mexico's Landscapes and Legends* (1884); the second volume, *Traditions and Customs,* was published in 1949.

Cuéllar

The novel of customs, properly speaking, is represented in this period by Don José Tomás de Cuéllar, who became extremely popular under the pseudonym of "Facundo" (Eloquent).

Cuéllar was born in Mexico City on September 18, 1830. In the schools of San Gregorio and San Ildefonso, he studied the humanities and philosophy; later he was a student in the Military School of Chapultepec, and he took part in the defense of it, with other boy heroes, in the glorious and bloody action against the North American invader on September 8, 1847; and, lastly, feeling himself called to be a painter, he studied in the National Academy of San Carlos—surely not without profit, for he succeeded in producing excellent pictures. In 1848 he began his literary work, writing for the press and trying his hand in the theater. Consecrated to diplomacy, he filled various posts, among others that of first secretary of the Mexican legation in Washington and that of undersecretary of foreign relations. He died blind, in the City of Mexico, on February 11, 1894.

Although he cultivated dramatic literature and poetry, Cuéllar's fame is vested in the novel and the article dealing with customs. As a novelist, following the dominant taste of the time, he was attracted to the historical type; his first novel, *The Sin of the Century*, treating the colonial background of the eighteenth century, was published in 1869. Knowing his own abilities and considering that these did fit him for such a road, he came to devote himself entirely to the *costumbrista* type. Outstanding among his complete works, which were published in twenty-four volumes under the general title of *The Magic Lantern* (1889-92), are novels and sketches of this genre, such as *Chicken Salad, History of Chucho the Fop, Baile y cochino (Bailiff and Hog), The Little Husbands, Las jamonas (The Big, Middle-Aged Women), The People That Are So, Los fuereños (The Ones from the Provinces), Christmas Eve,* and *Gabriel the Locksmith or My Father's Daughters.*

In Cuéllar, the observer and the satiric humorist were united with the moralist, although the latter never came to predominate over the former or to smother the picturesque inspiration under the didactic purpose. He followed Fernández de Lizardi in a way, but is a thousand leagues from the persistent sermonizing of the author of *Little Miss Quixote.* Cuéllar's novels are short, dynamic in plot, free and quick in execution; and the doctrinaire intention—the moralizing— is hidden in the very incidents of the story (it should be recalled that before he was a writer, he was a painter). His field of observation is limited to the middle class. Instead of their vices—presented with a view to correcting them—he likes to exaggerate their follies and eccentricities for the sake of arousing open laughter, and for this reason he resorts frequently to caricature. He pictures customs soberly; and in preference to exploring complex characters, he paints the distinct and characteristic types of the society he studied: the spoiled child, the coarse, brutal individual that reaches high positions with the help of the revolutions, the roguish schemer, the affected girl . . . The dialogue is animated, the narration lively and pleasing, the reproduction of atmosphere and people accurate—so much so, indeed, that a contemporary, Guillermo Prieto, referring to the last item, could say it was to be suspected that Cuéllar simply parodied the actual people he had in front of his easel.

Rabasa

Under the pseudonym "Sancho Polo," Don Emilio Rabasa introduced realism into the Mexican novel. In Cuéllar, *costumbrismo* stood out as the primary element; as said in the foregoing, the author of *The Magic Lantern* was a *costumbrista* with a sense of humor and a cautious moralizing tendency. Rabasa went farther: without ignoring atmosphere, without failing to present in an artistic manner the background of customs, he was inclined toward character study, and he gave a political and social meaning to the novel.

In "Sancho Polo," the man of science prevailed over the artist of fine sensibility. Perhaps this explains why his stay in the field of fiction was brief and why in the end he devoted himself to another kind of writing. Born in the town of Ocozautla, Chiapas, on May 22, 1856, he studied in Oaxaca and took the law degree there in 1878. Soon after finishing his studies, he devoted himself to professional practice, politics, and teaching. As a very young man, he served in the local legislatures of Chiapas and Oaxaca; he directed the Institute of San Cristóbal las Casas in his home state; in 1886 he came to Mexico City and began journalistic work; in 1891 he was elected governor of Chiapas and, later, senator in the national Congress. As a journalist and sociologist, he became the master of two generations of lawyers and produced as the fruit of his meditations such works as *The Constitutional Trial, The Political Organization of Mexico,* and *The Historic Evolution of Mexico.* The last two works were reprinted in 1956 by Editorial Porrúa.

Literature represents the briefest parenthesis in Rabasa's life; it is said that writing was a sin of his youth, into which, unfortunately, he never again lapsed. His work consists of a series of four novels: *La Bola, The Great Science, The Fourth Estate,* and *Counterfeit Coins,* the first two published in 1887 and the other two in the following year, under the general title of *Mexican Novels.* In *La bola,* placing the action in a small village and combining it with an innocent idyl,

Rabasa shows how a small, local revolution (the kind that our people have christened with the generic name of *bolas*) is generated, develops, erupts, rises to a climax, spreads, and triumphs, under the direction of rustics and petty politicians. The second novel of the series, *The Great Science* ("the great science of always winning, which in my country is called politics"), is a waggish, picturesque chronicle of the official, bureaucratic life in the capital of the same state, to which the author brings his protagonists, the principal actors in the little revolution above mentioned. *El cuarto poder (The Fourth Estate)* and *Counterfeit Coins* deal with the experiences of the original *bolistas*—one of them victorious, the other ruined—in the fields of politics and journalism in the capital of the Republic. The end of the conflict is brought about through the quiet idyl begun in the faraway little village, to which the "counterfeit coins" return at last—in reality, they were worth nothing and meant nothing, and they owed to the revolutionary storm, alone, the fact that they were swept from their town to rise deceptively and then to be hurled down and destroyed. A new edition of these four novels has been published in *Collection of Mexican Authors* by Porrúa.

If we could search out the controlling force behind "Sancho Polo," we would find it in the great Spanish novelists of his epoch, and in particular in Galdós, whom he followed in construction and style. The Mexican writer possessed a satirical vein and, as an avowed portraitist, has left in his novels an excellent copy of the very human types that are characteristic of the society he reflected. He narrates with vivacity, writes dialogue with ease, is concise in the descriptive passages, and, by quick strokes, gives here and there beautiful landscapes. His prose, plain, unvarnished, with a certain classical flavor sometimes, is not free from slovenliness. Perhaps, in order to have material for four novels, he overdiluted what could have been put in one or two. Nevertheless, they are among the most distinctive in flavor that our literature has produced; and, without doubt, *La bola* is one of the best Mexican novels.

Rabasa died in Mexico City on April 25, 1930. One of his novels —*The Three Years' War*—was printed in 1931 for the first time in book form, having been originally published in the columns of the *Universal* in 1891. Surely it deserves a place among the most beautiful works of its kind.

López Portillo y Rojas

Another representative of realism and the first Mexican who cultivated the novel of rural atmosphere is Don José López Portillo y Rojas.

The son of a prominent family of Jalisco, he was born in Guadalajara on May 26, 1850. He studied in his native city and in Mexico City, and took a law degree. His natural inclination and his diligence in acquainting himself with letters made it possible for him, while a student, to acquire a literary culture not at all common—a culture that he refined and perfected, as soon as he had finished his course of study, by extensive travel through England, France, Italy, and the Orient and that he increased constantly through the study of the Spanish, French, and English literatures, which he knew thoroughly. Without forsaking the practice of his profession, from his youth he did not disdain journalistic and political activities; he became a distinguished teacher; his excursions into public life brought him the responsibility of various offices, now in the judiciary, again in Congress, then as governor of Jalisco, and, finally, as secretary of foreign relations. He died in Mexico City on May 22, 1923.

López Portillo wrote on diverse topics; nevertheless, literature was his chief preoccupation. He cultivated poetry, drama, the travel narrative, criticism, and history. But neither his *Travel Impressions* (1873), his first book, nor his poems, which were collected in one volume under the title of *Fugitive Harmonies* (1892), nor his studies of a critical and historical character, like *Rosario la de Acuña* (1920) and the *Rise and Fall of Porfirio Díaz* (1921), were to give him the acclaim and renown that his fiction brought him. By calling and by nature, he was a novelist first of all.

His fiction is composed of short narratives and novels. To the first group belong *Six Legends* (1883), *Short Novels* (1900), *Incidents and Short Novels* (1903), and *Histories, Short Stories, and Little Tales* (1918); to the second *A Plot of Ground* (1898), *The Precursors* (1909), and *The Strong and the Weak* (1919). Having trained himself first in the technique of the short narrative, it was not until very late that he attempted the composition of long fiction. Perhaps he felt more at his ease, more master of himself, in the first type. Because of their diversity, perfection of plan, freshness of style, and the originality of the subjects, some of the short narratives are per-

haps the best work that came from his pen. In inspirations from romance of mere fantasy such as "Adalinda," "The Mirror," "The
Harp," "A Pact with the Devil"; in the transcription of events
("The Flight"); in mildly realistic pictures in which sometimes the
inclination of the *costumbrista* fraternizes with the emotion of the
poet ("Snows," "The First Love," "The Last of His Shoe"): in all
of these the writer seems to be entirely at home as in his own dominions.

He was also in his own realm when, with perspective broadened,
he gave to Mexican literature its best model of the rural novel: *A
Plot of Ground*, a work that the author himself never succeeded in
surpassing, or even in equaling, for his two other great novels are
far inferior to it. The theme is very simple; a dispute between two
neighboring ranchers over a little piece of rough, wooded land gives
the novelist the excuse for tracing a living, luminous, animated picture of the life of the Jalisco countryside. The narrative is fluent; the
descriptions are well handled; the principal characters are presented
in strong relief and the minor characters depicted with great exactness—a true picture of reality. The novelist transcribes the regional
speech and is revealed as a minute and careful observer of customs.
A Plot of Ground radiates love, as Salado Alvarez has noted, love
which is revealed in "warm humanity, affection for people and
things, faith in life, in progress, in the fulfillment of all the great
and good that inspires and pervades the author."

Though he was devoted to the English novelists, López Portillo
was influenced above all by contemporary Spanish novelists, and very
markedly in *A Plot of Ground* by Pereda. Opposing the French
literary currents that had been introduced at that time into Mexican
literature, he proclaimed the necessity of accentuating our nationalism without violating the genius of the mother tongue. "The only
thing we need in order to exploit the rich elements that surround
us," he said, "is to withdraw into ourselves and to dissipate ourselves
less on foreign material."

Delgado

Rabasa, López Portillo, and Rafael Delgado form the triumvirate
of Mexican novelists who, as realists, developed from Spanish influence. Intensely Mexican, like the first two, Delgado is distinguished

from them by a more delicate sensibility, which animates his pages with a pleasing breath of poetry; by his regionalism and sense of the picturesque, accentuated still more than theirs; and very particularly by his remarkable descriptive powers that, so far as feeling for nature and ability to create a living, breathing landscape are concerned, give him first place among Mexican novelists.

Delgado was a native of Córdoba, Veracruz, where he was born on August 20, 1853. He studied in his native city and in Orizaba, and received a profoundly religious education, which is definitely reflected in his literary work. Almost without leaving his own plot of ground, he devoted his quiet, humble life to teaching and to letters, until death came to him, in Orizaba, on May 20, 1914.

He produced drama, poetry, criticism, and textbooks, but his literary reputation is strictly confined to fiction. Delgado wrote four novels: *The Lark* (1891), *Angelina* (1895), *Rich Relatives* (1903), and *Common Story* (1904). And to these should be added his short narratives, collected under the title of *Stories and Notes* (1902).

If Delgado seldom succeeds in the short narrative—it is said that he found himself at ease only on an expanded stage and that his spirit, analytical in essence, took delight in detail—on the other hand, few writers can show, in what pertains to the novelist's art, a work so harmonious and spirited, without rough spots or lapses, as his. In *The Lark,* his first novel, he is revealed as he was; his later books hardly surpass it in technique and style. His choice of subject matter always shows his love of simplicity. The tragedy of the poor girl who, wavering between the love of a man of her own class and that of a lewd dandy, chooses the latter and weaves her own fate; the idyl of the student who returns to the village life, an idyl that is transformed, through erotic memories, into a conflict between two loves, neither of which comes to fruition in the end; the exciting moments and mishaps of a family that abandon the provincial home, trusting in the protection that wealthy relatives can offer them—such are the themes, respectively, of *The Lark, Angelina,* and *Rich Relatives.* The interest and beauty of the Veracruzan's novels depend, not on the intrinsic significance of these "simple, common stories, more real than imagined," but on the little, incidental details with which he clothes them. That constant procession of types "seen"; that detailed, and, nevertheless, temperate and powerful manner of reproducing local surroundings (so well did he paint the provincial cities he disguised under assumed names, "Pluviosilla" for Orizaba, "Villaverde" for Córdoba, that there are some who call the actual cities by the imaginary names); that masterful ability which reproduced in *The Lark,* on a magnificent canvas, the mountain ridge of Veracruz; that charm and art of storytelling; and, above all, that inexhaustible, communicable emotional faculty: these are the things that make the novels of Delgado—all written with great beauty and at the same time with rich fulness—both genuine works of art and documents of the purest nationalism.

Angel de Campo

In the foreground among our *costumbristas* should be placed Angel de Campo.

Like the lives of the contemporary writers in general, his is a life without a story. He was born in Mexico City on July 9, 1868, and he died in the same city on February 8, 1908. After his primary and preparatory studies, he intended to follow the career of medicine; but, lacking a real calling, he renounced that career in order to enter the field of journalism and letters. Employed in the Treasury Department, he divided his energies between his official tasks, fiction, and the humorous articles on current themes which he sent week by week to the newspapers. The humorist, under the pseudonym of "Tick-Tack," produced a copious amount, all of it scattered today in the press; this part of his work is terse, admirable on many counts, but uneven. The popular storyteller, on the other hand, known under a different pseudonym, that of "Micrós," accumulated only three volumes: *Idle Thoughts and Memoranda* (1890), *Things Seen* (1894), and *Cartoons* (1897). He also wrote one novel, *The Rumba,* which was first published serially in the *National,* and, in 1958, in an edition prepared by María del Carmen Millán for the Porrúa *Collection of Mexican Authors.*

Angel de Campo, by the nature of his literary work, follows in direct line from the "Mexican Thinker," "Fidel," and "Facundo"; but because of the feeling of deep tenderness and human pity that animates him, Don Federico Gamboa finds, not without reason, great similarities to Dickens and Daudet. Nevertheless, just as it is necessary to discount all direct foreign literary influence on "Micrós"—since he was, above all, a spontaneous product of his environment—so also his relationship to our preceding *costumbristas* does not prevent him from having a personality of his own, genuine, distinct, and even, in some respects, opposite to theirs. Unlike Fernández de Lizardi, he is an artist; diametrically different from Prieto, he has pure, well-developed taste; the reverse of Cuéllar, he never allows humor to reach the bounds of caricature.

Close to the humorist in "Micrós" was the poet; his tenderness is shown toward the humble and the suffering and is even broadened into pity for birds and animals, which, purposely and delightfully, he is in the habit of presenting as the protagonists of his stories: the canary eager to abandon the sweet prison of its cage; the stray dog; the *picador*'s horse. For this reason, he arouses the feeling of pathos along with a smile. In his little pictures of national life, "Micrós" is revealed as a psychologist who, without effort, searches the soul; a diligent painter who knows how to see and how to transmit his vision of the actual spectacle. He is, indeed, as Urbina says, an admirable genre painter. "He does not see in the large, but in detail and clearly. His drawing is wonderful; his color, brilliant and lively."

He knew the low class of society well, although, as a *costumbrista*, his preference was for the middle class. From both groups he drew scenes and character studies of marvelous accuracy. And if his style is far from being correct and pure, it is, nevertheless, vivid and picturesque, precise and balanced in description, highly faithful in the reproduction of the common speech, and purposeful with irony.

Rising above all our *costumbristas*, Angel de Campo undoubtedly carried this type of literature to its highest artistic perfection.

Gamboa

The French influence, which toward the end of this period made itself felt in the poetry and also the fiction of some of our poets—Gutiérrez Nájera, Nervo—and even in storytellers as Mexican as "Micrós," reached its culmination in the work of Don Federico Gamboa.

Born in Mexico City on December 22, 1864, he suffered the blows of adverse fortune during childhood and adolescence. Struggles, premature and hard, prepared his spirit and refined his feelings. He learned to make his own way; he had a firm conviction of his calling, as well as a strong will. While he was very young, in 1888, he entered diplomacy, to which he consecrated the greater part of his life, rising slowly and methodically from the modest post of second secretary to the high positions of minister plenipotentiary, ambassador, and secretary of foreign relations. Serving his country thus honorably in foreign lands, feted often, decorated not a few times, Gamboa never forgot that he was, before everything else, a literary man; and, to the beat of a diplomat's tasks, he unwound the work of the writer.

He divided his time among three literary types: the novel, the autobiography and memoirs, and the drama.

It is in the first, particularly, that Gamboa excels; and, as novelist, he can be considered the most prolific writer and the one that exhibits the most harmonious and vigorous production among the writers of his time. His first book, *From Nature* (1888), is a series of short narratives in which the minute observer of contemporary life is already visible. Soon thereafter, with *Appearances* (1892), he attempted the long novel, the type that he would continue to write. Although this novel can be called an experiment—it does not show the desired balance between construction and style—the author appeared fully developed and revealed his definitive literary character, four years later, in *Supreme Law* (1896). This second novel—which deals with the insane passion of a little court clerk for a murderess, a passion that besides destroying his humble home leads him to despair and death—shows, both in inspiration and technique, the influence of French naturalism and especially of two of its leaders: Zola and the Goncourts. The starkness of the analysis; the excessive delight in detail; the profuseness and vigor of the descriptions; the precise reproduction of atmosphere, now sinister, as in the scenes in the prison and the amphitheater, now filled with painful sweetness, as in the family scenes in Ortegal's house: these reveal its antecedents. Daring in theme—dealing with the nun who is transformed into a woman in the arms of the man that abducted her—and superior in style to *Supreme Law* is *Metamorphosis* (1899), a novel that gives a living reproduction of Mexican rural atmosphere in the colorful pages that describe a *"coleadero"* [the daring feat of a horseman who seizes the bull by the tail and throws the animal to the ground]. *Santa* (1903), Gamboa's most popular book, came next in order: it is the novel of a courtesan, and its expository chapters, because of the mastery with which they are written, the powerful intonation, and the plasticity of style, are the best and most beautiful the author ever wrote. Unwholesome curiosity brought it many readers; no other Mexican novel has received so much publicity; it has been reproduced continually on the stage and in motion pictures and printed and reprinted through thousands and thousands of copies. Nevertheless, in spite of its crudenesses, it is a chaste book; emphasizing the hideousness of the sin, it seeks to edify. The moralizing and sermonizing aim, implicit in the story itself, and the fondness for treating social and moral problems predominate in the author's last two novels: *Reconquest* (1908), a book of religious inspiration—the return of the indifferent to the Christian faith—and *The Ulcer* (1910), in which the convict hero, who preserves the light of goodness in his soul, struggles to rebuild his life on love.

Autobiographical books and memoirs occupy no small place in Gamboa's work, and, as well as his novels, show his intimate literary relationship with the French naturalists. *Impressions and Memories*, the first of this type and the most beautiful Mexican book of its kind, was published in 1893; it suggests Daudet in the quality of its inspiration, which, nevertheless, was highly personal. Memories of childhood and adolescence, episodes at the beginning of his literary life, journalism, his first friends, impressions of travels: these furnish the author with material for separate chapters of intimate character. This intimate note is accentuated in *My Diary*, memoranda recorded with the warmth of a moment's impression, like the similar work done by Edmond and Jules de Goncourt. Begun in 1892 and faithfully continued throughout his noble and laborious life, this work of Gamboa's represents something more than a synthesis of daily existence: it constitutes the reflection of the most varied atmospheres; a commentary on events; a picture, made with quick strokes, of men and things; and—for many reasons and in many ways—a very valuable document for our literary history. Up to the present, only five volumes of *My Diary* (1907-38) have been printed; these cover the years 1892 to 1911.

The theater, lastly, did not fail to attract the novelist—and Gamboa is a novelist even in his plays because of the peculiarities of his method that tends always to minuteness of analysis rather than brief synthesis. A social comedy, *The Last Campaign* (1894), marked his debut as playwright with remarkable success. This was followed much later by two other dramas: *The Serf's Revenge* (1905) and *Part Payment* (1907). Though all three are of literary significance, the second can doubtless be considered the most important because it is the first attempt at rural drama that our stage records. Finally, with his last play, *Among Brothers*, a contemporary Mexican tragedy, produced in 1928, Don Federico Gamboa attained, in regard to all that constitutes theatrical technique, his greatest success in the theater.

This renowned writer died in his native city on August 15, 1939.

Salado Alvarez

In Don Victoriano Salado Alvarez (a native of Teocaltiche, Jalisco; born September 30, 1867), literary activity predominated over every other kind, and he took delight in the severe disciplines of the art. Instead of the law, the profession that he was licensed to enter at an early age, he practiced teaching, journalism, and literature. Politics, and later diplomacy, in which he was to occupy high posts, though they made him a wandering pilgrim through various lands, did not separate him from letters, but brought him at last to confine himself to them.

Because of his broad literary culture and his fervent devotion to that archetype of beauty that is dependent on clarity, proportion, and harmony, Salado Alvarez can be called a humanist in the modern sense of the word. He did not confine himself to one genre, nor did he follow one exclusive range of studies. He cultivated equally literary criticism, the novel, history, and philology; an experienced essayist, pursuing the practice of journalism, he was accustomed to peep into every question of live interest.

His work is voluminous and multiform, though up to the present the greater part of it remains scattered in newspapers and reviews. Of the published volumes, the first was *Of My Own Invention* (1899), a collection of critical studies devoted to contemporary Mexican authors, in which the outstanding pieces are the controversial articles that define the author's position in opposition to the "modernist" movement in our poetry. Next came a book of stories, *De autos* (1901), and the two great narratives of fictionized history *From Santa Anna to the Reform* (3 volumes, 1902) and *The Inter-*

vention and the Empire (4 volumes, 1903). After a long interval and dedicated to a very different theme—philology—another of his books appeared: his study of the *Mexicanisms Surviving in the English of North America* (1924), which, under the title of *Migratory Mexico,* constituted his speech of acceptance into the Mexican Academy.

It was to be the last book that he published. In a manner almost unforeseen, while he was still carrying his crushing journalistic work and it was to be hoped that he would live for many years, making his luminous spirit shine before men, Salado Alvarez died in Mexico City on October 13, 1931. A posthumous book—though it had not been polished, revised, or prepared for the printer by the author, since death would not permit—was published in 1933 in Madrid: *The Unlucky and Romantic Life of Don Carlos María de Bustamante.* As a spectator of the events of his day and of his own personal deeds, he shows his talent, cleverness, and pleasing manner in *Memoirs,* also published posthumously (1946).

To literary criticism, to philology, and especially to history, Salado devoted himself by preference and with singular success; but the novel and the short story were, so to speak, the first manifestations of his mature genius.

As early as in *De autos* the stylist was revealed. In these stories, it is the author's manner that is fascinating and outstanding rather than the quality of inventiveness or the emotion. The prose artist of calm clarity appears in them—a writer with a slight archaic flavor but eminently modern in finish, in richness of shading, in beauty and flexibility of style. He reproduces types and customs with wit and charm. His narratives are seasoned with suave humor, and in some of them the inquisitive student of history is revealed—the scholar who does not atrophy but, on the contrary, enhances and exalts the artist's innate qualities. His short stories have been collected by his daughter in a volume entitled *Short Stories and Narratives,* published by Porrúa in their *Collection of Mexican Authors.*

Precisely this fusion of artist and historian is made evident in the two series of episodes that form the thick volumes entitled *From Santa Anna to the Reform* and *The Intervention and the Empire.* Together, they constitute an animated, picturesque chronicle of Mexican life in the dramatic period that extends from the dictatorship of His

Most Serene Highness to the tragedy of the Hill of Campanas, that is, from 1851 to 1867. These historical novels are far from resembling other historical novels published in Mexico in this or the preceding period; and if any literary parentage could be assigned to them, it would be Galdós' *Episodes*. Unlike the novelists who preceded him, the author did not propose to entertain the reader with a "newspaper serial" accumulation of wild, dramatic episodes—the kind in which history, generally, is falsified and distorted; instead, faithful to history and to the standards of art, he brings to life in a delightful style the culminating moments of the past, exhumes environments and customs, and creates characters and types with such richness of detail and such a semblance of reality that his work would appear to be that of an eyewitness.

With these books, the cycle of Mexican historical novels closes; and precisely because their author was able to carry the genre to its highest degree of perfection, they are outstanding in our literary history.

Minor Novelists

Along with the above-mentioned figures, who are the most prominent in the fiction of this period, we should name some others of minor importance.

The historical novel, which enjoyed a special vogue, had numerous cultivators. Among these Don Juan A. Mateos (1831-1913) stands out; he was a prolix writer without style, but his chief novels—*May Sun, Priest and Chief, The Insurgents, Sister Angelica,* and *Mexico's Dramas* (written between 1868 and 1887)—have a certain historical value because of their documentation. Don Ireneo Paz (1836-1924), journalist and author of the copious and interesting memoirs entitled *Some Campaigns,* likewise produced historical novels in abundance; besides *Love and Anguish* and *Doña Marina,* the most celebrated, he wrote six historical stories of the epoch of Independence and thirteen more devoted to personages of the period from the Reform to the 1920's. Of historical character, and picturesque in addition, is *Los Plateados de Tierra Caliente* (1891) by Pablo Robles. Don Enrique de Olavarría y Ferrari (1844-1918), Spanish by birth but a naturalized Mexican, followed Galdós' method in a series of *Mexican Historical Episodes,* which comprises thirty-six novels in which the national life from 1808 to 1838 is painted. Lastly, and considerably later, Don Heriberto Frías (1870-1928), among other novels of historical character, composed *Tomóchic* (1894), dealing with the Yaqui uprising; and Don Rafael de Zayas Enríquez published his historical novel *The Lieutenant of the Gavilanes* (1902).

In the field of the sentimental novel should be noted Pablo Zayas Guarneros (1831-1902), author of *Sublime Love* (1899); Pedro Castera (1838-1906), who, following in the footsteps of Jorge Isaacs, the Colombian, composed the romantic *Carmen* (1882); and José Rafael Guadalajara (born in 1863), author of *Amalia, Pages of First Love* (1899).

Conspicuous in the novel of customs were Manuel Sánchez Mármol (1839-1912), a clear and pure prose writer, who shows the direct influence of Juan Valera and who wrote three books of fiction, *Juanita Sousa* (1901), *Antón Pérez* (1903), and *Previvida* (1906); Rafael Ceniceros y Villarreal (1855-1933), author of a regional novel, *The Harvest* (1905); Dr. Porfirio Parra (1856-1912), Barreda's disciple and enthusiastic propagator of positivism in Mexico, author of a novel, *Ventures* (1900); Salvador Cordero (born in 1876; died in Mexico City, February 18, 1951), author of *Memories of a Justice of the Peace* (1910) and *Village Types* (1917); and, lastly, Cayetano Rodríguez Beltrán (1866-1939), who devoted himself to regional novels of Veracruz and produced, among other books, *Seaside Stories* (1905) and *Little Bird* (1908).

Among the novels of this period, stories of social or political tendency were not uncommon. We shall mention only Manuel H. San Juan (1864-1917), who may be called a disciple of Rabasa in *The Lord Governor* (1901); and the caustic Salvador Quevedo y Zubieta (1859-1935), author, among other novels, of *The Band of Thieves* (1912).

The psychological novel was cultivated by Ciro B. Ceballos (1873-1938), literary critic and caustic pamphleteer, author of *A Case of Adultery* (1903); and by María Enriqueta (born 1875), the poet already mentioned, whose fiction is beautiful and abundant: *Blackbird* (1918), *A Bit of the World*, and *The Secret*, novels, and *Life's Surprises*, *In the Dust of a Castle*, *The Mystery of His Death* (1926), *The Irremediable*, and *The Box of Colors* (1929), short stories. Nearly all of María Enriqueta's work was written abroad and, except for the very personal feeling that inspires it, has no Mexican color or flavor.

Under the excessively vague and indefinite heading of cosmopolitan novels may be placed the works of José Manuel Hidalgo (died in 1896), an imperialist who was a member of the commission that offered the crown to Maximilian at Miramar and who, having gone to Europe to spend the rest of his days, wrote *The Thirst for Gold* (1891), *Victims of Chic* (1892), *Lelia and Mariana* (1894), and *The Confession of a Worldly Woman* (1896). In 1960 Editorial Porrúa published a volume of letters of Hidalgo, with a summary, prologue, and notes by Sofía Verea de Bernal (*Biblioteca Porrúa,* Number 16).

As short-story writers, the following should be named: Carlos Díaz Dufoo, author of the volume entitled *Vigorous Tales* (1901); Alberto Leduc (1867-1908), who wrote the brief narratives *Mary of the Consolation* (1894), *Little Frigate* (1896), and *A Calvary* (1900); and the short-lived José Bernardo Couto Castillo (1880-1901), who was inspired by the very modern French writers in *Asphodels* (1897). Also, though he was not a novelist, Antonio García Cubas (1832-1912) should be mentioned here because of the picturesque appeal that he has as a *costumbrista* in *The Book of My Memories,* a delightful series of narratives dealing with history, personal experiences, and Mexican customs—a book unique of its kind.

THE DRAMA

Nineteenth-Century Writers

Although the other literary types came to a full flowering in this period, the drama did not meet with similar good fortune. And this was not caused by any failure to cultivate it. During this epoch, as perhaps never before, writing for the stage was abundant. Immediately after the restoration of the Republic in 1867, plays began to be produced with unusual frequency: dramas and comedies, some in prose, others in verse; some of historical background, others dealing with tendencies or circumstances of the times; the majority, indeed, inspired by hollow theatricality and out of touch with reality. The drama remained stationary, if not vacillating; and—except for one late attempt to restore romanticism and an occasional isolated work of merit—all its manifestations, up to the last of the century, were mere trials and experiments, which it may be presumed had very little significance as, in the main, they never reached publication.

The three main figures of this period are discussed below.

José Rosas Moreno, who has already been considered as a lyric poet, was one of the writers of the day who cultivated the drama with a plausible artistic bias. His drama in verse, *Sor Juana Inés de la Cruz* (1876), because of the impassioned mood of its heroine and, above all, because of its fluent versification, was perhaps the best produced in his time. He also wrote the following: two comedies, one of them *(The Relatives)* a satire in prose, and the other *(Daily Bread)* a *costumbrista* play in verse; the one-act farce *A Plan of Divorce,* also in verse; and the drama entitled *Netzahualcóyotl, the Bard of Acolhuacán.* Except for the farce, which was published, none of these latter works is extant; the two comedies were staged but not published, and *Netzahualcóyotl* was neither performed nor printed. Nevertheless, as evidence of the theatrical abilities of the poet, we have, besides *Sor Juana,* some attempts at drama for children—the first of the kind in Mexico. Rosas Moreno, who always enjoyed writing for children, composed a dramatic allegory in verse, *The New Year,* and a comedy and a funny farce, both in prose: *A Geography Lesson* and *Filial Love.* These three pieces were published in 1874.

Alfredo Chavero (1841-1906), a lawyer and politician who held high political posts and who, as a writer, was to devote himself particularly to archeology and history, was led by literary dilettantism to join himself to all the literary genres: poetry, the novel, and the drama. The last, however, was his favorite. His inspiration was far from being high, and as poet and prose writer he fell often into the sin of dulness. Notwithstanding, he knew the technique of the drama, and striving for effect commonly took the place of emotion in his plays. He is considered one of the most prolific playwrights of the period. He brought indigenous materials to the stage with a play in verse called *Xóchitl* (1877) and an attempt at tragedy, also in verse, entitled *Quetzalcóatl* (1878). He likewise experimented with the reconstruction of colonial history in *The Sister of the Avilas* and *The Loves of Alarcón* (1879); the latter is considered his best play. Between 1877 and 1881, he wrote a quantity of comedies and dramas: *Blessed Are Those Who Hope, The Hermitage of Santa Fe* (in collaboration with Peón y Contreras), *The Valley of Tears, Without Hope, The Hat, Love of Unhappiness, The Hurricane of a Kiss, The World of Today,* and even comic operas and a musical comedy, since he was indefatigable. That Chavero's work—with the exception of the historical plays—could have little significance from a national point of view may be deduced from the fact that the action of his comedies and dramas generally is unfolded in Paris, Madrid, or Rome, or even in Guanabacoa [Cuba]—in fact, anywhere in the world except Mexico.

José Peón y Contreras, a personality much superior to any of the other writers of this group, is doubtless the most important playwright of the period, considering the whole of his work.

He was born in Mérida, Yucatán, on January 12, 1843, and died in Mexico City on February 18, 1907. Belonging to a distinguished family and educated at home, he turned out to be as precocious in scientific studies as in poetry. At nineteen he had already received a degree in medicine; still a youth, he wrote a fantastic story, *The Cross on the Wall,* under the influence of Zorrilla, and composed three dramatic works: *Mary the Lunatic, God's Punishment,* and *The Count of Santiesteban.* In 1863 he moved to Mexico City, where he resumed his medical studies, devoted himself to his profession, and several times represented his native state in Congress, both as deputy and as senator.

He published his *Poems* in 1868. They show ease, delicacy, sensitiveness of feeling. He is outstanding for descriptive ability in *"El Grijalva"* and *The Tilapa River*; his "Meditation Dedicated to the Memory of My Mother" is filled with deep melancholy; gentleness and sweetness are displayed in his love songs, philosophic understanding in his elegy "To Don Leopoldo Río de la Loza," elevated thought, robustness of conception, and vigorous spirit in the "Ode to Hernán Cortés." In 1871 he published his *Mexican Historical Ballads,* which includes "The Fall of Atzcapotzalco," "Texcotzinco," "The Lord of Ecatepec, "Tlahuicole," "Montezuma," "Xocoyotzin," and "The Last Aztec"; in these, imitating the Duke of Rivas, he continued the type of indigenous poetry that Pesado and Roa Bárcena had introduced, writing with beauty and fluency of versification, but, like his models, being unable to avoid the artificial and rhetorical elements inherent in the genre. To the poems already mentioned should be added the following: the *Dramatic Ballads,* similar in form to the preceding, but Spanish, not indigenous, in subject matter; the *Little Dramas,* a collection of twenty more ballads in the same style; the *Columbian Ballads,* poems based on the life and fortunes of Christopher Columbus; and, lastly, the series of poetic meditations called *Echoes,* in which it seems Bécquer's influence can be detected. He also cultivated the novel; we are indebted to him for two works in this genre: *Taide* (1885) and *Fickle Woman* (1891).

His literary field, however, was the theater; in the lyric poet—and his excessive fondness for ballads reveals the fact clearly enough—was a fertile dramatic poet. He became known in this role in 1876 with the performance of *As High as the Sky!,* a tremendous melodrama in prose, dealing with colonial material, which earned a success for him, nevertheless. In the same year he made artistic amends with *The King's Daughter,* a three-act drama in verse, beyond any doubt his best work and perhaps the freshest, most beautiful flower of Mexican romantic drama. For this play he well deserved the honor that the writers of Mexico conferred upon him the night of May 7 of the same year—1876. In the theater of his triumph, they presented him with a gold pen and a diploma in which they proclaimed him "the restorer of the theater in the homeland of Alarcón and Gorostiza."

This high homage was a powerful stimulus to the playwright. Peón y Contreras, suddenly possessed by brilliant inspiration, gave to the theater the following works in the very brief period from 1876 to 1879 (in addition to the two plays already mentioned): *The Sacrifice of Life; Gil González de Avila; A Love Affair of Hernán Cortés; Juan de Villalpando; Antón de Alaminos; Struggles of Honor and Love; Hope; Impulses of the Heart; The Count of Peñalva; Because of the Jeweled Ornament on the Hat; Captain Pedreñales; Between My Uncle and My Aunt; Doña Leonor de Sarabia, Dead or Alive.* To these we should add *The Head of Uconor, For Fatherland, Father Joseph,* and *The Eternity of a Moment,* which must surely have been written later.

After this burst of activity, by virtue of which Peón y Contreras should be considered our most fruitful dramatic writer, a long silence followed. But in 1890 the poet returned to the stage with *Gabriela,* and after it came *Solitude* (1892), *A Storm at Sea* (1893), *Laureana* (1893), and *On the Threshold of Happiness* (1895). And still, to this abundant dramatic output, unparalleled in our letters, it is necessary to add the dramas and comedies that he left unpublished: *Margarita, Paul and Virginia,* and *Gertrudis*; and perhaps there are others of which we have no record.

The dramatic work of Peón y Contreras is uneven. According to all the evidence, the Yucatecan deserves the palm among our romantic playwrights for his works of colonial inspiration, the outstanding ones—not counting *The King's Daughter,* which is much superior to all the others—being *Gil González de Avila, Antón de Alaminos,* and *Because of the Jeweled Ornament on the Hat.* But the same cannot be said for his plays of contemporary setting, in which he sins through weakness and weariness as to both subject matter and technique. He was a better playwright in verse than in prose; and he was far better when his verse dealt with the viceregal period, which constituted his true realm and which no one has exploited in the theater with greater ability.

The poet, indeed, came late; the romantic drama, which he set out to revive, was already touching the western horizon or had passed completely. To this, apart from other material factors of the theater, must be attributed the fact that the extensive, very prolific work of the author of *The King's Daughter* has not had the influence that might have been expected. Would that Peón y Contreras had been born forty years earlier. Then his work would have been contemporary with that of Fernando Calderón—and perhaps a different fate would have befallen our dramatic literature.

Unfortunately, the dramatic works of Peón y Contreras have not been properly collected; only eleven of his dramas appear in the two volumes of the Agüeros Collection. A third volume of the collection contains his *Ballads, Little Dramas,* the *Columbian Ballads,* and *Echoes.*

Alongside the writers already mentioned, we should place—mainly under the pretext of historical curiosity—some others who are much less important, because of either the questionable literary value of their production or the scantiness of the work now available in published form.

The very prolific and scathing Don Juan A. Mateos, who after 1864 tried his hand in the theater in collaboration with Riva Palacio, filled the stage for long years with dramas and comedies of all kinds.

Prior to 1867 he wrote *Hereditary Hate, The Political Mania, The Stonecutter's Daughter, Niagara Falls, Martin the Demented,* and *Dangers of an Overcoat*—the titles of which are in themselves sufficiently suggestive. In 1867 he won notice for a factual drama, *The Death of Lincoln*; and between that time and 1881 came *The Official Bridegroom, The Kidnapping, The Other Man, The Great Gamblers,* (1877), *The Nun Alférez* (1877), *The Blonde and the Brunette, The Black Bird,* all of which were performed on the stage with varying fortune, some—like *The Other Man*—enjoying singular notoriety. Only those listed in the first group have been published.

Since almost the whole of the theatrical production of this epoch was not published and is not now extant, as said above, it is scarcely possible for us to know more than the titles of the works and the names of the authors. Among those who were fairly well known are the following: Manuel Peredo, celebrated theatrical critic, author of *He Who Wants All* (1868); Enrique de Olavarría y Ferrari, who wrote the comedy in verse *The Missionaries of Love* (1868); Justo Sierra, who accidentally peeped into the theater with a piece called *Piety* (1870); Roberto A. Esteva, who set the action of his play *Los Maurel* (1875) in France; Gustavo Baz, who treated the colonial theme in *Woman's Desires* (1876) and *The Conspiracy of Mexico*; and, lastly, Manuel José Othón, who hardly ever left his native province and yet, yielding to the prevailing mode, used Madrid (where he had never been) as the setting for his magnificent drama in verse, *After Death* (1885), dealing with contemporary material.

Next are the names that have remained in the shadow, if not buried in full obscurity. Jesús Echáiz (died in 1885) refurbished a melodrama, *Sahara of Córdoba, or The Inquisition in Mexico* (1867). Tragedies and dramas of foreign background were not lacking: Joaquín Villalobos (died in 1879) introduced *Sappho* in 1872, and Manuel María Romero (died in 1889) the same year presented *Catharine of Sweden.* Not lacking, either, were the authors who tried to turn the theater into a speaker's rostrum: for instance, a certain violent drama called *Martyrs of the People* (1876) brought persecutions to Alberto Bianchi; years later, he wrote another, probably of the same kind: *Social Vampires* (1887). Among the relatively prolific authors can be counted Bianchi himself and Ramón Manterola, who produced, in the year 1875 alone, four pieces, among them one

Isabel Lupouloff—with a Russian setting, as may be deduced from the title (though Sardou had not yet made that type the style). It is to be supposed that works of mere theatricality predominated and that they held the stage almost exclusively; of this type are *The Foundling* (1874) and *The Slave* (1876), by Rafael de Zayas Enríquez (1848-1932); *Vanity and Poverty, Luisa* (1874), by Francisco Lerdo; *Sofía* (1879), by Vicente Morales; *As There Are Many* (1881), by Javier Santa María (1843-1910); *Abysses of Passion* (1884) and *The Last Drama* (1887), by Miguel Ulloa; *Magdalena* (1884), by Jesús Cuevas; *Slander, Margaret* (1885), and *The Branch of Orange Blossoms* (1886), by Julio Espinosa; *The Best Revenge* and *A Trip to the Other World*, by Eduardo Noriega; *Cristóbal de Olid* (1887), a drama in verse, and even a translation of *Hamlet* (according to the notices, the only one in Spanish verse that has been made in Mexico), by Manuel Pérez Bibbins.

The preceding simple enumeration is sufficient to show that, in regard to quantity, the national production for the theater left nothing to be desired; it will be recalled that in the year 1876 alone—the richest in this respect—the Spanish actor Enrique Guasp gave forty performances of plays by Mexican authors, a thing unheard of until then, and that probably there was no Mexican actor, or foreign actor among those who came to Mexico during that period—Merced Morales, Manuel Estrada, Gerardo López del Castillo, Concha Méndez, Concha Padilla, José Valero, Salvadora Cairón, and la Jacinta Pezzana herself—who did not introduce new works by Mexican authors.

But the nationality of the authors hardly made these plays Mexican; ordinarily, they had as little to do with the national atmosphere or Mexican customs and character as with art. A drama of imitation, a drama without soul or character and not even, in compensation, adorned with the trappings of style—such was our drama in that epoch of feverish activity. Is it strange, then, that it should perish and be forgotten! After 1890, however, few comedies by Mexican authors appeared. As always, foreign plays dominated the stage. Alberto Michael (born 1865) alone built up a repertory of two hundred works by translations and arrangements from the French, the English, and the Italian, though in that figure should be included the original plays of this author, among which were the comedies *Ad majorem Dei gloriam, The Suitor Number Thirteen,* and *Cunning*

Tricks. Above all, especially prepared for the "hour theater"[1] were one-act farces with music and musical dramas in imitation of the Spanish type called *género chico*; but, in spite of the irremediable literary poverty of the theater, there was never lacking some little glimpse of customs or popular types in the musical dramas of the delightful comic writer Rafael Medina, the excellent humorist and poet José F. Elizondo, and, lastly, Aurelio González Carrasco.

Twentieth-Century Dramatists

The twentieth century had barely begun when, under the influence of Virginia Fábregas, the best Mexican actress of her time, a new effort was registered—an effort inspired solely by the desire to give at last a genuine national character to the drama. Marcelino Dávalos and José Joaquín Gamboa attained this goal.

Marcelino Dávalos was born in Guadalajara, Jalisco, on April 26, 1871, and died in Mexico City on September 19, 1923. Although he was a lawyer by profession and a politician now and then, it might be said that he devoted himself entirely to literature for the stage. His first work, *The Last Picture*, an impassioned drama not free from Echegaray's influence, reached the stage in 1900. This was followed by *Guadalupe* (1903), a popular regional drama, with naturalistic trimmings because of the subject treated—the hereditary transmission of alcoholism. His other works were *Thus They Pass . . .* (1908), the tragedy of the actress who grows old; *Tragic Gardens* (1909); *Marciano's Crime* (1909), a dramatic story inspired by a popular tradition; *Hail the Master!* (1910), a little rustic comedy in which the author tries to reproduce the rural speech; *The Old* (1911) and *Indissoluble* (1915), dramas of social themes; and, finally, *Eagles and Stars* (1916).

All of this work is in prose and is invariably on Mexican themes; consequently, it represents, in its homogeneity, a new, original note, in comparison with all that had gone before. Marcelino Dávalos lacked artistic finish and literary taste, but he had, instead, a command of theatrical technique that the dramatists preceding him did not attain. This, plus the fact that he always found his inspiration in Mexican

---

[1] A theater where several plays were given in one evening. The spectator could purchase admission to any one or all of the performances.—Translators' note.

people and things, makes him outstanding in the dramatic production of this epoch.

With more refined literary taste and superior literary ability, José Joaquín Gamboa (born in Mexico City on January 20, 1878; died in the same city on January 29, 1931) also toiled for the national theater.

He was well acquainted with foreign literatures. After a trip through Europe, while quite young, he studied to be a lawyer; but he finally gave up this career to devote himself to journalism and letters. He made his debut in the theater with a musical comedy, *Solitude* (1899). In his first drama, *The Flesh*—or *Teresa*, as it was called at its opening (1903)—the heroine is torn between mystic aspiration and sensual desire. In *Death* (1904)—its subject, at that time fashionable in the theater, is adultery in high society—one thought fills the whole drama: humanity's horror before the final transition, horror symbolized by the physician who, trying to defeat death, is at last conquered with his own weapons. *The Hearth* (1905) presents a young man from the provinces who, tired of life in the capital—which had converted him from an optimist into a skeptic—and eager to recover his moral health in the place where he had spent his childhood, returns to his home, only to find it shadowed and darkened by his sin. The high dramatic tone maintained in the preceding works was abandoned by Gamboa in his next play, *Judgment Day* (1908), a comedy of very delicate psychological analysis.

With this piece the dramatist's activities ceased, and there opened for him a long parenthesis of diplomatic life and of experiences abroad. It must have seemed that he had definitely retired from the stage. He returned to it, nevertheless, in 1923, with *The Devil Is Cold*, a dramatic comedy, which was followed by *Los Revillagigedos* (1925), *Via Crucis* (1925), and *If Youth Only Knew!* (1927). From the first, Gamboa had been characterized by his ability to reproduce the Mexican scene soberly, by his knowledge of the things and classes that he painted, and by the flexibility of his dialogue, well adapted for characterizing a type or a person with a few strokes; and these qualities are all heightened in his later works. He blends delicately. He constructs powerfully. Close to his principal characters, supplying a touch of bright *costumbrismo*, the minor figures stand out. In the dramatist is a poet of restrained tenderness, whose expressions of feeling are quickly brought into balance by the lightly ironical humorist. Finally—and this is the most important factor for its effect on the creation of a Mexican drama—in such comedies Gamboa refines and purifies the nationalistic inspiration, observing and sincerely interpreting Mexican life. And just as in *The Devil Is Cold* he succeeded in giving a picture filled with picturesque expression of the life of our humble middle class, so in the remaining plays he turned his eyes to the social drama and extracted from it powerful dramatic elements, as in *Via Crucis*, or studied the changes of environment in a class of Mexican society, as in the other works cited. The result—a thing never before recorded in our very badly deteriorated drama—is that his dramatic works not only are situated naturally in the very atmosphere in which they were created, but also are connected in an intimate manner with a definite moment of the national life.

Not to his second manner—in which the preceding were written—but to a third belong the works that came later. Being dissatisfied with his own mastery and insatiable in his desire for originality, Gamboa searched without ceasing for new roads—a continual shifting of technique. In *The Same Case* (1929), he shows us a veritable parade of stagecraft. A tormented psychologist, he pries into a soul in the enigmatic drama *She* (1930). Two short farces, meanwhile, had slipped from his pen: *Old Story* and *Spirits*; they constitute an interlude of good humor that the poet imposed on himself. Even at that time, in a bright midday that seemed very far from the tints of twilight, it would seem that he looked into the final mystery. The theater became too small for him. The stage seemed narrow. His thought and his inspiration went beyond them. And lo, with a prodigious leap, he conceived, planned, and executed his last great fresco —without an equal in our drama—*The Gentleman, Death, and the Devil* (1931), a work of inspired symbolic purpose, in which the thought, poetic and profound, dominates the imagination and sings the most mysterious and fascinating of songs.

This was his greatest work and also his last—something of a presentiment or a call from the beyond. Twenty days after the first performance, given January 9, 1931, the dramatist died.

The *Dramatic Works* of José Joaquín Gamboa were published in three volumes (Mexico, 1938).

XIX

History and Other Types of Prose

THE cultivation of history followed new directions. In this period the historians no longer were men tormented by political passion. Great investigators arose. There was not lacking the thoughtful artist who attempted a co-ordinated, harmonious work of synthesis. The brief picturesque chronicle appeared. Critics of history accomplished works of restitution or correction.

EMINENT HISTORIANS

Manuel Orozco y Berra

Don Manuel Orozco y Berra deserves a place among the great investigators of Mexican history and archeology.

He came into this world in the City of Mexico on June 8, 1816; and it might be said that his existence was a constant adjustment between the official duties that gave him a living and the disciplines that his calling delighted in. "Continually," he wrote on one occasion, "I was reduced to a sad alternative: if I had bread, I did not have time; if I had enough time, I lacked bread." To how many Mexican writers would the same painful formula apply!

Having passed through the College of Mining, Orozco y Berra took the degree of topographical engineer; and later, in 1847, after having studied in the Seminary of Puebla, he obtained the law degree. It was in Puebla during these years that he was initiated into literary work; and with his brother, Don Fernando, the novelist, he attempted journalism. Settled in Mexico City after 1851, he discharged successively the duties of various public offices, among others the office of director of the General Archives of Mexico, which he obtained through his natural bent toward scholarship and the active sponsorship of Don José Fernando Ramírez. Likewise, he undertook arduous scientific commissions. He made the map of the Valley of Mexico; he deciphered the original record books of the Municipal Council of Mexico City; he supervised the transfer to the state of the libraries belonging to the suppressed religious orders; he was professor of history and geography; in 1857, under the liberal government, he became minister of public works, and afterward occupied a seat on the Supreme Court. When the French Intervention—against which he had protested—occurred, he refused to become a member of the Assembly of Notables, since he would thereby be obligated to remain in the capital. Later, however, he was impelled by poverty to accept service under the Empire, and took various positions related to his training and profession; he attained signal distinctions, and came finally to be counsellor of state. After the fall of Maximilian, the eminent historian found himself in prison; but his great merits were such that the republican government showed itself merciful to him and gave him his liberty after he had spent two months in prison; and he was even reinstated in the Society of Geography and Statistics and the Academy of Literature and Sciences, organizations from which he had been expelled along with his imperialist colleagues. Notwithstanding all this, he never again held public office. At last he had time, but the bread was lacking. Powerful friends provided him with some resources so that he was not entirely without the means of life. Then the great scholar applied himself to writing his masterpiece, the *Ancient History of Mexico and the Conquest,* which was printed by the order and at the expense of the national government. It was in the process of publication when Orozco y Berra died on January 27, 1881, in his natal city.

Despite numerous official activities, Orozco y Berra devoted his whole life to historical studies, specializing in our early history. Guided by his friend and teacher, Don José Fernando Ramírez, he delved deep into archeology, devoting himself to deciphering the hieroglyphics, reading the writing on the ancient monuments, seeking the meaning of the Indian manuscripts—drawing help in all this from the old chroniclers, the missionary philologists, the historians and linguists of the early period. As a result, no one else has had so profound a knowledge of the ancient people of the Valley of Mexico —a field of study in which he is recognized as a primary authority of worldwide reputation. In him were united the qualities essential for the cultivation of history: immense knowledge, a powerful analytic mind, brilliant faculties of synthesis, and a clear, serene judgment.

His complete work has not yet been collected, and no small part of it is formed by monographs, memoranda, and studies scattered among official publications, periodicals, and reviews. Of the part printed in books, mention should be made of his outstanding contributions to the *Universal Dictionary of History and Geography,* on which he collaborated and for which he wrote the *Appendix* in three volumes (1855-56). Among his works requiring more sustained power in the handling of material are the following: *Historic Information about the Conspiracy of the Marqués del Valle* (1853), a faultless study of that epoch; *Geography of the Languages of Mexico and an Ethnographic Map* (1864), which includes an attempt to classify the indigenous languages, a study of the migrations of the tribes of Mexico, with information pertaining to their origin, formation, differences and affinities, civilization and customs, and, lastly, the geography of the languages, that is, the places in Mexico where the different indigenous languages and their dialects are still spoken; *Memoranda for the Map of the City of Mexico* (1867), which contains the cartographic history of the city along with interesting data about its most notable institutions and buildings; the *Materials for a Mexican Cartography* (1871), in which are explained the geographical ideas of the Aztecs and their manner of representing water and land, as shown in their geographic and topographic drawings, of which as many as 3,400 of various kinds are on record; and, lastly, the "Study of Mexican Chronology," published as a preface to Tezozomoc's chronicle—an erudite work, the first of its kind in Mexico, in which the scholar, after explaining one by one the diverse chronological systems that different authors have created, showing the defects of each and determining their origins, enters fully into the question, analyzes it, and establishes the bases on which we must rely in a matter so very enigmatic and confusing.

But the author's best claims rest, above all, on his last and excellent work: the *Ancient History of Mexico and the Conquest* (4 vols., 1880-81), the fruit of the investigations carried on throughout his laborious life and the book in which he concentrated all his learning. This work is divided into four parts. In the first—*The Civilization—*

he deals with mythology, customs, education, military and civil organization, legislation, commerce, agriculture, arts, hieroglyphic writing and system of numbers, calendar, and geography of the Aztec Empire and the distribution and languages of the families of Indian tribes. The second—*Prehistoric Man in Mexico*—tells of the original fauna and primitive man, of the monuments and the elements in common with the Ancient World. The third—*Ancient History*—is concerned with the Mayans, Michoacán, the Toltecs, the emigration of the Aztecs, the Chichimecas, the founding of Tenochtitlán, and the history of the Valley of Mexico up to the arrival of the Spaniards. In the fourth and last book, he outlines the history of the Conquest from the arrival of Diego de Velázquez in the Indies to the rebuilding of Tenochtitlán. Marvelous, in truth, is the picture enclosed in this monument of our letters. Employing a standard far from all prejudice and rigorously scientific, refining the enormous materials from which it was built, making use of his own investigations and discoveries, correcting errors, laying aside false theories, clearing up doubtful points, Orozco y Berra, with keen discernment, succeeded in purifying all the sources of our ancient history.

A worthy supplement to the preceding work is the *History of the Spanish Rule in Mexico,* now included in four volumes of the *Mexican Historical Library of Unpublished Works* (1938). In 1960 the *Ancient History of Mexico and the Conquest,* with a prior study by Angel María Garibay K., and a biography of Orozco y Berra, plus three bibliographies on his work by Miguel León Portilla, was published in the *Collection Porrúa.*

García Icazbalceta

Don Joaquín García Icazbalceta belonged to the same intellectual stock as Orozco y Berra, and few have served Mexican history with the wisdom, the zeal, and the noble generosity with which he served it. "The great master of all Mexican learning," Menéndez y Pelayo called him; and he is accepted not without reason as the leading authority on American affairs.

It might be said that this historian's pure, quiet existence knew only one austere passion: the love of investigation and study. His life holds no picturesque incidents or anything else not related to his exemplary intellectual activity. García Icazbalceta was born in Mexico

City on August 21, 1825. His family, who enjoyed a plentiful fortune, thought themselves obliged to move to Spain in 1829, fleeing from the political disturbances. They returned in 1836. The future writer studied at home, and he learned several languages in the free time left him after doing his work in his father's office. Soon, under the influence and counsel of Alamán, the desire to be a historian was awakened in him. He translated and published (1849-50) Prescott's *History of the Conquest of Peru,* adding new chapters and notes; next, his first works appeared in the *Universal Dictionary of History and Geography* (1852-56), and even at that time was revealed the scholarly investigator, the historian who combined clarity of style with clarity of judgment. He established a little printing press in his home. He formed a magnificent library. He devoted himself to collecting rare and valuable editions, manuscripts, and documents, some unknown, others that had been considered lost. "If some day the history of our country is to be written," he thought and later was to say, "it is necessary that we make haste to find the scattered materials that can still be recovered." Soon thereafter he launched the initial volume of his first collection of documents—a volume of which he was at once collector, editor, and printer. This was the first step. Such would be his whole life: to investigate, to study, to publish, until death came to him in the midst of his task, in his native city on November 26, 1894.

The works of García Icazbalceta can be divided into two categories: his editions of rare or unknown books, manuscripts, and documents important for the history of Mexico, and original works.

In the first classification—besides the editions of works by Mendieta, Cervantes de Salazar, González de Eslava, and Father Alegre, which have been mentioned in the sections devoted to these authors—the following works figure: the *Collection of Documents for the History of Mexico* (2 vols., 1858-66) and the *New Collection of Documents for the History of Mexico* (5 vols., 1886-92). These contain reports, letters, narratives, itineraries, ordinances, all being most important for the study of our history in the sixteenth century; and, as García Icazbalceta was accustomed to do in printing this type of work, each volume is preceded by erudite introductions, a true series of critical judgments and historico-literary dissertations revealing profound knowledge of the material discussed.

Among the original works the following belong in the first group: the *Memoranda for a Catalogue of Writers in the Indigenous Languages of America* (1866), *Don Fray Juan de Zumárraga, First Bishop and Archbishop of Mexico* (1881), and the *Mexican Bibliography of the Sixteenth Century* (1886). The book about Zumárraga, instead of being a biography, is an admirable pageant of Mexican history at the beginning of the colonial era. Editorial Porrúa has published in their *Collection of Mexican Authors* a new edition of all the documents collected by García Icazbalceta and several others, recently discovered, relative to Zumárraga. The picture is completed by the *Bibliography,* "a work ranking with the most perfect and excellent works of its kind that any nation possesses," according to Menéndez y Pelayo. This was the fruit of forty years of marvelous investigation and constitutes an itemized catalogue of books printed in Mexico in the period from 1539 to 1600, with biographies, explanations, facsimiles of old title pages, extracts from rare books, bibliographical notes, etc. A new edition by Agustín Millares Carlo was published in 1954. To the preceding should be added the 104 biographies, including that of Zumárraga, which form four volumes of the *Agüeros Collection,* and the numerous monographs, booklets, and articles (constituting another six volumes of the same collection) that came from the pen of the great and learned historian—the biographies destined to rescue from oblivion the figures of the workers for Mexican civilization; the other works dealing with the most varied questions related to our history in the sixteenth century: the press, public instruction, medicine, the religious orders, theatrical performances, fiestas, the earliest buildings and the appearance of the City of Mexico in the sixteenth century, studies of poets, printers, and bibliographers, and even very curious monographs like the ones devoted to cattle and the cacao tree in the history of Mexico.

If the expression is permissible, García Icazbalceta was the author of our sixteenth century. He disinterred it from the dust in which it lay forgotten. With his scholarly works, he began a new type of activity in the investigation and study of our history, showing that military and political events do not constitute all, or even the major part, of our past; instead, it is necessary to go deeper, to dig into the knowledge of customs, culture, and even the smallest aspects of the life of other times, and to present, finished and complete, the picture of civilization, in order to give a report of the formative process and the vicissitudes of a people.

And that the learned man succeeded in this, there can be no doubt. When he died while working on the *Vocabulary of Mexicanisms*, his posthumous work, which remained unfinished and was so published in 1905, he left a work and an example: the work and example of a historian of the greatest conscience and solidity, of the largest critical sagacity, scrupulousness, precision, and clarity of which Mexican literature boasts.

Justo Sierra

Don Justo Sierra was historian in a different manner. He did not investigate history; however, teaching it in the classroom or breathing life into it in books and addresses through the combined power of thinker and artist, he shaped the spirit of two generations. In him the historian was inseparable from the teacher.

Embracing the whole picture of human development, he aspired in his *School Manual of General History* (1891) "to show the social organism subjected—as all organisms are—to the universal law of evolution, without omitting the concrete factor that marks and vivifies the personality of a people and constitutes the meaning of an epoch." But, since for him "the love of country includes all the human loves—a love that is felt first and explained later," he took delight in giving this explanation to Mexican children in a *Catechism of Mexican History* (1896), a work admirable for clarity and simplicity. Later, elevating the tone and widening the perspectives, he made a synthesis of our political history, which appears in the second part of *Mexico: Its Social Evolution* (1900-1901), without doubt the most luminous and profound material written on this subject. This second part was published in a separate volume in 1940 under the title *Political Evolution of the Mexican People*. And, finally, he crowned his work as historian by raising a monument in magnificent prose to the man whose life he considered "a lesson, a supreme lesson in civic morality": *Juárez, His Work and His Time* (1905), a book that he wrote in good part but that was finished by Don Carlos Pereyra because the author's duties as minister of public instruction did not leave him time for completing it.

As Antonio Caso has observed, in Don Justo Sierra's historical books "the understanding of humanity throbs below the surface of a sincere optimism"; and, under the impetus of passion and enthusiasm, his ability to evoke scenes and people is so great that "the resurrection of the past is accomplished with the deceptiveness of psychological hallucinations." He turns history into a work of art in which profundity and nobility of thought are mated with magic of style, for this historian was probably the leading Mexican prose artist of his epoch in the abundance, completeness, and harmonious majesty of his work.

Inseparable from Justo Sierra's historical works are his addresses. It is sometimes said, not without justification, that the master's best pages may be found in his speeches. And, lastly, in order to complete the enumeration of his prose works, there should be mentioned all those important pieces still scattered in official publications and in periodicals devoted to pedagogy, politics, literary criticism, travels, etc., and, in this last genre, the book entitled *In Yankee Land* (1898). In Justo Sierra, the traveler unites the poet, the historian, and the public speaker, and these three come together to form a narrator always easy, as ready to be familiar and picturesque as to be profound and deeply significant.

Apart from its intrinsic value, the prose work of Justo Sierra is no less important for the study of the currents of thought that swayed his epoch. At first a fervent revolutionist, Justo Sierra was afterward converted to positivism, and, finally, as Antonio Caso expresses it, he confronted the absolutism of science with "the formidable question raised by contemporary criticism; and the enthusiasm for the religion of science with the incoercible wavering of the skeptic." His spirit was maintained in eternal youth by a restless desire to renew itself, and his work as historian is always characterized by its noble optimism.

The *Complete Works* of Justo Sierra have been published by the National Autonomous University, in fifteen volumes, with an excellent preliminary study—the best biography of the great historian—by Agustín Yáñez.

Bulnes

Another skeptic—during his whole life, not at the last moment only—Don Francisco Bulnes, unlike Justo Sierra, was a destroyer.

Born in the City of Mexico on October 4, 1847, he made a very brilliant record as a student in the School of Mining, where he obtained a degree in civil and mining engineering. In 1874 he went to Japan as member of a scientific commission headed by the scholar Díaz Covarrubias. But his purely intellectual inclinations separated him from the practice of his profession. From his youth he possessed substantial knowledge of various fields of science, and he applied himself to enrich that knowledge throughout his life. His training in mathematics, which taught him to reason clearly and exactly, enhanced the powers of the formidable logician. He was essentially a thinker and a sociologist.

Teaching, journalism, and politics absorbed nearly all his energies. On the floor of Congress, in which he served as deputy and senator for the space of thirty years, he was the most powerful orator of his day. In the role of consultant to various secretaries of state, he took part in drawing up the banking laws and the legal code for mining. His controversial articles in the press, no less than his speeches, had their moment of celebrity.

Prodigious memory, power of keen observation, clear, quick understanding: such were the characteristics of Bulnes' mind, in the opinion of Don Federico Gamboa. Three qualities, likewise, distinguish him as a publicist: independence of judgment, patriotic courage, and love of truth. Add to the preceding his encyclopedic culture, and it seems obvious that the orator and controversialist was largely endowed. As a writer, though far from measuring up to any standard of correctness, he was extraordinarily original and very personal. He enjoyed paradox and knew the art of cultivating it—he used it brutally. His verbal eloquence is transmitted whole to the written lines. "He is neither a conformist nor a purist in language," Gamboa observes;

on the contrary, his style, whether he speaks or writes, is weakened by unrestrainable, almost boorish independence, by preconceived, purposeful departure from good taste. In his character of thinker, he was absorbed in the thought, believing it must predominate and carry conviction; hence, his style, picturesque and coarse, suggestive and convincing, bulging with knowledge and bristling with ironies, which at times are cruelly sarcastic, is unruly and iconoclastic. If nothing gets in the way, the style usually is smooth and submissive toward the laws of the language; but at the least opposition or resistance, it leaps barriers, scorns rules, overthrows grammarians, and gibes at examples and precedents.

Bulnes wrote his first book in 1875. Having been named historian of the Mexican commission sent to Japan to observe the passage of Venus through the disk of the sun, he recorded his impressions as a traveler in *Eleven Thousand Leagues Over the Northern Hemisphere,* a work which reveals the peculiarities already discussed. In 1899 the sociologist appeared when he published *The Future of the Latin American Nations,* which served as a forum for his serious points of view.

But he turned quickly from the general study of the Spanish countries of the western hemisphere to the exclusive and very special study of his own country; both taste and talents confined him to historical criticism. He had been the high priest of positivism in Mexico; and like another great positivist—Hippolyte Taine, his inspirer, and, in a way, his master, who, absorbed in the problems of his country, gave himself to the study of the origins of contemporary France —Bulnes accomplished, "though in a fragmentary and disjointed way, with no few repetitions of events and points of view, and without that unity and harmony that are not the least virtues of Taine's great work," the study of the origins of contemporary Mexico in the series of books entitled, respectively, *The War of Independence: Hidalgo-Iturbide* (1910), *The Great Lies of Our History: The Nation and the Army in Foreign Wars* (1904), *The True Juárez and the Truth about the Intervention and the Empire* (1904), and *Juárez and the Revolutions of Ayutla and the Reform* (1905).

As has been said, Bulnes was a skeptic and a destroyer. His love of truth guided him, but it did not prevent him from falling sometimes into passion and sophistry. Hence, though much of his work still stands firm, no little part has been rejected as unreliable or even false, both because of its emotional origin and because of his reliance on and presentation of insufficient and incorrectly interpreted information.

His last works were *The Whole Truth about Mexico* (1916) and *The True Díaz* (1920). Even in extreme old age, he fought gallantly in the press, as his campaigns in the *Universal* bear witness, as well as the posthumous selection of his last articles, which was published as a book under the title of *The Great Problems of Mexico* (1927). He died in his native city on September 22, 1924.

González Obregón

In a way, through his special activity in historical matters, Don Luis González Obregón stems from García Icazbalceta.

Born in the city of Guanajuato on August 25, 1865, he was brought by his parents to Mexico City at two years of age. He studied first at home; still an adolescent, he entered the National Preparatory School, and, on leaving it, intended to pursue the study of law; but he soon renounced it, convinced that he had no calling for the law. His inclinations and tastes carried him in other directions. Altamirano, of whom he was a favorite pupil, awakened in him the love of letters. Beginning as a *costumbrista*—a phase of his literary character that he was to preserve permanently—he went on to the fields of history. In 1888 his first work appeared: biographical and bibliographical details concerning *Don José Joaquín Fernández de Lizardi*. In 1889 he started the *National Bibliographical Yearbook*, an enterprise that was not continued beyond the one issue; and he also published, during the same year, a *Brief Account of the Mexican Novelists in the Nineteenth Century*. From 1890 to 1891 he wrote for the *National* a weekly series of articles concerning the picturesque history of the City of Mexico. These, gathered into two series, each filling a volume, compose his very popular work *Old Mexico City* (1891-95), later rearranged in one volume in the Parisian edition of 1900. From that time on, his production became more and more abundant: *Captain Bernal Díaz del Castillo, Conquistador and Chronicler of New Spain* (1894), *Don José Fernando Ramírez, Bio-bibliographical Data* (1898), *Historical Sketch of the Drainage Works of the Valley of Mexico* (1903), *The Forerunners of Independence in the Sixteenth Century* (1906), *Don Justo Sierra, Historian* (1907), *Don Guillén de Lampart: The Inquisition and Independence in the Seventeenth Century* (1908), *Fray Melchor de Talamantes: Biography and Posthumous Writings* (1909), *The National Library of Mexico* (1910), *Life in Mexico in 1810* (1911), *Antiquities* (1917), *The Streets of Mexico City* (2 vols., 1922-27), *Cuauhtémoc* (1923). In 1937-38 some of the above works and others not previously collected (including articles on history and customs) appeared in the volumes entitled *Little*

Chronicles of New Spain, Chroniclers and Historians, and *Mexican Novelists.*

Like García Icazbalceta, González Obregón concentrated his investigations very definitely in the colonial epoch, the period least explored up to the time of these two noted historians; like Icazbalceta, again, he devoted himself to collecting materials for history, sometimes delving into archives and publishing rare and interesting books. And, lastly, following the route opened up by his predecessor in regard to the fundamental manner of understanding and interpreting history, he did not confine himself to military and political aspects, but penetrated deeply into the details of life in other times and threw a clear light on culture, manners, customs, and picturesque peculiarities.

Notwithstanding all this, González Obregón created a manner of treating history that is very personal and very much his own. In his hands, history turns away from the coldness and monotony of scholarly narratives and becomes a smooth, familiar story appealing to all. The unrelated fact, the frigid date, the colorless name regain life and warmth. Strange to say, he did not bow down before the great figures, nor before extraordinary deeds only. It might be said that he paused with a purer love before things, persons, and events that other historians, blind or indifferent, had passed by. He devoted his persistent attention to reconstructing the life of other days, with all its minute, captivating details, in an easy, fast-moving chronicle; and he popularized history by giving it color and literary meaning.

Literary history is indebted to him for very important bio-bibliographical investigations. But much more is Mexico City indebted to him; he is properly considered her best and most zealous modern chronicler.

González Obregón died in Mexico City on June 19, 1938.

Pereyra

Placed at the end of this group, which includes two great investigators, the powerful analyst who attempted the first important synthesis of Mexican history, the controversialist who cultivated historical criticism, and the picturesque expositor of life in former days, Don Carlos Pereyra represents the spirit of restitution and fair correction of history in behalf of the Spanish tradition.

A native of Saltillo, Coahuila, where he was born on November 3, 1871, Pereyra received his early education in his natal city. Later he continued his studies in Mexico City in the Preparatory School and the School of Jurisprudence. He took a law degree. He was professor of history and sociology, respectively, in those institutions, deputy to Congress, and diplomat. After retiring from political life and diplomacy, he remained for some time in Switzerland and later made his residence in Spain. He died in Madrid, June 30, 1942.

Very early in life, he acquired a fondness for history; he did research, collaborated in the publication of documents, and wrote a brief *History of the Mexican People*. Not only the best, however, but practically the whole of his work was done in Spain. The sum of accumulated learning, the experience acquired in his brief passage across the stage of politics and diplomacy, the view of new countries, the persistent study in libraries and archives, and, above all, the meditation at a distance, which widens perspectives and emphasizes outlines: these made it possible for him to construct a historical work truly substantial and comprehensive and to establish himself, by virtue of this work, as a leading authority on Hispano-American affairs.

Pereyra's work in this new period is sustained by a prevailing purpose: first, to show the character of the civilization that Spain brought to America, going to the documentary sources to clear up the truth and destroy the falsehoods that passion or ignorance has piled up; second, in a comparable way, and in intimate relationship with the preceding, to study some special historical problems of the American republics of Spanish origin; and, last, heedful of the racial struggle developing in the western hemisphere, where the powerful Anglo-Saxon was trying to fasten his claws in the countries of Spanish civilization, to reveal the truth about the United States in its attitude toward the Hispanic-American people and very especially toward Mexico.

The first of these objectives was attained in the following books: *The Work of Spain in America, The Conquest of the Oceanic Routes, Hernán Cortés and the Epic of the Valley of Mexico, The Footprints of the Conquistadors, Hernán Cortés* (a thorough study published in 1931), *Francisco Pizarro and the Treasure of Atahualpa*, and *Humboldt in America*. To the second category belong *Rosas and Thiers: European Diplomacy on the Plata River; Alberdi's Political Ideas;*

Bolívar and Washington: An Impossible Parallel; and *Francisco Solano López and the Paraguayan War*. And the crowning point of both the preceding groups is reached in the *Short History of America* (1930) and the *History of Spanish America* (1920-26); the latter comprises eight volumes and gives the most complete picture that has been made of the development of civilization in Spanish America, from the discovery of the New World, its exploration, and the formation of the Spanish Empire to the birth of the peoples now independent and their subsequent development up to the present. Lastly, the following books are concerned with the third of the objectives indicated above: *The Monroe Myth* (1931); *Texas: The First Dismemberment of Mexico*; *The Constitution of the United States as an Element of Plutocratic Rule*; and *The Crime of Woodrow Wilson*.

In Pereyra, extraordinary analytical powers and dialectical vigor were united with a rigid scholarship that would not permit him to write a line unless he had the documentary evidence before him. He mastered "the manly and concise style of history," though his work is full of vivacity and finely shaded with irony. His vehemence in argument, full of honesty and courage, was well tempered by a powerful critical spirit. To all this were added the art and originality of his method; and his works, without losing their strict historical character, hold the life and the interest of fictional narratives, and constitute, for the same reason, a powerful instrument for the dissemination of his views. He aspired "to give to the past the living touch of the present and to the present the feeling of perpetuity inspired by the things of the past."

MINOR HISTORIANS

Abundant, but not always important, is the production of history in this period. In order to avoid a long enumeration, we name only the following among other great personalities: Don Vicente Riva Palacio, under whose direction and with the collaboration of Don Alfredo Chavero, Don Julio Zárate, Don Enrique de Olavarría y Ferrari, Don Juan de Dios Arias, and Don José María Vigil, the important work entitled *Mexico Through the Centuries* (5 vols., 1884-89) was brought to completion; the versatile Dr. Agustín Rivera y Sanromán (1824-1916), author of *Philosophy in New Spain, Critical Introductory Chapters on the Viceroyalty and the War of Indepen-*

dence, and the *Annals of the Reform and the Second Empire;* Don Manuel Rivera Cambas (1840-1917), author of *The Rulers of Mexico* and *Mexico: Picturesque, Artistic, and Monumental;* Don José María Marroqui (1824-1908), whose work *The City of Mexico,* in three thick volumes, constitutes a rich arsenal of data for the understanding of the old metropolis; and Don Luis Pérez Verdía (1857-1914), author of a *Compendium of Mexican History* (1883), which might be considered the first valuable work of the kind that was written in Mexico.

In historic research and scholarship, Don Francisco del Paso y Troncoso (1842-1916) stands out—the scholar to whom Mexican history and ethnology owe much. He was a diligent explorer of the archives of Europe, a collector of documents, the editor of capital works for the understanding of our past, a man of numerous and vast enterprises—though he began many and finished few. Because of this peculiarity, which greatly impaired his gigantic work, García Icazbalceta humorously called him "a scholarly library of incomplete works." Among important works that he left unfinished was a monumental edition of Sahagún. The best of his original productions, consisting of monographs and archeological studies, are found in the *Annals of the National Museum;* and the work of the investigator is seen in the *Volume of Letters from New Spain,* rich in documents, which was published, after his death, in sixteen volumes.

Because of his systematic industry and his severe methodical spirit, Don Genaro García (1867-1920) performed excellent service for history. His principal historical works are the study of the *Character of the Spanish Conquest in America and in Mexico* (1901) and the very scholarly work concerning *Don Juan de Palafox y Mendoza* (1918). As publisher he is responsible for *Two Accounts of Florida* (1902) and the only edition that has been made from the original autographed manuscript of Bernal Díaz del Castillo's *True History of the Conquest of New Spain* (1904). Still greater, if possible, are his merits as a collector: to him are due the very important collection of *Unpublished or Very Rare Documents for the History of Mexico* and the *Mexican Historical Documents,* published under his direction by the National Museum to celebrate the first centenary of Independence.

Among the bibliographers should be mentioned Father Vicente de P. Andrade (1844-1915), for his *Essay on Mexican Bibliography of the Seventeenth Century* (1899), and Dr. Nicolás León (1859-1929), for his *Mexican Bibliography of the Eighteenth Century* (5 vols., 1902-06). The works of these men complement the masterly work of García Icazbalceta.

Lastly, in this period regional histories were abundant: Joaquín Arróniz, Jr., wrote of Orizaba (1867); Manuel Rivera Cambas, of Jalapa (1869-71); Alejandro Prieto, of the state of Tamaulipas (1873); Eligio Ancona, of the state of Yucatán (1878-80); Agustín R. González, of the state of Aguascalientes (1881); Antonio Carrión, of the city of Puebla de los Angeles (1896-97); Eduardo Ruiz wrote *Michoacán: Scenes, Stories, and Legends* (1900); Luis Pérez Verdía, the *History of the State of Jalisco* (1910-11); Manuel Muro, the history of the state of San Luis Potosí (1910); and J. A. Gay, that of Oaxaca.

CRITICISM

The growth of literary magazines and the press and the rise of artistic and scientific societies brought with them the development of criticism. Altamirano was the first to practice it, publishing his articles in the *Renaissance* soon after the restoration of the Republic; but his work had value as a model and an inspiration rather than intrinsic value, as is shown by the essays and reviews collected in the three volumes, with the title of *The National Literature*, and published in the Porrúa *Collection of Mexican Authors*. In the *National Review of Sciences and Letters*, founded in 1888 under the direction of Don Justo Sierra, literary criticism was plentiful. It was abundant, also, in the *Azure Review* and the *Modern Review*.

Nevertheless, few are the figures that stand out in this type of writing. "In Mexico, a country conceived in liberty," if we can believe "Brummel," who wrote this passage in 1888:

The Republic of Letters had been transformed into a Monarchy . . . or, to be more exact, into a Church. It had pontiffs and priests, and, according to the circumstances or the needs of the cult, various hack-writers discharged the duties of eunuchs of the Sistine Chapel, intoning in a very thin voice dithyrambs to the saint of the day, or, on other occasions, acting the rôle of sacrificers, flagellating dissenters and heretics mercilessly.

Puga y Acal

It was Don Manuel Puga y Acal, who, under the pseudonym

given above, set out directly to remedy this state of affairs, fighting
for the laws of good taste and provoking numberless polemics. Born
in Guadalajara, Jalisco, on October 8, 1860, he went as a boy to
France for his education. His father wished to make him a mining engineer. He took the work for the bachelor's degree in sciences and
letters in the School of Juilly in Paris; he then went to Belgium, where
he entered the Provincial School of Mines at Monza. But he soon exchanged mining for literature—which is far from being the same
thing. In Brussels he knew Verlaine and Rimbaud; he lived the
Bohemian life of Paris; he devoted himself to writing French verses
and was probably the first to translate Bécquer into the language of
Racine. And, at last, in 1883, he returned to his own country. From
that time on, sometimes in Guadalajara and sometimes in San Luis
Potosí or Mexico City, he devoted his time to political and literary
journalism, engaged in teaching, and was, for a short time, deputy
to the local Congress of Jalisco and the national Congress. The period
of his greatest activity as a critic corresponds to the period of his
connection with the *National Banner* and the *Liberal Party*. No
few of his articles, however, are to be found in the numerous periodicals and reviews that he founded and directed or in which he collaborated until his death; these include many articles of historical
character, which, if collected, would make thick volumes. As a
critic, he "dared to look straight at some of the suns of our literary
heaven." He was caustic, satirical; and his judgments, characterized
by a penetrating analytical spirit, were given consistency by his
broad, solid culture. Only the first series of "Brummel's" critical
essays has been published, appearing under the title of *Mexican Contemporary Poets* (1888); it contains interesting studies of Díaz
Mirón, Gutiérrez Nájera, and Juan de Dios Peza.

Puga y Acal died in Mexico City, September 13, 1930.

Icaza

Don Francisco A. de Icaza's main calling was that of critic, rather
than poet. Born in the City of Mexico on February 2, 1863, he took
his education and formed his spirit there. Consecrated to diplomacy,
he went to Spain in 1886 with General Riva Palacio when the latter
was designated minister plenipotentiary in Spain. Although he held
various diplomatic posts in the Old World—among others, the posi-

tion of Mexican representative in Germany for many years—Don Francisco spent the greater part of his life in Madrid. There he established his home, and there he won respect and fame with his literary works. He died in Madrid on May 28, 1925.

In addition to his poetry, which has already been mentioned, he produced an abundance of prose. He began with a *Survey of Critics* (1894), a synthesis of contemporary literary criticism. He then had a similar impulse to examine and interpret some of the greatest figures of the Spanish Golden Age. He became a consummate student of Cervantes. To the greatest genius of Castilian letters he dedicated his principal books: *The Exemplary Tales of Cervantes* (1910) —in the opinion of Foulché-Delbosc, "the best, nay, the only good book that has been published" on this subject; *How and Why "The Pretended Aunt" Is Not by Cervantes* (1916); *Cervantian Frauds and Errors* (1917); *El Quijote Through Three Centuries* (1918). Alongside these works should be placed *Real Happenings That Seem to Be Imaginary in the Works of Gutierre de Cetina, Juan de la Cueva, and Mateo Alemán* (1919), an essential book in that it treats the affairs of these writers in America; *Lope de Vega, His Loves and His Hates* (1919); and his critical editions of Spanish classics, with notes and prefaces. "In these books," Alfonso Reyes says, referring to Icaza's works,

we always find elaborate scholarship, for in matters of knowledge and of style he never confused his means and his ends; we always find that the materials are assimilated and interpreted, the dates corrected by laborious criticism, everything digested; that the books are really books, properly cooked and free from lumps of disintegrating material; we also find the joy of discrimination and the desire to attain, so far as it can be attained, freedom from error.

Icaza's prose work was completed by the following: his study of *The German University* (1915), his translations of Hebbel and Turgenef, and the much-discussed *Autobiographical Dictionary of Conquistadors and Settlers of New Spain* (1923). He had vast plans for devoting the rest of his life to investigations and historical and literary studies of the colonial era. These were interrupted by death.

Other Critics

Our literary history owes an incalculable debt to Don Enrique de Olavarría y Ferrari for his *Historical Sketch of the Theater in Mexico* (4 vols., 1895), which covers the period from the beginnings to 1896; to Don Francisco Sosa (1848-1925), for his important biographical works: *The Mexican Episcopate, Biographies of Distinguished Mexicans, Historical and Biographical Ephemerides, Contemporaries,* and *Manual of Yucatecan Biography*; and to Don Francisco Pimentel (1823-1893). The last named contributed much to the study of American linguistics with his *Descriptive and Comparative View of the Indigenous Languages of Mexico* (1874-75), and to the study of the national literature with his *Critical History of Poetry in Mexico* (1885) and *Mexican Novelists and Orators,* which appears in Volume V of his *Complete Works,* published in 1904. Pimentel was a man without style, taste, or critical discrimination, but his deplorable literary judgment can be pardoned in view of the abundance of information he collected. Extensive, but in large part not collected, is the critical work of Don José María Vigil (1829-1909): it comprises a diversity of monographs, speeches, sketches, and prologues, as well as the following books: the anthology of *Mexican Poetesses* (1893), that of *Mexican Poets* (1894), a scholarly study of *Lope de Vega* (1904), and the *Historic Sketch of Mexican Literature,* which he left unfinished. The academician Don Manuel G. Revilla (1863-1925) served the national art with special devotion and zeal; his critical labors in this respect are represented in the volume of *Biographies* (nearly all of them of painters) published in the *Agüeros Collection* and in the masterly book entitled *Art in Mexico* (1893), which is already a classic. The following authors should also be mentioned in this rapid enumeration: the eminent philologist Don Rafael Angel de la Peña (1837-1906), some of whose critical studies are to be found in the proper volume of the *Agüeros Collection*; and his son, Don Antonio de la Peña y Reyes (1869-1928), a disciple of Altamirano, who is responsible for *The Living and the Dead: Articles and Discourses* (1903), *Moral Anthology* (1920), and the *Biographical Dictionary of Mexican Writers,* unfortunately not finished, and who is also the author of many of the scholarly prefaces to the publications of the Mexican Historic-Diplomatic Archives. In conclusion, we shall mention two journalists: Dr. Manuel Flores (1853-1924), a man of vast culture, a distinguished educator, and, as a prose writer, one of the most copious (he left innumerable articles in periodicals, but the only ones that have been collected are the travel articles that form the volume entitled *Italy*, 1916); and Don Victoriano Agüeros (1854-1911), one of the most illustrious journalists of his generation and the forceful propagator of Mexican letters by means of his biographical studies of *Contemporary Mexican Writers* (1880) and—mainly, we might say remarkably—by his *Library of Mexican Authors*, a work often incorrect, but unique, which he edited and which reached a total of seventy-eight volumes (1896-1911).

ORATORY

Oratorical ability has never been characteristic of Mexican genius and character. As we have seen in this and preceding periods, however, there have always been personalities worthy of praise in the fields of both sacred and secular oratory. To those already pointed out—Altamirano and Ramírez, Bulnes and Sierra—it would hardly seem necessary to add any more; but there is one other—the most elegant of his period.

Jesús Urueta (born in the city of Chihuahua on February 9, 1868; died on December 8, 1920, in Buenos Aires, where he was representing his country in the capacity of minister plenipotentiary) united rigorous artistic training with spellbinding eloquence. In Mexico his name stands for "the orator," the artist of Apollo. Words were changed to music on his lips, and his periods had the grace and harmony of ancient marble. Though he was affiliated with the writers of the *Modern Review*, little of his work has been collected. His books, not counting the prologue for *Dulcinea* (a work that he unfortunately never carried beyond the stage of planning), include the volume entitled *Soul-Poetry: Lectures on Greek Literature* (1904); the little book of *Literary Discourses* (1919), selected by the author himself and published in the "Culture Collection"; a book of essays, *Fresca (Fresh Air)*, published in 1903; and *Political Satires and Diversions* (1911).

A spirit all flame, Urueta was consumed before he had created for Mexican letters the legacy that was appropriate to his genius. Without being a humanist—a circumstance that detracted from his "Hellenism"—he had a poetic and exuberant passion for Greece and everything Greek. As a result, he succeeded in giving us an interpretation of the ancients that is at least original and beautiful—although a like fondness for Hellenism has had a dismal effect on his imitators, both contemporary and later, and resulted in a very widespread and cheap type of oratory from which we still suffer. Familiar with the French literature of his time, Urueta turned, in his last days, to the great Spanish prose writers of the Golden Age. His prose—which belongs with the best produced at that time—has a delightful classic flavor with a fine modern blending.

Conclusion

XX.

Twentieth-Century Renascence

THE DICTATORSHIP AND THE REVOLUTION

THE YEAR 1910 marks the end of one cycle and the beginning of another in the history of Mexico. For thirty years General Porfirio Díaz had ruled the destinies of the country. Having come to power in 1876, he built a dictatorial government—a *paternal* dictatorship, as it has been called, based on the passive, lazy, indifferent acquiescence of the people rather than on the force of arms.

Two facts were made to coincide with this period: the peace and the prosperity of Mexico. The former is evident: the nation lived in uninterrupted peace for more than three decades. The latter is more apparent than real.

With peace established and the administration reorganized, material progress followed. Mexico opened her doors to the foreigner for the exploitation of her natural resources, attracting capital by means of great concessions and unusual privileges. Railroads began to cut through the country. Mining was revolutionized. Great industries were created. Commerce was expanded. The public treasury was put on a sound basis and credit established. Important public works were carried to completion in the capital and various seaports. Nevertheless, was this material progress actually a splendid thing? Did it correspond to a fair economic condition of the country in general and, more particularly, of the social classes as a whole? Also, was it consistent with moral progress?

"The whole economic condition of the country," Carlos Pereyra says, "dazzling as it was when seen from a distance, constituted an indefinite postponement of programs of reform, among which should be counted the building of a political structure on institutional

361

bases."[1] Thus, under a personal government with the outward appearance of a democracy, Mexico lived for thirty years in complete political stagnation. And in regard to social welfare, if we omit the privileged groups, the situation of the middle and lower classes was precarious when not wretched. Cities and towns, with the fountains of life slowly drying up, were depopulated so that their inhabitants might swell the mass of bureaucratic job-seekers in the capitals of the various states and, especially, in the national capital. Industry and commerce were in foreign hands. Rural property was controlled by a class lacking the means, if not the ability, to increase production; and the enormous mass of peons "with their salary of hunger" continued to exist without security in the present or hope for the future— either waiting for revolution or eligible to serve as "cannon fodder" when the moment came.

In 1910 General Díaz' administration had reached the height of its splendor. When the spectacular fiestas commemorating the centenary of Independence were celebrated, the regime he had built up during thirty years seemed impregnable and indestructible. Nevertheless, it was on the verge of disintegration. Institutional governments renew themselves and last a long time; personal governments grow old, decline, pass away. Mexico, in thirty years of peace, had not created a government of institutions; and the government of Díaz, at the height of its glory and solid in appearance, crumbled and dissolved within a period of months, overthrown by the impact of a revolution whose force rested more on public opinion than on arms.

The Revolution of 1910, which in its first impulse acted in obedience to ostensible political causes, involved also—in fact, chiefly involved—the stern reassertion of social goals. In reality, it continued and completed the two great revolutionary movements of the preceding century—Independence and the Reform—and with them it divides the modern history of Mexico into three great cycles.

We shall not follow the Revolution through its vicissitudes, for these belong to political history and not to letters. Let us limit ourselves solely to pointing out that it is the most important event—the fundamental fact that conditions the course of Mexican life—in the present period.

[1] *Historia de la América Española* (*History of Spanish America*), Mexico, III, 333.— Author's note.

THE NEW GENERATION

Though it is true that the three decades of peace under Díaz were not favorable to the creation of a permanent, self-renewing government and the regime collapsed as a result, it is no less true that this period of continued tranquillity was extremely beneficial to culture and letters.

Culture developed as in no other period of our history. The educational work of Justo Sierra at the head of the Secretariat of Public Instruction meant not only the beginning of public education in Mexico but also the introduction of the spirit of higher learning into public instruction. The great leader, when his efforts were crowned by the founding of the National University in 1910, speaking at the opening of that institution, denounced those groups that, having been initiated into human knowledge, form themselves into a gigantic pyramid and, "desiring to be able to see the stars better and to be seen by an entire people," build at the top a pagan temple around which is constructed "a kind of science, always farther removed from its earthly function, always farther from the soil that sustains it, always more indifferent to the pulsations of social reality."

In so speaking, the illustrious thinker quite fittingly did no more than voice ideas and feelings that were already in the minds and hearts of the youth of that day. For long years, the directors of culture had shut themselves within an intellectual faith; absorbed in the religion of science, they had made a god of it and expected everything from it. But a new generation had arrived: a generation that doubted and was beginning to fight. From this generation came the first attacks on positivism—made by a youth, Antonio Caso, who seems to have been nourished on the new philosophical doctrines; and by a restless, nervous dialectian, Ricardo Gómez Robelo.

Just as, years before, a group formed around the *Azure Review* and, later, around the *Modern Review*, so in this period a new group formed around another literary publication: the review called *Savia Moderna*, founded in 1906 by Alfonso Cravioto and Luis Castillo Ledón. Besides the young Mexicans who were trying out their literary talents, the group included two young writers foreign in nationality but not in spirit: the Dominicans, Pedro and Max Henríquez Ureña; and to these two was later added the Spaniard José Escofet, who became as Mexican as they. The first act of these youths was the public protest they led against the reviving, on a commercial basis, of Gutiérrez Nájera's famous review mentioned earlier; this innocent cry constituted the first "mutiny" in many years to be registered against the peace of the country. "It was that literary group, that little army," Alfonso Reyes writes, "which first raised in the streets the banners of free art—which assembled a multitude of university students in the plazas." "For the first time in Mexico," he adds,

there was a band of youths marching in the streets, demanding the rights of beauty—disposed, if need should arise, to defend beauty (oh sacred folly!) with their fists. They were the same ones who later summoned the nation to celebrate the anniversary of Barreda, the liberal educator, and then delivered, along with the announcement of a new literary era, the sign and token of a new political conscience.

From this memorable occasion on March 20, 1908, at which Justo Sierra condemned the official positivism, Antonio Caso dates the beginning of a new epoch in Mexican ideology.

That generation, spawned in the early years of the century and young at the time of the Revolution, showed profound differences from preceding generations. Philosophers, critics, novelists, and poets stood out. And representatives of other artistic activities were not lacking. In the broad literary organization of the period—the *Athenaeum*—the orators José María Lozano and Nemesio García Naranjo and the painters Diego Rivera and Angel Zárraga were an integral part; so also were Saturnino Herrán, another painter, and the composer Manuel M. Ponce in the latter days. Unlike the preceding generation, they did not seclude themselves in an ivory tower: they wanted direct contact with the public and the people, and for this reason founded the Society of Lectures, established the *Athenaeum of Youth*—afterward called the *Athenaeum of Mexico*—and instituted the first University of the People. Opening the eyes of the mind and spirit toward all horizons, they aspired to universality of culture. The predominating foreign influence up to that time had been French, but in the new generation this exclusiveness no longer existed: the young nourished themselves directly on all the great literatures and cultivated the Castilian with love and ardor; the study of the latter they fought to introduce, and in fact did introduce, into the preparatory schools and the curriculum of the university recently opened.

In short, the youth of that day, disciplined, serene, inclined toward laborious, persistent study, though they began by being combative and boisterous, came of their own accord to condemn the romantic Bohemianism still more or less continuing to exist. Disdaining the ivory tower and sympathizing with humanity, to quote Alfonso Reyes again, they worshiped "Athena Promachos, the Science that defends the fatherland, as Justo Sierra would have desired."

The winds of change were blowing. The faith of the intellectual had disappeared; positivism, which served to co-ordinate, to discipline, had fulfilled its mission. "The fetish made into a god by Barreda," as Antonio Caso has written, "joined the other broken idols in the pantheon of history."[2] The torch of the spiritual began to burn. A question stood before the future. A deep restlessness stirred. What was to come? "In the strange anguish of waiting," José Vasconcelos could say with something like prophetic vision, in September, 1910, "a glimpse of the future, quick and tragic, shows us the incomprehensible and far-off thing we lack: we feel the uselessness of our individual existence, and we sacrifice it in desire for the future, with that feeling of catastrophe that accompanies all grandeur."[3]

We stand in the midst of a cycle that is not yet ended. Throughout the tragic blows of civil strife, the workers for Mexican culture have carried their work forward. Not for an instant, in the last four decades, have the noble efforts of thinker and artist halted. An elaborate literature has come into existence in this long lapse of time. Nevertheless, to attempt an analysis of it would be premature and perhaps futile. Perspective is lacking; the general features are still incomplete.

Arriving at the threshold of the present and attempting to complete the picture of the history of Mexican literature (though it be with provisional strokes that the historians of the future will alter or erase), let us be content with a brief, superficial enumeration, rather than a critical résumé, of the books and men of our time.

PHILOSOPHY AND CRITICISM

Having come to maturity in a period of philosophical agitation,

---

[2] *El Problema de México y la Ideología National* (*The Problem of Mexico and National Ideology*).—Author's note.

[3] *Don Gabino Barreda y las Ideas Contemporáneas* (*Don Gabino Barreda and Contemporary Ideas*).—Author's note.

a period that earnestly desired a complete literary reform, philosophy and criticism were conspicuous activities of the generation of 1910.

Among those who consecrated themselves to these disciplines, one luminous personality stands out: that of Antonio Caso (born in the City of Mexico, December 19, 1883; died in the same city, March 6, 1946). It was he who introduced the courses in philosophy into the curriculum of the National University. In his work, thought and word have the life and warmth of fire. Even as a schoolboy, he commanded respect, and while he was still a youth, he was called "The Master." "There is no theory," Alfonso Reyes said, "no affirmation or doubt that he has not understood and made his at least for an instant. He has lived the history of philosophy. And with such experience of ideas and the logical power that unifies them, his lecturing is rightly the pride of our university world." Reyes wrote this in 1914. After that time, Caso did something more than make history and philosophy live and ennoble the classroom: as writer and thinker, he produced a vast, powerful work containing original philosophic doctrines; as critic and essayist of marvelous culture and the greatest clarity and eloquence, he examined a multiplicity of problems and analyzed the greatest figures of human thought; he revealed his lyrical gift in two volumes of verse; he composed treatises on aesthetics and sociology; and lastly, he participated, with austere ardor, in the battle of ideas and forces that stirred not only Mexico but the world, opposing historical materialism, fighting for "social-nationalism," and making himself a vigorous defender of freedom of thought and therefore of academic freedom also. This multiform intellectual activity is contained in the volumes entitled *Philosophic Problems* (1915), *Philosophers and Moral Doctrines* (1915), *Life As Economy, Unselfishness, and Charity* (1919), *Dramma per musica* (1920), *Brief Comment on Fray Luis de León's Ode to Music* (1921), *Addresses to the Mexican Nation* (1922), *Critical and Controversial Essays* (1922), *The Concept of Universal History* (1923), *Doctrines and Ideas* (1924), *The Problem of Mexico and National Ideology* (1924), *Heterogeneous Addresses* (1925), *Principles of Esthetics* (1925), *History and Anthology of Philosophic Thought* (1926), *Genetic and Systematic Sociology* (1927), *Alchemy* (poems, 1931), *El Acto Ideatorio* (1934), *Husserl's Philosophy* (1934), *New Addresses to the Mexican Nation* (1934), *El políptico de los días del mar* (poems, 1935), *The*

Philosophy of Culture and Historic Materialism (1936), *The Human Being and the Totalitarian State* (1941), *The Danger of Man* (1942), and *Mexico, Notes on Native Culture* (1943).

At the height of his intellectual and physical vigor, when much could be expected from his noble thought, fervent action, and high apostleship, Antonio Caso passed from the scene. He is the first great figure of the contemporary age who, issuing from the frame of an epoch which is yet to be concluded, remains to be evaluated definitely for his contribution to literature. Caso not only left an admirable and powerful work, but set a high example, an example of integrity, excellence, and spiritual courage. He was essentially a creative person and a teacher. He is rightfully considered the most eminent Mexican thinker, a strong personality in which were epitomized the culture and conscience of our time.

Another philosopher, a thinker and a man of action who was as original in his ideas as he was impetuous and impassioned in the expression of them, was José Vasconcelos (born in the city of Oaxaca in 1882; died in Mexico City, 1959). His spirit dwelt in perpetual restlessness. As the head of the Secretariat of Public Education, he accomplished a great and noble work. The fire of revolution burned in his spirit from his early years, impelling him not only to destroy but also to build; and in that fiery crucible, during more than half of his life, no few changes occurred, rising, colliding, flashing in the tortured spirit. Having begun his activities as a writer with a lecture on *Don Gabino Barreda and Contemporary Ideas* (1910), he did not continue them farther until 1918, when, after many vicissitudes, he published his essay on *Esthetic Monism.* This was followed by *Literary Digressions* (1919), *Prometheus Victorious* (a modern tragedy, 1920), *Pythagoras* (1921), *Hindu Studies* (1922), *The Cosmic Race* (1925), and *Indology.* He was a stormy writer, supple and vigorous, abounding in ideas—an untiring fighter. His literary production increased in amount and in strength during his last years. In four books filled with passion, stark sincerity, and picturesque strength, he told his own tempestuous life: *A Creole Ulysses* (1935), *The Tempest* (1936), *The Disaster* (1938), and *The Proconsulship* (1939). His *Short History of Mexico* (1937), though it cannot be considered a complete picture, nor even, in some respects, a fair view, constitutes a very personal interpretation of the national development. Vasconcelos was no stranger to the field of philosophic speculation, as is shown by the volumes entitled *Treatise on Metaphysics* (1929), *Ethics* (1932), *Esthetics* (1936), and *History of Philosophic Thought* (1937). Lastly, in addition to his incessant periodical writing, the following books give testimony to the roving vigor of his genius: *The Magic Sonata* (stories and narratives, 1933), *Bolivarism and Monroeism* (1934), and *What Is Communism?* (1936).

Alfonso Reyes (born in Monterrey, May 17, 1889; died in Mexico City, December 27, 1959) typifies the humanist par excellence. Possessing immense intellectual curiosity and the broadest culture, as a writer he became—in fact, he was from the beginning—the perfect model of humanism. He had the gift of style; he created a delightful individual type of prose. He was a penetrating, shrewd critic, an original storyteller abounding in surprises, a poet—in Antonio Castro Leal's judgment—of sharp sensibility, grounded in Góngora and Mallarmé, familiar with the classics ancient and modern, an artist "who adorns his song—the echoes of a hidden torrent, affectionate illuminations, the variegated colors of the mind—with the jewelry of precise, delicate words." He took delight in scholarly investigation. After long residence and study in Spain, he became recognized as an authority on various questions related to Castilian literature. Foulché-Delbosc—with whom he collaborated in publishing the works of Góngora—considered him "the leading Gongorist of the new generations." Moreover, his editions of the *Poem of the Cid* and of Alarcón's works are a model; and of equally great value are the prologues, notes, and commentaries for his other editions of classic and modern writers: the Archpriest of Hita, Quevedo, Gracián, Lope de Vega, Antonio de Fuente la Peña, Fray Servando Teresa de Mier, and Amado Nervo. Wandering through Europe and America on incessant diplomatic missions as representative of Mexico, he must never have allowed his pen to be idle. His original writings were vast and learned. They comprise, in the fields of criticism and essays, the following: *The "Rustic Poems" of Manuel José Othón* (a study published in the "Centenary Lectures," 1910), *Esthetic Questions* (1911), *Landscape in Mexican Poetry of the Nineteenth Century* (1911), *The Suicide* (1917), *Cartoons of Madrid* (1917), *Vision of Anáhuac* (1917), *Portraits Real and Imaginary* (1920), *Similarities and Differences* (five series, the last two with the titles *The Two Roads* and *Sundial*, 1921-26), *The Hunter* (1921), *Almanac* (1924), *Questions Relating to Góngora* (1927), *Address in Behalf of Virgil* (1931), *By Return Mail* (1932), *On the American Day* (1932), *Athenian Politics* (1932), *Tren de Ondas* (1932), *A Vote for the University of the North* (1933), *The Fall: An Exegesis in Ivory* (1933), *The Passing of Amado Nervo* (1937), *Goethe's Political Idea* (1937), *Spanish Evenings* (1937), *Lope de Vega's "The Pilgrim in His Own Country"* (1937), *The Influence of the Arthurian Cycle on Castilian Literature* (1938), *Concerning Descartes' Esthetics* (1938), *Chapters Concerning Spanish Literature* (First Series, 1939; Second Series, 1945), *The Seven over Deva (Dream of an August Afternoon)*, *Criticism in the Age of Athens* (1941), *Rhetorical Anguish* (1942), *The Demarcation: Foreword to Literary Theory*, *Literary Experience*, *Ultima Thule* (1942), *North and South* (1944), *Works and Days* (1945), *Written in Pencil*, *Among the Books*, *Panorama of Greek Religion*, *About a Writer Censured in the "Quixote,"* and *Pleasing Company* (1948).

The storyteller, the traveler, and the writer of memoirs, endowed always with subtle, imaginative charm and rare sensibility are revealed in *The Oblique Plane* (1920), *May Night* (1924), *Flight from Christmas* (1929), *Juan Peña's Testimony* (1930), *The Two Augurs: The Beginning of a Novel* (1931), *The Arrow* (1931), *In the Little Window of Toledo* (1931), *Hours Spent in Burgos* (1932), and *Where Indalecio Appears and Disappears* (1932). The poet, the difficult, inconstant poet, all quintessence—who writes "as life goes, in step with the soul, without turning the eyes"—is found in *Footprints* (1922), *Repose* (1926), *Five Almost Sonnets* (1931), *Ballad of January River* (1933), *To the Memory of Ricardo Güiraldes* (1934), *Grasses of Tarahumara* (1934), *Gulf of Mexico* (1935), *First Draft*, *Poetic Game* (1935), *Infancy* (1935), *Again* (1936), *Cantata at the Tomb of Federico García Lorca* (1937), *Ballads and Related Verse* (1945), and also social verses written for an album and other miscellaneous verse, which are in a volume entitled *Courtesy* (1948)—all this without taking into account that the poet and humanist join hands in the magic evocation of Greece: *Cruel Iphigeneia* (1924), a dramatic poem with a prose commentary. To the above works the following more recently published books should be added: *Perils, In a Loud Voice, Meeting of Shadows* (1949), *Marginalia, Anchorages, Gunpowder Tree, Memoir of Kitchen and Cellar, Berkeleyania* (1953).

Reyes made some translations of foreign writers—Sterne, Chesterton, Robert Louis Stevenson, and Chekhov—into Spanish and wrote numerous studies of various kinds, printing them in pamphlets and reviews, as well as his own "literary mail," *Monterrey*, which he began to publish in 1930. It should be said, also, that among the Mexican contemporary writers, he is the one that has been most often translated into foreign languages.

Jesús T. Acevedo (1892-1918) belonged in his generation to the type of writers "who do not write." A lover of good books, he took delight in cultivating the art of serious, intelligent lecturing. "His malicious insinuations, his aesthetic taste, the quickness of his thought, his resolute attitude toward life," Alfonso Reyes explains, "made him an exceptional person, the fruit of a civilization superior to that of the world in which he lived." The only reflection that remains to us of that noble, unfortunate spirit is a volume entitled *Dissertations of an Architect,* in which were collected some of his studies and lectures. It was published in a posthumous edition.

An outstanding figure in literary criticism, Antonio Castro Leal was born in the city of San Luis Potosí, March 2, 1896. He received his law degree from the Law School of the National University of Mexico, became a distinguished professor of literature and international law in the same university, and was named its rector. He has held several diplomatic posts with distinction, being noted for his broad understanding and firm convictions. His true calling, however, is literature. He is an accomplished humanist of universal culture which has been enriched by his diplomatic activities, understanding of various languages, contact with various peoples, and knowledge of foreign literatures. "His attention was first directed," Genaro Fernández MacGregor has said,

toward the matchless world of Castilian letters. Then he turned toward his native land. Just as navigators and cartographers trace on paper lands recently discovered, so has he retraced the map of our letters, pointing out its line of development, its geological genesis, so to speak, which consists of listening closely to the innermost recesses and meaning; he has measured the heights, gauging them exactly; sometimes he has climbed them in order to know them completely. His method of interpretation is exacting and judicious, leading him to long searching in old papers and ancient editions to correct texts and data.

This accounts for the vigor and excellence of his works. His affinity for literature bore fruit early: in 1914, in collaboration with Manuel Toussaint and Alberto Vásquez del Mercado, he published *The Hundred Best Mexican Lyric Poems*, an excellent anthology that was followed in 1939 by *The Hundred Best Modern Mexican Poems*; and in 1953 by *Modern Mexican Poetry* (anthology, preliminary study, and notes), which examines and reveals the evolution of our lyric poetry from Gutiérrez Nájera to the present time. He is the director of the series entitled *Collection of Mexican Authors*, published by Editorial Porrúa, which has already published eighty-four volumes that now replace the *Collection of Mexican Authors* edited by Victoriano Agüeros, a collection selected with slight aesthetic criteria and printed badly. Castro Leal's most important work, *Juan Ruiz de Alarcón: His Life and Works* (1943), is the finest and best-documented study that has been made of our great dramatist. In 1953, Castro Leal won, because of his study of the work of Díaz Mirón, the first prize in the international competition sponsored by the municipal government of Veracruz in celebration of the first centenary of the birth of that poet.

Literary criticism was also cultivated with dignity and great persistence by Francisco González Guerrero (1889), who has published some of his criticism in one volume: *The Books of Others* (1947). Likewise, literary criticism is indebted to José Luis Martínez for important critical works, among which is the volume entitled *Mexican Literature: Twentieth Century* (1949).

In the field of art criticism, we should mention the following: Federico E. Mariscal (born in Querétaro, November 7, 1881), for his work entitled *The Fatherland and the National Architecture* (1915); the enigmatic Dr. Atl[4] (a native of Guadalajara, although he says facetiously that he was born in Paris on the day when Leopoldo Lugones christened him with the above name), author of *The Folk Arts in Mexico* (1920), *Churches of Mexico* (6 volumes, 1926), and *The Landscape: An Essay* (1933); Francisco Díez Barroso, who

[4] Pseudonym of Gerardo Murillo.—Translators' note.

studied colonial painting, architecture, and ornamentation in the volume called *Art in New Spain* (1921); Rafael García Granados (1893-1956) and Luis MacGregor, for their book *Huejotzingo: The City and the Franciscan Monastery* (1934); Francisco de la Maza, for his work *San Miguel Allende, Its History, Its Monuments* (1939); the ethnologist D. Antonio Cortés, for his splendid monographs *Valenciana* (1933) and *Wrought-Iron Ornaments* (1935); and Justino Fernández, author of various works of great interest, among which are *Modern Art in Mexico* (1937), *José Clemente Orozco: Form and Idea* (1942), and *Coatlicue: Esthetics of Ancient Indigenous Art* (1954). Manuel Toussaint (born in Puebla on May 29, 1890; died in New York, November 22, 1955) also produced some excellent works in this field: *Saturnino Herrán and His Work* (1920), *The Cathedral of Mexico* (1924), *Taxco* (1931), *Painting in Mexico during the Sixteenth Century* (1936), *Colonial Avenues* (1939), *Muslim Art in America* (1946), *Colonial Art in Mexico* (1948), in addition to his literary studies—many of them masterly, but not yet collected into volumes—and his travel impressions such as *Phantom Voyages* (1924) and *Oaxaca* (1926); and finally, the historical work entitled *The Conquest of Pánuco* (1948). Travel literature, by the way, has been abundant in this period: besides other such books that will be mentioned incidentally in the following pages, we should note these: *In Our Cousins' Home . . .* (1918) by Alejandro Quijano (born in Mazatlán, January 5, 1883; died in Mexico City, February 17, 1957), a learned writer of polished prose, who has also cultivated linguistics, history, and literary criticism in his monographs and in his lectures for the university and learned societies, although only one volume of these (entitled *On the Rostrum*) has appeared; Manuel Gómez Morín (1896), author of *Loyal Spain* (1928), which is interesting because it shows the love and devotion of the new generation toward the cradle of our civilization—a feeling far different from the revolutionary spirit that formerly predominated; and, lastly, Alfredo Maillefert (1889-1941), who, in 1937, published *Praise of Michoacán*, followed by *Anchor in Time* (1940), and a posthumous work, *The Books I Have Read* (1942).

Philosophical criticism occupied no little part of the work of the educator Ezequiel A. Chávez (born in the city of Aguascalientes,

September 19, 1868; died in Mexico City, December 2, 1946); he wrote a penetrating study of the *Psychology of Adolescence* (1928) and also the most ample and scholarly study that has been made of Sor Juana Inés de la Cruz (1931). The name of Bernardo J. Gastélum is outstanding in more recent philosophic production because of his books *Intelligence and Symbol* (1927), *Philosophy of the Attitude and the Dehumanization of Man* (1936). The dedication to philosophy of Dr. Enrique A. Aragón, an eminent psychologist and psychiatrist (born in Mexico City, March 22, 1880; died in Veracruz, June 16, 1942), is seen in his *Complete Works*, the second volume of which, *History of the Soul*, was published in 1944. Samuel Ramos (born in Zitácuaro, Michoacán, June 8, 1897; died in Mexico City, 1959), founder of the Chair of History of Philosophy in Mexico, in the National University, wrote many works: *Hypothesis* (1928), *The Profile of Man and Culture in Mexico* (1934), *Diego Rivera* (1935), *Beyond the Ethics of Kant* (1938), *The Stravinsky Case* (1939), *Toward a New Humanism* (1940), *Twenty Years of Education in Mexico* (1941), and *History of Philosophy in Mexico* (1942). José Romano Muñoz (born in Villa de Cos, Zacatecas, August 9, 1890) also has distinguished himself in the discipline of philosophy: *The Ethics of Values* (1932), *Initiation into Culture* (1936), *Beyond Husserl* (1937), *The Secret of Good and Evil* (1938), and *Toward an Existential Philosophy*. Jesús Guisa y Azevedo (born in Salvatierra, Guanajuato, October 15, 1900), an impetuous controversialist, is the author of a small volume called *Louvain, Where I Come from* ... (1934), in which, since he believes that "the Middle Ages have a sense of the eternal that must be put into relationship, into contact, we might say, with the spiritual states of the present," he discusses briefly the thirteenth century, the philosophy of Saint Thomas, Neo-Thomism, and the work of Cardinal Mercier.

In the field of philology, we mention the following: Pablo González Casanova (born in Mérida, June 29, 1889; died in Mexico City, March 24, 1936), a very scholarly investigator though he died at the height of his powers and very few of his works have been printed; the humanist Francisco de P. Herrasti, prominent in philology and interpretative criticism, especially in Latin texts; and Miguel Salinas (born in Toluca, February 12, 1858; died in Mexico City, December 18, 1938), author of valuable works in linguistics, as well as the volumes entitled *Stories and Landscapes of Morelos, Data for the History of Toluca, Picturesque Places in Mexico,* and *Philological Lectures and Articles.* Classical learning has a distinguished representative in Gabriel Méndez Plancarte (born in Zamora, Michoacán, 1905; died in Mexico City, December 16, 1949), who, besides cultivating poetry in beautiful and original strophes, in his book *Horace in Mexico* (1937) studied the influence of the great Latin poet on Mexican literature of the sixteenth and seventeenth centuries and listed the translators and imitators of Horace from the eighteenth century to the present. He also published a critical edition, with introduction and notes, of *Unedited Poems* (1942) by the Jesuit humanist J. Juan Luis Maneiro, who was at the time unknown as a poet. In conclusion, lexicography and the study of proverbs constitute the field in which Darío Rubio (born in Mineral de la Luz, Guanajuato, December 8, 1879; died in Mexico City, January 21, 1952) made important investigations; his books include *The So-called Mexicanisms of the Spanish Academy* (1917), *Nahuatlan Expressions and Barbarisms* (1919), *The Anarchy of Language in Spanish America* (1925), *Mexican Popular Speech,* and *Mexican Adages, Proverbs, Sayings, and Slang* (1937). We should include a work valuable in its genre, the *General Dictionary of Americanisms,* composed by Francisco J. Santamaría and published in 1942, and his monumental *Dictionary of Mexicanisms,* which has been edited and published in one volume of more than one thousand pages (1959) by Editorial Porrúa, S.A. Lastly, regarding language used by horsemen and usages and customs of the *charros,* we should mention Carlos Rincón Gallardo, Marquis of Guadalupe (born in Mexico City, July 29, 1874; died in the same city, June 7, 1950), who wrote two important works: *Equestrian Dictionary* (1945) and *Book on the Mexican Charro* (1946).

ORATORY

Oratory, so far as its accomplishments in the first decades of this century are concerned, would hardly deserve a separate chapter. On the stage of politics, the art of eloquence was never widely practiced during the long regime of Díaz; except for Bulnes and Juan A. Mateos—strongly antithetical—few or none distinguished themselves in the practically nonexistent parliamentary debates. In the last days of the Díaz regime, however, literary and artistic oratory—if not political oratory—developed; and at the beginning of the Revolution the oratory of patriotic ardor flourished to some extent. In the latter, Querido Moheno and Luis Cabrera were outstanding: the one fluent, ingenious, overflowing; and the other very agile, dry, and of cutting irony on the floor of Congress; both of extraordinary power as political writers and controversialists. Not only civic oratory but also the oratory devoted to the exaltation of art was mastered by Jesús Urueta, who has already been discussed. And close to these three would stand José María Lozano and Nemesio García Naranjo.

Lozano (born in San Miguel el Alto, Jalisco, October 28, 1878; died in Mexico City, August 7, 1933) was a born orator, who enthralled and conquered his audiences—a man of the most facile speech, perhaps, that Mexico had known in many years. If for others—for instance, Moheno—oratory was the fruit of patient study, it was for him a natural and unfailing gift. Unfortunately, the little of his work that he left in written form has been scattered and is still uncollected.

On the other hand, Nemesio García Naranjo (a native of Lampazos, Nuevo León, where he was born March 8, 1883; died in Mexico City, December 21, 1962) is characterized by repose, by reflective preparation, though these qualities do not eliminate impetuosity or lyrical brilliance. A volume of his *Addresses* appeared in 1923. Devoted to journalism and history, he published a study of *Porfirio Díaz* (1930) and another of *Simón Bolívar* (1931). Also, attracted to the theater, he composed and produced a comedy, *The Dealer in Dolls* (1937). He was a graceful, vigorous prose writer.

THE NOVEL

Fiction plays an important and brilliant part in the literary production of this period. The novel, becoming more and more fully nationalized, penetrating deeply into the soul and life of Mexico, has followed the most varied courses and has assumed in many instances rare artistic beauty in both form and style.

Belonging to the group centered around the *Athenaeum of Youth* and, later, to the Mexican Academy, Carlos González Peña (born in Lagos de Moreno, state of Jalisco, July 7, 1885; died in Mexico City, August 2, 1955) had given his first novels to the press before 1910—*At Night* (1906), *The Little Girl* (1907), and *The Bohemian Muse* (1909)—and in 1919 published *The Chimera's Flight*, and later a travel book, *The Tumultuous Life: Six Weeks in the United States* (1920). Between 1945 and 1952 he published books which reflected his activities as an essayist, musical, literary, and dramatic critic, traveler, chronicler of the past and present: *Moonlight Patio (Scenes and Landscapes with Lakes), Flowers of Passion and Melancholia, Musical Enchantment, My People, The Illuminated Niche, To Spend One's Life Looking, Clearness in the Distance, The Soul and the Mask, Beyond the Sea, Paris and London* (travel scenes), *Through Italy, Portugal, and Spain.*

Martín Luis Guzmán (born in Chihuahua, October 6, 1887), a member of the generation of the *Athenaeum of Youth,* is the greatest writer produced by the Revolution. An author of diaphanous prose, a discerning observer and researcher with a restless and penetrating mind, Guzmán is a man in whom thought and action are one. Excepting his first two essays, *On the Banks of the Hudson* (1920) and *The Complaint of Mexico,* and the excellent fictional biography, *The Youthful Mina, Hero of Navarre,* all of his work was inspired by and dedicated to that great historical event in which he was both participant and witness. In 1928 he published *The Eagle and the Serpent,* the most vivid and powerful book written about the Revolution. This is a book of memoirs in which he narrates his own adventures and fortunes, but which is called a novel because of the aesthetic treatment of the most varied incidents, the impassioned plot, and the colorful depiction of customs. The best political novel in Mexican letters, *The Shadow of the Caudillo* (1929), reveals Guzmán's consummate skill and exposes the painful reality of one of the darkest periods of the post-revolutionary epoch, an epoch characterized by the desire for power and the struggle to obtain it. His ability as historian, memoir writer, and novelist is fully utilized in his remarkable work, *Memoirs of Pancho Villa,* the initial volume of which he published in 1938-39. In this original and unique book Guzmán, assuming the person of the terrible warrior and his peculiar picturesque speech, relates the story of Villa's life, giving us, from Villa's viewpoint, an animated, vital, and dramatic story of the Revolution in its most turbulent period. Finally, Guzmán's academic discourse entitled *Note on a Personality* is a beautiful and valuable autobiographical document that permits us to enter into the very being of the writer himself.

Alfonso Teja Zabre (native of San Luis de la Paz, Guanajuato, born December 23, 1888; died in Mexico City, February 28, 1962), after trying his hand with *Poems and Fantasies* (1914), turned to fiction in *Open Wings* (1920) and *Hope and Hatiké* (1922), both vividly original and the latter charmingly exotic. Later he devoted himself to history. In addition to a *Life of Morelos* (1917), the *History of Cuauhtémoc*, and the *Tragedy of Cuauhtémoc*, he published his *Essays on the History of Mexico, History of Mexico: A Modern Interpretation,* and *Theory of the Revolution.*

Artemio de Valle-Arizpe (born in Saltillo, Coahuila, January 25, 1888; died in the City of Mexico, November 15, 1961) is the creator of the artistic novel of colonial background. He had an inborn love of the past; "old furniture, the chinaware and ivory and jewels of bygone beauty, the old textiles" delighted him. Through sentiment and through knowledge—for no one else searched so avidly in musty chronicles and yellowed papers—he revivified the past with ardent sensibility in stories, novels, monographs and studies, articles, and anthologies. Among his works of fiction are the following: *Example* (1919), *Miraculous Lives* (1921), *Doña Leonor de Cáceres y Acevedo y Cosas tenedes* (1922), *Three Niches of an Altarpiece* (1936), *Lilies of Flanders* (1938), *Stories of Old Mexico* (1939), *Canillitas* (1942), *Restless Anxiety, In Mexico and in Other Centuries* (1948). His "Traditions, Legends, and Events of Viceregal Mexico"—which constitutes a vast, animated world, fictional also in that the imaginative fuses with the historical and the legendary—is an important series containing the following volumes: *Concerning Time Past* (1932), *Loves and Knavery* (1933), *Viceroys of New Spain and Their Wives* (2 volumes, 1933), *Book of Engravings* (1934), *Stories of the Living and the Dead* (1936), *Fortunes of Hernán Cortés and Other Excesses* (1940), *Mexican Legends* (1943), *Modest Little Garden* (1944), *Mirror of Time, Room of Tapestries, Hazy Distances* (1951), *Old Stones in the Sun,* and *Inquisition and Crimes* (1952). He also wrote a delightful study called *Don Victoriano Salado Alvarez and Conversation in Mexico* (1932), which is filled with data for our literary history; he further presented a good part of our history—primarily in its anecdotal aspect—in his monograph

The National Palace of Mexico (1936); and he gracefully described
the life of Mexico City from the early days of the colony to the present by giving the history of one street in *On the Old Causeway of
Tlacopan* (1937) and *Old Street and New Street* (1949); by giving
the history of a rich traditional art in *Notes on the Silversmiths'
Trade* (1931); by describing the customs in *Pictures of Mexico*
(1943); and by picturesque characters in *The Blonde Rodríguez*
(1950) and *Friar Servando* (1951). Finally, one other book of Valle-
Arizpe should be pointed out: *The Very Noble and Loyal City of
Mexico* (1924), an anthology of the most beautiful pages written in
former years about the city; a new edition, enlarged and rearranged,
was published in 1939 under the title of *History of the City of Mexico According to the Narratives of Its Chroniclers.*

Certainly the novel of colonial inspiration has not been neglected
in this epoch. Julio Jiménez Rueda (born in the City of Mexico,
April 10, 1896; died in the same city, 1960), though he devoted himself chiefly to the theater, showed his inclination toward viceregal
fiction in some pages of his first book—*Stories and Dialogues* (1917)
—and he yielded to it completely in the beautiful novel *Sister Adoration of the Divine Word* (1923) and in *Moisén* (1924), another
novel. Much later he wrote a novel of humorous character: *The Misfortune of Count Kadski* (1935). His brief diplomatic experience
furnished him with material for a volume giving his impressions of
a trip through South America: *Under the Southern Cross* (1922).
He also made an important contribution to the knowledge of our
letters in *History of Mexican Literature* (1928). To this should be
added his studies of *Juan Ruiz de Alarcón* (1934) and *Lope de Vega*
(an interpretative essay, 1935), his masterly book *Juan Ruiz de
Alarcón and His Times* (1939), published as a most valuable contribution to the celebration of the tercentenary of the great dramatist's death, his biography of *Don Pedro Moya de Contreras, First
Inquisitor of Mexico, Mexican Letters in the Nineteenth Century*
(1944), and *Heresies and Superstitions in New Spain (Heterodoxies
in Mexico,* 1946).

Francisco Monterde (born in Mexico City, August 9, 1894), a
playwright, a restless writer who has delighted in treading the most
diverse roads, likewise tried to evoke the viceregal era in two short
novels, *Cetina's Madrigal* and *The Secret of the Ladder* (1918).

Though afterward he pursued other goals in fiction—*A New Author* (1925), *Mexican Stories* (1936), and *Hall of Mirrors* (1937)—he returned to the colonial theme with *Fear of Hernán Cortés* (a book of short stories, 1943) and *Montezuma of the Golden Chair* (1946), his most recent fictional work. He also wrote the following books in the field of criticism and history: *The Viceroys of New Spain* (1922), *Manuel Gutiérrez Nájera* (1925), *Amado Nervo* (1929), *In Defense of a Work and a Generation* (1935), and *Mexican Culture* (1946), as well as *Meditative Journey* (1933), a book of poems, and *Profiles of Taxco* (1928), a travel narrative. Ermilo Abreu Gómez (born in Mérida, Yucatán, in 1894), a writer of the same restless kind, was attracted by the viceregal theme in *The Hunchback* (1924) and *The Miraculous Life of the Servant of God, Gregorio López* (1925). Later, he published a volume of short stories, *Mayan Heroes* (1942), and a volume of criticism, *Classicists, Romanticists, Moderns*; and contributed to the study of the personality and work of Sor Juana Inés de la Cruz both through new editions of such works as the *Reply to Sister Filotea* and the *Lives* written by Juan José Eguiara y Eguren and by Father Diego Calleja—for which he supplied notes and prologues—and through his own erudite work entitled *Sor Juana Inés de la Cruz: Bibliography and Works* (1934).

Mariano Azuela belongs to the period before 1910 both because of his age (he was born in Lagos de Moreno, Jalisco, January 1, 1873; died in Mexico City, March 1, 1952) and because the first part of his work—*Marie Louise* (1907), *The Ones Who Fail* (1908), and *Mala yerba* (*Weeds*, 1909)—was published in the earlier period. But he is placed in the present by his novels inspired by the scenes of the Revolution and those of psychological and *costumbrista* character, which he later wrote: *Andrés Pérez, Follower of Madero* (1911), *The Underdogs* (1916), *The Flies* (1918), *The Troubles of a Decent Family* (1918), *The Evil Hour* (1923), *Revenge* (1925), *The Firefly* (1932), *Comrade Pantoja* (1937), *Regina Landa* (1939), *The Outpost* (1940), *The New Bourgeoisie* (1941), *The Proprietess* (1944), *The Subdued Woman* (1946), *Forbidden Paths* (1949), *The Curse* (1955). To these should be added the beautiful, fictional biography he dedicated to the rebel Pedro Moreno; a volume of *Theater*, which contains the plays entitled *The Underdogs, The Night Owl, Concerning the Llano Brothers*; and a volume of criticism,

One Hundred Years of the Mexican Novel (1947). Azuela is distinguished by his vigor and the acuteness of his observation, and has been one of the most widely translated of modern Mexican novelists.

Martín Gómez Palacio (born in Durango in 1893) has written beautiful poetry—see the volume *Flush with Life* (1921)—but, nevertheless, he has devoted himself almost exclusively to novels: *The Mad Imagination* (1915), *One, Two, and . . .* (1923), *The Holy Horror* (1925), *The Best of All Possible Worlds* (1927), *The Bandage, the Scales, and the Sword* (1936), and *The Colt.* He is a robust prose writer, a shrewd analyst, a narrator full of irony and wit; in pages filled with life and color he has reflected scenes and types from Mexican life. Both the psychological novel (*Dilemma,* 1921) and the regional novel, cultivated with singular success (*Mexican People,* 1924), have occupied the attention of Xavier Icaza. His later work, *Panchito Chapopote* (1928)—we hardly know whether it belongs in the field of fiction—is a "tropical picture."

The novel of customs has had a representative in Esteban Maqueo Castellanos, author of *The Ruin of the Great House* (1921), and has been prolifically cultivated by Eduardo J. Correa, among whose principal works are *Lonely Souls, The Miracle of Miracles,* and *The Impostors.* The novel of social thesis is represented by *The Defiled Sister* (1927), by José Manuel Puig Casauranc (born in Laguna del Carmen, Campeche, January 31, 1888; died in Havana, May 9, 1939), who launched his career with a volume of highly dramatic stories, *Concerning Life* (1922), and wrote one later—*His Revenge* (1930). Finally, Genaro Estrada (born in Mazatlán, June 2, 1887; died in Mexico City, September 29, 1937), who composed in neat prose a book of colonial sketches, *Visionary of New Spain* (1921), flourished also in the field of the novel, as the malicious and subtle *Pero Galín* (1926) bears witness.

The short story has attracted no few writers. In the front rank of these stands Genaro Fernández MacGrégor (born in the City of Mexico, May 4, 1883; died there, December 22, 1959); his *Trivial Novels* (1918) are brief narratives of sharp analysis and salty style. He afterward turned his attention to criticism, in which he was outstanding as much for strict taste as for profound, varied, refined culture. He published in this field a *Critical Sketch of Contemporary Art* (1931), *The Sanctification of Sor Juana* (1932), *Díaz Mirón*

(1935), *Masks* (1935), *Genaro Estrada* (1938), and *Mora Restored* (1938). He returned, nevertheless, to the story—and surely in a masterly way—in a new book: *Late Harvest* (1939). Recent travel in Europe inspired his *Notes on an Unexpected Voyage* (1952).

Julio Torri (born in Saltillo, Coahuila, June 27, 1889)—"a humorist," according to Alfonso Reyes, "of cruel, perverse humor, an excellent stylist"—is author of a small but celebrated book of *Essays and Poems* (1917) and a volume of short stories, *Musket Shootings* (1940). Carlos Díaz Dufoo, Jr., a clever and unfortunate writer (born in Mexico City, November 28, 1888; died in the same city, April 30, 1932), like Torri in many respects, cultivated the essay and the sharp, ironic prose style in his book, *Epigrams*. Mariano Silva y Aceves (born in La Piedad Cabadas, Michoacán, June 26, 1886; died in Mexico City, November 24, 1937) may be considered "*the* short-story writer" by popular acclaim; a transparently clear writer, of restrained emotion and sometimes of shrewd humor, is revealed in *Ivory Box* (1916), *Virgin's Face* (1919), *Animula* (1920), *Little Silver Bells* (1925), and *Puppets* (1937). Dr. Atl, who was mentioned in the section devoted to criticism, figures among the cultivators of the short story and the brief prose piece by virtue of the following volumes: *Onward, Upward!* (1927), *Barbarous Stories* (1929), and *Stories of All Complexions* (1933); furthermore, his odd book *A Man Outside the Universe* (1935) should be mentioned. Guillermo Jiménez (born in Zapotlán, Jalisco, March 9, 1891) is outstanding in the short narrative and the chronicle: *Restless Souls* (1915), *Concerning the Past* (1916), *She of the Slanting Eyes* (1922), *and Notebook* (1929). He has published, also, two books of a different type, *Zapotlán* (1931) and *The Dance in Mexico* (1932), as well as various anthologies and selections. Lastly, Isidro Fabela (born in Atlacomulco, state of Mexico, June 24, 1884) showed a preference for the rural story in *The Master's Grief* (1915), though later he abandoned it in order to devote himself to works on international law and diplomatic history: *The United States versus Liberty, The Forerunners of Mexican Diplomacy* (1916), and *Belice: Defense of the Rights of Mexico* (1944).

The colonial theme—persistent in the literature of our day—has even cast its spell on the short narrative. Manuel Horta (born in the City of Mexico in 1897), a delicate stylist who began his literary ca-

reer with a volume of stories called *Chapel Windows* (1917), has
written *Sketches of Yester Year* (1919), *Exemplary Life of Don José
de la Borda* (1928), and a curious and picturesque book, interesting
for the study of the customs of an entire epoch: *Ponciano Díaz:
Silhouette of a Bullfighter of Yester Year* (1943). Jorge de Godoy
(born in Popotla, Federal District, in 1894) shows himself to be a
writer of pleasing wittiness in *The Book of the Roses of the Viceroy's
Lady* (1923). We shall name last another prose writer, and a poet,
too, of rare elegance: Francisco Orozco Muñoz (born in San Francisco del Rincón, Guanajuato, October 3, 1884; died in Mexico,
March 8, 1950), who, having received his education and passed a
good part of his life in Belgium, dedicated two beautiful books to
that country—the *Invasion and Conquest of Martyred Belgium*
(1915) and *Belgium at Peace* (1919)—and afterward gave to the
press two volumes of inspired poetry: *¡Oh, tú que comienzas a tener
un pasado!* (*Oh, Thou Who Art Beginning to Have a Past!*, 1932),
and *Lines from Seville* (1947).

The writing of fiction, far from slackening in amount or quality,
has maintained a singular splendor in recent years.

Gregorio López y Fuentes (born at the hacienda of "El Mamey"
in the former canton of Chicontepec in Huasteca, Veracruz, November 17, 1897) first devoted himself to lyric poetry, publishing two
volumes of verse, *The Crystal Flute* (1913) and *Forest Glades*
(1922), but ended by taking up the novel. His first work of this
type, *Encampment* (1931), was followed by *Earth* (1932), *My
General* (1933), *The Indian* (1935), and *Muleteers* (1937)—lively
evocations of Mexican life in the epoch of the Revolution, presenting
that life sometimes in its military aspect, at other times in terms of
agrarian and racial background, and sometimes, as in the last-named
book, in the strong flavor of rural tradition. López y Fuentes is one
novelist who is all vigor; frequently, for this very reason, his work is
coarse though forceful. He responds in a lively way to the sights and
sounds of the country—what impressions his eyes must have received
from childhood on!—and he reproduces his impressions with unadorned color. *The Indian* won the National Prize for Literature in
1935, and has been repeatedly translated. In his novel, *Huasteca*
(1939), he has dramatized a controversial question: Mexican oil.
With sarcasm rather than irony, he enters the political arena with

Accommodation: Novel of a Politician with Convictions (1943); in *The Immovable Pilgrims* (1944), he reveals with accentuated, almost "folkloric" provincialism, certain symbolic effects that can also be observed in *Mezzanine* (1948). *Cornfield, Cattle Ranch, and Upland,* his most recent fictional work, describes the rural families which, through lack of security in some regions, take refuge in cities or go to the United States and lose their Mexican identity.

José Rubén Romero (born in Cotija de la Paz, Michoacán, September 25, 1890; died in Mexico City, July 4, 1952) also began his literary career filled with lyrical emotions. His first poetic efforts, published in his province, were followed by works of luxuriant maturity, as *Tacámbaro* (1922) and *Old Verses* (1930). Afterward, "far from the fatherland, remembering it every hour," turning his eyes toward his own Michoacán, where he had spent the years of childhood and those of his unlucky youth, he devoted himself to recalling them in four books—"novels, stories, narratives of things lived, or whatever you want to call them," as he himself says petulantly: *A Villager's Notes* (1932), *Disorder* (1936), *The Innocent People* (1936), and *My Horse, My Dog, and My Rifle* (1936). To these should be added, by the strict right of brotherhood, *The Useless Life of Pito Pérez* (1938), composed on his return to Mexico. All these are regional novels with the very special mark of originality; the feeling for the picturesque, the accentuated note of *costumbrismo*, the picaresque outline, and the steadiness and attractiveness of the form are fused with a grace that is no less Mexican because it is very much the author's own. In two later books, *Anticipation of Death* (1939), a caprice humorous as well as doleful, and *Once I Was Rich*, a contemporary story of metropolitan life, he withdrew from the regional scene, although he returned to it in his most recent book, *Rosenda* (1946). Some of Romero's works, also, have had the honor of translation into various languages.

Teodoro Torres (born in Villa de Guadalupe, San Luis Potosí, January 4, 1891, died in Mexico City, September 26, 1944) is one of the most interesting and fascinating figures in the field of Mexican fiction. He won his spurs in journalism in 1914. His first literary endeavors, inspired by characters and events of the revolutionary era, are represented by *Pancho Villa: A Life of Romance and Tragedy* (1924). Then came the humorist, shrewd and sagacious, in *Like*

Cats and Dogs (1925). Next he wrote a book of anecdotes in which the journalist was revealed: *Origins of Customs* (1934). The journalist became the historian and critic in *Journalism* (1937), followed by the humorist in *Humor and Satire in Mexico* (1943). Teodoro Torres, however, was chiefly a novelist interested in people and places. His first novel, *The Lost Country* (1935), dealing with Mexican emigration to the United States, presents a picture that through vigor of execution, brilliance of coloring, the clear torrential power of the prose, the well-sustained dramatic force, the lyrical exuberance, and the sensation of pulsating, swarming humanity that throbs within it, is more than a work of art; its social significance makes it a pureblooded, national work. This novel would have been unsurpassed and perhaps unsurpassable if Torres, at the height of his powers and threatened by death, had not composed in his last years a still better work, his masterpiece: *Swallow* (1944), which was published the day after his funeral. It is a magistral work by all standards because its content, form, and style served as the vehicle for an important social theme: the depopulation of small villages, occasioned by our revolutionary convulsions. It is a vigorous song of the soil, dramatically contrasting the countryside with the cities. Types and customs are painted with vitality and tenderness, and even with irony and grace. Rich in details, animated in the succession of scenes, *Swallow* charms us with its variety, its delightful and noble harmony as a marble carved by the hand of a great artist. It was Torres' best and last book. As he was lowered into the sepulchre, Teodoro Torres attained the fullest literary glory.

It becomes increasingly apparent that the Revolution has had decisive influence on the Mexican novel of this period. Another illustration is Rafael Felipe Muñoz (born in the city of Chihuahua, May 1, 1899). The figure of the tremendous guerrilla chief attracted him to attempt a biography, and the result was *Francisco Villa* (1923). The same figure has continued to dominate nearly all his fiction, which includes the following books: *The Fierce Leader* (stories of the Revolution in the North, 1928); *The Bad Man* (short stories and narratives, 1930); *On with Pancho Villa!* (a novel, 1932), which has been translated, you may be sure, into English and German; *If They Should Kill Me Tomorrow* . . . (1933); and *They Carried Off the Cannon for Bachimba* (short novels and short stories, 1924).

To keen observation and familiarity with environment, which give profound realism to his narratives, Muñoz has joined a delicate poetic instinct. Lastly, turning to the past, he has written a beautiful fictionized biography, vigorous in style and blended with light irony, that was published, in abridged form, in Madrid in 1936 under the title of *Santa Anna: He Who Gained All and Lost All*; and, in complete form, in Mexico City the following year, under the title of *Santa Anna: Biography of a Dictator*.

Another novelist with a strong personality, Jorge Ferretis (born in Rioverde, San Luis Potosí, in 1902) also satirized the times with heightened relief. Employing crude, biting realism, he has taken up the theme of the Revolution and studied the revolutionaries who, once in power, forgot the Revolution. His works comprise four novels: *Hot Land, The Sun Scorches, When the Quixote Increases in Size, Saint Automobile*; and a volume of stories, *Men in Tempest*.

Mauricio Magdaleno (born in Villa del Refugio, Zacatecas, May 13, 1906) is outstanding for his intense activity, fertile inspiration, and especially for vigorous and colorful Mexican characteristics. At first he was interested in the stage as is shown by the plays *Pánuco 137, Emiliano Zapata*, and *Tropic*, contained in the volume *Mexican Revolutionary Theater* (1933). He has dedicated his robust personality mainly, however, to the novel, in which he has made a considerable contribution: *Celis Field* (1935), *Concha Bretón* (1936), *The Splendor* (1937), *Sonata* (1941), *The Extensive Land*, and *Corn Silk* (1949). He has also written two volumes of essays: *Rank* (1941) and *Land and Wind* (1948), the latter being notable for its forceful description and faithful depiction of the landscape.

Among the novelists and short-story writers who are likewise in full activity at the present time, we should mention the following: Dolores Bolio, a Yucatecan writer born in Mérida, who, though she began her work in the field of the lyric and has persisted in cultivating it (*Intimacy*, 1917, *Confidentially*, 1918, *Fragrant Herbs*, 1924), is also the author of *Tropical Perfume* (stories, 1917) and the novels *A Leaf from the Past* (1919), *In Secrecy* (1936), and *A Single Love* (1937), all of them the fruit of deep femininity; Rubén Salazar Mallén, a serious prose writer, a critic of wide vision, who has devoted himself principally to clarifying the huge social problems of our day and to whom we owe two novels of fine psychological

analysis: *Road to Perfection* (1937) and *Water Eye* (1949); Eduardo
Luquin, who reveals remarkable originality in his narrative *Shadowy
Water* (1937); Rosa de Castaño for her novels: *Estradeño Ranch*
and *Consequences of Blood*; Agustín Yáñez, author of a volume of
fictional narratives, *Archipelago of Women* (1943) and a soul stirring novel, *The Edge of the Storm* (1947); Leonor Llach for her
book of short stories, *Prominent People* (1933); Lucio Mendieta y
Nuñez, who, though dedicating himself to sociological works, is also
an able writer of short stories as seen in *The Endless Caravan* (1942);
and Rafael Solana, whose literary activity has found expression in
poetry: *Hillside* (1934), *Sonnets* (1937), *Trick Mirrors* (1944), *The
Same Sonnet One Hundred Times Over* (1948); in the novel, *The
Poisoned One* (1939); but principally in the short stories that he has
written with elegance and ease: *The Trumpet* (1942), *The Music
Inside* (1943), *The Innocent Saints* (1944), *The Crimes of the Three
Gangs* (1945), and *Dead Slaves* (1947).

The Miguel Lanz Duret Award, given annually by the daily news-
paper the *Universal*, greatly invigorated novelistic genres. The award-
winning novels are: *City* (1941), by José María Benítez; *The Man
of Clay* (1942), by Adriana García Roel; *The Large Pool in the
Ruins* (1943), by Sara García Iglesias; *Pensativa* (1944), by José
Goytortúa; *The Islands Also Are Ours* (1945), by Gustavo Rueda
Medina; *Paradise Beach* (1946), by Gilberto Chávez; *The Hidden
One* (1947), by Miguel N. Lira; *Human River* (1948), by Rogelio
Barriga Rivas.

POETRY

In a way, the poets of the *Savia Moderna*, who afterward became
a part of the *Athenaeum* group, continued the "modernist" tendency, but each in the way proper to his own forceful personality.

Roberto Argüelles Bringas (born in Orizaba, Veracruz, July 2,
1875; died in Mixcoac, Federal District, November 1, 1915) was the
poet "of blended fortitude and pain," as Luis Castillo Ledón expressed it. Vigorous, elegant, and gloomy at the same time, he had a
superior mastery of technique. His work is scattered—most of it in
the pages of the *Modern Review*—but on the day when it is classified
and collected, he will stand forth fully revealed as one of the most
interesting figures of the lyric poetry of our time.

The verses of Rafael López (born in the city of Guanajuato, December 4, 1875; died in Mexico, July 16, 1943) have majestic sculptural beauty; and his prose, scattered liberally in periodicals and reviews, is rich in images. Alfonso Reyes has called him "a poet of apotheosis and the sculptor's caress, of marble and sunlight." But this is not the whole of him: sometimes—as Eduardo Colín justly observes—"his Pindaric excess and chromatic fever are appeased." Then appears the "natural" poet, the poet that flees from "the brilliance and ostentation of Venetian colors and takes the eternal road to Florence." His collected poems are published in two volumes: *With Open Eyes* (1912) and *Poems* (1941).

The nine poems of *The Untouched Life* (1916) are the only known poetic works of Eduardo Colín (born in the City of Mexico, June 19, 1880; died in Cuernavaca, March 20, 1945). They are trim verses filled with youthful life—a strong, robust type of poetry, all equilibrium and health. According to Genaro Estrada, they give, in their choice of subject matter, "the sensation of actual, accessible experience—things we have all seen and felt on every hand; but the poet gives them a warm, expressive form, with emotional tones suggestively interpreted; sometimes he changes the mood and brings, to a recurring theme, delightful, inspired variations resulting from change of meter or accent." Colín's later activities have been almost exclusively in the field of criticism: *Seven Leaders* (1921), *Choice Word* (1922), and *Rasgos* (*Flourishes*, 1934). "Language in his hands," Baldomero Sanín Cano points out, "has metallic brilliance and the elasticity of organic matter." "The lucid intelligence of the appraiser in matters of art," the Colombian Eduardo Castillo notes, "is vivified in him by the poet's exquisite sensibility." His last book is a work of fiction: *Women* (a fable, 1934).

A thoughtful, impassioned, lyrical soul (simplicity and sincerity, beauty and melancholy are inseparably compounded in it) is revealed in another poet who soon deserted the lyric: Luis Castillo Ledón (born in Santiago Ixcuintla in what is now the state of Nayarit, January 17, 1879; died in Mexico City, October 7, 1944), author of *What I See and Feel* (1916). Beautiful construction, the note of intimacy, and a certain sensuality resulting from the influence of D'Annunzio stand out in these poems of early youth. Later, Castillo Ledón devoted himself with ardor to criticism and history. In addition to revealing the treasures of a rich sensibility, to discovering the beauty of the present, and to observing other people closely, he was passionately attracted to the changing events of the past. He was a strict investigator, a scrupulous, tenacious analyzer. Few others have dug as deeply as he into certain periods of our history, particularly the epoch of Independence. At the request of Justo Sierra, then minister of public instruction and fine arts, he retraced, beginning in 1908, the itinerary of Hidalgo, from the birthplace to the scene of the martyrdom of the Liberator, taking photographs, gathering documents and data in the very places where great events occurred. That long historical pilgrimage led him to decide to follow a literary career. He dedicated himself to investigation and study of everything related to the Father of the Country. He wanted to show the Mexicans, he repeatedly said, a great historical figure not completely known even today. For more than thirty years—with interruptions caused primarily by frail health—he worked at this task so tenaciously and decisively that we may well believe his only hope was to finish it in order to die. The monumental work, with the title of *Hidalgo: Life of the Hero,* was published in two thick volumes (1948). Among his other historical works—leaving out that part which has not yet been collected or published—we should note the following: *Mexican Authors of Operas* (1910), *Chocolate* (1917), *Ancient Indigenous Mexican Literature* (1917), *Origins of the Novel in Mexico* (1922), *The National Museum of Archeology, History, and Ethnology* (1924), *The Avenue of Viga and Saint Anita* (1925), *The Founding of the City of Mexico* (1925), *The Conquest and Spanish Colonization in Mexico: Their True Character* (1932), and the excellent study that serves as preface to Juan de la Granja's *Letters* (1937).

The deep note of intimacy is accentuated even more in Manuel de la Parra (born in Sombrerete, Zacatecas, March 29, 1878; died in Mexico City, September 9, 1930). His is a poetry of crystalline purity. In his verses, Alfonso Cravioto notes, life is refracted without rudeness or harshness. "Color changes into melancholy, passion into nostalgic longing. There are no lamentations—only sighs; no despairs —only nostalgias. It is all in the minor key—soft-hued, languid, suave, muted." Manuel de la Parra's poems were published in one volume, *Far Visions,* in 1914.

Not poetry, but prolix prose was cultivated by Alfonso Cravioto (born in Pachuca, Hidalgo, January 24, 1883; died in the City of Mexico, September 11, 1955) at the beginning of his career. Among his first works are two monographs devoted to the criticism of painting: one on Eugenio Carrière and the other on Germán Gedovius. Cravioto took delight in artistic prose. His pen was a palette. The aesthetic desire for perfection that tormented him clashed sometimes with his characteristic sallies of sly humor. He plunged into the civil strife: politics absorbed him. Though his activities left him hardly a moment of repose, he wrote, in a parenthesis, the only verses that he collected: *The New Soul of Old Things* (1921), poems of rare virtuosity, the inspiration drawn from the background of New Spain.

Joaquín Méndez Rivas (born July 20, 1888, in the City of Mexico) unites vigor and sonorousness with a breath of ancient poetry; his *Georgics* (1923), in their modern restlessness, show classic inspiration. Two other collections of lyrics preceded this work: *Student Poems* (1921) and *Madrigals Written with Blood* (1922). To Méndez Rivas we also owe the only tragedy in verse—*Cuauhtémoc* (1925)—recorded by our drama in this last period, although the play has never been performed on the stage.

With Rafael Cabrera (born in the city of Puebla, May 5, 1884; died in the City of Mexico, February 21, 1943), the group of poets within the *Athenaeum* is completed. "A writer of delicate sentiment and subtle emotions, with a style that is pure and elegant, chaste and modern," in Pedro Henríquez Ureña's phrase, Cabrera—like some of the preceding—is the poet of a single volume: *Omens* (1912).

José de J. Nuñez y Domínguez (native of Papantla, Veracruz, born April 27, 1887; died in Santiago, Chile, 1959) devoted his life to journalism and letters. He reveals himself as a poet of romantic delicateness, all intimacy and feeling; in sentiment and often in "stage settings" he is very Mexican. In his style, which is quite polished and modern, it is true, as Colín observes, that an "inclination toward a certain musical and pictorial brilliance" is shown, but we notice, much more often, as Urbina points out, "caressing softness, muted music, veiled half tones." He published five volumes of poetry: *Holocausts* (1915), *Titian's Hour* (1917), *Soft Music* (1921), *The Useless Pain* (1924), *Sea Foam* (1935); and in 1937 a volume of

Selected Poems was issued. His work in prose was no less abundant. As chronicler, he entered his marginal annotations on everyday life in *The Open Wings* (1925) and *The Fancy of Love* (1927). In his *Mexican Stories* (1927), he painted national types and customs gracefully. And in the field of history and literary criticism, his books, abounding in firsthand information and offering original points of view, deal with the most varied subjects: *The Shawl* (1914), *The Young Poets of Mexico and Other National Studies* (1918), *On the Margin of History* (1927), *A Liman Viceroy in Mexico: Don Juan de Acuña, Marqués de Casa Fuerte* (1927), *Gests of the Solar-Born: Historical Narratives of the State of Veracruz* (1931), *Martí in Mexico* (1933), *Ventura García Calderón* (1938), *Contemporary French Writers* (1941), *History and Bullfighting in Mexico, Rómulo Gallegos and the Hispanic-American Novel, The Coalition of Oriente* (1944), and his last book, *The Mexican Vicereine.*

Enrique Fernández Ledesma (born in Pinos, Zacatecas, April 15, 1888; died in the City of Mexico, November 9, 1939) was revealed in full maturity in his first book of verses: *With Thirsty Lips* (1919), which has an inspiration similar to that of the first works of López Velarde (the innovator who is discussed a little later in this section) —similar, that is, in respect to the themes and atmosphere that attract the poet—though Fernández Ledesma, in style and emotion, had an individuality of his own. Later devoting himself to the practice of literary criticism and the evocation of the past, he published two volumes of prose: *Trips to the Nineteenth Century* (1933) and *Gallery of Ghosts: Years and Shadows of the Nineteenth Century* (published posthumously, 1939), in which there pass in review the figures and figurines, colorful and breathing, that belong to the spiritual atmosphere of that very individual epoch of Mexican life; and the *History of Typography in Mexico: Nineteenth-Century Publications* (1935), which is very rich in data and appraisals relative to the development of our letters in that period.

Francisco Castillo Nájera (born in Durango, November 25, 1886; died in Mexico City, December 21, 1954), physician and prominent diplomat, devoted no small part of his energies to literature. In 1906 he published his first book of verse, *Dawns*; in 1931, his valuable translation of *A Century of Belgian Verse, 1830-1930*; and in 1934, his famous popular ballad, *The Sparrow-Hawk.* These were followed by *Considerations Relative to Spanish Spoken in Mexico* (1936); *Lyrical Intermissions* (1946), and a volume of criticism, *Manuel Acuña* (1950).

Francisco González León (born in Lagos, Jalisco, September 10, 1862; died in the same city, March 9, 1945) should also be counted as a member of López Velarde's school or, if one prefers, as a precursor of it. Though he secluded himself lovingly and permanently in the province that he vividly characterized and reflected, his poetry won national interest and regard because of its novelty of technique and its very individual inspiration. The spirit of González León breathes the fragrance "of the things that were," absorbed in the stillness of his native ground. He espoused that stillness; he transmits it to us, makes us feel it in his verses. "His originality," says Ramón López Velarde, "is true poetic originality: the originality of sensations felt and communicated." The first book of González León to reach the public was *Evening Bells* (1922), followed by *Megalomanias* and *Clay Models,* both published in Lagos (1908) and exceedingly rare. His last two books were *From My Book of Hours* (1937) and *Agenda* (1946).

Alfonso Junco (born in Monterrey, February 25, 1896) has yielded an abundant lyrical harvest: *Along the Smooth Path* (1917), *The Sacred Star* (1920), *Possession* (1923), *Eucharistic Anthology* (1926), and *The Divine Event* (1938). He is a poet of vigorous inspiration and careful style; burning religious fervor shines within him. He is a tireless fighter in defense of the Catholic faith, a chronicler, a critic of varied and pleasing literary culture, and a writer, lastly, on questions of history and politics. His prose work includes: *Physiognomies* (1927), *The Treason at Querétaro* (1930), *Christ* (1931), *A Fundamental Guadaloupan Problem* (1932), *Mexican Motives* (1933), *Inquisition Concerning the Inquisition* (1933), *A Century of Mexico* (1934), *Burning Matters* (1934), *Carranza and the Origins of His Rebellion* (1935), *Universal Lope* (1935), *People of Mexico* (1937), *Splendor of Mexico* (1938), *Savia* (1939), and *Hispanic Blood.*

Among the poets who flourished contemporaneously with the generation of the *Athenaeum of Youth,* or at no great distance from it, we should consider briefly the following: Samuel Ruiz Cabañas (born in Mexico City, August 20, 1886), whose extreme delicacy, elegance, and mastery are outstanding in the three volumes he has published: *Lyrical First Fruits* (1904), *The Tree of Life Is Bare* (1906), and *The Songs of Pierrot* (1907); Carlos Barrera, a poet of lively lyrical intonation, author of *Country Odes and Other Poems, Facing the Sea,* and the *Ballad of Monterrey*; Francisco González Guerrero; Joaquín Ramírez Cabañas (*Diversion*, 1925); Antonio Moreno y Oviedo (native of Lagos, Jalisco, born September 2, 1862), who very late culled and collected his beautiful lyric production in the volume called *Incense on the Embers* (1935), which was followed by a volume entitled *Pátina* (1940); José D. Frías (1891-1936), restless, original, a volume of whose *Selected Poems* was published; Pedro Requena Legarreta (1893-1918), like Frías, already dead, surely in the flower of life; Guillermo Prieto Yeme (born in Tacubaya, August 9, 1890), author of one volume of verses, *States of Mind* (1919) and translator of Rabindranath Tagore; Ricardo Mimenza Castillo, in whom archeology and poetry have blended to evoke the remote past of his native Yucatán and from whose vast work, begun in 1906 with *May Violets,* we should select for citation *Insubordination* (1915), *The Ballads of Yucatán* (1926), *Inscriptions of Mayab* (1935), *Elytrons* (1937), and the *Book of Teresita* (1938); and, lastly, José Gómez Ugarte (native of Ciudad Guzmán, Jalisco, born January 17, 1874; died in Mexico City, March 24, 1943), a prominent journalist and one of the rare humorous poets who, very Mexican and very loyal, draw us back to the traditional vein of poetry. His work—signed with the pseudonym of "The Kindly Abbot"—has been collected in the volumes called *Our Daily Bread* (1920), *Beads of My Rosary* (1922), and *Preaching in the Desert* (1926).

A revolution in Mexican poetry was begun by Ramón López Velarde (born in Jerez, Zacatecas, June 15, 1888; died in Mexico City, June 19, 1921). Though he cultivated prose with great originality—as his posthumous work *The Minute Hand* (1923) bears witness—the Muses were his chief devotion. He began by bringing the regional theme, the provincial note, into lyric poetry. In the first book of verse he produced—*The Devout Blood* (1916)—he gave to his poems the sensations of smell and color, the austere rhythm, the muted cry, the deep feeling, the grace, and the melancholy of his native spot of ground. His poetry then, as Fernández MacGregor observes, was purely objective; afterward, it became subjective and used the outer things only as symbols. "It is made deliberately small (reduced to a chaste trifle) and the interior drama is explained with a gesture resigned and deliberate. He adorns it with all that is detailed and insignificant, and he succeeds thus in renovating the literary baggage with which the emotions are expressed . . . even love." Neither in rhythm nor in ideas, in the opinion of the same critic, "does he fear the seventh discord, and he obtains tremendous effects from it: dissonances that give a unique enchantment to his verse." He lays hold, finally, on "his inner feelings one by one, describes them ambiguously, and is sometimes unintelligible to the uninitiated." This change may be seen in his second book of poems *Anguish* (1919) and in the poems included in the volume published after his death: *The Sound of the Heart.* He had broken entirely with tradition; he had followed a new road, but the end of it, unforeseen death prevented him from reaching. If he did not discover a style that we can call definitive, or even attain the full development he dreamed of, at least he had the power to influence his contemporaries, being, in many ways, the precursor of the next group of poets. *Complete Poems* and *The Minute Hand* of López Velarde were published in one volume by Antonio Castro Leal in the *Collection of Mexican Authors* (Editorial Porrúa, S.A.—1953).

Writers belonging entirely within the limits of the twentieth century compose the next group. The influence of very modern poetry—principally French—is more or less noticeable in them; all of them are marked by the desire to revolutionize both feeling and technique. Jaime Torres Bodet (born in the City of Mexico, April 17, 1902) is the member of this group who has produced the largest amount; in his first phase, he did not turn his back on tradition, nor did he close his eyes to the new perspectives. In his initial verse he is seen as a poet of fine sensitivity who reveals his sentiments in an attractive and melodious manner. Later, his lyrical emotion becomes more profound, being expressed in subtle, mysterious, and exacting lines, rejecting the facile and reveling in the complex. The following constitute his lyric work: *Fervor* (1918), *The Delirious Heart* (1922), *Songs* (1922), *New Songs* (1923), *The House* (1923), *The Days* (1923), and *Poems* (1924); all of these books reflect his first manner. The second is reflected in *Poetry* (1926), *Exile* (1930),

Crypt (1937), and *Sonnets* (1949). In addition to articles of criticism written for *Contemporáneos* (1928), he has written fiction with original techniques, seeking new ways of expression in the following novels: *Margarita of Niebla* (1927), *The Sentimental Education* (1929), *Proserpina Redeemed* (1931), *January the First* (1934), *Shadows* (1937), and *Birth of Venus and Other Stories* (1941). His clear, powerful prose is characterized by rhythmic dignity and plasticity. He has devoted much time to diplomatic work in this country and abroad. From 1943 to 1946 he was secretary of public education; in this position he performed, with magnanimous spirit, a remarkable work of renovation, co-ordination, and unification of educational facilities that will bear excellent fruit in the schools and in the culture. The principles and guidelines of his work can be seen in his volume entitled *Mexican Education: Speeches, Interviews, Messages* (1944). The dominant thought in this book is expanded and his perspective of the immediate past is greatly broadened in *Education and International Agreement, Speeches, and Messages* (1948). On his return to the Department of Foreign Relations, he was appointed minister; and in the last-named book, the diplomat and the educator join hands. Finally, this great Mexican writer has achieved international importance and influence by his appointment as director of UNESCO, the organization of the United Nations whose purpose is to work through science, education, and culture for peace and understanding among the peoples of the world.

Enrique González Rojo (born in the town of Sinaloa, in the state of the same name, August 25, 1899; died in Mexico City, May 9, 1939), took special delight in free verse and in the ballad, which he mastered with rare grace; he is the author of *The Harbor and Other Poems* (1924) and *Space* (1926). In Bernardo Ortiz de Montellano (born in the City of Mexico, January 3, 1899; died in the same city, April 13, 1949), subtle fantasy is attuned with perverse wit and grace, without excluding hidden melancholy. He published *Covetousness* (1921), *The Spinning Top of Seven Colors* (1925), *Snare* (1928), *First Dream* (1931), *Dreams* (1933), *Death from the Blue Sky* (1937), *Five Heartless Hours* (a volume of narratives, 1940), *The Huge Hat* (a fantasy, 1946), *Image, Love, and Death of Amado Nervo* (a biographical and critical study, 1943); and also an *Anthology of Mexican Stories* (1926). In the work of José Gorostiza (born in 1901), feeling blends with transparency of style; his *Songs to Sing in Boats* (1925) brings us a penetrating aroma of the traditional, along with healthful sweetness; and in *Endless Death* (1939), his poetry achieves remarkable transparency and depth.

In the writers just discussed, the voices of the old—the eternal—poetry can still be heard. But another part of this same group is composed of poets who could be called openly revolutionary in both technique and feeling. One of these, Carlos Pellicer (born in Villahermosa, Tabasco, November 4, 1899), is all dazzling brightness in *Colors in the Sea and Other Poems* (1921), *Sacrificial Stone* (1924), *Six, Seven Poems* (1924), *Twenty Minutes After One* (1927), *Highway* (1929), and *June Hour* (1937). Antonio Castro Leal says of him that "the unexpectedness of things gave him voice, and he sang the color, the light, the waters, and the mountains of America"; that "there is always in his poetry the delight in the big outline, the orchestral color," although "his sure instinct saved him from the great American civil pride." At the opposite extreme is Xavier Villaurrutia (born in Mexico City, December 3, 1903; died in the same city, December 25, 1950), who delighted in the minor tone, the subtle shading; his, it is said, is "poetry built upon the sense of touch and sight." His poetic work is contained in several volumes: *Reflections* (1926), *Nocturnes* (1933), *Nostalgia for Death* (1938), and *Song to Spring and Other Poems* (1948). He cultivated criticism, also; but though he wrote a great deal in this field, only one of his works has been published as a book: a study of *The Poetry by the Youths of Mexico* (1924). He composed a story in prose, *Dame of Hearts* (1928); translated Gide and William Blake; and, lastly, was outstanding in the theater for various works of extraordinary originality: *It Is Incredible* (an enigma in one act, 1934), *About What Are You Thinking?* (a mystery in one act, 1938), *Be Brief* (farce in one act, 1938), *Ivy* (comedy in three acts), *Invitation to Death* (drama in three acts, 1944), *The Burning Word* (1945), *Poor Blue Beard* (1948), and *Dangerous Game* (1950). In 1953 the *Complete Poetry and Drama* of Xavier Villaurrutia appeared in an attractive volume. The personality of Salvador Novo (born in Mexico City, July 30, 1904) has reached great heights in recent years. Though his first volume of verses, *Twenty Poems* (1925), could be said to copy the French ultraists, it can be stated that his later ones—*New Love*

(1933), *Mirror* (1933), and the most recent, *Seamen Rhymes* [the original title is in English], *Ballad of Angelillo and Adela*, and *Decimas* [ten-line stanzas] *on the Sea* (all of these privately printed in 1934)—depart from his initial manner and reveal another that is very personal and very much his own. His prose work, disclosing the essayist, the critic, and the traveler, comprises *Essays* (1925), *Return Ticket* [original title is in English, 1928], *The Literary Education of Adolescents* (1928), *The Youth* (1928), *Jalisco-Michoacán* (1933), *Song to Teresa* (1934), *Empty Continent* (1935), *In Defense of the Worn-Out* (1938), *New Mexican Grandeur (Essay on Mexico City and Its Environs in 1946)*, and *Birds in Castilian Poetry* (1953). All of his prose is characterized by neatness, richness of blending and coloring, and beauty of style. *New Mexican Grandeur* is marked by local color gracefully and ironically depicted. Recently, he has written for the theater a very interesting dramatization of the *Quixote* and another, *Astuteness*—remarkably faithful to the theme—of the famous novel of Valle Inclán. He has also published translations and anthologies—two of the latter of special importance: *Modern North-American Poetry* (1924) and *Modern French Poetry* (1924). The influence of English culture, for which he shows a singular preference, is evident; also, his humor stands out as one of his individual traits, sometimes changing into cutting sarcasm. He has written a short tragedy in French—*Le troisième Faust* (1934), published in a private edition.

This group of revolutionary poets also includes the following: Genaro Estrada, author of four books published between 1928 and 1934: *Crucifer (Transept)*, *Stairway*, *Level Passage*, and *Senderillos a ras (Smooth Pathways)*; Miguel Martínez Rendón (born in 1891); and Manuel Maples Arce (born in 1898), creator, in *Interior Scaffolds*, 1922, and *Metropolis*, 1924, of a "new manner" in poetry that he christened with the name—perhaps the logical one—of "stridentism," a style that he has ceased to cultivate.

Among the poets of the final group we shall name Leopoldo Ramos (born in El Triunfo, Baja California, June 8, 1898; died January 5, 1956), a limpid poet of rare exquisiteness, noble and robust spirit, who tends toward a new technique—personal and original in verse: *City, Country, and Sea* (1932), *Figures* (1937), *Bauprés* (1942), and *The Divine Altar Cloth* (1950); Enrique Carniado, whose book of poems *Tiny Soul* (1936), childlike in inspiration, though it is in reality for both children and adults, expresses a noble tenderness; Miguel N. Lira (born in 1905), a poet impregnated with folk poetry, as he reveals in his *Ballad of Domingo Arenas;* Vicente Echeverría del Prado, whose poetry—as he himself says—"strives to be only poetry, a game of shadows in impossible glassworks; without melodrama, but with drama and melody," and whose work, published between 1927 and 1949, is considerable: *Multiple Voices, Bewildered Life, Desirable Material, Sprouts from the Abyss, Inviolate Profiles, Bordering Love, In Gazelle's Time;* Carlos Gutiérrez Cruz (1897-1930), whose poetry aspires to social significance; Alfonso Gutiérrez Hermosillo (1905-1935), who died, like the preceding poet, in his youth, and whose brief work, of extreme delicacy, is gathered into a posthumous volume called *Itinerary* (1938); Octavio Paz (born in 1914), who, after publishing *Origin of Man* and *Beneath Your Bright Shadow* (both published in 1937), has given excellent samples of his poetry in *Between the Stone and the Flower* (1941), *On the Edge of the World* (1942), and *Liberty Under Oath* (1949); Humberto Magaloni, author of a delightful sheaf of crystal-clear poems, *Place of Many Springs.* With respect to the lyric harvest, we should mention, in conclusion, two women poets: Esperanza Zambrano, author of *Secret Rhythms* (1931) and *The Songs of Perfect Love* (1938); and Caridad Bravo Adams, who has published two volumes which are entitled *Reverberation* and *Tropic.*

THE DRAMA

The drama had few proficient writers at the beginning of the present period. Nevertheless, and especially in recent years, it has attracted no small number of authors.

In the aggregate of their work, a lively preoccupation with stage technique is noticeable, though an equal interest in style is not generally apparent; a unanimous nationalistic tendency, however, is an important characteristic. Mexican playwrights of the present period are trying to reproduce Mexican life through the depiction of types and customs; there are even a few who would grant admission to the dramatic conflicts that are concerned with social themes or that draw inspiration from incidents connected with present history.

José F. Elizondo (born in Aguascalientes, January 29, 1880; died in Mexico City, April 20, 1943) was one of the authors who worked hardest for the theater in Mexico. No one has equaled him in musical comedy and revue, generally frivolous in character, although often marked by *costumbrismo* and rich in Mexican types and reflections of popular speech. About forty productions of this kind, in prose and verse, came from his pen; some of them (like *Chin-Chun-Chan*, written in collaboration with Rafael Medina and staged in 1904) had such a resounding success that more than ten thousand performances were given. His principal works include *The Furrow* and *The Seller of Kisses.*

Affiliated with modernism, Elizondo began his career as a lyric poet; his first volume of verse was *Castanets* (1903). He cultivated light verse with a grace beyond all praise, commenting in epigrammatic style on the events of the day; poems of this type comprise the book called *More Than a Hundred Epigrams of Kien* (his lucky pseudonym), published in 1932. He is, in short, the most delightful of the present-day *costumbristas*, developing in direct line from "Facundo," "Micrós," and "Juvenal"; sure observation and good, sane humor without bitterness enable him to depict the comic and the ridiculous in events, dress, and types of Mexican life today. His numerous articles of the same inspiration—signed with the pseudonym of "Pepe Nava"—have been collected in two volumes: *Life in Jest* (1934) and *With Rose Colored Glasses* (1937). Under the same pseudonym, the humorous poet is revealed in a delightful book, *Stupidities* (1938).

Antonio Mediz Bolio (born in Mérida, Yucatán, October 13, 1884; died, September 15, 1957), a good poet, as his book *In the Middle of the Road* (1917) revealed, was a writer who brought from his own land an inner devotion to the Mayan legends, shown in *Evocations* (1904), *The Land of the Deer and the Pheasant* (1922), and *Song of the Son of Yucatán* (1953). In the first decade of the century, he composed dramas, comedies, operettas, and musical comedies, and was outstanding in the comedy of social thesis with *The Wave* and in the dramatic poem of indigenous subject matter with *The Arrow of the Sun* (1917). Imbued with love for the mysterious race that once peopled his native region, he translated, arranged, and published *The Book of Chilam Balam de Chumayel* (1930);

and in an academic discourse he dealt with *The Intermingling of the Maya and the Spaniard of Yucatán.*

In the field of the modern-society play and the drama of psychological analysis, Julio Jiménez Rueda, who has already been discussed as a novelist, has done his work, and to that general classification belong *As in Real Life* (1918), *Tempest on the Heights* (1922), *The Fall of the Flowers* (1923), and *His Wife's Rival.* He is also author of a beautiful scenic poem of colonial theme, *Sister Adoration,* based on his novel of the same title. He followed very modern theatrical orientations in *The Smoke Silhouette* (1927); later, inspired by one of the most impassioned tragedies of contemporary history—the Second Mexican Empire—he produced in 1932 the dramatic poem entitled *Miramar.*

Francisco Monterde, who, as we have seen, was active in the novel and criticism, did his share for the theater, beginning with a little regional drama, *In the Whirlpool* (1924). He followed it with plays of psychological analysis, *She Who Returned to Life* (1926) and *I'll Live for You,* and with a play of social theme *Black Gold* (1927), dealing with the exploitation of oil. He has also performed eminent service for our dramatic literature, greatly facilitating the study of it with his *Bibliography of the Drama in Mexico* (1934). The brothers Lázaro and Carlos Lozano García (born in Mexico City, May 6, 1899, and July 12, 1902, respectively) joined with the two preceding writers and José Joaquín Gamboa in attempting a theatrical revival in 1925, the effort resulting in a season of six months of Mexican repertory. They themselves wrote a beautiful drama, *Woman at Last* (1925), as well as *La incomprendida (The Misunderstood Woman),* and *Estudiantina (Band of Students),* plays of the same general type. They also produced the dramatic spectacle *The Little Boy,* of marked Mexican flavor.

Restlessness, lusty and perennial, was always the driving force behind the alert mind of Victor Manuel Díez Barroso (born in Mexico City, January 1, 1890; died there on August 30, 1936). Exquisitely cultured, constantly attentive to the worldwide stir in the theater, he followed the new lines of theatrical development both in critical articles and in his own creations. His first work was *The Passions Command* (1925), a drama conceived within the usual, current technique. The same year he jumped from this to *Control*

Yourself, a work in which Freudian theories provide him with an opportunity for constructing a strange, original, powerful dramatic conflict. In the following years, besides a little comedy called *Good Luck,* he composed and produced *A Tear* (1926), *A Farce* (1926), *The Broken Doll* (1927), and *En "El Riego"* (1929). All of these, in addition to the plays contained in the volume entitled *Seven Works in One Act* (1935)—even the ones that have not been performed—reveal Díez Barroso's constant desire to investigate new roads, though not as a faithful servant or vulgar imitator of foreign trends; on the contrary, he is a sound, vigorous playwright, delighted with originality, who renews his art by the process of experimentation, without ever neglecting the development of his own originality. Linked with this characteristic are direct observation and an inner nationalism, directed toward giving a genuine, individual aspect to characters and settings. A desire, likewise, to interpret—to grasp—not only the present, but the past, both immediate and remote, is apparent in *Sketches* (1932), a "meditation" in four acts with beautiful musical accompaniment by Leonor Boesch, his wife. Dying in the prime of life, Díez Barroso perhaps did not succeed in satisfying the ideal of art he had set for himself. The last work he gave to the stage was *He and His Body* (1934).

Premature death came also to Carlos Noriega Hope (born in Tacubaya, Federal District, November 6, 1896; died in the City of Mexico, November 15, 1934), whose period of production was short. He began with the novelette and went on to devote himself to the theater, staging some of his own fictional narratives. The fruits of this work are *Miss Goodwill, Una Flapper (A Flapper),* and *Che Ferrati.* His last dramatic creation—an original story for the stage—is *Margarita of Arizona,* produced in 1929. Kindly, picturesque, sensitive, with touches of wit and irony, is Noriega Hope's work. It is distinguished, no less, by the sprightliness of the form. In the first of the plays cited, he presents, through his heroine, an excellent study of woman; the second, in spite of its foreign title, is a charming love story set against a Mexican rural background. The young playwright's early passing robbed our stage of a personality rich in gifts.

To the same group as the preceding writers belongs Ricardo Parada León, who has been a valiant fighter in the theater. His first work, *Agony,* had its premiere in 1923. This was followed, in the same year, by *The Slave* and *An Autumn Night*; and later by *The Guilty Ones* (1925), *Other People's Sorrows* (1929), and *The Future of Doctor Gallardo* (1936). Parada León is distinguished for his dramatic power. In *Royal Road* (1949), he experiments with folklore in the regional theater.

Enrique Uhthoff (born in Atlixco, October 1, 1885; died in Mexico City, May 20, 1950), whose principal activities were in the field of journalism, his excellent articles reflecting his impressions of the roving life, also wrote plays. Two of his short plays, *Nopal* and *My Buddy the Boss,* and a longer one, *Ignorant Old Pancho,* have a popular Mexican flavor. His play *To Love, That Is Everything* is based on the life of Amado Nervo; and his powerful play *Thunderbolt on the Oak Tree* reveals his dramatic impression of the recent war in Spain.

When the Comedia Mexicana was reopened for the season of 1929, a veteran writer made his entrance into the theater with all the force and freshness of youth. This was Carlos Díaz Dufoo, a writer mentioned earlier. He was born in the city of Veracruz, December 4, 1861; died in Mexico City, September 5, 1941. His father, Dr. Pedro Díaz Fernández, was Spanish by birth but was a naturalized Mexican and was connected with our navy; his mother, Doña Matilde Dufoo, was a Veracruzan. Díaz Dufoo went to Spain at the age of six and did not return to Mexico until he was twenty-three. In Madrid he studied as he pleased. He did his first writing for the *Globe,* the periodical directed by Castelar, and for Sinesio Delgado's *Madrid Cómico.* On his return to Mexico, in July, 1884, he devoted himself to journalism, writing for the *Press* (Agustín Arroyo de Anda's publication), and the *National* (Gonzalo Esteva's). After a brief stay in Veracruz (1886), which he spent in journalistic labors, he returned to the capital in order to continue the identical kind of work on the daily he had previously worked for, as well as the *Universal* (directed by Rafael Reyes Spíndola). With Gutiérrez Nájera, he founded the *Azure Review* in 1894; after the poet's death the following year, he directed the magazine until 1896. The same year, serving as deputy to Congress, he founded the *Impartial* with Reyes Spíndola as his collaborator, and he continued on its editorial staff until 1912. He also directed the High School of Commerce and Administration in 1910; he was at the head of the weekly called *El Economista Mexicano* from 1901 to 1911; and, after a deliberate pause in his journalistic work, he returned to it in 1917. Meanwhile, during the whole period up to 1929—except for his first book, *Vigorous Stories* (1901)—Díaz Dufoo published only works of an economic nature: "The Industrial Evolution of Mexico" (in *Mexico: Its Social Evolution,* 1900); *Limantour* (1910); *A Financial Victory* (history of the Mexican treasury from 1891 to 1910, published in 1913); *Mexico and Foreign Capital*; and, last, *Economic Life.* Surely one would have supposed that he was exclusively and permanently confined to disciplines of that nature; but, in the depths of old age, almost blind, he rose up again for literature—in the theater. His first play was *Padre mercader (Father Merchant),* presented in 1929. Then came *Quixote's Fountain* (1930), *Words* (1931), *The Woman Chief,* (1931), and *Shadow of Butterflies* (1936). He made his appearance as an accomplished dramatist: there were no practice shots or vacillations; he had complete assurance in construction, command of scenic technique, and the depth of thought and ripeness of experience that give the force and flavor of living reality to his work. Because of the energy and flexibility of the dialogue, his success in creating types—some of them of marked comic quality—the careful development of situations and climaxes, and the meaning and irony with which he treats social problems, he stands out as one of the figures in high relief in the Mexican theater. His *Padre mercader* alone reached and passed the mark of one hundred performances— surely an evidence of robustness in the renascent theater.

If the preceding is not sufficient to prove that the theatrical movement registered in the last few years is of interest, let us mention the fact that a number of women writers are participating in contemporary dramatic writing. In this as in no other period, women are writing plays. Teresa Farías de Issasi is the author of *Head and Heart, Like the Birds, Religion of Love, Creative Force, Pages from Life,* all of these being serious plays and comedies; she is also author of *Nuptial,* a novel, and *Before the Great Enigma* (1938), a philosophic essay. Eugenia Torres (actress and writer; died in Mexico City, August 7, 1935) wrote, among other dramas, the following: *Conquered, The Sister, The Broken Puppet, Around the Chimera, Class Honor,* and *The Unforeseen.* Catalina d' Erzell (born in Silao,

Guanajuato, 1897; died in Mexico City, January 3, 1950), who published a novel, *The Immaculate Woman* (1920); a volume of stories, *Passionately*; and one of poetry, *He* (1938)—especially concerned herself with the social and moral problems of her sex in numerous plays: *Snow-capped Peaks* (1923), *Chanito* (1923), *Those Men* (1924), *The Sin of Women* (1925), *The Blue Shawl* (1925), *The Woman without Honor* (1926), *The Reason for the Sin* (1928), *The Other Woman's Sons* (1930), *What Only Man Can Stand* (1936), and *Maternity* (1937). It is worth noting that the performances of the last two of these works have passed the hundred mark. A fine feeling for dramatic creation characterizes Amalia de Castillo Ledón (born in Santander Jiménez, Tamaulipas, in 1902); her *When the Leaves Fall* (1929) is surely one of the most beautiful and finished plays—in construction and content—that has appeared on the Mexican stage of this period; *Well Buckets* (1934), her second work of the same type, is an original study of the background and customs of a certain class of Mexican society in this period. María Luisa Ocampo (born in Chilpancingo, Guerrero, in 1908), whose first play, *Life's Tricks* (1923), made her very favorably known, has continued her work for the theater, writing many plays: *The Bonfire* (1924), *The Pack of Hounds* (1925), *Without Wings* (in collaboration with Ricardo Parada León, 1925), *Thirst in the Desert* (1927), *The Ballad of Juan Saavedra* (1929), *Far Beyond Men* (1929), *Castles in the Air, the House in Ruins* (1936), and *A Woman's Life* (1938).

Lastly, Miguel N. Lira, in whose works prose and poetry alternate, has, in *Return to the Soil* (1940) and *Beautiful* (1942), introduced in the theater a new poetic form in a popular setting; and he has published *Carlotta of Mexico* (1943), a simulated history written in his peculiar style.

To show the Mexican public what directions theatrical production—or, to be more accurate, a certain type of production, the so-called "Vanguard"—is taking in the world at large, Celestino Gorostiza (born in Villahermosa, Tabasco, in 1904) founded the "Theater of Orientation," with a company of amateur actors formed and directed by him. In his role as dramatist, he produced some of his own works in the new theater; two of his plays were published in one volume in 1935: *To Be or Not to Be* and *The School of Love*.

In late years he has successfully presented *The Color of His Skin* and *Social Column*.

Finally, a vigorous personality, an outstanding figure in the contemporary theater, is Rodolfo Usigli (born in Mexico of an Italian father and Polish mother, November 17, 1905). His unmistakable calling to write drama came early, his first work, *The Apostle,* being published in 1931. This was followed by many plays, almost all of which were staged: *Secret State* (one of three nonpolitical plays, 1936), *Half Tone* (1937), *Woman Does Not Work Miracles, Day Dream* (1939), *Vacations* (1940), *The Family Dines at Home* (1942), *Phantom Crown* (1943), and *The Gesticulator* (1944). Strength and delicacy, refinement and originality, a penetrating spirit of close observation, a peculiarly ardent manner which is purposely concealed by cold objectivity and biting irony, are characteristics of Usigli. His remarkable dramatic skill and gloomy outlook have increased in his recent works, making him a controversial figure. These recent works include *Summer Night, The Fugitives* (1950), *The Child and the Fog* (1951), *Stagnant Waters* (1952), *Jano Is a Girl* (1952), and *One of These Days . . .* (1954). He has made translations of Corneille, Racine, Molière, Musset, Barrie, Galsworthy, Behrman, O'Neill, Maxwell Anderson, Schnitzler, and Chekhov. Except for one volume of poems, *Hopeless Conversation* (1939), his literary efforts have been concentrated in the field of dramatic art as historian, chronicler, dramatist, and critic. He is the author of *Mexico in the Theater* (1932) and *Itinerary of the Dramatist* (1941).

HISTORY

Literary activity during this period having been considerable in the fields already discussed, it is no matter for surprise that history has been cultivated with no less devotion, ardor, and success. Above all, in recent years, in addition to the original works of contemporary authors, we should especially note the continual publication both of historical documents and of very valuable works that had remained incomplete or previously unpublished.

Alberto María Carreño (born in Tacubaya, Federal District, August 7, 1875; died in Mexico City, 1962) is notable for his industry. He did research and studied in a number of fields. His work comprises *Economic and Social Studies, Biographical Studies, Histori-*

cal Studies, Historico-Geographical Studies, Philological Studies, and *Literary Studies,* besides a collection of *Diverse Works* (fourteen volumes of biographical sketches, monographs, addresses, lectures, and bibliographical essays). His last book, *The Chronicler Luis González Obregón* (1938), presents material given him orally by the great historian on the eve of his death—González Obregón's own memories and impressions of his life and experiences.

Following in the footsteps of González Obregón, though with a genuine individuality of his own, Manuel Romero de Terreros y Vinent (born in Mexico City, March 24, 1880) has devoted himself to reconstructing the colonial past. Better known by his title than by his name, the Marquis of San Francisco has brought into existence a copious, singularly valuable body of work. He first showed his devotion to letters in the field of fiction and drama, writing *Among the Flowers* (a play, 1907), *Anthology* (stories, 1909), *The White Woman* (a tragedy, 1910), and *The Bronze Door* (stories, 1921). From the beginning, however, he devoted his chief energies to the study of history and customs, particularly to matters concerning the colonial era and the two empires in the nineteenth century [Iturbide's and Maximilian's]. The following books are the fruit of these studies: *Synopsis of Heraldry* (1906), *Biographical Notes concerning Don Juan Gómez de Parada* (1911), *The Military Orders of Mexico* (i.e., the orders of knighthood, 1913), *Little Flowers of San Felipe de Jesús* (1916), *The Corregidors of Mexico* (i.e., magistrates representing the royal government, 1917), *The House of Parada* (1917), *Royal Tournaments, Masquerades, and Fiestas in New Spain* (1918), *The Epistolary Style in New Spain* (1919), *Hernán Cortés, His Sons and Grandsons, Knights of the Military Orders* (1919), *A Bibliophile in the Holy Office* (i.e., the Inquisition, 1920), *The Court of Agustín I* (i.e., Iturbide, 1922), *Viceregal Mexico* (1925), *Bibliography of Chroniclers of the City of Mexico* (1926), *Mexican Traditions and Legends* (with introduction, notes, and vocabularies, 1927), *Silhouettes of Other Years* (1937), *Things That Were* (1937), and *Sketches of Social Life in New Spain* (1944). Of all past and present Mexican writers he is doubtless the one who has done the most extensive research and writing on Mexican art. His books in this field include *The Colonial House* (1913), *Colonial Art* (three series, 1916-21), *The Engravers of Mexico during the*

Colonial Epoch (1917), *Colonial Residences in the City of Mexico* (1918), *The House of the Glazed Tiles* (1918), *The Gardens of New Spain* (1919), *Synthesis of Colonial Art* (1922), *Industrial Arts in New Spain* (1923), *Tres Guerras the Architect* (1929), *Brief Notes on Colonial Sculpture of the Seventeenth and Eighteenth Centuries* (1930), *The Medallions Commemorating the Proclamation of Independence and the First Empire* (1931), *Artistic Mexican Bookbinding* (1932), *The Art of Engraving in Mexico* (with preamble and notes, 1933), *The Painter Alonso López de Herrera* (1934), *The Colonial Tlacos* (coins, 1935), and *Art in Mexico during the Viceroyalty* (1951). He published, in the field of literary history, *Ideas Concerning Castilian Literature* (1926). Lastly, as editor of reprinted books, collections of documents, and letters, he has given to the press the following: *The Voyage of the Marquise de las Amarillas* (with notes, 1914), *Travel-Notes of Don Juan Romero de Terreros* (with introduction and notes, 1919), *Maximilian and the Empire* (based on contemporary letters, 1926), *Mexican Money during the Revolution* (translation and notes, 1933), *Loa about the Borda Garden* (introduction and notes, 1933), *Report concerning Japan* (introduction and notes, 1934), *Maximilian's Court* (Don Ignacio Algara's Letters, with foreword and notes, 1938). In his books, the Marquis of San Francisco unites richness of documentation—all of it usually firsthand—with such a complete knowledge of periods and subject matter that he is not counted in vain as an authority on the subjects to which he has consecrated himself.

Historic investigation and church history owe much to the scholarly Father Mariano Cuevas, S.J. (born in Mexico City, February 18, 1879; died there on March 31, 1949). He received his early education in his native city, attended the Conciliar Seminary, and went to Spain in 1893; two years later, he became a Jesuit; he studied rhetoric, the humanities, and philosophy in Burgos; theology and canon law in St. Louis, Missouri; preparatory historical studies in Rome; and methodology in Louvain, where he received the doctor's degree. He taught literature, history, and philosophy in various schools of the Jesuits, both in Mexico and in Spain. His principal activities, however, were in the field of history. For long years he did research in the Mexican archives, both ecclesiastical and civil, as well as among the records preserved in Seville, London, Rome, Bologna, Brussels, Paris, Madrid, New York, Philadelphia, California, and Texas. The fruit of his first research was the very important *Unpublished Documents of the Sixteenth Century for the History of Mexico*, which he collected and annotated and the National Museum published in a thick volume in 1914. Besides numerous tracts and articles of historical character not yet collected, he wrote a unique work called the *History of the Church in Mexico* (5 volumes, 1921-28), *Historic Album for the Fourth Centennial of Guadalupe* (1930), and *History of the Mexican Nation* (1940). We should also mention his most interesting and erudite study, *Monk and Mariner: Urdaneta* (1944), and *The Liberator* (about Iturbide, 1947).

Among those who have most greatly distinguished themselves in the cultivation of history in recent years, it is appropriate to include Vito Alessio Robles (native of Saltillo; born June 13, 1879; died in Mexico City, June 11, 1957). To him is due a work that is important for an understanding of the great colonizing enterprise in a vast part of our country: *Francisco de Urdiñola and the Northern Part of New Spain* (1931). No little part of his efforts as historian was devoted to his native province: his works concerning it include *Bibliography of Coahuila, Historical and Geographical* (1927), *How the History of Coahuila Was Written* (1931), *The First Printing Press in Coahuila* (1932), *Some Mislaid Pages of the History of Coahuila* (1932), *Etymologies of Uncertain Origin: Coahuila* (1934), and *Coahuila and Texas in the Colonial Epoch* (1938). He also studied noted personalities, some of them unjustly forgotten or insufficiently known: *Fray Agustín de Morfi and His Work* (1935), *Ramos Arizpe* (1937), *The Illustrious Master Andrés Manuel del Río* (1937). He evoked the past of certain cities, presenting for us their history and legend in three original books: *Acapulco* (1932), *Saltillo* (1934), and *Monterrey* (1936). Moreover, some of his work is devoted to contemporary events: *Blood-stained Files of Men* (1936), *Bucareli's Treaties* (1937), and *My Experiences with Our Ulysses* (1938). To the foregoing should be added the *Historic Sketches* (1938) and his annotated editions of works by Miguel Ramos Arizpe, Fray Juan Agustín de Morfi, and Pedro Tamarón y Romeral.

A brother of the preceding writer, Miguel Alessio Robles (born also in Saltillo, his birthday being December 5, 1884; died in Mexico City, November 10, 1951) devoted himself primarily to writing the history of the Revolution (in which he was an actor and an eye-witness), chiefly in its anecdotal aspect. Among his works of this class are the following: *Obregón As a Military Man* and *Political History of the Revolution* (1938), in addition to the volumes *Battle Cries, Fallen Idols, Ideals of the Revolution,* and *The Responsibility of the High Officials.* He cultivated the delightful genre of memoirs in *My Generation and My Epoch* (1949), *Half Way,* and *Looking at the Past.* His impressions and memories of his natal city are gathered in *The City of Saltillo* and *Profiles of Saltillo.* His Spanish sympathies are displayed in *Races* and *Hispanic Matters.* The tragedy of war which shook the world, beginning in 1939, gave him material for books in which he defended the cause of liberty against the totalitarian invader.

To complete the picture, brief notice should be given to other outstanding writers and works. Nicolás Rangel (born in León, Guanajuato, 1864; died in Cuernavaca, June 7, 1935) was a devoted servant of history, both as teacher and investigator. He collaborated with Luis G. Urbina and Pedro Henríquez Ureña in preparing the *Centennial Anthology* (1910); and because of his lucky, persistent searches in the archives, Alarcón's biography can now be reconstructed on a firm basis. Alfonso Toro (born in Zacatecas, 1873; died in Mexico City, June 7, 1952) wrote some interesting historical studies: *Compendium of Mexican History* (1926) and a *Colonial History of Spanish America,* whose three volumes begin with *The Voyages of Columbus* (1946). Juan B. Iguíniz (born in Guadalajara, Jalisco, 1881), another scholarly investigator, brought forth the mature fruit of his efforts in his excellent *Bibliography of Mexican Novelists* (1926), which was followed by a small volume on *The Printing Press in New Spain* (1938). Alfonso Caso (born in Mexico City, February 1, 1896), whose valuable studies and investigations in archeology culminated in the discoveries of Monte Albán, is the author of six important works: *The Teocalli of the Holy War* (1927), *The Zapotecan Stelas* (1928), *The Religion of the Aztecs* (1937), *Explorations in Oaxaca* (1938), *Thirteen Master Works of Mexican Archeology* (1938), and *Urns of Oaxaca* (1952). We should not omit the magnificent archeological work of Salvador Toscano— notable and lamented investigator—entitled *Pre-Columbian Art of*

Mexico and Central America (1944). Genaro Estrada gave generous, effective impetus to the study of Mexican bibliography by encouraging and directing the very useful series of *Mexican Bibliographical Monographs* that were published by the Secretariat of Foreign Relations beginning in 1925; the first in the series was prepared by Estrada and dedicated to Amado Nervo. José C. Valadés (born in Mazatlán, Sinaloa, 1901) has composed a well-documented volume on *Alamán: Statesman and Historian* (1938). Héctor Pérez Martínez (born in Campeche, 1906; died in Veracruz, 1948) is outstanding because of the lively evocation in *Cuauhtémoc (Life and Death of a Culture)* and *Juárez the Impassive*. General Rubén García (native of the city of Puebla; born February 14, 1896), having specialized in military affairs, has written about *Morelos' Campaigns against Acapulco and the Attack and Siege of Cuautla* (1933); in the field of biography should be mentioned his *Bio-bibliography of the Historian Francisco Javier Clavijero* (1931) and his *Biography of the General of the Division, Don Mariano Escobedo* (1932); and, lastly, to the study of our remote past he devoted the volume called *Ancient Mexico: Origin and Development of the Aboriginal Civilizations* (1927).

Next, for historical activities in the field of art, we should mention Alba Herrera y Ogazón (born and died in Mexico City, 1885-1931), a woman who was distinguished in musical criticism and the author of an excellent *History of Music* (1931); Gabriel Saldívar, who, restricting the picture, wrote the *History of Music in Mexico* (1934); Higinio Vázquez Santa Ana (born in Atemajac de las Tablas, Jalisco, October 25, 1889; died in the City of Mexico, January 19, 1962), who, besides collecting three volumes of *Canciones, Lays, and Ballads,* published a *History of the Mexican Canción*; Vicente T. Mendoza (born in Cholula, Puebla, in 1894), author of a comparative study, *The Spanish Ballad and the Mexican Popular "Ballad"* (1939); Daniel Castañeda (born in Mexico City, 1898) who theorizes on the same subject in *The Mexican Popular "Ballad," Its Literary and Musical Technique* (1943); Manuel Mañón, author of the *History of the Principal Theater of Mexico* (1932), a work abounding in data and of great value for the study of related illustrations and art work; José María González de Mendoza (born in Seville, Spain, June 23, 1893), essayist, short-story writer, and art and literary critic, of whose prolific work only a small part has been collected.

Lastly, as if the consideration and examination of our own materials were not enough, the critical spirit has turned even to the newest and the foreign; of this phase let the book entitled *The Theater in the U.S.S.R.* (1938) stand as testimony. Written by the eminent Mexican actor Alfredo Gómez de la Vega (1890-1957), it presents his direct, individual observations on the present Russian stage. So great, in short, has been the flocking of writers into the field of history that not even by making a separate study of it could we be sure of not omitting some name or work worthy of being taken into account.

In conclusion, the National Autonomous University of Mexico (the UNAM) undertook some time ago the publication of the *Library of the University Student,* a rich collection of Mexican authors, which has become an excellent auxiliary to the knowledge and diffusion of our literature. Of prime importance, too, in the study of our literature is the *Collection of Mexican Authors* that Editorial Porrúa is publishing, and of which eighty-four volumes of the most outstanding lyric poetry, fiction, criticism, and history have been printed. A similar effort is represented in the *Stylo Collection of Ancient and Modern Mexican Authors,* directed and published by Antonio Caso, Jr., which comprises twenty-seven volumes, almost all of contemporary authors. Finally, let us mention the most recent collection, *Mexican Letters,* published by the Foundation of Economic Culture, which is of great importance in the national literary output with its widely varying genres, augmenting the broad panorama of our contemporary literature.

From this summary of what has been accomplished since 1910, it is clear that the literary activity of Mexico is far from being sluggish or sterile. Of all the works mentioned, which will live, and which will pass away? ¡*A' posteri l'ardua sentenza!*

It is time to stop. The journey has been long; and it is right for us, like the legendary wanderers, to sit down by the side of the road on a little slope that commands a view of the road other historians or future wanderers will have to travel. The evening is fresh and the air serene. In the sky there have been storms—perhaps there are still—

that come to disturb the most excellent calm. It does not matter. Conflict and change constitute the law of life. The fatigue of our stubborn march across the centuries is resolved for us now into an optimistic conviction, soothing and peaceful: a conviction that we are not only a race but a tradition and a culture—a race that we must strengthen, a tradition that we should love supremely, finding in that love our own immortality.

Appendices

Appendix A:
Our Own Day

POETRY

THE POET Enrique González Martínez was throughout his long life the last *modernista* and the first to react against this movement. Because of his attention to the new directions in poetry he was considered the patriarch of modern Mexican poetry, even after his death in 1952. Nevertheless, it is with Ramón López Velarde, closer in age to the writers of the generation of the *Athenaeum*, that contemporary Mexican poetry begins. His short but valuable work, revealing his deep feeling for Mexico, claimed attention because it was inspired by his homeland and not patterned on European models. The generation of the *Contemporáneos*, named for the most important literary review published between 1928 and 1931, followed the generation of the *Athenaeum*. The *Contemporáneos* sought to place Mexican poetry on the level with universal poetry; and their eagerness to know and popularize the literature of other countries, especially French literature, characterized their work. The generation of the *Taller (Workshop)*, a review published from 1938 to 1941, opposed the aesthetic position of the *Contemporáneos*, with a revolutionary point of view addressed to social problems. Its principal members were Octavio Paz, Efraín Huerta, and Neftalí Beltrán. Around *Tierra Nueva (New Earth,* 1940-42) a new generation formed whose most definite purpose was "to seek a middle ground between tradition and modern ideas, between the iconoclastic enthusiasm of youth and the acceptance of a strictness in literary form." Belonging to this group were the critic José Luis Martínez, the philosopher Leopoldo Zea, and the poets Alí Chumacero, Jorge González Durán, José Cárdenas Peña, and others. The poets of the *Taller* and *Tierra Nueva* are the necessary antecedents of the two most important nu-

415

clei of young Mexican poets: the first group represented by Rubén Bonifaz Nuño, Rosario Castellanos, and Jaime Sabinas, all with a somber lyric intonation, whose background persistently reflects concern for the destiny of man; and the second group, more recent, in which Marco Antonio Montes de Oca, José Emilio Pacheco, and Homero Aridjis are outstanding.

As indicated in the Mexican Publishers' Note prefacing this edition, the following pages include both native poets and foreign poets with long residence in Mexico, briefly discussed in chronological order. When the place of publication is not given, the work was published in Mexico.

Poets Born Before 1900

León Felipe Camino y Galicia (1884) was born in Tábara, Zamora, Spain. Prior to 1940 he traveled in Mexico and the United States, and since that time he has been living in Mexico. Subsequent to World War II he visited Latin America, with brief stops in Argentina and Uruguay, where he gave anti-imperialist lectures. After his first book, *Verses and Prayers of a Traveler* (1920), his poetry acquired a revolutionary tone, in the form of harangues written in simple, free verse. The dramatic struggle of his country and the triumph of injustice and oppression have deeply wounded the heart of this upright and sensitive man. He is the author of *The Insignia* (Madrid, 1937), *The Clown with the Buffets and The Fisherman with the Pole* (1938), *The Spaniard of the Exodus and of Weeping* (1939), *The Great Responsible* (1940), *The Lizards* (1941), *You Will See the Light* (1942), *Call Me Publican* (1950), *The Deer* (1958), and *What Did King John Do?* (1962). Although he has written drama and other works in prose, León Felipe is above all one of the best Spanish poets in exile.

José Moreno Villa (1887-1955) was born in Málaga, Spain; he came to Mexico in 1939 as a political refugee and lived here until his death. He was a professor in the College of Mexico and wrote for national as well as foreign magazines and newspapers. He was poet and critic, painter and historian of art. Ortega y Gasset saw in his lyrics "an approximation to pure poetry." His painting is impressionistic; his work as a critic of art in general is of great value because of his orientation to and love for Mexico. Among his poetic works are the following: *Sheaf* (Madrid, 1913), *The Passenger* (Madrid, 1914), *Struggles of Sorrows and Joy and Their Transfiguration* (Madrid, 1915), *Changing Ideas* (Madrid, 1918), *Jacinta the Redhead* (Málaga, 1929), *Carambas* (Madrid, 1931), *Bridges without End, Drawing Room without Walls, The Unyielding Door* (Mexico, 1941), *The Night of the Word* (1942), *The Music in Him* (1913-47, Buenos Aires, 1950), *Voice in Flight to Its Cradle* (1961). His prose works include *Colonial Mexican Sculpture* (1942), *Life in Its True Light* (autobiography, 1944), *The Mexican Element in the Plastic Arts* (1948), and *Cornucopia of Mexico* (1952).

Juan José Domenchina (1898-1959), also Spanish and born in Madrid, came to Mexico in 1939 and remained here until his death. He contributed to various publications such as *Hoy (Today)*, *Mañana (Tomorrow)*, *Romance*, and wrote literary reviews in 1958 for the magazine *Tiempo*. His poetry, cerebral in his early works, changed greatly from the time of his exile, evolving toward expressive forms in which emotion and sincerity predominate. His poetry as an emigrant is permeated by anguish and nostalgia occasioned by grief for his lost homeland. In Mexico he published *Selected Poems* (1940), *Exile* (1942), *Third Jubilant Elegy* (1944), *Passion of Darkness* (sonnets, 1944), *Three Jubilant Elegies* (1946), *Collection of Oriental Poems of Abz-ul-Agrib* (1945), *Exul umbra* (1948), *Shadow in Exile* (1950), *Nine Sonnets and Three Ballads* (1952), *The Estranged* (1958).

Emilio Prados (1899-1962) lived as a political exile in Mexico from 1938 until his death. It can be said that his poetic work is one long poem with differing frequencies and modulations. His poetry written in exile shows him to be a master of metaphors, sometimes magical and sometimes religious. *Memory of Oblivion* (1940) depicts oblivion as the source of anguish and hope. *The Inscribed Stone* (1961) discovers the integration between the external world and the internal self, between life and death, between the world of the senses and the mythical world. He also wrote *Slight Death* (1942), *Closed Garden* (1946), *Natural River* (Buenos Aires, 1957), *Circumcision of the Dream* (1957), *Sonorous Enigma* (Spain, 1958), *Acceptance of the Word* (Spain, 1961), *Signs of Being* (Spain, 1962), and *Transparencies* (Málaga, 1962).

Carlos Pellicer (1899) is one of the greatest contemporary Mexican poets; his work represents "the defense of the word with its music and color as the poetical element, material, and essence of the poem." His rich, varied lyric poetry is the most resonant in modern Mexico. Carlos Pellicer came from the tropics; his home was the sea and the forest, and he brought to poetry a delight in nature. "Savage glorification of the senses" is Torres Bodet's characterization of this poetry which follows that of the descriptive poets initiated by Balbuena. This poet of landscapes and great American themes later becomes the poet of desolation and love, and finally, in his book *The Practice of Flight* (1956), reveals his profound piety in treating sacred themes. The National Autonomous University of Mexico has published his complete works under the title, *Poetic Material 1918-1961*; and in 1964 he was awarded the National Prize for Literature. His recent production includes *With Words and with Fire* (1963), and *Teotihuacán and August the 13th: the Destruction of Tenochtitlán* (1965).

Poets Born in the Decade 1900-1910

Pedro Garfias (1901) was born in Salamanca, Spain, but reared in Osuna, Seville, and considers the latter his place of origin. Residing in Mexico since 1939, he has given recitals and lectures in the universities of Guanajuato, San Luis Potosí, Monterrey, Guadalajara, and Mexico City. In 1919 he became known through Madrid periodicals and, along with others, launched the *Ultra,* a manifesto to literary youth, from which the movement *ultraísmo* emerged. He was at first very enthusiastic about the *"ismos"* (isms): *ultraísmo, dadaísmo, creacionismo*; being extraordinarily lyrical, however, he was able to save himself from these isms and to develop a strong personality, profound and capable of appealing to the emotions of his readers. With the exception of his first book, *The Wing of the South* (1926), which was published in Seville, the rest of his work has been published in Mexico: *Poems of the Spanish War* (1941), *Spring at Eaton Hastings* (1939), *Elegy to the Dnieprostoi Dam* (1943), *Old and New Poems* (1951), and *River of Bitter Waters* (1953).

Germán Pardo García (1902) was born in Choachi, Department of Cundinamarca, Colombia, but has lived in Mexico since 1931, where for many years he has been the editor of the cultural gazette *Nivel.* He has been called "the most Mexican of the Colombian poets." He is the prolific author of some twenty books of poetry, most of which have been published in Mexico City. Because of his having lived in the Colombian wilderness, in his first period he was a poet of solitude and interpreter of solitary places; but, being influenced later by the Mexican scene, he abandoned his early anguish and became interested in the problems of Spanish America. Among his works should be mentioned *Morning Star without Limits* (1952), *Poetic Act* (1953), *U.Z. Calls Out to Space* (1954), *Eternity of the Nightingale* (1956), *There Are Stones like Tears* (1957), *Centaur to the Sun* (1959), *Prelude of Osiris* (1960), *The Southern Cross* (1960), *Glass Angels* (1962), *The Cosmonaut* (1962), *The Defender* (1964).

The Sevillian poet Luis Cernuda (1902-1963), after a prolific career in colleges and universities of France, England, and the United States, settled in Mexico in 1951 and lived there until his death. He occupied various chairs in the Faculty of Philosophy and Letters of the UNAM, and shortly before his death he was paid homage in Jalapa, Veracruz, for his meritorious intellectual work. In the first period of his poetic career, Cernuda was cold and speculative, slightly nihilistic, but a remarkable artisan of verse. His two most notable works are *Reality and Desire* (Madrid, 1936; third, enlarged edition, Mexico, 1958) and *Desolation of Fancy* (1962), his last book. He also wrote *Profile of the Air* (Málaga, 1927) and *Wherever Oblivion Resides* (Madrid, 1935).

Juan Rejano (1903), born in Puente Genil, Córdoba, Spain, has lived since 1939 in Mexico, where all of his work has been written and published. He has served on the editorial staff of the review *Taller* and was founder and director of such magazines as *Litoral* (1944), and *Romance* and *Ultramar* (1947). From 1947 to 1957 he directed the "Mexican Review of Culture" of the *National*, in which appeared his weekly column "Notebook of Signs of the Times." Like the poetry of the majority of Spanish poets who suffered exile, the songs of Juan Rejano are impregnated with Spain and her tragedy. In other poems he interprets popular aspirations and his strong desire for peace in a world without shadows. His first book, *Fidelity of the Dream* (1943), was followed by *The Genil River and the Olive Trees* (1944), *Heroic Prelude* (1947), *The Obscure Limit* (1948), *Night Within* (1949), *Spanish Ode* (1949), *Minor Constellation* (1950),

Songs to Peace (1955), *The Reply* (1956), *The River and the Dove* (1960), and *The Book of Tributes* (1961).

Jorge Cuesta (1903-1942) was born in Córdoba, Veracruz. About 1922 he came to Mexico City to study chemical sciences. His first essays appeared in the review *Ulises* (1927-28), and in 1928 he became editor of the *Anthology of Modern Mexican Poetry*. He affiliated with the group known as *Contemporáneos* (1928-32) and was a contributor to the principal publications of his time. After he became insane, he took his own life in Mexico City. He left a work, short in length but intense in content, which speaks of dissatisfaction, constant conflict, the suppression of emotions, and a tortured search for unattainable perfection. As a critic of contemporary literature and art in general, he wrote many essays of undeniable value and depth. The UNAM has published his work in a collection entitled *Poems and Essays* (4 volumes, 1964).

Elías Nandino (1903), born in Cocula, Jalisco, is a physician by profession, but a poet from early youth by dedication. From 1956 to 1960 he directed the literary review of *Estaciones (Seasons)*; and from 1960 to 1964, the review *Cuadernos de Bellas Artes (Notebooks of the Fine Arts)*. His poetic work reveals a continuous increase in depth of sentiment as he frees himself of rhetorical and discursive trappings. His serious poetry sings of desolate love and death, and crystallizes the story of a tortured man whose deepest desire to believe finds obstacles everywhere. With this subjective manifestation, Nandino ably expresses the collective anxiety of man in our time. In *Poetry I* (1947) and *Poetry II* (1949), he has compiled several of his books. Recently he has published *Shipwreck of Doubt* (1950), *Triangle of Silences* (1953), *Nocturnal Summary* (1955), *Nocturnal Love* (1958), *Nocturnal Day* (1959), and *Nocturnal Word* (1960).

Gilberto Owen (1905-1952), grandson of an Irish miner, was born in El Rosario, Sinaloa, and died in Philadelphia, where he was engaged in the diplomatic service. At the National Preparatory School he met Jorge Cuesta, who had a great influence on his intellectual development. Likewise influenced by Xavier Villaurrutia, he wrote for the reviews *Ulises* and *Contemporáneos*. He was, as all the "Contemporáneos," a cultivated man of rigorous judgment, essentially a poet, even in his *Novel Like a Cloud* (1928). His only available book is *Poetry and Prose*, published by the UNAM in 1953, though his *First Poems* (Toluca, 1957) is to be found in the *Memoranda of the State of Mexico*.

To the same decade belong also the Spaniards Manuel Altolaguirre, Agustí Bartra, and Ernestina de Champourcín.

Manuel Altolaguirre (1905-1959) was born in Málaga. Shortly after his exile, he and his wife, Concha Méndez, published *La Verónica*, in Havana. After 1943 he made his home in Mexico, where, with Juan Rejano, Luis Cernuda, Emilio Prados, and others, he published the review *Litoral* (1944). While visiting in Spain, in 1959, he was killed in an automobile accident. His work includes poetry, drama, a novel, unedited essays, scenarios, translations, articles, and contributions to European and American magazines, in addition to his work as publisher and editor of several literary magazines. He published numerous volumes of poetry: *The Guest Islands* (Málaga, 1926), *Example* (Málaga, 1927), *Poetry* (1931), *A Poem for a Girl Friend* (Paris, 1931), *Loneliness Together* (Madrid, 1934), *New Poems of the Guest Islands* (Madrid), *Slow Freedom* (Madrid), *Transitory Cloud* (Havana, 1940), *More Poems of the Guest Islands* (1944), *New Poems* (1946), *End of a Love* (1949), *Poems in America* (Málaga, 1955).

Agustí Bartra (1908) was born in Barcelona. He was fighting at the front as a republican soldier when his first book of poems, *Cant corporal* (*Corporal Song*, 1938), was published. At the close of the Civil War he spent some time in France, the Dominican Republic, Havana, and Haiti; in 1941 he settled in Mexico, where he has done most of his work. He has written several plays; the novel, *The Christ of 200,000 Arms* (*Field of Algiers*, 1958); and stories such as *Demeter* (1961). Bartra is above all a humanistic poet who offers to a suffering world an enduring faith and hope in the future of mankind. One of his chief works, *Odysseus*, was translated from Catalan into Spanish (1955), as was his poem *Marsias and Adila* (1962). Lastly, we mention his long poem *Quetzalcóatl* (1960), *Ode to Catalonia from the Tropics*, and *Behold the Man* (1964).

Ernestina de Champourcín (1905) was born in Victoria, Alava, Spain. In 1939 she and her husband (the poet Juan José Domenchina) were invited by Alfonso Reyes and La Casa de España in Mexico to live in Mexico City. Ernestina's poetry is characterized by a yearning for perfection and an erotic-mystic tone which relate her to several

Spanish-American women poets such as Alfonsina Storni and Guadalupe Amor. She has published literary criticism, several translations, and a novel, *The House Across the Street* (Madrid, 1936). Her poetic work includes *In Silence* (Madrid, 1925), *Now* (Madrid, 1928), *The Voice in the Wind* (1931), *The Useless Song* (Madrid, 1936), *Figure in the Dark* (Madrid, 1952), *The Name You Gave Me* (1960), and *Prison of the Senses* (1964).

Poets Born in the Decade 1910-1920

Concha Urquiza (1910-1945) was born in Morelia, Michoacán, and lived in New York from 1928 to 1932. On returning to her native town, she entered as a postulant in the Congregation of the Daughters of the Holy Ghost. A short while later she chose to dedicate herself to teaching in San Luis Potosí, and later on to studying in the School of Philosophy of the UNAM. In 1945 she was invited to teach in the School of the Daughters of the Holy Ghost in Tijuana. While on an excursion to Ensenada, Baja California, she was drowned. Her prose and poetry were published posthumously in *Works* (1946), to which Gabriel Méndez Plancarte wrote an extensive introduction, presenting her as a remarkable mystic poet constantly engaged in spiritual conflict.

The poet Miguel Bustos Cerecedo (1912) was a native of Chicontepec, Veracruz, and a graduate of the Normal School for Teachers. He was one of the publishers of the literary review *Moment* (Jalapa, 1933), and later editor of the review *Cone* (Mexico, 1938). He belongs to the important group of modern poets who have known how to express not only their sorrow and happiness but also their sympathy for the freedom of the individual and society. He has written *Night on Its Knees* (1933), *River Bed* (collective poems, 1934), *Revolution* (1934), *Three Revolutionary Poems* (1935), *Hunger* (1937), *Distant Love* (1942), *Rumors about Héctor Pérez Martínez in Five Sonnets* (1948), *Elegies to Remember a Love* (1950), *Supplication to Enrique González Martínez* (1952), *Specifications* (*Pliegos*, 1953), *Sonnets* (1953), *An Open Road* (1957), *Words to Cultivate a Love* (1958), *When We Were Children* (1958), *Memory of Your Steps* (1961).

The poet and essayist Octavio Paz (born in Mixcoac, D.F., 1914), along with Efraín Huerta, Neftalí Beltrán, Alberto Quintero Alvarez, and others, belongs to that literary generation that first became known in the reviews *Barandal* (Railing, 1931-32), *Cuadernos [Notebooks] of the Valley of Mexico* (1933-34), and *Taller Poético (Poetic Workshop,* 1936-38), and then confined itself to the *Taller* (1938-41). He entered the diplomatic service in 1943. In 1963 he won the Grand International Prize for Poetry in the Sixth Competition of the International Congress of Poetry in Knocke, Belgium. His works have attained universal renown and have been translated into various languages. If as a poet he occupies an outstanding place among his contemporaries, as an essayist he is author of sharp, penetrating books such as *Labyrinth of Loneliness* (1950), which is an attempt to explain the character and personality of man in Mexico; *The Bow and the Lyre* (1956), a book on aesthetics and on his own poetry; and *Pears from the Elm Tree* (1957), valuable essays on Mexican poetry and other subjects. His first collection of poems was *Origin of Man* (1937), followed by *Beneath Your Bright Shadow* (Spain, 1937), *Between the Stone and the Flower* (1941), *On the Edge of the World* (1942), *Liberty Under Oath* (1949), *Liberty Under Oath,* Second Edition (a poetic work, 1935-58, published in 1960), *Eagle or Sun?* (prose poems, 1951), *Thoughts for a Hymn* (1954), *Sun Stone* (1957), *The Violent Season* (1958), *Water and Wind* (1959), *Two and One Three* (1961), *Salamander* (1962), and *The Day of Udaipur* (Spain, 1963).

Efraín Huerta (born in Silao, Guanajuato, 1914) has been a professional journalist since 1936. He has traveled throughout the United States of America and Europe. In 1945 the French government awarded him the Academic Palms, and in 1952 he visited Poland and the Soviet Union. Like Octavio Paz, Efraín Huerta belongs to the generation of the *Taller,* a group distinguished by their rejection of aesthetic and subjective lyricism in order to follow wider roads of universal solidarity. He has written *Absolute Love* (1935), *Line of the Dawn* (1936), included in *The Men of the Dawn* (1944), *Poems of War and Hope* (1943), *The Primitive Rose* (1950), and *Poetry* (1951). In his *Poems of Voyage, 1949-1953* (1956), the themes are peace, struggle against racial discrimination, the music of the Negroes and their customs. The following complete the list of his work: *Star on High and New Poems* (1956), *To Enjoy Your Peace* (1957), *My Country, Oh, My Country!* (1959), *Elegy to the Mounted Police* (1959), *Tragic Farce of the President Who Wanted an Island* (1961), *The Bitter Root* (1962), and *The Tajín* (1963).

Neftalí Beltrán (born in Alvarado, Veracruz, 1916) was also a member of the *Taller* group. He was director of the review *Poetry* (1938), which was edited by Angel Chápero. Already considered an excellent writer of sonnets, he published when he was twenty years old his first book, *Twenty-One Poems* (1936). In 1937 he published *Two Sonnets* and *Song of the Wind*; and, in 1941, *Poetry*. In *Unfriendly Solitude* (1944), he again demonstrates his predilection for the sonnet; in 1949 this work was published in an enlarged second edition. His most recent work is entitled *Some Songs of Neftalí Beltrán* (1953). He has written some plays and scenarios for the radio and cinema.

The Guatemalan poet Raúl Leiva (1916) won the First International Prize for Poetry in Central America in 1941. He belongs to the group that in his country, about 1940, began to publish the review *Accent*; and in 1945 he founded, with Luis Cardoza y Aragón, the *Review of Guatemala*. In his first sojourn in Mexico (1942-43), he published his initial book of poetry, *Anguish* (1942); and, since 1954, when he returned to this country, he has frequently contributed poetry, essays, and literary criticism to most of the reviews and to literary supplements in Mexico and abroad. A prolific and painstaking poet, Raúl Leiva is the author of more than fifteen books of poetry, some of which, including *Dance for Cuauhtémoc* (1955) and *Dark Eagle, Poems to Benito Juárez* (1959) have been dedicated to Mexican heroes. In *Imagery in Contemporary Mexican Poetry* (1959), he gathers a series of essays on Mexican poets from the postmodernist period up to the generation born between 1922 and 1925.

Although born in San José, Costa Rica, Alfredo Cardona Peña (1917) has done most of his writing in Mexico and because of this is considered an integral part of Mexican letters. An inspired poet, his poetry has been published in Hispanic America and in the United States; and since the publication of his first book, *The World That You Are* (1944), he has been acclaimed one of the best contemporary poets of Hispanic America. Enrique González Martínez says of him, "Master of style, he depicts much of the landscape and soul of Mexico." His talent as a narrator is evident in his short stories: *Talking*

Mask (1944), *The Secret of Queen Amaranta* (1946), and *Death in a Vase* (1962). He has won plaudits in Mexico and abroad because of his intellectual labors, and particularly because of his essays on Pablo Neruda, Alfonso Reyes, and others. He has published more than a dozen books of poetry, among them *The Loving Gardens* (1952), *Zapata* (1954), *First Paradise* (1955), *Occasional Verse* (1959), and the anthology of his work, *Greater Harvest* (1964).

Margarita Michelena (born in Pachuca, Hidalgo, 1917) studied in the School of Philosophy and Literature of the UNAM, and for a time was director of the literary review *El Libro y el Pueblo (The Book and the People)*, the organ of the Secretariat of Public Education. At the present time she is editing the political magazine *Respuesta (Reply)*. A keen sensitiveness and lyrical excellence of well-defined poetic symbols are found in her books of poetry: *Paradise and Nostalgia* (1945), *The Angel's Laurel Wreath* (1948), *Three Poems and an Autobiographical Note* (1953), and *Terrestrial Sadness* (1954).

Francisco Giner de los Ríos (born in Madrid, 1917) has been living in Mexico since 1939, with the exception of an interval of some years in Chile. He published his first poems in the review *Floresta (Collection of Fine Things)*, which Juan Ramón Jiménez was editing in the Spanish capital, but the true poet was formed in the civil war and matured in exile. His first book, *The Living Bough* (1940), belongs to Mexico, as do all his later works: *First Passion* (1941), *Small Collection of Ballads of Faith* (1941), *The Laurel Trees of Oaxaca, Notes and Poems of a Voyage* (1948), *Perfect Journey* (poetry from 1934 to 1952), and *Mexican Poems* (1958). These books contain beautiful poetry, composed with affection, tenderness, and simplicity.

Emma Godoy (born in the city of Guanajuato, 1918) studied philosophy and theology in the Institute of Feminine Culture, the Normal School, and the School of Philosophy and Letters of the UNAM. She has traveled through Europe and the Middle East, contributed to the review *Abside (Apse)*, and, in recent years, has been teaching in the Normal School and in the junior high school. In religious as well as erotic poetry, she has excelled because of the intensity of her song. Lately she has cultivated the narrative in her first novel, *He Was a Five-Faced Man* (1961), which won the 1962 prize awarded by the William Faulkner Foundation at the University of Virginia. For the theater she has written *Cain and Man* (1950); her poetry has been collected in *Pauses and Sand* (1948).

Griselda Alvarez (born in Guadalajara, Jalisco, 1918) was graduated from the Normal School qualified to teach in junior high school; she also studied psychopathology in the Normal School of Specialization. Her most recent book is *Erotic Litany for Peace* (1963), but she has become known since 1956 for her amorous poems in *Cemetery for Birds*. Later she sang of corn and countryside in *Two Songs* (1959). *Solitary Company* (1961), her third volume, talks about the world, things, and the solitary being of the author herself.

José Cárdenas Peña (1918-1963) was born in San Diego de la Unión, Guanajuato, and spent his last days there. He was educated in Mexico City; in the service of the Secretariat of Foreign Affairs, where he worked until his death, he traveled in Europe and South America. His poetry is essentially amorous. *Dream of Shadows* (1940) was his first book. *Subterranean Weeping* (1945), testimony of anguish and despair, reveals that love is the only salvation. *The City of the Birds* (1947) was followed by *Amorous Conversation* (1950), an elegiac lamentation on the passage of time, in which only love makes one forget oneself. *Broom of Oblivion and Other Poems* (1954) is a song to death, which contrasts with the youthful spirit of *Adonis or the Elegy of Love and Song of Dionysus* (1961). New poems were collected for the posthumous edition of *The Numbered Days* (1964).

Alí Chumacero (born in Acaponeta, Nayarit, 1918) belongs to the group centered around the review *Tierra Nueva* (*New Land,* 1940-42), of which he was the co-director. Occasionally, he directed *Letras de México* (*Mexican Letters*). Since 1964 he has been a member of the Academy of Language, and at present, he is general manager of the Foundation of Economic Culture. As a poet, strict, aware, and lucid, he expresses, in a manner more confidential than imaginative, the essence of being rather than the sensual, making thereby the most valuable contribution of his group. *Desert of Dreams* (1944) and *Exiled Images* (1948) show careful work, disciplined sentiment, and a keen sense of the meaning of a poem. *Exiled Images* is one of the most sensitive amorous testimonies in contemporary Mexican poetry. In *Words in Repose* (1956), his third and last book published to date, he reveals anguish in the presence of the enigma of death, desire, love, and solitude. Besides being an excellent poet, he is a magnificent critic, sagacious and well informed, as is shown in his numerous contributions to newspapers and magazines.

Tomás Díaz Bartlett (1919-1957) was born in Tenosique, Tabasco. He received his medical degree in 1945 but practiced his profession only two years. Then he became gravely ill and was confined to his bed until his death. His poetic vocation was born on the sick bed; he created poems filled with the enchantment of the tropics such as those in his first book *Low Tide* (1951), colored by a pain discreetly concealed but nevertheless intense. The necessity of fortifying himself in pain and loneliness is found in his second book, *With the Indifference of a Tree* (1955). Serene and resigned, he culminated his work with the central theme of death in *Office of Cadaver* (1958).

Poets Born in the Decade 1920-1930

Guadalupe Amor (born in Mexico City, 1920) studied in Catholic schools in the Federal District and in Monterrey. Praised or censured, she always holds the interest of the public because of the dramatic conflicts of life and death that her poetry traces decisively and soberly. In her work are combined the longing to appear before God and the anguish of our day, expressed in direct, harsh language, and an admirable feeling for classical forms. The themes constantly employed are God, death, nothingness and dust, loneliness and anguish, vanity and love. In 1951, in *Complete Poems,* she collected her poetry written since 1946, and later she published *Decimas to God* (1953), *Another Book of Love* (1955), *Serving God As a Flame* (1958), and *All the Ages of the World* (1959). Guadalupe Amor also has written two works in prose, the novel *I Am My House* (1957) and the stories of *Puppets' Gallery* (1959).

Margarita Paz Paredes (born in San Felipe Torres Mochas, Guanajuato, 1922) studied journalism in the Workers' University of Mexico and literature in the School of Philosophy and Literature in the UNAM. Her first book, *Jingles* (1942), appeared when she was very young; and, thanks to an uninterrupted creative period of work, she now has more than fifteen published works, among which are *The Plural Yearning* (1948), *Mean Origin* (1949), *Scaffoldings of Shade* (1950), *Dimension of Silence* (1953), *The Image and Its Looking Glass,* and the most recent ones, *Adam in the Shade, Final Night,* and *Seven Prayers* (1964).

Jesús Arellano (born in Ayo el Chico, Jalisco, 1923) studied first in New Mexico, and then in the School of Law and the School of Philosophy and Letters of the UNAM. As a critic he has been interested in the study and diffusion of modern Mexican poetry, as may be seen in his *Anthology of the 50* (1952), *Young Poets of Mexico* (1955), and in his tireless promotion of young writers in the reviews that he has founded or edited: *Fuensanta (Sacred Source), Letters, Poetry and Letters,* and *Metaphor.* He is, however, a poet faithful to his vocation, a nonconformist showing continuous growth as a writer from 1950, the time of the publication of his first book, *The Sign of Light.* In his melancholy poetry of *Now and in the Dawn* (1951), *New Day* (1956), and later works, bitterness and desolation give way before a new lyricism exalting man and justice.

Rubén Bonifaz Nuño (born in Córdoba, Veracruz, 1923) received his law degree from the University of Mexico in 1950. He is professor of Latin in the School of Philosophy and Letters, Director of Publications of the University, and member of the Academy of Language. He is one of our most important poets because of his delicate sensitivity and mastery of expressive material. His work *Images* (1953) is in impeccable classical form. In *The Devils and the Days* (1956) he has come nearer to the people in poems with social content and forms approaching prose. *The Mantle and the Crown* (1958) counterbalances these two manifestations of his lyricism and becomes one of his most perfect works. In his most recently published book, *Fire of the Poor* (1961), he approaches the social problem with sincere emotion.

Dolores Castro (born in Aguascalientes, 1923) became known with the publication of her poem, *The Transfigured Heart* (1949). Since then she has continued to evince a sensitive spirit in beautiful short poems that have been collected in *Two Nocturnes* (1952), *Seven Poems* (1952), *The Land Is Ringing* (1959), and *Songs of Vigil* (1960), in which she has proved her mastery of a personal, mature, and penetrating expression. Recently, she essayed the novel in *The City and the Wind* (1962), describing provincial life in Mexico in the years following the Revolution of 1910.

Jaime Sabines (born in Tuxtla Gutiérrez, Chiapas, 1925) lived in Mexico City for some years, dedicating himself to the study of the humanities, and then returned to reside in his home state. He treats the themes of love and death in his first book, *Horal* (1950), employing the poetic device of a vigorous romantic duel. In his volume, *The Sign* (1951), the despair in his previous work is accentuated in a permanent clash with bourgeois and hostile reality. *Confusion* (1956), in which the language is clear, direct, and objective, adds further proof of the inflexibility and loneliness of the poet. *Weekly Journal and Poems in Prose* (1961), presenting Sabines' universe, coherently arranged, places the author among the best contemporary Mexican poets. *Inventory of Poems*, published by the UNAM in 1962, is a collection of everything Sabines has written to date.

Poets Born in the Decade 1930-1940

Mauricio de la Selva was born in Soyapango, San Salvador, in 1930, but has been living in Mexico since 1951. He has written essays, short stories, and criticism in literary publications of Hispanic America. His poetry, with a varied technique and spontaneous musical quality, deals with the eternal themes of being, death, happiness, and loneliness, without overlooking the collective despair of the epoch in which he lives. His essays in particular show preference for the burning problems that affect Latin America. He has written in collaboration *Our Song to Guatemala* (1954), *Word* (1956), *Two Poems* (1958), *Poems to Recite at a Distance* (1958), and *Fever of the Eyelids* (1963).

Luis Rius (born in Tarancón, Spain, in 1930, and living in Mexico since 1939) received the degree of Master of Letters from the School of Philosophy and Literature in 1954. He is known as a poet and critic of Spanish literature in general. As essayist he has written *The Amorous World of Cervantes and His Characters* (1954) and studies on Pellicer and León Felipe. He has published *Songs of Vigil* (1951), *Songs of Absence* (1954), *Songs of Love and Shadow* (1965), books of poetry in which he has been able to re-create the ever current topics of love, solitude, and hope.

Horacio Espinosa Altamirano (born in Mexico City, 1931), after completing his preparatory studies, has devoted himself to journalism and the writing of poetry. He became known in 1953 with *Testi-*

mony of America in Blood and *Flock of Doves* (1954). In addition he has published *Human Song* (1955), *Beaches of the Sun* (1959), *Mexico City* (1961), *The Signs of Exile* (1962), and *Oratory of the South* (1965), books in which the author combines his lyrical emotion with his social and political preoccupation.

Marco Antonio Montes de Oca (1932) is likewise a native of Mexico City. He appears as a poet with *Ruin of the Infamous Babylon* (1953), receiving acclaim immediately as a valuable member of the group of young poets. *Counterpoint of Faith* (1955) is a search for original expression, disclosing an avid interest in metaphors and youthful dynamism. *A Bundle of Testimonies* (1956) presents the rebellious poet who is already master of peculiar ways of handling artistic form. *Birds Sing Before Dawn* (1959) includes his previous works and adds "Offerings and Epitaphs." Recently, he has published *Songs to the Sun Which Does Not Rise* (1961), *Basis of Enthusiasm* (1963), and *The Plot of Ground in Eden* (1964).

Because of his youth, Jaime Augusto Shelley (born in Mexico City, 1937) belongs to that group of young poets who became known in *The Rebellious "Ear of Corn"* (1960), a collection of poems by Juan Bañuelos, Jaime Labastida, Oscar Oliva, Eraclio Zepeda, and Shelley. Up to the present he has published *The Great Ladder* (1961) and *Song of the Cities* (1963), books of simple poetry and of vigorous optimism even in despair.

José Emilio Pacheco (1939) is, as the three former poets, a native of Mexico City. He studied in the School of Law and the School of Philosophy and Literature of the UNAM and is at present editorial secretary of the review *University of Mexico*. His poetry, written between 1958 and 1962, is published in the collection *The Elements of Night* (1963). In his poetry we see a closeness to Octavio Paz; and in the short stories, *Medusa's Blood* (1959) and *The Distant Wind* (1963), he follows Jorge Luis Borges.

Lastly, we should mention Homero Aridjis (born in Contepec, Michoacán, 1940), who studied journalism in the Carlos Septién García School and who enjoyed a fellowship to the Mexican Center of Writers in 1959-60. He is the author of five books of poetry: *The Red Muse* (1958), *Wide Open Eyes* (1960), *The Difficult Ceremony* (1963), *Before the Kingdom* (1963), and *Watching Her Sleep* (1964); and one of narratives, *The Tomb of Filidor* (1961).

Aridjis has achieved an early intellectual independence, and is, without doubt, one of the young Mexican poets of most definite personality.

THE NOVEL

Contemporary Mexican literature begins with the Revolution of 1910, a movement which serves as a necessary antecedent. It is a heartening task to record the culmination of the narrative genre during the last twenty years, and particularly the notable growth attained by the novel. Departing from the documental and historical character of the novel of the past, the contemporary novel is characterized by eagerness to acquire aesthetic qualities. In the beginning of this insistence on excellence and universality, an important role was played by Agustín Yáñez' novel, *The Edge of the Storm* (1947), with which a new cycle of novels originated after the novel of the Revolution. Yáñez is the forerunner and teacher of the present generation of novelists: Rosario Castellanos, Sergio Galindo, Carlos Fuentes, Juan Rulfo, and others, a constellation of young writers of diverse tendencies, who are constantly seeking to express more adequately their respective visions of the present-day world.

Novelists Born Before 1900

General Francisco L. Urquizo (born in San Pedro de las Colonias, Coahuila, 1891) began his literary career in 1914 by writing books for use in the army. Later, he wrote about his travels in *Central Europe in 1922, Argentine Affairs,* and *Madrid in the 'Twenties.* His first novel, *The Unrecognizable,* published in Madrid, is written in the well-defined style he uses later to describe his revolutionary experiences. His true talent, however, is revealed in his later works which describe what he has seen and experienced as a soldier of the Revolution: *México Tlaxcalantongo* (1932), *Venustiano Carranza the Man, the Politician, and the Caudillo* (1935), *Seven Years with Carranza* (1959), and others. The literary work of Urquizo comprises the short story and the fictional narrative. Though he has written short fiction, his best writing is of narrative character, sketches or memoirs of his revolutionary days that constitute a valuable documental and historical source. *Old Soldiers* (1943), considered "one of the best novels of the Revolution" because of its realism and its interest, merits for the author the title of "the soldier's novelist."

José Mancisidor (1894-1956, born in Veracruz and died in Monterrey while teaching in the summer school) was an active revolutionary all of his life and one of the most important stimulators of literature with social content. He is important mainly as a novelist, but he also cultivated the short story, of which he published two useful anthologies: *Mexican Short Stories of the Nineteenth Century* and *Mexican Short Stories by Contemporary Authors* (1946). His revolutionary affiliation is seen in his essays on Zola, Marx, Lenin, Juárez, Hidalgo, Morelos, Guerrero. His first novel, *The Tumultuous Crowd* (1931), shows him as an uneven but vigorous narrator, a characteristic that is again evident in *The Red City* (1932). One of his most significant works is *Frontier by the Sea* (1953), which describes the heroic struggle of the people of Veracruz against the North American marines. *Dawn in the Pit* (1953) describes the struggle for the national recovery of Mexican petroleum. In addition, Mancisidor left a volume of short stories, *The First Stone* (1950), and three incomplete novels.

The "Cristero" novel has a devoted representative in Fernando Robles (born in Guanajuato, 1897), who published his first novel in Buenos Aires in 1934: *The Virgin of the "Cristeros,"* on the theme to which the title alludes; his *The Saint Who Murdered* is about León Toral. *When the Eagle Lost His Wings* (1951) refers to the mutilation of the Mexican Republic in 1848 by the United States. His last published novel is *The Star That Refused to Live* (1957). Generally speaking, the works of Fernando Robles are characterized by historical focus and undeniable documentary value.

Novelists Born in the Decade 1900-1910

Francisco Rojas González (born, 1904, and died, 1951, in Guadalajara) served in the Secretariat of Foreign Affairs from 1920 until 1935. Beginning in 1934, he completed his ethnic and sociological studies in the Institute of Social Research of the UNAM and became a professional research worker. His frequent trips through different parts of the country put him in direct contact with indigenous groups, experiences which he utilized in producing original literary works of great aesthetic value. Rojas González became known as a short-story writer in 1930 when he published *History of a Dress-*

coat. Later he published . . . *and Other Stories* (1931), *The Bird Catcher* (1934), *Thirst, Little Novels* (1937), *Chirrín and Cell 18* (1944), and *Stories of Yesterday and Today* (1946). *The Maker of Gods* (1952), a posthumous collection of short stories that depict the life and customs of the Indians of Mexico, placed him among the outstanding writers of Mexican short stories. His first novel, *The Negress Angustias* (1944), presents the unusual theme of the intervention of women in the Revolution. His second novel, *Lola Casanova* (1947), has an indigenous theme and describes the life of the Seri Indians in the state of Sonora.

Agustín Yáñez (born in the city of Guadalajara, 1904), a prolific researcher, essayist, and government official, has dedicated his entire life to literary and cultural pursuits. He received both the Master's and Doctor's degrees in philosophy from the National University of Mexico, where he has filled important teaching and administrative posts. He has edited *The Complete Works of Justo Sierra.* He is a former member and president of the Seminary of Mexican Culture, a member of the Academy of Language and of the National College, and at present is secretary of public education. Love of his province is the keynote of most of his works, including *Representative Types and Figures of Guadalajara* (1941), *The Flower of Ancient Games* (1942), *The Spiritual Climate of Jalisco* (1945), *Yahualica* (1946), *The Edge of the Storm* (1947), *Prodigal Land* (1960), *Sterile Land* (1964), and others. In *The Edge of the Storm,* Yáñez offers us a faithful picture of life in a typical Jalisco village, in which love and religion are the two great determining forces. Ideas and concepts revolve around sentiments and customs; the characters talk about this and lament about that, they live and die, and dream, "just because." This work is both a prelude to the Revolution and a justification for it; it is the first manifestation of a "current" toward a national literature, and the first novel, since *The Underdogs,* which merits universal recognition. Other novels by Yáñez are *Passion and Convalescence* (1943), *Creation* (1959), and *Holloweyed and Painted* (1960). His recent production in the field of the short story and narrative comprises *Three Stories* and *The Feelings of the Air* (1964).

Miguel N. Lira (born in Tlaxcala in 1905 and died there in 1961), a lawyer by profession, became a poet, dramatist, biographer, and novelist. His work as editor, printer, and director of various publications has left a definite mark as much on the history of typography as on that of literature. On his own press he published his books and those of others under the trade name of Editorial Fábula. His courier was the small literary review *Huytlale.* In the diverse genres that he cultivated, Miguel N. Lira had Mexican authenticity as his source of inspiration. A poet at twenty, his lyrics followed popular themes and forms, and he knew how to dignify them by virtue of art and human emotion. The rich harvest of legends and Mexican *corridos* was rescued by the theater of Lira. His first novel, *Where the Tepozanes Grow* (1947), is the legendary story of a "Nahual" in a Tlaxcaltecan village, with scenes of customs and indigenous witchcraft. It is considered one of the best indigenous novels that have been published in Mexico. His second novel, *The Hidden One* (1948), deals with the Revolution. His next book, *A Woman in Solitude* (1956), is an epistolary novel. His last work is *Waiting for Death, Novel of the Revolution* (1958).

María Lombardo de Caso (born in Teziutlán, Puebla, 1905, and died in Mexico City, 1964) became known for her book of short stories, *Puppets of Mist,* ten stories in which the author evokes figures and scenes of life in Puebla, especially in her home village. Her first novel, *A Light on the Other Bank* (1959), depicts the struggle for the spiritual freedom of women against the littleness and bigotry of provincial life. *The Snake That Stopped Up the River* (1962) tells the story of a child and his dog who identify with each other, through tenderness and loneliness, in the alien world of adults.

Miguel Angel Menéndez (born in Izamal, Yucatán, 1905) published his first book, *Hollywood without Pajamas,* in 1928. This was followed by three books of poetry: *Another Book* (1932), *Song of the Revolution* (1933), and *The Direction of the Verses* (1936). The work that gave him prominence, however, was his novel *Nayar* (1940), which won the National Prize for Literature, on the life and environment of the Cora Indians in the state of Nayarit. In spite of his prolixity in the descriptive parts, he is redeemed by his narrative gifts and poetic tone. Deep reflection and emotional warmth, reserved and restrained, are characteristics that make *Nayar* one of the most felicitious fruits of its genre. Recently, Angel Menéndez has written *Malintzin* (1963) and *Life and Death of Kennedy.*

Novelists Born in the Decade 1910-20

Alberto Bonifaz Nuño (born in Niltepec, Oaxaca, 1911) is at present working as a publicist for General Direction of Publications of the University of Mexico. Since 1945 he has been known for his short stories and articles published in newspapers and magazines in the capital and elsewhere, but he did not publish any books until 1959, when his short stories were collected in a volume entitled *Game of Mirrors*. He has written one play, *The Right of the Master* (1960), a work of sentimental and political intrigue that shows the dirty tricks employed by the white syndicates. He is best known, however, for his novel, *Southeastern Cross* (1954).

Jesús R. Guerrero (born in Numarán, Michoacán, 1911) has written short stories and novels in which is revealed a limited, bitter vision of life, notwithstanding his qualities as a good observer and precise painter of vigorous, rugged traits. Luis Buñuel made a cinema of Guerrero's best novel, *The Forgotten Ones* (1944), a work in which the author presents a series of cruel, painful scenes of the life of the destitute classes in Mexico. Other works he has written are the novels *The Deputy Taffoyat* (1939), *White Gold* (1941), *Dull Days* (1946), *The Final Point* (1953), *The Painted Enclosure* (1953); and a book of stories, *Reflections of Human Light* (1948).

Héctor Raúl Almanza (born in San Luis Potosí, 1912), a lawyer, and presently consul for Mexico in Lebanon, belongs to the group of novelists who are interested in the solution of social and political problems in Mexico. Almanza lived in Matamoras from 1944 until 1946, and that milieu gave him material for his first novel, *White Strike* (1950), a work in which he attacks the exploitation of the Mexican day laborers by Texas farmers and false Mexican leaders. In *Candlemas of the Ducks* (1952), the action takes place in a section by that name, a suburb typical because of the wretched conditions of life. *Breach in the Rock* (1955) denounces the exploitation of Mexican workers and the outrages to which they were submitted by the petroleum companies of Huasteca until the nationalization of that industry in 1938. In his last published novel, *Back of the Mirror* (1962), Almanza relates the life of Gabriel Sosa, who, at the death of Madero, joined those opposed to the usurpation and reached such a high place in society that economic temptations influenced him to modify his previous noble ideas.

Rogelio Barriga Rivas (born in Tlacolula, Oaxaca, 1912; died in Mexico City, 1961) wrote four novels employing *costumbrista* themes. The first, *Guelaguetza* (1947), describes the customs in his native state and abuses by the bosses. The fifteen years he worked in Mexico as an agent of the Federal Public Ministry gave him the subject matter for *Human River* (1948), which won the Lanz Duret Prize. This novel depicts the suffering of those who have to seek justice at the railing of the deputy's office. *Learned Judge* (1952) and *Stewardship* (1952) came from the memories and personal experiences of his youth in Oaxaca. The last book cited, which also won the Lanz Duret prize in 1951, was filmed under the title of *Sunset Bells Trujano*.

Ramón Rubín (born in Mazatlán, Sinaloa, 1912), a prolific author preoccupied with the problems of his country, has written eight volumes of short stories and ten novels, the majority of them being inspired by the life and customs of rural Mexico. His first works were collections of short stories: *Stories About the Mexican Rural Environment* (1942), *Mestizo Stories of Mexico, II* (1948), *Third Book of Mestizo Stories* (1948), *Ten Bubbles in the Sea, a String of Salty Stories* (1949). One of his most popular novels, *The Silent Grief of the Tzotziles* (1948), relates the manner of dress, customs, and traditions of the Indian tribe living in the mountains of the state of Chiapas. *The Fog Turns It Blue* (1954) deals with the primitive existence of the Huichole Indians; and *The Song of the Cricket* (1952), with the Coras in the Nayarit mountain range. His most recent novels are *When the "Táguaro" Is Dying* (1960), *The Bosom of Hope* (1964), and *Where My Shadow Is Frightened* (1964).

Since her youth Magdalena Mondragón (born in Torreón, Coahuila, 1913) has devoted herself to journalism, a genre in which she has been outstanding because of her activity and efficiency. She has published six novels, several plays, two volumes of poetry, one volume of chronicles, one of essays, and one of newspaper articles. Her first published book was the novel *Perhaps Another Year* (1937). One of her novels, *I As a Poor Person . . .* (1944), shows the wretched life of those who live in the dump heaps of Mexico City; it was translated into English with the title *Some Day the Dream,* and in 1947 won a prize in New York for the best book of the month.

Other novels of hers are *Barbaric North* (1944), *Land Exists Farther On* (1947), *The Day Does Not Arrive* (1950), *We Are Thirsty* (1954), and two others unpublished as yet.

José Revueltas (born in Durango, 1914) is one of the militant, active leftist authors in Mexico. He is a controversial and restless writer whose work, saturated with intense personal and ideological views, not infrequently disconcerts even his co-religionists. Accused of twenty years of subversive activity, he was deported to the prison on Maria Islands, which gave him the theme for his first novel, *The Walls of Water* (1941). His literary renown, however, begins with the publication of *El luto humano* (*Human Mourning,* 1943), undoubtedly one of his best novels because of the poetic world which he succeeds in vivifying in his clear, warm prose.[1] *God on the Earth* (1944), his first volume of short stories, contains "some of the best short narrations written in present times," a quality confirmed in his second book of stories, *To Sleep on the Land* (1960). In addition to essays and scenarios and other theatrical works, he has published the following: *Earthly Days* (1949), *In Some Valley of Tears* (1956), *The Motives of Cain* (1957), and *The Mistakes* (1964).

Josefina Vicens (born in Villahermosa, Tabasco) has written on political affairs in various weeklies and has been, occasionally, plot writer and adapter for the cinema. She is known, though, in Mexico and abroad for her one book published to date, *El libro vacío* (*The Empty Book,* 1958), a novel which won the Villaurrutia Prize and was translated into French under the title of *Le cahier clandestin* (1964), with a prologue by Octavio Paz.

Sara García Iglesias (born in Mexico City, 1917) studied chemistry at the National University; she has traveled widely in Europe and the United States, and since 1955 has been living in Ozuluama, Veracruz, where she was mayor from 1958 to 1961. She became known by her novel *The Large Pool in the Ruins* (1943), which won the Miguel Lanz Duret prize in 1943. *Exile* (1957), her second and last published book, reveals anew her excellent qualities of style, art, and skill. In this book she deals with Spaniards who, exiled because of fascism in the Peninsula, live together in Mexico and there have to

---

[1] This novel was translated by H. R. Hays and published by Reynal and Hitchcock, in 1947, under the title *The Stone Knife.*—Translators' note.

come to grips with the consequent problems of adaptation and comprehension.

The Novelists Born in the Decade 1920-30

Jorge López Páez (born in Huatusco, Veracruz, 1922) received the law degree from the National Autonomous University of Mexico and also studied in the School of Philosophy and Literature. He began his literary career as a short-story writer with *He Who Hopes . . .* (1950) and *The Masts* (1955); in 1951, he tried the dramatic genre with *The Last Visit.* His most successful work is his novel *The Solitary Atlantic* (1958), a psychological study that delves into the magical and personal world of the child. His last published works are the volume of short stories, *The Stone Guests* (1962), and the novel, *Toward the Bitter Sea* (1965).

Rosario Castellanos was born in Mexico City in 1925, spent her childhood in Comitán, Chiapas, and at the age of sixteen returned to the capital where, in 1950, she received the Master's degree in philosophy from the University of Mexico. She also studied at the University of Madrid, visited several European countries, and, on her return to Mexico, worked on some cultural assignments and continued her creative literary endeavors. She became known as a poet in 1948, when she published *Trajectory of Dust* and *Memoranda for a Declaration of Faith.* These were followed by *About the Sterile Vigil* (1950), *Two Poems* (1950), *The Ransom of the World* (1952), *Presentation in the Temple* (1951), *Poems, 1953-1955* (1957), *Salome and Judith* (1959), *Literally* (1959), *Livid Light* (1960). Rosario Castellanos is considered the present-day poet with the most intimate and purely feminine accent. Social preoccupation and love of her native soil are permanent notes in her poetry and prose. Using the thread of childhood memories, she, in her first novel, *Balún-Canán* (1957), weaves a story in which surges the complicated, badly-organized social life of Chiapas, with its class prejudices and exploitation of the Indians. Throughout the story there is a dramatic play of sentiments and passions, and in the foreground there is always the sensitiveness of the child around whom the story revolves. *Powers of Darkness* (1962) is another excellent example of the devotion of the author to her place of origin, and this highly successful work is the best in a long line of indigenous novels. She has published two books of short stories, *Royal City* (1960) and *The August Guests* (1964). Her most recent novel is *Initiation Rite* (1965).

In his long career in journalism Luis Spota (born in Mexico City, 1925) has developed an obvious narrative ability and has become a keen observer of persons and events. Perhaps this explains why his novels tend to emphasize the spectacular. He finds his favorite themes in the far from perfect social order in Mexico. For example, *They Died in the Middle of the River* (1948) deals with the exploiting and killing of day laborers on the frontier; *The Violent Hours* (1958) depicts the corrupt world of well-known leaders of the workers; *Enemy Blood* (1959) describes the lives of men and women who are without hope because they were born of men and women who had no hope. *Almost Paradise* (1956), considered his best novel, "paints with faithful and incisive cruelty the 'hide skinners' of Mexican so-called high society." To his fictional work belong *The Colonel Was Thrown into the Sea* (1947), *Mas cornadas da el hombre* (*Man Gives More Thrusts than the Bull*, 1950),[2] *Vagabond* (1950), *The Vacuous Star* (1950), *The Great Waters* (1954), *The Time of Wrath* (1960), *The Tender Age* (1964), and *The Cat's Guffaw* (1964).

Since 1955 Sergio Fernández (born in Mexico City, 1926) has been a professor in the School of Philosophy and Literature in the National Autonomous University of Mexico, where he received his doctorate in Spanish literature. He has written penetrating essays such as *Five Hispanic American Writers* (1958) and *Essays on Spanish Literature in the Sixteenth and Seventeenth Centuries* (1961). In 1958 he published his first novel, *The Lost Signs*, which shows bitterness and disillusionment, and dramatizes the problem of living with other people and of loneliness. *Doubtful Success* (1964) has the same characteristics as his first novel, the same delving into the personalities of the characters, and the same tendency to minimize plot. The importance of this novel lies not in the story but in the manner in which it is told—the rich and copious descriptions of the most minute details.

Sergio Galindo (born in Jalapa, 1926) studied in the School of

[2] This novel was translated by Barnaby Conrad and published by Houghton Mifflin, in 1957, under the title *The Wounds of Hunger.*—Translators' note.

Philosophy and Literature of the University of Mexico and in France. He was chairman of the Editorial Department of the University of Veracruz and director of the review *The Word and the Man* until 1964; at present he is chief co-ordinator of the National Institute of Fine Arts. His first published volume was a collection of short stories, *The Idle Machine* (1951). Years later he published his first novel, *Rice Powder* (1958), a work of sober realism dealing with the life of a conservative, provincial bourgeois family. *Justice in January* (1959) relates the intertwined stories of various migration agents. In *The Border* (1960) the still unexhausted tremors of the tragic shock of the Revolution are felt, and Galindo skilfully creates the surroundings of a provincial family shut up in their big house in Las Vigas, Veracruz. *Carnival Masquerade* (1964) again takes up the provincial theme; in this novel the city of Jalapa, freed of moral restraints during Carnival, forgets the outward show and reveals itself in its nakedness.

Armando Ayala Anguiana (born in León, Guanajuato, 1928) has been a journalist and correspondent for *Vision,* and as such has traveled in Europe and the United States. His experiences in the border city of Tijuana, where he lived for a time, gave him sufficient material for his first novel, *Desire to Believe* (1958), in which he presents the turbulent life of that city and its inhabitants who are capable of accumulating large fortunes and are inconsistent in their apparent love for their country and their scorn of tourists. *The Step from Nothingness* (1960) recounts the experiences of the author as a traveling correspondent.

Carlos Fuentes (born in Mexico City, 1928) has his law degree and has studied in Switzerland. He has worked in the diplomatic service of the Secretariat of Foreign Affairs, and is a contributor to numerous reviews and periodicals. As short-story writer, novelist, essayist, and political writer, he published in 1954 his first book of stories, *The Masked Days,* in which objective reality is confused with the disturbed world of fantasy. His first important novel, *The Most Transparent Region* (1958), made an impact on literary circles and caused him to be regarded as one of the best of the young writers. In his second novel, *Good Consciences* (1959), he deepens his exploration of life in Mexico, begun in the former work, but he omits the scenic effects found in that novel and undertakes the clarification of national life by added depth and perspective. In *The Death of Artemio Cruz* (1962), Carlos Fuentes presents the picture of a middle-class citizen who, having shared in some of the skirmishes of the Revolution, later succeeds in amassing a large fortune and acquiring immense power, thanks to methods so disgraceful that he cannot confess them. He has also written the short story volumes *Aura* (1962) and *Song of Blind Men* (1964); his most recent work, *The Lifeless Hero*, describes the last day in the life of Emiliano Zapata.

Novelists Born in the Decade 1930-40

Tomás Mojarro (born in Jalpa, Zacatecas, 1932) published in 1960 his initial volume, *Canyon of Juchipila,* a group of eight short stories, written in a very elaborate style, about the milieu of the provinces in the southern part of Zacatecas. His characters, theological students and day laborers, are depicted as victims of misery and fanaticism. Mojarro reaffirms his narrative ability in his novel, *Mating Place* (1963), in which he returns to the theme of the province, the transformation in Margil de Minas when a highway links it with the rest of the country. Well structured, written in a suggestive and synthetical style, and with lifelike characters, this work is a contribution to present-day Mexican fiction.

Vicente Leñero (born in Guadalajara, Jalisco, 1933) is, with Tomás Mojarro, one of the youngest novelists writing today. He received his degree in engineering at the National University and in journalism from the Carlos Septién García School of Journalism. He began his literary efforts as a short-story writer with *The Cloud of Dust and Other Stories* (1959), in which he ably treats themes of the city and countryside. In *The Heartsick Voice* (1961), his first novel, he finds his own style, clearing the way for the voice of his character who narrates, dreams, and reports. In *The Bricklayers* (1964) the author makes an incursion into the different social and economic strata of Mexico City, describing them by using the method of counterpoint—the work and idleness, problems and satisfactions, love, friendship, and resentment of the construction workers, bricklayers, architects, engineers, and such. The story is narrated effectively, the interest of the reader is captured from the beginning, the characters are possible, and the universe in which they live has its own existence.

The Short Story

Short-Story Writers Born Before 1900

Antonio Robles (born in Robledo de Chavela, Madrid, 1897, and better known as Antoniorrobles) has been living since 1939 in Mexico, where he has continued his profession as journalist and writer of children's literature, teaching the latter in the National Normal School, the Oral Normal School, and the Manuel Acosta Training School. Through his works for children, he has received many awards and has acquired merited fame. His stories are outstanding because of their deep human understanding, grace, and delicacy; their literary quality adds importance to their educational nature. His writings in Mexico comprise several volumes: *Hallelujahs and Heel Stompings, A Sparrow in the War of the Wild Beasts* (1943), *The Fawn Waddles, Doña Paz the Witch* (1959), *Eight Stars and Eight Mockingbirds, The Child with the Orange, Heel Stompings and 100 Other Stories* (Volume I, 1962; Volume II, 1964), and the novel, *Flores, the Refugee Centaur.*

Arqueles Vela (born in Tapachula, Chiapas, 1899) has been a journalist since 1920 and one of the more resonant voices in the *estridentismo* movement. After studying in several European universities, he directed the literary supplement of the *National* in Mexico, and thereafter his activities have been closely related to innumerable educational projects. He cultivated poetry in *The Gray Path and Other Poems, 1919-1920* (1921) and *Cantatas to the Strong and Happy Maidens of Mexico* (1940). He is the author of various books and essays dealing with art, aesthetics, universal and Mexican literatures, and *modernismo*. His *Songs of Day and Night* (1945) gave him a preeminent place among contemporary short-story writers in Mexico. His last published novels are *The Volanda* (1956) and *The Hummingbird* (1961).

Short-Story Writers Born in the Decade 1900-1910

Juan de la Cabada (born in Campeche, 1903) published his first works, which always deal with the social problem, in the *Machete*, the organ at that time of the Mexican Communist Party, and later in the review of the League of Revolutionary Writers and Artists, of which he was the founder. He became known as a short-story writer with his book *Parade of Lies* (1940), a collection of varied tales— full of surmises and flattering promises—in which the author is seen as a man of decisive action and profound experience. His second book, *Melodic Incidents in an Irrational World* (1944), is, according to José Luis Martínez, "an extraordinary fantasy of indigenous inspiration." His movie scenario, *The Strong Arm* (1963), is an incisive satire on corrupt political leadership, but at the same time is wholesome, overflowing with humanity and truth.

Max Aub was born in Paris, France, in 1903, of a German father and a French mother, but he is Spanish in education and cultural development. He came to Mexico in 1942 and has written most of his works here. He has been a professor in the UNAM and in the Cinematographic Institute, executive member of University Television, director of Co-ordinated Services of Radio, Television, and Recording of the UNAM, and one of the founders of the review *Los Sesenta (The Sixty)*. Max Aub has written in almost all the genres: poetry, novel, short story, drama, essay; in all of these are united passion and talent, versatility and exuberance, humor and sobriety. His best-known books are *Closed Country* (1944), *They Are Not Stories* (1944), *Field of Blood* (1946), *Waiting Room* (three volumes, 1949, 1950, 1951), *I Live* (1953), *Mexican Short Stories with Frontispiece* (1959), *Fields of the Moor* (1963), and *The Vulture and Other Mexican Stories* (1964).

César Garizurieta (born in Tuxpan, Veracruz, 1904; died in Mexico City, 1961) studied law in the School of Jurisprudence, was magistrate of the Superior Court, and served in the diplomatic corps until his death. He wrote various stories with social content, in which the inhabitants of his native state of Veracruz move freely. His work is distinctive because of his keen, humorous spirit. He wrote *Days Run* (1937), *Undertow* (1939), *The Apostle of Idleness* (1940), *The Chess Player Dances in Heaven* (1942), *The Devil, the Priest, and Other Frauds* (1947), *Memories of a Child in Long Trousers* (1952), *Juanita "the Drizzler"* (1956), and two interesting essays: *Catharsis of the Mexican* (1946) and *Introduction to the Mexican* (1952).

Efrén Hernández (born in León, Guanajuato, 1904; died in Tacubaya, D.F., 1958) began the study of law but abandoned it later to devote himself to literary pursuits. He was an enthusiastic illustrator for the "anthology magazine" *America,* for which he had the title of subdirector. He first became known through his magnificent story *Flaws* (1928); and in this genre he has had his greatest success. Later, he published *The Wooden Master* (1932) and *Short Stories* (1941). He wrote some of the most refined prose in modern Mexican literature. His lucid imagination and keen sensibility permitted him to profit by the conquests of the masters of the contemporary novel. He wrote two novels, *Cloudy Weather on the Nicómaco* (1946) and *The Dove, the Underground Cellar, and the Tower* (1949), and two books of poetry in which is seen the classical origin of his intellectual development: *Hour of Hours* (1936) and *Between Faded Walls* (1943). His *Complete Works* (1965) was published by the Foundation of Economic Culture.

Andrés Henestrosa (born in Ixhuatán, Oaxaca, 1906) was director of the reviews *El Libro y el Pueblo* and *Letras Patrias,* chairman of the Department of Literature of the National Institute of Fine Arts (1952-58), and representative to the National Congress (1958-61). He has been a member of the Mexican Academy of Language since 1964. He has made an outstanding contribution to the study of indigenous elements in Mexico. In *The Men Who Broke Up the Dance* (1929), he re-creates and fabricates, in forceful prose and narrative efficiency, the popular stories and legends of his native Zapotec soil. His book, *Portrait of My Mother* (1940), is one of the most beautiful in our literature. In his extensive work—the major part of which has not yet been published—Henestrosa has followed a line parallel to that of his published books: the exaltation of the people and their indigenous past, the defense of the liberal spirit, and the study and evaluation of national expressions.

Luis Córdova (born in Orizaba, Veracruz, 1908) studied law in Mexico City and at present is lending his services to the Secretariat of Foreign Affairs. In 1935 he published the satirical story *Mr. Parker, Mr. Jenkins* that was followed by other volumes of stories: *The Screens* (1954), *The Mockingbird and Other Stories* (1955), *Lupe Lope and Other Stories* (1959), *The Punctual Siren* (1960); and three plays, *Palace Business Goes Slowly* (1944), *Scissors and Ribbons* (1956), and *Great Lake* (1962).

Nellie Campobello (born in Villa Ocampo, Durango, 1909) was very young when she arrived in Mexico City, where her first book,

I, Verses for Francisca (1928), was published. She soon became a professional dancer and is now considered an authority in teaching and research in this field. She is at present director of the School of the Dance, which is a part of the National Institute of Fine Arts. She wrote two novels; the first, *Cartridge* (1931), gathers together sketches and individual portraits of revolutionaries, generally *villistas*. In her stories she uses unornamented expression with clear, direct, short, and even brutal phrases. Her second novel, *The Hands of Mama* (1937), is a homage to her mother and to all mothers who suffered during the revolutionary epoch.

Short-Story Writers Born in the Decade 1910-20

Gabriel López Chiñas (born in Juchitán, Oaxaca, 1911) received the law degree from the National University. He has worked in the Radio Section of the University and in the Administration of Cultural Broadcasting. He has written poetry: *Song of Man to the Earth* (1951), *Poems* (1953), *The Beguiled Looms* (1953), *Sea* (1960), and *Filigrees of the Dream* (1961); but he owes his prestige as a writer to his short stories, in which he projects the regional spirit of his native soil. *Vinnigulasa* (1940), stories of Juchitán, has merited three editions, the last being published by the University Press of the UNAM.

Francisco Peláez (born in Mexico City, 1911) is now living in Madrid, Spain. His first two volumes appeared in 1943: the novel *Down Here* ironically dramatic, and his short stories, *Night,* under the pseudonym of "Francisco Tario." In his stories, which have original titles such as "The Night of the Coffin," "The Dog's Night," "The Night of the Doll," animals and objects have the gift of speech. His use of an adjective contrary in meaning to the accompanying noun leads us to suppose he has had some knowledge of the work of Jorge Luis Borges and the *Anthology of Fantastic Literature*. His other short stories show his excellence as a writer of this genre: *What I Knew About Love* (1950) and *Tapioca Inn: Mansion for Ghosts* (1952). He also wrote *Short Diary of a Lost Love* (1951) and *Acapulco in the Dream* (1951).

Fernando Benítez (born in Mexico City, 1912) is important in journalism because of his numerous articles, essays, and critical works, and as initiator and director of the cultural supplements of the

National, Novedades (Novelties), and the review *Siempre*. Having traveled in Europe, Asia, and America, he relates his experiences in such books as *China in View* (1953), *The Battle of Cuba* (1960), and *Journey to Tarahumara* (1960). Benítez began his literary career with *Horse and God* (1945), a volume of short stories on death. Later, he tried his hand at drama with *Christopher Columbus* (1951). His true calling, though, is revealed in works that combine reporting and the essay, two of these being on colonial themes, *The Route of Hernán Cortés* (1950) and *Creole Life in the Sixteenth Century* (1953); another, about the events of the Independence, *The Path of Liberty* (1960); and, still another, of the significance and drama of sisal hemp in Yucatán, *Ki: the Drama of a People and a Plant* (1956). Recently, he has published works of fiction such as *The Old King* (1959) and *Poisoned Water* (1961).

Since his early youth Edmundo Valadés (born in Guaymas, Sonora, 1915) has lived in Mexico City, where he has devoted himself to journalism. Since May, 1964, he has directed the imaginative review *El Cuento* (The Short Story), which has alleviated to a certain extent the lack of good popular reviews of this genre. The book that has brought him the most renown as a short-story writer is *Death Has Permission* (1955), of which five editions have been printed to date. This work contains fourteen excellent stories, written in direct and pleasing style. Other stories by him are *Adriana* (1957), *The Disturbed Roots* (1957), *Antipodal* (1961), and *Rock* (1963).

From infancy María Elvira Bermúdez (born in Durango, 1916) has lived in Mexico City, where she received her law degree in 1939. Since 1954 she has published essays on literary criticism and reviews of contemporary Mexican books in newspaper supplements and magazines in the capital. She represents the unusual in Mexican letters, being a writer interested in detective literature. In 1953 she published a novel of this type, *Death Has Different Reasons*, a good example of its genre, as are also her short stories, *Soliloquy of a Dead Person* (1951), and others scattered in reviews, annual publications, and anthologies; these have considerably enriched narrative fiction of this type.

Gastón García Cantú (born in Puebla, 1917) studied law in his native city and was director of the periodical library in the University of Puebla. In 1953 he came to live in Mexico City and has been director of the cultural supplement of *Novedades*. At present he is undersecretary of the National Institute of Indigenous Studies. He is the author of some essays such as *The American Mediterranean* (1960), *Notebook of Notes* (1961), and *Public Papers* (1961); these have been collected and enlarged in *Mexican Utopias* (1963). As a short-story writer, in his *False Rumors* (1955) he has included sixteen stories on the general subject of provincial Puebla life, which is opaque and apparently simple, but complex under the surface and filled with prejudice, tedium, and ignorance. The book is bitter and contains a protest woven with humor and satire.

Juan José Arreola (born in the city of Guzmán—Zapotlán the Great—Jalisco, 1918), along with other writers, edited in his home state the reviews *Eros* and *Pan*. In Mexico City he studied the theater and became an actor; in France he studied the technique of acting and oratory. He has won the Jalisco (1953) and the Xavier Villaurrutia (1963) literary prizes. With Héctor Mendoza, he directed some of the magnificent theatrical programs of "Poetry Read Aloud," initiated in 1956; and he has founded and directed the collection *Los Presentes (The Presents)*, and that of *Cuadernos y Libros del Unicornio (Notebooks and Books of the Unicorn)*. He became known as an excellent short-story writer with the story *He Did Good While He Lived* (1943), one of the cleverest and most faultless *costumbrista* stories in Mexican literature. Possessor of a craft and master of the secret techniques of the short narrative, Arreola has developed a new type of short story in his two volumes, *Varied Invention* (1949) and *Confabulario* (1952). His dramatic work, *Everyone's Hour* (1954), won the first prize in the Drama Festival of the INBA and attracted attention because of its original composition, dramatic force, and emotion. His novel, *The Fair* (1963), thematically and stylistically recapitulates his complete work.

Juan Rulfo (born in Sayula, Jalisco, 1918) from early childhood came into contact with rural environment and later witnessed some of the events of the *"Cristero"* Rebellion. At present he has charge of the Editorial Department of the National Institute for Indigenous Studies. His first stories appeared in the review *Pan*, of Guadalajara; but it was his book *The Burning Plain and Other Stories* (1953) that won acclaim for him as one of the best contemporary short-story writers. The subject matter deals with the province, but he uses techniques that have given the present-day novel and short story new directions: monologue, simultaneous planes, introspection, the slow pace. In his novel *Pedro Páramo* (1955), there pass in review elemental characters of dark passions, without happiness or magnanimity, filled with covetousness, lust, and remorse, hewn with vigor and created with artistic mastery.

Short-Story Writers Born in the Decade 1920-30

Guadalupe Dueñas (born in Guadalajara, Jalisco, 1920) published her first stories in anthologies, reviews, and literary supplements of the capital; some of these were included in the collection entitled *Female Rats and Other Stories* (1954) under the trade name of *Abside*. The best of her work has been compiled in *The Night Has A Tree* (1958). She is characterized by subtle spirit, love of minute things and repulsive beings, the strength and originality with which she constructs the scaffolding of her fantastic creations, and the ingenious methods she uses to introduce us to a world in which no horror is impossible.

Eugenio Trueba (born in Silao, Guanajuato, 1921) is a lawyer by profession. He lives in the capital of his native state and has been rector of the University of Guanajuato as well as professor and director of the Law School in that university. He directed, there, two important publications, *Garabato (Scribble)* and *El Umbral (The Threshold)*, publishing his first stories in the former. He is the author of *Stories* (1951), *Anteroom* (1956), and *Cat's Eye* (1957), in which he reveals the two constant directions of his prose: the fantastic and the realistic. His play *Collective Interests* (1960) is a political farce. His first novel, *The Indistinct Image* (1962), describes the conduct of four adolescents—in an ultra-provincial city—whose family background is in inverse proportion to their economic success.

Augusto Monterroso (born in Guatemala, 1921) has lived in Mexico City since 1944. He served in the diplomatic corps from 1945 to 1954. Broadly cultured and self-taught, he founded the group and the review *Acento* and also is one of the founders of *Revista de Guatemala*. At the present time he is associated with the Foundation of Economic Culture and the University Press of the UNAM. He has written some essays, but he is outstanding as one of the most skilful and intelligent fiction writers of his generation. As a short-story writer, he is the author of *The Concert and the Eclipse* (1952), *One Out of Three and the Centenary* (1954), *Complete Works and Other Stories* (1959), all stories revealing a fine sense of humor and a clear-cut style.

Ricardo Garibay (born in Tulancingo, Hidalgo, 1923) studied in the School of Philosophy and Literature of the UNAM. He was a professor of literature and held a fellowship in the Mexican Center for Writers. He is the author of one essay, *Our Lady of Solitude in Coyoacán* (1955), and the short stories *The New Sweetheart* (1946), *Notebook* (1950), and *Stories* (1952). He is outstanding in his work *Mazamitla* (1955), a long short story or a short novel in which he treats, with resources unusual in Mexican prose, the murder of a humble rural man.

José Luis González (1926) was born in Santo Domingo, Dominican Republic, but as a child went to San Juan, Puerto Rico, where he later was graduated as a licentiate in political science. At different times he has traveled in Europe and the Middle East, and on his last tour he visited Russia. In Mexico he received the Master's degree in literature from the School of Philosophy and Literature of the UNAM, and has been a professor in the University of Guanajuato. His books of short stories, *In the Shade* (1943), *Five Stories of Blood* (1945), and *The Man in the Street* (1948), were published in Puerto Rico. He has published only two works in Mexico: the short stories *On This Side* (1954), written in simple poetic style, and a novel entitled *Paisa* (1950), a "story of emigration," as the author calls it, in which he ably intertwines a plot and an evocation.

Raquel Banda Farfán (born in San Luis Potosí, 1928) devoted herself to teaching in various places in her native state. At present she is studying in the School of Philosophy and Literature of the National University. Her frequent contact with country people gave her material for many of her short stories and novels. To the first-mentioned genre belong *Scenes of Rural Life* (1953), *The Engagement* (1957), *A Slice of Life* (1959), *The Secret* (1960), and *Poppy* (1964), written in light, dynamic narrative. She captures the simple daily life of the people of the countryside; but out of the social background there emerges a denunciation of the grievous condition in which these men and women are forced to live. In her first novel, *Green Valley* (1957), she continues the theme of her short stories;

but in the second, *Downhill* (1958), her vision changes direction and turns toward the negative ambient of the city.

Carlos Valdés (born in Guadalajara, Jalisco, 1928) has been a contributor to the review *Ariel,* in his native city, and editor, with Huberto Batis, of the literary review *Cuadernos del Viento (Notebooks of the Wind).* In *Absences* (1955), his first book of short stories, the imaginative element is dominant along with the fantastic and a feeling of loneliness and weariness of soul confronted by the meanness of the world. Nevertheless, his stories give evidence of faith in the final triumph of the human spirit. Other short stories by Carlos Valdés are *Two Fictions* (1958), *Two and the Dead* (1960), and *The Name Is the Least Part* (1961). In his novel *The Ancestors* (1963), the author presents the history of a family through four generations from Mexican Independence to the time of Porfirio Díaz and the Revolution.

María Amparo Dávila (born in Pinos, Zacatecas, 1928) studied in San Luis Potosí, where she wrote three books of poetry: *Moonlight Psalms* (1950), *Profile of Lonely Places* (1954), and *Meditations on the Edge of a Dream* (1954). Her prestige, however, is due to her short stories, some of which have been included in anthologies and some translated into English. In her stories in *Squandered Time* (1959), we notice the influence of Kafka and Poe, and, among contemporary writers, that of Bioy Casares and Julio Cortázar. Her second book of short stories is called *Real Music* (1964). The ease with which Amparo Dávila manipulates her characters and the intelligence with which she moves them between the two planes, the real and the fantastic, make her books two of the best collections of short stories in which the unreal element is stronger than the real.

Short-Story Writers Born in the Decade 1930-40

Arturo Souto Alabarce (1930) was born in Madrid, Spain, and has lived in Mexico since 1942. In 1955 he received the Master's degree in the School of Philosophy and Literature of the UNAM. He has been professor of literature and, from 1957, chief of public relations of the university bookstore. He was founder, editor, and contributor to the reviews *Ensayos Científicos (Scientific Essays),* *Clavileño,* *Segrel,* and *Ideas de México.* Since 1947 Souto has been known for his short stories, published in literary supplements and magazines in the capital. Later, he collected some of them—among which "Coyote 13" and "The Pinto" are outstanding for their significant profundity—in *The Plague of the Chrysanthemum* (1960). "Coyote 13" has been translated into various languages and included in anthologies.

Juan Vicente Melo (born in Veracruz, 1932) received a degree in medicine from the National Autonomous University of Mexico; but literature is his true vocation and he is at present devoting himself to letters. He contributes criticism and musical reviews to various magazines and literary supplements. His first volume of short stories appeared in 1956 under the title of *The Night Deluded*. In *The Unfriendly Walls* (1962), he uses themes—ever inspirational—such as love, death, time, grief, profound preoccupation with the destiny of man and the triumph of liberty. The most interesting aspect of his third book, *Weekend* (1964), is the skill with which he takes us from the real world to the fantastic. His knowledge of music has enabled him to give a characteristic rhythm to his prose.

Juan García Ponce (born in Mérida, Yucatán, 1932) studied dramatic art in the School of Philosophy and Literature of the UNAM. He became known as an intelligent critic of art, the theater, and literature. Three of his plays—not all of them published—have been staged: *The Song of the Crickets, The Distant Fair,* and *Twelve and One Three.* His short stories, *First Image* (1963) and *Night* (1963), placed him among the best short-story writers of his generation. In reality, however, they foreshadow the novelist in the excellent characterization, psychological depth, and unusual way in which he treats the environment and circumstances that influence his characters. These characteristics—accompanied by objectivity and simplicity in order to capture the environment—appear also in his first novel, *Straw Figure* (1964).

Eraclio Zepeda (born in Tuxtla Gutiérrez, Chiapas, 1937) has taught literature in the University of Veracruz and, at present, is teaching the same subject in the University of Oriente, Cuba. Among the short-story writers who have appeared in Mexican literature in recent years, he is outstanding because of his rich contribution. The world of his stories is the indigenous world of his native state; he delves into landscapes or scenes which border on the magical; he becomes an accomplice of the spell of the totem and a sharer of miraculous beliefs. *Benzulul* (1959), in addition to its anthropological interest, contains a collection of various types of primitive psychology, where death is the common denominator. Selections of his poems have appeared in the *Revista Mexicana de Literatura* during 1960, and in the collective volume *The Rebellious "Ear of Corn"* (1960).

THE THEATER

The flowering of Mexican literature in general, as has been said, begins with the novel, *The Edge of the Storm* (1947) by Agustín Yáñez; in the theater it was initiated by the generation of the *Contemporáneos*—principally with Rodolfo Usigli's *The Gesticulator*, presented for the first time in 1947—and culminated in the University Theater that was born of the experimental renewal of the theater in Coapa, in 1954.

Dramatists Born in the Decade 1900-1910

María Luisa Ocampo (born in Chilpancingo, Guerrero, 1905) has been in charge of the Department of Libraries of the Secretariat of Public Education, and is at present assistant director of the School of Librarianship of that Secretariat. A novelist and author of a large number of plays, she has written the novels *Under Fire* (1941), based on childhood memories of the Revolution; *The Little Teacher* (1949), considered her best work; *Dr. Benavides Has Died* (1954); *Atitlayapan* (1955); *Shadows in the Sand* (1957); and *The Lord of Altamira* (1963). Nevertheless, it is as a dramatist that she has stood out as much for her creative work as for the impetus she has given to the theater during some epochs in which that art seemed to be bankrupt. Many of her plays have been staged since 1923. Her published plays are *Things of Life* (1926), *The Masks* (1933), *The Romance of Juan Saavedra* (1934), and *The Strong Virgin* (1943).

Dramatists Born in the Decade 1910-20

Carmen Toscano (born in Mexico City, 1910) studied in the School of Philosophy and Literature. She founded the review *Rueca (Distaff)*, and has collaborated with Mexican television and the film industry. She has written two books of verse, *Incomplete Sketch* (1934) and *Unattainable and Mine* (1936); one essay, *Rosario of Acuña, Romantic Myth* (1948); and various plays, an outstanding one being the reworking of *The Mourner,* a well-known Mexican legend, which was staged in the open-air theater of the Plaza of Chimalistac in 1958 and published in 1959.

Federico S. Inclán (born in Mexico City, 1910) has produced to date some twenty plays, many of them prizewinners. He began in 1950 with *Carbide Lights,* in which he portrays the life of the miners in a moment of crisis. Later, in 1955, he had the premiere of his comedy, *Today the Blond Solicits,* considered at that time the best play of the year. In that play, as in *Hidalgo,* produced for the first time in 1953, he uses historical subject matter; and in *Carbide Lights, Wet Backs Cross the Bravo,* and *The Duel,* he treats social themes.

Edmundo Báez (born in Aguascalientes, 1914) studied medicine for five years, but abandoned that career to devote his time to literature. He has specialized in the technique of film scenarios and has won many trophies for his work as scenarist and as adapter of books written by others. He wrote one book of verse, *Reason of the Dream* (1949). His play *The Rancor of the Land* (1943) shows an interlocking of cultivated and strange forms, and of typically Mexican feeling for the soil, open country, and province. In *A Pin in the Eyes* (1952), considered his best work, overwhelming passions play an important role. Presented first in 1959, *A Male!* fails as drama because it is chiefly a scenario.

Rafael Bernal (born in Mexico City, 1915) is serving at the present time in the Mexican Embassy in the Philippines. As a poet he has written *Reproach to New York and Other Poems* (1943). He has also written short stories, compiled in *Tropic* (1946) and in *Three Detective Novels* (1946). These stories, a short novel called *The Strange Case of Aloysus Hands* (1946), and his novels *A Dead Man in the Tomb* (1946) and *His Name Was Death* (1947) are all of the detective and fantastic type. His last published novel, *Land Grant* (1963), takes place in the region of the Orinoco and in the city of Caracas, Venezuela, during the dictatorship of Pérez Jiménez. To his list of plays belong the following: *The Cadaver of Mr. García, The Letter, Antonia, Solitude, The Idol, Peace with You or The Martyrdom of Father Pro* (1961), and *Corn in the House* (1961).

Rafael Solana (born in Veracruz, 1915) studied in the Schools of Law and of Philosophy and Literature in Mexico City. Since 1940 he has collaborated with the film industry, for which he has written various scripts, and recently he has been involved in radio and television work. From 1958 to 1964 he was private secretary of Jaime Torres Bodet, minister of the Secretariat of Public Education. A prolific writer, Rafael Solana has attempted many genres: seven books of verse, four of essays, two of chronicles, seven of short stories, three novels, and some plays. He directed the *Taller Poético* and was one of the group that edited the *Taller*. His first book of poetry was entitled *Hillside* (1934); some of his later ones are *The False Mirrors, All the Sonnets* (1963), and *I Wish to Speak* (1964). His first collection of short stories appeared in the volumes *The Music Within* (1943) and *The Oficleido and Other Stories* (1960); and recently another volume has appeared, *All the Stories of Rafael Solana*. In the novel, Solana has written *October Sun* (1959), *The House of the Most Holy* (1960), and *The Maderna Palace* (1960). His plays—like his poetry and stories—tend toward the fantastic, as seen in *The Golden Isles* (1952) and *To Her Image and Likeness* (1957), or their themes come from the show world, as for example *The Fading Star* (1954), *The Celebrated Cradle* (1954), and *Lazarus Has Returned* (1955).

Dramatists Born in the Decade 1920-30

Luis G. Basurto (born in Mexico City, 1920) studied in the School of Philosophy and Literature and received the law degree from the School of Jurisprudence. He has written literary articles, chronicles, theatrical criticism, scripts, and film adaptations. To date he has composed twenty plays, in which he follows the traditions of lofty Spanish *comedia*, with a certain melodramatic accent. His first play, *The Dialogues of Suzette,* was staged by Rodolfo Usigli in 1940. His success as a playwright, however, did not begin until *A Perfect Lady* was performed in 1954. In this play he deals with a conflict in marriage relationships, with unfulfilled emotions and ambitions in the upper middle class. A more harmonious work, *To Each His Own Life,* is, on the other hand, a broad mural, painted in raw colors, of a ward in a Mexican city. His definite dedication dates from 1956, from his *Ash Wednesday,* a work which received the Juan Ruiz de Alarcón prize as the best play of the year. Since then he has written *The Madness of the Angels* (1957), *The Kings of the World* (1959), *The Scandal of the Truth* (1960), *Intimate Enemies* (1962), *The Gov-*

erness (1963), and a farce in three acts, *And All Ended Up Barking* (1964).

Elena Garro (born in Puebla, 1920) studied in the School of Philosophy and Literature of the UNAM. Choreographer, journalist, and writer of cinemagraphic material, she has lived abroad many years, especially in France and the United States. Several of her works have been translated into other languages and presented in different countries. She became known through three plays that were read by the group called "Poetry Read Aloud": *To Beat About the Bush, The Pillars of Doña Blanca,* and *A Solid Hearth*; they were later published in one volume called *A Solid Hearth* (1958). These plays reveal originality in dramaturgy and poetic sensitiveness with a parabolic surrealistic tendency. *The Lady on Her Balcony,* staged in 1963, has as its theme the frustration, loneliness, lack of communication, and anguish so very prevalent in our day. In *The Memories of the Future* (1963), her first novel, she uses a village in the south, Ixtepec, as the narrator of its life. *The Week of Colors* (1964), a series of short stories not inferior to her novel, parades her poetic ability.

Carlos Solórzano (1922) was born in Guatemala, but has been living in Mexico since 1939. He received his Master's and Doctor's degrees in literature in the School of Philosophy and Literature in the UNAM and studied dramatic art in France. On his return to Mexico he served as director of the University Theater from 1952 to 1962. At present he is teaching Iberoamerican Drama at his alma mater. He began his work as a dramatist with the historical *auto, Doña Beatrice, The Unfortunate One,* staged first in 1952. After that he wrote *The Sorcerer,* presented first in 1954, whose action unfolds in a small, conquered city. With this work he incorporates the new outstanding values in dramatic art. *The Hands of God* (1957) shows the struggle between rebellion and submission, and more properly belongs to the theater of ideas than to that of character. Later, he has staged or published *The Crucified One* (1957), *The Puppets* (1959), *Cross Roads* (1959), *The Angel's Dream* (1960), and *The False Demons* (1964), some of them being translated into French, Russian, German, and English.

Carlos Prieto (born in Mexico City, 1922) studied in the Schools of Law and of Philosophy and Literature of the UNAM and in several universities in North America. He has devoted himself to making documentary films. He was initiated successfully into the theater with his work *Outraged Modesty,* first produced in 1952, a popular play, filled with witty sayings, in which he denounces the privileged class's constant abuse of those who have nothing. Later, he attracted the attention of the judges of the Festival of the INBA with *Halfway* (first presented in 1954), a play with a revolutionary theme. In 1955 he staged his most elaborate work: *Through the Eye of a Needle,* depicting the difficulties the rich experience when trying to enter heaven. He staged *The Imprisoned Cat* in 1956, using a detective plot. His later productions are *The Wretched One* (1957), *Ashes for Bread* [original title in English, 1957], *The Substance of the Earth* (1959), *The Cackle of the Hens* (1962), *and The Rebellion of the Tepehuanes* (1963).

Wilberto Cantón (born in Mérida, Yucatán, 1923) has studied in the School of Philosophy and Literature and received his law degree in the School of Jurisprudence. He founded and directed the review *Espiga (Ear of Corn).* He has served as chairman of the Editorial Department of the UNAM, director of the *Diary of the Southeast,* of Mérida, and of *Cuadernos de Bellas Artes.* He has written two books of verse, *Second Season* (1943) and *Two Poems* (Argentina, 1955). He became known as a playwright with his work *Whenever the Boat Weighs Anchor,* produced in 1946. In 1950 he staged his second play, *To Know How to Die,* in which he tried to show, by means of some harangues, the existential theories much in vogue at that time. In 1954 he produced the farce *The School of the Courtesan,* which has its setting in the colonial epoch but directly alludes to current political situations. Since then he has published *Nocturne to Rosario* (1956), *Mortal Sin* (premiere in 1957), *The Accursed Ones* (1959), *The Garden of the Gorgons* (1960), *So Near to Heaven* (first staged in 1961), *Unforgettable* (1961), *We Are God* (first presented in 1962), *We All Are Brothers* (first staged in 1963), *Red Note* and *He Died for the Country* (both staged in 1964).

Sergio Magaña (born in Tepalcatepec, Michoacán, 1924) has studied science, mathematical physics, social sciences, law, and literature. He gained prominence as a dramatist in 1951 with his play, *The Signs of the Zodiac,* which is considered one of the best works in the contemporary Mexican theater. With the premiere of *Montezuma II,* in 1953, Sergio Magaña entered the field of tragedy, portraying a refined, discerning Montezuma whom the gods must destroy because he is ahead of his time. In *The Little Case of Jorge Lívido* (premiere in 1958), another facet of the creative ability of the author is shown: he attacks the problem of justice and the "psychological" procedures used by representatives of the law to obtain a confession from a criminal. Still to be staged are his last two plays, *The Motives of the Wolf* and *Medea* (1965). He has also written the short stories included in *The Broken Angel* (1946) and *Our Father* (1947) as well as two novels, *The Supplicants* (1942) and *The Wind Mill* (1954).

Fernando Sánchez Mayans (born in Campeche, 1924) has been, since 1944, a journalist and editor of the most important reviews and literary supplements in the capital. In the National Institute of Fine Arts he organized the "Poetic Fridays," and published the material from them under the rubric of Poetic Christmas Gift. In 1958 he became chairman of the Department of Literature of the Institute. He gained prominence in the theater with *The Wings of the Fish,* which won both the *National* prize and the Juan Ruiz de Alarcón prize. He has recently written *Lewd Quartet* (premiere, 1961), *The Gardener of Ladies-in-Waiting* (1963), and *Youthful Drama* (1965). A poet of intense emotional power, he has published several books of poetry: *Leaves in the Wind* (1946), *Pause for Silence* (1950), *To Say All About Spring* (1951), *Poems* (1955), and *Propitious Act* (1958).

Emilio Carballido (born in Córdoba, Veracruz, 1925) earned the Master's degree in literature at the National University, specializing in dramatic art and English literature. At present he is teaching in the University of Veracruz and is a member of its editorial council. Carballido has written short stories, short novels, monologues, libretti for opera and ballet. Many of his plays have won prizes in various competitions; others have been adapted to the cinema. Nevertheless, it is as a dramatist that he has attained an important place among the young writers of Mexico. In 1950 he became known, through Salvador Novo, with the play *Rosalba and the Llaveros*, which, along with *The Intermediate Zone,* showed the two tendencies that have been revealed in his work since then: a kind of scenic neo-realism, on the one hand, and an attempt at fantasy and poetic imagination, on the other. He is the author of *To Write, for Example* . . . (1950),

The Domestic Symphony (premiere, 1953), *The Dance That the Tortoise Dreams* (premiere, 1955), *Happiness* (premiere, 1955), *The Golden Thread* (premiere, 1956), *The Ivory Statues* (1960), *A Little Day of Wrath* (1962), *Theseus* (premiere, 1962), and *Be Quiet, Plucked Chickens, They're Throwing Corn to You* (premiere, 1963); two novels, *The Oxidized Weather Vane* (1956) and *The North* (1958); and a book of short stories, *The Empty Box* (1962).

Luisa Josefina Hernández (born in Mexico City, 1928) studied English literature and drama in the School of Philosophy and Literature, beginning in 1951, and received the Master's degree in literature, with dramatic art as her major subject, in 1955. She has studied in North America and Europe, and has taught in the School of Philosophy and Literature and in the Fine Arts Theatrical School. She was recognized as a dramatist when her play *Rum* (1951) was given a prize in the "Spring Festivals." In spite of her youth, she departs from practices of other writers. Her capacity for reflection dominates her creative work and controls sudden bursts of sentiment or romanticism. Her dramatic works, perhaps harsh and too gloomy, are written in excellent style. In 1954 she won the prize offered by the *National* with her play *Model Apothecary's Shop* and, in 1957, that of the Drama Festival of the INBA with *The Fallen Fruit*. Her other plays are: *The Royal Guests* (1958), *White Harps . . . Golden Rabbits* (premiere, 1959), *Fictitious Peace* (premiere, 1960), *History of a Ring* (1961), and *The Street of the Grand Occasion* (1962). She has written four novels: *The Place Where the Grass Grows* (1959), *The Square of Puerto Santo* (1961), *Deserted Palaces* (1963), and *Secret Anger* (1964).

Jorge Ibargüengoitia (born in Guanajuato, 1928) studied engineering but abandoned that career in 1949 to study, from 1951 to 1954, dramatic art in the School of Philosophy and Literature of the UNAM. He revealed his ability as a dramatist in 1954 with a play using a student background, *Suzanne and the Young People*, which was staged during the meeting of the National Union of Authors. *The Struggle with the Angel* (1955) received special mention in the Competition of the Latin American Theater of Buenos Aires; *The Conspiracy Betrayed* (premiere, 1960) won the City of Mexico Prize, and *The Attempted Abuse* won a prize offered by the House of the Americas in Cuba, in 1963. Many of his short stories are scattered in annuals and literary reviews. Recently, he published his first novel, *August Lightning* (1964), which also won the annual prize of the House of the Americas in Cuba. In this novel he humorously presents the inconsistency and degradation of some of the political leaders of the Mexican Revolution.

Dramatists Born in the Decade 1930-40

Héctor Azar (born in Atlixco, Puebla, 1930) studied law in the National University and received the Master's degree in the School of Philosophy and Literature. In 1958, 1959, and 1961, he won the Xavier Villaurrutia Prize in Experimental Theater. In 1964 the company of the University Theater, which he directs, won the first prize in Nancy, France, with Valle Inclán's play *Words Divine*. Héctor Azar is director general of the theater of the UNAM and chairman of the Department of Theater of the INBA. His talent and renewing spirit provoke immediate interest in the cultural and artistic media when his name appears in connection with a production; likewise, much can be said for his ability to organize and direct plays, and for his work in literary diffusion through his adaptation of works of Mexican writers. His work as director of the theater in Coapa, worthy of the highest praise, has inspired the organization of many other experimental theaters and is responsible for the triumph of the present University Theater. Azar became known first as a poet with *Dwellings* (1951), *Windows of France* (1951), and his book of prose and poetry, *Holy Days* (1954), but he has been outstanding because of his dramatic productions, of which we shall cite several works: *The Passionate Woman* (1958), the stage version of *Picaresque* (premiere, 1958), *The Potter* (1959), *The Lean Cows* (1959), *The Vengeance of the Godfather* (premiere, 1959), *"Corrido" of Pablo Damián* (1960), *Olympic* (premiere, 1964).

Miguel Barbachano Ponce (born in Mérida, Yucatán, 1930) studied in Mexico City in the Law School and took several courses in the School of Philosophy and Literature. At present he is directing the production of short films, and since 1955 he has directed the broadcasts "Tele-revista" and "Cine Verdad." He became known as a playwright in 1954 with *The Maker of Gods*, based on a short story of the same title by Francisco Rojas González. His most important works are *The Broken Lances* (1959) and *The Birds* (1961). The first refers to the political events occurring in Cuba in recent times, and the second contains five one-act plays dealing with the problem of sex. *Examination of Dead People* (premiere, 1955) and *Eleven Moons and One Pumpkin* (premiere, 1958) constitute all of his published plays. Recently, he has written his first novel, *The Diary of José Toledo* (1964).

Antonio González Caballero (born in Celaya, Guanajuato, 1931) abandoned the study of accounting to devote himself to painting and, after having exhibited in Mexico and abroad, he embarked upon a career as playwright. In 1960 his play *Young Ladies Against Their Will* was presented and, in 1964, two others were staged, *Half Hair* and *One Without . . . and Two with Salt*. He belongs to the *costumbrista* school of the Mexican theater. Because of his power of observation and the freshness and spontaneity of his dialogue, his plays—especially *Half Hair*—communicate a full sensation of life.

Héctor Mendoza (born in Apaseo, Guanajuato, 1932) received the Master's degree from the School of Philosophy and Literature of the UNAM. He has organized student groups in the University Theater and was director and actor in some of the programs of "Poetry Read Aloud." For several years he has been directing, always successfully, professional plays, and became a recognized dramatist in 1952 with *Suffocated Ones*, a strong, realistic play of social character, whose action takes place in the railroad yards of Buenavista. In *The Simple Things*—a prizewinner as was the former—he deals with the "small, great juvenile conflicts" among students of the National Preparatory School. Recently, he has written *Sprinkle Me with Love* (premiere, 1964) and *Here's to Boeotia!*, a one-act play published in a capital daily.

THE ESSAY

The flowering of the contemporary essay begins with *The Labyrinth of Loneliness* (1950) by Octavio Paz. Within the framework of Mexican literature in the first half of this century, the essay is the genre that first experienced a transformation caused by the effect of the Mexican Revolution of 1910—and even farther back than that, because in the years 1908-9, immediately before the armed struggle began, through the essay a reaction had been initiated against the official doctrine of Porfirio Díaz. The *Athenaeum of Youth*, which as a group lasted only a few years—from 1909 to 1914—brought about in the cultural field a revolution similar to that in the political and social fields. Its distinguishing feature was its philosophical spirit and its moralizing purpose. Out of the *Athenaeum* group came first the exclusively philosophical tendency, originated by Caso and Vasconcelos and continued by Samuel Ramos, Leopoldo Zea, and others; another tendency which followed the example of Pedro Henríquez Ureña in the critical-historical essay; and still another which took its direction from Alfonso Reyes in the free, original interpretative type. The nucleus of essayists who gave new and original directions to this genre has already been discussed by González Peña. We shall confine ourselves—as in the previous pages of this Appendix—to adding names of some essayists who have given prestige to our literature.

Essayists Born Before 1900

Enrique Díez-Canedo (born in Badajoz, Spain, 1879; died in Mexico City, 1944) lived in Mexico from 1939 until his death. He was a professor in the UNAM and the College of Mexico. His critical work represents the most keenly intelligent of his epoch. Of extraordinary culture and exquisite taste, Díez-Canedo was an outstanding authority in all literary fields. Enrique González Martínez said of him: "Mexican writers had no better friend in Spain, no man better informed, and no defender more determined and enthusiastic." His first books were poetry: *Verses of the Hours* (Madrid, 1906) and *The Visit of the Sun* (Madrid, 1907), in which incipient *modernismo* and the spirit of the generation of 1898 are to be observed; but his personal, lasting voice is heard in *American Epigrams* (Madrid, 1928). Joaquín Díez-Canedo published a selection of Enrique Díez-Canedo's poems under the title of *Little Garden of E.D.C.* (Mexico, 1945). His work as an essayist comprises several books such as *Room of the Portraits* (San José de Costa Rica, 1920), *Literary Conversations* (Madrid, 1921), *The Gods in the Prado* (Madrid, 1931), *The Theater and Its Enemies* (1939), *The New Poetry* (1941), *Juan Ramón Jiménez in His Work* (1944), *American Letters, Continental Literatures* (1944). The complete edition of his works was begun in 1964 by Joaquín Mortiz.

Juan B. Iguíniz (born in Guadalajara, Jalisco, 1881) settled in Mexico City and, since 1910, has held various posts in the National

Museum, in the National School of Librarians and Archivists, in various libraries in the city, and in the Secretariat of Foreign Relations. From 1951 to 1956 he was director of the National Library; and since 1956 he has been a research worker in the Institute of History of the UNAM. For nearly fifty years he has held teaching posts in his specialty in various institutions, and at present he is carrying on his meritorious work of teaching in the School of Philosophy and Literature. His bibliography is most extensive and varied: the graphic arts, bibliology and bibliography, librarianship, biography, literary criticism, genealogy, heraldry, and history. His bibliographical work has greatly facilitated the labor of investigators, critics, and students in general. Of particular importance are *The Bibliography of Mexican Novelists* (1926), *The Bibliography of Mexican Biography* (1930), *Bibliography of Writers of the Jesuit Society* (1945), and *Bibliographic Mexico* (1959).

Francisco González Guerrero (born in San Sebastián—today Gómez Farías—a village in the southern region of Lake Chapala, Jalisco, 1887; died in Mexico City, 1963) studied in Mexico City at the Normal School; he founded and directed the interesting review *Nosotros* (1912-14); he served as representative to the National Congress (1922-24) and worked in the diplomatic service (1936-44). He was a member of the Mexican Academy of Language, a persevering journalist, and director of the publishing section of the technical services (Servicio Técnico Editorial) of the UNAM until his death. During his lifetime he published only one book of verse, *Ad altere Dei (To the High God,* 1930), written in the manner of the later *modernista* current. Some of his unedited poems have recently been published under the title, *Pursuing a Dream* (1964). He successfully devoted himself to a detailed study of such poets as Manuel Gutiérrez Nájera and Amado Nervo, to some of whose works he wrote prologues that were incomparable essays. These works, his extensive knowledge of Mexican *modernista* poetry, and his essay *The Books of Others* (1947) give him a place among the best critics of our literature.

Angel María Garibay K. (born in Toluca, state of Mexico, 1892) was ordained as priest in 1917. Because of his long ministry in different indigenous and rural communities in the state of Mexico, he was able to understand the soul of the inhabitants, to know their language, and to delve into the customs and traditions of pre-Hispanic origin. In 1941 he was designated prebendary of the Basilica of Guadalupe; in 1952, Professor Extraordinary of the School of Philosophy and Letters of the UNAM; and since 1956 he has been director of the Seminary of Nahuatl Culture. Awarded the National Prize for Literature in 1965, Angel María Garibay K., specialist in Nahuatl, Hebrew, and Greek, is the most competent expert in the literature of the ancient Mexicans, as is shown by his *History of Nahuatl Literature* (two volumes, 1953-54) and other research: *Indigenous Poetry of the High Plateau* (1940), *Literary Panorama of the Nahua Peoples* (1963), and *The Literature of the Aztecs* (1964). An eminent humanist, he has also made excellent translations of Aeschylus, Sophocles, and Euripides.

José María González de Mendoza (born in Seville, Spain, in 1893, and now a naturalized Mexican) came to Mexico in 1910, and entered the diplomatic service in 1928; he was also employed in the secretariats of the Treasury and of Agriculture. He is a member of the National Academy of History and Geography and of the Mexican Academy of Language, and correspondent of the Spanish Royal Academy. At present he is connected with the Secretariat of Foreign Relations. González de Mendoza—also known as the Abbe Mendoza —after his brief work in creative poetry and fiction, has done excellent work as chronicler, essayist, and literary and art critic, activities in which he is distinguished because of his measured judgment and solid knowledge of Mexican literature. In the field of research in our indigenous literary monuments, he translated into Spanish, in collaboration with the Guatemalan Miguel Angel Asturias, the French versions of Georges Raynaud's *Popol Vuh or Book of Counsel* (1927) and *Annals of the Xahil* (1928). He has written magnificent essays such as *The Painting of Angel Zárraga* (1941), *Some Painters of the Salon of Autumn* (1942), and *Biographies of Cervantes and Critics of the Quijote* (1955). At midcentury he had published more than 2,500 newspaper articles in Mexico and abroad. Presently he is preparing, in a seminar of the Center for Literary Studies, the complete works of José Juan Tablada.

Francisco Monterde (born in Mexico City, 1894) received the doctorate in Spanish literature from the School of Philosophy and Literature. He has been chief of the Office of Publications and of the

Department of Libraries of the Secretariat of Education, librarian of the National Museum of History and Archaelogy, and associate director of the National Library. He is a member and president of the Mexican Academy of Language, and a member of the Mexican Society of Geography and Statistics and of other literary and scientific associations. With other writers he has participated in the re-establishment of the Union of Dramatic Writers. He was, in 1925, one of the Group of Seven Authors who established the Comedia Mexicana. In 1950, with Antonio Magaña Esquivel, he founded the Group of Theater Critics, of which he is honorary president. His vast work comprises poetry, drama, biography, narratives, critical studies, the novel, short story, fable, essay, and history of Mexican literature, in which he is one of the most knowledgeable experts. Writers—such as Navarrete and Cuenca—and periods of transition have interested him; he has written studies on Balbuena, Lizardi, Prieto, Fernando Calderón, Payno, Rafael Delgado, Amado Nervo, Gutiérrez Nájera, Díaz Mirón, López Velarde, and modernism. In contemporary literature he has promoted important movements such as that which awakened Mexican interest in the literature of the Revolution, for it was he who rescued from oblivion a work up to that time forgotten, *The Underdogs* of Mariano Azuela. With *The Madrigal of Cetina and the Secret of the Stairway* (1918), he was one of the initiators of the colonial style in Mexico.

Essayists Born in the Decade 1900-1910

Salvador Novo (1904) was born in Mexico City but lived, between the ages of six and twelve, in Torreón, center of the revolutionary storm. He later began the study of law in Mexico City but abandoned that career to devote himself to literature. In 1925 he assisted in the preparation of the excellent *Classical Readings for Children*, and since then he has published anthologies of Mexican and Hispanic-American short stories, and of North American and French poetry. From 1927 to 1928 he directed the review *Ulises* with Xavier Villaurrutia and assisted in founding the "Theater of Ulises," serving as translator, director, and actor. He has traveled in the Americas, Europe, and Asia. Lately he has devoted himself very successfully to journalism, in which, with notable skill and talent he has created styles of writing still in vogue. From 1946 to 1952 he was head of the Department of Theater of the INBA, and in that same institution he directed, in 1956, the School of Dramatic Art. He has belonged to the Mexican Academy of Language since 1952. Of his generation Salvador Novo is one of the writers of greatest culture and keenest literary sense. In his first verse, *XX Poems* (1925), the predominant note is irony, an accent which he later succeeds in sublimating in a lyrical depth which at times coincides with the modulations of the best poetry of our time. Later, he employed the amorous theme with such fortunate results that he has left us some of the most profound, sensitive, and lasting poetry. In 1955 he published a collection of his poetry written from 1915 to that date, under the title *Poetry*, and another in 1961 with the same title. Novo has constantly written essays, now those of literary intent as found in his first book *Essays* (prose and verse, 1925), and again those included in the volume called *In Defense of Usage* (1938); now delightful travel notes and descriptive narratives such as those in *The Youth* (1928) and *New Mexican Grandeur* (1946). Most of his prose works have been published recently in *All the Prose* (1964). In 1947 he began to devote himself to the theater, but his real success began in 1951 with the presentation of *The Cultivated Lady* and continued with *To Eight Columns* (1956), *Jocasta, or Almost* (1961), *Ulysses Has Returned* (1962), *The War of the Fat Women* (1963), and other plays.

Andrés Iduarte (born in Villahermosa, Tabasco, 1907) received his law degree from the National University of Mexico and the doctorate in philosophy from Columbia University. He taught in the National Preparatory School and was director of the review *Universidad de Mexico* and a member of the University Council. Since 1940 he has been living and working in the United States, with the exception of the period from 1952 to 1954 when he was director of our National Institute of Fine Arts. The great figures of Hispanic-American letters and culture are the proper field for the essays of Andrés Iduarte. In literary criticism his excellent study, *José Martí, Writer* (1945), portrays Martí's method and ability and is perhaps the best study dealing with this aspect of the Cuban apostle. The pages he has dedicated to Gabriela Mistral, Rómulo Gallegos, and Alfonso Reyes show a spirit in which fervor is always allied with intelligence. Outstanding in his creative work are the terse and moving pages of *A Child in the Mexican Revolution* (1951), an autobiographical book that takes the author from his birth to his preparatory studies. The following is a partial list of Andrés Iduarte's books: *Hispanic-American Speeches* (1951), *Twenty Years with Rómulo Gallegos* (1954), *Alfonso Reyes: the Man and His World* (1956), *Don Pedro de Alba and His Time* (1963), and *Gabriela Mistral, Saint on Horseback* (1958).

Luis Leal (born in Linares, Nuevo León, 1907) did his graduate work in the United States, where he has been living for some years. He has taught at Northwestern University and in the universities of Chicago, Mississippi, Emory, and Illinois. Luis Leal has devoted himself to the study of Hispanic-American literature, and particularly of the Mexican short story, in his books *Brief History of the Mexican Short Story* (1956), *Anthology of the Mexican Short Story* (1957), and *Bibliography of the Mexican Short Story* (1958). His predilection for the contemporary period in our literature is evident in his essay on the short story of the Mexican Revolution, *The Revolution and Letters* (in collaboration with Edmundo Valadés, 1960), in the anthology of the best short stories of Amado Nervo (1951), and in the prologue to the *Annual of the Mexican Short Story* (1960), published by the INBA.

Antonio Magaña Esquivel (born in Mérida, Yucatán, 1909) went to Mexico City in 1927 to study law but later abandoned that career to devote himself to specialized studies in the theater and literature. Since 1935 he has contributed to the *National* and the review *Tiempo*. He was founder and president of the Group of Drama Critics in Mexico, member of the Academy of Cinematographic Arts and Sciences, and head of the Theater Foráneo of the INBA. He is a novelist, playwright, critic, and essayist. His first novel, *The Ventriloquist* (1944), placed him as a new Mexican writer of influence. *The Reddened Earth* (1951), his second novel, won the City of Mexico Prize in Literature. His *Image of the Theater* (1940) is outstanding as a reference book that reveals his ability as critic and researcher. He is also the author of *Dream and Reality in the Theater* (1949), *Brief History of the Mexican Theater* (in collaboration with Ruth S. Lamb, 1958), and *The Theater and the Cinema* (1962). He became known as a dramatist with his two plays, *Seed from the Air* (premiere, 1956) and *The Place and the Hour* (staged, 1961).

Antonio Acevedo Escobedo (born in Aguascalientes, 1909) came to Mexico City in 1925 and began his career as a journalist on *El Universal Ilustrado*. Later, he contributed to *Revista de Revistas* (*Review of Reviews*, 1932-38), *El Nacional* (from 1934 to the present time), *Fábula, Letras de México* (1937-46), and *El Hijo Pródigo* (*The Prodigal Son*). Since 1959 he has been head of the department of literature of the INBA. His first book of short stories, *Siren in the Classroom*, appeared in 1935, and he published *At the San Marcos Fair* in 1951, *The Days of Aguascalientes*, 1952, and *Letter Perfect*, 1953. In 1941 he wrote a popular farce for a puppet show, *Here Comes Gregorio Esparza!* In *Sulphur in Mexico*, he pointed up some aspects of the foreign exploitation of sulphur. Through innumerable articles and reviews published in magazines and newspapers in Mexico and abroad, he has distinguished himself as a recorder of the pulse of the national literature.

Essayists Born in the Decade 1910-20

José Rojas Garcidueñas (born in Salamanca, Guanajuato, 1912) received his degree of Licentiate in Law in 1938 from the National School of Jurisprudence of the UNAM, and in 1954 the Master's degree in literature from the School of Philosophy and Literature. During 1947-48 he was head of the Department of Information of the Secretariat of Foreign Relations, and in 1953-54 he was professor and director of the School of Philosophy and Literature of the University of Guanajuato. Since 1939 he has been a research writer in the Institute of Aesthetic Research of the National University and professor in the School of Philosophy and Literature; since 1956, legal consultant of the main office of International Boundaries and Waters of the Secretariat of Foreign Relations; and since 1961, member of the Academy of Language. Expert on the culture of the colonial period, Rojas Garcidueñas has recorded his research on the history of the theater, of literature, and of Mexican art in that period. He has produced basic works such as *The Theater of New Spain in the Sixteenth Century* (1935), *Don Carlos de Sigüenza y Góngora, Baroque Scholar* (1945), *The Old College of San Ildefonso* (1951), *Bernardo de Balbuena, Life and Work* (1958), and some important studies on Sor Juana Inés de la Cruz, Genaro Fernández MacGregor, and Bernardo Couto. In 1959, in collaboration with John S. Brushwood, he published a *Short History of the Mexican Novel,* a valuable manual for the student and researcher working in our literature.

María del Carmen Millán (born in Teziutlán, Puebla, 1914) received the Master's and Doctor's degrees in Spanish Language and Literature from the School of Philosophy and Literature of the National University, where, since 1954, she has been a full-time teacher and secretary of the school. As director of the Center for Literary Studies, she has been the guiding spirit in a period of advanced research by several persons working together in Mexican literature, stimulating and directing works that are published by that institution. Her own literary labors, collected in books or scattered in numerous publications in Mexico and abroad, place her among the most respected authorities in her field. Her extensive information and critical objectivity have been recognized in university circles not only in Mexico, but in Hispanic-America, Europe, and the United States. Her first volume, *Landscape in Mexican Poetry* (1952), merited eulogies from Alfonso Reyes and Salvador Novo. In *Ideas of the Reform in the Native Literature,* she presents a succinct review of the novelists, poets, and journalists of that period. She has written essays on *The Modernismo of Othón* (1959), *The Generation of the Athenaeum and the Mexican Essay* (1961), and a history and anthology of Latin American essayists, not yet published. In addition to two anthologies, *American Short Stories* (1946) and *Mexican Romantic Poetry* (1957), she has edited and written prologues for the work of Angel de Campo: *Pastimes and Notes and the Rhumba* (1958) and *Things Obvious and Cartoons* (1958). Her last book to date, *Mexican Literature* (1962), is a useful work devoted to undergraduate students; in it the author synthesizes clearly the literary evolution of Mexico.

José Luis Martínez (born in Atoyac, Jalisco, 1918) completed his secondary and preparatory studies in the University of Guadalajara, and the course in literature at the National Autonomous University of Mexico. He was co-director of the review *Tierra Nueva* (1940-42), director of *Letras de México* (1943), editor of *El Hijo Pródigo* (1943-46) and of the *Nueva Revista de Filología Hispánica (New Review of Hispanic Philology),* director of the *Revista Mexicana de Literatura,* and co-director of *Estaciones* (1956). He has been professor of literature in various educational institutions, among others the School of Philosophy and Literature, ambassador from Mexico to

Peru (1961-63) and to UNESCO (1964), member of the Academy of Language since 1958, and at present is director of the National Institute of Fine Arts. José Luis Martínez had already produced commendable work as a critic and literary historian when he published, in 1949 and 1950, the two volumes of his *Mexican Literature in the Twentieth Century,* in which he gathers the most complete information up to that time on Mexican writers, Spaniards resident in Mexico, anthologies, bibliographies, critical studies, and literary reviews, as well as various studies written by himself since 1941. In his two volumes of *The Modern Mexican Essay,* he presents the panorama of our prose from the moment it began to move away from traditional molds. *The National Expression* (1955) is a valuable collection of works that he published from 1947 to 1952, and is an indispensable source for the understanding of the literature of the nineteenth century, a gestative period for "the maturation of intellectual independence and the creation of an original national expression." His work is complemented by the monographs on Mexican literature that he has written in prologues, notes, and various editions.

Essayists Born in the Decade 1920-30

Antonio Alatorre (born in Autlán, Jalisco, 1922) did his graduate work in the School of Philosophy and Literature of the National University and in the College of Mexico. He has been a professor in the university and a research worker in the college. From 1953 to 1960 he was secretary of the *Nueva Revista de Filología Hispánica,* and since 1960 he has been director. At present he is director of the Center of Linguistic and Literary Studies of the College of Mexico. Alatorre has earned distinction as a research worker, philologist, essayist, and teacher. His works of literary theory and criticism are still scattered in periodicals here and abroad. He is the author of *The "Heroides" of Ovid and His Imprint on Spanish Letters* (1950), *The Ballads of Hero and Leander* (1956), *For the History of a Problem: The Mexican Characteristics of Ruiz de Alarcón* (1956), and *Note (dispensable) to Some Sonnets of Sor Juana* (1964).

Salvador Reyes Nevares (born in Durango, 1922) studied law in the National University and took some courses in the School of Philosophy and Literature. He was a member of the *Hiperión* group, and founded, with several friends, the publishing house of *Los epi-*

grafes which, from 1951 to 1952, published some twenty small books of young writers. The work of Reyes Nevares comprises the essay, the short story, and literary criticism published in the principal reviews and literary supplements of the capital. He wrote a book of short stories, *Indecisive Frontier* (1955), essays such as *Love in Three Poets* (1951), and *Love and Friendship in the Mexican Man* (1952), and the chapter on Mexico in *Panorama of the Literatures of Ibero-America* (Coimbra, Portugal, 196?).

Ernesto Mejía Sánchez (born in Nicaragua, 1923) studied law in his native country in the University of Oriente y Mediodía. He has lived in Mexico since 1944, at which time he entered the School of Philosophy and Literature of the UNAM. He received the Master's degree in Spanish literature in 1951. He has undertaken special studies in the Central University of Madrid and has done research in the College of Mexico. At the present time he is in charge of the publication of the *Complete Works* of Alfonso Reyes. He received the Rubén Darío National Prize for Poetry for his collection of previously unpublished poems *Impurity* (1950), and in 1955 he won second place in the Central American competition in El Salvador with his book, *European Meditations* (1957). As researcher and essayist, Mejía Sánchez has been outstanding because of the profundity of his criticisms and his interpretation of the work of Rubén Darío, to whom he has dedicated such volumes as *Complete Stories of Rubén Darío* (1950), *The First Stories of Rubén Darío* (1951), and *Poetry of Rubén Darío* (1952).

Henrique González Casanova (born in Toluca, state of Mexico, 1924) studied in the Law School of the UNAM, the College of Mexico, and the National School of Anthropology. From 1955 to 1961 he was general director of publications for the National University. He is a titular professor in the National School of Political and Social Sciences. As a journalist, he was interim director of the cultural supplement, "Mexico en la Cultura" (1951), co-ordinator of the review *Universidad de México* (1953-61), editor of the *Gaceta de la Universidad* (*University Gazette*, 1954-61). Presently, he is a member of the editorial board of the review *Cuento (Story)*, founded in 1964. He is distinguished for his love of contemporary Mexican literature and for his literary criticism, essays, prologues, and articles. In 1964, because of his work he was designated an expert in the fields of humanities and journalism by the Council of the World Association of Universities. We shall mention only three of his many works not yet in collection: "Review of Mexican Poetry of the Twentieth Century" (1953), "Present State of Mexican Literature" (1953), and "Mexican Novelists of the Revolution" (1953).

Ramón Xirau (born in Barcelona, Spain, 1924) has lived since 1939 in Mexico City, where, in 1946, he received the Master's degree in philosophy. He was associate director of the Mexican Center for Writers (1953-64) and editor of the Center's *Boletín.* In 1945 he traveled in England and Cuba; in 1956 he visited in France and the United States, lecturing and teaching in various universities. At present he is directing the review *Diálogos,* of which he was one of the founders. Ramón Xirau has written poetry in Catalan and prose in Spanish. He is doubtless one of the best critics of poetry written in Spanish, as witness his books, *Three Poets of Loneliness* (1955), *Hispanic-American and Spanish Poetry* (1961), *First Fruits As Introduction* (1962), *Poets of Mexico and Spain* (1962). The remainder of his work includes *Method and Metaphysics in the Philosophy of Descartes* (1946), *Endurance and Existence* (1947), *The Pendulum and the Spiral* (1959), and *Introduction to the History of Philosophy* (1964).

Miguel León Portilla (born in Mexico City, 1926) has the Master's degree (1951) from Loyola University, Los Angeles, and the doctorate in philosophy (1956) from the UNAM, where he has taught the history of Nahuatl culture since 1957. He has been secretary, associate director, and director of the Inter-American Indigenous Institute. Since 1962 he has been a member of the Academy of Language and, since 1963, director of the History Institute of the UNAM. As historian and philosopher, León Portilla has devoted himself to the study of ancient Mexico, the pre-Hispanic culture and literature. His books, *Vision of the Conquered* (1959), written in collaboration with Dr. Garibay K., and *Seven Essays on Nahuatl Culture* (1958), are an indispensable source for a complete understanding of our culture. In addition to the above-mentioned books, his bibliography comprises *Rites, Sacrifices, and Accoutrements of the Gods* (1958), *The Ancient Mexicans in Their Chronicles and Songs* (1961), *The Nahuatl Philosophy Studied At Its Source* (1956), *Images of Ancient Mexico* (Argentina, 1963), *Pre-Columbian Lit-*

eratures of Mexico (1964), *The Reverse of the Conquest* (1964), and other works.

Emmanuel Carballo (born in Guadalajara, Jalisco, 1929) studied in Guadalajara and directed the reviews *Ariel* (1949-53) and *Odiseo* (1952). In Mexico City he was editorial secretary of the review *Universidad de México*. He founded, with Carlos Fuentes, the *Revista Mexicana de Literatura* (1955). He was chief editor of the *Gaceta* of the Foundation of Economic Culture. Presently, he is director of the Sunday supplement of *Ovaciones* and president of the José Martí Institute of Mexican-Cuban Cultural Relations. He became known as a poet for his work, *It Is Called Love* (1951), published in Guadalajara; later, he was recognized as a prose writer when his book of short stories, *Great Hindrance to Hope* (1954), was given to the press. Since 1950 he has published numerous works of criticism, reviews, and interviews that show him to be one of the best-informed writers of contemporary Mexican literature. He wrote the prologues for *Complete Stories* (1952) by José López Portillo y Rojas and for *The Three Years' War* and *Unpublished and Unknown Poems* (1955) by Emilio Rabasa. He is the author of *López Velarde in Guadalajara* (1953) and two anthologies, *Modern Mexican Short-Story Writers* (1956) and *The Mexican Short Story of the Twentieth Century* (1964). The prologue to his last book—his best—is an excellent study of contemporary Mexican literature.

Appendix B:
Mexican Works in English

A SELECTED LIST

ALTAMIRANO, IGNACIO MANUEL. *Christmas in the Mountains*. Translated by H. L. JOHNSON. Gainesville: University of Florida Press, 1961.

———. *El Zarco the Bandit*. Translated by M. ALLT. London: Folio Society, 1957.

ARREOLA, JUAN JOSÉ. *Confabulario and Other Inventions*. Translated by GEORGE D. SCHADE. Austin: University of Texas Press, 1964.

AZUELA, MARIANO. *"The Flies," "The Bosses," Two Novels of Mexico*. Translated by LESLEY B. SIMPSON. Berkeley: University of California Press, 1956.

———. *Marcela, a Mexican Love Story*. Translated by ANITA BRENNER. New York: Farrar and Rinehart, 1932.

———. *The Underdogs*. Translated by ENRIQUE MUNGUÍA, JR. New York: Brentano's, 1929.

BENÍTEZ, FERNANDO. *In the Footsteps of Cortés*. New York: Pantheon Books, 1952.

BLACKWELL, ALICE STONE. *Some Spanish American Poets*. Philadelphia: University of Pennsylvania Press, 1937.

BULNES, D. FRANCISCO. *The Whole Truth About Mexico*. Translated by DORA SCOTT. New York: M. Bulnes Book Company, 1916.

CASO, ALFONSO. *The Aztecs: People of the Sun*. Translated by LOWELL DUNHAM. Norman: University of Oklahoma Press, 1958.

———. *The Religion of the Aztecs*. Mexico City: Central News Company, 1937.

———. *Thirteen Masterpieces of Mexican Archaeology*. Translated by EDITH MACKIE and JORGE R. ACOSTA. Mexico City: Editoriales Cultura y Polis, 1938.

CASTELLANOS, ROSARIO. *The Nine Guardians.* Translated by IRENE NICHOLSON. London: Faber and Faber, 1959; New York: Vanguard Press, 1960.

CERVANTES DE SALAZAR, FRANCISCO. *Life in the Imperial and Loyal City of Mexico in New Spain, and the Royal and Pontifical University of Mexico.* Translated by MINNIE LEE BARRETT SHEPARD. Austin: University of Texas Press, 1953.

Codex Mendoza. Edited and translated by JAMES COOPER CLARK. 3 vols. London: Waterlow and Sons, 1938.

CORTÉS, HERNÁN. *The Fifth Letter.* Translated by DON PASCUAL DE GAYANGOS. London: Printed for the Hakluyt Society, 1868.

——. *Five Letters, 1519-1526.* Translated by J. BAYARD MORRIS. New York: Robert M. McBride & Co., 1929.

——. *Letters of Cortés.* Edited and translated by FRANCIS A. MACNUTT. New York: G. P. Putnam's Sons, 1908.

DÁVALOS, BALBINO. *The Great North American Poets.* Translated by OWEN W. GILLPATRICK. Mexico City: Oficina Impresora del Timbre, 1901.

DÍAZ DEL CASTILLO, BERNAL. *The Bernal Díaz Chronicles: The True Story of the Conquest of Mexico.* Translated and edited by ALBERT IDELL. Garden City: Doubleday & Co., 1956.

——. *The Discovery and Conquest of Mexico.* Translated by A. P. MAUDSLAY. London: G. Routledge & Sons, 1928.

FERNÁNDEZ DE LIZARDI, JOSÉ JOAQUÍN. *The Itching Parrot* (33 selected chapters). Translated by KATHERINE ANNE PORTER. Garden City: Doubleday, Doran & Co., 1942.

FUENTES, CARLOS. *The Good Conscience.* Translated by SAM HILEMAN. New York: Ivan Obolensky, 1961.

——. *Where the Air Is Clear.* Translated by SAM HILEMAN. New York: Ivan Obolensky, 1960.

GÓMARA, FRANCISCO LÓPEZ DE. *The Conquest of the Weast India (1578) by Francisco López de Gómara.* Translated by THOMAS NICHOLAS. New York: Scholars' Facsimiles & Reprints, 1940.

GONZÁLEZ MARTÍNEZ, ENRIQUE. *Three Poems.* Translated by ALICE STONE BLACKWELL. Washington, D.C.: Pan American Union, March, 1927.

GONZÁLEZ OBREGÓN, LUIS. *Legends of the City of Mexico*. Translated by THOMAS A. JANVIER. New York: Harper & Bros., 1910.
———. *The Streets of Mexico*. Translated by BLANCHE C. WAGNER. San Francisco: George Fields, 1937.

GUZMÁN, MARTÍN LUIS. *The Eagle and the Serpent*. Translated by HARRIET DE ONÍS. New York: Alfred A. Knopf, 1930; Garden City: Dolphin Books, 1965.
———. *Memoirs of Pancho Villa*. Translated by VIRGINIA H. TAYLOR. Austin: University of Texas Press, 1965.

LEE, MUNA. *Some Contemporary Latin American Poets in English Version*. Washington, D.C.: Pan American Union, July, 1925.

LÓPEZ Y FUENTES, GREGORIO. *El Indio*. Translated by ANITA BRENNER. New York: Bobbs-Merrill Co., 1937; F. Ungar Publishing Co., 1961.

MAGDALENO, MAURICIO. *Sunburst*. Translated by ANITA BRENNER. New York: Viking Press, 1944.

MEDIZ BOLIO, ANTONIO. *The Land of the Pheasant and the Deer*. Translated by ENID E. PERKINS. Illustrated by DIEGO RIVERA. Mexico City: Cultura, 1935.

MENÉNDEZ, MIGUEL ANGEL. *Nayar*. Translated by ANGEL FLORES. New York: Farrar & Rinehart, 1942.

MONDRAGÓN AGUIRRE, MAGDALENA. *Some Day the Dream*. Translated by SAMUEL PUTNAM. New York: Dial Press, 1947.

MOTOLINIA, PADRE TORIBIO DE. *History of the Indians of New Spain*. Translated by FRANCIS BORGIA STECK. Washington, D.C.: Academy of American Franciscan History, 1951.

NERVO, AMADO. *Confessions of a Modern Poet*. Translated by DOROTHY KRESS. Boston: Bruce Humphries, 1935.

NOVO, SALVADOR. *Nuevo Amor*. Translated by EDNA WORTHLEY UNDERWOOD. Portland, Maine: Mosher Press, 1935.

PAZ, OCTAVIO. *Anthology of Mexican Poetry*. Translated by SAMUEL BECKETT. Bloomington: Indiana University Press, 1958.
———. *The Labyrinth of Solitude; Life and Thought in Mexico*. Translated by LYSANDER KEMP. New York: Grove Press, 1962.

RAMOS, SAMUEL. *Profile of Man and Culture in Mexico*. Translated by PETER G. EARLE. Austin: University of Texas Press, 1962.

REVUELTAS, JOSÉ. *The Stone Knife*. Translated by H. R. HAYS. New York: Reynal & Hitchcock, 1947.

REYES, ALFONSO. *Criticism and the Roman Mind*. Translated by
RICHARD A. MAZZARA. New York: Collier Books, 1963.
————. *The Position of America*. Translated by HARRIET DE ONÍS.
New York: Alfred A. Knopf, 1950.
ROBLES SOLER, ANTONIO JOAQUÍN. *The Refugee Centaur*. Trans-
lated by EDWARD and ELIZABETH HUBERMAN. New York: Twayne
Publishers, 1952.
ROMERO DE TERREROS Y VINENT, MANUEL, and ROSENBERG,
S. L. M. *Mexico Virreinal*. New York: Alfred A. Knopf, 1925.
ROSENBERG, S. L. M., and TEMPLIN, E. H. *A Brief Anthology of
Mexican Prose*. Palo Alto: Stanford University Press, 1928.
————. *A Brief Anthology of Mexican Verse*. Palo Alto: Stanford
University Press, 1928.
RULFO, JUAN. *The Burning Plain and Other Stories*. Translated by
GEORGE D. SCHADE. Austin: University of Texas Press, 1967.
SAHAGUN, FRIAR BERNARDINO DE. *A History of Ancient Mexico*.
Translated by FANNY R. BANDELIER. Nashville: Fiske University
Press, 1932.
SPOTA, LUIS. *The Enemy Blood*. Translated by ROBERT MOLLOY.
Garden City: Doubleday & Co., 1961.
————. *The Time of Wrath*. Translated by ROBERT MOLLOY. Gar-
den City: Doubleday & Co., 1962.
————. *The Wounds of Hunger*. Translated by BARNABY CONRAD.
Boston: Houghton Mifflin, 1957.
STARR, FREDERICK. *Readings from Modern Mexican Authors*. Chi-
cago: Open Court Publishing Co., 1904.
TEJA ZABRE, ALFONSO. *Guide to the History of Mexico; a Modern
Interpretation*. Translated by P. M. DEL CAMPO. Mexico City:
Press of the Mexican Ministry of Foreign Affairs, 1935.
TORRI, JULIO. *Essays and Poems*. Translated by DOROTHY M. KRESS.
New York: Publications of the Institute of French Studies, 1938.
TOUSSAINT, MANUEL. *Colonial Art in Mexico*. Translated by ELIZA-
BETH W. WEISMANN. Austin: University of Texas Press, 1967.
UNDERWOOD, EDNA WORTHLEY. *Anthology of Mexican Poets*. Port-
land: Mosher Press, 1932.
USIGLI, RODOLFO. *Crown of Shadows*. Translated by WILLIAM F.
STIRLING. London: A. Wingate, 1946.
VASCONCELOS CALDERÓN, JOSÉ, and GAMIO, MANUEL. *Aspects of*

Mexican Civilization. Chicago: University of Chicago Press, 1926.

VASCONCELOS CALDERÓN, JOSÉ. *A Mexican Ulysses; an Autobiography.* Translated and abridged by W. REX CRAWFORD. Bloomington: Indiana University Press, 1963.

WALSH, THOMAS. *Hispanic Anthology.* New York: G. P. Putnam's Sons, 1920.

YÁÑEZ, AGUSTÍN. *The Edge of the Storm.* Translated by ETHEL BRINTON. Austin: University of Texas Press, 1963.

ZAYAS ENRÍQUEZ, RAFAEL DE. *The Case of Mexico and the Policy of President Wilson.* Translated by ANDRÉ TRIDON. New York: A. and C. Boni, 1914.

Bibliographies

Latin American Poetry in English Translation. Compiled by CLAUDE L. HULET. Washington, D.C.: Pan American Union, 1965.

Latin American Prose in English Translation. Compiled by CLAUDE L. HULET. Washington, D.C.: Pan American Union, 1965.

Appendix C: Original Titles of Works in Text and Appendix A

Abad, Diego José: *De Deo.*

Abate Mendoza; *see* González de Mendoza, José María.

Abreu Gómez, Ermilo: *El corcovado*; *La vida milagrosa del venerable siervo de Dios Gregorio López*; *Héroes mayas*; *Clásicos, románticos, modernos*; *Sor Juana Inés de la Cruz: bibliografía y biblioteca*; edited new editions of *Respuesta a Sor Filotea* and *Las Vidas* of Sor Juana, by D. Juan José de Eguiara y Eguren and P. Diego Calleja.

Acaico, Ipandro; *see* Montes de Oca y Obregón, Ignacio.

Acevedo, Jesús T.: *Disertaciones de un arquitecto.*

Acevedo Escobedo, Antonio: *Sirena en el aula*; *En la feria de San Marcos*; *Los días de Aguascalientes*; *Al pie de la letra*; *¡Ya viene Gregorio Esparza!*; *El azufre en México.*

Acosta, José de: *Historia natural y moral de las Indias.*

Acuña, Manuel: "Ante un cadáver"; "El hombre"; "Entonces y hoy"; "Hojas secas"; "La vida del campo"; "La ramera"; "Lágrimas"; "Letrilla"; "Nocturno."

Achosa y Ucaña, Atanasio de; *see* Ochoa y Acuña, Anastasio María de.

Agüeros, Victoriano: *Biblioteca de Autores Mexicanos, Escritores mexicanos contemporáneos.*

Aguilar y Morocho, Ignacio: *La batalla del Jueves Santo.*

Alamán, Lucas: *Disertaciones sobre la historia de México*; *Historia de México.*

Alarcón y Mendoza, Juan Ruiz de: *El Anticristo*; *El desdichado en fingir*; *El dueño de las estrellas*; *El examen de maridos*; *El semejante a sí mismo*; *El tejedor de Segovia* (segunda parte); *Ganar amigos*; *La amistad castigada*; *La crueldad por el honor*; *La cueva*

478

de Salamanca; *La culpa busca la pena, y el agravio, la venganza*;
La industria y la suerte; *La Manguilla de Melilla*; *La prueba de las
promesas*; *La verdad sospechosa*; *Las paredes oyen*; *Los empeños de
un engaño*; *Los favores del mundo*; *Los pechos privilegiados*; *Mu-
darse por mejorarse*; *No hay mal que por bien no venga*; *Quien
mal anda, mal acaba*; *Todo es ventura*.

Alatorre, Antonio: *Las "Heroidas" de Ovidio y su huella en las letras
españolas*; "Los romances de Hero y Leandro"; "Para la historia de
un problema: La mexicanidad de Ruiz de Alarcón"; "Nota (pres-
cindible) a unos sonetos de Sor Juana."

Alcaraz, Ramón Isaac: *Las estaciones*.

Alegre, Francisco Javier: "Nysis"; *Opúsculos inéditos latinos y castellanos del P. Francisco Javier Alegre*; revised and completed Francisco de Florencia's *Historia de la Provincia de la Compañía de
Jesús de Nueva España*.

Alemán, Mateo: *El pícaro Guzmán de Alfarache*; published in New
Spain his *Ortografía castellana* and *Sucesos de D. Fray García
Guerra, Arzobispo de México*.

Alessio Robles, Miguel: *Asuntos hispánicos*; *Historia política de la
Revolución*; *Ideales de la Revolución*; *Idolos caídos*; *La ciudad de
Saltillo*; *La responsabilidad de los altos funcionarios*; *Las dos razas*;
Obregón como militar; *Perfiles del Saltillo*; *Voces de combate*; *Mi
generación y mi época*; *A medio camino*; *Contemplando el pasado*.

Alessio Robles, Vito: *Acapulco*; *Bibliografía de Coahuila: histórica y
geográfica*; *Bosquejos históricos*; *Coahuila y Texas en la época
colonial*; *Cómo se ha escrito la historia de Coahuila*; *Desfile san-
griento*; *El ilustre maestro Andrés Manuel del Río*; *Etimologías
bastardeadas: Coahuila*; *Francisco de Urdiñola y el norte de la
Nueva España*; *Fray Agustín de Morfi y su obra*; *La primera
imprenta en Coahuila*; *Los tratados de Bucareli*; *Mis andanzas con
nuestro Ulises*; *Monterrey*; *Unas páginas traspapeladas de la historia de Coahuila*; *Ramos Arizpe*; *Saltillo*.

Almanza, Héctor Raúl: *Huelga blanca*; *Candelaria de los patos*;
Brecha en la roca; *Detrás del espejo*.

Alpuche, Wenceslao: *Hidalgo*.

Altamirano, Ignacio Manuel: "Al Atoyac"; "Antonia"; *Antonia y
Beatriz*; *Atenea*; *Clemencia*; *El Zarco*; "Flor del alba"; *Julia (Una
noche de julio)*; *La navidad en las montañas*; "Las abejas"; "Las

amapolas"; *Las tres flores (La novia)*; "Los bandidos de la Cruz"; "Los naranjos"; *Paisajes y leyendas, Tradiciones y costumbres de México*; *Rimas*.

Altolaguirre, Manuel: *Las islas invitadas*; *Ejemplo*; *Poesía*; *Un verso para una amiga*; *Soledades juntas*; *Nuevos poemas de las islas invitadas*; *La lenta libertad*; *Nube temporal*; *Más poemas de las islas invitadas*; *Nuevos poemas*; *Fin de un amor*; *Poemas en América*.

Alva, Fernando de; *see* Ixtlilxóchitl, Fernando de Alva.

Alvarado, Francisco de: *Vocabulario en lengua mixteca*.

Alvarez, Griselda: *Letanía erótica para la paz*; *Cementerio de pájaros*; *Dos cantos*; *Desierta compañía*.

Amieva, Ignacio: *La hija del Senador*; *Valentina*.

Amor, Guadalupe: *Poesías completas*; *Décimas a Dios*; *Otro libro de amor*; *Sirviéndole a Dios de hoguera*; *Todos los siglos del mundo*; *Yo soy mi casa*; *Galería de títeres*.

Ancona, Eligio: *El conde de Peñalva*; *La cruz y la espada*.

Andrade, Vicente de: *Ensayo bibliográfico mexicano del siglo XVII*.

Anglería, Pedro Mártir de: *De Orbe Novo*.

Anónimo (El) o Códice Ramírez: *Relazione d'un gentiluomo di Ferdinando Cortés* (Italian version); *Relación del origen de los Indios que habitan esta Nueva España según sus historias*.

Anunciación, Juan de la: *Sermones*.

Aragón, Enrique A.: *Obras completas*; *Historia del alma*.

Arango y Escandón, Alejandro: "En la Inmaculada Concepción de Nuestra Señora"; *Ensayo histórico sobre Fray Luis de León*; "Invocación a la bondad divina"; "La piedad divina"; *Versos*.

Arias, Juan de Dios: collaborated on *México a través de los siglos*.

Aridjis, Homero: *La musa roja*; *Los ojos desdoblados*; *La difícil ceremonia*; *Antes del reino*; *Mirándola dormir*; *La tumba de Filidor*.

Arrangoiz, Francisco de Paula: *Breve reseña*; *México desde 1808 hasta 1867*.

Arreola, Juan José: *Varia invención*; *Confabulario*; *La hora de todos*; *La Feria*.

Arróniz, Marcos: *Manual de biografía mexicana*; *Manual del viajero en México*.

Asbaje, Juana de; *see* Cruz, Sor Juana Inés de la.

Astanio; *see* Ochoa y Acuña, Anastasio María de.

Atl, Doctor: *¡Arriba, arriba! Cuentos bárbaros*; *Cuentos de todos* *colores; El paisaje: un ensayo; Iglesias de México; Las artes popu-lares en México; Un hombre más allá del universo.*

Aub, Max: *Campo cerrado; No son cuentos; Campo de sangre; Sala de espera; Yo vivo; Cuentos mexicanos (con pilón); Campos del moro; El Zopilote y otros cuentos mexicanos.*

Ayala Anguiano, Armando: *Las ganas de creer; El paso de la nada.*

Azar, Héctor: *Estancias; Ventanas de Francia; Días santos; La ap-passionata; Picaresca; El alfarero; Las vacas flacas; La venganza del compadre; Corrido de Pablo Damián; Olímpica.*

Azuela, Mariano: *María Luisa; Los fracasados; Mala yerba; Andrés Pérez, maderista; Los de abajo; Las moscas; Las tribulaciones de una familia decente; La malhora; El desquite; La luciérnaga; El camarada Pantoja; Regina Landa; Avanzada; Nueva burguesía; La marchanta; La mujer domada; Sendas prohibidas; La maldición; Teatro; Los de abajo; El buho en la noche; Del Llano Hermanos, S. en C.; Cien años de novela mexicana.*

Báez, Edmundo: *Razón del sueño; El rencor de la tierra; Un alfiler en los ojos; ¡Un macho!.*

Balbuena, Bernardo de: *Bernardo o Victoria de Roncesvalles; Com-pendio apologético en alabanza de la poesía; El siglo de oro en las selvas de Erifile; La grandeza mexicana.*

Banda Farfán, Raquel: *Escenas de la vida rural; La cita; Un pedazo de vida; El secreto; Amapola; Valle verde; Cuesta abajo.*

Barbachano Ponce, Miguel: *El hacedor de dioses; Las lanzas rotas; Los pájaros; Examen de muertos; Once lunas y una calabaza; El diario de José Toledo.*

Barquera, Juan Wenceslao: "A Fernando VII"; "A la libertad"; *Salu-tación a la primavera.*

Bartra, Agustí: *Cant corporal; Cristo de 200,000 brazos (Campo de Argelés); Deméter; Odiseo; Marsias y Adila; Quetzalcóatl; Oda a Cataluña dels tropics; Ecce Homo.*

Barrera, Carlos: *Corrido de Monterrey; De cara al mar; Odas cam-pestres y otros poemas.*

Barriga Rivas, Rogelio: *Guelaguetza; Río humano; Juez letrado; La mayordomía.*

Basalenque, Diego de: *Crónica de Michoacán.*

Basurto, José Ignacio: *Fábulas morales para la provechosa recreación de los niños que cursan las escuelas de primeras letras.*

Basurto, Luis G.: *Los diálogos de Suzette*; *Toda una dama*; *Cada quien su vida*; *Miércoles de Ceniza*; *La locura de los ángeles*; *Los reyes del mundo*; *El escándalo de la verdad*; *Intimas enemigas*; *La Gobernadora*; *Y todos terminaron ladrando*.

Batís, Huberto: edited *Cuadernos del Viento* (with Carlos Valdés).

Baz, Gustavo: *Celos de mujer*; *La Conjuración de México*.

Belmonte Bermúdez, Luis de: *Vida del Padre Maestro Ignacio de Loyola*.

Beltrán, Neftalí: *Veintiún poemas*; *Dos sonetos*; *Canto del viento*; *Poesía*; *Soledad enemiga*; *Algunas canciones de Neftalí Beltrán*.

Bello, Andrés: *Silvas*.

Benavente, Toribio de; *see* Motolinia.

Benítez, Fernando: *China a la vista*; *La batalla de Cuba*; *Viaje a la Tarahumara*; *Caballo y Dios*; *Cristóbal Colón*; *La ruta de Hernán Cortés*; *La vida criolla en el siglo XVI*; *La ruta de la libertad*; *Ki: el drama de un pueblo y de una planta*; *El Rey Viejo*; *El agua envenenada*.

Benítez, José María: *Ciudad*.

Beristáin y Souza, José Mariano: *Biblioteca hispano-americana septentrional*; *Diálogos entre Filopatro y Aceraio*; *El verdadero ilustrador americano*; "Sermón del Domingo de Ramos"; compiled *Cantos de las musas mexicanas*.

Bermúdez, María Elvira: *Diferentes razones tiene la muerte*; *Soliloquio de un muerto*.

Bernal, Rafael: *Improperio a Nueva York y otros poemas*; *Trópico*; *3 novelas policíacas*; *Un muerto en la tumba*; *Su nombre era muerte*; *El extraño caso de Aloysus Hands*; *Tierra de gracia*; *El cadáver del señor García*; *La carta*; *Antonia*; *Soledad*; *El ídolo*; *La paz contigo o El martirio del Padre Pro*; *El maíz en la casa*.

Betancourt, Agustín de; *see* Vetancourt, Agustín.

Bianchi, Alberto: *Martirios del pueblo*; *Vampiros sociales*.

Bocanegra, Matías de: *Canción alegórica a la vista de un desengaño*.

Bolio, Dolores: *A su oído*; *Aroma tropical*; *De intimidad*; *En silencio*; *Una hoja del pasado*; *Un solo amor*; *Yerbas de olor*.

Bonifaz Nuño, Alberto: *Juego de espejos*; *El derecho del señor*; *La cruz del sureste*.

Bonifaz Nuño, Rubén: *Imagénes*; *Los demonios y los días*; *El manto y la corona*; *Fuego de pobres*.

Boturini Benaduci, Lorenzo: "Catálogo"; *Cronología de las principales naciones de la América Septentrional*; *Idea de una nueva historia general de la América Septentrional.*

Bramón, Francisco: *Los sirgueros de la Virgen sin original pecado.*

Bravo Adams, Caridad: *Reverberación*; *Trópico.*

Bravo, Francisco: *Opera Medicinalia.*

Bringas y Encinas, Diego Miguel: "Sermón de la reconquista de Guanajuato."

Brocar, Juan de: *Obras que Francisco Cervantes de Salazar ha hecho, glosado y traducido.*

Brummel; *see* Puga y Acal, Manuel.

Brushwood, John S.: collaborated with José Rojas Garcidueñas on *Breve historia de la novela mexicana.*

Bulnes, Francisco: *Sobre el Hemisferio Norte Once Mil Leguas*; *El porvenir de las naciones latino-americanas*; *La Guerra de Independencia: Hidalgo-Iturbide*; *Las grandes mentiras de nuestra historia: La Nación y el Ejército en las guerras extranjeras*; *El verdadero Juárez y la verdad sobre la Intervención y el Imperio*; *Juárez y las revoluciones de Ayutla y de Reforma*; *The whole truth about Mexico*; *El verdadero Díaz*; *Los grandes problemas de México.*

Burgoa, Francisco: *Descripción geográfica de la América Septentrional y de la Nueva Iglesia de Occidente*; *Itinerario de Oaxaca a Roma y de Roma a Oaxaca*; *Palestra historial o Historia de la Provincia de San Hipólito de Oaxaca.*

Bustamante, Carlos María de: *Apuntes para la historia del gobierno del general Santa Anna*; *Campañas del general D. Félix María Calleja*; *Cuadro histórico de la Revolución Mexicana*; *El Gabinete mexicano durante el segundo período de la administración del Presidente Bustamante*; *El nuevo Bernal Díaz del Castillo, o sea historia de la invasión de los anglo-americanos en México*; *Galería de príncipes antiguos mexicanos*; *Historia del emperador D. Agustín de Iturbide*; *Mañanas de la Alameda de México.*

Bustillos, José María: "Colibríes"; "En la noche"; "Junto al río"; "La gruta de Cicalco"; "Nocturno de estío."

Bustos Cerecedo, Miguel: *La noche arrodillada*; *Cauce*; *Revolución*; *Tres poemas revolucionarios*; *Hambre*; *Remoto amor*; *Se dice de Héctor Pérez Martínez en cinco sonetos*; *Elegías para recordar un* amor; *Oración a Enrique González Martínez*; *Pliegos*; *Sonetos*; *Un camino abierto*; *Palabras para cultivar un amor*; *Cuando éramos niños*; *Memoria de tus pasos*.

Cabada, Juan de la: *Paseo de mentiras*; *Incidentes melódicos del mundo irracional*; *El brazo fuerte*.

Cabrera, Cristóbal: *Manual de Adultos*.

Cabrera, Rafael: *Presagios*.

Cabrera y Quintero, Cayetano: *El Iris de Salamanca*; *Escudo de armas de la ciudad de México*; *La Esperanza malograda*.

Calderón, Fernando: *A ninguna de las tres*; "A una rosa marchita"; *Ana Bolena*; *Armandina*; "El soldado de la libertad"; "El sueño del tirano"; *El torneo*; *Hermán o la vuelta del Cruzado*; *Hersila y Virginia*; *Ifigenia*; "La vuelta del desterrado"; *Los políticos del día*; "Los recuerdos"; *Ramiro, conde de Lucena*; *Reinaldo y Elvira*; *Zadig*; *Zeila o la esclava indiana*; *Dramas y Poesías*.

Calderón de la Barca, Señora de: *Life in Mexico*.

Calleja, Diego: *Vidas*.

Camarillo de Pereyra, María Enriqueta: *Album sentimental*; *El arca de colores*; *El misterio de su muerte*; *El secreto*; *Entre el polvo de un castillo*; *Jirón de mundo*; *Lo irremediable*; *Mirlitón*; *Rincones románticos*; *Rumores de mi huerto*; *Sorpresas de la vida*.

Camino y Galicia, León Felipe: *Versos y oraciones de caminante*; *La insignia*; *El payaso de las bofetadas y el pescador de caña*; *Español del éxodo y del llanto*; *El gran responsable*; *Los lagartos*; *Ganarás la luz*; *Llamadme publicano*; *El ciervo*; *¿Qué se hizo el rey don Juan?*.

Campo, Angel de: *Cartones*; *Cosas vistas*; *La rumba*; *Ocios y apuntes*.

Campobello, Nellie: *Yo, Versos por Francisca*; *Cartucho*; *Las manos de mamá*.

Campos, Rubén M.: *Aztlán, tierra de las garzas*; *Chapultepec: su leyenda y su historia*; *Claudio Oronoz*; *Cuentos mexicanos*; *El Bar (la vida literaria de México en 1900)*; *El folklore literario de México*; *El folklore musical de las ciudades*; *El folklore y la música mexicana*; *La flauta de Pan*; *La producción literaria de los aztecas*; *Las alas nómadas*; *Tradiciones y leyendas mexicanas*.

Cantón, Wilberto: *Segunda estación*; *Dos poemas*; *Cuando zarpe el barco*; *Saber morir*; *La escuela de cortesanos*; *Nocturno a Rosario*; *Pecado mortal*; *Los malditos*; *El jardín de las Gorgonas*; *Tan cerca del cielo; Inolvidable; Nosotros somos Dios; Nota roja; Todos somos hermanos; Murió por la patria.*

Carballido, Emilio: *Rosalba y los Llaveros; La zona intermedia; Escribir por ejemplo* . . . ; *La sinfonía doméstica; La danza que sueña la tortuga; Felicidad; La hebra de oro; Las estatuas de marfil; Un pequeño día de ira; Teseo; Silencio, pollos pelones, ya les van a echar su maíz; La veleta oxidada; El Norte; La caja vacía.*

Carballo, Emmanuel: *Amor se llama; Gran estorbo la esperanza; López Velarde en Guadalajara; Cuentistas mexicanos modernos; El cuento mexicano del siglo XX.*

Cárdenas, Juan de: *Primera parte de los problemas y secretos maravillosos de las Indias.*

Cárdenas Peña, José: *Sueño de sombras; Llanto subterráneo; La ciudad de los pájaros; Conversación amorosa; Retama del olvido y otros poemas; Adonais o la elegía del amor y Canto de Dionisio; Los contados días.*

Cardona Peña, Alfredo: *El mundo que tú eres; La máscara que habla; El secreto de la reina Amaranta; La muerte cae en un vaso; Los jardines amantes; Zapata; Primer paraíso; Poesía de pie; Cosecha mayor.*

Carniado, Enrique: *Alma párvula.*

Carpio, Manuel: *El Popocatépetl; "El turco"; La Anunciación; La cena de Baltasar; La pitonisa de Endor; La Virgen al pie de la Cruz; México; Napoleón en el Mar Rojo.*

Carreño, Alberto María: *El cronista Luis González Obregón; Ensayos literarios; Estudios biográficos; Estudios económicos y sociales; Estudios filológicos; Estudios histórico-geográficos; Estudios históricos; Obras diversas.*

Casas, Bartolomé de las: *Brevísima relación de la destrucción de las Indias; Historia apologética; Historia de las Indias.*

Caso, Alfonso: *El teocalli de la Guerra Sagrada; Exploraciones en Oaxaca; La religión de los aztecas; Las estelas zapotecas; Trece obras maestras de arqueología mexicana; Urnas de Oaxaca.*

Caso, Antonio: *Comento breve de la Oda a la Música de Fray Luis de León; Crisopeya; Discursos a la Nación Mexicana; Discursos heterogéneos; Doctrinas e ideas; Dramma per música; El acto ideatorio; El concepto de la Historia Universal; El políptico de los días del mar; El problema de México y la ideología nacional; En-*

sayos críticos y polémicos; Filósofos y doctrinas morales; Historia y antología del pensamiento filosófico; La existencia como economía, como desinterés, y como caridad; La filosofía de Husserl; La filosofía de la cultura y el materialismo histórico; Nuevos discursos a la Nación Mexicana; Principios de estética; Problemas filosóficos; Sociología genética y sistemática; La persona humana y el Estado totalitario; El peligro del hombre; Mexico: Apuntamientos de cultura patria.

Caso, María Lombardo de: *Muñecos de niebla; Una luz en la otra orilla; La culebra tapó el río.*

Castañeda, Daniel: *El corrido mexicano; su técnica literaria y musical.*

Castaño, Rosa de: *Rancho Estradeño; Fruto de sangre.*

Castellanos, Rosario: *Trayectoria del polvo; Apuntes para una declaración de fe; De la vigilia estéril; Dos poemas; El rescate del mundo; Presentación en el templo; Poemas: 1953-1955; Salomé y Judith; Al pie de la letra; Lívida luz; Balún-Canán; Oficio de tinieblas; Ciudad Real; Los convidados de agosto; Rito de iniciación.*

Castera, Pedro: *Carmen.*

Castillo, Florencio M. del: *Amor y desgracia;* "Botón de rosa"; *Corona de azucenas; Culpa; Dos horas en el Hospital de San Andrés; ¡Hasta el cielo!; Hermana de los Angeles; La clase media.*

Castillo Ledón, Amalia de: *Cubos de noria; Cuando las hojas caen.*

Castillo Ledón, Luis: *Antigua literatura indígena mexicana; El chocolate; Museo Nacional de Arqueología, Historia y Etnología; El paseo de la Viga y de Santa Anita; La conquista y colonización española en México: su verdadero carácter; La fundación de la ciudad de México; Lo que miro y lo que siento; Los mexicanos autores de óperas; Orígenes de la novela en México; Hidalgo: la vida del héroe;* and preface to *Epistolario* by Juan de la Granja.

Castillo Nájera, Francisco: *Albores; Un siglo de poésia belga; El gavilán; Consideraciones sobre el español que se habla en México; Treguas líricas; Manuel Acuña.*

Castillo y Lanzas, Joaquín María del: "A la victoria de Tamaulipas"; *Ocios juveniles.*

Castro, Agustín de: *La Cortesíada.*

Castro, Dolores: *El corazón transfigurado; Dos nocturnos; Siete poemas*; *La tierra está sonando*; *Cantares de vela*; *La ciudad y el viento*.

Castro, José Agustín de: *El Charro*; *Exhortación privada a una novicia*; *Los remendones*; *Miscelánea de poesías sagradas y humanas*; *Vidas*.

Castro Leal, Antonio: *Las cien mejores poesías mexicanas modernas*; *La poesía mexicana moderna*; *Juan Ruiz de Alarcón: su vida y su obra*; collaborated on *Las cien mejores poesías (líricas) mexicanas*.

Cavo, Andrés: *Historia civil y política de México (Los tres siglos de México durante el gobierno español)*.

Ceballos, Ciro B.: *Un adulterio*.

Ceniceros y Villarreal, Rafael: *La siega*.

Cepeda, Francisco de: *Artes de los idiomas chiapaneco, zoque, tzendal y chinanteco*.

Cernuda, Luis: *La realidad y el deseo*; *Desolación de la Quimera*; *Perfil del aire*; *Donde habite el olvido*.

Cervantes de Salazar, Francisco: *Academia Mexicana*; *Civitas Mexicus interior*; *Crónica de Nueva España*; *Diálogos* (Vives); *Mexicus exterior*; *Obras que Francisco Cervantes de Salazar ha hecho, glosado y traducido*; *Túmulo imperial de la gran ciudad de México a las obsequias del invictísimo César Carlos V*.

Cetina, Gutierre de: *Flores de varia poesía*; *Paradoxa en alabanza de los cuernos*.

Clavijero, Francisco Javier: *Diálogo entre Filateles y Paleófilo*; *Disertaciones*; *Historia antigua de México*, translated into Italian as *Storia antica del Messico*; *Historia de la Antigua o Baja California*.

Clearco, Meonio; *see* Pagaza, Joaquín Arcadio.

Clímaco, San Juan: *Escala espiritual para llegar al cielo*.

Codex Ramírez; *see* Anónimo (El).

Cogolludo, Fr. Diego López de: *Historia de Yucatán*.

Colín, Eduardo: *La vida intacta*; *Mujeres*; *Rasgos*; *Siete cabezas*; *Verbo selecto*.

Cordero, Salvador: *Memorias de un juez de paz*; *Semblanzas lugareñas*.

Córdoba, Juan de: *Arte*; *Vocabulario zapoteca*.

Córdova, Luis: *Mr. Parker, Mr. Jenkins*; *Los alambrados*; *Cenzontle y otros cuentos*; *Lupe Lope y otros cuentos*; *La sirena precisa*; *Los negocios de Palacio van despacio*; *Tijeras y listones*; *Gran lago*.

Cortés, Antônio: *Hierros forjados*; *Valenciana*.

Cortés, Hernán: *Cartas de relación sobre el descubrimiento y conquista de la Nueva España*.

Cortina, Conde de la; *see* Gómez de la Cortina, José Justo.

Correa, Eduardo J.: *El milagro de milagros*; *Las almas solas*; *Los impostores*.

Couto, José Bernardo: *Diálogo sobre la historia de la pintura en México*; *Discurso sobre la constitución de la Iglesia*; contributed to *Diccionario universal de historia y geografía*.

Couto Castillo, José Bernardo: *Asfodelos*.

Cravioto, Alfonso: *El alma nueva de las cosas viejas*.

Cruz, Sor Juana Inés de la: "A la rosa"; *Amor es más laberinto*; *Athenagórica*; *Cetro de San José*; "Detente, sombra"; *El Divino Narciso*; "Hombres necios"; "Liras"; *Loa*; *Loa a la Concepción*; *Filotea*; "Romance de la ausencia"; *San Hermenegildo*; *Sonetos*; *Los empeños de una casa*; *Neptuno alegórico*; *Respuesta a Sor Sor Juana Inés de la Cruz, Obras escogidas*; *Sueño*; *Obras completas*.

Cuéllar, José Tomás de: *La Linterna Mágica*, general title of twenty-four volumes, including: *Baile y cochino*; *El pecado del siglo*; *Ensalada de pollos*; *Gabriel el cerrajero o las hijas de mi papá*; *Historia de Chucho el Ninfo*; *Las gentes que son así*; *Las jamonas*; *Los fuereños y la nochebuena*; *Los mariditos*.

Cuenca, Agustín F.: "A orillas del Atoyac"; "Carmen"; "La calleja"; "La montaña"; *Poemas Selectos*; "Rosa de fuego"; "Sol de agosto"; *La cadena de hierro*.

Cuesta, Jorge: *Ulises*; *Antología de la poesía mexicana moderna*; *Poemas y ensayos*.

Cueva, Juan de la: *Epístola*; *Obras*; contributed to *Flores de varia poesía*.

Cuevas, Jesús: *Magdalena*.

Cuevas, Luis Gonzaga: *Porvenir de México*.

Cuevas, Mariano: *Album histórico guadalupano del IV Centenario*; *Documentos inéditos del siglo XVI para la historia de México*; *Historia de la Iglesia en México*; *Historia de la nación mexicana*; *Monje ye marino: Urdaneta*; *El Libertador*.

Cumplido, Ignacio: *Presentes amistosos*.

Champourcín, Ernestina de: *La casa de enfrente*; *En silencio*; *Ahora*;

La voz en el viento; *El cántico inútil*; *Presencia a oscuras*; *El nombre que me diste*; *Cárcel de los sentidos*.

Chavero, Alfredo: *Bienaventurados los que esperan*; *El amor de su desdicha*; *El huracán de un beso*; *El mundo de ahora*; *El Sombrero*; *El valle de lágrimas*; *La ermita de Santa Fe* (in collaboration with Peón y Contreras); *La hermana de los Avilas*; *Los Amores de Alarcón*; *Quetzalcóatl*; *Sin esperanza*; *Xóchitl*; collaborated on *México a través de los siglos*; edited *Historia chichimeca*.

Chávez, Ezequiel A.: *Psicología de la adolescencia*; *Sor Juana Inés de la Cruz*.

Chávez, Gilberto: *Playa Paraíso*.

Chumacero, Alí: *Páramo de sueños*; *Imágenes desterradas*; *Palabras en reposo*.

Damón; *see* Ochoa y Acuña, Anastasio María de.

Dávalos, Balbino: *Las ofrendas*.

Dávalos, Marcelino: *Aguilas y estrellas*; *Así pasan . . .*; *El crimen de Marciano*; *El último cuadro*; *Guadalupe*; *Indisoluble*; *Jardines trágicos*; *Lo viejo*; *¡Viva el amo!*.

Dávalos Mora, Rafael: "*El Jorullo.*"

Dávila, María Amparo: *Salmos bajo la luna*; *Perfil de soledades*; *Meditaciones a la orilla del sueño*; *Tiempo destrozado*; *Música concreta*.

Dávila Padilla, Agustín: *Historia de la provincia de Santiago de México de la Orden de Predicadores*.

Delgado, Juan B.: *Canciones surianas*; *Poemas de los árboles*; *París y otros poemas*; *Bajo el haya de Títiro*; *El cancionero nómada*; *El país de Rubén Darío*.

Delgado, Rafael: *Angelina*; *Cuentos y notas*; *Historia vulgar*; *La Calandria*; *Los parientes ricos*.

D'Erzell, Catalina: *Apasionadamente*; *Cumbres de nieve*; *Chanito*; *El pecado de las mujeres*; *El rebozo azul*; *Esos hombres*; *La inmaculada*; *La razón de la culpa*; *La sin honor*; *Lo que sólo el hombre puede sufrir*; *Los hijos de la otra*; *Maternidad*.

Díaz Bartlett, Tomás: *Bajamar*; *Con displicencia de árbol*; *Oficio de cadáver*.

Díaz Covarrubias, Juan: *El diablo en México*; *Gil Gómez el Insurgente o la hija del médico*; *Impresiones y sentimientos*; *La clase media*; *La sensitiva*; *Páginas del corazón*.

Díaz de Gamarra, Benito: *Elementa Recentioris Philosophiae.*

Díaz del Castillo, Bernal: *Historia verdadera de la conquista de la Nueva España.*

Díaz Dufoo, Carlos: *Cuentos nerviosos*; *La evolución industrial de México*; *La fuente del Quijote*; *Limantour*; *La jefa*; *La vida económica*; *México y los capitales extranjeros*; *Padre mercader*; *Palabras*; *Sombra de Mariposas*; *Una victoria financiera.*

Díaz Dufoo, Jr., Carlos: *Epigramas.*

Díaz Mirón, Salvador: "A Byron"; "A Gloria"; *Astillas y Triunfos*; *Lascas*; "Oda a Víctor Hugo"; "Sursum"; *Poesías completas.*

Díez Barroso, Francisco: *El arte en Nueva España.*

Díez Barroso, Víctor Manuel: *Buena suerte*; *El y su cuerpo*; *En "El Riego"*; *Estampas*; *La muñeca rota*; *Las pasiones mandan*; *Siete obras en un acto*; *Una farsa*; *Una lágrima*; *Véncete a ti mismo.*

Díez Canedo, Enrique: *Versos de las horas*; *La visita del sol*; *Epigramas americanos*; *Jardinillo de E.D.C.*; *Sala de retratos*; *Conversaciones literarias*; *Los dioses en el Prado*; *El teatro y sus enemigos*; *La nueva poesía*; *Juan Ramón Jiménez en su obra*; *Letras de América*; *Literaturas continentales.*

Dorantes y Carranza, Baltasar: *Sumaria Relación.*

Dueñas, Guadalupe: *Las ratas y otros cuentos*; *Tiene la noche un árbol.*

Duque Job (El); *see* Gutiérrez Nájera, Manuel.

Durán, Diego: *Historia de las Indias de Nueva España y islas de Tierra Firme.*

Echáiz, Jesús: *Sahara de Córdoba o la Inquisición en México.*

Echeverría del Prado, Vicente: *Voces múltiples*; *Vida suspensa*; *De la materia suspirable*; *Tallos de abismo*; *Perfiles inviolados*; *Lindero Amor*; *En tiempo de Gacela.*

Eguiara y Eguren, Juan José de: *Anteloquia*; *Biblioteca Mexicana*; *Vidas.*

Elizondo, José F.: *Con las gafas alegres*; *Crótalos*; *Chin-Chun-Chan* (in collaboration with Rafael Medina); *El surco*; *Gansadas*; *La vendedora de besos*; *La vida en broma*; *Más de cien epigramas de Kien.*

Escobedo, Federico: *Poesías*; *Cauces hondos*; *Rapsodias bíblicas*; *Siempre antiguo y siempre nuevo*; *Aromas de leyenda*; *Geórgicas mexicanas.*

Escolano y Obregón, Francisco: *El miserable engañado o la niña de la media almendra.*

Eslava; *see* González de Eslava, Fernán.

Espinosa, Julio: *El ramo de azahar*; *Margarita*; *Calumnia.*

Espinosa Altamirano, Horacio: *Testimonio de América en la sangre*; *Haz de palomas*; *Canto humano*; *Playas del sol*; *Mexico City*; *Los signos del destierro*; *Oratorio del Sur.*

Esteva, José María: "El jarocho"; *La mujer blanca*; *Poesías*; *Tipos veracruzanos y composiciones varias.*

Esteva, Roberto A.: *Los Maurel.*

Estrada, Genaro: *Crucero*; *Escalera*; *Paso a nivel*; *Pero Galín*; *Senderillos a ras*; *Visionario de la Nueva España*; directed publication of *Monografías bibliográficas mexicanas.*

Fabela, Isidro: *La tristeza del amo*; *Los Estados Unidos contra la libertad*; *Los precursores de la diplomacia mexicana*; *Belice: defensa de los derechos de México.*

Facundo; *see* Cuéllar, José T. de.

Farfán, Agustín: *Tratado breve de medicina.*

Farías de Issasi, Teresa: *Ante el gran enigma*; *Cerebro y corazón*; *Como las aves*; *Fuerza creadora*; *Nupcial*; *Páginas de la vida*; *Religión de amor.*

Fernández, Justino: *El arte moderno en México*; *José Clemente Orozco: forma e idea*; *Coatlicue: estética del arte indígena antiguo.*

Fernández, Sergio: *Cinco escritores hispanoamericanos*; *Ensayos sobre literature española de los siglos XVI y XVII*; *Los signos perdidos*; *En tela de juicio.*

Fernández de Lizardi, José Joaquín ("El Pensador Mexicano"): *Auto Mariano para recordar la milagrosa aparición de Nuestra Madre y Señora de Guadalupe*; *El negro sensible*; *El Periquillo Sarniento*; *El unipersonal don Agustín de Iturbide*; *Fábulas*; *La noche más venturosa o el premio de la inocencia*; *La Quijotita y su prima*; *La Tragedia del Padre Arenas*; *Vida y hechos del famoso caballero D. Catrín de la Fachenda*; *Noches tristes y día alegre*; "Polaca en honor de Nuestro Católico monarca el señor Don Fernando Séptimo".

Fernández de Oviedo y Valdés, Gonzalo: *Historia general y natural de las Indias.*

Fernández de San Salvador, Agustín Pomposo: *Desengaños que a los insurgentes de Nueva España, seducidos por fracmasones agentes de Napoleón, dirige la verdad de la religión católica y la experiencia; El modelo de los cristianos presentado a los insurgentes de América;* "La América llorando por la temprana muerte de su amado, su padre, su bien y sus delicias, el Excmo. Sr. D. Bernardo de Gálvez, Conde de Gálvez"; *Las fazañas de Hidalgo, Quixote de nuevo cuño, facedor de tuertos . . . .*

Fernández Granados, Enrique: *Margaritas; Mirtos.*

Fernández Ledesma, Enrique: *Con la sed en los labios; Historia crítica de la tipografía en México: impresos del siglo XIX; Viajes al siglo XIX; Galería de fantasmas: años y sombras del siglo XIX.*

Fernández MacGrégor, Genaro: *Apunte crítico del arte contemporáneo; Carátulas; Díaz Mirón; Genaro Estrada; La santificación de Sor Juana; Mies tardía; Mora redivivo; Novelas triviales; Notas de un viaje extemporáneo.*

Ferretis, Jorge: *Tierra caliente; El Sur quema; Cuando engorda el Quijote; San Automóvil; Hombres en tempestad.*

Fidel; *see* Prieto, Guillermo.

Florencia, Francisco de: *Historia de la Provincia de la Compañía de Jesús de Nueva España.*

Flores, Manuel: *Italia.*

Flores, Manuel M.: "A Carmen"; "A Clementina"; "A Ramona"; "A Rosario"; "Bajo las palmas"; "Eva"; *Pasionarias;* "Tu imagen"; "Ven."

Frías, Heriberto: *Tomóchic.*

Frías, José D.: *Poesías escogidas.*

Fritz, Andrés: *Penélope.*

Fuente, Agustín de la: *Comedia de los Reyes.*

Fuentes, Carlos: *Los días enmascarados; La región más transparente; Las buenas conciencias; La muerte de Artemio Cruz; Aura; Cantar de ciegos; El héroe sin vida.*

Galindo, Sergio: *La máquina vacía; Polvos de arroz; La justicia de enero; El Bordo; La comparsa.*

Gallardo, Aurelio: *Adah o el amor de un ángel.*

Gallardo, Bartolomé José: *Ensayo.*

Gamboa, Federico: *A buena cuenta; Apariencias; Del natural; Entre hermanos; Impresiones y recuerdos; La llaga; La última campaña; La venganza de la gleba; Metamorfosis; Mi diario; Reconquista; Santa; Suprema ley.*

Gamboa, José Joaquín: *Cuento viejo; El caballero, la muerte y el diablo; El día del Juicio; El diablo tiene frío; El hogar; Ella; El mismo caso; Espíritus; La carne—o Teresa; La Muerte; Los Revillagigedos; ¡Si la juventud supiera!; Soledad; Teatro; Via Crucis.*

Gaona, Juan: *Colóquios de la paz y tranquilidad del alma.*

García, Genaro: *Carácter de la conquista española en América y en México; Documentos históricos mexicanos; Documentos inéditos o muy raros para la historia de México; Dos relaciones de la Florida; D. Juan de Palafox y Mendoza;* edited *Historia verdadera de la Conquista de la Nueva España.*

García, Rubén: *Bio-bibliografía del historiador Francisco Javier Clavijero; Biografía del General de División don Mariano Escobedo; Campañas de Morelos sobre Acapulco; Ataque y sitio de Cuautla; México antiguo: origen y desarrollo de las civilizaciones aborígenes.*

García Cantú, Gastón: *El Mediterráneo Americano; Cuadernos de notas; Papeles públicos; Utopías mexicanas; Los falsos rumores.*

García Cubas, Antonio: *El libro de mis recuerdos.*

García de Palacio, Diego: *Diálogos militares; Instrucción náutica.*

García Granados, Rafael: collaborated with Luis MacGrégor on *Huejotzingo: la ciudad y el convento franciscano.*

García Icazbalceta, Joaquín: *Apuntes para un catálogo de escritores en lenguas indígenas de América; Bibliografía Mexicana del Siglo XVI; Colección de documentos para la historia de México; Diccionario Universal de Historia y Geografía; Don Fray Juan de Zumárraga, Primer Obispo y Arzobispo de México; Nueva colección de documentos para la historia de México; Vocabulario de mexicanismos.*

García Iglesias, Sara: *El jagüey de las ruinas; Exilio.*

García Naranjo, Nemesio: *Discursos; El vendedor de muñecas; Porfirio Díaz; Simón Bolívar.*

García Ponce, Juan: *El canto de los grillos; La feria distante; Doce y una tres; Imagen primera; La noche; Figura de paja.*

García Roel, Adriana: *El hombre de barro.*

Garfias, Pedro: *El ala del sur; Poesías de la guerra española; Primavera en Eaton Hastings; Elegía a la presa Dnieprostoi; Viejos y nuevos poemas; Río de aguas amargas.*

Garibay K., Angel María: *Historia de la literatura náhuatl*; *Poesía indígena de la Altiplanicie*; *Panorama literario de los pueblos náhuas*; *La literatura de los aztecas*; *Historia Antigua y de la Conquista de México*; collaborated with Miguel León Portilla on *Visión de los vencidos*.

Garizurieta, César: *Singladura*; *Resaca*; *El apóstol del ocio*; *Un trompo baila en el cielo*; *El diablo, el cura y otros engaños*; *Memorias de un niño de pantalón largo*; *Juanita "la lloviznita"*; *Catarsis del mexicano*; *Isagoge sobre el mexicano*.

Garro, Elena: *Andarse por las ramas*; *Los pilares de doña Blanca*; *Un hogar sólido*; *La señora en su balcón*; *Los recuerdos del porvenir*; *La semana de colores*.

Gastélum, Bernardo J.: *Deshumanización del hombre*; *Física de la actitud*; *Inteligencia y símbolo*.

Gilberti, Maturino: *Diálogo de la Doctrina Cristiana*; *Gramática*; *Tesoro espiritual*; *Vocabulario*.

Giner de los Ríos, Francisco: *Floresta*; *La rama viva*; *Pasión primera*; *Romancerillo de la fe*; *Los laureles de Oaxaca*; *Notas y poemas de un viaje*; *Jornada hecha*; *Poemas mexicanos*.

Godoy, Emma: *Erase un hombre pentafácico*; *Caín y el hombre*; *Pausas y arena*.

Godoy, Jorge de: *El libro de las rosas virreinales*.

Gómara, Francisco López de: *Historia general de las Indias*; *Historiadores primitivos de Indias*.

Gómez de la Cortina, José Justo: *Biografía de Pedro Mártir de Anglería*; *Diccionario de sinónimos castellanos*; *Diccionario manual de voces técnicas castellanas en Bellas Artes*; *Euclea o la griega de Trieste*; *Leonor*; *Life in Mexico*; *Nociones elementales de numismática*.

Gómez de la Vega, Alfredo: *El teatro en la U.R.S.S.*

Gómez Morín, Manuel: *España fiel*.

Gómez Palacio, Martín: *A flor de la vida*; *A la una, a las dos y a las . . .* ; *El mejor de los mundos posibles*; *El santo horror*; *La loca imigración*; *La venda, la balanza y la ejpá*; *El potro*.

Gómez Ugarte, José: *Cuentas de mi rosario*; *El pan nuestro de cada día*; *Predicando en el desierto*.

González, José Luis: *En la sombra*; *Cinco cuentos de sangre*; *El hombre en la calle*; *En este lado*; *Paisa*.

González Caballero, Antonio: *Señoritas a disgusto*; *El medio pelo*; *Una pura . . . y dos con sal.*

González Casanova, Henrique: "Reseña de la poesía mexicana del siglo XX"; "Estado actual de la literatura mexicana"; "Los novelistas mexicanos de la Revolución."

González Dávila, Gil: *Teatro eclesiástico de las Iglesias de Indias.*

González de Eslava, Fernán: *Coloquios espirituales y sacramentales y poesías sagradas*; "El bosque divino"; "Coloquio de la Consagración del Arzobispo Moya de Contreras."

González de la Puente, Juan: *Crónica de Michoacán.*

González de Mendoza, José María: *La pintura de Angel Zárraga*; *Algunos pintores del Salón de Otoño*; *Biógrafos de Cervantes y Críticos del Quijote.*

González de Sancha, José: *Fabiano y Aurelia.*

González Guerrero, Francisco: *Poesías completas*; *Los libros de los otros*; *Ad altere Dei*; *Persiguiendo un sueño.*

González León, Francisco: *Campanas de la tarde*; *Megalomanías*; *Maquetas*; *De mi libro de horas*; *Agenda.*

González Martínez, Enrique: *Algunos aspectos de la lírica mexicana*; *Ausencia y canto*; *El diluvio de fuego*; *El libro de la fuerza, de la bondad y del ensueño*; *El romero alucinado*; *Jardines de Francia*; *Lirismos*; *La muerte del cisne*; *La palabra del viento*; *Las señales furtivas*; *Los senderos ocultos*; *Parábolas y otros poemas*; *Poemas truncos*; *Preludios*; *Silénter*; *Poemas*; *Bajo el signo mortal*; *Segundo despertar*; *Vilano al viento*; *Babel*; *El hombre del buho: Misterio de una vocación*; *La apacible locura.*

González Obregón, Luis: *Anuario bibliográfico nacional*; *Breve noticia de los novelistas mexicanos en el siglo XIX*; *Croniquillas de la Nueva España*; *Cronistas e historiadores*; *Cuauhtémoc*; *D. José Fernando Ramírez, datos bio-bibliográficos*; *Don Guillén de Lampart: La Inquisición y la Independencia en el siglo XVII*; *Don José Joaquín Fernández de Lizardi*; *Don Justo Sierra historiador*; *El Capitán Bernal Díaz del Castillo, conquistador y cronista de Nueva España*; *Fray Melchor de Talamantes, biografía y escritos póstumos*; *La Biblioteca Nacional de México*; *Las calles de México*; *La vida en México en 1810*; *Los precursores de la Independencia en el siglo XVI*; *México viejo*; *Novelistas mexicanos*; *Reseña histórica de las obras del desagüe del Valle de México*; *Vetusteces.*

González Peña, Carlos: *De noche*; *La chiquilla*; *La fuga de la quimera*; *La musa bohemia*; *La vida tumultuosa: seis semanas en los Estados Unidos*; *El patio bajo la luna* (*Escenas y paisajes laguenses*); *Flores de pasión y de melancolía*; *El hechizo musical*; *Gente mía*; *El nicho iluminado*; *Mirando pasar la vida*; *Claridad en la lejanía*; *El alma y la máscara*; *Más allá del mar*; *París y Londres*; *Por tierras de Italia, Portugal y España*.

González Rojo, Enrique: *El puerto y otros poemas*; *Espacio*.

Gorostiza, Celestino: *La escuela del amor*; *Ser o no ser*; *El color de su piel*; *Columna social*.

Gorostiza, José: *Canciones para cantar en las barcas*; *Muerte sin fin*.

Gorostiza, Manuel Eduardo de: *Apéndice al teatro escogido*; *Cartilla política*; *Contigo pan y cebolla*; *Don Bonifacio*; *Don Dieguito*; *Indulgencia para todos*; *Las costumbres de antaño*; *Obras de D. Manuel Eduardo de Gorostiza*; *Tal para cual o las mujeres y los hombres*; *Teatro escogido*; *Teatro original*; wrote introduction to "Contestaciones habidas entre la Legación extraordinaria de México y el Departamento de Estado de Estados Unidos"; adapted *Bien vengas mal si vienes solo* (*También hay secreto en mujer*); *El amigo íntimo*; *El Jugador*; *Emilia Galotti*; *Lo que son mujeres*; arranged *Estela o el padre y la hija*; *La hija del payaso*; *La madrina*; *Paulina o ¿se sabe quién mueve los alambres?*; *Un enlace aristocrático*; *Vale un apuro*.

Goytortúa, José: *Pensativa*.

Granados, Joaquín: *Tardes americanas*.

Granja, Juan de la: *Epistolario*.

Grijalva, Juan de: *Crónica de la Provincia de México*; *Historia de San Guillermo, Duque de Aquitania*.

Guadalajara, José Rafael: *Amalia, páginas del primer amor*.

Guadalupe, Marqués de; *see* Rincón Gallardo, Carlos.

Guerra, José; *see* Mier, Servando Teresa de.

Guerrero, Jesús R.: *Los olvidados*; *El diputado Taffoyat*; *Oro blanco*; *Los días apagados*; *El punto final*; *El corral pintado*; *Reflejos de luz humana*.

Guevara, Juan de: collaborated on *Amor es más laberinto*.

Guisa y Azevedo, Jesús: *Lovaina, de donde vengo* . . . .

Guridi y Alcocer, Miguel: *Apuntes de su vida*; *Arte de la lengua latina*; *Cantos de las musas mexicanas*; *Curso de filosofía moderna*; *Discurso sobre los daños del juego*.

Gutiérrez, Alonso; *see* Veracruz, Alonso de la.

Gutiérrez Hermosillo, Alfonso: *Itinerario*.

Gutiérrez Najera, Manuel: *Cuentos color de humo*; *Cuentos frágiles*; "De blanco"; "Dios"; "Hamlet a Ofelia"; "Historia de un peso falso"; "La Cruz"; "La Duquesa Job"; "La fe de mi infancia"; "La serenata de Schubert"; "María"; "Mariposas"; "Monólogo del incrédulo"; "Mis enlutadas"; "*Non omnis moriar*"; *Odas breves*; "¿Para qué?"; "*Pax animae*"; "Rip-Rip"; "Tristissima Nox"; *Poesias completas*.

Guzmán, Martín Luis: *A orillas del Hudson*; *El águila y la serpiente*; *La sombra del caudillo*; *Memorias de Pancho Villa*; *Mina el Mozo, héroe de Navarra*; *La querella de México*; *Apunte sobre una personalidad*.

Henestrosa, Andrés: *Los hombres que dispersó la danza*; *Retrato de mi madre*.

Henríquez Ureña, Pedro: collaborated on *Antología del Centenario*.

Heredia, José María de: Cuban author of "Al Níagara"; "El Teocalli de Cholula."

Hernández, Efrén: *Tachas*; *El señor de palo*; *Cuentos*; *Cerrazón sobre Nicómaco*; *La paloma, el sótano y la torre*; *Hora de horas*; *Entre apagados muros*; *Obra completa*.

Hernández, Luisa Josefina: *Aguardiente de caña*; *Botica Modelo*; *Los frutos caídos*; *Los huéspedes reales*; *Arpas blancas . . . conejos dorados*; *La paz ficticia*; *Historia de un anillo*; *La calle de la gran ocasión*; *El lugar donde crece la hierba*; *La plaza de Puerto Santo*; *Los palacios desiertos*; *La cólera secreta*.

Herrera y Ogazón, Alba: *Historia de la Música*.

Herrera y Tordesillas, Antonio de: *Décadas o Historia general de los hechos de los castellanos en las islas y tierra firme del Mar Océano*; *Historia general de Indias*.

Hidalgo, José Manuel: *La confesión de una mundana*; *La sed de oro*; *Lelia y Mariana*; *Víctimas del chic*.

Hinojosa, Antonio de: *Vida y milagros del glorioso San Jacinto*.

Horta, Manuel: *Estampas de antaño*; *Vida ejemplar de D. José de la Borda*; *Vitrales de capilla*; *Ponciano Díaz: silueta de un torero de ayer*.

Huerta, Efraín: *Absoluto amor; Línea del alba; Los hombres del alba; Poemas de guerra y esperanza; La rosa primitiva; Poesía; Poemas de viaje; Estrella en alto y nuevos poemas; Para gozar tu paz; ¡Mi país, oh mi país!; Elegía de la policía montada; Farsa trágica del presidente que quería una isla; La raíz amarga; El Tajín.*

Ibargüengoitia, Jorge: *Susana y los jóvenes; La lucha con el ángel; La conspiración vendida; El atentado; Los relámpagos de agosto.*

Icaza, Francisco A. de: *Cancionero de la vida honda y de la emoción fugitiva; De cómo y por qué la Tía Fingida no es de Cervantes; Diccionario autobiográfico de conquistadores y pobladores de Nueva España; Efímeras; El Quijote durante tres siglos; Examen de críticos; La canción del camino; La Universidad Alemana; Las novelas ejemplares de Cervantes; Lejanías; Lope de Vega: sus amores y sus odios; Sucesos reales que parecen imaginados de Gutierre de Cetina, Juan de la Cueva y Mateo Alemán; Supercherías y errores cervantinos.*

Icaza, Xavier: *Dilema; Gente mexicana; Panchito Chapopote.*

Iduarte, Andrés: *José Martí, escritor; Un niño en la Revolución Mexicana; Pláticas hispanoamericanas; Veinte años con Rómulo Gallegos; Alfonso Reyes: el hombre y su mundo; Don Pedro de Alba y su tiempo; Gabriela Mistral, santa a la jineta.*

Iguíniz, Juan B.: *Bibliografía de novelistas mexicanos; La imprenta en la Nueva España; Bibliografía biográfica mexicana; Bibliografía de los escritores de la Compañía de Jesús; México bibliográfico.*

Inclán, Federico S.: *Luces de carburo; Hoy invita la güera; Hidalgo; Espaldas mojadas cruzan el Bravo; El duelo.*

Inclán, Luis G.: *Astucia, el Jefe de los Hermanos de la Hoja o los charros contrabandistas de la Rama.*

Ipandro; *see* Montes de Oca y Obregón, Ignacio.

Ixtlilxóchitl, Fernando de Alva: *Historia chichimeca; Relación de pobladores; Relaciones.*

Jiménez, Guillermo: *Almas inquietas; Cuaderno de notas; Del pasado; La danza en México; La de los ojos oblicuos; Zapotlán.*

Jiménez Rueda, Julio: *Bajo la Cruz del Sur; Como en la vida; Cuentos y diálogos; Don Pedro Moya de Contreras, primer Inquisidor de México; El rival de su mujer; Herejías y supersticiones en la Nueva España (Los Heterodoxos en México); Historia de la literatura mexicana; Juan Ruiz de Alarcón; Juan Ruiz de Alarcón y su tiempo*; *La caída de las flores*; *La desventura del Conde Kadski*; *La silueta de humo*; *Letras mexicanas en el siglo XIX*; *Lope de Vega*; *Miramar*; *Moisén*; *Sor Adoración*; *Sor Adoración del Divino Verbo*; *Tempestad en las costumbres*.

Junco, Alfonso: *Carranza y los orígenes de su rebelión*; *Cosas que arden*; *Cristo*; *El alma estrella*; *Fisonomías*; *Florilegio eucarístico*; *Gente de México*; *Inquisición sobre la Inquisición*; *La divina aventura*; *La traición de Querétaro*; *Lope ecuménico*; *Lumbre de México*; *Motivos mexicanos*; *Por la senda suave*; *Posesión*; *Sangre de Hispania*; *Savia*; *Un radical problema guadalupano*; *Un siglo de México*.

Kino, P.: *Libra astronómica y filosófica*.

Lagunas, Juan Bautista de: *Arte*; *Diccionario breve*.

Lamb, Ruth S.: collaborated with Antonio Magaña Esquivil on *Breve historia del teatro mexicano*.

Landívar, Rafael: *Rusticatio Mexicana*.

Leal, Luis: *Antología del cuento mexicano*; *Anuario del cuento mexicano*; *Bibliografía del cuento mexicano*; *Breve historia del cuento mexicano*; *La Revolución y las letras*.

Leduc, Alberto: *Fragatita*; *María del Consuelo*; *Un Calvario*.

Leiva, Raúl: *Angustia*; *Danza para Cuauhtémoc*; *Aguila oscura*. *Poemas a Benito Juárez*; *Imagen de la poesía mexicana contemporánea*.

León, Nicolás: *Bibliografía mexicana del siglo XVIII*.

León Felipe; *see* Camino y Galicia, León Felipe.

León Portilla, Miguel: *Siete ensayos sobre cultura náhuatl*; *Ritos, sacerdotes y atavíos de los dioses*; *Los antiguos mexicanos a través de sus crónicas y cantares*; *La filosofía náhuatl estudiada en sus fuentes*; *Imágenes del México antiguo*; *Las literaturas precolombinas de México*; *El reverso de la Conquista*; collaborated with Angel María Garibay K. on *Visión de los vencidos*.

Lerdo, Francisco: *Luisa*; *Vanidad y pobreza*.

Lira, Miguel N.: *Corrido de Domingo Arenas*; *La escondida*; *Vuelta a la tierra*; *Linda*; *Carlota de México*; *Donde crecen los tepozanes*; *Una mujer en soledad*; *Mientras la muerte llega: Novela de la Revolución*.

López, Rafael: *Con los ojos abiertos*; *Poemas*.

López de Cogolludo, Fr. Diego; *see* Cogolludo, Fr. Diego López de.

López de Gómara; *see* Gómara, Francisco López de.

López de Hinojoso, Alonso: *Suma y recopilación de Cirugía.*

López Páez, Jorge: *El que espera . . .*; *Los mástiles*; *La última visita*; *El solitario Atlántico*; *Los invitados de piedra*; *Hacia el amargo mar.*

López Portillo y Rojas, José: "Adalinda"; *Armonías fugitivas*; "El arpa"; "El espejo"; "El primer amor"; *Elevación y caída de Porfirio Díaz*; *Fuertes y débiles*; *Historias, historietas y cuentecillos*; *Impresiones de viaje*; "La horma de su zapato"; *La parcela*; *Los precursores*; "Nieves"; *Novelas cortas*; *Rosario de la Acuña*; *Seis leyendas*; *Sucesos y novelas cortas*; "Un pacto con el diablo"; "La fuga"; *Cuentos completos.*

López Velarde, Ramón: *El minutero*; *El son del corazón*; *La sangre devota*; *Zozobra*; *Poesías completas.*

López y Fuentes, Gregorio: *Arrieros*; *Campamento*; *Claros de selva*; *El indio*; *Huasteca*; *La siringa de cristal*; *Mi general*; *Tierra*; *Acomodaticio: novela de un político de convicciones*; *Los peregrinos inmóviles*; *Entresuelo*; *Milpa, potrero y monte.*

Lozano García, Carlos and Lázaro: *Al fin mujer*; *El Chacho*; *Estudiantina*; *La incomprendida.*

Luquín, Eduardo: *Agua de sombra.*

Llach, Leonor: *Gente conocida.*

MacGrégor, Luis: collaborated with Rafael García Granados on *Huejotzingo: la ciudad y el convento franciscano.*

Magaloni, Humberto: *Hontanar.*

Magaña, Sergio: *Los signos del zodíaco*; *Moctezuma II*; *El pequeño caso de Jorge Lívido*; *Los motivos del lobo*; *Medea 1965*; *El ángel roto*; *El padre nuestro*; *Los suplicantes*; *El molino del aire.*

Magaña Esquivil, Antonio: *El ventrílocuo*; *La tierra enrojecida*; *Imagen del teatro*; *Sueño y realidad del teatro*; *El teatro y el cine*; *Semilla del aire*; *El sitio y la hora*; collaborated with Ruth S. Lamb on *Breve historia del teatro mexicano.*

Magdaleno, Mauricio: *Pánuco 137*; *Emiliano Zapata y Trópico*; *Teatro revolucionario mexicano*; *Campo Celis*; *Concha Bretón*; *El resplandor*; *Sonata*; *La tierra grande*; *Cabello de elote*; *Rango*; *Tierra y viento.*

Maillefert, Alfredo: *Laudanza de Michoacán*; *Ancla en el tiempo*; *Los libros que leí.*

Maldonado, Francisco Severo: *Contrato de asociación para la república de los Estados Unidos del Anáhuac*; *El triunfo de la especie humana*.

Mancisidor, José: *Cuentos mexicanos del siglo XIX*; *Cuentos mexicanos de autores contemporáneos*; *La asonada*; *La ciudad roja*; *Frontera junto al mar*; *El alba en las simas*; *La primera piedra*.

Maneiro, Juan Luis: *Vidas de varones ilustres mexicanos*; *Poemas inéditos*.

Manterola, Ramón: *Isabel Lupouloff*.

Mañón, Manuel: *Historia del Teatro Principal de México*.

Maples Arce, Manuel: *Andamios interiores*; *Urbe*.

Maqueo Castellanos, Esteban: *La ruina de la casona*.

María Enriqueta; *see* Camarillo de Pereyra, María Enriqueta.

Mariscal, Federico E.: *La patria y la arquitectura nacional*.

Marqués de San Francisco; *see* Romero de Terreros, Manuel.

Martí, Manuel: *Cartas latinas*.

Marroqui, José María: *La ciudad de México*.

Martínez, José Luis: *Literatura mexicana: siglo XX*; *El ensayo mexicano moderno*; *La expresión nacional*.

Mata, Filomeno: edited Altamirano's *Cuentos de invierno*.

Mateos, Juan A.: *Borrascas de un sobretodo*; *El ave negra*; *El novio oficial*; *El otro*; *El plagio*; *El sol de Mayo*; *La catarata del Niágara*; *La hija del cantero*; *La Monja Alférez*; *La muerte de Lincoln*; *La Politicomanía*; *La rubia y la morena*; *Los dramas de México*; *Los grandes tahures*; *Los insurgentes*; *Martín el demente*; *Odio hereditario*; *Sacerdote y caudillo*; *Sor Angélica*.

Maza, Francisco de la: *San Miguel Allende: Su historia: Sus monumentos*.

Medina, Baltasar de: *Crónicas de la Provincia de San Diego de México*.

Medina, Rafael: collaborated with José F. Elizondo on *Chin-Chun-Chan*.

Mediz Bolio, Antonio: *El Libro de Chilam Balam de Chumayel*; *En medio del camino*; *Evocaciones*; *La flecha del Sol*; *La ola*; *La tierra del faisán y del venado*; *Canto del hijo de Yucatán*; *Interinfluencia del maya con el español de Yucatán*.

Mejía Sánchez, Ernesto: *Obras completas* (de Alfonso Reyes); *La impureza*; *Contemplaciones europeas*; *Cuentos completos de Rubén*

Darío; *Los primeros cuentos de Rubén Darío*; *Poesía de Rubén Darío*.

Melo, Juan Vicente: *La noche alucinada*; *Los muros enemigos*; *Fin de semana*.

Méndez Plancarte, Alfonso: published Sor Juana Inés de la Cruz's *Obras completas: Lírica personal*; *Villancicos y letras sacras*; *Teatro sacro y profano*; *Prosa*.

Méndez Plancarte, Gabriel: *Horacio en México*.

Méndez Rivas, Joaquín: *Cuauhtémoc*; *Geórgicas*; *Los poemas estudiantiles*; *Madrigales escritos con sangre*.

Mendieta, Jerónimo de: *Cartas*; *Historia eclesiástica indiana*.

Mendieta y Núñez, Lucio: *La caravana infinita*.

Mendizábal, Luis de: "El asno, el caballo y el mulo."

Mendoza, Héctor: *Ahogados*; *Las cosas simples*; *Salpícame de amor*; *¡A la Beocia!*.

Mendoza, Vicente D.: *El romance español y el corrido mexicano*.

Menéndez, Miguel Angel: *Hollywood sin pijamas*; *Otro libro*; *Canto a la Revolución*; *El rumbo de los versos*; *Nayar*; *Malintzin*; *Vida y muerte de Kennedy*.

Mexía, Luis: "Apólogo de la ociosidad y el trabajo."

Michael, Alberto: *Ad majorem Dei gloriam*; *El novio número 13*; *Monerías*.

Michelena, Margarita: *Paraíso y nostalgia*; *Laurel del ángel*; *Tres poemas y una nota autobiográfica*; *La tristeza terrestre*.

Mier, Servando Teresa de: *Apología y relaciones de su vida*; *Historia de la revolución de Nueva España*; *Memorias*.

Millán, María del Carmen: *El piasaje en la poesía mexicana*; *Ideas de la Reforma en las letras patrias*; *El Modernismo de Othón*; *La Generación del Ateneo y el ensayo mexicano*; *Cuentos americanos*; *Poesía romántica mexicana*; *Ocios y Apuntes y La Rumba*; *Cosas vistas y Cartones*; *Literatura mexicana*.

Mimenza Castillo, Ricardo: *Elitros*; *El libro de Teresita*; *El Romancero de Yucatán*; *Laúdes del Mayab*; *Rebeldía*; *Violetas de mayo*.

Mojarro, Tomás: *Cañón de Juchipila*; *Bramadero*.

Molina, Alonso de: *Arte mexicano*; *Vocabulario castellano-mexicano*; *Vocabulario mexicano-castellano*.

Mondragón, Magdalena: *Puede que l'otro año*; *Yo como pobre*; *Norte bárbaro*; *Más allá existe la tierra*; *El día no llega*; *Tenemos sed*.

Monterde, Francisco: *Amado Nervo*; *Bibliografía del Teatro en México*; *Cuentos mexicanos*; *El madrigal de Cetina*; *El secreto de la escala*; *En defensa de una obra y de una generación*; *En el remolino*; *Galería de espejos*; *Itinerario contemplativo*; *La que volvió a la vida*; *Los virreyes de la Nueva España*; *Manuel Gutiérrez Nájera*; *Oro negro*; *Perfiles de Taxco*; *Un autor novel*; *Viviré por ti*; *Agustín F. Cuenca: el prosista, el poeta de transición*; *Cultura mexicana*; *El temor de Hernán Cortés*; *Moctezuma, el de la silla de oro*.

Monterroso, Augusto: *El concierto y el eclipse*; *Uno de cada tres y El Centenario*; *Obras completas y otros cuentos*.

Montes de Oca, Marco Antonio: *Ruina de la infame Babilonia*; *Contrapunto de la fe*; *Pliego de testimonios*; *Delante de la luz cantan los pájaros*; *Cantos al sol que no se alcanza*; *Fundación del entusiasmo*; *La parcela en el Edén*.

Montes de Oca y Obregón, Ignacio: *A orillas de los ríos: Cien sonetos*; *Fiesco*; *Nuevo centenar de sonetos*; *Obras de Píndaro*; *Obras pastorales y oratorias*; *Ocios poéticos*; *Otros cien sonetos de Ipandro Acaico*; *Poetas bucólicos griegos*; *Recuerdos y meditaciones de un peregrino en el Castillo de Miramar*; *Sonetos jubilares*.

Mora, José María Luis: *Catecismo político de la Federación Mexicana*; *Disertación sobre la naturaleza y aplicación de las rentas y bienes eclesiásticos*; *México y sus revoluciones*; *Obras sueltas*.

Morales, Vicente: *Sofía*.

Moreno Villa, José: *Garba*; *El pasajero*; *Luchas de Penas y Alegrías y su transfiguración*; *Evoluciones*; *Jacinta, la pelirroja*; *Carambas*; *Puentes que no acaban*; *Salón sin muros*; *Puerta severa*; *La noche del Verbo*; *La música que llevaba*; *Voz en vuelo a su cuna*; *La escultura colonial mexicana*; *Vida en claro*; *Lo mexicano en las artes plásticas*; *Cornucopia de México*.

Moreno y Oviedo, Antonio: *Incienso en el rescoldo*; *Pátina*.

Mota Padilla, Matías de la: *Historia de la Nueva Galicia*.

Motolinia (Toribio de Benavente): *Camino del Espíritu*; *Carta al Emperador Carlos V*; *Carta de Fr. Toribio de Motolinia y Fr. Diego de Olarte a D. Luis de Velasco, Virrey de la Nueva España, sobre los tributos que pagaban los indios antes de su conversión*; *Doctrina cristiana en lengua mexicana*; *Guerra de los Indios de Nueva España*; *Historia de los Indios de Nueva España* (published in Lord Kingsborough's *Antiquities of Mexico*) ; *Memoriales*; *Tratados de materias espirituales y devotas*; *Venida de los doce primeros padres y lo que llegados acá hicieron.*

Muñoz, Rafael Felipe: *El feroz cabecilla*; *El hombre malo*; *Francisco Villa*; *Santa Anna, biografía de un dictador*; *Santa Anna, el que todo lo ganó y todo lo perdió*; *Si me han de matar mañana*; *¡Vámonos con Pancho Villa!*; *Se llevaron el cañón para Bachimba.*

Muñoz Camargo, Diego: *Historia de Tlaxcala.*

Muñoz Camargo, Pedro: "Exaltación magnífica de la Betlemítica rosa de la mejor americana jericó, y acción gratulatoria por su plausible plantación dichosa, etc., etc."

Muñoz de Castro, Pedro: "Ecos de las cóncavas del Monte Carmelo y resonantes balidos tristes de las Raqueles ovejas del aprisco de Elías carmelitano sol con cuyos ardores derritidos en llanto sus hijas las religiosas carmelitanas de México lamentan la pérdida de su amantísimo benefactor el Excmo. Sr. D. Fernando de Lencastre Noroña y Silva, Virrey que fue desta Nueva España."

Navarrette, José Manuel Martínez de: *Entretenimientos poéticos.*

Nervo, Amado: *Almas que pasan*; *Amnesia*; *Cuentos misteriosos*; *El arquero divino*; *El Bachiller*; *El diablo desinteresado*; *El diamante de la inquietud*; *El donador de almas*; *El estanque de los lotos*; *El exodo y las flores del camino*; *El sexto sentido*; *Elevación*; *En voz baja*; *Juana de Asbaje*; *La amada inmóvil*; *La Hermana Agua*; *Lira heroica*; *Los jardines interiores*; *Mañana del poeta*; *Místicas*; *Obras completas*; *Pascual Aguilera*; *Perlas negras*; *Plenitud*; *Poemas*; *Serenidad*; *Una mentira*; *Un sueño.*

Noriega, Eduardo: *La mejor venganza*; *Un viaje al otro mundo.*

Noriega Hope, Carlos: *Che Ferrati*; *La señorita Voluntad*; *Margarita de Arizona*; *Una Flapper.*

Novelo, José I.: *Abril*; *El hombre y otros poemas*; *Ultimo abril*; *Ultimas rosas.*

Novo, Salvador: *A ocho columnas*; *Canto a Teresa*; *Continente vacío*; *Décimas en el mar*; *El joven*; *En defensa de lo usado*; *Ensayos*; *Espejo*; *Ha vuelto Ulises*; *Jalisco-Michoacán*; *La culta dama*; *La educación literaria de los adolescentes*; *La guerra de las gordas*; *La poesía francesa moderna*; *La poesía norteamericana moderna*; *Le troisième Faust*; *Nuevo amor*; *Poesía*; *Return Ticket*; *Romance de Angelillo y Adela*; *Seamen Rhymes*; *XX Poemas*; *Nueva grandeza mexicana (Ensayo sobre la ciudad de México y sus alrededores en 1946)*; *Las aves en la poesía castellana*; *Toda la prosa*; *Yocasta, o casi*; assisted in the preparation of *Lecturas clásicas para niños*.

Núñez y Domínguez, José de J.: *Al margen de la historia*; *Cuentos mexicanos*; *El inútil dolor*; *El rebozo*; *Espuma de mar*; *Gestas del solar nativo: relatos históricos del Estado de Veracruz*; *Holocaustos*; *La hora del Ticiano*; *Las alas abiertas*; *Los poetas jóvenes de México y otros estudios nacionalistas*; *Martí en México*; *Música suave*; *Poesías selectas*; *Un virrey limeño en México: D. Juan de Acuña, marqués de Casa Fuerte*; *El imaginero del amor*; *Ventura García Calderón*; *Escritores franceses contemporáneos*; *Historia y tauromaquia mexicana*; *Rómulo Gallegos y la novela hispanoamericana*; *La coalición de Oriente*; *La Virreina Mexicana*.

Obregón, Baltasar de: *Historia de los descubrimientos antiguos y modernos de la Nueva España*.

Ocampo, María Luisa: *Castillos en el aire*; *Cosas de la vida*; *El corrido de Juan Saavedra*; *La casa en ruinas*; *La hoguera*; *La jauría*; *Más allá de los hombres*; *Sed en el desierto*; *Sin alas*; *Una vida de mujer*; *Bajo el fuego*; *La maestrita*; *Ha muerto el doctor Benavides*; *Atitlayapan*; *Sombras en la arena*; *El señor de Altamira*; *Cosas de la vida*; *Las máscaras*; *La virgen fuerte*.

Ochoa y Acuña, Anastasio María de: *Don Alfonso*; *Poesías de un mexicano*.

Ochoa, Antonio: *Sucesos de Fernando o La caída de Fernando*.

Olaguíbel, Francisco M. de: *Canciones de bohemia*; *Rosas de amor y de dolor*.

Olavarría y Ferrari, Enrique de: *Episodios Históricos Mexicanos*; *Los misioneros del amor*; *Reseña histórica del teatro en México*; collaborated on *México a través de los siglos*.

Olmos, Andrés de: *Gramática mexicana*; *Juicio Final*.

Orozco Muñoz, Francisco: *Bélgica en la paz*; *Invasión y conquista de la Bélgica mártir*; *¡Oh, tú que comienzas a tener un pasado!*; *Renglones de Sevilla*.

Orozco y Berra, Fernando: "Al sepulcro de una niña"; *La guerra de treinta años*.

Orozco y Berra, Manuel: *Apéndice* to *Diccionario Universal de Historia y Geografía*; *Estudio de cronología mexicana*; *Geografía de las lenguas y Carta y etnográfica de México*; *Historia antigua y de la conquista de México*; *Historia de la dominación española en México* (published in four volumes of *Biblioteca Histórica Mexicana de Obras Inéditas*); *Materiales para una cartografía mexicana*; *Memoria para el plano de la ciudad de México*; *Noticia histórica de la conjuración del Marqués del Valle*.

Ortega, Francisco: "A Iturbide en su coronación"; "A los ojos de Delia"; "La venida del Espíritu Santo"; *México libre*; drafted *Bases orgánicas*; prepared notes and appendix for Veytia's *Historia antigua de México*.

Ortiz de Montellano, Bernardo: *Antología de cuentos mexicanos*; *Avidez*; *El trompo de siete colores*; *Muerte de cielo azul*; *Primer sueño*; *Red*; *Sueños*; *Cinco horas sin corazón*; *El Sombrerón*; *Figura, amor y muerte de Amado Nervo*.

Othón, Manuel José: *Después de la muerte*; *El último capítulo*; *La gleba*; *Lo que hay detrás de la dicha*; *Poemas rústicos*; *Poesías*; *Obras completas*.

Owen, Gilberto: *Novela como nube*; *Poesía y prosa*; *Primeros versos*.

Pacheco, José Emilio: *Los elementos de la noche*; *La sangre de Medusa*; *El viento distante*.

Pagaza, Joaquín Arcadio: *Algunas trovas íntimas*; *María: fragmentos de un poema descriptivo de la tierra caliente*; *Murmurios de la selva*; *Reto*.

Parada León, Ricardo: *La esclava*; *Los culpables*; *La agonía*; *Una noche de otoño*; *El dolor de los demás*; *El porvenir del Doctor Gallardo*; *Camino real*; collaborated with María Luisa O'Campo in *Sin alas*.

Pardo García, Germán: *Lucero sin orillas*; *Acto poético*; *U. Z. llama al espacio*; *Eternidad del ruiseñor*; *Hay piedras como lágrimas*; *Centauro al sol*; *Osiris preludial*; *La cruz del sur*; *Los ángeles de vidrio*; *El cosmonauta*; *El defensor*.

Parra, Manuel de la: *Visiones lejanas*.

Parra, Porfirio: *Pacotillas*.

Paso y Troncoso, Francisco del: *Anales del Museo Nacional*; *Epistolario de la Nueva España*.

Payno, Manuel: *El fistol del diablo*; *El hombre de la situación*; *Los bandidos de Río Frío*; *Tardes nubladas*.

Paz, Ireneo: *Algunas campañas*; *Amor y suplicio*; *Doña Marina*.

Paz, Octavio: *Raíz del hombre*; *Bajo tu clara sombra*; *Entre la piedra y la flor*; *A la orilla del mundo*; *Libertad bajo palabra*; *El laberinto de la soledad*; *El arco y la lira*; *Las peras del olmo*; *¿Aguila o sol?*; *Semillas para un himno*; *Piedra de sol*; *La estación violenta*; *Agua y viento*; *Dos y uno tres*; *Salamandra*; *El día de Udaipur*.

Paz Paredes, Margarita: *Sonaja*; *El anhelo plural*; *Génesis transido*; *Andamios de sombra*; *Dimensión del silencio*; *La imagen y su espejo*; *Adán en sombra y Noche final y Siete oraciones*.

Peláez, Francisco: *Aquí abajo*; *La noche*; "La noche del féretro"; "La noche del muñeco"; *Antología de la literatura fantástica*; *Yo de amores qué sabía*; *Tapioca Inn: Mansión para fantasmas*; *Breve diario de un amor perdido*; *Acapulco en el sueño*.

Pellicer, Carlos: *Camino*; *Colores en el mar y otros poemas*; *Hora de Junio*; *Hora y 20*; *Piedra de sacrificios*; *Seis, siete poemas*; *Práctica de vuelo*; *Material poético 1918-1961*; *Con palabras y fuego*; *Teotihuacán, y 13 de agosto: ruina de Tenochtitlán*.

Peña y Reyes, Antonio de la: *Antología moral*; *Diccionario biográfico de escritores mexicanos*; *Vivos y muertos*; *Artículos y discursos*.

Pensador Mexicano (El); *see* Fernández de Lizardi, José Joaquín.

Peón y Contreras, José: "A don Leopoldo Río de la Loza"; *Antón de Alaminos*; *Doña Leonor de Sarabia*; *Vivo o muerto*; *Ecos*; *El capitán Pedreñales*; *El castigo de Dios*; *El conde de Peñalva*; *El Conde Santiesteban*; "El Grijalva"; *El Padre José*; "El río de Tilapa"; *En el umbral de la dicha*; *Entre mi tío y mi tía*; *El sacrificio de la vida*; "El Señor de Ecatepec"; "El último azteca"; *Esperanza*; *Gabriela*; *Gertrudis*; *Gil González de Avila*; *¡Hasta el cielo!*; *Impulsos del corazón*; *Juan de Villalpando*; *La Cruz del Paredón*; *La eternidad de un minuto*; *La hija del Rey*; "La ruina de Atzcapotzalco"; *Laureana*; *Luchas de honra y amor*; *Margarita*; *María la Loca*; "Meditación dedicada a la memoria de mi madre"; "Moctezuma"; "Xocoyotzin"; "Oda a Hernán Cortés"; *Pablo y Virginia*; *Pequeños dramas*; *Poesías*; *Por el joyel del sombrero*; *Por la patria*; *Romances históricos mexicanos*; *Romances dramáticos*; *Soledad*; *Taide*; "Texcotzinco"; "Tlahuicole"; *Trovas colombinas*; *Un amor de Hernán Cortés*; *Una tormenta en el mar*; *Veleidosa*; *La cabeza de Uconor*.

Pepe Nava; *see* Elizondo, José F.

Peralta Castañeda, Antonio de: *Historia de Tobías.*

Peredo, Manuel: *El que todo lo quiere.*

Pereyra, Carlos: *Bolívar y Wáshington: un paralelo imposible; Breve historia de América; El crimen de Woodrow Wilson; El mito de Monroe; El pensamiento político de Alberdi; Francisco Pizarro y el tesoro de Atahualpa; Francisco Solano López y la guerra del Paraguay; Hernán Cortés; Hernán Cortés y la epopeya del Anáhuac; Historia de la América Española; Historia del pueblo mexicano; Humboldt en América; La conquista de las rutas oceánicas; La Constitución de los Estados Unidos como elemento de dominación plutocrática; La obra de España en América; Las huellas de los Conquistadores; Rosas y Thiers: la diplomacia europea en el Río de la Plata; Tejas: la primera desmembración de México.*

Pérez Bibbins, Manuel: *Cristóbal de Olid.*

Pérez Martínez, Héctor: *Cuauhtémoc (Vida y muerte de una cultura); Juárez el Impasible.*

Pérez Ramírez, Juan: *Desposorio espiritual entre el Pastor Pedro y la Iglesia Mexicana.*

Pérez Verdía, Luis: *Compendio de la Historia de México; Historia del Estado de Jalisco.*

Pesado, José Joaquín: *Alabanzas a la Santísima Virgen;* "Al ángel de la guarda de Elisa"; *El Cantar de los Cantares;* "El hombre"; "El sepulcro"; "El valle de mi infancia"; *Jerusalem;* "La primera impresión de amor"; *La princesa de Culhuacán; La Revelación; Los Aztecas;* "Mi amada en la misa de alba"; *Moisés; Rimas amorosas.*

Peza, Juan de Dios: *Algunos versos inéditos; Benito Juárez; Canto a la Patria; Cantos del hogar; El arpa del amor;* "En mi barrio"; *Flores del alma;* "Fusiles y muñecas"; *Hogar y Patria; Hojas de Margarita; Horas de pasión; La beneficencia en México; La ciencia del hogar; La Lira Mexicana; La Lira de la Patria; La musa vieja; Leyendas históricas, tradicionales y fantásticas de las calles de México; Memorias, reliquias y retratos; Monólogos y cantos a la Patria y a sus héroes; Poesías; Poesías completas; Poesías escogidas; Poetas y escritores mexicanos; Recuerdos y esperanzas; Tradiciones y leyendas mexicanas; Ultimos instantes de Colón; Un epílogo de amor.*

Pimentel, Francisco: *Cuadro descriptivo y comparativo de las lenguas indígenas de México; Historia crítica de la poesía en México;*

Novelistas y oradores mexicanos (included in his *Obras completas*).

Portilla, Anselmo de la: *De Miramar a México*; *La Revolución de Ayutla*; *México en 1856-57*; *Virginia Steward*; *Biblioteca histórica*.

Prieto, Carlos: *Atentado al pudor*; *A medio camino*; *Por el ojo de una aguja*; *El gato encerrado*; *El lépero*; *Ashes for Bread*; *El jugo de la tierra*; *El pregón de las gallinas*; *La rebelión de los tepehuanes*.

Prieto, Guillermo: "A Cristo crucificado"; "Romance de Iturrigaray"; *El romancero nacional*; *Lecciones de historia patria*; "Los cangrejos"; *Los San Lunes de Fidel*; *Memorias de mis tiempos*; *Musa callejera*; *Poesías escogidas*; *Versos inéditos*; *Viaje a los Estados Unidos*; *Viajes de orden suprema*.

Prieto de Landázuri, Isabel: "A mi hijo dando limosna"; "Bertha de Sonnenberg"; *¿Duende o serafín?*; *La escuela de las cuñadas*; "La madre y el niño"; "La Plegaria"; *Las dos flores*; *Las dos son peores*; *Oro y oropel*; *Un lirio entre zarzas*.

Prieto Yeme, Guillermo: *Estados de ánima*.

Puga, Vasco de: *Cedulario*.

Puga y Acal, Manuel: *Baladas lúgubres*; *Lirismos de antaño*; *Los poetas mexicanos contemporáneos*; *Otelo ante Dios*.

Puig Casauranc, José Manuel: *De la vida*; *Su venganza*.

Quevedo y Zubieta, Salvador: *La camada*.

Quijano, Alejandro: *En la tribuna*.

Rabasa, Emilio: *El cuarto poder*; *El juicio constitucional*; *La bola*; *La evolución histórica de México*; *La gran ciencia*; *La guerra de Tres Años*; *La organización política de México*; *Moneda falsa*.

Ramírez, Ignacio: "A Josefina Pérez"; "Al amor"; "A mi musa"; "A Sol"; "Por los desgraciados"; "Por los muertos."

Ramírez, José Fernando: *Adiciones a la Biblioteca de Beristáin*; *Notas y esclarecimientos a la historia de la Conquista de México de Prescott*; *Vida de Motolinia*; discovered the manuscript known as *El Anónimo o Códice Ramírez*.

Ramírez, José María: *Una rosa y un harapo*.

Ramírez Aparicio, Manuel: *Los conventos suprimidos en México*.

Ramírez Cabañas, Joaquín: *Esparcimiento*; wrote introduction and notes to *Historia verdadera de la conquista de la Nueva España*.

Ramos, Leopoldo: *Presencias*; *Urbe, campiña y mar*; *Bauprés*; *El mantel divino.*

Ramos, Samuel: *Hipótesis*; *El perfil del hombre y la cultura en México*; *Diego Riviera*; *Más allá de la moral de Kant*; *El caso Stravinsky*; *Hacia un nuevo humanismo*; *Veinte años de educación en México*; *Historia de la filosofía en México.*

Rangel, Nicolás: collaborated on *Antología del Centenario.*

Rea, Alonso de la: *Crónica de la Provincia de San Pedro y San Pablo de Michoacán.*

Rebolledo, Efrén: *El desencanto de Dulcinea*; *Hojas de bambú*; *Joyeles*; *Libro de loco amor*; *Rimas japonesas*; *Saga de Sigrida la Blonda.*

Remesal, Antonio: *Historia de la Provincia de San Vicente de Chiapa y Guatemala.*

Revilla, Manuel G.: *Biografías*; *El Arte en México.*

Revueltas, José: *Los muros de agua*; *El luto humano*; *Dios en la tierra*; *Dormir en Tierra*; *Los días terrenales*; *En algún valle de lágrimas*; *Los motivos de Caín*; *Los errores.*

Reyes, Alfonso: *A la memoria de Ricardo Güiraldes*; *Atenea política*; *A vuelta de correo*; *Calendario*; *Cantata en la tumba de Federico García Lorca*; *Capítulos de literatura española*; *Cartones de Madrid*; *5 casi sonetos*; *Cuestiones estéticas*; *Cuestiones gongorianas*; *Discurso por Virgilio*; *Donde Indalecio aparece y desaparece*; *El cazador*; *El paisaje en la poesía mexicana del siglo XIX*; *"El peregrino en su patria" de Lope de Vega*; *El Plano oblicuo*; *El suicida*; *El testimonio de Juan Peña*; *El tránsito de Amado Nervo*; *En el Día Americano*; *En el ventanillo de Toledo*; *En torno a la estética de Descartes*; *Fuga de Navidad*; *Golfo de México*; *Horas de Burgos*; *Huellas*; *Idea política de Goethe*; *Ifigenia cruel*; *Infancia*; *Influencia del Ciclo Artúrico en la literatura castellana*; *La caída: exégesis en marfil*; *La saeta*; *Las vísperas de España*; *Los dos augures: arranque de novela*; *Los dos caminos*; *Los "Poemas Rústicos" de Manuel José Othón*; *Minuta, juego poético*; *Noche de mayo*; *Otra vez*; *Pausa*; *Reloj de Sol*; *Retratos reales e imaginarios*; *Romance del Río de Enero*; *Simpatías y diferencias*; *Tren de ondas*; *Visión de Anáhuac*; *Voto por la Universidad del Norte*; *Yerbas del Tarahumara*; *Los siete sobre Deva (Sueño de una tarde de agosto)*; *La crítica en la edad ateniense*; *La angustia retórica*;

El deslinde: Prolegómenos a la teoría literaria; La experiencia lite-raria; Ultima Tule; Norte y sur; Los trabajos y los días; A lápiz; Entre libros; Panorama de la religión griega; De un autor cen-surado en el "Quijote"; Grata compañía; Romances; Cortesía; Sirtes; De viva voz; Junta de sombras; Marginalia; Ancorajes; Arbol de pólvora; Memoria de cocina y bodega; Berkeleyana; edited *Poema del Cid* and works of Archpriest of Hita, Quevedo, Gracián, Lope de Vega, Fuente la Peña, Mier, and Amado Nervo.

Reyes, Antonio de los: *Arte.*

Reyes Nevares, Salvador: *Frontera indecisa; El amor en tres poetas; El amor y la amistad en el mexicano; Panorama de las literaturas de Iberoamérica.*

Reyna Zeballos, Miguel: *La elocuencia del silencio.*

Reynel Hernández, Marcos: *El peregrino con guía y medicina uni-versal de la alma.*

Rincón, Antonio del: *Arte mexicano.*

Rincón Gallardo, Carlos: *Diccionario ecuestre; El libro del charro mexicano.*

Rius, Luis: *El mundo amoroso de Cervantes y sus personajes; Can-ciones de ausencia; Canciones de amor y sombra; Canciones de Vela.*

Riva Palacio, Vicente: "Al viento"; *Calvario y Tabor; Cuentos del General*; "El Escorial"; "La vejez"; *La vuelta de los muertos; Las dos emparedadas; Los Ceros; Los piratas del Golfo; Martín Gara-tuza; Memorias de un impostor, D. Guillén de Lampart, Rey de México; Monja y casada, virgen y mártir;* collaborated on *México a través de los siglos.*

Rivera y Sanromán, Agustín: *Anales de la Reforma y el Segundo Imperio; La filosofía en la Nueva España; Principios críticos sobre el Virreinato y la Guerra de Independencia.*

Rivera Cambas, Manuel: *Los gobernantes de México; México pinto-resco, artístico y monumental.*

Rivera y Río, José: *Fatalidad y Providencia; Los misterios de San Cosme; Mártires y verdugos.*

Roa Bárcena, José María: *Acopio de sonetos castellanos*; "Aminta Rovero"; "Buondelmonti"; *Catecismo de historia de México*; "Combates en el aire"; "Diana"; "El rey y el bufón"; *Ensayo de una historia anecdótica de México; La princesa Papantzin*; "La quinta modelo"; "Lanchitas"; *Leyendas mexicanas, cuentos y baladas del Norte de Europa y algunos otros ensayos poéticos*; "Noche al raso"; *Novelas; Poesías líricas; Recuerdos de la invasión norteamericana; Ultimas poesías;* "Una flor en su sepulcro"; *Xóchitl.*

Robles, Antonio: *Aleluyas de Rompetacones; Un gorrión en la guerra de las fieras; La fauna se columpia; La bruja doña Paz; Ocho estrellas y ocho cenzontles; El niño de la naranja; Rompetacones y 100 cuentos más; El refugiado Centauro.*

Robles, Fernando: *La virgen de los cristeros; El santo que asesinó; Cuando el águila perdió sus alas; La estrella que no quiso vivir.*

Robles, Pablo: *Los Plateados de Tierra Caliente.*

Rodríguez Beltrán, Cayetano: *Cuentos costeños; Pájarito.*

Rodríguez Galván, Ignacio: "El ángel caído"; "El insurgente en Ulúa"; *El privado del Virrey;* "El tenebrario"; "Eva ante el cadáver de Abel"; *La capilla;* "La visión de Moctezuma"; "Mora"; *Muñoz, visitador de México;* "Profecía de Guatimoc."

Rojas Garcidueñas, José: *El teatro de la Nueva España en el siglo XVI; Don Carlos de Sigüenza y Góngora erudito barroco; El antiguo Colegio de San Ildefonso; Bernardo de Balbuena, la vida y la obra.*

Rojas González, Francisco: *Historia de un frac; . . . y otros cuentos; El pajareador; Sed. Pequeñas novelas; Chirrín y La celda 18; Cuentos de ayer y de hoy; El diosero; La negra Angustias; Lola Casanova.*

Rejano, Juan: *Fidelidad del sueño; El Genil y los olivos; Víspera heroica; El oscuro límite; Noche adentro; Oda española; Constelación menor; Canciones a la paz; La respuesta; El río y la paloma; El libro de los homenajes.*

Romano Muñoz, José: *La ética de los valores; Iniciación en la cultura; Más allá de Husserl; El secreto del bien y del mal; Hacia una filosofía existencial.*

Romero, José Rubén: *Apuntes de un lugareño; Desbandada; El pueblo inocente; La vida inútil de Pito Pérez; Mi caballo, mi perro y mi rifle; Tacámbaro; Versos viejos; Anticipación a la muerte; Una vez fui rico; Rosenda.*

Romero, Manuel María: *Catalina de Suecia.*

Romero de Terreros y Vinent, Manuel: *Apuntaciones de viaje de D.*

Juan Romero de Terreros; Apuntes biográficos de D. Juan Gómez de Parada; Arte colonial; Bibliografía de cronistas de la ciudad de México; Breves apuntes sobre la escultura colonial de los siglos XVII y XVIII; Cosas que fueron; El arquitecto Tres Guerras; El estilo epistolar en la Nueva España; El grabado en México; El pintor Alonso López de Herrera; Encuadernaciones artísticas mexicanas; Entre las flores; Florecillas de San Felipe de Jesús; Florilegio; Hernán Cortés, sus hijos y nietos, caballeros de las órdenes militares; Historia sintética del arte colonial; La casa colonial; La casa de los Azulejos; La casa de Parada; La corte de Agustín I; La corte de Maximiliano; La moneda revolucionaria de México; La mujer blanca; La puerta de bronce; Las artes industriales en la Nueva España; Las medallas de la proclamación de la Independencia y del Primer Imperio; Las órdenes militares de México; Loa del Jardín de Borda; Los corregidores de México; Los grabadores de México durante la época colonial; Los jardines de la Nueva España; Los tlacos coloniales; Maximiliano y el Imperio; México virreinal; Nociones de literatura castellana; Relación del Japón; Residencias coloniales de la ciudad de México; Siluetas de antaño; Sinopsis del blasón; Torneos, mascaradas y fiestas reales en la Nueva España; Tradiciones y leyendas mexicanas; Un bibliófilo en el Santo Oficio; Viaje de la Marquesa de las Amarillas; Bocetos de la vida social en la Nueva España; El arte en México durante el Virreinato.

Rosado Vega, Luis: *Alma y sangre; Libro de ensueño y de dolor; Sensaciones.*

Rosas Moreno, José: *Amor filial; El año nuevo; El pan de cada día;* "El valle de mi infancia"; "El zentzontle"; "La vida del campo"; *Los parientes; Netzahualcóyotl, el bardo de Acolhuacán; Ramo de violetas; Sor Juana Inés de la Cruz;* "Tristeza del crepúsculo"; *Una lección de geografía; Un proyecto de divorcio.*

Rubín, Ramón: *Cuentos del medio rural mexicano; Cuentos mestizos de México, II; Tercer libro de cuentos mestizos; Diez burbujas en el mar, sarta de cuentos salobres; El callado dolor de los tzotziles; La bruma lo vuelve azul; El canto de la grilla; Cuando el táguaro agoniza; El seno de la esperanza; Donde mi sombra se espanta.*

Rubio, Darío: *El lenguaje popular mexicano; La anarquía del lenguaje en la América Española; Los llamados mexicanismos de la*

San José, Antonio María de: *Baluarte de México.*

San Juan, Manuel H.: *El Señor Gobernador.*

Sánchez de Tagle, Francisco Manuel: *Obras poéticas.*

Sánchez Mármol, Manuel: *Antón Pérez; Juanita Sousa; Previvida.*

Sánchez Mayans, Fernando: *Aguinaldo poético; Las alas del pez; Cuarteto deshonesto; El jardinero de las damas; Joven drama; Hojas al viento; Pausa al silencio; Decir lo de la Primavera; Poemas; Acto propicio.*

Sancho Polo; *see* Rabasa, Emilio.

Sandoval y Zapata, Luis de: *Panegírico de la paciencia; Poesías varias a Nuestra Señora de Guadalupe.*

Santa Ana, Antonio: *El blanco por fuerza.*

Santa María, Javier: *Como hay muchos.*

Santamaría, Francisco J.: *Diccionario de Mejicanismos.*

Santa Rosa, Conde de; *see* Calderón, Fernando.

Sartorio, José Manuel Mariano Aniceto: "Liras"; *Poesías sagradas y profanas.*

Sedano, Francisco: *Noticias de México.*

Selva, Mauricio de la: collaborated on *Nuestro canto a Guatemala; Palabra; Dos poemas; Poemas para decir a distancia; La fiebre de los párpados.*

Serán, Carlos Hipólito: *Ceros sociales.*

Shelley, Jaime Augusto: *La espiga amotinada; La gran escala; Canción de las ciudades.*

Sierra, Justo the Elder: *La hija del judío; Un año en el Hospital de Lázaro.*

Sierra, Justo the Younger: "A Cristóbal Colón"; "A Dios"; "Al autor de los 'Murmurios de la Selva' "; "Aníbal"; *Catecismo de Historia Patria;* "César Nero"; *Confesiones de un pianista; Conversaciones del Domingo; Cuentos románticos; Discursos;* "El Beato Calasanz"; "El funeral bucólico"; "En Jerusalem"; "En la apoteosis de los héroes de la Independencia"; *En tierra yankee;* "Florencia"; *Historia política; Juárez: su obra y su tiempo;* "La novela de un colegial"; "La sirena"; *Manual escolar de historia general;* "María Antonieta"; "Marina"; *México: su evolución social;* "Otoñal"; *Piedad;* "Playera"; "Spirita"; *Evolución política del pueblo mexicano.*

Sigüenza y Góngora, Carlos de: *Calendario de los meses y fiestas de los mexicanos*; *Canción*; *Genealogía de los reyes mexicanos*; *Glorias de Querétaro*; *Historia del imperio de los chichimecas*; *Infortunios de Alonso Ramírez*; *Libra astronómica y filosófica*; *Manifiesto filosófico contra los cometas*; *Mercurio volante con la noticia de la recuperación de las provincias de Nuevo México*; *Oriental planeta evangélico: Epopeya sacro-panegírica*; *Paraíso occidental*; *Primavera Indiana: Poema sacro-histórico de María Santísima de Guadalupe*; *Relación histórica de los sucesos de la Armada de Barlovento*; *Teatro de las grandezas de México*; *Theatro de virtudes políticas que constituyen a un príncipe*; *Triunfo parténico*; *Trofeo de la Justicia española*.

Silva y Aceves, Mariano: *Animula*; *Arquilla de marfil*; *Campanitas de plata*; *Cara de virgen*; *Muñecos de cuerda*.

Solana, Rafael: *Ladera*; *Los sonetos*; *Los espejos falsarios*; *Cien veces el mismo soneto*; *El envenenado*; *La trompeta*; *La música por dentro*; *Los Santos Inocentes*; *El crimen de tres bandas*; *Trata de muertos*; *Todos los sonetos*; *Pido la palabra*; *El oficleido y otros cuentos*; *Todos los cuentos de Rafael Solana*; *El sol de octubre*; *La casa de la Santísima*; *El palacio maderna*; *Las islas de oro*; *A su imagen y semejanza*; *Estrella que se apaga*; *La ilustre cuna*; *Lázaro ha vuelto*.

Solís, Antonio de: *Historia de la Conquista de México*.

Solórzano, Carlos: *Doña Beatriz, la sin ventura*; *El hechicero*; *Las manos de Dios*; *El crucificado*; *Los fantoches*; *Cruce de vías*; *El sueño del ángel*; *Los falsos demonios*.

Soria, Francisco: *Guillermo Duque de Aquitania*; *La Genoveva*; *La Mágica mexicana*.

Sosa, Francisco: *Biografías de mexicanos distinguidos*; *Efemérides históricas y biográficas*; *El Episcopado Mexicano*; *Los Contemporáneos*; *Manual de biografía yucateca*.

Souto Alaborce, Arturo: *La plaza del crisantemo*.

Spota, Luis: *Murieron a mitad del río*; *Las horas violentas*; *La sangre enemiga*; *Casi el paraíso*; *El coronel fue echado al mar*; *Más cornadas da el hombre*; *Vagabunda*; *La estrella vacía*; *Las grandes aguas*; *El tiempo de la ira*; *La pequeña edad*; *La carcajada del gato*.

Suárez de Peralta, Juan: *Libro de alveitería*; *Noticias históricas de la Nueva España*; *Tratado de la caballería de la gineta y brida*; *Tratado del descubrimiento de las Indias y su conquista*.

Tablada, José Juan: *Al sol y bajo la luna*; *Artes plásticas mexicanas*; *El florilegio*; *El jarro de flores*; *Hisroshigué*; *Historia del arte mexicano*; *La feria*; *La feria de la vida*; *La resurrección de los ídolos*; *Li-Pó*; *Los días y las noches de París*; *Un día*.

Tamiro Micenco; *see* Escobedo, P. Federico.

Teja Zabre, Alfonso: *Alas abiertas*; *Ensayos de historia de México*; *Historia de Cuauhtémoc*; *Historia de México: Una moderna interpretación*; *La Esperanza y Hatiké*; *Poemas y fantasías*; *Teoría de la Revolución*; *Tragedia de Cuauhtémoc*; *Vida de Morelos*.

Tello, Antonio: *Crónica miscelánea en que se trata de la conquista espiritual y temporal de la Santa Provincia de Xalisco*.

Teresa de Mier, Fr. Servando; *see* Mier, Fr. Servando Teresa de.

Terrazas, Francisco de: *Nueva Mundo y Conquista*; *Tratado de mar y tierra*.

Tezozomoc, Hernando de Alvarado: *Crónica mexicana*.

Tick-Tack; *see* Campo, Angel de.

Toro, Alfonso: *Compendio de Historia de México*; *Historia Colonial de la América Española*; *Los viajes de Colón*.

Torquemada, Juan de: *Monarquía indiana*.

Torres, Eugenia: *El muñeco roto*; *En torno de la Quimera*; *Honra de clases*; *La hermana*; *Lo imprevisto*; *Vencida*.

Torres, Teodoro: *Como perros y gatos*; *La patria perdida*; *Orígenes de las costumbres*; *Pancho Villa: una vida de romance y de tragedia*; *Periodismo*.

Torres Bodet, Jaime: *Canciones*; *Cripta*; *Destierro*; *El corazón delirante*; *Fervor*; *La casa*; *La educación sentimental*; *Los días*; *Margarita de Niebla*; *Nuevas canciones*; *Poemas*; *Poesías*; *Primero de enero*; *Proserpine rescatada*; *Sombras*; *Sonetos*; *Contemporáneos*; *Nacimiento de Venus y otros relatos*; *Educación mexicana: discursos, entrevistas, mensajes*; *Educación y concordia internacional*; *Discursos y mensajes*.

Torri, Julio: *Ensayos y poemas*; *De fusilamientos*.

Toscano, Carmen: *Trazo incompleto*; *Inalcanzable y mío*; *Rosario la de Acuña, mito romántico*; *La Llorona*.

Toscano, Salvador: *Arte precolombino de México y de la América Central*.

Toussaint, Manuel: *En casa de nuestros primos*; *La Catedral de México*; *La pintura en México durante el siglo XVI*; *Oaxaca*; *Saturni-*

no Herrán y su obra; *Tasco*; *Viajes alucinados*; collaborated on *Las cien mejores poesías (líricas) mexicanas*; *Paseos Coloniales*; *Arte Mudéjar en América*; *Arte Colonial en México*; *La conquista de Pánuco*.

Tovar, Pantaleón: "A una niña que llora por unas flores"; *Ironías de la vida*; *Justicia del cielo*; *La gloria del dolor*; *La hora de Dios*; *La conjuración de México*; *Misterios del corazón*; *Una deshonra sublime*; *¿Y para qué?*.

Tuerto (El); *see* Ochoa y Acuña, Anastasio María de.

Trueba, Eugenio: *Garabato*; *El Umbral*; *Cuentos*; *Antesala*; *La pupila del gato*; *Los intereses colectivos*; *La turbia imagen*.

Ulloa, Miguel: *Abismos de la pasión*; *El último drama*.

Urbina, Luis: *Bajo el sol y frente al mar*; *Cuentos vividos y crónicas soñados*; *El cancionero de la noche serena*; *El corazón juglar*; *El glosario de la vida vulgar*; *Estampas de viaje*; *Hombres y libros*; *Ingenuas*; *Lámparas en agonía*; *La vida literaria de México*; *Los últimos pájaros*; *Luces de España*; "Poema del Lago"; *Psiquis enferma*; *Puestas de sol*; *Versos*; *Vespertinas*; collaborated on *Antología del Centenario*.

Urquiza, Concha: *Obras*.

Urquizo, Francisco L.: *Europa Central en 1922*; *Cosas de la Argentina*; *Madrid de los años veinte*; *Lo incognoscible*; *México Tlaxcalantongo*; *Venustiano Carranza, el hombre, el político, el caudillo*; *Siete años con Carranza*; *Tropa vieja*.

Urueta, Jesús: *Alma poesía: conferencias sobre literatura griega*; *Discursos literarios*; *Fresca*; *Pasquinadas y desenfadas políticos*; "Prológo" to *Dulcinea*.

Usigli, Rodolfo: *Medio tono*; *México en el teatro*; *El Apóstol*; *Estado de secreto*; *La mujer no hace milagros*; *Sueño de día*; *Vacaciones*; *La familia cena en casa*; *Corona de sombra*; *El gesticulador*; *Noche de estío*; *Los fugitivos*; *El niño y la niebla*; *Aguas estancadas*; *Jano es una muchacha*; *Un día de éstos*; *Conversación desesperada*; *Itinerario del autor dramático*.

Uhthoff, Enrique: *Nopal*; *Mi compañero el gallo*; *Pancho Macho*; *Amar, eso es todo*; *Rayo en la encina*.

Valadés, Edmundo: *La muerte tiene permiso*; *Adriana*; *Las raíces irritadas*; *Antípoda*; *Rock*; collaborated with Luis Leal on *La Revolución y las letras*.

Valadés, José C.: *Alamán: Estadista e historiador.*

Valdés, Carlos: *Ausencias; Dos ficciones; Dos y los muertos; El nombre es lo de menos; Los antepasados.*

Valdés, Octaviano: *Por los campos de México.*

Valencia, Juan de: *Teresiada.*

Valenzuela, Jesús E.: *Almas y cármenes; Lira libre; Manojo de rimas.*

Vallarta, Ignacio L.: *Discurso sobre la abolición de la Compañía de Jesús.*

Valle, Juan: "El infortunio"; "La guerra civil"; "La muerte de mi madre"; "Mi historia"; *Misterios sociales;* "Tu ausencia."

Valle-Arizpe, Artemio de: *Amores y picardías; Cuentos del México antiguo; Del tiempo pasado; Doña Leonor de Cáceres y Acevedo y Cosas tenedes; Don Victoriano Salado Alvarez y la conversación en México; Ejemplo; Historias de vivos y muertos; El Palacio Nacional de México; La muy noble y leal ciudad de México,* published in *Historia de la ciudad de México según los relatos de sus cronistas; Libro de estampas; Lirios de Flandes; Por la vieja calzada de Tlacopan; Tres nichos de un retablo; Virreyes y virreinas de la Nueva España; Vidas milagrosas; El Canillitas; La movible inquietud; En México y en otros siglos; Andanzas de Hernán Cortés y otros excesos; Leyendas mexicanas; Jardinillo seráfico; Espejo del tiempo; Sala de tapices; Lejanías entre brumas; Piedras viejas bajo el sol; Inquisición y crímenes; Calle vieja y calle nueva; Notas de platería; Cuadros de México; La Güera Rodríguez; Fray Servando.*

Vasconcelos, José: *Breve historia de México; Bolivarismo y monroísmo; Don Gabino Barreda y las ideas contemporáneas; Divagaciones literarias; El desastre; El monismo estético; El proconsulado; Estética; Estudios indostánicos; Etica; Historia del pensamiento filosófico; Indología; La raza cósmica; La sonata mágica; La tormenta; Pitágoras; Prometeo vencedor; ¿Que es el comunismo?; Tratado de metafísica; Ulises criollo.*

Vásquez del Mercado, Alberto: collaborated on *Las cien mejores poesías (líricas) mexicanas.*

Vásquez Santa Ana, Higinio: *Canciones, cantares y corridos; Historia de la canción mexicana.*

Vela, Arqueles: *El sendero gris y otros poemas 1919-1920; Cantatas a las muchachas fuertes y alegres de México; Cuentos del día y de la noche; La volanda; El picaflor.*

Veracruz, Alonso de la: *Dialectica Resolutio*; *Physica Speculatio*; *Recognitio Summularum*; *Speculum Conjugiorum.*

Vetancourt, Agustín: *Arte*; *Teatro mexicano: descripción breve de los sucesos ejemplares, históricos, políticos, militares y religiosos del Nuevo Mundo*; "Crónica de la Provincia del Santo Evangelio" (fourth part of *Teatro Mexicano*) supplemented by "Menologio franciscano."

Veytia, Mariano: *Historia antigua de México*; *Baluarte de México*; *Historia* (de Puebla).

Vicens, Josefina: *El libro vacío*; *Le cahier clandestin.*

Vigil, José María: *Flores de Anáhuac*; *Lope de Vega*; *Poetas mexicanos*; *Poetisas mexicanas*; *Realidades y quimeras*; *Reseña histórica de la literatura mexicana*; collaborated on *México a través de los siglos.*

Villalpando, Luis: *Arte y Vocabulario.*

Villaseñor y Cervantes, José María: "Deseado"; *Festivas aclamaciones de la villa de Jalapa a Fernando VII*; *La gloria de la nación por su rey y por su unión*; *Libertad.*

Villaseñor y Sánchez, José Antonio: *Teatro americano, descripción general de los reinos y provincias de la Nueva España.*

Villaurrutia, Xavier: *Dama de corazones*; *¿En qué piensas?*; *La poesía de los jóvenes de México*; *Nocturnos*; *Nostalgia de la muerte*; *Parece mentira*; *Reflejos*; *Sea usted breve*; *Canto a la Primavera y otros poemas*; *La hiedra*; *Invitación a la muerte*; *El verbo candente*; *El pobre Barba Azul*; *Juego peligroso*; *Poesía y teatro completos.*

Xirau, Ramón: *Tres poetas de la soledad*; *Poesía hispanoamericana y española*; *Primicia de introducción*; *Poetas de México y España*; *Método y metafísica en la filosofía de Descartes*; *Duración y existencia*; *El péndulo y la espiral*; *Introducción a la historia de la filosofía.*

Yáñez, Agustín: *Obras completas*; *Archipiélago de mujeres*; *Al filo del agua*; *Genio y figuras de Guadalajara*; *Flor de juegos antiguos*; *El clima espiritual de Jalisco*; *Yahualica*; *La tierra pródiga*; *Las tierras flacas*; *Pasión y convalecencia*; *La creación*; *Ojerosa y pintada*; *Tres cuentos*; *Los sentidos del aire.*

Zambrano, Esperanza: *Las canciones del amor perfecto*; *Los ritmos secretos.*

Zárate, Julio: collaborated on *México a través de los siglos*.

Zarco, Francisco: *Historia del Congreso Extraordinario Constitu-yente*.

Zavala, Lorenzo de: *Ensayo histórico de las revoluciones de México*; *Memorias*; *Viaje a Bélgica y Holanda*; *Viaje a los Estados Unidos*; *Viaje a Suiza*.

Zayas Enríquez, Rafael de: *El esclavo*; *El expósito*; *El Teniente de los Gavilanes*.

Zayas Guarneros, Pablo: *Amor sublime*.

Zepeda, Eraclio: *Benzulul*.

Zumaya, Manuel: *El Rodrigo*; *Parténope*.

Index

Index

525

DATE DUE